To Mark
Best Wishes
[signature]

BARNSLEY F.C.
1887 - 1998
THE OFFICIAL
HISTORY

By:

Brian Dennis

John Daykin   Derek Hyde

Published by:
Yore Publications
12 The Furrows, Harefield,
Middx. UB9 6AT

© Brian Dennis 1998

....

British Library Cataloguing-in-Publication Data
A catalogue record for this book
is available from the British Library

ISBN 1 874427 87 9

YORE PUBLICATIONS specialise in football books, normally of an historic nature...
Club histories, Who's Who books, etc. plus non-League football.
Three free Newsletters are issued per year, for your first copy,
please send a S.A.E. to the address above.

Printed and bound by The Bath Press

Dedicated to:

Julie and Sarah

******

The memory of Chris Hollis,
who would have been watching
from the Oakwell outpost in the sky
as the events of the 26th April 1997 unfolded.

****

The Reverend Tiverton Preedy, who started it all.

FOREWORD
HAROLD DENNIS (DICKIE) BIRD. MBE. LLD. DR.

I was born in Barnsley on the 19th April, 1933, and educated at Raley Secondary Modern School. One of my school mates was the late Tommy Taylor, and we played together in the school soccer team, and later for Barnsley Boys. I played at inside-right and Tommy played at left-back. Even from an early age, Tommy had phenomenal pace and timing, and his heading of the ball was unbelievable. Tommy's career, which was tragically cut short in the Munich air disaster, has been well documented, and, in my opinion, he was the most gifted player ever to have graced this wonderful game. I often visit his resting place at Monk Bretton Cemetery, to spend some time with my old friend.

Whilst Tommy's soccer career blossomed, my own hopes of making it in the game were dashed by a damaged knee when I was 15, so I turned my attentions to my second love, cricket, and in the interim period, I worked in the fitting shop at Monk Bretton Colliery.

I learned my cricket trade with Barnsley Cricket Club, where I met and played with Michael Parkinson and we have been friends ever since. I made my debut for Yorkshire CCC 2 nd eleven when I was 19. However, I had to wait until 1956 before I was selected for the first team, but between then and 1959 my first team appearances were limited because of the enormous amount of talent in the club at that particular time. I decided to seek pastures new, but not before I made my maiden first class century playing against Glamorgan at Bradford.

I joined Leicestershire in 1960, and was awarded my county cap in my first season with the club, and spent five happy seasons there. I was already thinking in terms of qualifying to become an umpire when I left Leicestershire in 1965 to coach cricket at Plymouth College Preparatory School, and was appointed to the first class umpires list in November 1969 after a spell as professional with Paignton Cricket Club.

As I embark on my last season on the County circuit, I think about the wonderful life I have led visiting all the cricket playing countries in the world, and meeting a host of exciting and talented players and personalities.

I have achieved every honour humanly possible in the umpiring world, culminating in being made a Member of the Most Excellent Order of the British Empire by Her Majesty Queen Elizabeth II in her Birthday Honours List in June 1986.

But yet, I am just an ordinary Yorkshire lad, born and bred in Barnsley and proud of it. No matter which part of the Globe my job takes me, I always look forward to coming back home to my roots, to my beloved Barnsley, and to my football team.

I have supported the 'Reds' since I was a lad, and no one was prouder than me when Danny led us into the Premiership. I feel particularly pleased for the unsung heroes, the 2,000 odd supporters who turned up at Oakwell in the dark days of the old 4th Division, the tea ladies, the office and backroom staff, and of course, the players and officials of this lovely little club.

I was nowt but a lad of six when my Dad took me to Oakwell for the first time, and I used to sit on his shoulders and watch the skills of Binns, Bullock and Bokas, names which are but a distant memory. I recall the wizardry of Johnny Kelly and Gavin Smith in that great side of the late forties/early fifties, and in particular an F.A. Cup match against Blackpool, who had the silky skills of Matthews and Mortenson at their disposal. Gordon Pallister was marking the legendary Matthews, and that Barnsley lost 1-0 is history, but many years later I met the two gentlemen in question, and Stanley Mortenson confessed to me that the winning goal came off his shin pad.

I could talk about cricket and Barnsley F.C. until the cows come home, but my mate 'Parky' summed it up in a newspaper article he wrote after he accompanied Gordon Pallister and myself to a meeting of the 'Wombwell Cricket Lovers Society'. Michael wrote *"Nostalgia dwells on things past but it makes them seem like next door neighbours rather than visitors from a distant land. The wondrous quality of nostalgia is that it is unchallengeable. Like beauty, it rests in the eye of the beholder. Moreover, no matter what they might tell you, there are still characters in sport worth remembering. I was looking at Dickie Bird and thinking that as far as umpires and Barnsley are concerned, nostalgia is in very good hands."*

DICKIE'S MAJOR ACHIEVEMENTS
First class cricket career:
1956/59 Yorkshire CCC   1960/65 Leicestershire CCC
93 matches   3314 runs.average 20.71 - 2 centuries.
Highest score - 181 not out v Glamorgan at Bradford in 1959

International Umpire career:
67 Test Matches (a world record)
92 one day International Matches (a world record)
3 World Cup Finals: West Indies v Australia at Lords (1975)
West Indies v England at Lord's (1979)
West Indies v India at Lord's (1983)
4 World Cup Tournaments

Awards:
Yorkshire Personality of the Year (1977)
Awarded the MBE (1986)
Honorary Life member of Yorkshire CCC (1995)
Yorkshireman of the Year (1996)
Honorary Life member of MCC (1996)
Honorary Life member of Leicestershire CCC (1996)
Honorary Doctorate Degree at Sheffield Hallam University (1996)
Honorary Doctorate Degree in Laws at Leeds University (1997)
General: Dickie is the author of the following best-selling books: *"Not Out"*, *"That's Out"*, *"From the Pavilion End"*.
His recent autobiography has sold over 375,000 copies worldwide.

INTRODUCTION AND ACKNOWLEDGEMENTS BY BRIAN DENNIS

There have been various publications over the years about Barnsley Football Club, but since Grenville Firth published his excellent *"Oakwell - The Official History"* in 1978, little has been done on that particular scale. This was partly remedied in 1996 when, with the help of Derek Hyde, I compiled *"The Definitive Barnsley F.C."* which was published by the Association of Football Statisticians. Derek and I then decided that the time was right to embark on a more major project, which has culminated in the publication of *"Barnsley F.C. 1887-1998 - The Official History"*. I also solicited the help of John Daykin, and the three of us have spent many hours burning midnight oils to produce the first ever complete history of the Club. Although myself and my two co-authors are life-long supporters of the Club, we are all exiles - John emigrated to America 15 years ago and is now residing in California. Derek is settled in Cardiff, and I live in Orpington, Kent.

My initial thanks then, go to John for his absorbing and well written narrative from the early days to the promotion season of 1980/81, to Keith Lodge for his excellent review of 1997/98 and to 'eagle-eyed' Derek Hyde for his concise player 'Who's Who', and his meticulous checking and double checking of most aspects of the book. I penned the narrative from 1981/82 to 1996/97.

Every effort has been made to ensure accuracy, but typographical errors are inevitable, and I apologise for these in advance. The views expressed in the narrative are the authors', and are not necessarily the views of Barnsley Football Club.

Acknowledgments and grateful thanks are due to the following, who have assisted during the compilation of this book:
Michael Spinks, General Manger/Secretary of Barnsley F.C. for his continuous support: John Dennis, Chairman: Danny Wilson (ex-Manager): John Hendrie (Manager), and Norman Rimmington.
Dickie Bird, who gladly accepted my invitation to write the foreword for the book.
Keith Lodge for the loan of numerous colour photographs.
Mr. & Mrs. Blackborough (Norfolk), Bob Davies, Steve Emms, Jerry Fisher, Sam Goulding, Diana Gilfillan, Damian M.Green, Miriam Harper, Benny Hill, Mr. and Mrs. Hook (London N1), Michael Joyce, Brian March, Andy Ramsden, Ian Roberts, David Wake, David Woods.
Malcolm Hanson (Managing Director) and Ian Davies (Marketing Manager) of ORA Electronics for their help and support.
My wife, Christine, for her patience and understanding.

BOOKS

Oakwell: The Official History of Barnsley Football Club 1887-1979	*Grenville Firth*
Oakwell Heroes: A Who's Who of Barnsley Footballers 1945-1986	*Graham Noble*
Oakwell Centurions	*David Watson*
Barnsley: A Study in Football 1953-59	*Andrew Ward, -[an Alister*
Oakwell Saints Go Marching On!	*Keith Lodge*
The Definitive Barnsley F. C.	*Brian Dennis*
The Cult of the Manager	*Jeff King, John Kelly*
Jack Charlton: The Autobiography	*Jack Charlton*
Bill Shankly: The Biography	*Stephen F. Kelly*
Football Daft	*Michael Parkinson*
Association Football and English Society 1863-1915	*Tony Mason*
A History of the Church in England	*JR.H. Moorman*
The Victorian Church	*Owen Chadwick*
History Of British Society: Britain in the Nineteen-Twenties	*Noreen Branson*

NEWSPAPERS & PERIODICALS (from personal collections & reference libraries):
Islington Gazette, Islington & Holloway Press, The Star, North London Press, Church Times, St. Silas with All Saints Newspaper, London Diocesan Magazine, Barnsley Independent, Barnsley Chronicle, Sheffield Morning Telegraph, Star Green 'Un, Daily Mail, Sunday People, Sunday Express, Sunday Pictorial, Sunday Post.

PAMPHLETS & OTHER PUBLICATIONS
Barnsley F. C. Official Yearbooks, Barnsley F.C. Official Programmes, Barnsley FC Supporters' Club (London Branch) Newsletters, Lifting the Cup: Barnsley's Wonderful History (*Pub. J.Lodge & Sons 1912*), Barnsley Football Club (From the Book of Football 1906) (*F.Lodge*), History of Barnsley Football Club (*Argus*), Conditions of Labour in Yorkshire Coal Mines (*James Evison*), St. Peter's Church, Barnsley - Jubilee Youth Festival Booklet

PUBLIC RECORDS
Chancellor's School, Lincoln: Registers of Scholae Cancellarri Lincolniensis. Report of the Guild of St. Hugh 1893-94
Ripon Diocesan Registry: Diocesan Registers
Greater London Council Records Office: Archives of All Saints Mission. Archives of St. Silas Church
Barnsley Reference Library: 1881 Census Returns.
Registrar General: Tiverton Preedy: Birth, Death & Probate Records.

My final thanks go to Dave Twydell of Yore Publications for publishing the book, and for his friendly, but professional attitude and his excellent publishing skills.

SPECIAL THANKS: Without the assistance of Arthur Bower, the Club historian, this publication would not have been possible. I will be eternally grateful to Arthur, who loaned me his unique photo collection (teams and players), and his extensive records and files, programmes and memorabilia. Arthur, his wife Rosalie and son Tim, made me very welcome on my many visits to Locke Avenue, and my heartfelt thanks go to the Bower family.

CONTENTS

Page

CHAPTER 1

✤ FOOTBALL, BEER, MINERS AND CHURCH ✤

They lined the streets and cheered as the team made its way through town, waving to applause on all sides. Men spilled out of pub doors, families came with babes in arms and sat young 'uns on their shoulders; they clapped, sat at open upstairs windows, and called out to the players by name; they draped flags, swung from the street lights, waved streamers of red and white. The town streets were furrowed fields of upturned faces, all trying to glimpse the heroes of Oakwell as they passed through a canyon of noise. Surely nothing like it had ever been seen in Barnsley before.

The scene may have been the centre of Barnsley on Monday, May 5th, 1997, after the Reds had won promotion to the Premier League for the first time in their 110-year history. But it was also the scene on Wednesday, April 24th, 1912, when Archie Taylor held aloft the F.A. Cup on behalf of the only team ever to carry off that famous trophy with a victory in Yorkshire, as he led the team's return from their win at Bramall Lane against West Bromwich Albion.

When the club's founder, Rev. Tiverton Preedy, spoke of the F.A. Cup at a banquet held to honour the 1912 success, he said to a chorus of cheers, *".... I was not astonished. We set out to win it, and meant to win it."* With regard to the First Division, as it then was before the Premier League, his confidence was a little more misplaced: *"...see to it that we get into the First Division next year,"* he cried. *"*If you cannot do it next year, see that you do it the next, and take the place of Blackburn Rovers. Be determined not to rest until you are at the top of the tree.*"

It took a little longer than Preedy, or anyone else in Barnsley, could have imagined but when manager Danny Wilson led Barnsley to the Premier League in 1997 he carried a baton that Preedy had first passed so many years ago. The Barnsley Football Club of Preedy's time, like its modern counterpart, was built on determination, defiance of the odds, and an unstoppable wave of enthusiasm that fired up the locals and lit up the town.

The Reverend Tiverton Preedy

It also had a terrible reputation in the southern press, which Preedy found *"a disgrace and a shame."* Somehow, a modern day fan is entitled to muse, the more things change the more they stay the same.

Preedy himself was the source of the club's determination and enthusiasm but the full story of the club's beginning is much more than simply assigning credit to one man. The history of Barnsley Football Club is a social history of industrial England at the end of the 19th century, exposing the roots of football clubs the length and breadth of the land. In the heart of towns like Barnsley, economics, religion and working conditions mixed together like powder in a gun. Chance was the fuse. In Barnsley, Preedy lit the match.

In the late 1800's, Barnsley was an ebony black jewel in Yorkshire's coal crown. One in four men in a population of 50,000 was a miner. The collieries, by 1888, had 'favourable' working hours and the miners brought home up to five shillings per day, wages which on the whole were considered good for the times. Miners were beginning to have some time on their hands and a little spare change in their pockets. They were ready to turn over their threepences and sixpences for admission to entertainments such as football if only such entertainment could be found.

Miners' families, of course, saw little of the 'new affluence'. The sudden upswing in the mining industry had unloaded them into cramped cottages in crowded closes. Five or six people lived in one and two room dwellings; two-up-two-down was a luxury. Conditions were squalid. Rather than go home to this and bawling babies after a shift underground, miners often loitered on street corners and spent their little extra money on drink. Gambling and knurr and spell were their other biggest distractions.

Inevitably, drink and the devil found use for such idle hands. The Barnsley Chronicle reported in 1875 that Baker Street in Barnsley was a *"hell of debauchery"*, and the West Riding Constabulary felt that at least one village in the Barnsley area, Staincross, was so rough in the 1880's that *"it was a good place to send men to be broken in."*

Slum conditions throughout all the major cities of England, in new areas away from established parish churches, were facing the same kind of problems. The Church was responding by setting up 'missions' staffed by a new breed of people's priest who, while living frugally among the people, introduced social welfare with one hand while waving a bible in the other. In 1872, St. Mary's (the Parish Church of Barnsley) created a mission only a stone's throw from the part of town that the Chronicle found so distressing. By 1887, Rev. John Lloyd Brereton had built the mission up from a single room to the point where he had been granted a license as minister of a new district, St. Peter's, and raised funds to build a nave. The social work was obviously going well, but Brereton needed help.

When Tiverton Preedy stepped down from the train and took his first look at Barnsley he was barely 24 years-old, a small, fresh-faced, wiry, young man with a twinkling steely eye, a smile on his thin lips, and a bold, jaunty stride, about to set out on his first curacy. Newly ordained Deacon by the Bishop of Lincoln, he had just completed two years at Lincoln Theological College and was being unleashed on an unsuspecting world as St. Peter's Assistant Stipendiary Curate at a rate of one-hundred-and-twenty pounds per year. His chosen vocation; to enrich the lives of England's poor and downtrodden masses. The fact that he had studied at Lincoln was fortunate for the future of football in Barnsley.

The Church of England which Preedy represented was undergoing many revolutions. A new breed of Christian, the 'Muscular Christian', believed that an emphasis on physical activity and enjoying life in all its robustness and variety was morally correct and therefore good; in other words, playing sport was preparation for ascent to Heaven. At Lincoln, this belief was incorporated into theological training. As a scholar there, Preedy was expected to play sports and recognize the spiritual benefits of physical exercise.

Another revolution had already given Mission priests their charter, namely the idea that the church should minister to ordinary people in a language they could understand, in a way they could relate to, instead of hiding under antique steeples. At Lincoln, Preedy had studied under Benson, later to become perhaps the greatest Archbishop of Canterbury, who encouraged this view. Preedy was to find that the language of the ordinary man was often the language of sport, and easily embraced it. *"Father Preedy,"* said the Bishop of London at his funeral many years later, *"was a sportsman. He could talk to sportsmen."*

Some cynics, of course, could also detect another deliberate hand in the Missions' timely social work. The relief they offered to the working classes helped preoccupy entire communities at a time when trade unions and fledgling political parties competed for attention. At the Missions, men were given sport for their energies, and children soup, leaving social agitators less fuel for unrest. All around the country, priests were organising social clubs and sports events. Attracting men, and saving them from drink, was a priority. Prayer-meeting chairs were moved back to hold boxing contests; cricket, soccer and rugger were offered up after morning Mass; the working classes flocked in. Religion may have become the panacea of the masses, but it also gave birth to the modern football club. Aston Villa, Bolton Wanderers and Everton are just three of the many clubs which began with church sponsorship. In later years, Church teams such as Regent Street Congregational (The 'Congs') and the Kilnhurst Bible Class helped to produce star players for Barnsley's ranks. At one time, it was estimated that 25% of all the football clubs in England were affiliated with places of worship.

When Preedy had unpacked his bags and set out to get acquainted with Barnsley, he was quickly introduced to the Rugby Club. Having been raised in a middle class home in Hunstanton, Norfolk, he was familiar with rugby during his youth, and the gentlemen of the town who made up the Barnsley club were no doubt proper company for him to be introduced to.

Preedy's short association with Barnsley Rugby Club is now legendary. He was happy to play on Saturdays, but when they arranged a fixture on Good Friday, he quit. In an interview with the Church Times in 1926, Preedy recalled that he resigned from the Rugby Club *"...in protest, and walked down the street to where some young men at a public house corner were making plans for a soccer side...."*, so he joined them. A memoir printed in 1898 recalls: *"Said he to a number of his working-class chums, we will start an Association club such as the Rugbyites will not crush out."*

The break with Barnsley Rugby Club was a stroke of good fortune. Preedy's involvement there was probably social, but his chance meeting with the fledgling soccer club was a practical opportunity to begin his ministry, a vent for his enthusiasm. By taking the team under the wing of St. Peter's, he was able to put into practise his ideas about the role of the church. Barnsley St. Peter's Football Club was underway, and the 'Sporting Parson' began to earn his reputation.

Rugby Union, since its break with Association Football in 1864, considered itself the more elite of the two sports, with a 'snob' value that has of course continued down until this day. The more affluent types in Barnsley favoured the rugby game and disdained 'footer'.

Association Football was a game soiled by the common man, and by incursions of professionalism. Notably, in 1887, rugby was played in Barnsley on Huddersfield Road, on the nice side of town about as far away as you could get from the slums of St. Peter's, under the auspices of St. Mary's Church where the leading lights of the town worshipped.

Here then was one reason why the Association game had not taken hold in Barnsley up until this time. Many miners had left school before the age of twelve. They could get themselves to a field on time to play an occasional game, but they lacked the organisational skills and finances needed to run a continuing activity involving schedules, record-keeping, travel and playing expenses, skills which in Barnsley were the domain of the middle classes playing rugby. In Sheffield, where the game was strong, it was driven by a core of merchants and trades people who saw an opportunity to make money. In Barnsley, small teams such as the Casuals, Farriers, and Amateurs, played and folded with regularity and without much support.

Preedy brought the required organisational skills and an entrepreneur's drive to the St. Peter's club. He was also probably the first person in Barnsley with any social standing to try and organize a soccer club among working

men; those middle classes who had any leanings at all towards the Association game played on 'old schoolboys' teams such as the Barnsley Wanderers, who also played at the Huddersfield Road site. The Wanderers bothered little about attracting spectators, but played for fun in the amateur spirit of the game.

Preedy, on the other hand, saw the direction of football's popularity since the F.A. legalized professionals in 1885, and from the outset had no qualms about achieving either commercial success or success on the playing field. It did not seem out of the ordinary to him that a working man should make life a little more comfortable by picking up some reward for his athletic skill. Little wonder then that he *met with more ridicule than support for identifying himself with such a task". "Our success was by no means instantaneous,"* he recalled, *"Rugger was the game up to then and the new style met with strenuous opposition. The Press, the people, everyone seemed to be against us. But we fought on."*

By beginning the club under the auspices of St. Peter's Church, he earned some credibility and respect, and eventually the support of important people in town. As Association Football's popularity and acceptance gradually swelled throughout the area, Preedy steered his club to the crest of the wave.

The earliest traced item relating to the Club
A fixture card for the 1894/95 season

CHAPTER 2

✤ TIVERTON PREEDY'S RANGERS ✤
1887 - 1898

"Play up St. Peter's, white and blue,
I shall always stick to you;
When the season's nearly up
I hope you'll win the Barnsley Cup.
You're playing now in splendid style,
To the game no strangers,
Play up my lads,
You're all their dads,
For you're Tiverton Preedy's Rangers."

Anon. c.1893

Tiverton Preedy's leadership imprinted itself on Barnsley St. Peter's to such an extent that the 'Saints' became known locally as Preedy's team in much the same way that, on a grander scale, Shankly was to become identifiable with Liverpool, Busby with Manchester Utd., Clough with Derby and Nottingham Forest. *"It was his intention from the start that the Club should have more than a parochial appeal, and his free, frank and generous nature, coupled with unrelenting energy, soon made the club talked about over a wide area,"* said one club commentator, writing within living memory of the events.

Preedy did everything at the club. He played, he raised money, he recruited players and officials, he mediated disputes, he set the tone and the style of leadership that put the club on course for the Football League and the F.A. Cup. By the time he left in 1893, the club had generated a life of its own without him but his legacy was so strong that it took four more years before the club could officially drop 'St. Peter's' from its title and finally acknowledge a parting of the ways from its church origins.

For the first three years of its life Barnsley St. Peter's Football Club lived on a diet of 'friendly' games that often turned out to be not so friendly, spiced with challenge cup competition. The Sheffield Challenge Cup, which St. Peter's entered in their second year, was at that time the biggest competition in the area with more local prestige than the F.A. Cup, but the Saints also played smaller contests, such as a challenge tournament at Barnsley's Queen's Ground for a prize of eleven gladstone bags in 1889. They won the bags.

The club was initially too small to engage in league play, which at that time meant district competition against strong, established clubs, but each one of the first three years of friendly games on a widening local circuit was a successful season, and each raised standards on the playing field from the year before.

The very first game played by Barnsley St. Peter's Football Club took place quite some time after Preedy had walked out on the rugby crowd. First of all, on Tuesday, September 6th, 1887, the club recorded an inaugural meeting at which its first officers were elected. Rev. J.L.Brereton, the priest in charge of St. Peter's Church, was made President. Vice President was A. Fieldsend. R.Chappell was voted Captain, and A.Thompson vice-Captain. Rev. Preedy became Financial Secretary, and G. Bevitt Corresponding Secretary. Elected to a Committee were Messrs. Harrod, Fieldsend, Mason, Dryden, Jackson and Beckett. Eleven days later, the club put a team on the field for the first time. Inevitably, they were nick-named 'The Saints'.

On Saturday 17th September 1887, Barnsley St. Peter's ran out against Manor House at Ward Green wearing maroon and navy blue striped jerseys, which would be the club colours for the next two years. At the start of the third season, the club changed to chocolate and white. Their famous red and white uniform was not adopted until 1898, on their entry to the Football League.

The club's initial depth of personnel is illustrated by the presence of several newly elected officers turning out as players as well, but nonetheless the first page of the club's history book falls proudly open at a 4-1 victory. Scorer of the club's first goals were R. Chappell, Steven Denton(2) and A. Thompson, and the historic line-up was:

J. Mason
G. Walker   R. Chappell
A. Armitage   G. Beckett   S. Harrison
T. Preedy   A. Thompson   S. Denton   S. Thompson
A. Harrison

Within a few weeks, there were enough players to form a second team. During the next three years personnel changed so much that none of the players who started that day would be on the field when Barnsley St. Peter's began its first season of league play in 1890-91. Every season, players came and went in droves. In those days, players casually went from one club to another looking for a game. Player registration was not a formality, and only those who were openly professional were restricted to playing for one club in a season. At St. Peter's, the door was always open to prospective players who could offer something more. Better ones stayed to become the foundation of a successful club, and others made way for them. The club's early success was built on the mettle of these players.

Tom Nixon, for example, was one of the first quality players to arrive, just three games into St. Peter's first season. He was perhaps the first 'Mr. Barnsley', becoming club captain and trainer and enjoying a playing career that saw Barnsley all the way through to the Second Division. His last game for the club, after only a brief break in service, was on January 6th, 1900. Born at Lundhill Row, near Wombwell, he moved to Barnsley when only a nipper. He started his career at fifteen, was captain of the Gladstone team at Worsbro' Common only a year later, and played for the Shakespeare Hotel in Barnsley before going to Sheffield as a professional with the 'Zulus'. He was quickly back, and playing at Ardsley. His reputation as a player was widely known, and many clubs across South and West Yorkshire, including Sheffield Wednesday, tried to entice him but he wanted to remain in the Barnsley area. He chose St. Peter's. Over the course of his career he was many times offered financial inducements to leave but *"I was one of the first to join the St. Peter's club, and I mean to stick to it,"* he once said, typifying the kind of attitude that ensured Barnsley St. Peter's was going to endure. In 1890, Nixon became the first player to represent the County while on Barnsley's books in a match against Cheshire at Macclesfield.

Another player of the kind who made sure the Saints survived was Tom Hirst, *".....as fearless as he was big,"* noted one journalist. *"...No line of forwards ever gave Tom the shivers, and it was an exception when he failed to hold his own..... Nothing annoyed him more than to see a 'wishy-washy' individual on a team...."* Hirst was another town lad, and all his football had been played in the district before joining St. Peter's from the Young Vics. Like Nixon, he stayed with St. Peter's until injury ended his playing career, in this case seven years later in 1894-95.

Sam Hunt was an extremely popular acquisition during the early days. He was a centre-forward who, as well as being a deadly shot, could command the ball and switch play with excellent distribution across the width of the field. Another Barnsley lad, he spent two years as a professional with Doncaster Rovers before moving to Lincoln, and then back to Barnsley. He later went on to train not only St. Peter's but also Sheffield United.

Celebrity goalkeeper Arthur Mallinson also had a fleeting engagement with the club, making one appearance for them at Sheffield Clinton on New Year's Day 1889. Mallinson, a former amateur with Barnsley Wanderers, had played for the County team against visitors from Glasgow at Bramall Lane in 1875 when he was chaired from the field by spectators applauding his performance. Considered by some to be the greatest goalkeeper of his day, Mallinson found out in his one appearance for Barnsley, that his best days as a player were gone. He conceded four goals and Barnsley notched only one. Over the next few years he continued to be an active booster of St. Peter's cause.

From local friendlies, the club's rise through the Sheffield District League starting in 1890-91, to regional competition in the Midland League of 1895-96, was a rapid journey that required constant refuelling in the recruiting of new players. The club had to cast its net both wide and deep in the search for talent to sustain growth. Turnover continued year after year with sometimes a dozen or so new players signed to the club at the start of a new season. Some were never seen again, but others like Donald Lees, of Lincoln City and Celtic, or Jack Drummond of Liverpool, and Fred Woolhouse of Ecclesfield, provided backbone for a year or two.

In 1892 Barnsley signed the club's first Scottish players, breaking open a seam of talent that still runs rich and deep at Oakwell a hundred years later. Alec Black came from Berwick-on-Tweed to make a lasting impression on the club as player and Secretary. Roy Vickers and John Hastie came at the same time from north of the border. A dour defender who only lasted one season with the club, Hastie is perhaps best remembered as a player only because of his name, although he later managed the club for two years just before the Great War. Charlie Taylor of Kilnhurst once challenged Hastie's abilities as a full-back during post-match hospitality. *"Tha wants to get moor hastey pudding into ther, and then talk abaht being a back",* cried Taylor. Hastie was angry at the use of his name until Tom Nixon translated. He didn't mean anything wrong, said Nixon; hasty pudding was simply the name for porridge in those parts.

In addition to recruiting journeyman players, Barnsley also looked to fresh local talent. In October 1894 they advertised for promising juniors and received 32 replies. One of them, Hanson from Ward Green, quickly earned respect and a regular place in the first team for the rest of the season. In 1897 a future England international, goalscoring Harry Davis, was signed from local rivals Ardsley, and the namesake of another future international, Tommy Taylor, arrived from Staincross in 1893.

Barnsley's rising stature, which made the constant hunt for new players so necessary, is well illustrated by a look at the club's geographically expanding fixture list.

In 1887-88, their first year, St. Peter's travels barely took them out of town. Honeywell, Birdwell, Ardsley, Carlton, Silkstone Common and Worsbro' Bridge, Monk Bretton, Manor House and Gawber, local villages now part of the Barnsley conurbation, were about as far as they went. The team paid only one visit to the Sheffield area, to play Broomhill.

The following year, the team had to travel to the Sheffield-Rotherham area on several occasions, including Heeley, Staveley, Ellesmore, and Clinton, and to Doncaster as well. By the third year, St. Peter's schedule pitted the club further afield against teams from Sheffield, Wath, Wombwell, Greasborough, Mexborough, Leeds, Wakefield, Stocksbridge, Staincross and Wentworth. After 1895-96, league competition took Barnsley into Derbyshire, Nottinghamshire, Lincolnshire and West Yorkshire. On November 23rd. 1895, a friendly game against Woolwich Arsenal took them to the nation's capital for the first time, the furthest they had ever travelled to complete a fixture. It created a real stir in town when local folk heard that St. Peter's were actually going to play in London. After giving the Arsenal a run for their money in the first-half, they lost 4-1.

It was an exciting climate that produced the perfect conditions for this kind of expansion to flourish. The club was nothing but a seedling in terms of development. Money watered it, players nutrified it, officials tended it, but it could not have grown to full maturity without the climate provided by the glass-house of simultaneous social change. Football was booming among working class communities throughout the country. 'Half-day off' on Saturdays had become widespread, giving thousands of working men the opportunity to enjoy a Saturday afternoon football ritual. The recognition of professional players as employees encouraged development of clubs into small businesses, and the sport's commercial prospects and emerging prestige attracted entrepreneurs in every town and village.

To take full advantage of the expanding market for football, countless new leagues sprang up. The 'bowler hats', who counted takings, recognized that competitive football brought paying customers through the turnstiles. League play, with its emphasis on season-long competition, was in; friendlies, with their notions of amateurism, were out. No league exemplified this more than the newly formed Football League, which Barnsley would shortly join. Beginning in 1888, it represented the ideals of north v. south, professionalism v. amateurism. It was a direct rival of the Football Association, the southern based amateur bastion, and confirmed commercialism as the force which would shape the game's destiny.

Barnsley's widening travels came about largely through their involvement in a number of the new leagues. The Sheffield and District League, which was host to South Yorkshire teams, developed into the Sheffield Challenge Cup League, which the Saints played in until 1895. By then it was large enough to be broken down into Divisional play, with Barnsley in Division One. In 1895-96, the Midland League became Barnsley's main source of competition, but they also continued to play in the Sheffield Cup, later known as the Wharncliffe Cup League.

The club also signed up for a new United League in 1895, which was disallowed by the Football Association before it even kicked off. In 1897-98, they joined the Yorkshire League with Leeds, Bradford, Huddersfield, Doncaster Rovers, Hunslet and the reserves of Sheffield United and Wednesday. Barnsley Reserves, established under the name St. Peter's Swifts, played their games through the Barnsley Football Union and the Sheffield Alliance League.

Without the booming interest and increasing commercialism that fuelled the game, competition could not have existed at all these different levels. Not all seedlings in the greenhouse grew as proficiently as Barnsley, however, who while never championing their leagues (except for the minor Wharncliffe Cup in 1896) nearly always posted winning records over the season.

Barnsley's growth was secured, when others' was not, by performances beyond the playing field. It was in the committee rooms where groundwork for continued success was laid. Guest speaker at the club's first annual dinner was Mr J. S. Rose, Chairman of the Rugby Club for 21 years. There is no doubt he was invited by Reverend Preedy; the two of them maintained a friendship which must have begun with Preedy's introduction to the rugby club and to St. Mary's Church, and continued after Preedy left Barnsley to live in London. Rose complimented the club on having such good officers, and predicted that *"the large company present and the enthusiasm displayed meant that they intended to make their club a great success in the future."* Significantly, Rose was to become one of the most important figures in Barnsley, an Alderman, and Mayor of Barnsley. He was once voted third in a poll to decide the 12 most popular residents in Barnsley. Although he was *"up to his neck in rugby"* at the time of his introduction to St. Peter's football club, he must have been suitably impressed; he later became Chairman of Barnsley Football Club, and held the post for twenty-five years.

The early interest and connections of people like Rose were instrumental in bringing credibility and, eventually, much needed finances to the club. It is perhaps no coincidence that in direct reply to Mr. Rose's speech, club captain Joe Raley suggested that if townspeople could find the money, he and the Reverend Preedy would find the players.

Other notables recruited by Preedy to bolster the business side of the club were Guy and Arthur Senior. The Senior family were owners of Barnsley Brewery Company, and again from Preedy's introduction grew a long and beneficial relationship for Barnsley Football Club, even if at times it was to have its difficulties. The most obvious benefit to the club was acquiring the use of a field on property owned by the Seniors as a venue to play St. Peter's home games.

Adjoining the north side of Barnsley Brewery was a series of open fields in an area known as Oakwell, from which the famous Oakwell Ales took their name. This was the property owned by the Seniors which Preedy could see across the valley from the steps of St. Peter's Church. Whether the club played its very first games there is uncertain. It is known that the players changed in the Dove Inn, which was the club's early headquarters directly across Doncaster Road from St. Peter's. One account suggests that the team then played on a field near the Dove, but gives no specific detail. It is possible that the players walked over the railway line and across Pontefract Road to play on one of the Seniors' fields.

The Oakwell site certainly figures very early in the club's history. F. Lodge, a Barnsley Football Club Director writing in 'The Book of Football 1906' says that the Oakwell ground is the original club enclosure, but matchday programme notes from the 1923-24 season say, *"the original ground of the Club was the field adjoining the present Oakwell enclosure."* A 1937 matchday programme also reports that the first playing pitch was behind the 'low stand' of the current playing area; in other words, perhaps the flat area now under concrete as VIP parking at the back of the East Stand, or the parking lot behind the ORA Stand.

The reason for the move to the present stadium site was clear. Although visitors would complain about the playing surface of the first pitch, the gently sloping field above it where the Oakwell Stadium now stands was more attractive to the club not simply because of the field quality but because of its potential for accommodating larger numbers of paying spectators in a controlled setting. Gate receipts, at threepence per head for regular games, quickly became very important.

Another programme note from the 1937-38 season reports that *"But for (Preedy's) work, it is doubtful whether the Club would ever have found its home at Oakwell. His first application for the field adjoining the present one was turned down by Mr. Guy Senior, and in many subsequent interviews he met with no better success."*

It is said that Reverend Preedy then turned to Mrs. Senior, Arthur's wife. Tiverton Preedy was certainly a man who could charm ladies with ease when it came to extracting a contribution for one of his causes. He won Mrs. Senior

over and husband Arthur eventually consented to let St. Peter's have use of the vacant ground.

At the close of the second season, Arthur and Guy Senior were made vice-Presidents of Barnsley St. Peter's Football Club. At a meeting of the club on Tuesday, August 12th, 1890, the condition which Guy Senior had applied in letting the ground to the St. Peter's was finally made known: *"You can have the field so long as you behave yourselves!"*

Both on and off the field there were lots of adventures during the years of 'Tiverton Preedy's Rangers'. When St. Peter's travelled to play Heeley Olympic on October 27th, 1888, in the Sheffield Challenge Cup competition, the Barnsley players were forced to pay the same admission price as spectators to get into the ground before they could play. In an exciting game, Barnsley levelled the scores at 3-3, and their travelling supporters celebrated by hugging the local bobby so much they knocked his helmet off. On September 15th, 1888, the Saints played at Sheffield Ellesmere where an over-enthusiastic journalist delighted the Barnsley fans. He appeared on the field with pencil and notebook in hand and chased the play, dodging players and the ball as he scribbled down notes. On October 19th, 1889, it rained heavily at a cup-tie between St. Peter's and Sheffield Clinton. The referee attracted even more barracking than usual from the forty or so supporters who had made the trip from Barnsley; he ran the game carrying an open umbrella. However, he was happy to point out to the vocal Barnsley fans that he was enjoying the last laugh on them. St. Peter's lost 5-1.

In those days, the home team provided the referee and each club provided someone to run the line. At Park Grange, only two weeks after the Ellesmere game, the home-appointed referee allowed a goal by St. Peter's 'Dodger' Whyke to stand despite appeals for offside. Park Grange had appointed the referee so, disliking the job he was doing, they fired him. The replacement official didn't meet with St. Peter's approval, so they demanded another change. As the game closed with Barnsley 3-2 winners, the home team expressed dissatisfaction with Barnsley's choice of the third official. He let the game run eight minutes over time.

In the 1889-90 season, the Saints racked up their biggest ever score, a victory of 13-0 at home to Leeds Steelworkers. It somewhat made up for one result the previous year when the club went down in its biggest defeat, 12-0 to Staveley in the Second Round of the Sheffield Challenge Cup. Staveley, however, were regarded as one of the best teams in the country at the time.

Tiverton Preedy once recalled how the game was played in those days. *"I remember playing honest, robust and straightforward football,"* he said, *"when the sporting press were not frightened of seeing honest, good, sound, shoulder charging. Those were the days when we had a good charge and a knock head over heels. Those were the days when referees did not blow the whistle so often, and those were the days when football was real football and shoulder charging was real charging without any nasty tricks of the trade...."*

In a game against Ecclesfield in 1891, St. Peter's veteran 'Con' Needham fractured a shoulder shortly after the start of the game, but played through to the end, and in 1892 broke a leg playing against the same opponents. Tom Nixon dislocated his shoulder in a game against Rotherham United in 1892. Fred Woolhouse was knocked out by Wharton, Rotherham United's black goalkeeper at Clifton Park, Rotherham, in the same game and did not recover consciousness until he arrived back home in Cemetery Road, Barnsley, fifteen miles away. Jack Hellewell got a broken nose at Attercliffe. So much for honest shoulder charging!

The fierceness of competition on the field sometimes spilled over into players' tempers during play, inflamed the spectators, and set the scene for intense local rivalries. On November 19th 1887, in the 10th game of their first season, the Saints played at Gawber and came away 2-0 winners. Angry villagers rained a volley of stones at them. In the next to the last game of that season the Saints left the field in the second half of a game because of *"the questionable tactics"* of their opponents, Silkstone Common. In 1891, referee S.Allerton of Kilnhurst allowed a Mexborough goal which St. Peter's claimed was off-side. One Barnsley player hit the referee, and another left the field in protest. In 1898, the club posted a warning to spectators about violence towards referees at Oakwell.

The club's first keen rivalry was with Ardsley Old. The village of Ardsley supplied several teams to local competition, such as Ardsley Wanderers, Ardsley Nelson and Ardsley Woodman, but Ardsley Old were the top local club, and they quickly identified St. Peter's as a threat to their supremacy. Games against all Ardsley teams were "life and death struggles, neither side flinching in the least", even in the Saints' first year, reported one observer, when St. Peter's and Ardsley Old battled out two 0-0 draws.

The following year, when St. Peter's entered the Sheffield Challenge Cup for the first time, they were mistakenly drawn in the Junior Competition while Ardsley Old were drawn in the competition proper. There was a lot of derisive taunting of St. Peter's by Ardsley Old until the matter was straightened out, but feelings were already so high between the two clubs that Reverend Preedy decided they should not meet on the playing field at all during the 1888-1889 season.

This decision led to a brouhaha of accusations fanned by the local press. Preedy wrote a public explanation:

"SIR - For some weeks past, paragraphs have appeared in your football notes with reference to the relative positions of the Ardsley and Barnsley St. Peter's Football Clubs, and as your last week's issue contained a letter from an Ardsley supporter I feel it is time that we (St. Peter's) placed before the public our views on the subject.

"In the first place, we should not have the slightest objection to meet the Ardsley club in a friendly game; but I am sorry to say that, owing to the high party feeling at present existing among the supporters of the respective clubs, this is almost an impossibility in an ordinary club match.

"Again, at the commencement of the present season, I talked the matter of home and away matches over with our committee and two or three of the Ardsley players, and we all agreed that, under the circumstances, it would be better to let the fixture lapse for the present.

"However, rather than stand in the way of any possible benefit accruing to such a deserving institution as the Beckett Hospital, and also with a view of testing which club should hold the premier position in the district, the St. Peter's committee has authorised me to say that they are perfectly willing for their club to play Ardsley on neutral ground, with umpires and referee appointed by Mr. Haigh, the Secretary of the Sheffield and Hallamshire Football Association, on either the 30th of November or the 25th January, the profits of the match to be given to the Beckett Hospital. The best neutral ground I can suggest is the Queen's Ground, which, I have very little doubt, the proprietors would, if asked, give the use of for the occasion.

"I regret I am unable to advise my committee to consent to the match being played on the Ardsley ground, but I cannot satisfy myself that, judging from past experience, the conduct and language of a large portion of spectators would be such if the match was played there - i.e. on a party ground - as to be conducive of either a pleasant or a well-played game, and several of the Ardsley players agree with me in this.

"We cannot too strongly bear in mind that if we allow the football field to degenerate simply into a resort for people who will not conduct themselves aright, we shall lose the support of those people who encourage football for the game's sake, and who are its only true supporters.

"I am quite certain too that unless the committee of such clubs as Ardsley and St. Peter's - leading clubs in the district - use every endeavour to put down the disagreeable and offensive language too frequently heard on football fields, respectable people will have no alternative but to stay away altogether.

Tiverton Preedy."

As it turned out, Barnsley St. Peter's met Ardsley Old once that season in a fixture tacked onto the end of the list on April 22nd, 1889. They lost 3-1.

As Barnsley outgrew their squabble for local dominance with Ardsley, they grew into a rivalry with Mexborough. Mexborough were one of the top district teams outside of Sheffield, a prominence that Barnsley was rapidly challenging. Games between the two clubs generated tremendous interest for miles around. When they met in the 1893 Barnsley Charity Cup Final, which Barnsley won after a replay, special trains carried over 2,000 spectators to the games.

The rivalry came to a head in 1894 when Barnsley won 3-1 at Mexborough in a league encounter. Riotous scenes at the end of the game resulted in Mexborough being reported to the Sheffield Association, who staged an enquiry. The home team were ordered to pay one pound to Barnsley for expenses, and offered a public apology. The Association decided that one female spectator had to be banned from Mexborough's ground, and a reward of one pound was offered for any information leading to the conviction of more offenders.

Although league play provided the club with its bread and butter, cup competition was much sought after jam. During these years Barnsley made their debut in the English Cup competition (now known as the F.A. Cup) and became giant killers for the first time. Their first campaign, in 1893-94, fizzled out in the first qualifying round with a 5-4 loss to Gainsbro' Trinity after the Trinity winger, Ward, thumped the ball into the net with his hand for the winning goal, and Barnsley had their late equalizer disallowed. But the following year, Barnsley launched a cup run that brought them national attention.

Two and a half thousand people showed up at Oakwell to see Barnsley knock out Grantham Rovers in the first qualifier, then Leeds were disposed of 8-0, and Mexbro' after a replay. Worksop were defeated 3-1 to bring on Liverpool of the Football League in the First Round Proper at Oakwell. At the end of ninety minutes in front of five thousand people the scores were level at 1-1. For reasons best known to himself, the referee decided to play extra time. Liverpool scored again, but Barnsley's protests about the unofficial extra time were upheld by an F.A. Consultative Committee and the game went to a replay at Liverpool, Barnsley thereby becoming perhaps the only team to lose an F.A. Cup tie and not be immediately eliminated from the competition. It did not do them much good. In the replay they slumped 4-0.

The following season they failed to get past their first game again, but in 1896-97 Barnsley reached the first round proper once more with an upset of Football Leaguers Lincoln City, winning 2-1 away from home, after first despatching Hunslet and the Sheffield Club. Their reward for this giant killing act was a meeting with Derby County, whose pedigree players trounced the Oakwell men 8-1.

Appearances in the first round proper of the F.A. Cup represent a milestone in the club's history, but they could not have advanced that far without learning the art of winning in the proving grounds of local competition. Curiously enough, rugby football was once again involved when Barnsley St. Peter's set about securing their dominance of the local football scene, and Preedy was again at the heart of it.

In 1890 local rugby clubs put up a cup for competition, but they upset the 'footer' crowd with the manner they raised subscriptions to cover costs. For one thing, they promoted their competition by falsely implying in the newspapers that Barnsley St. Peter's would be competing for the trophy.

This incident prompted Reverend Preedy to get together with the leaders of the Ardsley club and propose that the local association clubs should have a cup of their own to compete for. As a result, on March 19th, 1891, the Barnsley Charity Association Football Union held its inaugural meeting at the Kings Head Hotel, and the purchase of a silver cup costing 75 pounds, and weighing 140 ounces, was arranged. St. Peter's once again demonstrated how influential they had quickly become on the local scene. Not only did the initiative come from Reverend Preedy, but he was made the Union's first Secretary, and W. Raley, brother of the St. Peter's captain, was made its first president. Reverend Preedy used the inaugural meeting and the launching of the cup competition to make a speech in which he again emphasized his determination to see that Barnsley became a footballing centre.

The Barnsley Charity Cup was first played for in the 1891-1892 season, with Barnsley determined to take it at the first attempt. After defeating Wombwell Main (away), Kilnhurst (home), and Hoyland Town and Parkgate after replays, St. Peter's entered the first Barnsley Charity Cup Final on March 19th, 1892, at Shaw Lane Cricket Ground, Barnsley. St. Peter's took the game seriously, and put their players through special training for a full week. Nobody gave their opponents much of a chance, not even their own followers, but Ecclesfield scored a shock 3-2 victory that sent the local football world reeling with surprise. Barnsley officials had been so confident about winning that they had hired a band to play their team triumphantly back to Cup headquarters at the King's Head in town; instead, Ecclesfield led the procession to the tune of 'See the Conquering Hero Comes' at Barnsley's expense; literally!

The under-rated Ecclesfield crew so impressed Barnsley that Preedy went out and signed six of them over to St. Peter's ready for the start of the new season, along with another half dozen new players. With the pick of the new signings in the team, Barnsley beat Kilnhurst and Wombwell Town to advance again to the Charity Cup Final, still determined to land the trophy. To tighten the squad in the game against Mexbro' and prevent a repeat of the previous year's disaster, they signed a goalkeeper called Hadfield from Sheffield Wednesday. He played an important role in holding Mexbro' to one goal in the final and in the replay, then returned to the Owls.

Barnsley scored four in the replay game to lift the trophy after the initial match had ended in a 1-1 draw. Celebrations went on until late at night.

The following year Barnsley won the cup again, defeating Wombwell Town 6-3, and sealed their position as the district's top club. These Charity Cup victories crowned an era. The 1893 win was the club's first championship, establishing a large following for the club in town and generating lots of excitement and attention throughout the district. The 1894 win marked the club's departure from the competition to seek bigger rewards elsewhere; local competition had become small fry.

This period saw the end of another era too. In 1893 Tiverton Preedy said farewell to Barnsley and headed for London to advance his church career with a curacy at St. Clement's Church, City Road, Islington. In 1897, he moved to the newly founded All Saints Mission in Pentonville and continued his sporting work, not through football, for there was little open space to play in the slums of London, but through wrestling and boxing and the foundation of the Ashdown Athletic Club, with a full-sized boxing ring and two billiard tables under the crypt of his church.

What Preedy accomplished in London demonstrates the kind of man that St. Peter's football club began life with. The Ashdown Athletic club produced Olympic wrestlers and national boxing champions from a poor working class neighbourhood; Preedy became a respected Prebendary of St. Paul's Cathedral. There is not a single account of the early days of Barnsley Football Club in which Preedy is not mentioned with respect. It took a special charisma not only to launch St. Peter's Football Club but to see the Association game firmly established in Barnsley. Without his spark the Football League and the F.A. Cup may never have become part of the town's history.

The Barnsley Football Union which Preedy helped found gave him a purse of sixty pounds to send him off to London. The players, as working men did for the next thirty-five years, found him unpretentious, straightforward and supportive. They saw him off with unpretentious working men's gifts; a walking stick, a pipe and a tobacco pouch.

When Preedy left for London, his ties with the club were far from severed. On a Saturday evening, the Reverend would come out of his study in White Lion Street, Pentonville, in his shirtsleeves, squinting up and down the pavement with steely blue eyes, peering through the smokey haze of a Gold Flake cigarette jammed into the corner of his mouth. A couple of boys would be hanging around waiting for the errand that was coming. He would call one over, give him a few 'coppers', and send him off to a vendor at the corner of the street to pick up the late edition of a newspaper. Folding the paper over, Preedy would stand in the street and scan the 'Stop Press' column for Barnsley's results before returning inside, hopefully with a smile, but sometimes with a grunt of disappointment. He complained to anyone who would

listen that Barnsley never got a fair *"write-up"* in the southern press.

When Barnsley played a match in the London area he would try and get to the game and visit with any old friends travelling with the club. After a game in the capital Barnsley players were invited to his Mission to mingle with the crowds at his Saturday night boxing bouts; among the cockneys they bumped into Lords, Admirals and statesmen, friends of Preedy's from London's West End. Occasionally, Preedy enjoyed a trip north to watch Barnsley at the 'Well, and he hated to miss a good cup-tie. Before every F.A.Cup tie up until his death in 1928, he sent the team a good luck telegram. He was a guest at the 1912 Cup Final and the ball from that conquest of West Bromwich Albion was proudly displayed in his London study after being donated to him by the club. Although Preedy left Barnsley in 1893, obviously something about Barnsley never left him.

With his departure the club's last real connection with St. Peter's Church was severed. The advance of professionalism and playing success on the field had already driven the club way beyond its beginnings. And so, in the summer of 1895, Mr. E. Jaeger led a *"small army"* in support of changing the club's name. No-one at the church, he said, except the President, was any longer connected with the club, and if they broke the affiliation with St. Peter's the objection against playing games on Good Friday would be removed. They ought to be the town's club, and have the mayor as President, and call themselves Barnsley Town Association Football Club. Mr. D. J. Barron agreed with most of what Mr. Jaeger said, but thought they should be simply Barnsley Association Football Club, and not have the word 'Town' in the title. The club's ruling committee voted 18 to 11 in favour of Mr. Barron's suggestion, but the name could not be adopted immediately on a point of order; it was not on the agenda.

The name change failed again the following year, when a bid to follow Mr. Jaeger's suggestion in electing the Mayor as President failed by 28 votes to 20. The club had to wait until the following year, 1897, for a name change when Mr. I. Fox rose to make the motion. His only idea in changing the name, he said, was to put the club in its proper place. There was no Barnsley Club, and so lest somebody got the name before they did, he thought they should take the opportunity and put themselves in proper position by name as well as by play. At the beginning of the 1897-98 season, St. Peter's officially became known as Barnsley Football Club.

The era of 'Tiverton Preedy's Rangers' had drawn to a close. The club was now Barnsley F.C. *"frum t'tarn"*, acknowledged as a Barnsley institution. They played on a field with a covered grandstand, attracted thousands of paying spectators, played in national competition, and brought some of the biggest names in English football to Oakwell. Only one year later, the club that had begun life ten years before as a rumbustious church football team was a member of the elite Football League.

CHAPTER 3

✤ PIONEERS OF PROFESSIONALISM ✤

When Reverend Tiverton Preedy organized the first Barnsley St. Peter's football team in 1887 he was looking to provide an interest that promoted his social work in the parish, not start a commercial enterprise. His only stated goal was to make the best job of it that he could, but the changing nature of the times meant that making the best job quickly meant coming to terms with financial reality. There was to be no escaping the early importance of professionalism if the football team was to amount to something more than just a day out for the choir. If you wanted a decent player on your team you had to recruit him, and to recruit him you had to find him a little something to make it worth his while. That's what everybody did.

Preedy might have been able to suggest eternal salvation as a reward but other clubs offered more immediate paybacks. Although professionalism may have started out at Barnsley as the promise of a little charity here and there it quickly had to match the harder terms on offer everywhere else. Fortunately, Preedy was a man of the times who apparently saw no conflict with either his religious or sporting ambitions when working men took a little extra on the side to make life more comfortable.

His post as Financial Secretary grew from the recording of subscriptions to the proffering of a hat for collections, and ended with carefully ledgered payments to documented professional players, even before the team ever kicked a ball in organized league play. Barnsley St. Peter's may have had a church connection but it was undoubtedly a professional club in a small way almost from its inception.

Professionalism however did not mean the same then as it does now. The club was not professional for many years by today's standards; its history is littered with missed trains, broken down charabancs, players failing to show for games, teams taking the field short of players, and erstwhile spectators pulling on a jersey to level the numbers. Neither was it professional in the sense that it paid its players a living wage, or provided them with their main source of employment. In 1892, when Scotsman Alec Black signed for the club, he came to town primarily to follow his occupation as a schoolteacher, not to play football. Black, by the way, demonstrated his professionalism by walking 25 miles to Glossop when he missed the train to play a Christmas Day game. The legendary Tom Nixon is also known to have had a 'day job', because in 1897 the possibility of it preventing him from playing for Barnsley was dragged into his contract negotiations.

Professionalism in those days simply meant any kind of payment made to a player. However the officers of the club did have a professional outlook in another sense in that they had the highest aims and the determination to see them through.

The players who trotted out with Preedy at Manor House to start the club's first season in 1887 were not the kind seeking to make money. They *"took delight in their club's welfare"* and wanted no more than a good afternoon's sport. Many of the early players paid subscriptions to the club and bought their own uniforms. *"The pioneers of soccer at St. Peter's were a band of young men,"* recalled Preedy. *"They didn't trouble about 'gates'; what they wanted were goals. Spectators could come and were welcome. The lads were pleased to see them, but they did not in any way depend upon them."* Yet among the first real players to arrive at the club, and displace the earliest pioneers, were players with known professional backgrounds.

Tom Nixon, for example, was lured from Ardsley after St. Peter's had played only a few games. It was a bit premature to suggest he was swayed by results. Maybe Preedy's silver tongue enticed him, but surely it didn't get him to stay for thirteen years in the face of offers from clubs all over the north of England. Players like Tom Hirst (1887) and Sam Hunt (1889) were not whistled for at the top of a pit shaft either, they came with solid playing careers, and a history of being paid for their services on the field.

Newspaper columnist 'Argus' writing in 1898 confirms that no large sums of money were immediately available in the earliest days of the club's existence, but some players were rewarded with offers of employment and small handouts

Preedy recalled that *"the first time we made a collection we got 2s-6½d "* (13p), but fairly soon the collection had to become a bit more organized. The club showed a deficit of sixteen pounds on its first season. Once St. Peter's started playing outside of Barnsley they found other clubs charging for admission to the game, and it was not long before 3d. became the standard donation to watch St. Peter's on the fields of Oakwell. This is one reason why, by the 1890-91 season, after just three years of play, St. Peter's had managed to grow from a neighbourhood team to an established district club with a reputation big enough to attract talent from all over Yorkshire. Without income at the gate, they could not have done it.

By then the players obviously considered themselves a professional outfit. Bad weather forced postponement of some games, and they came up with this little ditty about themselves:

"We've got no work to do-oo-oo
We've got no work to do-oo-oo
We're all froze out, poor football pro's,
We've got no work to do."

By the start of the 1890's, and Barnsley's first foray into league play, partisan support and a winning performance could no longer be the only motivations at any club if it was to survive. The presence of professional players required income to pay them. Revenue, which Preedy says his pioneers disdained, now became critical. Its importance can be judged by intense competition among clubs to earn 'gate money' and by Barnsley's sorry record of unbalanced balance sheets.

The eighteen-nineties was the age of the 'protest', an attempt by a club to cancel out a result it did not like on the basis of a technicality. Although pride was often at stake, the 'protest' more often indicated how desperately cut-throat clubs could be when threatened by the loss of revenue. The protest was a commonplace tactic used to try and increase a club's income, by using any excuse to try and get a result overturned or a game replayed, and stay in a knock-out competition until the more lucrative final rounds. This was in the days before League play became a club's bread and butter when contests of elimination brought in the crowds and generated the season's real excitement in an otherwise steady diet of 'friendlies'. Usually, protests centred on the eligibility of players appearing for the other team, but no claim on the authorities was too bizarre if it meant not losing a game and so remaining in competition, because continuing in competition meant not only recognized success but more income.

Barnsley St. Peter's, for example, were losing a cup-tie at Kilnhurst by five goals to two on January 7th 1893, when one of the Barnsley players had the idea of protesting to the referee that the ground was unfit for play because it was covered by several inches of snow. Amazingly, the referee upheld the objection, and declared the game that day a 'friendly'. When the cup-tie was replayed, Barnsley won by one goal with almost the last kick of the match in disputed extra time. In revenge, Kilnhurst launched a protest about three of St. Peter's players, but the complaint was dismissed. Regardless of who progressed, the clubs had already doubled their takings by playing the fixture twice and generating a lot of interest.

On November 7th 1891, before a first round Sheffield Cup-tie against old rivals Ardsley at Oakwell, some of the opponents' followers inspected all the goal-lines and touch-lines around the playing field. When the referee came out the Ardsley captain lodged a protest that three of the goalposts were the wrong height and asked for them to be measured. So keen were they to have an excuse for another game that they lodged a protest even before the game started. The referee of course did not have a tape measure with him, but asked for one to be available at half-time. At half-time, the referee and both captains went out and measured the goalposts, finding that three of them were fine, but one was actually two inches too high. The referee instructed play to continue to the end of the game, which Barnsley won 3-2, but as far as Ardsley were concerned, it was not over. The protest went to a hearing.

The chairman of the commission which heard Ardsley's complaint was the same referee who had officiated at the game, Mr. J.C.Clegg, a widely respected man and President of the Sheffield and Hallamshire Football Association. Representing Ardsley, was Mr. Ward, and in Barnsley's corner, the Reverend Tiverton Preedy. The proceedings show how seriously clubs took their protests.

Initially Mr.Ward objected to Barnsley goalkeeper Sammy Harrison, claiming he was ineligible to play in the Oakwell fixture because he had played for St. Peter's against Hexthorpe the previous season while still a professional on Ardsley's books. On hearing this complaint, Reverend Preedy pulled out a letter from the English Football Association stating they knew about the matter and were prepared to overlook it. Mr. Clegg turned to his committee and said, *"Can we, as the committee of the Sheffield and Hallamshire Association, take any step in opposition to the English Association?"* No-one made any motion otherwise, and so the first objection was dismissed.

The second objection was the height of the goalposts. Mr. Clegg gave his account to the Committee in his capacity as referee of the game, and asked whether the Committee considered the match ought to be re-played or awarded to Ardsley. The Committee conversed for a few moments, but again declined to make any motion, so Mr. Clegg, this time as Chairman, announced that the second objection was also dismissed.

Mr.Ward then tried to make another objection but Mr. Clegg stopped him, saying that he had not given prior notice of it, and therefore if Mr. Ward wanted to go ahead with it, it would cost him ten shillings. Reverend Preedy, perhaps tongue-in-cheek at the prospect of his rival having to come up with the money, said he did not mind if Mr. Ward wanted to proceed with the case that evening as he did not want to be coming to Sheffield every week. The case was closed and Ardsley went away not only sore at losing the tie to a hated rival, but miffed that they were out of the cup and had lost out on future income.

To Barnsley, the result of this hearing was so important that St. Peter's secretary Sam Ruston immediately sent off a telegram from Sheffield to the Dove Inn at Barnsley: *"Ardsley lost. Would not move any resolution in respect to it. (Cup) Draw will follow. Ruston"*

While rivalry was obviously an important issue, Sam Ruston was eager to send news of the draw back to St. Peter's administration in Barnsley for the same reason that small clubs look to the F.A. Cup today; they would be keeping their fingers crossed for a money-spinner in the next round as well.

Perhaps the most famous protest of all occurred when Barnsley were drawn against Liverpool in the English Cup in 1894. Liverpool were a highly regarded 'big club', and Barnsley were still not even a Football League team. Liverpool did not want to play at Oakwell. Presumably they felt more assured of passing to the next round if they played at Anfield Road. Shortly after the draw was made they lobbied the Football Association to see if there was any way they could avoid playing at Barnsley, claiming Oakwell was unsuitable for a cup-tie because of *"the privacy of the enclosure, surface, and touch-lines."* An F.A. Emergency Committee visited the ground, and Liverpool's protest was dismissed because it was found to have not been made within the proper time frame allowed by the rules.

Liverpool then telegraphed the F.A. with another protest, this time against Barnsley's practice of charging boys half price admission. F.A. rules said that admission to cup-ties had to be sixpence, and Barnsley were preparing to charge boys only threepence. Barnsley received the following letter from Mr. W.E.Barclay, the Liverpool secretary:
"We object to boys being admitted for less than sixpence for a very good reason. You know as well as I do that your ground will not enable a large crowd to see the game. Why, then, should boys take up the best places at 3d? On a ground like ours, where there is plenty of room to spare, it would be different."

St. Peter's stuck to their guns and insisted they were going to charge the boys half price, resulting in another letter from Mr. Barclay:
"The Council of the Football Association has decided (please see end of Cup rules) that the minimum charge for admission shall be 6d. I am surprised to hear from our treasurer that after being refused, you are going to do so. Please note that we shall require half gate at 6d. per head after the legal deductions. If you like to admit boys at 3d., you must bear the cost."

If there was any doubt that this issue was not about money, Barclay's telegrams cleared it up. The Saints opted for the goodwill of their customers and did bear the cost, receiving national publicity in their David and Goliath battle with Liverpool. Interestingly, Barnsley drew a 5,000 attendance to Oakwell and the replay at

Liverpool attracted only 3,000. No doubt local passions in Barnsley were aroused by Liverpool's heavy handed attitude. The two games grossed about £210.

Liverpool's attempts to change the venue of the first game was not an unusual occurrence. It was fairly commonplace for a wealthy club to change the venue of a cup-tie to their home ground to secure passage to the next round or guarantee a larger attendance. However, this was usually done by offering financial incentives to the smaller club, not by protesting, a move taken by Liverpool which the press reported as *"unsportsmanlike."*

In 1897, when Barnsley drew Derby County at home in the first round proper of the English Cup, Derby immediately enquired how much it would take for the Club to switch the fixture away from Oakwell. Taking a sound negotiating posture, club Secretary Walter Taylor wrote back: *"In reply to your telegram, my committee instruct me to say that no offer which you may make will induce them to play the cup-tie at Derby."* Derby counter-offered with a guarantee of £80, plus half the gate. Barnsley came back with a request for £100 and half the gate, and a deal was struck. The club came away with a badly needed financial boost, having appeared before a crowd of 8,000, but this time only after damaging the goodwill of their supporters.
"The Saints of Blackest Barnsley,
who have sold their choice of ground,.
Will be missing from the contest
when we reach the second round.
And Derby, it is possible, will give those Barnsley men
A double-figure thrashing, with a margin, say, of ten."

The poet was ever so close, Derby won 8-1. Cup-ties of all kinds were a major source of income and helped to keep the Barnsley club afloat. The thrill of knock-out cup competition drew good crowds and brought the opportunity of multiple encounters, each one more profitable than the last as the club progressed. In fact, sizeable takings were sometimes considered as much a victory as a win on the field. The press, for example, would always report the amount taken at the gate as a matter of public interest. Losing in the early rounds of a cup competition reduced a club's means of attracting and keeping professional players for the coming season, and therefore reduced its ability to compete, and, ultimately to survive.

The balance sheet of the protested Ardsley cup-tie of 1891, mentioned above, read thus:

Tickets sold	£5-11s -0d
Gate receipts	£9-15s-10d
Gross Total:	£15-6s-10d
Expenses.	
(Police, printing, etc.)	£ 3- 8s - 0d
Net Total:	£11-18s-10d

Ardsley's and St.Peter's Share: £5-19s-5d each.

In other words, the clubs took home from a first round local cup-tie about the equivalent of what was then a miner's monthly income. This equates, at the time of writing, to several hundred pounds.

Just how quickly financial considerations of the game mushroomed is shown by looking at cup-tie takings over the next few years. On March 18th and 23rd, 1893, when Barnsley conquered Mexborough at the Queen's Ground in the final of the Barnsley Charity Cup - which went to a replay - the combined takings for the two games was just over £266. That converts to a gross of about £25,000 at mid-1990's prices. At the 1897 Derby cup-tie mentioned above, Barnsley took home as their share £184 (about £18,000).

Obviously there was money in football, and obviously St. Peter's was up to the neck in it. The amounts involved increased rapidly, but even though gate receipts soared from the tens of pounds to the hundreds, and attendance figures climbed into thousands, most of the money that flowed into Barnsley Football Club through the turnstiles flowed out in expenses just as fast.

The main reason was increased player costs. Barnsley had sixty-four of them on their books by 1891, some receiving payments, some requiring outfitting with uniforms, all requiring travel to games. At the end of the 1893 season, payments 'To and For Players', amounted to £314; but the club took only £356 at the gate. Other expenses easily tipped the club into the red.

The more success that was achieved, the greater became the price of maintaining it. Once payments became the expected norm, successful players demanded higher returns. Harry Davis can be used as an example. When the club started out, players came and went freely and were satisfied with a few shillings to cover expenses. In 1897, ten years later, club secretary Alec Black broke new ground by persuading the committee to let him spend £5 to secure Davis's transfer from Ardsley, with Barnsley's first openly recorded payment of a transfer fee. The club thought this was a lot of money to spend *"but with many misgivings they gave way to their impetuous and extravagant secretary"*, says an old programme. Davis's contract was for two pounds ten shillings a week in the first season, two pounds a week summer wages, and three pounds a week in his second season. Top players' earnings were obviously getting closer to a living wage, and Davis was a top player. He was transferred to Sheffield Wednesday for £175, and went on to play for England.

Earning opportunity did not pass established players by either. Tom Nixon, who in earlier days once said he *"meant to stick with this club"*, wandered off to Darwen in Lancashire for a year. When he came back for the 1897-98 season, before a ball was kicked he publicly

announced that the club and himself had not agreed terms, and further, *"he positively declined to play with the Barnsley team unless he received a proper salary."*

Things were so bad in 1895-96 that midway through the season, when the club realized they were not taking enough money at the gate to meet all their commitments to players, they gave notice to three of them in an attempt to cut expenses. One of them, Drummond, accepted the economics. Rather than be transferred to another club he offered to play for Barnsley for expenses only.

In addition to player costs, a continual rise in the level of competition forced the club into ground improvements. Money from the Liverpool cup run of 1893-94 was converted into Oakwell's first grandstand, on the 'top side' of the ground. The structure was constructed in wood in three tiers, with a corrugated iron back and roof; it blew over in a gale not long after being put up. Money from the 1896 Derby County cup run was used to re-roof the grandstand and provide the first press box.

These kinds of demands on the club's purse were reflected in financial statements year after year. At the end of the club's last season of friendly competition, in 1890, Barnsley St. Peter's had a deficit of only £6. This amount increased seven-fold in four years, and two years later, it was £150. Friendly games no longer covered their costs and were abandoned as fund-raisers. To make up the difference the club tried selling subscription memberships and holding bazaars and smoking concerts, but income, however it was earned, never seemed to want to meet expenditure.

In 1894, the annual meeting saw heated discussion over the question of finances. One member alleged that the club was not run on a proper business footing and moved that Barnsley F.C. should become a limited company. The suggestion was derisively shouted down. How could they go public with an overdraft and no security?

The move towards full blown professionalism moved one step nearer when the club was elected to the Football League in 1898. The change in status meant not just a leap in playing standards but also in finances. Club members knew that payments to players would have to rise, and that the club would face added expense in ground improvements and travel arrangements without being able to guarantee enough success to secure attendances any better than they already were in the Midland League. It was the first time the cry *"they can't afford. to go up"* was heard around Oakwell, but certainly not the last.

With only four days to spare before a Football League meeting which would decide the League membership for the coming season, the Barnsley club held a special Committee meeting behind closed doors on 23rd May,

1898. The motion to apply for membership of the Football League was passed by only 8 votes to 7. The importance of finances was emphasized when the club announced it had *"turned professional"*, and put up a guarantee fund of £800 as credentials to support its membership petition. The Football League existed as a commercial proposition and the 'professional' tag was essential even though it simply meant that the club openly acknowledged it had a payroll. Payments to players were regularized instead of cash contracts being offered to some and expense money to others. Using this expression told the world that Barnsley Football Club was serious about its ambitions and organized on the right kind of footing to do business in the Football League. In practical terms, it had been professional for years.

Barnsley's application was helped by the fact that the Football League had decided to expand in 1898 and four vacancies were available in the Second Division. Bottom-placed Darwen in the 1897-98 season were re-elected and eight clubs clamoured for the remaining three places. New Brighton polled 30 votes, Glossop earned 24 and Barnsley got 10, each more than the remaining five applicants.

Joe Greaves
Barnsley player 1898-1902

Once in the Second Division the inevitable next step of becoming a limited company was completed on July 9th, 1900, when the club's officials realised their personal credit was in danger. By this time, Barnsley F.C.'s overdraft at the bank had risen to over £500, and the officials had personally guaranteed it. The opening capital was fixed at £1,000 with shares offered at ten shillings (50p) each. The future directors of the company went from door to door and raised about half the start-up capital, but the town was not really interested in investing in Barnsley Football Club Limited. To make the scheme float, Mr. Senior covered the remaining half of the capital and personally guaranteed the club's overdraft at the bank.

With this move, and the club's presence in the Second Division of the Football League, Barnsley F.C. confirmed its existence as a thoroughly professional football club and commercial business. It was set on a course that would carry it through the next century. From its very first days the club was barely ahead of the wolf at the door and never quite able to get ahead of the pack on the field either. Barnsley F.C. had begun life in a vicious circle which would dominate many of the next hundred years, chasing itself financially without ever being quite able to catch up.

J. BETHUNE

Signed for Barnsley in 1906, he was to become an influential player.

CHAPTER 4

✤ MILKING THE CASH COW ✤

When Barnsley Football Club entered the Football League, the timbers for a successful launch had been laid in Tiverton Preedy's era; few adjustments were needed to trim the sails to a cut they carried for most of the next hundred years. But after the hurly-burly of football's explosion at the end of the nineteenth century, the pace of progress began to slow and as Barnsley drifted into the twentieth century their own advance was in danger of being becalmed. In fact, they might have floundered altogether had not an astute Scotsman, namely John McCartney, stepped up to the helm.

The biggest change in Association Football during the early part of the century was the introduction of a manager with responsibility for the team. In this, Barnsley Football Club were among the pioneers. When John McCartney was appointed team manager at the beginning of the 1901-02 season, it was at the start of a trend which much more illustrious clubs took many years to follow. While Manchester United, for example, appointed J.E.Magnall as their first manager in 1906, Aston Villa, among football's most prominent early teams, never appointed a manager until 1958. Others such as Everton, Blackburn Rovers, and Newcastle United waited until the twenties and thirties. For Barnsley, hiring McCartney as manager was a move which established them in the twentieth century, saved them from extinction, and ultimately paved the way for their F.A.Cup successes at the end of the decade.

Early football clubs, such as Barnsley St. Peter's, were run by a committee which attended to all matters of player affairs, including team selection. As clubs became more professional and were turned into limited companies, the board of Directors took over the role of the committee. In some cases, a Chairman whose money kept the club afloat became a complete autocrat in all matters off the field and on. Aston Villa never appointed a team manager because of domineering chairman Will Cuff, for example. At Barnsley however, where the Directors were small town tradespeople, no one member of the Board had deep enough pockets or sufficient influence to take the whole club by the scruff of the neck.

Across the country, Boards of Directors at emerging professional football clubs faced up to the same dilemma. Their Directors were, by and large, men who had arrived at their position because they had the luxury of their own full-time businesses and enjoyed the sociality and prominence that football connections gave them. While they knew the inside-out of brewing, drapery or grocery worlds, they were often naive about the business of football, which was a new and uncharted territory. Perhaps their involvement in the game had begun as a hobby, but the growth of the game soon placed such pressures on them that they were forced to step back and start to delegate the affairs involved in running a club.

Club Secretaries became Directors' workhorses. They became most involved in player affairs, acting as a liaison between players and management. Their role evolved into Secretary/Manager, but in most cases the Board still retained rights over team selection and other important decisions. This was the case at Barnsley before Arthur Fairclough offered his resignation as Secretary at the end of the 1900-01 season. Fairclough, however, was not resigning as a result of personal difficulties. He had the foresight to make his resignation conditional on the acceptance of John McCartney as a manager with full control of team affairs, and became a Director himself.

Another dilemma facing Directors, as attendances and press coverage increased, was dealing with public attention which more often than not was unfavourable towards them. The Secretary/Manager grew to be the Directors' spokesperson to the public as well. This also became McCartney's role. When the club sold his star players he was called on to answer to the public on behalf of the club.

The idea to give McCartney a free rein was as much common sense as it was ground-breaking. Neither Fairclough nor any other member of the Board at that time had played the game professionally, but McCartney, after arriving at Oakwell as a player from Luton Town for Barnsley's first League season in 1898-99, was a hardened and accomplished professional whose 'stout heartedness' quickly marked him as a team leader and club favourite.

McCartney began his own playing career at the age of fourteen with Cartvale, in Renfrewshire. He captained the Scottish Corinthians against Sunderland and was a member of the Glasgow Rangers team in the English Cup. He signed with Newton Heath (Manchester United) as a professional and spent three more years with Luton Town, the first club in the metropolitan area to employ professional footballers. A hefty full-back who made 70 appearances in two years for Barnsley, scoring four goals, he became team captain before breaking a leg against Blackpool in September 1900. The fracture prematurely finished his career; he played only once again after that.

In those days, the role of team manager was different from today. This was largely because of the way the game was played; there were no tactics as we understand them and managers were not usually held responsible for the way a team played, except when a Board needed a scapegoat for total failure. It was understood that, by and large, players won and lost games by themselves. Although football's modern framework was falling into place through rule changes and the relentless march of professionalism, the amateur notion of each man simply giving his best for the team prevailed.

By 1901, wooden posts and crossbars had nets to give a better indication of when the ball had gone into the goal. Referees with whistles and two linesmen ran the games, awarding penalty kicks, two-handed throw-ins, and free-kicks for unfair play and illegal handling of the ball. Players wore shorts, long socks and shinpads. But perhaps surprisingly, until 1912, goalkeepers were allowed to handle the ball anywhere on the field.

Despite the fairly modern appearance of the game, the spirit in which it was played still reflected the sport's amateur beginnings when it was not appropriate to be seen to try too hard to win. At Tottenham Hotspur, a Luton team which had included a younger John McCartney was attacked by supporters of the home club for trying too hard to beat their favourites. Teams rose and fell on individual skill, which was honourable, but not by intricate teamwork, which was still unexplored.

The only team strategy was to kick the ball forwards as much as possible; players chased it in a cavalry charge, dribbling to their opponents goal in numbers, and the best men won the stampede. The only real development in the previous thirty years, introduced by Scots, had been the spread of players across the field, encouraging the notion of passing the ball more, and breaking up the one big scrimmage that used to last an entire game. It was a very simple, direct style of play which required a lot of fitness but no special instruction. You had to be strong, fast, and have good endurance. Technical ability, such as dribbling and shooting, was felt to be God-given, not something to be learned. While fitness was something that could be built up in training, organized skill development was never even considered.

Even in 1912, when Barnsley won the F.A.Cup, training consisted of little more than hard discipline and stamina-building. Retired army sergeant Bill Norman, who was first introduced to the club by McCartney in January 1904, had never played the game and couldn't even lace up a football, but was a stickler for military-style preparedness. When Norman barked, *"Report at 10 o'clock!"* no-one dared be a minute after. He drilled the players in preparation for the 1912 Cup Final not with a ball but with 50 or 60 laps of the field in a morning, and back for more in the afternoon, ten miles at a time. To add a little variety to their routine, he marched the players for miles over the moors around Penistone.

What McCartney brought to the club as manager was not then the superior tactical knowledge or motivational skills that would be expected today. In fact it is likely that he spent little time watching his own team play. Once the team had been pinned to the notice board on Friday, his responsibility to the players was done. On game days he was likely to be out scouting for new talent. The line between management and worker was as clearly drawn at

the football club in those days as it was in the colliery yard. A manager at Oakwell belonged in an office, wearing waistcoat and watch chain, just as much as his counterpart did at Barnsley Main. As the colliery manager did not fraternize with the miners, so the Barnsley manager did not wear football kit and mix with his players. With such little emphasis on tactics, he had no need to build a relationship with them. Instead of travelling to a game with the team, the manager found himself more often than not alone in a railway carriage on the way to make a new signing. And that was where McCartney's strength lay. He had the ability to locate and recruit raw talent both by his strong network of football connections built across a lifetime in the game and by the canny judgement of his own eye.

The importance of McCartney's three-year contribution as manager to Barnsley's existence, and ultimately good fortune, can only be appreciated by looking once more at the club's books where red continued to be an all too popular colour of ink. Entry to the Second Division of the Football League did not bring any financial windfall, but only made worse the problems of balancing expense against income. After one year in the Football League the club showed a deficit of £256, and by the end of its second year the deficit had more than doubled to £521. League football continued to produce insufficient takings at the gate to meet the club's every day running costs, and those costs continued to become ever greater.

In 1908, the club needed to make £150 per week to break even but could only manage £100 to £120 per week over the League season. As fast as money poured in, it flowed out of two ever-open taps - ground improvements and player expenses. Just as much as in pre-League days, the club relied on good Cup runs to butter its bread. Until 1910 cup takings were thin on the ground and what there was invariably went straight into ground upkeep.

As part of the conditions of Barnsley's entry to the League in 1898, the club had to guarantee some ground improvements, and the same condition occurred again in 1900 when the club had to apply for re-election, following a finish of third place from bottom. In addition to these mandated developments, the club also recognized that Oakwell would have to be upgraded to make conditions safer and more attractive for paying customers, and to increase capacity. Although Oakwell had been the club's playing arena since almost the very beginning, the scope of the developments meant that it was by no means cut and dried that Oakwell would remain Barnsley F.C.'s permanent home. With one eye to the future, the club's management considered other alternatives. When the expense of making changes to enter the League came up, Col.Arthur Senior suggested that the club should take over the lower part of Queen's Ground instead. His plan was for Barnsley F.C. to rent the field, pay 10% of the costs of preparing a new playing surface with grandstands, and allow the proprietors to make money by having rights over the sale of refreshments. But a deal could not be worked out and the first Second Division campaign in the club's history opened as previous seasons had, at Oakwell.

After re-election, the club once more looked long and hard at putting more money into the Oakwell ground. Buildings and land adjoining Queen's Road became available. The property was occupied by the Conservative Club, and included a field called 'The Midden'. Barnsley were presented with a good offer to purchase, but proposals involved diverting a cart road around some adjoining cottages, and in the end arguments over the right of way proved a stumbling block. Many thought the club had 'shot themselves in the foot', because of the land's value and location close to the town centre. It was subsequently bought by Barnsley Corporation, and probably included the area adjacent to, and partly underneath, the present town centre relief road which the council at one time developed into council houses, Langdale Road, and a Building Department depot.

Oakwell continued to be the club's home and developments begun in 1898 were consolidated when Barnsley purchased the site for £1,376 in 1907. For entry into the Football League, the playing field had to be levelled and modern changing rooms provided for players and officials. Upon re-election, the old stand was improved, new railings added, and a covered area built on the low side of the ground, the site of the present ORA Stand. For the start of the 1903-04 season a new stand was built on the same site.

On 10th September 1904, the Mayor of Barnsley, Alderman T. Bray, opened the new stand before the first home match of the season, against Blackpool. It was a project costing £600, led by Chairman Tom Fisher, and seated 1,200 people. Over these years, the official ground capacity was raised from 8,000 to 10,000 although thousands more were squeezed in for the biggest games. Limits set by safety or fire restrictions did not exist then; capacity was set by physical limitation, and when it was impossible to move the ground was declared full. Therefore 'official capacities' tended to be no more than estimates. Unless a ground had ever been filled, a guess had to be made as to its capacity. In Barnsley's case, the best Oakwell attendances of early in the century more than doubled the official capacity. By 1912, the club claimed, their *"well equipped"* enclosure could hold 35,000, and estimated that over the years it had spent close to £10,000 on development.

In addition to the costs of ground improvements, player expenses climbed as well. When the club officially accepted professionalism, its wage bill became a regular and necessary overhead regardless of results on the field and takings at the gate. This heavy commitment almost crippled the club. In 1904, the club's entire wage bill was less than £40 pounds per week, and by 1912 it had grown in excess of £50 weekly. Performance bonuses were also offered on top of salary. The F.A.Cup final of 1910, for example, helped to put over a thousand pounds on the following season's annual wages bill when trainer Bill Norman and each of the players were each given £100. Management problems were made harder because professional players under contract could no longer be dealt

with summarily to cut costs. The Players Union became affiliated to the Federation of Trades Unions in 1909, and militancy against unfair employer practices became as real a threat in football dressing rooms as in coal mines and steel mills across the north of England.

In addition to League-wide issues such as the transfer system and wage ceilings, clubs had to deal one-on-one with players demanding their rights. In 1908, Barnsley's regular inside-forward Len Griffiths was dropped into the Reserves, but went on strike standing on the field with his arms folded and refusing to play. After being cajoled to play by the rest of the team, he missed two open goals and was subsequently suspended by the Directors. Aside from hurt pride, playing for the Reserves also meant a loss of income to a player whose wages were already kept at a low level relative to other working class trades. In 1912, Barnsley's F.A. Cup winners received £2-15s (£2·75) a week as a first team player, and only £2 as a reserve.

Relying on a good cup run to fill the coffers was putting fate entirely in the hands of the gods, so Barnsley had to come up with more practical solutions to closing the gap between income and expenses. First of all, the club looked at raising money from activities away from the playing field. They continued to sell memberships in the club, then in 1900 they came up with the idea of becoming a limited company and selling shares. The club's lady supporters held bazaars; one such event at the Civic Hall in 1900 raised £200.

A second idea was to pare down costs. Volunteers assisted with ground improvements, moving three thousand cubic feet of soil from one side of Oakwell to the other to level the playing field in the summer of 1898.

Since neither of these measures ever made up the deficit, the club had to review its efforts on the playing field as well. In 1899, the club competed in both the Second Division and the Midland League. In 1900, the club pulled out of the Midland League to save money. What else was left? In January 1900, the Board set a precedent that was to be repeated, to the anger and frustration of its supporters for the next century. Harry Davis, a talented local youngster and a crowd favourite for the previous two years, the only bright light in an otherwise gloomy season for Barnsley fans, was sold for £175. He had played 56 games for Barnsley in the Football League and F.A. Cup, and scored 25 goals. The club made a profit of £195 on the transaction, having paid Ardsley only a fiver for him before entering the League. Davis went on to play for England and enjoy a career in the First Division, while Barnsley remained in the Second. But at least they stayed alive. In 1901, the club sold centre-forward Andrew Swann to Arsenal after he scored 19 goals in only 32 appearances, and the pattern of selling to make money was firmly established as a means of survival.

The following season John McCartney took over as manager, combining a frugal financial sense with a keen eye for football. Even with the sale of Davis and Swann and others, and despite all its other efforts, the club was £338 in debt, having failed to turn a profit in its first three years of League existence. Keeping the club afloat was a desperate priority, but McCartney had the ability to see it through.

If Barnsley were to sell their best players to survive, the player pool had to be constantly replenished with new blood of equal or preferably greater ability. Obviously, the replacements could not be bought at much cost. McCartney's answer was to start the club's first 'youth policy' and develop his own talent. As no coaching other than fitness was involved at this time, all that meant was finding young players likely to succeed before anyone else could get to them, and then simply letting them play to the full extent of their ability. But if the scheme was to succeed it needed a trained eye which people like Arthur Fairclough recognized he and others in the Boardroom did not possess, but which McCartney did. During his three seasons in charge, McCartney rarely signed a player over 22 years of age, and all his signings made at least one first team appearance. To balance the inexperience of his young players McCartney made a practice of adding a couple of older, presumably wiser heads to the formula, selecting veterans with solid ability rather than star quality.

McCartney's first move was to head north and come back with eight youngsters from the mining communities of north-east England and his native Renfrewshire for an outlay of £10, less than the signing-on fee usually demanded by one English professional. Of this batch, Hay made his debut in 1901 and played for seven seasons, making a total of 158 appearances for the Reds before going to Chesterfield, Welch made 67 appearances over three seasons, and Seymour made 69 first team appearances before going to Bradford City. All the others also made the first team, but had limited appearances before moving on.

McCartney made repeated trips north and made what was perhaps his best signing ever on one of these journeys, on 28th November 1903, when he signed 18-year-old George Wall from non-League Jarrow. After 80 appearances for Barnsley, with 25 goals, the young winger was transferred to Manchester United early in 1906 and became another England international who 'got away' from Oakwell.

Youngsters like Hay and Wall could expect to begin their careers under McCartney in the Midland League Reserve team and to prove their worth before moving up. The same Reserve team was also a hothouse for South Yorkshire talent as well. Arnold Oxspring from Doncaster Rovers and Benny Green from Penistone Juniors F.C. quickly made a name for themselves, and forced themselves through into the first team.

Green was only 18-years-old when he made his first full appearance in December 1901, but he had to wait until March 15th the following year to establish his place by scoring the winning goal in a 3-2 away victory at Stockport in his third full outing with the club.

The following week, at home to Newton Heath (soon to be renamed 'Manchester United'), Green endeared himself to the Oakwell crowd as Barnsley fought back from an early 2-0 deficit. Green took the ball from just over the opponents' halfway line, beat two players and smashed home his shot, before setting up the winner with a cross to inside-left Herbert Dartnell. The fans loved him instantly. The following year he scored 16 goals for them in 30 League appearances.

Other clubs in the Midland League also had great talent waiting to be discovered. McCartney spotted and signed Ilkeston's young full-back Alf West. He was only 20-years-old when he signed in the close season, but he moved straight into Barnsley's first team line-up for the opening game of the 1902-03 season.

Having established a youth policy, McCartney took another step reflecting the pressures of a regular wage bill. After a year in charge he cut the playing staff to just 12 with the announcement of his retained list, bringing his total playing staff to only 18 by the start of the next season. The club could no longer afford to sign players in bulk as they had in pre-League days, when tremendous 'wastage' was accepted. Offering contracts on a tight budget meant that each signing had to be worth his weight if not in gold, then at least in goals.

McCartney's policies cut down expenses by making the payment of large transfer fees unnecessary and by avoiding large salaries perhaps expected by more experienced players. After two years in charge 'Mac', as the shrewd Scot was known around town, had converted a £338 overdraft into a £152 credit balance while keeping the team, with 11th and 8th place finishes, at its highest positions in the League up until that time. It was a brilliant and unprecedented performance by the manager. Unfortunately, this was still not enough for the club's Directors.

On 14th October 1903, with the Reds riding in second place in the Division behind Arsenal - after three wins, two draws and only one loss from their first six games - the fans' favourite, goalscorer Benny Green, was transferred to Birmingham City for the club record sum of £500 pounds. Not only Barnsley fans but the entire footballing nation sat up and spluttered. One First Division manager remarked that he would expect an entire team for that sort of money. Barnsley fans didn't care about that, they had lost their hero and they demanded to know why.

The club called an emergency public meeting at its Clarence Hotel headquarters, where manager John McCartney stood up to present the Board's position. They could not afford to turn down that amount of money, and they could not stand in Benny Green's way when Birmingham offered him £4 a week. A packed hotel vented its anger and booed club officials. But only a few weeks later the club sold McCartney's full-back discovery Alf West to Liverpool for the same amount. The Reds finished in 8th place again.

The club announced plans to build a commodious new grandstand, obviously assisted by the proceeds. McCartney announced he had been offered a job with Paisley St. Mirren and he was going for the start of the new season.

McCartney's contribution was important not merely in terms of what he accomplished immediately, saving the club when it appeared ready to drown in its own financial mess, but because he gave it a blueprint for survival in a climate where big money already seemed the only key to success. Programme notes some years later recall that *"Barnsley owe him a debt of gratitude for the services he rendered, not only as a player and captain, but subsequently as Secretary and Manager of the Club."*

When his good friend Arthur Fairclough took over again after McCartney's departure at the end of the 1903-1904 season, he picked up the reins where McCartney had left off and drove the club down the same route, galloping all the way to the 1912 Cup Final. During Fairclough's tenure, as under McCartney, no vast sums were spent on recruiting new players. The emphasis remained on acquiring youngsters and supporting them with a couple of experienced players brought in to do a specific job, usually filling a gap left by the sale of a player, until a replacement could be brought up. For these reasons, the veterans sometimes stayed at the club only a year.

The coal-mining communities of the north-east were constantly revisited in search of young talent, resulting in finds like Jackie Mordue, from Spennymoor, a 19-year-old left-winger who moved to inside forward and scored 12 goals in his 25 games for Barnsley. The local area was tapped for new talent such as Tommy Boyle and George Utley, both from Elsecar. Boyle signed as an 18-year-old in 1906, and made 178 appearances for the Reds, becoming centre-half and captain of the side which went to the 1910 Cup final. Utley signed as a 21-year-old, appeared in the 1912 Cup Final team during his 196 first team outings, and became the only man to represent England whilst still a Barnsley player. The Midland League was scouted for youngsters like George Reeves. Reeves, an inside-right, arrived as a 22-year-old from Sutton Town in 1906. In his first season he scored 13 goals in 18 League appearances, and the following year he put away 14 goals in only 12 outings.

When Barnsley won the Cup in 1912, Fairclough's team echoed McCartney's winning formula. It comprised five Geordies, three players from the North Midlands, two from the Barnsley area, and one Scot. Two of these players, captain Archie Taylor and centre-half Phil Bratley, were signed as veterans - both aged 29 - to lend experience to the side. The other nine joined the club as youngsters with an average age of under 21. The whole cup-winning team was assembled for less than £250; it was dismantled for five thousand.

Unfortunately, the Board of Directors had learned from the sale of Davis, Swann and West, that good players could quickly be converted into cash. Perhaps the sale of some players was essential for survival during the crisis of the early 1900's, but perhaps also the Directors were naive in believing that a football club had to be run like their own small businesses, where hands were set to turn a profit, and a restrictive eye was always kept on the balance at the bank.

Despite an improved financial situation after McCartney's reign they marched Barnsley's brightest stars to the bank year after year, breaking transfer records all the way, and plundering the youthful assets that had given them their greatest successes. Fortunately for them, the supply of young talent coming through seemed inexhaustible.

Jackie Mordue was sold to Arsenal for £600 in 1906-07, and he later played for England. George Reeves went to Aston Villa in 1907-08 for a fee of £700 to £900. Tommy Boyle went to Burnley for £1,250 in 1911. A similar fate even met the club's Cup winning heroes. The 1912 side was dismantled in 1913 when Bob Glendenning went to Bolton Wanderers for £1,200, George Utley to Sheffield Utd for £2,000 and George Lillycrop also joined the Burnden Park club for £1,300.

The club made itself richer off the field and perhaps for the first and only time in its existence appeared financially sound, but irate supporters seethed at what they saw to be the bankruptcy of playing talent and the inconsideration of their rights as paying customers. In 1912, fans who had bought season tickets on the back of the previous season's Cup success were not to know what lay ahead. Expecting to see the club launch an assault on getting out of the Second Division and into the First, they were appalled to see their heroes peddled off one by one. In a letter to the press one wrote, *"We have paid good money to see Barnsley Football Club this season and I now find it has been like paying for strawberries and cream and being served with gooseberries and skimmed milk and we are expected to eat it and say nowt. I will never go to Oakwell again."*

The club missed promotion to the First Division in 1913 by five points. They were four points out of the race the following year, and in 1915 finished in third place for the first time in their history. But it was too late. War ended League competition in 1915 and no-one will ever know how great the club might have been, or how badly it might have floundered over the long term, as a result of the Directors' policies.

As the world became immersed in catastrophe, football for once became of secondary importance. When League Football resumed the world was a different place. What is certain is that supporters of the time were soured by the experience, and that generations of Barnsley fans began to hand down grudges from father to son. Supporters' entrenched cynicism about the ability and motives of the Board of Directors had begun even while the club revelled in its best ever placing in the Football League.

CHAPTER 5

✤ WE'RE UP FO'T'CUP ✤

The greatest single achievement of the pre-1915 era, and in most of Barnsley's history, was winning the F.A. Cup in 1912. Despite an unremarkable League history up to that point, and without ever leaving the Second Division, the Reds proudly won what was then the most prestigious trophy in the country with a team that was homespun and cost next to nothing to assemble. Taking a tortuous route that pitted them against old rivals they set a series of records on the way, some of which stood for many years.

Until Barnsley won promotion to the top Division for the first time in their history in 1997, they were the only club to have won the Cup without ever playing in the top flight since the inception of the Football League in 1888, and with the replay of the 1912 Final being played at Bramall Lane, they are the only team ever to have won the Cup in Yorkshire. Barnsley's marathon of twelve games required to lift the trophy still stands as a record. The 11 goals for and three against which took them there was also the best goal average of any team winning the Cup until 1976. On the way to the final, they helped break the record for receipts at a Cup semi-final with takings of £2,985 when they played Swindon Town in front of 48,507 at Stamford Bridge, and posted a best-ever home attendance up until that time of 24,987 for the fourth round quarter-final tie against Bradford City.

Cup glory raised the club's reputation as competitors onto a national stage but still managed to earn them little real respect. The national press, based in London, played up the novelty angle of coalminers from a little Yorkshire town rolling up their sleeves and battling their way to the Cup through pluck rather than talent by coining the phrase 'Battling Barnsley', a phrase which has stuck like a limpet to every piece of good fortune the club enjoyed on the field for the rest of this century. Barnsley supporters revelled in the image; a 1912 picture of the team portrayed them as: "BRIGHT NUTS FROM BARNSLEY'S HARD SEAM .... GUARANTEED TO GIVE YOU A HOT TIME AND LAST WELL" and the club adopted 'The Colliers' as a nickname. The F.A.Cup brought an intensity of excitement to Barnsley that no-one had ever experienced before, and the club found that there really was a pot of gold at the end of the rainbow as Cup success rained dreamed-of cash into the Oakwell coffers.

Such riches were little more than fancy for most of the preceding years. Despite being Football League members, Barnsley qualified automatically for the Cup first round proper only once before 1906. Up until that time each Cup campaign usually began with qualifying encounters, often against non-League opposition, which made the ladder to the more glamorous rounds longer and harder to climb. Attendances for games against the likes of Doncaster, Gainsborough Trinity, Ilkeston and Belper Town drew only one to four thousand paying spectators, no more than those for League games, numbers with which the club barely broke even at the turnstile.

In 1902-03, with McCartney's emerging youngsters beginning to find their form, the club finally earned its first significant Cup windfall in many years, but once again upset their supporters in the process. The Reds had arrived at the first round proper for only the third time in their history. The attendance at Oakwell jumped to 7,000, double the home average, for the visit of League rivals Lincoln City. Barnsley fans already had long memories. From the year before, they remembered a Lincoln shove on the Barnsley goalie which led to a disputed equalizer for Lincoln, a goal which they believed helped put Barnsley out of the Cup. When Barnsley full-back Chris Welch clogged a long ball from the halfway line in the Oakwell tie, two Lincoln defenders bumped into each other going for it, the 'keeper misjudged the bounce, and the ball looped into the net. The crowd howled with derision, believing they were seeing just revenge. Barnsley won 2-0 and for the first time ever the club's name went into the hat for the second round.

When they were drawn against Aston Villa at home the town was almost delirious with excitement. Aston Villa had a team full of stars, were three times winners of the trophy, and were one of the country's biggest clubs. It was a plum draw from the supporters' point of view. Villa immediately flexed their financial muscle and asked for the tie to be moved to Birmingham, offering £100 and half the takings at the gate. The club looked at their own Oakwell ground, holding an official capacity of 8,000, and were sorely tempted. They countered with a request for £300, half the gate, and a friendly at Oakwell. Villa's final offer was £250 and half the takings. The Directors publicly turned them down and the town began to buzz with excitement, looking forward to the biggest game ever to be held in Barnsley.

In the week before the match the Directors' mettle cracked. They decided they needed the income they would get from a switch of grounds far too badly. Chairman Tom Fisher and Manager John McCartney made a secret visit to Birmingham and accepted Villa's offer; the match would be played at Villa Park. Barnsley F.C. hoped to appease their supporters by subsidizing special trains to take them to the game, but fans were

ENGLISH CUP TIE. FEB 23RD 190

BARNSLEY v BURY
THIRD ROUND.

RESULT. BARNSLEY 1. BURY. 0.

Postcard souvenir from a memorable F.A.Cup run

distraught when news leaked out. Four special train-loads of them, at half-a-crown each (12½p), made the journey from Court House Station to Birmingham and helped to make up a 28,000 crowd, the largest the Reds had played in front of up to that time. The club earned over £600 in cash, but not a trip to the third round, for they lost 4-1.

Barnsley made it to the second round again in 1905-06, when Liverpool were drawn at home again. With none of the palaver that had attended their last cup meeting in 1895, Barnsley agreed to switch the game to Anfield, hoping to cash in on the revenues from a large attendance. Barnsley's Directors were disappointed to find only 10,000 people there, a figure that provided no big financial advantage. They might have done better if the game had been kept at Oakwell. While the Directors were busy ruminating about the wisdom of the move, the only goal of the game was scored by Alf West, the full-back they had sold to Liverpool to raise more money two years before, and Barnsley were out. The failure of the switch to Liverpool had its effect, for the Directors decided they would never again change venues away from Oakwell to increase income, and they held their promise.

The following year they were rewarded with a series of home ties against Portsmouth, Bury and Arsenal after drawing away with Nottingham Forest in the first round and winning the replay. A record 13,781 squeezed into Oakwell to see the Arsenal game, willingly paying double admission prices rather than see it taken to London.

The club coined in over £800 and enjoyed a foretaste of success to come. If they won this game against First Division Arsenal, Barnsley would be in the Semi-finals. For the first time in its history the club could sense an F.A.Cup success just over the horizon. Inspired by a terrific home atmosphere, the Reds took their game to the opposition. O'Donnell soared to head home a Brooks corner in the first-half and put them in the lead. The crowd erupted onto the field. Play was held up until celebrating fans could be cleared back behind the lines. But two goals in five minutes midway through the second-half stole the game back for Arsenal. Although Barnsley hit the post and the crossbar in the final ten minutes during intense pressure, they couldn't find the equalizer. Beaten, but not disgraced, they had finally made their mark on the competition and given a hint of something to look forward to.

Cup magic deserted them for two more years with exits in the first round, giving little indication of what was to follow in 1909-10. When their Cup campaign began in January of that season, Arthur Fairclough's talented blend already had the town excited with some great performances over the first half of the League season. Goalkeeper Fred Mearns - standing in for the injured Cooper - and outside-left Tom Forman, lent their experience as 30-year-olds to a team that otherwise averaged a little over 22 years of age, drawn from the usual mix of regional backgrounds; Geordies, local lads, Midland League players and Scots.

There was enough potential among the youngsters to captivate, adoring fans and set them talking eagerly about where their promise might lead. Tommy Boyle, at centre-half, was only 5'-8" (1.73m.) tall, but was surprisingly good in the air and exceptionally fast. Still only 22-years-old, the fans talked enthusiastically about him as a future England player, a prospect all the more exciting for them because of his local roots. Fairclough spotted Boyle playing for Elsecar against Rockingham Colliery at Hoyland Common before bringing him to Oakwell as an 18-year-old. Boyle tried out for England but was not given full international honours - despite being listed as a reserve whilst with Barnsley - until 1913, by which time he was with Burnley.

Up front, the centre trio of Gadsby, Lillycrop and Tufnell could score goals almost at will. Twenty year old Ernie Gadsby already had two hat-tricks in the League before Barnsley started their Cup campaign; 24-year-old Geordie George Lillycrop had 18 goals in 20 League games at centre-forward, and 24-year-old Harry Tufnell from Burton-on-Trent was averaging one goal in every three appearances.

With wins of 7-0 away at Leeds and 7-1 at home to Wolves in October, the fans felt the team was capable of anything on their day; they had that exciting feeling that something was coming. Even a couple of League defeats over Christmas and New Year did little to dampen optimism, measured in bumper attendance at the first round ties. An exuberant army of 2,000 fans travelled to Blackpool on January 15th to see the Reds hold the home team to a 1-1 draw. In the return at Oakwell the mood of the fans could be judged when almost 14,000 showed up, half as big again as the largest League gate of the season thus far. Arthur Fairclough's aces did not disappoint. They ran rampant, demolishing Blackpool 6-0 with the terrible trio of Lillycrop (2), Tufnell (2) and Gadsby doing the damage; Tommy Boyle added a penalty.

Perhaps the Directors sensed something was possible too. When the draw for the next round pitted Barnsley away at Bristol Rovers they made a rare bid to bring the game to Oakwell, offering a guarantee of £500. Regular entrance prices were doubled (ground admission went from sixpence to one shilling - 5p) to make up the money guaranteed to Rovers as their share for switching the venue. Although increased prices kept some fans away the crowd of 10,285 was still larger than all but two League games that year. The club may have lost money at the turnstiles, taking only £593, of which five hundred was earmarked for the visitors, but the gamble paid off on the field.

Gadsby, Bartrop and Forman crushed their opponents with first-half goals to put Barnsley into the next round. Local youngster George Utley rounded off the team's performance with a spectacular individual goal, dribbling from midfield to beat three men and slam home a shot from 25 yards during the second-half. Barnsley triumphed 4-0.

West Bromwich Albion were drawn at home in round three. With no bribery required to switch venues this time, the Directors allowed prices to remain the same as for League games and the fans responded with a record 18,636 handing over sixpence each for ground admission at a time when the official capacity of Oakwell had been thought to be only 10,000. They saw Lillycrop chest down a long ball from full-back Dicky Downs and lay it off for Tufnell to slug home the 1-0 winner, bringing the Quarter-finals to Oakwell.

The visit of Queen's Park Rangers was one of the biggest and most anticipated events in town history. 23,574 crushed in and more remained locked outside as turnstiles closed with an hour to kick-off. With the game underway, Barnsley fans willed the winning goal into the net. Boyle put Bartrop through on the right, and the winger lofted his cross over the middle to the far post where it cannoned off the woodwork and dropped into the back of the goal. It may have been fluky, but it was the only goal of the game. Barnsley had sneaked through to the Semi-finals!

The English Cup was still by far the most prestigious competition in the land. Its lure was so captivating that Barnsley decided to put League play on a backburner, twice resting first team players from League fixtures.

THE WINNING GOAL
BARNSLEY -V- QUEENS PARK RANGERS March 5th 1910
ENGLISH CUP

Action from the F.A.Cup Semi-final replay versus Everton at Old Trafford (31 March 1910)

Twelve days before the Semi-final against Everton, on Saturday 26th March 1910, they had a Monday afternoon game away at Oldham, then after the Semi-final ended in a scrappy 0-0 draw at Elland Road, they were at home to Lincoln two days later. On both occasions Barnsley rested first team players. The Football League fined the club a total of £75 for fielding under-strength teams but the club felt this was a small price to pay if the players were allowed to rest and prepare for the Cup.

Barnsley already placed a premium on preparing players for big matches. Arthur Fairclough had some years before introduced the practice of taking the players away to train for important games at health and fitness resorts.

The spa town of Buxton was a popular retreat for the club. For the 1910 Cup run the team trained in the bracing sea air and muscle-busting sand dunes of Lytham St. Anne's.

In the Semi-final replay at Old Trafford, Barnsley's preparations paid off. In the previous year, First Division Everton had knocked Barnsley out of the cup with a 3-1 win at Goodison Park, but in Manchester the tables were turned. In a tense first-half, Tommy Boyle missed from the penalty spot at one end and Fred Mearns saved a spot-kick by Everton's Sharp at the other. Fifteen minutes into the second-half, Ernie Gadsby pounced on a knock-down of Boyle's long range shot to put Barnsley into the lead. With only six minutes left, Lillycrop set up Forman for a second goal, and Everton fell apart.

Action from the 1910 Final at The Crystal Palace.

Straight from the restart, Lillycrop regained possession and put Tufnell through to seal a 3-0 victory. Thousands of travelling Yorkshiremen danced with joy as the final whistle sounded Barnsley's arrival in the F.A.Cup Final. Returning home, they poured out of their trains and charabancs into Barnsley's streets and celebrated noisily until late into the night.

Barnsley travelled to London to meet Newcastle United in their first appearance at the nation's leading venue before Wembley Stadium became the traditional home of Cup Finals - the English Cup mecca of Crystal Palace - where 77,747 greeted the two teams before the start of the game. It was Newcastle's fourth visit to the Final in six years, and they had yet to win one. For thousands of Yorkshiremen in the crowd, many of whom had never ventured further than the coalfields, the weekend of April 23rd 1910 was a first opportunity to visit the nation's capital and visit its famous sights, but the sight they wanted most of all to see escaped them. Supporter Wilf Baxter reminisced 70 years later that *"...it cost me six shillings* (30p) *to get to London, one shilling return to the Crystal Palace, and another shilling to get in. Then it was so crowded inside that I had to climb a tree to see the game..."*

When Wilf Bartrop drove a low cross into the box and Harry Tufnell forced it home after 38 minutes it seemed as if Barnsley's dream could come true, but as the game edged nervously into the last minute of time a long ball found Newcastle winger Rutherford wide open in the Barnsley half. Shouts of *"off-side"* roared from the Barnsley contingent but Rutherford raced away unchecked by the referee and slotted in an equalizer. In one stunning moment, Barnsley's hopes crashed. Arthur Fairclough recalled, *"My wife had .removed the red ribbons from her umbrella to tie on the cup in celebration of our victory ....*

I had completed arrangements for the Barnsley M.P., Sir Joseph Walton, to receive the trophy. Just as I sat down Newcastle equalized...". One reporter wrote, *"Barnsley people will never be convinced that the cup was not in their keeping ... the opinion is not theirs alone either."*

Alf Ramsey's famous World Cup Final speech may have been just as appropriate to Barnsley at that moment, as it was at full-time to England in 1966...*"You've won it once, now go out and do it again."*

Despite the bitter disappointment, Barnsley were confident they could do it again when the teams met at Goodison Park on Thursday April 28th. Twenty thousand fans travelled from Barnsley. Fifteen thousand were locked outside when the ground's gates were closed with a capacity 65,000 people inside, creating a tremendous atmosphere. For Barnsley, it was too much. They struggled to find a rhythm and could hold Newcastle for only the first 51 minutes. When Shepherd put the Geordies ahead it made their uphill battle even harder. When Ness brought Shepherd down in the box and the striker got up and converted the penalty for Newcastle's second goal, it was all over.

Despite the disappointment of a 2-0 defeat, Barnsley fans found a silver lining. With a cartload of unknown youngsters and a shoestring budget, the little club may have arrived in the Final like unknown gatecrashers to the eyes of a startled nation, but to its fans the loss to Newcastle was merely a setback, not the end of the trail. For them, the team's youthful potential meant that Barnsley's future sparkled with promise as much as the last few months had sparkled with excitement. The club found a silver lining too, to the tune of £6,436 in gross game receipts over all the rounds before the Final, and a share of a record cheque of £5,980 for their participation in the Final itself.

The success carried over into the close season when Barnsley's newly-found celebrity status as Finalists earned them the chance to tour Europe with exhibition games in Austria, Germany, France and Hungary.

Photograph of shops in Barnsley after the Cup run, with a suggested 'monument' superimposed on the scene.

Supporters' expectations were shortlived however when the team returned to normal business. In 1911, not only did Barnsley announce a loss of £1,255 on their season following the bumper year of 1910, but they struggled in the League and finished second from bottom. Last year Cup finalists.... this year re-election. Their Cup run must have counted for something, however. Fellow League members gave them most votes in the re-election ballot, which was at least some measure of respect in an otherwise disappointing League season. The Cup was just as unkind, sending Barnsley to Watford in the first round and Burnley in the second, where their travels ended. First Division Burnley were able to have a good look at Barnsley's pretender for the England centre-half position, Tommy Boyle, and must have liked what they saw. Six months later he was a Burnley player.

Boyle's transfer caused the biggest furor of all the trades that the Directors had made thus far and continued to make as part of the club's financial policy. Season tickets were sent back, the club was attacked in the press, and even the players publicly shook their heads in disappointment and disbelief. With the 1911-12 season already underway and the team already struggling, the sale of Boyle, a key member of the squad, was a frustrating low point for supporters. By the time the first round of the Cup came around in January 1912, their League season was still not on fire and it was still hard to be too optimistic.

Veteran Phil Bratley had emerged over the first half of the season to take over Boyle's centre-half spot. The oldest member of the team at thirty-one, he had been signed the previous year from Rotherham County, and bided his time as a reserve. Fans had to make do with his consistency and experience in the middle of the field, rather than the youth, promise and excitement of his predecessor, but at 5'-10" (1.78m.) he was still one of the tallest players on the team and had the advantage to fans of being a South Yorkshire lad, from Rawmarsh.

Full-back Archie Taylor had taken over the captaincy. At twenty-nine, another veteran, Taylor arrived at the beginning of the season from Huddersfield Town. Born in Dundee, Taylor was a strong, squat, no-nonsense Scot who gave the back line the physical qualities of a brick wall, weighing in at 13 stone (83 kg.) despite being only 5'-9" (1.75m.) tall. John 'Dickie' Downs was his partner at right-back, a characterful 26-year-old Geordie with four years at the club, who established the sliding tackle as his trademark, delighting fans by appearing at just the right moment from nowhere, and diving in with his famous slide to clip the ball off a stunned opponent's toes. Downs became an England international after leaving Barnsley for Everton in 1919.

The playmakers of the team were Bob Glendenning, another Geordie, and local lad George Utley from Elsecar,

who as half-backs were charged with getting the ball down the field and out to the wings. Glendenning did not stand on ceremony. *"No haughty gesture marks his gait, no pompous tone his word"* is the way one poetic fan put it. On the field, this translated to rolling up his sleeves and getting on with the job in the traditional workmanlike fashion that Barnsley spectators have always expected and enjoyed. Glendenning was an ex-miner who played hard to win and was well respected by other players on the team because of it. 'Glenny', as the players called him, had a little trick of hooking his thumb inside an opponent's shorts to stop him jumping for the ball so he could get there first.

Utley, on the other hand, brought a defter touch and keener sense of style to Barnsley's play. Two years older than his fellow half-back, he signed the same year as Glendenning, in 1908, and both players broke into the first team almost simultaneously. By the start of 1909 both were two of the first names pencilled onto the team sheet for every game. A good dribbler and passer, Utley's class marked him out to become the first and only player to gain full England honours while playing for Barnsley.

Up front, with the departure of inside-right Gadsby to Bristol City in 1911, the right to partner Lillycrop and Tufnell had been won by James 'George' Travers. Gadsby's erstwhile replacement bought from Darlington during the close season, Matthew Cornock, had scored five goals in his first eight appearances, but was dogged by injury. There was no other ready-made successor, and Travers was fortunate to win his place at the end of December after spending most of his time in the Reserves. His call-up to the first team coincided with a good run of results and Fairclough left the winning team well alone; Travers retained his place for the rest of the year. He was not a natural goalscorer, getting only four in his 22 League games that season, but as inside-left he could be a thorn in opponents' sides with his quick pace and strong running.

The real goalscoring responsibility fell at the feet of Tufnell and Lillycrop, playing at inside-right and centre-forward respectively. George Lillycrop was by now the longest serving player on the team, having made his first appearance as a 20-year-old in 1907. Being also the smallest player on the squad, he was living evidence that attacking the ball in the air was not Barnsley's game plan. At 5'-6" (1.68m.) and 11 stone 4 lbs (72kg.) wringing wet, the wee Geordie made a name for himself by buzzing opposing defences like an annoying pest, seizing half-chances, snapping up loose balls, putting full-backs under pressure, and displaying a venomous sting in his finish. Lillycrop was the kind of player you couldn't give an inch to; creative, quick thinking, always in the right place at the right time, and not needing much room to work.

He and Harry Tufnell had been developing an understanding up front since the opening day of the 1909 season when they paired off together for the first time. Going into the 1912 English Cup with over 90 games side by side, each having missed only a handful of matches owing to injury in the past few years, they became one of Barnsley's most dangerous and consistent striking partnerships.

Perhaps the best example of their work was Tufnell's goal in the 1910 final. When Bartrop crossed, Lillycrop set Tufnell up by leaping over the ball and letting it run on to his partner. They read each other well and enjoyed playing off each other. Lillycrop ran out with more career goals for Barnsley (104 in 223 games) than his partner, but Tufnell, two years Lillycrop's junior, consistently averaged one goal every three games over his seven peacetime seasons at Oakwell.

Good ball service was one reason the pair were so successful. Wilf Bartrop joined them as a 20-year-old from Worksop Town in 1909, and his forages down the wing provided a third dimension to the striking partnership. In the tradition of great wingers, Bartrop whet the fans anticipation whenever the ball was played out to his side of the field. Everyone knew he was fast; in 1912, a picture of Bartrop was published with the caption 'I go, I go, look how I go, swifter than the arrow from the Tartar's bow'. He was also stockily built and hard to knock off the ball. This meant he could get off a good and reliable supply of crosses under pressure from opposing full-backs, and the goalmouth was always in danger of bombardment even if they forced him out to the corner flag.

On the other flank, Bert Leavey was first choice winger but he was to break a leg in one of the quarter-final replays against Bradford City. Up until that time, he had been an ever-present for the season but never played for Barnsley again. Leavey was brought in to replace 1910's Cup veteran Tom Forman, sold to Spurs during the previous season, and was a rarity at Oakwell; he was one of the first southerners ever to play for the club.

Taking over from Leavey in time for the Cup Final run-in was James Moore, the baby of the team, only a few months past his twentieth birthday and with just five previous first team outings. Moore, another native of the north-east, played inside-left for Boldon Colliery in County Durham but on the day Fairclough went to scout him he was switched to outside-left to replace an injured winger, and that was the position Fairclough signed him up to play. His first game for Barnsley as Leavey's replacement was the last Quarter-final replay with Bradford City. The selection of a young, inexperienced player for such a big game caused some controversy, but when Barnsley won, Jimmy's place was secured for the rest of the season.

Jack Cooper

Returning in goal was Jack Cooper, a Nottinghamshire native and another one of Fairclough's 'babe' signings, from Midland League Sutton Town. After his debut at nineteen in 1908, Cooper's career had been on hold because of injury. In November 1911 he found the right time to make a come-back, winning his place in time to be included in the Cup-winning team. One of the biggest and most physically developed players on the team at 5'-10" (1.78m.) and 12 stone (76kg.), Cooper's build reflected the demands on a goalkeeper in the days when charging the ball into the net was allowed, even if the 'keeper was still wrapped around it. Despite his big frame, Cooper was agile with quick reflexes and a shot-saving reputation.

Although the team had won four out of five League games in December 1911, they struggled against modest opposition in the New Year and failed to score a single goal in their first two games of 1912. The Cup had an attraction all of its own however. Both fans and team would answer its call, but confidence was muted when the campaign began in the First Round on January 13th.

Barnsley did take their cup preparations seriously once again, training at a cold and windy Lytham St. Anne's before travelling to meet Birmingham at St. Andrew's. For the third successive time since Christmas, the Reds failed to score a goal but neither did their opponents and a 0-0 draw brought Birmingham back to Oakwell. Snow delayed the replay by four days, but the biggest crowd of the season turned out in bitter cold to see Barnsley finally find the net three times without reply.

A home draw favoured Barnsley's encounter with Leicester Fosse in the second round, but it was not an attractive tie nor an easy one from the fans' point of view. Barnsley had not beaten Fosse since November 1909.

The last three encounters between the teams had all ended in draws, and except for the win against Birmingham, Barnsley had yet to score a goal in 1912. Over 15,000 turned out to watch the game with high hopes rather than confidence. When the teams went in at half-time it looked like yet another 0-0 draw was on the cards, but after half-time the game came alive. Only a minute after the restart, Phil Bratley brought down Leicester's King in the box.

Penalty! Currie stepped up to take the kick. He fired hard, but straight, at the Barnsley keeper. Cooper knocked the ball down; Currie charged the rebound but drove it wide. Sparked by the sudden excitement, Barnsley's game began to pick up. Bartrop used his speed to cut in from the right-wing and drive towards goal. His shot was blocked by the keeper but Lillycrop popped up to stab it home. One-nil, and Barnsley were on their way to the third round.

When Bolton Wanderers' name came out of the hat Barnsley were faced with a cup-tie in the best traditions, travelling as underdogs to meet a First Division club which had twice appeared in the Final. Over 4,000 fans crossed the Pennines to cheer the Reds. They were not to be disappointed. A giant third round crowd of 34,598 packed inside Burnden Park applauded both teams off at half-time after a thrilling but scoreless contest that was shortly to break open. Almost directly from the second-half kick-off Leavey broke down the left and centered into a crowded box. There was a scramble; almost inevitably the boot that found the ball belonged to Lillycrop, and Barnsley were 1-0 up. Leavey again broke clear, and this time cutting inside fired from an angle. A Bolton defender, Whiteside, swiped at the ball on the line but only succeeded in whacking it into the roof of the net. Leavey took credit for the goal and Barnsley were 2-0 ahead, conceding only one late goal to the home team as they slackened their pace. It was the kind of surprise result that makes the Cup special.

When the draw for the next round was announced, the town went crazy, for Barnsley were given a dream match. They were paired at home to First Division opposition, the current Cup holders, in an all Yorkshire derby. In 1907-08, the last season the two teams met, Bradford City beat Barnsley twice en route to winning the Second Division Championship. Since that time the two had been a Division apart. Barnsley had been applying for re-election while Bradford had done what the Reds had failed to do, beat Newcastle United in a Cup Final replay. Barnsley's record official attendance up to that time, 24,987, turned up at Oakwell to watch yet another 0-0 draw on Saturday 9th March. A replay at Valley Parade the following Wednesday attracted almost 32,000 spectators but ended in the same result. Barnsley were in a second replay for the first time in their history and Elland Road, Leeds, was selected as the location.

Anyone who thought that two 0-0 draws might have stifled interest in the third game would have been mistaken. Instead, the contest was reaping more and more interest as it rolled along. It was becoming the, biggest talking point in Yorkshire. From Barnsley, hundreds of under-employed miners marched on foot to the game; others pedalled heavy iron bicycles through the lanes of West Yorkshire and chugged along in chartered motor-charabancs, bells ringing, horns honking, waving their hats and scarves to each other in shows of support. Despite being gripped in a coal strike thousands of regular spectators scraped together enough coppers to pay for admission and a drink on the way home, pinning their hopes on Barnsley's success as a diversion from their own plight.

The streets around Elland Road were awash with rivers of supporters from West and South Yorkshire. The ground disappeared under a tide as they flooded inside. It had an official capacity of 35,000 but gate receipts indicated takings from 37,000 people and police estimated that between 45,000 and 50,000 actually got inside to watch the match. They milled along the edges of the pitch throughout the game and spilled onto the field. Taking corner-kicks was almost impossible because there was no room to step back and address the ball. The referee, feeling players were threatened by the advancing crowds as the game approached its end, called time five minutes early, with the score at 0-0. Compounding Barnsley's disappointment with the result, and the difficulty of their task, was a serious injury to Bert Leavey, hero of the previous round. After Bert was carried off with a broken leg, Barnsley had to continue with only 10 men; substitutions were not yet allowed. At the end of the day, the fact that they had earned another replay with a depleted side probably came as something of a relief.

A crowd of 38,264 arrived at Bramall Lane, Sheffield on Thursday afternoon, March 21st 1912, to see the grand finale of the Quarter-finals. Scrappy play and lack of goalmouth action had frustrated fans in the first three games but fireworks quickly exploded in this the fourth and final bout. George Travers shot Barnsley ahead with only his second goal for the club, and his first ever for them in the Cup. Bradford retaliated with two goals from Speirs and Devine.

The game pushed towards full-time. With five minutes left, Glendenning forced a corner on the left. Jimmy Moore floated the ball into the box and Lillycrop got his head there first. Two-two! Barnsley fans, who a moment ago were preparing gloomily for defeat, went ecstatic and the team re-launched themselves into extra time with new energy, searching for a winner. The minutes ticked by again with both sides hanging grimly onto the 2-2 scoreline and neither wanting to risk giving up a goal nor looking like scoring one at the other end.

With the referee looking at his watch, and the crowd looking at another replay, Wilf Bartrop powered a cross into the Bradford box from the right side. The defence knocked it down. It bobbled. They couldn't get it out .... Lillycrop!..... GOAL! The last kick of the game sent thousands of Barnsley supporters screaming wild. They were in the Semi-final for the second time in three years! Cheering crowds met the team's train on their return to Barnsley's Court House Station. George Lillycrop was scooped up and chaired down the stairs and away down Eldon Street on a tidal wave of boisterous supporters.

After the elation of the Bradford epic, a meeting with Southern League club Swindon Town at Stamford Bridge, Chelsea, in the Semi-final was almost destined to be something of a let-down. Both sides clogged and kicked their way through a bad tempered, scrappy match, the only item of merit being the fact that a crowd of 48,057 paid record receipts for a Cup Semi-final, over £2,985. The game ended 0-0. In contrast, at the other semi-final at Liverpool, Blackburn Rovers, perhaps the biggest team in professional football at that time, played in front of a smaller crowd (only 30,000) and took less than £2,000 at the gate. Their game with West Bromwich Albion also ended in a 0-0 draw.

Barnsley's replay was at Notts County on Wednesday April 3rd, where the effects of hard times in the mining industry on Barnsley's travelling support, a daylight midweek kick-off, and the travelling distance for Swindon's small contingent of supporters, kept the crowd to down to only 18,000. They did not have long to wait for some excitement though. After 35 minutes Swindon's Jefferson was fouled inside the Barnsley penalty area and the referee marched straight to the penalty spot. Big Jack Cooper stood on his line, spat on his hands and rubbed them together, kept his eyes on the ball. 'Thunk'! Cooper hurled himself to his right and tipped the ball away for his second penalty save of the competition. The rest of the team hurled themselves on Cooper and mobbed him with congratulations.

They were still in the game, and went in at half-time with scores level at 0-0. Going into the second half, Jimmy Moore was sent sprawling inside Swindon's box but Barnsley's cries of *"Penalty!"* were waved away by the referee and play continued. Only a few minutes later Travers headed against the bar, Bartrop lunged for the rebound and forced a save out of Swindon's 'keeper, Skiller. The ball went out for a corner on the right side. Fifty-seven minutes gone. Bartrop with the corner. Barnsley bring up their big guns; there's Phil Bratley, the tallest man on the team, on the edge of the box...Lillycrop's in there, Travers, Tufnell on the near post .... Here it comes now. Bratley makes a run ... BRATLEY! It's there! Phil Bratley, with his only goal of the season, runs in unmarked and meets it squarely with his head, beating the keeper to the ball .... Skiller, in goal,

has no chance and Barnsley are in the lead, one-nothing ... just look at the celebrations on the terraces, they think they're going to Crystal Palace and they might be right.....

They were going to Crystal Palace alright, to meet West Bromwich Albion in the Final. Once again, the importance of the F.A.Cup overshadowed all else at Barnsley Football Club. Having been fined and warned by the Football League for fielding understrength teams in the run up to the 1910 final, Barnsley obviously could not afford to officially rest their players in large numbers again but it is obvious from League results and from team changes that only one thing was on everybody's mind as winter turned to spring at Oakwell.

Barnsley's Quarter-final marathon with Bradford had begun on March 9th. They played seven League games between then and the final, winning only three, losing two and drawing two. Only Cooper, Downs, Bartrop and Moore of the Cup Final team played in them all; the others were in and out. The management was totally focussed on winning the Cup. Arthur Fairclough had the team train at Lytham and Matlock before cup-ties, and trainer Bill Norman put them through a fitness programme that would make a Royal Marine wince. They ran, ran again, and ran some more, just in case.

Barnsley left their Cup Final accommodations at London's Imperial Hotel and made their way to Crystal Palace on the warm, sunny afternoon of Saturday April 20th, 1912. At the ground the players were held up when no-one recognized them or believed who they were! They were locked outside until someone went and found the passes they should have been carrying in the first place. Once inside, they found a slightly disappointing crowd of only 54,556. Barnsley's travelling support was still limited by the financial predicament that many miners found themselves in because of continuing industrial action in the coalfields, and West Brom's. support may well have suffered from the same problem.

The crowd were treated to a poor game with little flair and finesse but lots of frustrating kick and rush on a hot, dusty afternoon. The Barnsley half-backs prevented good play by constantly booting the ball up into the air at every opportunity, according to 'The Times' of London. The Barnsley Chronicle blamed the heat and a bone-hard pitch for a poor game. In any case, Barnsley and West Brom played to a 0-0 draw, and at the close of Barnsley won the toss to choose the location of the replay. There was no hesitation in asking for Bramall Lane. After the Bradford encounters, the club thought of it as their 'lucky' ground. For the first time in history the F.A. Cup Final was coming to Yorkshire.

The replay in Sheffield on Wednesday April 24th made the final more accessible to many of the Barnsley faithful who had not been able to afford the longer journey to

London. Once again they walked, cycled, rode, and thronged the roads on their way to see the Reds. Approaching Bramall Lane, the streets became a sea of red and white. Fans clanged handbells, rattles chattered, bugles shrieked, as spectators milled excitely in their thousands.

The Barnsley players weaved their way through these boisterous crowds to arrive at the field about noon. The club's founder, Tiverton Preedy, had made his way north from London for the big game and was waiting at the ground to meet them. As guest of honour he led them out onto the field for a pre-match inspection. These were the days before irrigation kept a pitch green throughout the year and a hot spell across the whole country had left it as bone hard as the Crystal Palace surface had been a few days before. A bouncing ball or a scraped boot raised clouds of dust. Once more, the afternoon was uncomfortably hot with bright sunshine. Only a slight breeze towards the Bramall Lane end of the ground promised to bring any hint of relief.

The crowd inside Bramall Lane was still fewer than expected at 38,555, but most of them were Yorkshiremen, and thousands of them were from Barnsley. From West Brom's. point of view, the 'neutral venue' was more like playing an away game at Oakwell. They ran out first a little before 3 o'clock to a small cheer. When Barnsley emerged onto the field, Bramall Lane shook with a roar.

There was more to cheer in this game than in the first with near misses, blocked shots, and great saves, but even so, when regulation time ended the score was still frozen at 0-0. Extra time was called for, but both teams defences were the strongest part of the game and as the clock edged towards 118-minutes of play, fans with knots in their stomachs began to look at another goalless replay marathon as being the most likely, and perhaps preferred, possibility. The last minute loss to Newcastle in the final two years before must have been on many Barnsley minds. Bramall Lane's exit gates were open and some spectators were already edging out of the ground when full-back Dicky Downs played a ball down the right side to Bob

Glendenning in midfield. Glendenning dribbled it forward. Everyone expected him to feed Wilf Bartrop on the right, and Bartrop edged forwards ready to take on West Brom's international full-back and captain Jesse Pennington one more time. As Pennington moved over to cover the Barnsley winger, Glenny looked up and saw Tufnell breaking into space left open down the centre. He slid the ball through, Tufnell raced into the box, steadied himself and slammed a shot into the bottom right-hand corner.

GOAL!
Glendenning, following up, shrieked with excitement, jumped on Harry Tufnell, knocked him to the ground and bit through his ear with joy! As the blood dripped out, Glenny looked down at Tufnell and yelled with a big grin on his face, *"Tha' can put a ring in theer nah, Tuffy!"*

Pandemonium broke loose. Fans invaded the field, Tufnell was mobbed, and the game was over. The Reds had won the Cup! The Reds had won the Cup!
The Reds had won the Cup!
As order was restored, Mr. J.C.Clegg handed over the Cup to Archie Taylor and passed out medals to the players on the field. *"I hope they will wear their trophies for many years to come with pride and pleasure,"* he said. *"It will be legitimate pride. I hope they will continue to do as they have done up to present in maintaining the game as a real sport."*

The old Finals lacked the pomp and ceremony of a modern occasion and there was little formal celebration for the team immediately after the game. After changing, they climbed back onto their bus and headed out into the traffic winding its way back to Barnsley.

Telegraphs clattered out the news ahead of them, and according to the Barnsley Chronicle, *"...When the result of the game reached Barnsley there was great jubilation in the streets, which despite the mass exodus to Sheffield, were thronged. Sheffield Road from May Day Green to the Borough Boundary was thick with people. A large force of police, some mounted, took charge of the expectant crowd.... When the players' motor-charabanc was sighted approaching there was a scramble and a rush towards it, scores of people hanging on to the sides."*

As the crowd moved towards the town, the band of the Territorial Army struck up in front of the players' bus and marched with them. Hundreds of people hung out of bedroom windows, waving flags and red and white streamers.

The players display the F.A.Cup in their charabanc tour following their victory

Shouts rang out down the street. The players waved their hats to cheers and Archie Taylor balanced himself at the front of the motor, precariously waving the trophy aloft, just out of the grasp of jostling fans. In the spring dusk the team slowly forced its way in a crawling motorcade through masses of supporters pressing on all sides to the club's headquarters at the Clarence Hotel, where the Mayor of Barnsley, Councillor Cotterill, was waiting on the balcony to greet them.

The crush was so great that the players could barely dismount and get through the crowd to a reception inside. Taylor continued to hold up the Cup for the fans to see, but the crush forced him to lose his grip and the Cup fell onto the ground and rolled under a horse. There was a scramble to pick it up and take it inside, and no serious damage was done. Inside the Clarence Hotel the club presented Rev. Preedy with the match ball, which he proudly kept for the rest of his life.

But the reception had to be short; the following day Barnsley entertained Chelsea in the League at Oakwell. Not surprisingly, they lost 2-0. Somewhat surprisingly, only 7,000 turned out to salute them. Of the Cup-winning eleven only Taylor missed the game. The last game of the season on the following Monday at Oakwell saw Glendenning finish off lowly Glossop with a single goal in front of just 2,000 people. Now the club could hold a party!

The interior of the King's Head Hotel on Tuesday 30th April was a gleaming prism of gaslight, silver, glass, black suits and starched white collars. Players, officials and guests dined on a full banquet of courses before Barnsley's M.P., Sir Joseph Walton, rose with a toast to the Queen and the admonition, *"Gentlemen, you may smoke."* A smell of cigars began to drift across the room. Sir Joseph introduced the Mayor, and the company raised its glasses again to the club and the players.

Rising to his feet once more, Sir Joseph cleared his throat. *"The sporting parson,"* he said, *"will not be denied the pleasure of making a speech on this occasion."*

The company responded with applause and shouts of *"hear, hear!"*. *"When you remember that he was really the founder of the football club,"* Sir Joseph continued, *"we feel indebted more than we can tell to his uniting efforts in the initial stages of its formation. I give you Tiverton Preedy."*

Preedy rose to applause and shouts of *"Well done, Dove Inn!"* Preedy smiled, and as the noise subsided began his speech. ... *"As for seeing the English Cup at Barnsley, I was not astonished,"* he said. *"We set out to win it, and meant to win it. We never did anything but what we meant to be at the top of the tree. We have won the Cup, and when it comes to it my old friend Bill Norman has an honest duty to perform. He must see to it that we get into the First Division next season. If you cannot do it next year, see that you do it the next, and take the place of Blackburn Rovers. Be determined not to rest until you are at the top of the tree. Not many players, young or old, hold the number of honours the Barnsley team does. I hope you and I will meet again in two years time to congratulate the Barnsley team in getting into the First Division. We have seen the players, and know the grit and spirit within them. There is nothing that can keep them back. They have displayed a fine spirit of loyalty and when this is led by a player like Archie Taylor, then they cannot go wrong. He may not be a bow-legged collier, he might not be able to tumble about like him, but he has a head on his shoulders they all might be proud of..... Let us remember that the team's victories are due to their judgement and skill and knowing what to do and when to do it. ....May your forwards be the same magnificent shots as your magnificent defence..."*

Preedy sat down again to prolonged applause. He had voiced the hopes of all those in the room; little were they to know that their ambitions, now burning with Cup success, would flicker and fade like the gaslight in the globes around the room as they left the banquet.

While the F.A. Cup cast a warm glow across the club's history for many years, it would be another eight-and-a-half decades before the First Division dreams first cherished so long ago finally flared into life.

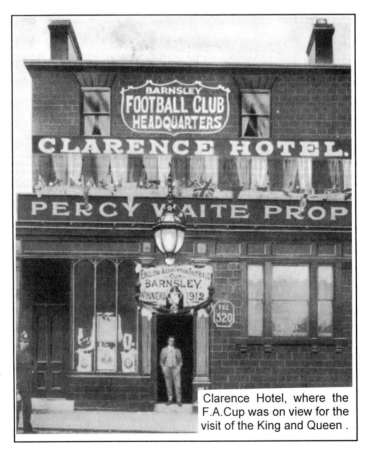

Clarence Hotel, where the F.A.Cup was on view for the visit of the King and Queen .

CHAPTER 6

OUTRAGEOUS MISFORTUNE

Followers of Barnsley Football Club often feel they are fighting an unfair battle. The Club has always been small and unfashionable, striking a note amongst supporters who themselves have more than once felt victims of a society bent on keeping them down, either by chance or by design. Perhaps this is because both club and fans are victims of circumstance. The growth of coal mining around Barnsley helped generate the growth of professional football. It also gave men a chance to work, but fate stopped short of allowing either club or townfolk a chance to get rich from their efforts. Both were provided with the means to get by, but not to succeed, enabling the supporter on the terrace to identify his own struggles with those taking place at Oakwell. Both club and supporters have seen that life is unfair with few rewards for the just; fortune may be supposed to favour the brave, but in Barnsley, she has sometimes been more of an enemy.

There are no better examples of how luck and circumstance have combined to shape the destiny of Barnsley Football Club than those found in the years between the two wars, 1919 and 1939. It was an era when the pace of rapid change in football began to slow, and Barnsley Football Club, after briefly threatening to settle amongst the leaders in the game, mellowed into an ordinary existence.

Barnsley had finished in third place in the Second Division in 1915 with a young team full of promise. In 1919, because of that third place finish before the War, the Club was excited at the prospect of being automatically invited, with Preston and Derby, to make up the numbers in the new First Division. Instead, the Football League decided to hold a ballot amongst its members to decide which other club should be allowed the last extra place with the elite.

Arsenal, who had finished in fifth place in the Second Division in 1915, four points behind Barnsley, polled 18 votes. Barnsley received only five. Arsenal were voted in; Barnsley were out. The Oakwell representatives stormed out of the meeting in protest, but the Club's fate was sealed. They began the period between the wars in the same place they were to finish, in the Second Division, victims of a class vote that favoured a potentially richer, more fashionable club, over a less glamorous one that had earned its right to promotion on the playing field. It was an attitude that Barnsley fans came to expect. They had been panned by a patronising press year after year even as they produced some of the best football players in Britain. While ever Downs, Tilson, Brook, Hines, Barson, Spence and company played for Barnsley, they were nobodies; as soon as they left, they were picked for England.

When the Football League met to organize its first season after the Great War, it was decided to expand the First Division from 20 to 22 clubs. Chelsea, who had finished next to bottom of the First Division in 1915, and who would normally have been relegated, were invited to stay put. Derby County and Preston North End, who had finished in the top two places in the Second Division in 1915, the last year of play, were automatically promoted.

(February 1922) A 3-2 win, to help the promotion challenge.

Two seasons after being passed over in favour of Arsenal, First Division status eluded Barnsley's grasp again. This time, it was the roll of fortune's dice that ended their dream. The 1921-22 season began with ten wins in the first twelve games, immediately singling Barnsley out as serious promotion contenders.

At the end of January, the Reds were resting in sixth place, had settled on a regular team, and were starting to put together a run of good results that kept them in touch with the leaders. In those days, a win was good for two points, and only the top two teams from Division Two were promoted to the First; a third place finish earned nothing. By mid-April, the Club needed maximum points from their last two games to have a chance of finishing in second place to gain automatic promotion.

Woods (Trainer) talking to Beaumont and Fell, prior to the Preston Cup-tie

Stoke, had been denied a place in the First Division by less than one tenth of a goal. It was incred-ible. Stoke's goal advantage over the Reds was made even more bitter when fans and players agon-ized over the glaring opportunities that had gone begging over the season. One more goal in any game would have sealed promotion. Instead of a celebration, the season became a commiseration over the goals that had been missed.

In the penultimate game of the season, away at Hull City, the Reds romped home 3-1 winners. A week later, in their final game, they beat Notts County 3-0 at Oakwell. The victory put them in second place in the table, two points ahead of Stoke. The town was in raptures, but Stoke's season wasn't over; they had one game left to play, at home to Bristol City, and a win would put them equal on points with Barnsley.

The scene was set for a classic end-of-season finale. Stoke's opponents, Bristol City, faced relegation to the Third Division South; they needed a win to vault over Bradford Park Avenue and Coventry City at the bottom of the table to save themselves from the drop. Stoke could go ahead of Barnsley on goal average, and claim the last promotion place, only if they won by three clear goals. It was the last day of the season; the two teams in the game still had everything to play for, and the fates of other clubs hung on this result. Barnsley were caught up in a terrific drama, but could do nothing to help themselves. They could only watch and wait.

The Reds had scored more goals than anyone that year, a total of sixty seven. No one could have faulted their ambition or their industry. Brough Fletcher, Russell Wainscoat and Ernest Hine spearheaded an attack which might well have surprised a few First Division defences; it had taken First Division Preston North End two attempts to knock them out of the Cup. Now, goals pulled the carpet from under Barnsley's feet. As the town hunkered down in anticipation, that warm May afternoon in 1922, excitement turned to stunned belief and then bitter disappointment. The result came through. Almost impossibly, Stoke had got the three clear goals they needed.

Newspaper reporters reached for their slide rules and raced to the presses. Barnsley, equal on points with

In the third to last game of the season, the Reds had visited first place Nottingham Forest. Over 1,200 expectant fans travelled from South Yorkshire to spur them on. Early in the game, with the score 0-0, Barnsley winger George Donkin was tripped whilst dribbling into the Forest penalty area. The crowd roared; the referee pointed to the spot. Brough Fletcher, already with seventeen goals in the season, placed the ball and strode back for his run up; a tense hush fell. Fletcher turned and ran, thumped the ball; the silence turned into a frenzy of agony and relief; he had hit it straight at the keeper, and Forest lived again. Ten minutes before half time, Forest took the lead themselves. It needed a second penalty kick, this time converted by Ernest Hine, to tie the game up for Barnsley and gain a point. Final score, 1-1.

One point for a draw was not enough; it had still left the Reds needing to win their last two games. If Fletcher had scored from the spot, not only would it have overturned Stoke's goal difference, it could have given Barnsley an additional point which would have knocked Stoke out of the race altogether. Supporters also looked back to November at Oakwell, when visitors Leicester City escaped with a 0-0 draw. Barnsley had failed to score from the penalty spot on two occasions in that game. If only one had gone in, it might have been enough to change the course of history at Barnsley Football Club. Fortune had not favoured them at all. Although the Club retained almost the same team the following year, with Hine belting home 24 goals, Barnsley never found themselves that close to the First Division again for the next 75 years, a long time to pay for the tiniest margin of error.

Ten years later, goal difference played its part again. This time, it cut the thread on which the Club had been twirling at the bottom of the Division for an agonising three years; the drop out of Division Two was the first in their history. In 1928, Arthur Fairclough had returned as team manager for the after spells at Huddersfield and Leeds. Two years in the position were enough to reveal how bad Barnsley's predicament was. He left in 1930 and Brough Fletcher was given his chance in management. Fletcher inherited an unhappy situation. The team was already struggling. In his first season in charge, 1930/31, Barnsley finished just two places above relegation.

In the last game of his second season, 1931-32, the Oakwell men earned a 2-2 draw at Oldham, to put them clear of the relegation zone by two points, but Port Vale, one place below them, had a game left. In a replay of events of 1922, but with terribly different consequences, Barnsley waited whilst two other teams played to decide their future. Leeds United were in second place in the League, and already promoted to the First Division. Barnsley were convinced that Leeds, playing at home, would beat Port Vale easily and keep them up, but once again a team from the Midlands twisted a knife into Barnsley's back in their last game of the season. Vale produced a shock 2-0 win to draw level on points with Barnsley. The slide rules came out again. Port Vale had a goal average of 0.6516 to Barnsley's 0.6043, a margin of less than one tenth. It was enough to send Barnsley down into the Third Division North.

Although their stay in the lower division was short, fate was not yet done throwing banana skins across Barnsley's path. They returned to the Second Division as Champions in 1934, but immediately struggled. They could not score goals anymore, even though they kept a reasonably tidy defence. Near the end of the 1937/38 season, Barnsley found themselves needing three points from two home games to stay clear of the relegation zone. The first of the games, an encounter with Norwich at Oakwell, was a dull 0-0 draw, setting the scene for a high stakes decider in the last game of the season against Nottingham Forest. Barnsley and Forest had 35 points, one point less than Swansea Town, who had an inferior goal average. A win for Barnsley was essential, although if Swansea Town had lost rather than won their last match of the season, a draw would have been good enough to keep both Barnsley and Forest up. One of the largest League gates of the season, sensing the possible sudden-death edge to the game, generated a fierce home atmosphere.

Forest jumped out to an early lead, but the Reds, inspired by their supporters, fought back. With three minutes remaining in the game, Barnsley were 2-1 up. The happy crowd, keeping one eye on the play, was beginning to shuffle confidently towards the exits, ready to let out a huge cheer and celebrate Second Division survival, when Forest launched an attack. Barnsley 'keeper, Cliff Binns, stepped off his goal line and collected the ball to his chest. A Forest forward barged into him and knocked him and the ball into the back of the net.

"Hey up, Ref! Foul! Come on." The referee blew his whistle and came running over.
"Aye up, he's given it, we're reit," the crowd muttered, puffing with relief.
"Wait a minute........No, he hasn't given it. He's given a goal. He can't have." But he had.

The players ran furiously down the field after the referee, arms windmilling in protest, shouting for the foul. The crowd bayed in disbelief, but it was no good. The ball was going back to the centre-spot in total chaos, and the score was level at 2-2.

Fired by anger, Barnsley stormed all over Forest as soon as the game re-started. They invaded the visitor's half with everyone except the goalkeeper, in a mad, frantic last effort to bombard the Forest goal with a winner. In the final minute, the ball fell to Bert Barlow, Barnsley's inside-right, the man whose go-ahead goal had been wiped out by Forest's shove. Not content with teasing Barnsley's goal average, fate now produced an amazing sleight of hand. Barlow shot. The ball beat the 'keeper. It hit the inside of the upright, ran across the front of goal, hit the foot of the other upright and bounced out for a goal kick. Absolutely unbelievable.

However, there was something even more awful that Barnsley had to believe. They had taken only one point from the game, leaving them with the same number of points as Forest who had a goal average of 0.78333 compared to Barnsley's average of 0.78125. Two-thousandths difference was enough to send Barnsley down.

A poor sportsman blames his luck, but supporters leaving the ground with heads down could perhaps be forgiven for cursing theirs, when they considered other factors beyond their control, and beyond the Club's ability to direct, had also played a part in fashioning destiny at Oakwell. The truth, although perhaps few saw it at the time, was that it seemed almost impossible for the Reds to become the big, successful club of their dreams, in the climate that existed. It is unlikely that even winning promotion to the First Division early in the century, when the wave of progress might have carried them further forwards, could have sustained them at the highest level for very long. After the Great War, when the pace of change slowed, football clubs seemed to consolidate only what they had achieved so far as the modern football's leagues began to take shape. In Barnsley's case, circumstances meant they could not look forward to being anything more than a small town club for the next few decades.

Without sponsorship, television revenue and licensed products, in those days, the only regular income any club could earn was from takings at the gate. The big successful clubs of the era drew enormous crowds, and the revenue from such large attendances enabled them not only to pay their bills, but to build dynasties by paying top price for everyone else's best players. In contrast, Barnsley FC had struggled to pay their way ever since they first started to keep accounts; the size of their home crowd was the main cause, and there was little they could do about it.

Attendances largely depended on three things; general trends that affected the whole country, the population of the area around the football club, and the team's performance. Barnsley could try and control only the last of these, and not always with success. Yet, without taking big money at the gate, the Club could not expect to seriously compete at the highest level.

In Barnsley, some local factors also played a small part in restricting day to day attendances, although they were not exclusive, other clubs had similar problems. Barnsley miners were restricted by a shift system, and a need to work, which sometimes were at odds with home games. Barnsley's traditional 3.15 p.m. kick-off (the rest of the country favoured 3.00 p.m.) was a tip of the hat to shift workers leaving the pit on Saturday mornings, encouraging them to come to the game.

At holiday times such as Christmas, Boxing Day and Easter, crowds were given a boost because pits were closed and all supporters had the day off. Attendances could sometimes double. Midweek games were difficult to attend; they were played during daylight hours in these pre- floodlights days. The working man did not own a car, and bus travel from surrounding districts was slow, adding expense to the afternoon. Many supporters walked from villages like Monk Bretton, Carlton and Dodworth, which were not too far out, but it is no wonder that cold weather and lean times were likely to keep attendances down, particularly when the team was not performing well.

Before the Great War, Barnsley FC had enjoyed their most successful years, yet even then average home gates in the League were only around five or six thousand. Immediately after the War, attendances boomed across the country; Barnsley took their share, doubling home crowds to ten and eleven thousand during the first half of the nineteen twenties. As the size of gates across the country levelled off, Barnsley felt the effects. Hard times for the working classes during the mid-twenties and early thirties did not help, but neither did Barnsley's failure to make an impact on the field. As the Reds struggled in the bottom half of the Second Division, they turned a national levelling off in attendances into a downhill slide at Oakwell. Home attendances fell into the six thousand range by the end of the twenties, and remained that way until Barnsley became Third Division Champions in 1934.

Crowds of over nine thousand celebrated their return to the Second Division. Attendances - partly reflecting a change in fortunes on the field as well as economic recovery - grew from then until the outbreak of the Second World War, when the Club enjoyed its best home average to that time, almost 14,000.

However, comparing Barnsley's attendances with those of larger clubs, not wary enough to escape a season or two in the Second Division, reveals a huge gulf between the sizes of the crowds that Barnsley could attract, and those of their rivals, even in good years:

1921-22	Barnsley v Nottm. Forest	18,000
	Nottm. Forest v Barnsley	28,000
1934-24	Barnsley v Sheffield Wed	16,000
	Sheffield Wed v Barnsley	25,000
1927-28	Barnsley v Manchester City	17,252
	Manchester City v Barnsley	38,226
1928-29	Barnsley v Chelsea	7,886
	Chelsea v Barnsley	34,793
1931-32	Barnsley v Tottenham	5,852
	Tottenham v Barnsley	28,585

Manchester, Sheffield and London clubs attracted large crowds because of the sheer numbers of people with easy accessibility to their grounds. The sad truth was that Barnsley's catchment area was simply not big enough to provide large numbers of regular supporters, even if the team had been the most successful club in the world. In 1936, when the visit of Stoke City in Round five of the FA Cup attracted a record attendance of 40,255 to Oakwell, the entire population of the Borough of Barnsley was only 60,000.

It was unreasonable to expect that Barnsley could sustain support in the region of twenty or thirty thousand at every game with such a small local population, but First Division clubs like Newcastle, Aston Villa and Arsenal did so easily. For important games, these clubs attracted home attendances which were larger than Barnsley's entire population.

By the time that transport became quicker, easier and more accessible, allowing Barnsley to draw support from a larger area, big clubs had established their followings and dominated the scene. Once this pattern was established, there was simply no way Barnsley could finance themselves into being the sort of club, supporters thought it should be. It was difficult enough simply keeping the Club alive. Inflation after the Great War, coupled with hardships in the mining industry, made it hard just to make ends meet.

The problem of paying players' wages on income from League games, for example, was still a recurring nightmare. Winger George Donkin had been paid the usual £2 a week when he first signed for the Club in 1913. by 1921, he was earning £8 per week and a pass to travel on the bus between Barnsley and Monk Bretton. The Club took only about £500 per week at the turnstiles that year. Although players wages rose considerably, admission prices did not keep pace. Even in the nineteen thirties, it still only cost sixpence (2½p) to stand on the terrace, and a shilling (5p) to sit in the wing stand, prices people had been paying to watch Barnsley for more than twenty years. With those sixpences, the Club had to support another twenty or so professional players like Donkin, and their trainer and manager; pay for travel to games as far apart as Bristol and Blackpool; maintain Oakwell, which now included offices, grandstand and covered standing areas, as well as the upkeep of the playing area; and in addition pay all the necessary Association and League fees and administrative costs required to keep teams on the field and the Club open for business. It came up around £100 a week short. In terms of attendances, that represented a minimum of 4,000 extra supporters every week just to keep the Club standing still.

In 1929, the Club lost £3,865 on the season, around half-a-million at to-day's prices. Income from Cup games was prayed for annually, not to fatten the purse, but to help the Club simply pay its way. Unfortunately, during the years between the wars, income from Cup games failed by a long way to bridge the gap between income and expenditure. Barnsley suffered through the leanest Cup years in their history, up to that time. On twelve occasions, they were eliminated at the first hurdle, and only once in twenty years, in 1935-36 when they won through from the third to the sixth round, did they even threaten to take their reputation as Cup battlers down from the shelf and shake the dust off it. For most of the period windfalls were few and far between. Only one resource was left to produce the kind of money which the Directors felt was needed to keep the Club afloat - the players. The Board did not sell the team's best players without considering alternatives, but there was no income to compare with selling one good player, and no cost-saving measure more effective than cutting the salary bill. Players like Hine, Brook, Barson and Tilson were sold to First Division clubs for cash; thirteen players were given free transfers after relegation in 1933.

On 1st December, 1929, the Club had tried to improve its financial standing by a different route. An extraordinary General Meeting was called at the Royal Hotel, Barnsley, to increase the share capital of the Club from £1,000 to £5,000 by issuing 8,000 new shares at 10 shillings each. Members had first chance of buying, the remaining balance was put on sale to the general public, but the response from the public was not good. Failure to raise capital in the town went to the root of the problem. Supporters complained loudly about the Club selling its

best players, but refused, or were not able, to be a part of the solution by either attending games in sufficient numbers or by contributing financially. Joe Richards, Chairman of the Financial Committee, spelled out the facts as the Directors saw them. *"We should not have to rely on the sale of our players to survive,"* he told the special meeting, *"but gates will have to improve. We have been criticised often enough for these transfers, but the transfers will continue, unless gate receipts go up."* We now know that it was unrealistic to expect gates to go up sufficiently enough to support the Club at the level the fans expected. Supporters saw it differently. They felt that if Barnsley had kept the first class players they had sold, they could have built winning teams which would have paid their way. However, the Directors experience of small businesses did not extend to speculation on that scale. They were more worried about the practical matter of whether ends would meet at the end of each week, when the payroll had to be counted and bills settled. They weren't millionaires, but their personal guarantees at the bank helped keep Barnsley FC afloat, and they feared ruin for both themselves and the Club. It was that fear that guided their policy.

They certainly could not have been driven by a desire to line the shareholder's pockets, as supporters sometimes suggested, for annual profits were as rare as an egg under a cockerel. In 1919, the very first year of renewed competition after the Great War, they did actually manage to make some money, but the £3,244 profit only corroborated the Director's point of view; if they had not sold Dickie Downs and Frank Barson during the season for a combined total of £5,700, the Club would actually have finished £2,500 out of pocket.

In the remaining years of the period, Directors continued to use the money from selling players as necessary income. However, they were unable to turn a profit like that again. With no surplus in hand, and regular income barely meeting overheads, it was obvious that not only would players continue to be sold, but that the team could not be supplemented by buying any additional players which might be required to boost its fortunes. Players could only be bought after others were sold.

It was extremely hard to be a Barnsley supporter. Fans on the terrace had seen their team scorned by football's elite, held down by a diabolical piece of refereeing, and fail to get any lucky breaks even when they tried hard to play good, attacking football. To fans of the future, this would seem like déjà vu. To make matters worse, any player who came along who was worth his salt, was likely to be gone before he had worn out his first pair of laces, and that the Directors were unlikely to venture any money to bring success to Oakwell. On reflection, it is not how small the Oakwell crowds were that is worth noting, but how well the fan's patience endured to keep attendances so high in the face of such discouragement.

CHAPTER 7

THE GREAT DEPRESSION

The small amount of finances available to Barnsley Football Club restricted their ambitions on the field. Each manager appointed by the Board had his own way of trying to cope, but circumstances were moving opportunity further and further out of Barnsley's reach. There were some highlights for the fans to enjoy between the wars, but for most of the period, Barnsley were trapped in a depression on the field just as great as the economic and social depression which gripped the country through the same period.

Peter Sant was first to try his hand as Manager at the start of the new age. Percy Lewis had been in charge of the team during the War, but he left to take over at Hull City. Sant was a Director of Barnsley Football Club before being appointed Secretary-Manager in 1919. He had no experience as a professional player, but had been a Football League referee. His credentials for the job came mostly through his administrative expertise. This was still an era when, at most clubs, players decided tactics for themselves, and the Manager was the man who bought the train tickets. For Barnsley, the appointment was something of a throwback to the times before McCartney, a manager who had, at least, brought some real football savvy to the role.

Sant, however, did carry some opinions of his own when it came to assembling a team. Little Jimmy Moore, who had played outside-left for Barnsley in the 1912 Cup Final, and was centre-forward in the third place finish team of 1915, remembered meeting Sant for the first time after being released from war work in the munitions factory on the Isle of Wight in 1919. He returned to Barnsley immediately, hoping to pick up his career. *"I had married a Barnsley girl and wanted to continue living in the town,"* recalled Moore. *"Percy Sant.......was the new boss, and told me without any more ado that he'd put me on the transfer list. Within two hours, I was fixed up with Southampton."* It was obvious that a fresh start after the new peace was on everyone's minds at Oakwell. When Sant took over, the Great War had already taken steps to break up a team that had looked so strong in 1915. Players were scattered far and wide. Some had joined the armed forces; others, like Jimmy Moore, had been relocated to work in reserved occupations. The Reds frequently needed the services of guest players just to put a team on the field between 1915 and 1919. While the League was suspended, they played in regional competitions designed to keep up spirits on the home front, but the games were more of an exhibition than a serious contest.

The pre-war momentum which had carried the Club to the brink of the First Division slipped away. Only five pre-war regulars returned to first team duty when the League opened again in August 1919.

Whatever Sant's opinions about the team he should put on the field, he was just as much a prisoner of club policy as his predecessors had been before the war. On 23rd October, 1919, Barnsley disposed of centre-half Frank Barson for a record fee of £2,700, and on 3rd March, 1920, the legendary full-back Dickie Downs was sold for a new record of £3,000. In fairness to the Directors, neither sale was made without the wishes of the players themselves. Barson, a player who knew his worth, was pushing for higher wages which the Club told him they would not pay, and Downs requested a transfer for 'family reasons'.

With the sale of Frank Barson, supporters believed that the Board had ripped out the heart of the Club. Frank arrived at Oakwell as a twenty-year-old in 1911, having been spotted while playing for a Cammell Lairds steelworks team in Sheffield. As soon as he gained a regular first team place in 1913, the fans loved him. Frank was a hard tackler and a strong header of the ball; he took no prisoners and brooked no slacking. He was a natural leader, and became team captain with a personality which dominated the centre of the field, delighting home crowds with characterful defending which sometimes left a less than favourable impression on visiting forwards. Some believe that the same fiery attitude which endeared him to fans is the reason why he made only one appearance for England after he left the Club for Aston Villa. Whilst at Villa, Frank claimed the longest headed goal ever in League football; a 30 yard bomb to beat Sheffield United at Bramall Lane on Boxing Day, 1921.

Cup winning veteran John 'Dickie' Downs, the originator of the sliding tackle, was, at thirty-three, getting a little long in the tooth, but he could still play. A few days before he signed for First Division Everton, he was selected to play in an England trial game, along with Frank Barson. After moving to Goodison Park, Downs also became a full England international.

With the loss of these two quality players from their defence, supporters could perhaps be forgiven for fearing the worst. They were wrong. The policy of selling established players for income, and filling the gaps with youth or experience, was still holding good for the time being.

Percy Beaumont, another local lad from Mexborough, emerged to run operations in the centre of the field. Jack Tindall provided stability at full-back, and 19-year-old Jack Gittins arrived from Bentley Colliery, initially to play at half-back and later to become a full-back partner to Jack Tindall.

It only took a couple of years for Sant's rebuilt team to rekindle hopes of the top flight. Barnsley ran a close race for promotion in 1921-22, their most successful season of the decade, which ended with that desperately close goal average which separated them from Stoke and a promotion place. Their success was owed to a trio of goalscorers, Brough Fletcher, Russell Wainscoat and Ernest Hine, supported from midfield by Joe Halliwell plus Charlie Baines, and from the wing by George Donkin.

The season before, Barnsley had scored only 48 goals. Suddenly they were on their way to racking up 67, more than any other team in the Division. It was obvious that these extra goals made all the difference in the world to the team's fortunes; they had conceded around the same number of goals in 1920-21 when they finished below mid-table.

Barnsley, like most teams, played with the predictable formation of five forwards, three half-backs and two full-backs, and, with the number of forwards overpowering the number of defenders, it was no surprise that spectators expected goals to be scored freely. By the same token, it was considered normal for a team to concede one or two goals now and then. This placed a higher premium on goalscoring than perhaps exists to-day. If you knew you were likely to concede fifty or so goals in a season, you had to have the players up front to score more than sixty - the emphasis was on attack.

The situation was fuelled by a popular understanding about how the game should be played. There were no team tactics designed to 'close down' opponents, play for a draw, or win games by making a priority out of stopping the other team scoring. Success depended on the one-against-one abilities of individual players; wingers against full-backs, centre-forwards against centre-halves, and so on. The importance of having strong players in key positions doubled. A player who was better, stronger and faster than the opponent he squared off against was worth his weight in gold.

In 1921-22, Barnsley were fortunate in putting together a whole batch of them. Brough Fletcher, a Geordie lad, came down from Shildon at the age of twenty-one in 1914, and made Barnsley his adopted home. He enjoyed his time at Barnsley so much that he came back to be coach and manager after his playing days ended. By 1921, he was an experienced 28-year-old with several years of Second Division competition behind him.

Brough Fletcher

Playing half the season at inside-right, and the remainder at centre-forward during 1921-22, he contributed 17 goals in 39 League games, his best production ever. Russell Wainscoat, at inside-left, came from non-League Maltby in 1919, aged 21, and equalled Fletcher's tally of seventeen goals in the season. He would later jump to the First Division with Middles-brough.

Ernest Hine

However, the real goal-scoring sensation of the year was Ernest Hine, a 20-year-old from Staincross, who burst into the first team midway through the season, and crashed home 12 goals in only 18 games during the vital end of season run-in. Like Barnsley's most famous inside-right predecessor, George Lillycrop, Hine was no giant. At 5 feet 7 inches (1.7m.), he was a pocket sized powerhouse with a shot so hard, he 'could send a ball through iron railings'. Ernest was eventually sold to First Division Leicester for £3,000 and played for England four times. He was later to join Manchester United.

George Donkin was another local lad, from Carlton, and proud of it, signing as a youngster on the eve of the Great War, and refusing to play for anyone other than his home town Reds, despite interest from the country's top clubs.

He thrilled down the right-wing with his pace and control and supplied most of the crosses for the terrible trio. Another England hopeful, he made it to the national team's trials, but poor health helped prevent selection as a full international. He died tragically at the young age of thirty-four.

In 1927, he leaped into the canal at Carlton to save a drowning girl, even though he could not swim, an act which earned him a bravery award from the Humane Society, but which also led to illness from which he never recovered.

Joe Halliwell, a versatile hard working forward who, jointly with Lol Chappell, holds the record for the number of hat-tricks scored in a season (three), signed for the club in 1913, around the same time as George Donkin. He dropped back to lend experience to the right-half position for the 1921-22 season, whilst Charlie Baines, renewing the Barnsley F.C. ties with Ardsley, claimed the left-half spot. Halliwell and Baines eventually clocked up more than 650 League and Cup appearances between them.

The exciting blend of youth and experience which almost propelled Barnsley into the First Division in 1922, stuttered badly the following year. A bright start suggested the team could continue where it left off, but when George Donkin's ill health forced him out of the team in December, the lustre wore off. Barnsley stayed in touch with the leaders but failed to join them. In April, when they should have been mounting their final push, they collapsed badly with losses to three clubs below them in the table, and only two wins out of their last seven games. They finished six points off a promotion place and never threatened to rush the door to the First Division again. In fact, as Barnsley's 'Great Depression' settled in, fans would have to wait a full eleven years for the next event worth cheering about.

Peter Sant did not wait that long. In 1926, with Barnsley floundering in the lower regions of Division Two, he made way for John Commins, an Irishman who had no previous connections with the club. Commins failed to improve Barnsley's position during his two seasons with the Club - 1926-27 and 1927-28 - and the Directors replaced him with Arthur Fairclough, whose experience they hoped would steady the helm. Fairclough had enjoyed a managerial career with Leeds United and Huddersfield Town after leading Barnsley to success

George Donkin

before the Great War. But by the time of his return he was ageing and did not have the stomach for a fight. In 1929-30, Barnsley lost a record number of away games in one season, eighteen, and finished just one point above the relegation zone. Fairclough saw that there would be no easy repeat of previous glory, and the task of managing Barnsley Football Club was more suited to a younger man; he recommended Brough Fletcher.

Brough Fletcher's appointment came as a break with recent custom. Brough had spent most of his playing career at Barnsley with only a short break at Sheffield Wednesday. Fairclough recognized the value of his experience as a player by making him first team coach during his second year in charge, and the Board appointed him Manager on the strength of Fairclough's recommendation and his service to the Club. McCartney had been the first Barnsley manager to take personal responsibility for the team, now Fletcher became the first not to simultaneously carry out the duties of Secretary to the Board. Obviously, the position of team manager at Oakwell was slowly evolving towards modern times. Unfortunately for Fletcher, progress was not smooth.

The new Manager did not inherit much in the way of a going concern to begin with, and his policies as Manager did not help to improve the situation. In his first year in charge, 1930-31, Barnsley failed to win a single game away from home and finished fourth from bottom, the last two teams being relegated. The following year, they were relegated from the Second Division for the first time in their history, after an unbroken membership of 34 years (30 playing seasons). Although they quickly bounced back from Division Three (North), Fletcher was unable to build a team capable of lasting success. His career at Oakwell ended as Barnsley prepared to slither back into the Third Division again.

Under Fletcher, the formula for team building took a turn for the worse. Since the early years of the century, the Club had largely survived on McCartney's system of signing teenagers from non-League clubs, and stabilising them with one or two experienced professionals. This was made possible by the fact that Barnsley had been one of the first clubs to operate a manager system. A manager with responsibility for a team, organized the scouting, recruitment and signing of young players. When Barnsley first started doing this, amateur and non-League football

F.A.Cup
1930/31

(Above)
Training before
the 5th round tie
at home to
Wolves...........

..............(Left)
Action from the
match, which
ended in a 3-1
defeat. The
Oakwell crowd
numbered over
33,000.

were unplundered sources of rich, undiscovered talent. The Club brought home as much as it could carry, and never had to worry about filling the gaps left by selling established players to other clubs. Needless to say, others began to realise what they were missing. With more clubs competing for unregistered players, and the effects of the Great War on population, the talent pool in junior and non-League football started to diminish. Quality replacements for the players Barnsley sold were getting harder to come by.

By the thirties, when Fletcher took over at Oakwell, many clubs had scouting operations in place. Managers of professional football clubs were active across the length and breadth of the country, and competition to sign young players was intense. Social historian Stephen Wragg wrote that managers *"..........now began to acquire a*

special mystique. They became canny wheeler-dealers, hanging furtively around railway platforms or hotel lobbies, waiting to conclude secret business. They were implied to be in a permanent battle of wits...........conning the parents of gifted young footballers into parting with their sons signatures, and so on. In the football folklore of the nineteen thirties, the manager always had a trick or two up his sleeve.........."

Young players not attracted away by the most famous clubs in the land were encouraged to sign for local clubs where they could enjoy the advantages of local popularity, and least disruption to their lives. Barnsley began to make the most of their junior signings in South and West Yorkshire where the Club was well known, and where juniors could start apprenticeships at local collieries whilst testing the waters of a football career.

The same kind of thing, working against Barnsley's interests, was happening in those regions where they traditionally had a strong recruiting base. Sunderland, Newcastle and Middlesbrough were all now actively capturing local talent before it got away; offers to join them looked more tempting to youngsters in the North East than did a trip down to Barnsley. The land that was once milk and honey became off-limits to Oakwell, and the flow of good quality recruits began to dry up.

With the Club forced to recruit more from a smaller geographical area, the talent available to them was reduced proportionately. Also, with more players tied to League clubs from an early age, Barnsley found themselves having to trade for players they might have once picked up for nothing. The transfer market had arrived. Unattached players of any worth became as rare as diamonds.

There is no better example of how times were changing than Barnsley's acquisition of George Henderson. George was a centre-half who came down from Sunderland in 1928 to bolster a defence that was in danger of shipping the team into Division Three. It was almost unheard of for Barnsley to spend money on acquiring players, but desperate circumstances caused the Club to break with tradition and splash out a record fee of £1,500. In a different age, Henderson might have already been at Oakwell, signed for nothing as a junior from his local colliery team; now, Barnsley had to pay a transfer fee. He made more than 270 appearances for Barnsley, but his price helped contribute to a huge financial loss at the end of the season.

As a result of the changes in football recruiting, almost half Barnsley's team on any given Saturday afternoon in the mid-thirties comprised players signed from other clubs; fewer and fewer were signed directly from colliery, works and district teams. At Oakwell, the effect gave a new twist to the composition of the team. Instead of a clutch of youngsters steadied by one or two experienced professionals, the opposite was the case. Fletcher's use of the transfer market, in the absence of available young talent and a Board that would not speculate, tended towards the 'quick fix' of veteran players supported by one or two up and coming youngsters.

George Caddick - over 170 appearances for Barnsley between 1925 and 1931.

Following relegation in 1932, Fletcher organized a major clear out and started to rebuild his side. By the time 1933-34 came around, he had assembled a team ready to challenge for the Championship, and a return to Division Two. A talented young goalscorer was one of the leading characters in a team that reprised the familiar mix of South Yorkshiremen, Geordies and North Midlanders, but the average age indicated that this was no 'Barnsley Babes' phenomenon. It was a team that did not have a long future, as the youthful pre-War teams had. Sure enough, within a couple of years, most of the players in the team that won the Third Division (North) Championship had to be recycled, and the scramble began again.

Abe Blight was a teenager working in a colliery in County Durham when Brough Fletcher first received reports about him; fortunately for Barnsley he was one of the increasingly few prospects that Oakwell scouts were able to snatch from under the noses of rival clubs. Playing for Blackhill, his local team, Blight knocked in 65 goals in one season. At Barnsley, he had big shoes to fill. Top scorer John Wallbanks, a lone ray of sunshine with 22 goals during the relegation struggle, and another 20 during the first year in Division Three, had just been transferred to Portsmouth. Fans were rolling their eyes again at the Management's ineptitude, and the Club's prospects without their best player, as a second year began in the lower division. Fortunately, Blight was an instant success, pummelling 31 League goals in the promotion season, a record high that stood for 17 years. Unfortunately, his career was cut short by a knee injury just a year later.

Blight was the exception rather than the rule, as Fletcher built his promotion push on experience, and not youth. Blight's inside-left partner was 30-year-old Harold Andrews, and when 31-year-old full-back Aneurin Richards went out with an injury, Fletcher brought in Sam Cookson, who was approaching his 37th birthday, as his replacement. Richards was capped for Wales whilst playing for Barnsley in the Second Division. He was a good player, but Barnsley managed to make him look ordinary; Richards missed only one game in Barnsley's worst ever defensive season when they went down from the Second Division in 1932, conceding 91 goals.

Club Captain, and crowd favourite 'Tubby' Ashton, was 27, and had already spent six years on the wing at Oakwell when he turned out to begin the season which saw them triumph over the Third Division. It would be fair to say that most of the other players in the team also had more career to look back on, than forward, to when the season kicked off in August. Players in the mid-twenties were babes in the team. To Fletcher's credit, they stood up robustly to the demands of a difficult year, and met the immediate challenge, but it was not a formula for long-lived success.

Promotion back to the Second Division was a serious challenge. In those days, the League consisted of national First and Second Divisions and two regional Third Divisions, North and South, each with 22 teams. Each year, the two clubs which finished bottom of Division Two were relegated, and their places were taken by the Champions of both Third Divisions. A second place finish in the Third Division was worth nothing, it was Championship or bust.

After a mediocre first season in Division Three (North) in 1932-33, Barnsley came out hot for the start of the new campaign. They scored 21 goals in their first 6 games, and dropped only one point. For most of the season, Chesterfield were ahead of them in first place, but Barnsley clung furiously to their coat-tails. At times, they were on fire. On 3rd February, 1934, they equalled the

Aneurin Richards

Club's record of goals scored in a League game with a 9-0 away win at Accrington Stanley. Abe Blight scored four, the most any Barnsley player has ever scored in an away game. The following week, they roared into a 'four-pointer' win at home against rivals Chesterfield. Despite the fact that Barnsley did not lose a single game after the last page of December 1933 was torn from the calendar, it was still a race to the wire. That run of 21 unbeaten games, from 1st January to 5th May, is still a Club record. Finally, Barnsley triumphed by one point.

For the fans, something to shout about had been a long time coming; there was finally a burst of light in the gloom of their depression. The Third Division Championship was the first thing the Club had won since 1912, and although it did not look particularly distinguished at the side of the FA Cup, it proved that following a winning team in a lower Division could be more fun than watching them struggle in a higher Division. Support at home had almost doubled compared to the previous season. The fans were also happy to travel to away games in noisy numbers; more than 3,000 of them journeyed by bus, train and car to the last game of the season at New Brighton, which Barnsley had to win to be sure of the title. They made up almost half the crowd. The little stadium, awash with red and white scarves, became like a home venue to help steer the Reds to a 1-0 victory.

Fans welcomed Barnsley's return to Division Two, but it was a pyrrhic victory for Fletcher and the Club. The horses that had hitched their wagon to a star had almost nothing left to offer. When Abe Blight was lost to injury, goals dried up. In their promotion push, Barnsley had scored 118 goals; in their first year back in Division Two, they scored just 60. Fletcher's solution was to bring in more 'quick-fix' veterans.

Ernest Hine was brought back from Manchester United to replace Blight midway through the season.

Formal kick-off at the Richards Testimonial match - 30 April 1934.

To strengthen the squad for another year, Brough Fletcher came back from Birmingham on 29th November, 1935, holding a contract with the name of Barnsley's most expensive signing on it. The Club had tipped up £2,000 for a 'star' player, Tom 'Pongo' Waring, of First Division Aston Villa, a prolific goalscorer who had made five appearances for England.

With these two ex-England internationals up front, Barnsley's attack acquired celebrity status. It was a coup for Brough Fletcher, but Hine was 33 years of age, and Pongo 29. Both players were veterans near the end of their careers, and their arrival did nothing to improve the Club's prospects over the long or short term. In

Big signing in 1935, 'Pongo' Waring

fact, Waring played only 18 League games for Barnsley. Hine struggled manfully on as leading scorer in both 1935-36 and 1936-37, but with little support, and the task of saving the Club was too much for one man. In the year that the two teamed up together, Barnsley only managed to score a meagre 54 League goals. At the other end, they were deluged with 80. Barnsley avoided relegation by one point, and Brough Fletcher faced the same problems at season's end as he had faced almost every year since taking over; what to do for the future?

Although the Club made a major departure from previous policy by signing Henderson, Hine and Waring during their lean years, it did not signal a change of heart in the Boardroom. In fact, the opposite was probably true. The Club's poor return on its expense was possibly noted by Joseph Richards, a young man who had served on the Financial Committee, and who was now Chairman, a position that lasted two and a half years (January, 1934 to July, 1936). Richards would become Chairman again twelve years later, and dominate the Club in a way no one else had since Tiverton Preedy's time.

During the years of Barnsley's great depression, he was learning the lessons that would shape his policy and the Club's destiny. The signings of Henderson, Hine and Waring confirmed what he already suspected, that throwing money about did not solve the Club's problems. However, his apprenticeship in football directorship with the ancient John Rose, the man under whose Chairmanship Barnsley had won the FA Cup in 1912, made him a firm supporter of selling to survive; he had seen it work with his own eyes.

Rose, who had seen the selling policy succeed in a different climate, when replacements were easily available, remained Chairman and advocate of selling the best players until his death in 1933.

The fans thought it was a good sign that the Board had actually parted with money to bring players to Oakwell, but they knew the money had been spent on the wrong players and at the wrong time. In the case of Hine and Waring, the signings were made out of desperation to solve an immediate problem, not as keystones for future team building. All the fans wanted to see, was Barnsley keep their suite of good players, and buy only the aces needed to turn the team into a winning hand. Instead, their depression deepened as quality players continued to be stripped from the ranks and sold, even when the Club needed all the help it could get from them. The supporters became increasingly frustrated as they saw good players leave to be replaced by ones of lesser ability.

Fred Tilson was twenty-two when he signed for Barnsley from Regent Street Congs, a church team that, over the years, became one of the best showcases of town talent. Going straight into the first team in 1926, he scored 23 goals in 61 League appearances before being signed by Manchester City, who were going into the First Division as Second Division Champions. With City, Fred won a Football League Championship and the FA Cup, scoring both goals in a 2-1 Wembley win, and played four times for England. After spells with Northampton Town and York City, he returned to Manchester City as coach, and progressed to Assistant Manager and finally Chief Scout before retiring in 1972.

His partner up front at Barnsley was Eric Brook, a nineteen-year-old from Mexborough. Barnsley bought him for £200 from Wath Athletic, and he quickly became the first team's left-winger. A few days after Tilson signed for Manchester City, Brook left Barnsley to join him at Maine Road. Eric played 18 times for England, and 494 League and Cup games for City in the First and Second Divisions, scoring 178 goals, with a League Championship and two Cup Final appearances to his credit.

Manchester City's Barnsley duo of Brook and Tilson plagued First Division defences for years; it was one of the most talked about topics in the Football League. Brook was built like the proverbial outhouse, a brave, hard player whose fierce determination was not a substitute for talent, but simply another facet of it. Tilson, playing alongside Brook at inside-left, diddled opposing defences with deft ball control, and fired a hard shot with either foot. Barnsley fans were under-standably angry when this lethal combination packed up their kit and headed over the Pennines in March 1928; their future careers, although then unknown, proved to them, over a period of time, absolute folly of the Club's Directors.

Dickie Spence played for Platts Common Working Men's Club, and earned a reputation as a prodigious goalscorer in Barnsley soccer circles, with 88 goals in one season. Fletcher brought him to Oakwell as a 24-year-old, and put him on the right wing during season 1932-33, Barnsley's first in Division Three.

He scored on his debut against Darlington, and the following year was an important part of the team which won the Third Division Championship, with 19 goals in 41 games, a rate of scoring that no other winger has ever duplicated, and which some Barnsley forwards have only dreamed about.

Frank Chivers scores in the 2-2 home draw with Blackpool. March 1935

Long-serving Manager, Angus Seed.

The move out to the wing paid dividends for Spence's career. He was able to showcase his strength in beating players one-on-one, whilst providing an extra quality which a lot of wingers lacked; instead of just booting the ball into the middle, he had the option of ending his runs by challenging the goalkeeper with a fierce shot.

This lethal combination of talent attracted Chelsea. They parted with £4,000 early in the 1934-35 season, and Spence was yet another player on his way from Oakwell to the First Division and two international appearances for England, leaving Barnsley a team still on the way to nowhere. Their young, England bound, First Division talent continued to leave, and older, less experienced veterans continued to arrive; it was a recipe which could lead to only one conclusion.

Barnsley fans sunk deeper into their depression as the Club headed for the Third Division once again. However, as Britain climbed out of its economic recession, a new seed of success was being planted at Oakwell; Barnsley prepared to lift spirits and stage their own long awaited recovery.

CHAPTER 8
SEEDS OF SUCCESS

No matter how low fortunes are in the League, the FA Cup always seems to inspire some hope of success. For Barnsley, during most of the nineteen twenties and thirties, even the slim hope of Cup glory managed to elude them. Not until 1935-36 did the Reds take their reputation as Cup battlers out of the closet and give it a good shaking. When the dust settled, they found themselves in a quarter-final tie with Arsenal, the biggest, richest club in the land.

A good cup-tie has a magical attraction. When First Division Birmingham visited Barnsley in Round Three of the 1936 competition, the crowd of almost 30,000 was easily the largest turnout of the season to date. When the Reds drew the game 3-3, the crowd milled philosophically up Grove Street on their way home; it had been a good match, but that was it. The Blues would surely finish Barnsley off in the replay at St. Andrews.

It turned out that Barnsley had a lucky charm. Centre-forward Pongo Waring, who had spent his career in the First Division before signing for Barnsley a few months earlier, had scored against England goalkeeper Harry Hibbs, who was in City's goal for the replay, just about every time he had played against him. Pongo's luck held out in the second-half of the replay. He seized onto a bouncing ball, and cannoned it into the top corner from 30 yards to seal a 2-0 win. Barnsley were absolutely brilliant on the day; they played their hearts out and earned praise from all corners. The victory was a major upset, one of those wonderful unexpected wins that supporters remember for a lifetime.

The next round took Barnsley to the other end of the Cup spectrum, Third Division Tranmere Rovers, away. They trained at the Lancashire seaside,

as Cup-winning teams had done before them, and running in heavy sand certainly prepared them well to play in the muddy quagmire that Tranmere's field became after heavy rain. Barnsley slogged their way to a 4-2 victory.

Cup fever became an epidemic when the draw for Round Five was made. *"Barnsley........at home to........Stoke City,"* intoned the radio announcer. Stoke City! Another First Division team, but more than that, the team of England's legendary winger, Stanley Matthews. On a damp and frosty afternoon on 15th February, 1936, the biggest crowd ever likely to be seen at Oakwell crammed itself into the ground. In the days before crowd safety restrictions, people pressed together so tightly that if you had your hands in your pockets before the game started, you would not be able to wipe your nose until you got to Barnsley bus station after the match. Oakwell, a grey sea of winter overcoats splashed with red and white cup rosettes, buzzed with a special cup-tie atmosphere of cheerful excitement, nerves and bravado.

Within seconds of the start, the 40,255 people inside the ground were in danger of exploding with excitement. Tubby Ashton got the ball from the kick-off, crossed from the left, and Frank Gallacher jumped to nod the ball home. What an amazing start! Shocked City fought to recover and quickly made their mark with a goal only eight minutes later, but with less than ten minutes gone, a capacity crowd had a game on their hands; they knew they were in for a real cup-tie.

Barnsley revelled in the home atmosphere and the famous opposition. At left-back, Harry Topping had the job of stopping Stanley Matthews. He had played only seven times before for Barnsley, and the 27-year-old had just twelve League games to his credit when he joined Barnsley from Manchester United.

A very mundane programme for the game which attracted an all-time record crowd to Oakwell. (Note the programme number!)

Topping had Matthews in his pocket for the entire game, and without him, the City attack rarely looked dangerous. Barnsley's right-half that day, Tom Holley, recalled in a newspaper article he wrote 20 years later, *"I'll bet Matthews, even after all the memorable occasions he has had in his career, has a spot in his memory for Harry Topping. Never before or since, not by all the famous continental full-backs who have opposed him, have I seen Stanley so subdued."* Full back partner Bob Shotton, later to become Barnsley trainer, helped stitch up the rest of Stoke's threats.

Meanwhile, Waring and Hine were a couple of menaces for Barnsley up front. Just before half-time, Tubby Ashton crossed the ball again. Waring shot; the ball was deflected. Gallacher pounced, his shot was beaten down, Hine charged, the loose ball flew into the net, and Barnsley were 2-1 up. That was good enough for a final result, and Barnsley trotted from the field to thunderous applause, proud giant-killers with another famous scalp to hang on their belts.

Their reward was a trip to Arsenal, the most successful club of the era. Arsenal had two League Championships and one FA Cup win to their credit in the previous five years. Wilf Copping was just one of their stars; they were known as the 'England Team' for all the internationals who turned out for them. Barnsley, meanwhile, were at the foot of Division Two, and the Third Division North Championship was the only thing they had won in 20 years. However, Barnsley fans, enthused by cup fever, still believed that the Reds could go marching on.

Unfortunately, injuries shattered Barnsley's chances of cup glory. Waring broke his arm in a League match a few days before the Arsenal game, and could not play, even though he offered to turn out with his arm in a splint. Full-back Topping went down in the second-half of the match, and Barnsley were forced into an emergency re-shuffle; no substitutes were allowed in those days. By then, Arsenal were already leading from a goal scored just three minutes into the game. The combination of injuries, a patched up team formation, and a cultured opposition playing at home in front of more than 60,000 people, proved too much; the game caved in on Barnsley's heads, and they trooped off the field to a 4-1 loss. Beaten, but not shamed, the fans had enjoyed their brief flirtation with success.

The F.A. Cup provided one more brief but memorable moment before the War. After beating Third Division Southend in the third round of the 1937-38 competition, Barnsley earned a home tie against Manchester United. Over 35,000 people went down to the 'Well for the big game. The talking point of the match turned out not to be the result, but a goal credited to Barnsley's Frank Bokas. United went ahead after only eleven minutes, and Barnsley charged at them from the kick-off, roared on by the big crowd. United tried to ease the pressure and a

Barnsley attack was broken up by kicking the ball out of play about fifteen yards from the corner flag.

Frank Bokas, Barnsley's right-half, strode up to take a long throw, not so commonly seen in 1938. The ball sailed through the air towards the Pontefract Road end goal, cleared the heads of everyone in the box, hit the underside of the bar, came down on goalkeeper Breen's hands, and dropped over the line.

It took everyone by surprise, including the stunned crowd, the majority of whom knew you could not score a goal directly from a throw-in. However, as United hoofed the ball out, the referee signalled a goal. He had seen the ball hit the 'keeper and cross over the goal line. For many years, Frank Bokas became the answer to a trivia question, "Who is the only player ever to score a goal from a throw-in". Not until Huddersfield were the visitors to Oakwell in 1996, when Barnsley 'keeper Watson was judged to have touched a Huddersfield throw-in that looped into the net, was anything like it seen before or since. Unfortunately for Barnsley, Bokas' good luck did not transfer to the result, a 2-2 draw. Barnsley lost the replay at Old Trafford, 1-0.

Despite the loss, and relegation from the Second Division yet again, there was finally a real seed of success down at Oakwell in Angus Cameron Seed. Seed was hired to replace Brough Fletcher as Manager in February, 1937. Fletcher's legacy of an ageing team struggling in the bottom half of the Second Division gave Seed little chance of effecting a quick cure. The Board did let their new manager spend £2,500 for Spurs' centre-forward Doug Hunt in March, 1937, but found once again that they could not buy their way out of trouble. The team finished in 14th place that year, and the following season were relegated. Hunt became top scorer, but with only 14 goals. It was obvious that problems ran deep and that changes had to be made.

Fortunately, as Angus Seed got into his stride, he had the effect of a new broom sweeping clean. His was the ideal appointment at the right time, rejuvenating a club which had become sterile after years in the doldrums, with fresh ideas and a notebook full of useful contacts throughout the country to help him carry them out. His very first signing, for example, was right-half Johnny Logan, a man he had first met some years before at his brother's club, Charlton Athletic, but who was now wasting away at Darlington. Signed within a few days of Seed taking over, Logan cost a bargain £750, and eventually made over 300 appearances, including 234 wartime games, for Barnsley.

Many think that Angus Seed was a Scot, which is hardly surprising given his name and his connections with Scottish players whom he called on to serve Barnsley well. He was actually born in Whitburn, County Durham, and his brother Jimmy played five times for England before becoming one of Charlton Athletic's most successful managers, taking them from the Third to the First Division in consecutive seasons. The Seed family was steeped in the game, but Angus was never a star player himself.

In 1914, he joined Leicester Fosse (later Leicester City), and then moved from one little club to another; Reading, Edinburgh St.Bernards, Mid-Rhondda, Workington, Broxburn United and Workington again. During the Great War, he served in the trenches and came back with the Military Medal for valour at Vimy Ridge. Although his playing career was undistinguished, it gave him a broad background of experience to draw on at clubs with limited resources, and his military service surely helped give him the mettle to be a strong leader. He began coaching and managing with Workington, and then moved to Aldershot, where he won the Southern League and London Combination, before taking them in to the League in 1932.

Mr. Seed arrived at Oakwell at the age of 44, after spending 10 years (1927 to 1937) as manager of Aldershot who joined the Football League in 1932. He had an appetite for the game, a keen eye for talent, the ability to carry through changes that worked, and the respect of his players, through a fatherly personality. After seeing the Club relegated during his first season in charge, he also had a plan. He decided to build a team with more future.

Seed's strong connection with players from north of the border resurrected a relationship with the Scottish game which Barnsley had not enjoyed since McCartney's time. The Reds had not done so well at signing new players since it became harder to recruit outside the local area, and more players came with a transfer fee.

Seed's access to talent from Scotland was like being given the key to a private storeroom. When the door was unlocked, out popped Johnny Lang from Aberdeen, Danny McGarry from Greenock Morton and Johnny Steele from Ayr United, three forwards who helped to transform a relegated team into Championship winners in 1938/39.

During the promotion season, Seed added depth to his player pool with Gavin Smith from Dumbarton and Arthur Baxter from Dundee. Such was the influence of the Scots at Oakwell that the Hull City Chairman once referred to Barnsley as 'The Glasgow Rangers of the Third Division North'.

Bert Barlow

In keeping with the times, Barnsley's new talent had a price. Danny McGarry cost £5,000 and Jock Steele £2,500. Another Scot, Jack Calder, who failed to make the impact of the other two, was signed from Bolton Wanderers for £3,000. However, the outlay of cash did not mean the Board had thrown caution to the wind; the money came largely from the sale of other players. For example, First Division Wolves paid £7,500 for inside-right Bert Barlow, a home-grown youngster, and a reserve called Myers. The cash from that deal financed the purchase of McGarry and Steele. Nevertheless, Seed did gamble; he relied on scouting reports to confirm details about players, and did not always see them play himself.

With Steele, it worked perfectly. When Wolves made their approach for Barlow, they whispered that a young Scot called Johnny Steele would be a good replacement if Barnsley could sign him. When Angus Seed heard the same story from a Manchester United scout, Steele was quickly signed without the Manager ever having set eyes on him. With Danny McGarry, it did not work so well. Seed was keen to sign younger players and thought McGarry was 22. When McGarry arrived at Oakwell, Seed found out he had just bought a 28 year old!

Fletcher's concept of stacking the forward line with players at the end of their careers had produced neither goals, in time of need, nor heirs apparent for the future. During this time, the defence had not particularly leaked goals, but Seed, in line with the popular understanding of the game, knew that in order to be successful and shoot the Club out of the Third Division, he had to set the forward line on fire. McGarry, at outside-left, and Lang, at inside-left, became two flame-throwers with 22 League goals between them. Johnny Steele, at inside-right, added seventeen by himself.

Besides their individual contributions, these players also threw off sparks that set other players burning. Right-winger George Bullock had managed only two goals in the previous year; now he grabbed ten. Twenty-eight-year old Beaumont Asquith, from Painthorpe near Wakefield, had signed for the Club as a 22-year-old, and had been knocking on the first team door for three years before finally edging his way in as a regular, the year the Club went down. Playing at inside-forward that season, he had bumped along with eight goals, although even that was good enough to make him the second highest scorer in a poor team. Alongside the invading Scots, he suddenly blossomed into a super hero at centre-forward with twenty-eight goals.

It jump-started his career, as Manchester United swooped for him at the end of the season, paying Barnsley £6,000, and off he went. Beaumont played only one League game for Manchester United due to the outbreak of war at the start of the next season.

In his wonder year at Barnsley, Asquith equalled the Club record for most goals scored in a game with five against Darlington at Oakwell. Five years earlier, Peter Cunningham had scored five at Oakwell against the same opponents, and in 1927, Eaton had set the ball rolling with five against South Shields. His 18 goals at Oakwell that year also equalled the Club record for the most goals scored at home by a Barnsley player in one season.

George Lillycrop had achieved the same feat in 1912-13. Beaumont was perhaps a sign that things were going right for Barnsley, at last. Those who remembered 1922, the year they lost out on promotion because of goal difference and missed penalties, would have been tearful watching Asquith clobber home all nine spot kicks which came the team's way that particular year. In fact, Asquith converted 29 consecutive penalties in all before finally missing one.

McGarry, Lang, Asquith and Bullock were all pretty much one year wonders through no fault of their own, for the outbreak of the Second World War closed their chapters. Johnny Steele, however, has remained at Barnsley almost as long as the ravens at the Tower of London, putting his heart and soul into the Club in a record of service unique to football. It was very nearly not the case. Steele was one of a series of prospective footballers who came to Barnsley over the years, took one look at the town, and thought, 'you must be joking'.

Johnny Steele and Danny McGarry had travelled down together from Glasgow in the summer and were staying in digs at Mottram Street. The first morning, they were woken up before dawn by a terrible noise in the street outside. Throwing back the curtains, they saw a parade of miners clattering over the cobblestones in clogs, off to a day shift at the pit. McGarry said *"I'm not going to be long here!"* and Steele quickly agreed with him. However, Steele is still at the Club today. On 26th April 1997, aged 80, in a place reserved for him by the Club, as a Vice-President for life, he was one of the tearful thousands who stood in pouring rain celebrating Barnsley's promotion to the Premiership, sharing the achievement of a one hundred and ten year dream, and his own 60 year part in that dream.

As a player, Johnny Steele was renowned as the man with the corkscrew dribble. Give him the ball, and he would run it right through the opposing team, if he could. In a game against Crewe in the 1938-39 promotion year, that's just what he did, scoring one of the best individual goals Barnsley fans have ever seen at the 'Well. Steele got the ball in his own penalty area, ran the length of the pitch, dribbling past five opponents on the way, rounded the 'keeper and booted it home to cap a 5-2 victory. At thirteen stone, Jock was not the kind of player you easily knocked off the ball. His speed and skill with the ball at his feet were belied by his powerful, stocky build, and the same size provided him with a rasping shot.

In 1938-39, there were few occasions when the team did not look good. It was a rampage for most of the year, with the Reds at one stage looking as if they would break the League record for number of points in a season. They missed by one, but they did score more goals (94) and concede less (34) than any other team in the four Divisions, and set new club records on their way to finishing eleven points clear of their nearest rivals, Doncaster Rovers.

Their 30 wins were the most number of games a Barnsley team had ever won in one season in the League, and their five losses were the fewest. Their 67 points, based on 2 for a win and 1 for a draw, were the most ever won in one season. They did the 'double' a record ten times. Although the 1934 promotion team scored more goals, this team gave up fewer than any other in Barnsley's history, conceding just 34 in a 42 game season.

The team that Seed had assembled was not by any means a 'babes' team, but it still had a future. Most players were in the fullness of their prime. Only goalkeeper Cliff Binns, full-back Jack Everest and forward Johnny Lang had pushed past thirty, and even their combined years failed to bring the average age of the team past 27. Given its clear superiority in the Third Division, and supplemented by more of Seed's shrewd additions, there was no reason why the team could not have continued its success at a higher level. Both on the field and financially, with the largest total league attendances in its history over the season (home gates averaged nearly 14,000), the Club was on an upward curve. Johnny Steele, looking back ruefully to the interruption caused by War, always felt that the 1938-39 team was, until recent years, the best ever seen at Oakwell. *"It was a very good team............I think that if war hadn't broken out, we would have gone up another Division,"* he said in a 1997 Yorkshire television documentary.

However, when war was declared in September 1939, the Government, sensing vulnerability to enemy bombing raids and a potential for tragedy, forbade any event drawing thousands of people together in one place. In a replay of 1915, when hostilities first curbed the progress of an aspiring Barnsley team, the Football League was temporarily discontinued. Fortune, for once having allowed the Club's cup to be filled, dashed it from Barnsley's lips before supporters could drink, leaving the Seeds of success with no chance to bear fruit.

CHAPTER 9

THE SUNSET OF OUR HOPES

When the Football League resumed after the Second World War, Barnsley picked up where they had left off in 1939, both literally and figuratively. The season's fixtures for 1939, which had been cancelled after only three games, were reproduced for the start of the first campaign after the war, in 1946. As the Reds kicked-off in games delayed seven years by events in Europe, they tried valiantly to reproduce the spirit, flair and enthusiasm which had characterised the last days of the pre-war years. For a while, it seemed as if they would succeed. Fans basked in the glorious enjoyment of entertaining football, and the prospect that the Club would eventually come good, little suspecting that in fact they were witnessing the sunset of their hopes, not a new dawning. A decade later, the well of star players would dry up, attendances would begin to fall, and financial hardship would become a crushing burden.

In 1946, Angus Seed was still manager. He had kept the flame burning at Oakwell throughout the war years, when Barnsley played in regional competitions designed to keep up national spirit, but reduce travel owing to war-time restrictions. In Barnsley, where the mining and glass industries offered reserved occupations, there was always an audience ready to support the local team, and employment to support the players.

Player registration rules were relaxed and players stationed in different parts of the country on war-time assignments, popped up on loan wherever they could get a game. Seed juggled combinations of old regulars, borrowed players and new hopefuls, to put a team on the field each week. On a couple of occasions, he even persuaded England internationals to turn out in Barnsley's colours; Ted Sagar of Everton played twice for Barnsley in 1940-41 and Ken Willingham, an international half-back, appeared five times in for Barnsley in 1943-44. Barnsley's own Bernard Harper, a Gawber lad, captain and centre-half of the 1938-39 team and a war-time regular, was himself called up to play for England in an international against Scotland in 1939.

When the League season re-opened in 1946, the effects of the war-time interlude could be seen as soon as Barnsley's team took the field. George Bullock, one of the exciting prospects of the 1938-39 team, had been killed in an accident while serving with H.M. Forces in the south of England. Johnny Steele, the stocky and exciting inside-forward, had injured his knee in a game at Oakwell in 1942, and then was posted with the R.A.F. to a boat patrol in the Bay of Bengal where he played only three games of football in two years; he returned a stone

and a half overweight and his career was effectively over. The hard man of the defence, Bernard Harper was missing too, considered too old now at nearly 34 to return as a player, despite retaining his fitness as a P.T. instructor in the R.A.F. Danny McGarry, after playing through the War, went back to play for smaller clubs in Scotland, and by now a 35-year-old. Johnny Logan, the fearless hard running half-back of the 1938-39 team, lasted only a few games. However, it was not the omissions, it was the new additions that set the town buzzing, and kept the fans flocking to Oakwell over the next few years.

In many ways, these were amongst the most exciting years to be a Barnsley fan. Although the Club had no real success, the years after the War were enjoyed as a honeymoon between club and town, as once again the country tried to return to normal after the War. Football was a familiar and comforting ritual which provided a sense of fun and hopefulness after the despair of recent years. Attendances boomed across the country, as they had done after the First World War, and particularly so at Oakwell where the Club averaged gates of over 19,000, including one memorable season in 1947-48, when this rose to over 21,000, their best home average ever. In the F.A. Cup, Barnsley played in front of 60,384 at Newcastle in 1946, and 38,000 at Oakwell against Blackpool in 1949 - the highest home attendance since the Stoke visit in 1936.

Fans flocked to enjoy themselves. The Barnsley players they watched were the last bloom of the rose, and the fans revelled in the glory of their play, and the richness of their characters. Without team success, it was an era in which the players themselves were definitely the main attraction. Blanchflower, Kelly, Robledo, Baxter and McCormack, every supporter had his favourite, and every game was an adventure. Packed tightly around Oakwell, supporters could call out to players on the field as if they were hailing them across the street. They bantered freely and humorously with each other on the terraces, 'ooohed' and 'aaahed' at every play, and clapped fiercely to applaud good play by both teams.

In those days, spectators at Oakwell could watch a parade of quality players performing in the Second Division, even England internationals. It was one of those periods when everything seemed to be comfortable, perhaps too comfortable. At Barnsley, the atmosphere bordered on complacency. For the sake of a little risk, the Club might have turned their last hurrah into a call to victory.

During these post-war years a good nucleus of players with which to mount a charge to the First Division passed through the gates of Oakwell for the last time in fifty years.

Up front, when the League season opened in 1946, a slightly built, loose-limbed Chilean youngster bombed three goals against Nottingham Forest in Barnsley's opening day game, his first appearance in the Football League, serving notice of the team's potential. George Robledo was a revelation. At a time when foreigners were unheard of in the English game, Robledo provided Barnsley fans with all the magic and enchantment that modern crowds expect from imported players, in the dour and unlikely setting of post-war Oakwell. Not that George was really all that foreign by this time, for he had lived in West Melton since he was five, but his foreign birth gave him a little romance, and he was always known as 'Barnsley's Chilean centre-forward'.

After playing for Dearne Valley Boys, and flirting with Huddersfield Town as an amateur, Robledo signed as a professional with Barnsley at the age of 17. He had actually first played for the Club in a friendly at the age of 15, and scored twice, reflecting both his tremendous promise and the difficulty of finding players to put teams together during the war. However, when real competition began again, Robledo quickly showed that, although he was only young, he could play a man's game. He scored 23 goals in his first 42 League games for Barnsley, and played 114 times for the Club before joining, in 1949, one of the all-time great Newcastle United sides that included legends like Jackie Milburn and Joe Harvey. Newcastle paid a fee of £26,000 which also included brother Ted Robledo, a Barnsley reserve who eventually won a place in United's 1952 F.A. Cup Final team.

Robledo was a sign of the future in more ways than one. He supplemented his talent with a tremendous work ethic,

(Above) George Robledo.................
.................(Below) Johnny Kelly

spending hours in extra training, working on meeting crosses and first-timing the ball, when training for most players still meant laps and practice games in which they were encouraged to 'save it fo' Setdi'. He was a harbinger of the future when natural ability alone would not be enough to survive, and new methods on the training field would increase in importance to a player's career. It fuelled his success, and perhaps did the same for another young, slightly built player signed as a youngster, except that this player was denied that kind of ball-training at Barnsley, and Oakwell was poorer when he left in search of it.

Danny Blanchflower cost Barnsley £6,000 when Angus Seed brought him from the Irish club Glentoran in 1949. By then, he had already played for the Irish League but, amazingly, no other English club had shown any real interest in him. Those that acknowledged his qualities as a skilful player thought he wasn't sturdy enough to survive in the English Football League. Ironically, it was a club which, over the years, put up a reputation for fielding a 'bunch of cloggers' that recognized his artful talent and gave him a stage to display his artistry. Unfortunately, it was the same lack of imagination that drove him away.

At the age of 23, Danny was already such a polished player, before his first try out with the reserves, the Barnsley staff decided he was one of the greatest wing-halves they had ever seen. At the end of his first game for the Club, the supporters rose to give him a standing ovation, and within a few months he had won his first full international cap. Blanchflower was a crafty footballer. An early experience of playing for the Irish League against a much better Football League XI, and his light physical build, inspired him to think about his game and work deliberately to improve it; he played with guile, not brawn.

His desire to develop as a footballer led him to leave Barnsley. Angus Seed, for all his fatherly interest in young footballers, was not a progressive coach. When Blanchflower asked if he could practice with a ball whilst other players lounged in the billiards room after regular training was over, Seed made his famous reply: *"I don't believe in it. If you don't see the ball during the week, you'll be more keen to get it on Saturdays."*

The refusal led to an argument, and Blanchflower left for Aston Villa for £15,000 after only 70 appearances for Barnsley, on condition that his new club would let him practice with the ball. He went on to captain the famous 'Spurs team of the early sixties, the first to win the League and Cup double in the modern era, and captain Northern Ireland in the World Cup Finals.

There were, however, more traditional players at Oakwell who gave Seed less trouble, and the crowds perhaps even more delight. When Seed asked Johnny Kelly whether he preferred to play on the right or left-wing, he replied, *"I'm not bothered boss. I can play just as badly on either one."* That was a classic piece of cheek from a player who must rank as one of the most popular ever to play at Oakwell, and the only Scot ever to gain full international honours whilst playing for the Club.

Danny Blanchflower at the
Barnsley Chronicle (1949/50 season)

Kelly was as impudent on the field as he was off, entertaining the crowd by dribbling past a player, waiting with his foot on the ball for the player to recover, then taking the ball back to beat him again. He loved to play for the fans, and the fans loved him back for it. Despite being born thin on top and slightly bandy-legged, and seeming to keep both characteristics most of his life, his charm on the field and his irrepressible grin made him a firm favourite. In 1985, he was the subject of a contest winner's entry in the matchday programme to nominate the 'Best Footballer ever to play for Barnsley'.

Kelly was the hero of one of the most unforgettable League games of the period played at Oakwell, on 2nd October 1948, when Southampton were the visitors. Alf Ramsey, considered by many to be one of the classiest, most polished full-backs in the country, was taunted, tantalised and tarnished by Kelly's genius as Barnsley drubbed the visitors 3-0. Kelly's shaming of Ramsey, as he beat him time after time, is one of Oakwell's legendary moments. As Ramsey sat defeated on the turf, daubed in mud after another failed challenge, Kelly virtually rolled the ball under his nose, and dared him to get up and have another go. The crowd roared with delight egging him on, and yelling such advice as *"Tha'd best learn to stand up if tha wants to play this game, Ramsey, lad."*

Ramsey, of course, after an international career, became England manager, and invented a team of 'wingless wonders' who won the World Cup for England in 1966; Barnsley fans will forever believe that a team without wingers was the vengeful outcome of Ramsey's humiliation at Kelly's feet that particular afternoon.

Kelly, even though he was something of a comedian, was not a player to be taken lightly. When Barnsley played Blackpool in the Third round of the F.A. Cup in 1949, it gave the football world a chance to see him side by side with, arguably, the greatest winger ever, Stanley Matthews, and he compared well. At the peak of his career, Kelly was perhaps the most sought after player in Great Britain. For once, Barnsley did not have to sell to survive, for bumper attendances and sales of other players were keeping the Club solvent.

They could afford to turn down offers like the £20,000 enquiry from Newcastle, but an approach from the Millonarios club in Bogota directly to the player, promising him cash payments no club in England could match, gave the Club the shivers.

From Kelly's point of view, he had fun at Barnsley. He was a celebrity, and because the Football League enforced a maximum wage limit, he could earn no more in a week anywhere else than he did at Barnsley, unless he moved to Bogota. So, he stayed. Over a period of 8 years, including the last war-time season, he made over 200 appearances, and supplemented his income with a business selling 'Kelzone' bleach, which he mixed in a garage in Worsbrough Dale. He peddled it around town in a series of rickety old vehicles. Driving down the road in an Austin with a loose steering wheel, he would pull the wheel off and hand it to gobsmacked passengers with the quip *"Here, take the wheel for a minute, will you."* Horace Pickering, one of the Club's Directors, was former Secretary of the Barnsley British Co-Operative Society, and was able to talk the Co-op into taking £25 worth of Kelly's bleach every week; in such devious ways, clubs navigated around the maximum wage rule to increase their star players' earnings.

Kelly's partner at inside-left was another Scot, a shy, skinny little lad called Jimmy Baxter, who arrived at Oakwell as a nine stone weakling. He was one of those who came to Barnsley, took one look around the town, and ran back home. It didn't help that in his war-time debut, where he played on the left side of defence, he was up against England winger Tom Finney, whose display demoralised the youngster's confidence. He hid in his Dunfermline home, and spun Barnsley a tale of fictitious injuries to avoid coming back while enjoying his soccer locally under assumed names.

Jimmy Baxter

However, Angus Seed believed in Baxter's future. He made a personal visit to find him, and brought him back under escort. The role of inside-left fell to Baxter by default, because no one else wanted to play in Johnny Kelly's shadow on the left side of the field. In Baxter's case, playing with Kelly gave him a chance to find his confidence, and to flourish into one of the most talented players of the era. He had always had good, tight control, developed playing alone as a youngster against walls. Partnering Kelly down the wing enabled him to add precision long passes to his repertoire. It was the quality of his passing out of midfield, where shyness dissolved into courage, and bold, adventurous play coupled with hard running throughout the game, that made him stand out and catch the eye of much bigger clubs.

Although the League did not begin until 1946-47, the F.A. Cup recommenced immediately after the war, and in an exciting tie against First Division Newcastle, Baxter established himself with the winning goal in front of 30,000 Oakwell fans. Two hundred and thirty five games and fifty-six goals later, Baxter became a team-mate of

the same Tom Finney who had so nearly scotched his career before it started, when he joined Preston North End. His seven seasons in the First Division with Preston included a Wembley final.

On the other side of the field, Kelly's skullduggery with the ball on the left was balanced by Gavin Smith's speed down the right. Smith, yet another wee Scot, was so fast it was rumoured he could 'catch pigeons'; his party piece was to race Yorkshire Traction buses between stops around town, and beat them. It was for him that Oakwell supporters invented the joke that the Club had special gates erected at the corners of the ground because once he got going, he didn't have room to stop; a tale since repeated for other players of lesser ability. Famous for his 50 yard runs, he also had a fierce shot, and despite the good natured taunting from the terraces, he often arrived at the other end of the field with enough control to make use of it; particularly as a youngster during the war years, when he could go past full-backs so quickly he was even too fast to 'get legged up' and left opponents blindly trying to kick a lump out of his slipstream. While the timid Baxter had been dubious about settling down in Barnsley, Gavin Smith fitted right in. He was at the Club for 15 years, and stayed in the town after his career finished.

As Baxter fed Kelly with precision passes down the left, so Steve Griffiths fed Smith down the right. Griffiths was born in Stairfoot, and enjoyed a career with four League clubs before coming back to his home town as a 33-year-old, with one eye on moving into coaching. To everyone's surprise, the move to Oakwell rejuvenated his playing career. As an inside-forward with lots of experience, and noted for diligence rather than flair, he balanced teams with young players like Blanchflower, and was wily enough to pop up and score the odd goal or two himself. As inside-right, he could hold the ball until Gavin Smith got ready to break down the wing, and then split the defence with a sweetly struck ball that Gavin, working on a full head of steam, could take in his stride like an express train sucking in a bag of mail on its way through a railway station at 90 mph.

After Robledo left, Cecil McCormack took over the centre of the attacking line, and dined on the crosses fed by Smith and Kelly. McCormack's passage across the Oakwell firmament was as blazing, and as short as a

1947: Goalkeeper Norman Rimmington in action at Leeds Road.

give defenders the slip; around the box he could feint for a shot or wrong foot opponents for a cross; inside the box, he could lose his marker with a sudden burst, and drive in a shot with reflexes faster than the 'keeper's. Johnny Steele, looking back over 50 years at the Club, once rated Cecil McCormack as the 'classiest' centre-forward during his time there.

Alongside McCormack was a big, six foot, thirteen stone goalscoring Irishman in the traditional centre-forward mould, who had to make way in the line-up for Cec in the centre position by playing inside-forward. It was probably the only thing Eddie McMorran ever willingly gave up on the football field. Eddie was a big man with a big personality, a big grin and a big presence. Supporters called him 'Tank' for the way he barrelled through opposing defences. He would plough through heavy mud and rain with his head lowered and his arms pumping, crash into the penalty area with the strength of a charging ox, and collide with the ball. If it didn't meet his head, he had a thumping shot and a fearsome challenge that put a goalkeeper and his centre-half under a lot of pressure. Eddie's form at Barnsley, where he was top scorer in 1951-52, rejuvenated his international career with Northern Ireland. After a layoff of four years, he was picked again to play for his country and made nine more appearances for them whilst a Barnsley player.

At the other end of the field, the very Irish-sounding Pat Kelly occupied the goal with a unique presence. Kelly was actually born in South Africa, where he was recruited by a touring Aberdeen team in 1939. Barnsley picked him up in 1946, and over the next few years he was the automatic choice between the posts. He was an extrovert, and an all-round athlete who came late to football, bringing with him a fresh perspective to the art of goalkeeping. In the water, an accomplished diver, he once launched himself from the deck of an ocean liner into the harbour to win a bet. He loved to show off his acrobatic abilities in leaping to make saves, and was so strong and agile, he could run on his hands.

Some fans loved his gymnastics. However, this being Barnsley, there were always some who thought he was a bit of a 'show-off', who should 'gi' oe'r muckin' abaht an' gerron wi' it'. His slightly eccentric, but exciting style, may have confirmed suspicions that goalkeepers were a bit odd, but it also earned him international honours with Northern Ireland during his time at Oakwell. Again, despite the extrovert exterior, like his namesake on the wing, Kelly took his football seriously. When Scotland hammered 8 goals past him on his international debut, it affected his form at Barnsley; he was

comet. Some cultures believe the passage of a comet is a bad portent. In this case, it may have been true. McCormack's coming lit the fans with rapture, in his departure, the death-knell tolled. A season after McCormack left, the Club was struggling to score goals, was relegated from the Second Division to the Third, and began a long, bitter struggle with obscurity.

The capture of McCormack was an astute piece of recruiting. A Geordie, and a former player with First Division Middlesbrough, he was playing with non-League Chelmsford because his southern wife had not settled in the North. At 28-years-old, McCormack missed the excitement of League football, and knew that if he wanted to enjoy any more of it, he would have to move quickly, for his age was working against him. Barnsley approached him at the right time, and he decided to join for the twilight of his career. He made his debut at the start of the 1950-51 season, and if anyone wondered what Barnsley were doing with an unknown, lightweight non-League player who was not exactly a spring chicken, wearing the number nine shirt, their questions were answered by an unexpected explosion of goals.

In the fourth home game of the season, McCormack became only the fourth Barnsley player ever to score five goals in a game, equalling the Club record in a 6-1 win over Luton. By the end of the season, he had notched a goalscoring record that stands to this day, with 33 goals in only 37 appearances, the most goals ever scored by a Barnsley player in one season. The following year, McCormack was on track again, with 9 goals in 13 games, when Notts. County offered Barnsley £20,000 for him. In this case, the lure of gold proved too much, and Cec McCormack was gone.

Following the tradition of successful goal scoring Barnsley forwards, McCormack was not a lumbering giant, but a slim man, 5 foot 8 inches tall, with a quicksilver touch who worked for the half chance. In tight spaces, he could bring the ball down on his toe and traumatised and depressed for weeks, even though it was the quality of players in front of him that lost the game, not his performance.

In front of Kelly at Barnsley was Gordon Pallister. Pallister signed for the Club as a 21-year-old before the War, and was one of the few players to bridge the gap to post-war years when he appeared as a regular at full-back, making a total of 232 appearances, many of them as captain. The War robbed him of the opportunity to make the most of his football career, but in 1950, at the age of 33, his contributions were at last acknowledged when he was chosen to play for a Football League XI against the Irish League.

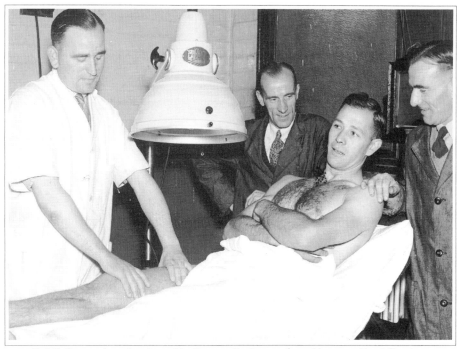
Pat Kelly receives treatment in the medical room from Masseur Fred Semley. Trainers Fleetwod and Shutton look on.

Long-serving Gordon Pallister.

As indicated by his regular selection and his long career, Pallister was a steady, reliable and calm defender - a model professional. Another native of County Durham, Pallister stayed in Barnsley when his playing career was over and later became a Director of the Club, serving for 30 years. Now a life Vice-President, Gordon still visits Oakwell to watch games in company with his old team mate and neighbour, Johnny Steele.

These then were some of the players who made a trip to Oakwell so enjoyable for many in the years immediately after the War, players who one by one, slipped over the horizon. Angus Seed had done his job

in bringing quality players to Oakwell, but the Club never capitalised on their potential. In the League, despite occasionally challenging the leaders, Barnsley never finished higher than 9th place in the Second Division between 1946 and 1953. In the F.A. Cup, they were knocked out at the first hurdle four years out of seven. In the other three years, they went out in the next round. With the addition of one or two other good players at any one time, the Reds may have climbed the table and stormed into the First Division, but once again they were victims of their times and the Director's policies. The Club never bought a proven First Division player because they all came with a price on their head, and Barnsley could not, or would not pay for them.

Ted Robledo: Unlike brother George, he only played a few games for Barnsley, before the pair moved on to Newcastle United in 1948.

CHAPTER 10

THE HOUSE THAT RICHARDS BUILT

Joseph Richards' Chairmanship played a large part in the Club's failure to spend money when it was needed, and in the continued sale of talent, policies which ultimately triggered the Club's slide to lower Divisions and to the brink of financial ruin. Richards succeeded George Tomlinson as Chairman in 1948. For the next 18 years, he ruled the Club with an iron fist and an uncompromising style. Even though he may have grasped enough about football and business to keep the Club ticking over in undemanding circumstances, he lacked the vision and drive necessary to fashion a flourishing football club out of increasingly limited resources.

credit was often considered a sign of weakness and bad business; spending money you had not got was socially frowned upon. Mr. Richards felt that overdrafts at the bank would help neither the good name of the Club nor his own, for it was on the good standing of his personal credit that the Club went to the bank for more when receipts dried up. Consequently, money to buy new players was rarely available, and when it was spent, such as £10,000 on George Spruce in 1952, the purchase was quickly followed by a transfer to recoup the outlay, in this case, the sale of Jimmy Baxter.

Eventually, Richards was devoured by a monster of his own making. His ambitions never seemed to extend further than keeping up the 'good name of the Club', and maintaining a balanced set of books. He never spoke publicly about his desire to create a footballing power at Oakwell, but he did talk about selling players in order to keep up with an overdraft at the bank, and chided the public for not showing up in crowds large enough to make sure that bills were paid. Ironically, it was financial disaster and the turning of Barnsley F.C.'s name into a national joke that, in the end, forced his retirement in 1966.

Richards was a great conservative who seemed to believe that maintaining the status quo was a respectable ambition despite his own amazing climb up the ladders of success. It was not in his nature to speculate or gamble with Club money, even though he consolidated his own wealth with dealings in stocks and shares. The Club was not allowed to run up its overdraft securing the services of players who might take them up a Division, because that was too much of a risk for Richards; there was no 'buy now, pay later' or 'speculate to accumulate' with him.

Such financial conservativeness was not out of place in the times. In the Britain of the early fifties, 'hire purchase' was only just gaining acceptance. Relying on

In 1955, after promotion from the Third to the Second Division, the Board made a rare promise not to sell any important young players for the next five years. The implication was that there would be no money to buy any significant new players either. The Club's future seemed reasonably rosy at that time. Although it paid its bills hand to mouth and ran an overdraft at the bank, there seemed to be plenty of promising talent coming through, and a chance of rising to the First Division with the personnel in hand. The plan went awry, when injuries and the failure of the talent to mature to previous standards left Barnsley bobbing up and down in the lower half of the Second Division for the next four years. By the end, almost everyone who could be sold, was sold. Once again, supporters believed that if the Club had genuinely felt that its chances of advancing upwards were good, a timely speculation may have been just the injection which the doctor ordered to inspire a full recovery. Of course, it was easy for them to speculate when they did not have to look a £20,000 overdraft in the eye every morning.

The preoccupation of Richards with finances led him to bicker over pennies as well as pounds. At one end of the scale he would inflate the asking price of a player, who attracted the interest of a wealthy club, by thousands of pounds; at the other end he would try to make niggling cut-backs at the expense of the players. When the Reds were relegated from Division Two to the Third Division

North in 1953, Richards sent a letter to captain Norman Smith telling him his wages would be cut by ten shillings (50p). Smith was insulted, and wrote back asking how Richards thought he could perform 'ten bob worse' on the field. Smith's wages were re-instated. Even so, Richards seemed generous to some. Tim Ward got a 50% pay increase after Barnsley's promotion from the Third Division North to the Second Division in 1955 when he refused tempting offers from other clubs.

The pecuniary pre-occupation of Richards did not endure him to supporters. Some shareholders at the Club thought Richard's efforts showed financial astuteness; some thought him just plain thrifty; on the terraces, it was suggested he could split a farthing with a butter knife, and would sell his own Grandmother if the price was right. It was even mooted amongst some disenchanted supporters during Richard's reign, that attendance figures were sometimes 'doctored' to show official receipts for less than the actual numbers inside the ground, but none could account for the reason or where the missing cash could have gone, unless someone was perhaps trying to beat the entertainment tax based on per head admissions. All the supporters knew, was that when they read the Sunday papers, they saw a smaller attendance reported than they felt they had seen at the game the day before, and they blamed the Directors anyway.

The fans had a deep distrust of the Board seated in its history of unpopular player moves, and Richard's own circumstances did little to help the feeling. He had begun working life as a miner at Barnsley Main, and moved to the offices after breaking a leg in an accident with a pit-tub; eventually, he held high office with the National Coal Board, and built up his own coal and coke business, allowing him to indulge his interests in the game by giving him the means to become a football administrator. A Director of Barnsley Football Club since 1920, he became, in addition to his Chairmanship of the Board, President of the Football League; founder of the Northern Intermediate League, F.A. Youth Cup and England under-23 team; and a selector and tour manager for the English F.A., in the days before the national programme was run by a coach. He was knighted for his services to football.

As an administrator, he brooked no equal. He wrote the rules at all levels of the game, and believed in living to the letter of them; he could dot the i's and cross the t's of any contract, and read a balance sheet upside down. However, despite such impressive credentials, there were many, from the fan on the terrace at Barnsley to men in football's corridors of power, who doubted Richard's real feel for and appreciation of the game. On one occasion, Derby County Manager Harry Storer, asked him to his face what right he had to be an England selector. Richards replied that he had been watching football for fifty years.

"Come off it." said Storer. *"We've got a corner flag at the Baseball Ground that's been there for fifty years, and it still knows nothing about the game."* In conducting the Club's affairs with the same meticulous attention to detail which he applied to the management of his own affairs, some supporters felt he missed the obvious point that it was quality on the field that mattered, not the quality of accounting.

The further up the scale that Richards progressed, and the further down that Barnsley slid, the wider the gulf became between the Boardroom and the fan on the terrace. Mr. Richards travelled to and from Oakwell in a chauffeur-driven Rolls-Bentley, smoked large cigars and dressed in expensive suits. These signs of affluence, as Barnsley struggled, sent mixed signals. Richard's executive positions in the world of football may have brought respect to the Club in some circles, but earned him few friends on the streets of the town. Ordinary people openly doubted that his passions were really for the game and for Barnsley Football Club. They thought his passion was for wielding the status and power he had acquired as a 'self-made' millionaire, and adding to his own fortune.

When the familiar tale of insufficient revenue was bleated again and again from the Boardroom, and axes hung over the future of favourite players, some wondered where Richard's 'brass' was when it was needed. The most the public saw of it was when he opened a fund to buy the Club's floodlights in 1957 with a donation of one hundred guineas, and asked the supporters to find the remaining £2,000. Inside the Club, he provided a new bar extension for the Director's boardroom, a gift which the Club marked not by one, but by two commemorative wall plaques recording Richard's name, and the generosity of his gift.

In 1955, when the Third Division North Championship trophy was awarded to Barnsley after their last home game of the season, supporters made their opinions clear. The Championship shield was handed to Richards in the Director's box. Fans, who had gathered around the tunnel entrance, let out such a spontaneous grumble that Richards quickly passed the shield to captain Norman Smith. In the fan's minds, the Club was going up because the team had earned it, and the Chairman had nowt to do wi' it.

One of the criteria which Richards looked at when evaluating prospective new Board members was whether or not they had 'enough wool on their back', in other words whether or not they were financially well off. It is hard to see why a Director's wealth mattered at the time, unless Richards believed that social and class barriers should be maintained for the 'good name of the Club'. Payments to players were strictly controlled by League regulations, and Directors were not openly encouraged by Mr. Richards to spend their own money on improving the

Club. Directors dipped their hands into their pockets to provide player perks such as a round of drinks, a free chicken at Christmas, a lift in a car or the offer of a job. Arthur Raynor was considered a good Director by the players because he provided chewing gum for games at Oakwell, and bags of sweets for away games.

Richard's fellow Directors on the Board were certainly not in his financial league, although most of them had good standing in the town. The gulf in status meant that they did not have the means to challenge his authority; more often than not they simply agreed with what the Chairman had to say. Horace Pickering, for example, Secretary of the Barnsley British Co-Operative Society, and John Hirst, a local butcher, had been Barnsley supporters since the turn of the century and were steeped in the conservative financialism of the small businessman, and the early success of 'sell to survive but don't buy' policy at Oakwell. Pickering had followed the Club since 1897. Colleague Billy Diggle, a former pit deputy, could lucidly recount details of his trip to watch the 1912 Final. New Directors, whilst having to meet Richards' approval of their financial situation, were also drawn from the traditional fan base. Local businessmen Ernest Dennis, Ralph Potter and Arthur Raynor were all nominated after first volunteering as officers of the new Supporters Club, which Dennis had begun in 1946, but they were not to make any impact until Richards resigned in the sixties.

In the early fifties, Richards' elderly cronies still dominated. With these kinds of hands at the helm, some of the best post-war players were sold while others were allowed to grow too long in the tooth to be of any use, except to draw faithful fans at the gate. In neither case were adequate reinforcements provided. In 1952, the Club finished 20th out of 22 in the Second Division, avoiding relegation by two points. The following year, they slumped to the foot of the table and were relegated to Division Three North with a record-breaking worst performance ever by a Barnsley side. The team not only lost more games in a season than ever before (29), but also won the least (only 5) while collecting the lowest points total as well (18). On the way, they began a record for the longest run without a win, which was only terminated the following season, 26 games later.

Barnsley's demise was paralleled by Angus Seed. Bad health progressively took its toll and in March 1953 he died after taking ill on the train travelling back from a Cup-tie in Plymouth. The need for a new manager and Barnsley's imminent fall into a Division below were catalysts for change, and an opportunity for the Club to breeze into a new era.

To Joe Richard's credit, he recommended a young manager with an excellent record as a professional player, a manager he saw as a man of the future. On the other hand, when the Board appointed Tim Ward as the youngest Manager in the Football League at the age of 34, Richards had someone in charge of the playing staff who respected him from their contact during a foreign tour with the Football Association; who was inexperienced, and likely to turn to him for advice; and who was indebted to him for the early opportunity to break into management. In other words, Richard's choice was a young man unlikely to rock the ship. True enough, they had few altercations. By and large, Ward managed the team and Richards the cheque book, but by 1957 Ward was more able to express dissatisfaction when their two paths crossed. He threatened his resignation when he felt Richards was inclined not to pay inside-right Sid Storey a bonus. Another incident suggests that Ward was however sometimes inclined to bow to Richard's pressure.

Goalkeeper Harry Hough believed his career with Barnsley was shortened by pressure from Mr. Richards on manager Tim Ward. A fitness fanatic who played professionally and semi-professionally for another 11 years after leaving Barnsley, Hough had been officially praised by the Board at their 1958 Annual Meeting, as a player the Club was fortunate to have on its books. However, after being dropped from the team following a 5-0 defeat at Sheffield United in February 1959, he was left out of the side, apart from one game, until the end of the season.

During his absence, the team slipped from a mid-table position to bottom place. At the end of the season, they were relegated. Despite a run of poor results, the experienced and popular goalkeeper had not been recalled for a single game since 21st February.

Hough thought this strange until he met with Richards to discuss a close season transfer request. It was only the third time in his Oakwell career that he had spoken with the Chairman. Richards told him, *"You've cut our profits to the bone since you started up."* Hough was taken aback. It turned out that Richards had an interest in a sporting goods store which had suffered in competition with a new sports business set up by the Barnsley goalkeeper and local businessman Bob Midwood. Despite Hough's wonderful record with the Club, Richards' conversation with his player centered on the loss he had taken to Hough's new sports supply enterprise. The goalkeeper believed he had at last found the real reason he was out of favour, and it had nothing to do with loss of form.

Harry Hough

Tim Ward had played twice for England in his Derby County days, his only other League club, when he signed for Barnsley as a player in March, 1951. Richards met him two years earlier on a Football Association exhibition tour of Canada when Ward was captain. When Danny Blanchflower was transferred to Villa, Richards suggested Ward to Angus Seed as a replacement. Both men knew that Ward had an eye towards coaching and management, and Richards ensured that, in addition to playing for the first team, Ward got an opportunity to work with the Oakwell juniors, already grooming him as Seed's successor. When Seed's position was offered, Ward beat off long-serving player Gordon Pallister and Harry Catterick, the man who would build Everton's dynasty in the nineteen-sixties.

Ward was in touch with new developments in the game, and was keen to chance his own hand with ideas he had been in contact with as a top player. While an England international, he had been exposed to the concept of instructional coaching rather than training just for physical fitness.

The Football Association had installed its first Director of Coaching in 1946, and Walter Winterbottom, with his chalkboard, spectacles and professional air, had begun to teach tactics to national players and a new breed of coaches. As a player in the First Division, Ward had also played against, and been impressed by the 'push and run' style, developed by the 'Spurs League Championship team of 1951, in which players worked the ball downfield with short, accurate passes along the ground.

At Oakwell, Ward found Barnsley locked into a style that was more like 'kick and rush', in which the job of the bread and butter players in the side was to get the ball to the feet of the masters as quickly as possible. Shouts of *"Booit it!"* and *"Get rid!"* echoed around both training field and spectator's enclosures on game days. A good defensive performance was one in which a defender cancelled out all attacks by "gi'in it some clog dahn t'field" at the earliest opportunity. Training still consisted of lapping the playing field, followed by more lapping, under the watchful eye of trainer Bob Shotton.

Ward, young enough that he could still relate to players, left his coat and tie in the office, and trotted out onto the practice field with his teams to become Barnsley's first 'track suit' manager. He tried to instil a sense of style and purpose through emphasising team-work rather than playing to one-on-one confrontations. He re-created situations from previous games, and talked the players through the options that they had to handle each situation differently. He even encouraged them to play games with a ball, but demanded short, direct passes instead of aimless clogging. In his team selection, he picked players most suited to the new style. Centre-half George Spruce, for example, was not typical of his breed in the Third Division, for he was not a heavyweight nor a bone-cruncher. Lithe and sharp, he had played as a winger earlier in his career, and brought a winger's close control and ball skills to his present role. He became a constructive play-maker at the heart of the defence, prepared to dribble down the centre and slide a useful pass out to his half-backs, instead of making an instinctive airborne clearance.

Ward was helping to create a team which would win the Third Division Championship, and return to the Second Division within two years of Angus Seed's legacy. One of Chairman Joe Richards' good points was his belief in a youth programme, although perhaps for the wrong reasons. Seed had helped to establish one for him after the war. A feeder system of young, local players was created when Barnsley Boys, a team selected from the best local school players, was organized by teachers Harold Rushforth and Ted Davies. Occasionally, the Club tried to sign the entire Barnsley Boys team on amateur or apprentice forms. Trials for players outside the school district might attract another 80 or so young hopefuls.

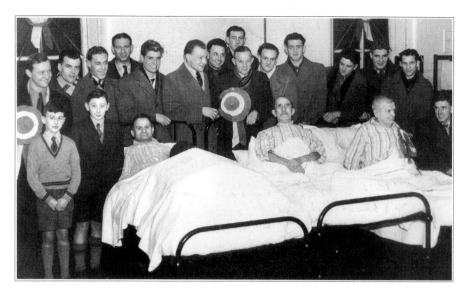

Visit to St. Helens Hospital, Barnsley in 1951.

Players (left to right): McCormack, Smith, Normanton, Pallister, Lambert, Hough, Innocent, Lindsay, (behind) Allen, Callaghan, McMorran, Taylor, Robinson, Deakin, Blanchflower (sitting).

As a result, the Club ran four teams; a first team, reserves, an 'A' team and the Juniors. In 1951, the Northern Intermediate League team had a pool of 30 youngsters from which to draw its starting eleven from, and the Club had over 90 players on its books. The juniors came, predominantly, from the local area. League clubs in other areas continued to develop youth programmes in their own backyards, and stopped clubs from outside taking the cream of the crop. Barnsley's scouting system in its traditional North-East hunting grounds, put in place by Angus Seed, was beginning to wear down. Harry Nattrass, unable to admit that Newcastle, Sunderland and Middlesbrough had already picked over the best talent, referred 68 players to Barnsley for trials in 1957. Obviously, the quantity of players sent down was a desperate attempt to mask the lack of quality; not one of the north-eastern lads made the cut.

Even so, there were still, occasionally, ones that got away, and Barnsley were grateful that Frank Bartlett from Chester-le-Street slipped the local net in 1950. Frank, who was picked up as a 20-year-old playing for Blackhall Colliery, worked his way through the Reserves to play a total of 325 times for the Reds between 1953 and 1963. A reliable workhorse who ran until he dropped, Frank could play all over the field. In 1955, he established a shortlived Club scoring record for a winger with a total of 17 goals in the season. Two years later, Arthur Kaye went one better as Bartlett dropped back to play a competent right-half role. In 1960, Frank became an inside-forward, and was the leading scorer for the next two years.

Johnny Steele organized and coached the younger players. From their ranks emerged a rare talent. A shy, skinny 16-year-old lad from Smithies named Tommy Taylor caught the Club's eye. After toughening up during National Service, he claimed the Barnsley centre-forward spot as successor to McCormack at the start of the 1952-53 season; seven months later, he was a Manchester United

man, and the most expensive player in England. Tommy was thrilled to have signed for the Oakwell Club. It's said that he loved being at Barnsley so much that they had to ask him to leave so they could lock up at night.

Tommy Taylor

Eventually, scouts from the biggest clubs in England dogged his every move. Some of the Barnsley coaches, sensing Tommy's potential for leading the Club to success, and knowing how proud he was to be playing for his home town team, encouraged him not to think about going anywhere else, despite the attention. When Joe Richards heard about this, he instructed his staff not to give any such advice because the Club needed the fee they could get for him. Tommy, upset and confused, sought an interview with his Chairman. *"I don't want to go, Mr. Richards,"* he pleaded, as they walked along the corridor outside the dressing room.

Richards replied, *"You've got to go Tommy, and that's the end of it."* In an amazing sweep, Taylor and the charismatic Irishman Eddie McMorran, the Club's only other recognized first team centre-forward, were both sold on the same day.

After just 44 League appearances and 26 goals, Tommy Taylor became one of Matt Busby's famous 'Babes'. Busby did not want Tommy to face the publicity of becoming football's first £30,000 player, so an agreement was made for £29,999, and Busby tipped the odd pound to Lily Wilby, the Oakwell receptionist who brought him tea during transfer negotiations. Shortly afterwards, the 21-year-old from Quarry Street, now Britain's most expensive player, arrived in Manchester, with his boots in a brown paper bag. Within ten weeks of arriving in the First Division, he was an England international. Tommy helped Manchester United lead the nation's first assaults on the European Cup, and their infamous tragedy at an ice-bound Munich airport in 1958, in pursuit of that trophy, ended Tommy's life and robbed English football of a legend.

Arthur Kaye from Higham was another product of Barnsley's youth system after the War. After signing as a 17-year-old in 1950, Arthur quickly became Barnsley's best and most popular player of the mid-fifties. The fans loved the way he ran at opposing defences, regardless of their size, challenging them to stop him. He was only five feet five inches tall and ten stones dripping wet, but packed terrific power. One day, while practising penalties, he broke a ground staff assistant's arm with one shot. Harnessed to his power were speed, lots of energy and slick control of the ball, qualities which made Arthur a natural choice to succeed Gavin Smith on the right-wing, and quickly attracted attention from big clubs, including Spurs and Chelsea. He had the class to play with either of them, but gave the best years of his career to Barnsley, a loyalty he perhaps came to regret more than once.

In 1955, Arthur was called up to play for the England under-23's, and the following year made the final twenty-two being considered for England's World Cup campaign in Sweden. Arthur was so sure he had made the cut, he bought himself a new suit for the trip. It was generally thought that a World Cup call did not come because he played

for Barnsley, an unfashionable team struggling in the Second Division. Arthur's place went to Peter Brabrook of Chelsea, a player who might have been in the reserves if Arthur had transferred there.

Despite this setback, Arthur still stuck with Barnsley, turning out a total of 280 times. His reward was a clash with Joe Richards over salary. In 1958, the maximum wage for professional players was raised by the Football League to £20 per week; Barnsley refused to give any player, including Arthur, more than £18, even though Arthur's name on the team sheet alone was enough to add hundreds of pounds a year to gate receipts. He was hurt by the Chairman's meanness after sacrificing his own career for the sake of the Club and it knocked the spirit out of him.

First Division Blackpool took advantage of the falling out to steal him for a knock-down price of £13,500, as a replacement for the ageing Stanley Matthews; that's how good Arthur Kaye was. As it turned out, Matthews still had some fire left in him, and Arthur finished up partnering the legendary England winger from an inside-right position, before signing for Second Division Middlesbrough, where he stayed for five years.

Besides the great talents of Taylor and Kaye, Oakwell's youth system turned out a consistent stream of other players for Manager Tim Ward to choose from. Arthur Kaye was replaced by Jackie Lunn, of Smithies, who capped his short 64 game career with Barnsley by becoming top scorer in 1959-60. Lol Chappell, from High Green, took over from Tommy Taylor and despite an injury prone career, scored almost one goal every two games, and on three occasions, he was the Club's leading scorer. A lad from Chapeltown was a fan favourite at the other end of the field. Harry Hough set a goalkeeping record with 346 League appearances before leaving for Bradford Park Avenue.

Two thirds of Barnsley's most famous defensive combination were also a product of the youth system. Short, Sharp and Swift described not only a defensive philosophy, but also an Oakwell line-up. Centre-half Duncan Sharp and left-back Colin Swift were partnered by right-back John Short, who was imported from Stoke City.

Lol Chappell

Sharp was a hard man. He was feisty, independent and physically powerful. At six feet tall (1.83m.) and thirteen stone (83 kg.), he appeared to be a classic, crunching centre-half. After one of his tackles left an opponent dazed on the ground, supporters would joke, "Ey up, was it murder or manslaughter, then"? Forwards' faces would drop when they knew Duncan Sharp was in the Barnsley line-up, but they might not have been so afraid had they thought of him as a Grammar School lad with School Certificates in Greek and Latin.

In actual fact, Duncan was unlike most players of his time, for he was highly intelligent, ambitious and driven. He quit the game when he was ready, not when his career dictated, at the age of only twenty-nine, and then successfully built up his own business interests. Duncan Sharp and Manager Tim Ward rarely saw eye to eye. During a reserve game as a youngster, Sharp had answered his Manager back, and Ward never forgot the incident. However, Duncan was determined to play for Barnsley, and not even the Manager could stand in his way when his mind was made up. Eventually, he captained the team and played over 200 games.

By 1957, stocky Colin Swift had earned his place as regular left-back, and the trio of Short, Sharp and Swift held court for the first time. Swift was perhaps not as apt a name for him as 'Steady' might have been. He was 'adopted' as a youngster at Oakwell by trainer Bob Shotton, who himself had been a full back, and advice from Shotton as they sat alongside each other watching senior games from the trainer's dugout, no doubt helped shape Colin's solid, no-nonsense style of play in the traditional full back mould. Colin was the last of the 1949 Barnsley Boys team which won the English Schools Trophy to pass through the Barnsley team. Whilst his career never became glamorous, he was always happy and proud to have passed all his professional playing days in the red shirt of his home town Club, for a total of 263 appearances.

Sid 'Skinner' Normanton, from Lundwood, also trod the long path from Oakwell juniors to the Second Division. Sid was nicknamed 'Skinner' from boyhood, long before he earned a reputation for 'skinning' opponents on the football field. In fairness, Skinner was an intense and committed competitor who marked closely and tackled with force, even though at times he may have been

Duncan Sharp

clumsy. He was certainly not 'classy'. Neither was he the celebrity that writer and broadcaster Michael Parkinson later made him out to be. In his book 'Football Daft', Parkinson recounts that the wing half "..........was a miner, and built like one. Billiard table legs and a chest like the front of a coal barge. He was so fearsome that there are those who will tell you that naughty children in and around Barnsley were warned by their parents, "If you don't be good, we'll send for Skinner".

In fact, the terrible things that people believe about Barnsley F.C. and Skinner, if they were not found entirely in Parkinson's boyhood imagination, most probably stemmed from the image created by Duncan Sharp. His 213 League games made a more substantial impression on opposing teams, and Barnsley's reputation at the time, than Skinner's 123 games spread over seven years with the Club.

However, to deny Skinner any credence at all is to ignore the fact that he became a national legend and a polished piece of Barnsley folklore during the peak of Parkinson's writings in the 'Sunday Times' in the late nineteen-sixties. Skinner came up to the first team in Angus Seed's time; when Tim Ward took over, with ambitions to play a more polished game, he was unprepared for the way Skinner 'got stuck in'. Even in practice, he used to play hard. On one occasion, the new manager sent Sid off for a bone-crunching tackle on his own winger, Johnny Kelly, much to the amusement of the other players. Ironically, Sid's career was ruined by a piece of dirty play that went unpunished. In the 1952 fourth round F.A. Cup tie at Arsenal, Alex Forbes went over the top in a tackle, as Skinner slid in for the ball, and just about took his knee off. As the Barnsley player rolled in agony on the ground, captain Gordon Pallister yelled to the referee, "Aren't you going to send him off? He might have broken this lad's leg." The referee snapped back, "Shut up or I'll send you off." Arsenal's First Division star was not even spoken to, whilst Skinner left the field on a stretcher. It has always been hard, and not always fair, playing for Barnsley.

It became harder still as the fifties began to fade towards the sixties. By the end of the 1958-59 season, Ward's ambitions at Oakwell had been soured by skimming off the cream of the talent, and the Club's refusal, or inability, to spend any money.

Pallister, followed by Hough and Jarman, leads the team out at Highbury for the 1951/52 Cup-tie.

The few players who had been imported to supplement home-grown talent during Ward's reign, had made little impression. Barnsley finished at the bottom of the Second Division, and dropped into the new, non-regional Division Three for the first time.

What made relegation a harder pill to swallow, was the feeling around town that the team had given up, and that the Club had lost its pride.

Johnny McCann

This mood was reflected by public finger-pointing over relegation to the Third Division at the 1959 Annual Meeting. Chairman Joe Richards accused the players of surrendering, and Manager Tim Ward said they were disloyal. John Boylin, Chairman of the Supporters Club in whose memory the current Player of the Year trophy is dedicated, stood up and told the Board that there was a lack of leadership at Oakwell. By the end of February 1960, there was certainly a lack of a manager; Tim Ward left the Club to take over at Grimsby Town.

Arthur Kaye scores with a penalty at Stoke City (1957/58 season).

CHAPTER 11

INTO THE ABYSS

When Tim Ward left Barnsley F.C., the Board considered replacing him with a player-manager, from outside the Club, repeating the precedent of installing a young and inexperienced man, who would come quite cheaply and who was unlikely to rock Joe Richard's ship. Instead, they found an equally comfortable solution without leaving home. Johnny Steele, a loyal club man, whose only desire was to see Barnsley return to Division Two, was promoted from Youth Coach to full Manager. Steele had already turned down a chance to coach at Birmingham City, for a salary three times what he earned at Oakwell, because he had become so attached to his Barnsley Juniors. He had never even considered becoming first team manager until a Director whispered in his ear that he should apply. As an insider, Steele knew the situation as well as anyone, and had shown that he was undeterred by it.

When he took office, the Club had already lost its way in the Third Division. In earlier years, a drop into the Third Division North had been like a fall on a trampoline, as the Club always bounced back with a quick return. Now, the drop was like falling into a swamp. Changing fortunes wrapped themselves around the Club, and pulled it further and further into the mire.

Thirty-six professionals were on Barnsley's books when they finished the last season in Division Two; only nineteen started the new campaign in Division Three, and only 12 of those were full-time. Players were disposed off at fire sale prices, thrown overboard to lighten the financial load as the ship went down, and few of the players lining the rails as the Oakwell ship sank into a lower Division matched the ability or potential of their predecessors swimming over the horizon. The Club pinned its hopes of reaching safety on Steele's diminished youth programme. It was like trying to save an entire ship's company with a couple of life-preservers and no lifeboat.

Fans, who could have given the Club some assistance at the turnstiles, stayed away in droves as the Club settled to the depths. After previous relegations, they had continued their support, with only a marginal drop or an increase as the team challenged for promotion. However, this time, dwindling attendances at the end of the Second Division season carried over into the new campaign. While the team was struggling at the bottom of the Second Division, Barnsley enjoyed average gates of 11,000. Now, attendances slumped by almost half to just over 6,000 in the first season in Division Three.

Since the austerity of the immediate post-war period, working classes had started to have a little more spare cash and had begun to turn away from football as a source of recreation. National trends showed a steady decline in attendances at football games. As the pop culture of the sixties flowered, the teen generation had more alternatives than ever before in television, cinema, music, dance and fashion. Meanwhile, mature adults spent more time and money on cars, their families and their homes. In Barnsley, where such changes came more slowly, they were, nevertheless, felt more acutely when compounded with supporters' feelings about the state of the Club. Embittered by distrust, disillusioned by the sale of their favourites and disappointed by attitudes on the field, relegation to the Third Division came as the last straw that broke the camel's back. An overwhelming number said "Bugger it!" to Oakwell; they finally decided they could find something better to do with their time.

Besides dangerously low attendances, the Club faced more expenses on the road because of the 'nationalisation' of the Third Division. Gate receipts at most venues were no larger than when the Clubs had played regionally, but now Barnsley had to travel to places like Bournemouth and Southampton for the same income as they received travelling to Bradford or York, a meagre 20% receipts after taxes, and the home club's game expenses were taken out. Long distances meant more expenses for the visiting team to eat up that 20%; there were gruelling bus journeys, meals for the players and sometimes a hotel to be paid for.

All in all, as the Club entered the sixties in the Third Division, its future looked bleak, but at least predictable. When in 1961, the maximum wage rule was overturned, and players were allowed to argue their contracts in an open market place, even that small consolation was lost. Payroll, which had been reasonably fixed and controllable, suddenly had the potential to be unpredictable and more dangerously elastic. At Barnsley, the elastic was in danger of snapping, for any player demanding an amount beyond which the Club, already weighed down with debt, could reasonably offer, would either have to be transferred or could not be signed in the first place.

This meant that Barnsley lost its hopes of getting and keeping the quality players needed to restore its pride. In South Yorkshire - although the Club could count on some local loyalty for as long as they were in the lower Division - the Reds had to compete to sign young talent, against four other League clubs, most of whom could now offer youngsters not only the prospect of playing at a higher level, but also prospects of earning more money. Sheffield had 'glamour' clubs in United and Wednesday, and even Rotherham and Doncaster looked a better bet than Barnsley.

Also, as rich clubs got richer and more successful, pressure on youngsters to turn away from local loyalties and sign with big clubs, also increased. In 1949, Barnsley F.C. captured every player in the Barnsley Boys team, yet by the end of the sixties, scouts from clubs outside the area, like Manchester United and Liverpool, were following promising Barnsley schoolboys home. Young lads playing for their school teams no longer dreamed of careers with the local club, they wanted to play for the famous teams which by the mid-sixties they began to see regularly on television. Coupled with the potential for more earnings, this meant there was always a danger that any good, young player who did come up through the Barnsley ranks, might be tempted to leave even more quickly than the Board could sell them off.

On the open transfer market, Barnsley had never put up the cash to sign better players. Now, they could not afford top players wages either. Free transfers and exchange deals were the best they could hope for, and the players involved in this kind of trading, without being unkind, were often what was left when the best had been picked over. To put the changes into perspective, Oakwell stars of international ability such as Arthur Kaye and Johnny Kelly had been content to stay at Barnsley, partly because they would not have been able to earn more at any other League club. Without the protection of the maximum wage, it seemed unlikely that players of their quality would ever be content at Oakwell.

Johnny Steele was under no illusions about the effect of the ruling. In a 1967 newspaper interview, he summarised how its impact had affected the Club. *"We cannot compete with some of the bigger clubs. At one time we could pay as well as any other club, and we could sign Second Division players. It has also had its effect at junior level, where, previously, there was little attraction for a schoolboy to leave home for another club, but now the outstanding boys, not unnaturally, are attracted to clubs in higher divisions. We still get our share of boys, even though competition is much fiercer now with clubs looking all over the country for 15-year-olds. Take Alan Woodward, Jimmy Greenhoff and Frank Casper, all local boys who had famous careers with famous First Division clubs,.............think what we could do if they were with us now"*.

Amazingly, in the face of all the odds, Johnny Steele still managed to find and develop some talent during the sixties. When he took over after Ward's departure, his appointment helped sew the thread of Barnsley's youth policy into the first team's fortunes.

With no money in the bank, the Club had to rely on passion and loyalty to motivate players; Steele, driven by his belief in the Club, set his players an example of dedication and pride. Hitching this example to years of experience as a player and youth coach, enabled the fatherly Scot to squeeze the most out of the comparatively little talent that now became available to him at Oakwell.

For example, Eric Brookes from Mapplewell, joined the Club as a schoolboy, made his debut at 16, won six England Youth caps and, in 1961, became the youngest player to win a regular place in the team. He turned out at left-back for the next nine seasons with a cool, unhurried and intelligent style which should have taken him to bigger and better things. He admitted that his own lack of ambition was the main reason he stayed at Barnsley, even though there was lots of transfer talk throughout his career. For Example, Northampton Town, who rose from the Fourth to the First Division in the early sixties, offered Barnsley £30,000 for him. At the time, that would have bought almost any defender already making regular appearances in the top flight.

Centre-half Eric Winstanley made his debut at 17, and made four appearances for the England Youth team before becoming Barnsley's youngest-ever captain, at nineteen. He was on the verge of signing for a First Division club when injury collapsed his career in 1965, aged only twenty-two. After a bitter year of rehabilitation, Eric began what amounted to a second career at Barnsley as the cornerstone of a new team. In both cases, the players loss, although unfortunate for their own careers, was Barnsley's gain in a time when good things were hard to come by.

Just how much of a contribution the youngsters made to the team is reflected by Brookes and Winstanley being considered so senior at the age of only twenty-three, that the Club arranged a testimonial, making them the youngest Barnsley players ever to receive such a benefit. When the testimonial game was played in 1968 against First Division Sheffield Wednesday, the youngsters already had over 500 appearances between them.

Of course, not all the talented players who came through Barnsley's youth system stayed to play their careers out at the Club, although starting them in the first team at such an early age meant that some could still make useful contributions to Oakwell campaigns, and still have plenty of years left to further their own careers with a move. Their transfers, as usual, brought in much needed cash. League attendances remained around 6,000 during the first half of the sixties, whilst occasional boosts from the transfer of developing players helped to maintain a financial pulse.

Alan Hill, from Ardsley, signed as a goalkeeper after leaving school. He made his debut at 17, and appeared

152 times over 6 seasons for the Reds. After taking the blame for some costly goals, he fell out of favour; as Barnsley slipped into the Fourth Division, he jumped to Division Two with Rotherham United, which brought a fee of £12,500, and embarked on a new career which eventually took him into the First Division with Nottingham Forest. Another goalkeeper, Alan Ogley from Darton, played six times for England schoolboys and then became an apprentice at Oakwell, making his first team debut as a 16-year-old in September 1962, and made 9 appearances for the Reds in the 1962-63 season. He became Barnsley's highest priced goalkeeper, at the time, when he was sold to First Division Manchester City for £7,000 in the close season.

There was even some success in acquiring players on the transfer market, and a few players picked up for nothing came good at Oakwell. Tony Leighton arrived from Doncaster Rovers on a free transfer in 1962, after being discarded because of cartilage surgery. He was leading scorer at Oakwell for the next three years before being transferred to Second Division Huddersfield Town for a profit of £20,000, and his 24 goals in 1963-64 set the Club's Third Division individual scoring record. Ken Oliver arrived as a part-time professional from non-League South Shields in 1960. Once he had broken into the first team as an inside-forward, he thrilled the crowd with his heading ability. He could stoop to lay off a beautiful pass with his head, or deflect a hard cross at the goal with knife-throwing accuracy. In 1961, he was the first Barnsley player to score a hat-trick in the newly formed League Cup competition. Two years later, he went to Watford, earning the Club £10,000. George Kerr was Johnny Steele's first professional signing in May 1960 from Scottish Junior club Renton Select, for the price of the paper his contract was written on. Six years later, he also brought in £10,000 when he left for Bury after 40 goals in 166 League games, after a season as top scorer in 1965-66.

Despite these individual success stories, the Club enjoyed no success as a team in the Third Division. Barnsley's few stars lacked a supporting cast of suitable ability. As a result, the team leaked goals like a colander, conceding 95 goals in 1961-62. From that season on, as the number of goals began to dwindle as well, every year was just a struggle to climb out of the relegation morass at the bottom of the Third Division, until finally, in 1965, the inevitable happened, and the Club slid into the Fourth Division. Thankfully for the Club and its supporters, the F.A. Cup injected some massive doses of relief into the League programme during the early sixties, and at the same time breathed a little life into the Club's ailing finances.

By November 1960, Steele's first full season, it was almost fifty years since Barnsley had won the Cup. The year of 1911-12 was also the last time they had even

enjoyed a really good run in the competition, although there had been some memorable encounters to brighten the years in between. The fans tinder of Cup expectation was dry as dust after all the years without success; little could they imagine that this year, with the Club lurking gloomily in the Third Division, a spark would ignite their imagination again.

Since joining the Third Division, Barnsley had been compelled to start the road to Wembley from the almost impossible distance of the first round. In that 1960-61 season, a 0-0 first round draw at non-League Gateshead on a cold, wintry afternoon, was about as far from glory as any team could get. Even tipping their opponents out 2-0 in the reply was just barely progress; there were fewer spectators at Oakwell to see the replay, only 5,099, than had been at the first game at the non-League club's home ground in the North-east. A second round trip to fellow strugglers Bradford City also failed to capture the fans imagination, but when a 2-1 win took Barnsley to Reading in the third round, a murmur of anticipation started around town. The Reds had reached the glamour stages of the competition. Even though fellow Third Division strugglers Reading were far from glamorous opponents, any straw of excitement was worth clutching, and excitement built at the very real prospect of Barnsley progressing to a dramatic conclusion.

Replay goal-scorer Frank Bartlett.

After a 1-1 draw at Elm Park, over 11,000 people turned out for the replay. In those days, Barnsley still did not play under 'lights at Oakwell, and an 11,000 crowd on a weekday afternoon was an exciting event in itself.

The game turned out to be an added thriller. Ken Oliver put the Reds in front, Reading equalized, and for the first time ever, an Oakwell crowd saw a game played into extra-time. Two more goals, from Bert Tindill and Frank Bartlett, pushed the Reds through.

The fourth round gave them a tough, but exciting draw. Second Division Huddersfield Town, with England international Ray Wilson at full-back, had dumped out Wolves in the previous round. At Leeds Road, confidence was brimful, and enthusiasm bursting out all over. Yorkshire rivalry added spice to the clash, and thousands of Barnsley supporters helped make up a packed crowd of 44,761 Cup-happy fans on a freezing cold February night, after snow had postponed the original Saturday game just an hour before kick-off.

In the second-half, the Reds jumped out into the lead with a goal that melted even their most frosty supporter. Bert Tindill got the ball in space down the inside-right channel in the Huddersfield half, and no defender came over to challenge him. Tindill had time to look up as he toed the ball forward, and he saw the Huddersfield 'keeper off his line. Scooping his foot under the ball, he sent it soaring over the stranded goalie. It looped down towards the net and the 'keeper, chasing back, threw himself at it.

Ken Oliver came leaping in over the top of the diving goalie, and nodded home the rebound as it fell off the bar. For a while, it looked as if the Reds, hanging grimly to their one goal lead, might pull off one of the upsets of the round, but with only 10 minutes left, Duncan Sharp

Match-winner, Bobby Wood

flattened a Huddersfield player inside the Barnsley box. It was never a foul, surely.........but the referee, ignoring furious Barnsley protests, pointed to the spot; 1-1.

At Oakwell, the following Monday afternoon, the fans demonstrated their hunger for excitement when over 29,000 scarf-wearing, hat-waving, rattle-churning spectators skipped their afternoons at work and school to see the replay. Bobby Wood shot Barnsley ahead just before half-time, and brought Second Division Luton to Oakwell in round five. *"The cheers.......could be heard in the town centre,"* reported the Barnsley Chronicle.

Almost 33,000 people clicked through the turnstiles on 18th February. The match was tense, as both teams cancelled each other out in midfield and there were few clear chances. The only goal of the game came during a second-half breakaway, when Houghton fed Jackie Lunn down the left. The Barnsley winger cut into the box, and as Luton's 'keeper came out to challenge, Lunn chipped over him into the empty net, sending the crowd wild. *"In the closing 22 minutes.....Barnsley fans scarcely dare breath,"* reported the Chronicle, *"The anxious thousands had one eye on their watches and the other on the match.........In the dying seconds, Barnsley supporters reminded Mr. Smith, the referee, that it was time for the final whistle by whistling themselves. Then, the final blast came........hundreds invade the pitch to mob the Barnsley players."*

For only the second time since they won the Cup, Barnsley were in the Quarter-finals. All over town the following Monday lunch-time, radios were tuned to the BBC to hear the Cup draw live from F.A. Headquarters at Lancaster Gate. Wooden balls, each with a number representing one of the teams left in the competition, clacked noisily in front of the microphone as an official jiggled them inside a cloth bag, and then drew them out one by one to announce the teams in each tie.

A loud breath was exhaled as Barnsley's name followed Leicester City out of the bag; tinges of disappointment at being drawn away from home gave way to excitement as the whole town became infected by Cup fever.

First Division Leicester, with Gordon Banks in goal, were one of the favourites to win the Cup. However, Old Moore's Almanac had predicted that a team in red and white would be cup-winners, and Barnsley were the only club left in the competition with those colours. Some fans, inhaling too much excitement, really believed Barnsley could set a record by becoming the first Third Division club ever to win the trophy. On the first Saturday in March, trains, buses and cars flying red and white scarves like the banners of a medieval army, streamed out of Barnsley, bound for the battle of Filbert Street.

The Reds rose to the occasion, earning a 0-0 draw that could have gone either way, and Bert Tindill missed one glorious chance that could have ended it all in their favour. The replay on Wednesday afternoon brought Barnsley to a standstill. Schools and businesses threw up their hands in defeat and closed officially, knowing they could not swim against the tide of absenteeism that an afternoon kick-off would bring. The result was a holiday atmosphere and a gate of 39,250, the second largest in Oakwell history.

Unfortunately, the excited crowd saw Leicester go ahead after 22 minutes in a ding-dong opening flourish. Barnsley, playing into the Pontefract Road end, quickly hit a post and claimed the rebound had crossed the line for a goal, but the referee waved play on. Then, England U-23 international Howard Riley, dodging down Leicester's right wing, checked outside young full-back Eric Brookes, came up the goal-line and slipped the ball inside the Barnsley 'keeper's near post. The shot was cleared, and the referee was waving play on when the linesman flagged to indicate the ball had gone over the line. Leicester were ahead.

Three minutes later, at the other end, a cross from Barnsley's right-winger Ron Smillie hit a Leicester defender on the hand inside his own penalty area; as the referee shook off appeals for 'hand ball', Oliver seized on the bounce and struck home Barnsley's equalizer from 12 yards out. The game progressed to extra time with no more scoring, and The Reds, struggling ambitiously against Leicester's class, began to stumble. After 107 minutes, Sharp ducked out of a cross in his own area, expecting 'keeper Leeson to come for it, but Leeson stayed back, the ball dropped onto the head of Leicester's Leek, unmarked in the box, and he plopped it into the net. Barnsley were out of the Cup.

The 1960-61 Cup run was a wonderful boost for the Club in more ways than one. Attendances showed that the town still wanted to love the Club even though, in the League, fans had protested recent fortunes by voting with their feet. Attendances brought in revenue, and total receipts from the ten games Barnsley played in the competition amounted to almost £40,000; the Club's share was over £10,000, enough to save them from having to sell a player for a while. Also, the excitement and publicity generated by the Cup run gave the players, town and Club a terrific boost.

The Sunday Pictorial newspaper awarded Barnsley F.C. their 'Giant Killers Cup', which was presented to captain Duncan Sharp on the field before a League game. The players were rewarded with a formal banquet at the Royal Hotel, as if they had won the F.A. Cup itself. Little old 'Battling Barnsley' of the Third Division had gripped the whole country's imagination for a brief, but exhilarating few moments.

Two years later, Barnsley reached the third round of the Cup again, and landed a plum home draw against star-spangled Everton, who went on to win the League Championship that year. Bad weather kept the crowd down to 30,011, and in a game that slithered and stumbled across freezing snow after being twice postponed, Barnsley's hopes were iced. The visitors kept their feet better with three second half goals to Barnsley's none.

The following season, 1963-64, the Reds were favoured with a draw which led them on a dance to the fifth round. After struggling to get past the early rounds, their reward was a fifth round home tie against F.A. Cup holders Manchester United. Despite a 38,076 crowd, and a terrific buzz of excitement around town, no one really expected a major upset, for the visit of one of the most famous teams in the land was simply a treat. The match programme records that the United team included an Irish youngster with promise, George Best, and a talented Scot who was also the most expensive player in Britain, Denis Law. There were seven internationals in United's line-up, including Bobby Charlton and Nobby Stiles, who two years later would help England carry off the World Cup. In a game with no surprises, United coasted to a 4-0 win.

Michael Parkinson wrote that, *"United played as if they had written the modern theory of the game, and Barnsley as if they had read it backwards..........Denis Law shimmered like quicksilver, and scored as he pleased, and a young lad called George Best played with the instinctive joy of a genius."* Barnsley failed to rise to the occasion, as their recently renewed battling Cup spirit deserted them. Even the Chronicle remarked, *"Barnsley's most attractive Cup tie for over 50 years turned out to be a damp squib from the point of view of a contest."*

Instead of a good Cup run inspiring refreshed performances in the League, it was the 'damp squib' effect that carried over. The Reds escaped relegation to the Fourth Division by only one point the year they met Manchester United in the Cup. Twelve months later, they finished bottom of Division Three, and slipped into the dungeons for the first time in their history.

The few remaining regular supporters had it in their hearts that the Club was too good for the Fourth Division and would quickly bounce back; the reality of the situation pained them. Even at this lower level, Barnsley struggled. After being knocked out in the first round of the League Cup and the second round of the F.A. Cup, their first season in the Fourth division was effectively over before Christmas. They were a terrifyingly ordinary team, distinguished only by centre-forward George Kerr who managed 17 goals, and he left for Bury before the end of the season. The team floundered, occasionally bursting into song with a small bagful of goals, but more often stumbling along in a ragged stupor. At the end of 1965-66, they finished just 3 points above the re-election zone.

For the first time in living memory, players made more noise than the crowd during a game at Oakwell. Attendances dropped to below 2,000, and the crowd of 1,577 on 10th May 1966 for the visit of Wrexham, was the lowest since 1932. When a second Fourth Division season opened in August 1966, little more than 2,500 spectators showed up at the first game. At the time, ground admission was two shillings (10p) for adults, and a shilling for boys, making it impossible for the Club to take much more than £250 a week at the turnstiles, of which 20% went to the visitors. Weekly expenses were about £200. Any small profit that the Club might show after a home game was quickly offset the following week, when it was Barnsley's turn to receive the visitor's percentage, as the away team. Despite Chairman Joe Richard's frugal measures, money was flowing out of the door like water from a leaky pipe. To make matters worse, there were no more players to sell, and no likelihood of success on the field to provide revenue to dam the flow.

At the start of the 1966-67 season, the Club was more than £43,000 in debt at the bank, and paying interest each week on the overdraft. Barnsley F.C.'s links to the town through its Directors, and its ability to keep the wolf from the door for the last 20 years by selling players, and in recent years attracting crowds in the Cup, had always managed to tease the bank and the Club's other creditors into keeping lines of credit open. Although it was expensive, it was the only way they had of coping with a negative cash flow.

However, if the manager of Barnsley's account at the Bank had sat down to open his newspaper over Sunday breakfast on 6th September, 1966, the truth of the situation would have dawned on him as he folded back the sports pages. He would have seen a football club chained to the bottom of the Fourth Division with no points from their first five games, no income at the gate, and no liquid assets to be converted into quick cash. A horrible vision would have flashed before his eyes, the Club was going to fail, and his bank would never recover the money it had advanced.

The fear was very real. The bank began to talk about recalling its loans to the Club. If Barnsley F.C. had to meet its overdraft in full, it either needed a rich benefactor or would have to cash in the only collateral it owned, which was the Oakwell ground, there was nothing else. If the ground was sold to any interest outside the game, it could spell the end of League football in Barnsley; outside interests would be thinking in terms of the commercial or residential development of the land on which the ground stood, and the Club could be out of a home. Obviously, the sale of Oakwell would mean defeat, and had to be avoided at all costs.

Rumours of the Club's serious financial difficulties spread like a disease. Suppliers of goods and services to the Club had experienced difficulty in getting paid for a number of years; Joe Richards, who checked every invoice, would deliberately hold up payment in a 'rob Peter to pay Paul' type of accounting. Now, local businesses feared never getting paid at all. Belgrave Road Co-op, who were owed £20, refused to deal with the Club anymore, and neither players nor officials were allowed to buy on 'tick' from them. Norman Rimmington, who was then the first team trainer and is currently in charge of the player's kit, remembers *"We couldn't buy any soap, matches or anything at all. We had only one strip to share between all the teams, and couldn't wash it properly because we had no washing powder".*

In September, Joe Richards forlornly addressed the Club's Annual General Meeting, *"Goodness knows where the money is going to come from,"* he said. *"I don't know the answer and the bank is now pressing us. I wish there was someone who could come to our assistance if they want League football to continue in Barnsley; I don't know what we will do, but we are certainly living from hand to mouth".*

One shareholder, Harold Wills, suggested that the Club considered refloating its status as a limited company. Basically, this meant selling more shares to raise the required amount of money. Share schemes for the Club had never gone down well with the Barnsley public, and this one would prove no different.

Representatives went door to door and assessed the level of interest; they figured they might sell only about 3,000 shares at ten shillings (50p) each when the sale of 80,000 was needed. The people of Barnsley were resigned to the fact that the Club was in its death throes, and they certainly would not throw good money after bad. *"The Directors have ruined the Club by doing nowt but sell all t'best players, and now they are asking us for money. Why should we gi'em owt,"* was a typical response.

Barnsley F.C. became the butt of countless jokes on the street, in the Clubs and even on television and radio. *"Who's the strongest team in the Football League?......Barnsley, they are holding all the others up". "What time does the game start at Oakwell?...... What time can you get there". "A bobby caught somebody climbing over the wall at Oakwell last week, but he threw him back in".* Barnsley's name was ridiculed in every old joke you could think of, even around town.

For Joe Richards, it must have been a terrible ignominy. His only ambition for the Club had been to stay solvent, and maintain the good name of the Club; circumstances heaped failure on both counts. His policy of selling good players for income, coupled with a failure to set proper goals, had finally come home to roost. In October 1966, the Club was destitute both on the field and at the bank. Barnsley F.C. faced extinction.

CHAPTER 12

THE BEGINNING OF THE FUTURE

At the beginning of October 1966, Barnsley had played ten games in the Fourth Division and lost eight of them. They were bottom of the table, already five wins behind the team in the first safe place above the re-election zone. Rumours of imminent bankruptcy spread from inside the Club to the town. The possibilities of Barnsley failing to be re-elected to the Football League at the end of the season, if the Club could stay alive that long, were already being mulled over. Either way, the townsfolk gloomily resigned themselves to the worst, like distant family expecting grim but inevitable news about a fading relative.

Chairman Joe Richards had nothing left to give. His policies were exhausted, and the Board of Directors, who for years had been used only to agreeing with Richards' plans, had no original ideas of their own. The cupboard, as well as the purse, was bare. Very few people felt that Barnsley Football Club would ever recover.

But then, there was Ernest Dennis, who was a local fruit and vegetable wholesaler and a lifelong supporter of Barnsley FC. His enthusiasm had got him involved with the Club as early as 1947, when he started up the Official Barnsley F.C. Supporters Club, after it had lapsed during the war. As Chairman of the Supporters Club, he built up a thriving association which raised money to supplement Barnsley F.C.'s income at the gate. The Club grew to a membership of 3,000, and shortly after Mr. Dennis stepped down as Chairman, it turned over five of the £6,000 the Club needed to build the old Brewery Stand on the site of the present East Stand, which was completed in 1954; old-timers sometimes referred to it as the 'Supporters Club Stand'.

Dennis moved up into the Boardroom as a Director of Barnsley Football Club under Joe Richards in 1951. He was ousted in 1954 after a single three-year term. In 1958, he returned for a second spell, but lost his seat at the Annual General Meeting in 1961 after the Club was relegated to the Fourth Division. By this time his frustration at the Club's lack of progress on the field was compounded by his disappointment with its leadership under Joe Richards. Mr. Dennis, as a fan and a Director, had been galled by the sale of Tommy Taylor to Manchester United in 1953. From then on, he rarely saw eye to eye with the old Chairman. The state of affairs into which the Club had been allowed to drift had, by October 1966, become too much for Dennis to take.

He proposed a scheme to his friend and fellow supporter Geoffrey Buckle, whereby they would make financial guarantees to the Club with secret provisions which they hoped would turn its fortunes around. First of all, he and Buckle would make money available to buy new players. Secondly, the two friends were to be co-opted onto the Board where they planned to use their joint influence to break prevailing policy, and thirdly, Joe Richards' days as Chairman would have to end.

Their offer put a pistol to the Club's head. The Board could ill afford to turn down the financial incentives they offered, but the changes that Dennis and Buckle insisted upon would turn their world on its head. Richards knew that, by agreeing to step down as Chairman, his fingers would be pried loose from the Club he had ruled with a rod of iron for the last eighteen years, even though he would be allowed to keep a seat on the Board. As far as he could see, it was the beginning of the end for him, and he was reluctant to go. If Buckle and Dennis had money to offer, they should turn it over, and the Board should direct how it was spent. It was rumoured that bitter words were exchanged before financial desperation prevailed, and the rest of the Board voted the deal through.

On Thursday 10th November, 1966, the town was agog when news broke out that Barnsley FC had splashed out £10,000 on two new forwards. The signings were rushed through to beat the transfer deadline which made them eligible for the next Saturday's home game against Port Vale. Barnsley's meagre home attendance swelled to nearly 5,000; the curiosity-seekers, eager to see Barrie Thomas and John Evans spearhead Barnsley's attack against a notoriously tough Vale defence, went away with good things to report. Midway through the second-half, winger Bob Earnshaw rifled home a goal for a one-nil victory. The revival on the field had begun.

Four days later, Barnsley visited middle-of-the-table Exeter; on the same evening, a small crowd gathered at Oakwell to watch a Barnsley Boys game. As the Oakwell announcer gave the up-to-the-minute score over the crackling public address system, the crowd burst into shouts of unmitigated glee; one-nil, two-nil, three-nil. It was unbelievable! New centre-forward Thomas scored twice in the first 12 minutes. A 2-2 draw away at Crewe the following Saturday, brought Barnsley back home to face Southport, fourth from the top of the Fourth Division, in the 1st Round of the FA Cup.

A buzzing crowd of 11,560 flowed into Oakwell to see for themselves the phenomenon of a team back from the dead. Thomas (2) and Evans sliced Southport open with their pace on the break, and their eagerness in front of goal. All of a sudden, football was fun again at Barnsley. The Cup run included a crowd of over 21,000 for a Third Round clash against Second Division Cardiff City, which Evans forced to a replay with the last kick of the game, and their League form saw them climb to 16th out of 24 by the end of the season, and average home attendances increased by over 1,000 on the previous campaign.

The signing of Barrie Thomas for £7,500 from Scunthorpe United, and Johnny Evans for £2,500 from Exeter City, vindicated the policy demanded by Ernest Dennis and Geoff Buckle. For Joe Richards, their success meant his defeat. On Monday 28th November, two days after Barnsley's exciting demolition of Southport in the FA Cup, he resigned from the Chair, to complete the secret provisions of the Board's take-over. Director Sid Edmundson, one of the Dennis backers, was elected in his place. A year later, the Board moved out of Richards' shadow completely. The Barnsley F.C. 1968 Annual Report recorded Joe Richard's death with an acknowledgment that didn't quite manage to be a compliment. It read simply, *"Sir Joseph's marathon years of service to the Club will never be forgotten..........."*

However, before new Chairman Sid Edmundson could take over, a tragic and momentous blow struck, when he collapsed and died suddenly in December 1966, leaving the Oakwell Chair vacant. It was a position which none of the Directors really wanted for themselves in the prevailing climate. Arthur Raynor, who had taken over the Supporters Club from Ernest Dennis in 1951, and had served on the Board of Directors for the previous 11 years, became acting Chairman until the next Annual General Meeting. Then, Ernest Dennis was voted the man to take over.

Ernest Dennis was unlike many of his predecessors on the Board of Barnsley Football Club in two major respects; he had a dream, and he had the courage to go out on a limb to achieve it. It is clear now, that his leadership was the cornerstone of Barnsley Football Club's long and subtle climb from the bottom of the Fourth Division to the F.A. Carling Premiership over thirty years later, although the arduous trail was not always so clear at the time.

Many in town, and some at the Club, had never set their ambitions any higher than simply seeing Barnsley out of the Fourth Division and back into the Second Division 'where they belonged', but Ernest Dennis was sure from the beginning that Barnsley FC should aim at even greater things. *"It is the biggest fallacy ever spoken or quoted that*

we are a Second Division club", he said in 1968, with the Club out of the Fourth Division just one season after he took office. *"We have the greatest potential of any club in South Yorkshire. We can command support for the highest quality of football that can be put on at Oakwell, and we have a ground which can be made equal to the best in the Country. There is no Second Division limit to our achievements. Our pride in the Club will never be complete until the ultimate objective has been reached".*

The ambitious vision of Dennis led him to reverse the policies which had crippled the Club for many years, shape a sound financial future and develop a philosophy of pride at Oakwell which more than once has spilled over into the hearts of players on the field. Ultimately, that vision passed along within the closely-knit club after his death in 1979, paving the way for Barnsley to reach the highest levels of the game. It was an incredible rise for a club which Dennis himself once described as *"ready to have the coffin lid screwed down on it."*

The Chairman's vision for Barnsley F.C. was conceived through the eyes of a fan, his determination to carry it through was steered by a businessman. *"I appreciate the public will not follow our team, or any team, just for the sake of doing so. They must have value for money."* Dennis told the Star Green 'Un. *"If the team plays well and wins, the fans will be satisfied. If they play well and lose, there could still be some satisfaction. But, if they play badly and win with a fluky goal, there is little satisfaction - and we want spectators to leave Oakwell with a feeling of satisfaction. When I became Chairman, I regarded two things as being of paramount importance. Firstly, the maintenance of a team to provide satisfaction for the thousands of football followers in this area. Secondly, the finances of the Club just had to be improved. The one follows the other. If you have a successful team, the money will come through the turnstiles".*

However, Dennis knew from his involvement with supporters' fund-raising that the Club needed more revenue than could come through the turnstiles alone, and with his authority as Chairman, he promoted new efforts to boost income. One of the first areas to be developed was marketing, which combined public relations, to create a new image for the Club, with the ability to make money and get people involved.

To launch the 1967 season, a cartoon mascot was created; a cheerful thumbs-up pup called 'Toby Tyke'. For the first time ever, the Club developed a range of official souvenirs.

Toby featured on a series of stickers, pennants and T-shirts. At first, the Club had no shop of its own; the official Barnsley souvenirs were made available at the Club Office and a supporter's home in St. George's Road. Eventually, a cabin was opened inside Oakwell behind the Pontefract Road end terrace; mid-week customers had to be escorted to the cabin and have it unlocked specially for them.

The second area to receive a boost was lottery fund-raising, run by a separate arm of the Club known as the Barnsley Development Association. Beginning in 1967, a bevy of 'Golden Girls' in hotpants and red-and-white plastic raincoats began to sell 'Golden Goal' tickets to spectators, who were hopeful of purchasing one with the time of the first goal printed on it in order to win a cash prize. Although the pretty girls did not endure for long, ticket sales did. The 'Tote Double Draw' attracted supporters with the offer of commission on sales, and cash prizes. With the development of a £12,000 social club in the Pontefract Road end car park in 1968, the Club created an even bigger and better venue for more supporters' social events, raffles and draws.

The third area for improvement was advertising and sponsorship. The Club programme, which had always carried local advertising for such local staples as Barnsley Bitter and Albert Hirst's pork pies, grew from a few flimsy pages the size of a square of toilet paper to a bulkier magazine format on glossy stock, encouraging more elaborate and expensive advertising. In the earliest experiments with sponsorship, supporters were encouraged to 'donate' a match ball; the donor's name being printed on the team sheet in the programme. By 1971, the combination of marketing, fund-raising and public relations had developed enough for the Club to appoint its first Commercial Manager in Johnny Evans, an ex-player forced into retirement through injury.

Mr. Dennis did more than just figure out ways to bring money into the Club. Marrying his own enthusiasm to the pride and loyalty of people already inside Oakwell, like Johnny Steele, trainer Norman Rimmington and captain Eric Winstanley, Ernest Dennis rolled up his shirt sleeves and set a tone of 'can-do' personal responsibility that permeated the entire organization. No detail was too small for the Chairman's attention. If a fan wrote a complimentary letter about the Club to a newspaper, Ernest Dennis sent a personal note of thanks. If a fan wrote to the Club with criticisms, Ernest Dennis answered at length. All of it was done quietly in the background, nothing was done for personal recognition. Dennis stressed that the Club was all about the players and the paying supporters, not about the people behind the scenes. The only reason he became Chairman, he said, was because he couldn't expect anyone else to accept the responsibility if he wasn't prepared to do so himself. *"I believe in Barnsley FC, and I would like everybody in Barnsley and District to believe in the Club with me"*, he said. It was as simple as that.

The example was a startling change from the leadership of the previous twenty years. At a small club like Barnsley, with limited resources, morale is vitally important, and sometimes it is the only means of getting things done. Too often, the Board had waited for performances on the field of play to raise spirits; too frequently they had been disappointed. When Ernest Dennis took over, optimism started at the top and worked its way down, for the first time in perhaps half a century. In 1968, Johnny Steele pointed out *"The drive, determination and dedication to put Barnsley Football Club where it belongs emanates from the top. The Chairman, Vice-Chairman and their colleagues on the Board have this season given us the encouragement and incentive we needed".*

Under Dennis, the Club learned to survive with nothing, a policy which put Barnsley F.C. in good stead to deal with financing in the future. Visitors might ask, *"How do you manage to get by on so little?"* *"Because we have nowt to get by on,"* was the stock reply. The Club developed an unwritten rule that money was for spending on players, first and foremost, and on anything else only if cash was left over, explaining why the Oakwell stadium was left substantially undeveloped for many years except for compulsory improvements.

Even in the Premiership in 1997/98, the lessons of years of hardship were still to the forefront when the Club refused to modernize its dressing rooms or its visiting supporters' enclosure in favour of keeping funds on hand to boost the team, but that is hardly surprising, for constant reminders abounded at Oakwell. The Chairman in 1997 was John Dennis, son of Ernest; the General Manager was Michael Spinks, who had learned his trade on a shoestring under Ernest Dennis; Steele, Pallister, Winstanley and Rimmington were all still at the Club; and the Board comprised long-time Club supporters with good memories. In this sense, the changes begun under Ernest Dennis from 1966 onwards were truly the beginning of the future for Barnsley Football Club.

The players of the time were also inspired by the changes. When they reported for pre-season training at Wharncliffe Woodmoor Sports Centre before the start of the 1967/68 season, they found themselves enjoying a new style of coaching based on the Football Association's camps at Lilleshall. In addition, they were promised double any previous pay bonuses if the team finished in the top four, a placing which would guarantee them promotion out of the Fourth Division. The combination of interest and motivation worked. They trained in high spirits and carried a new-found confidence on to the field at the start of the season.

A team which previously played like ragamuffins, trotted out on to the field looking sleek, fit and proud. Club captain Eric Winstanley explained the new spirit at Oakwell. *"We believe in ourselves now,"* he told a Sheffield Morning Telegraph reporter, *"........We've always seemed to be fighting against something rather than for it, and our supporters have had a lot to put up with, but things have changed at Barnsley.......We do a lot more talking and thinking amongst ourselves, and if a thing doesn't work out, we talk it over and try to find out what's happening to stop it from working. We're all trying to help each other, and there's a lot more understanding amongst us".*

That understanding led to remarkable success. At the end of 1967/68, Barnsley were promoted back to the Third Division in front of average home crowds of nearly 11,000, the largest for nine years; for the first time in fifteen years, the Club made a profit at the turnstiles, bearing out the Dennis theory that the town would support attractive soccer and a successful team. Over 140,000 fans watched the last 11 home games. It helped that in July 1966, England had hosted and won the World Cup, sparking a revival of interest in football throughout the Country, and raising attendances in general, but the boom at Oakwell had very much been earned by the Club's own amazing turnaround.

The revival's momentum carried the Reds forward into Division Three, driven by hopes of a quick return to the Second Division, 'where they belonged'. For a short while, they looked to be on the brink of fulfilling their dream. For three years in the Third Division, they finished each campaign in the top half of the table, but were never quite good enough. In 1972, the revival was derailed when they dropped back into the Fourth Division.

Action from the 1968/69 season versus Grimsby Town (note the packed Stand)

Blame for the Club's failure to capitalize on the ground it had gained could no longer be laid with the Board's lack of ambition, instead the Board's inexperience was a factor. Many fans believed the collapse was a sign of

'business as usual' at Oakwell. They could be forgiven for losing patience after watching some of the team's performances, but hindsight sheds a different light. Ernest Dennis and his Board had tried to remain true to their aims. They had made an effort to bring quality football back to Oakwell, making best use of the limited means available. Privately, they acknowledged learning a bitter lesson; they felt they tried to go too far, too fast. The sudden dive taught them that a new base level of support and organisation had to be built for each new level of success before the next tier could be attempted, a mistake they would rectify in the future.

One indication of the Board's continuing ambition, and perhaps of its over-eagerness, was a willingness to go out and buy new players. Unfortunately, the spending spree which brought a sequence of new players to Oakwell in the late sixties, eventually became as unproductive as it was unprecedented. It was poor judgement in the transfer market that helped turn the Club's fortunes back, and undid the work of the first few years.

The Directors' purchasing policy started well with Thomas and Evans. When Thomas was injured in December 1967, the Club spent £10,000 on centre-forward Jimmy Robson. The following season, they spent a further £10,000 on striker Norman Dean. When Dean broke his leg, they spent £10,000 on forward Eddie Loyden. The next season, they bought George Boardman for £7,000. A record £20,000 was paid to Cardiff City for wingers Les Lea and Frank Sharp in 1970. Another £10,000 went for forward Brian Mahoney, and £6,000 for forward Jimmy Seal in 1971-72. Perhaps little Johnny Evans and Les Lea were the best of the bunch. A nippy little inside-forward in the old Barnsley tradition, 5' 8" Evans worked hard and snatched chances in 170 League appearances (54 goals) between 1966 and 1971, twice finishing as top scorer. He was the fans' choice as the first 'Player of the Year' in 1970, the year the Boylin Trophy was introduced. *"He never gives up trying, and has lots of guts and determination"*, wrote one voter.

Feisty little Les Lea, an attacking midfielder and energetic forward, was also twice top scorer with the Club, and won the supporters' vote in 1971. However, neither of these two scored enough goals to make any significant difference. The problem was so bad that, in 1969, Eric Winstanley, playing from centre-half, was leading marksman with just 14 League and Cup goals.

Another sign that the Directors were holding their faith was the lack of transfer activity away from the Club. For the first time in living memory, not all the best players were marched straight

Alistair Millar makes his debut in the home game with Rochdale (6 March 1971)

to the Bank; Eric Winstanley and Pat Howard could have brought in a small fortune, but stayed at Oakwell. Even so, there were still some unpopular moments. When Stewart Barrowclough was sold to Newcastle United for a Club record £40,000 in 1970, there was a clamour of protest, but Barrowclough, a local teenager, had not even earned a regular place in the first team; he was a reserve who had turned out nine times whilst deputizing for the injured Bob Earnshaw. Barrowclough enjoyed a First Division career before returning to Oakwell eleven years later, when he helped the Reds win promotion to the Second Division under Norman Hunter.

Another unpopular move was the release of Eddie Loyden to his former club, Chester. Scoring goals was a nightmare for the team, and gangly Loyden had seemed a partial cure when he scored 10 times in his first 22 League appearances. The fans, perhaps remembering full-back Bob Parker's spot-kick attempt which once put a corner flag in danger, liked Loyden as soon as he rifled home a penalty on his debut on Boxing Day 1968, but he only found the net another 13 times in his last 43 League games for the Club. The supporters were hurt most by the timing of his transfer. Loyden scored a memorable hat-trick in a mid-week County Cup win against Sheffield United at Oakwell, and was gone the next day. The deal had already been arranged, but his performance against Yorkshire rivals from a higher division made his departure look very bad timing.

More importantly, the players who stayed showed tremendous loyalty to Barnsley Football Club. The failure of Barnsley strikers to find the net at one end of the field was counter-balanced at the other end by the talents of Eric Winstanley and Pat Howard, and the

doggedness of Barry 'Spud' Murphy. For four years, Winstanley and Howard anchored the team, and provided the essence of regular supporters' enjoyment; Spud turned in a Club record 567 appearances which lasted into the late seventies, many as captain.

Football changed rapidly when England won the World Cup in 1966 with a team that featured a 'back four' and no wingers. Success bred imitation, and the traditional five-forward system with a single centre-half disappeared from the Football League. Defensive formations of 4-3-3, 4-2-4 and 4-4-2 appeared; teams began to play strategically for a draw away from home, and learned how to 'shut up shop' instead of chasing goals at the other end, a development that Barnsley's inability to score, was painful treatment to. Although the Reds' attack may not have adapted well, the popular new idea of twin centre-backs provided Winstanley and Howard with a perfect stage on which to perform their double act.

Eric Winstanley was over six feet tall, and thirteen stone, a physically commanding presence as he strutted over the turf under a shock of curly black hair, with his chest out and head up, pointing, yelling and directing the game. Blonde-haired Pat Howard was smaller and lighter, but slick and fast with a crushing tackle. If Winstanley stepped up to meet the play, Howard swept up behind him; if Howard took off to wipe out a breaking forward with a sweetly timed long slide that cannoned the ball into the wall and sent the opponent skidding belly first along the grass, Winstanley covered the middle.

Winstanley, rising like a missile launch from Cape Canaveral, took everything in the air and Howard, purring across the turf like a combine harvester, took everything on the ground. It was incredible that Barnsley should have such talent available to them in the Third and Fourth Divisions.

Both Winstanley and Howard were local lads, who put their faith in Barnsley F.C., and gave the Club a chance before seeking advancement of their own careers. For Winstanley, loyalty to the Club was repayment for the patience Barnsley showed after his cruciate ligament injury in 1965.

A Harley Street specialist said that no one had recovered sufficiently enough to play again after that sort of injury; it certainly brought First Division clubs' interest in him to a speedy end. However, encouragement from Barnsley gave Eric the incentive to beat the odds. He suffered excruciating pain in training, but refused to give up, and when he regained his first team place, he became a permanent fixture for seven seasons. He was adored by supporters who loved to see him trot up the field for corners; he seemed to climb as high as The town Hall clock. When there was a rumour that he might be transferred to another club, fans handed a written petition to Barnsley demanding that he stayed, which he did until his career faded into the twilight, and then no one begrudged him the move.

'Winnie's' best performance perhaps was one of the most exciting individual displays ever seen at Oakwell. On 22nd April, 1969, Third Division champions Watford were leading 2-0 when Eric played a captain's game by promoting himself to centre-forward and scoring a

(Above) Eric Winstanley leads the team out on his 300th League appearance, versus Plymouth (28 November 1970). (Below) Barry 'Spud' Murphy.

second half hat-trick. He snatched victory almost single-handedly in the dying minutes. Eric was the fans' Player of the Year in 1973, and the Club's top goal-scorer in 1968-69, making 461 appearances for the Reds. He is currently first team trainer, after spending only a few years of his life away from Oakwell.

Pat Howard, from Dodworth, joined the Club as a sixteen-year-old, and made his debut at eighteen. At the age of nearly 20, he joined Eric Winstanley as centre-back in the team which was promoted from the Fourth Division, and became an automatic choice for over 200 games. Pat left at the beginning of the 1971-72 season during changes at the Club which brought relegation at the end of the year.

At Oakwell, he had always been the junior partner, toiling in Winstanley's shadow, but he had no trouble stepping from the Third Division to the First, and making a mark of his own, even though he did not begin until he was nearly 25. He made 237 appearances in the First Division with Newcastle, Arsenal and Birmingham, and also appeared in both an F.A. Cup Final and a League Cup Final. Howard's departure did not signal a change of heart by the Board. The player felt he had given Barnsley a fair chance, and that after four years as a first team regular, it was the right time to make a move in his own best interests. By and large, the fans agreed, and wished him luck.

Spud Murphy perpetuated Barnsley's link with the North-East. Signed for nothing from South Shields in 1962, he was also an example of how determination can pay off. Although he did not earn a regular place in the side until the age of 27, Spud made a record number of consecutive appearances (182), before being dropped for just one game, on the way to a total of 567, which is unlikely ever to be beaten, finally bowing out at the age of 38. A full-back not blessed with great speed, Murphy closed down opposing forwards with a characteristic open-legged stance likened to a cowboy just down from his horse, and stuck to his man like a limpet. He earned respect for his diligence and persistence from professionals in almost every club he played against. Spud was the first Barnsley player ever to come on the field as a substitute, replacing Brian Jackson on 29th October, 1965 against Doncaster Rovers at Oakwell, and was the fans' Player of the Year in 1972.

The late sixties saw the beginning of the future in ways beyond developments in the Barnsley F.C. Boardroom. Televised football and hooliganism both had their beginnings in the same period as Barnsley's revival. Television would eventually bring in revenue and the chance to earn national recognition; hooliganism would bring extra costs, security problems and bad publicity.

In the fifties, Barnsley players might have been lucky to see themselves briefly on a Pathé Newsreel at the cinema; by 1965, the Football League had authorized the showing of recorded game highlights on television, resulting in the BBC's launch of 'Match of the Day'. When the famous programme began to include regional coverage in addition to a top First Division match every Saturday night, Barnsley won their first 15 minutes of TV fame in a 3-2 defeat at Walsall on 20th December, 1969. Only a week later, Yorkshire TV's cameras featured Barnsley for the first time in their Sunday afternoon broadcast of a game from the previous day, against Doncaster Rovers. Barnsley won a scrappy Oakwell game 2-1 in front of over 17,000 fans.

There was a new audience for live football as well, when traditionally, good natured working class crowds began to be dominated by young, aggressive supporters. In the early nineteen-sixties, the Liverpool Kop vibrated with the 'Mersey Beat' pop music explosion, and spontaneously began to sing their own versions of the hits; their first was the 1962 Routers' song 'Let's Go', to which they substituted the name of their favourite player 'St. John' - in 1997-98 the chant was back in favour; Barnsley fans took it back to Anfield shouting 'The Reds' at the end of their rhythmic clapping. Around the Country, young fans gathered behind the goals at their home town stadiums and emulated the Liverpool sound from radio and television. At Barnsley, on a good day such as 10th September, 1969, when Oakwell hosted a game between the Football League and the League of Ireland, the Pontefract Road end became a choir stall of massed singers. Unfortunately, the development of chanting and 'home ends' quickly encouraged territorial displays between rival fans. Football's worst disease, hooliganism, was about to arrive at Oakwell.

Fortunately, Barnsley F.C. never experienced a serious football gang problem, but there were flashes of madness during the late sixties, and throughout the seventies. Most incidents were generated by imitation, spontaneous bravado and misguided football loyalty, triggered off by a charged atmosphere; the organized, coldly calculated soccer violence that infected bigger clubs never arrived at Oakwell.

For many years, police presence at Oakwell had been limited to a couple of rosy-cheeked bobbies walking the edge of the pitch, and the few regulars, known by name to many in the crowd, could easily deal with noisy youngsters who rained down toilet rolls and streamers of Yorkshire Traction ticket bobbins, to celebrate a home goal, which was the first signs of changing crowd behaviour in the late sixties. By the mid-seventies, in the days before clubs employed their own stewards, policing would be a huge operation; In 1981, at the end of season game against Rotherham United, hundreds of officers were involved, enough to circle the entire playing area.

On 13th August 1969, the first documented incident of real hooliganism took place after a League Cup-tie with Halifax Town. Ill-feeling against Halifax had begun two seasons earlier, in March 1968, when Manager Alan Ball Snr. disrupted a game at Oakwell during Barnsley's promotion run-in. Barnsley fans were incensed by Halifax's hard-tackling when Ball, disputing the sending-off of one of his players, came out onto the field and held up the game to yell at the referee, Johnny Steele, and anyone else within earshot, before being escorted away. When the League Cup came around over a year later, fans had not forgotten. Their anger boiled over when Halifax kicked, stamped and booted their way to a 1-0 League Cup robbery. Next day, the Daily Mail reported that the windows of visiting fans coaches had been smashed in the Queen's Ground car park.

Alan Ball was scheduled to return again for a League game on 1st November 1969, when he received a letter threatening to kill him with a cyanide-tipped dart if he showed up at Oakwell. It was a threat so ludicrous, and so far removed from the thuggery of real hooliganism, that it seemed laughable, but Ball's arrival at the game had to be guarded by plain clothed policemen, and Barnsley made national headlines.

By 1971, the height of the skinhead craze, rioting had become a football cult throughout the Country. Travel to away games was an excuse for visiting supporters to run rampant, particularly on 'Football Special' trains, when fans were dumped at a railway station often miles from the football ground. Barnsley fans visiting York for a routine Third Division match in November 1971, made newspaper headlines when they ran riot through the city centre before the game, and without provocation, smashing windows, bouncing cars, turning over sales displays and stealing merchandise. For Barnsley F.C., such incidents were rare, but for many years to come, almost every away game excursion was peppered with some acts of vandalism.

The worst incidents of crowd behaviour at Oakwell were most likely to happen when large numbers of travelling supporters came to town. Gradually, these incidents forced changes in spectators' accommodation. The

Johnny Evans, made nearly 200 appearances for Barnsley, and was 'Player Of The Year' in 1970.

games most likely to provide incidents on the terrace were local derbies, when rival passions added to short travelling distances for eager fans, but it was not exclusively so. On 12th September, 1970, Aston Villa, just relegated to the Third Division, and enjoying huge support, were Barnsley's visitors. Their early arriving supporters were allowed to occupy home turf on the 'Ponty End' - now the ORA Stand. As home fans arrived, only a line of police separated the two chanting groups. During the game, a charge by home supporters sent spectators scattering over the walls in search of safety. Two weeks later, there was a similar incident with Chesterfield fans.

Incidents such as these brought enforced fan separation to Oakwell, and an end to traditional free movement around the ground. For years, home fans had switched ends to stand behind whichever goal Barnsley were attacking, and mingled openly with any visiting supporters they may have found.

Now, the Spion Kop became reserved for away supporters, and home fans wishing to change ends with the play had to make do with the northern part of the Brewery Sand - now the East Stand. Within a few years, visiting supporters would be caged in completely by red metal fences, and movement into the Brewery Stand would be restricted.

Tighter measures inside Oakwell moved fan warfare into the streets, and to the bus and railway stations where opposing fans gathered to board special excursion buses and trains. Perhaps the most infamous day in the Club's history occurred after a game with Bradford City, a fixture which regularly brought out a large number of hooligans on both sides.

In a melee between rival groups at Barnsley's Jumble Lane railway crossing on 1st February 1975, a missile took out a police horse's eye, and catapulted Barnsley's 'inhumane' fans onto the front pages of every national newspaper.

Hooliganism at Barnsley was part of a national epidemic that would only end with the tragedy at Hillsborough in 1988. The death of Liverpool fans sobered football, brought down fences, and ushered in all-seater stadiums. Football lost its seedy image as seats became filled by a new generation of supporters. Rampant violence, which at one time had threatened to be a part of an inescapable future, even at Oakwell, quickly became a part of the past, and Barnsley F.C.'s own future began to speed along without it.

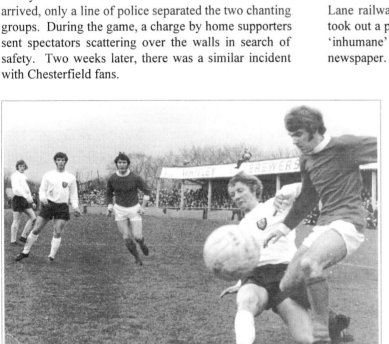

No hooliganism at Rhyl in the F.A.Cup (12 December 1970). Frank Sharp in action. The eventual outcome was an embarrassing defeat for Barnsley in the second replay!

CHAPTER 13

COMING HOME

Barnsley F.C.'s first attempt to regain a higher perch in the Football League ended with a slide back into the Fourth Division like a high jumper hitting the bar and falling unceremoniously to earth. Undaunted, the Club pulled itself together and set about its second attempt. It took until 1981 for them to finally soar over the top with style and passion. The Club's efforts were delayed by more years of frustration and financial hardship that dogged it like a bad hamstring. When success finally came, it was earned only after extinction had been looked in the eye, and beaten, for a second time.

In September 1971, Johnny Steele announced his retirement after 11 years as Manager. At the time, only Matt Busby at Manchester United had spent longer as a Manager with one club. Busby, however, had enjoyed success, conversely Steele, despite the 1968 promotion, had served through some of the most miserable times in the history of Barnsley Football Club. A stranger judging his record as Manager based on the success of his teams might find it difficult to understand why he was in charge so long, but Johnny Steele played a part beyond that achieved on the field. His patience, unselfishness and belief in the Club helped keep the ship afloat, even when there was almost no water under the keel, something that might not have been expected from an outsider with no special loyalty.

Steele, however, was a product of the nineteen thirties. He learned his trade in the days of baggy shorts, cropped hair and deadweight footballs. His abilities as a coach were rooted in the simple old traditions of flying wingers, dazzling dribbles and solid tackles. Despite years of experience, football was passing beyond his generation during the seventies, the era of bell bottoms and velvet jackets. The Board, looking to the future, hoped that a fresh injection of aggressive young management might stimulate the team in a way their signings in the transfer market had not.

Steele stepped down by mutual consent; the old trooper stayed on at the Club as its first General Manager, a position created for him not only to recognize his years of service, but also to take advantage of his experience and commitment to the Club. Later, he would become a Director. Taking his place as Manager was John McSeveney, another Scot seeking his first chance at management, whose aggressiveness had the opposite effect to that intended.

At Hull City, where Barnsley found McSeveney as an ambitious coach under Terry Neill, he had earned a reputation as a hard man with a fiery temperament. Oakwell terrace talk immediately reported that he had brought his reputation with him, and that feathers were ruffled on the training ground. When he signed his neighbour and old friend Paddy Greenwood for £10,000 in November 1971, it was rumoured that his abrasiveness had isolated him from the players and that he needed an ally amongst them to get the job done.

McSeveney's only full season in charge, 1971/72, was a disaster. Barnsley slumped back to the Fourth Division on goal average. Up front, it was still the old problem of ineffective strikers finding goals hard to come by. At the back, with Howard missing and Paddy Greenwood taking time to settle, the team conceded more goals than it had done since 1966-67, despite McSeveney's bargain buy of a capable and popular goalkeeper in Gerry Stewart. McSeveney's other forays into the transfer market, such as strikers Brian Mahoney and Kevin McMahon, were failures.

Only thirteen months after it began, one of Oakwell's shortest managerial tenures came to an end. The team were lacklustre, gates had tumbled into the two thousands, the Club was losing money and, neither the fans, the Board nor the players could see any hope of even stepping onto the bottom rung of an escape ladder. In 1972, with only 5 wins out of 16 games at the start of a new season in Division Four, fans angrily chanted "McSeveney out", and the Board agreed. Johnny Steele took charge of the team once more.

With Steele back in the Manager's office, it was too much like déjà-vu all over again. Somehow, the Club had slid back into the mire it thought it had escaped in the sixties; no income, no resources and no prospects. On the playing front, there were no star players either to sell, or to lift the team. Eric Winstanley, the only player on the books who could ever have been called outstanding, had passed Harry Hough's record of 346 League appearances in January 1972, and was aging gracefully near the end of his career; when he finally left in 1973, it was to Chesterfield for only £15,000, to give him experience with another club before moving on to a coaching career. The Juniors, meanwhile, continued to suffer from the aggressive scouting of Barnsley boys by bigger, richer clubs. For example, local lads Brian Greenhoff and Arnold Sidebottom signed for Manchester United. Barnsley had to settle for what the top scouts left. Fortunately, there were a few loyal local youngsters to provide first team backbone, even if another Tommy Taylor was out of the question.

One town lad, Kenny Brown, could have been the inspiration for a Lowry's 'matchstick men' scene when he made his debut in Barnsley's midfield at Torquay in 1970, aged 18. Set against the lower division heavyweights, his tiny, fragile-looking eight-and-half stone frame skittered over the field like a crisp bag blowing through a parade of lorries on the M1. Despite a body-building diet, Brown gained only about a stone in his 9 seasons and 303 games for Barnsley. His youth, skinny build and deadpan expression irritated spectators who, in frustration at the Reds' plight, would have preferred to see someone they thought more likely to 'get stuck in'. They frequently made Kenny a scapegoat, yelling abuse and derision, yet he never gave up trying. Six years after his debut, fans voted him Player of the Year for his work rate, dedication and overall professionalism.

Another couple of local boys, David 'Sam' Yates and Phil Chambers, paired off at full-back for the first-half of the seventies. Chambers had earned 6 England schoolboy caps while representing the town, but Yates was passed over by Barnsley Boys, and had to invite himself to a trial at Oakwell. Phil, stocky and compact, played a modern full-back's game, coming forward on the overlap. His crosses, floated in from the left, were a feature of countless Barnsley attacks.

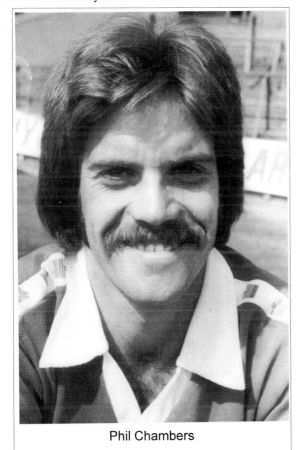

Phil Chambers

Phil stayed at Oakwell and became Club captain with 494 appearances over 15 seasons, eventually leading the Club back to Division Two in 1981.

'Sam' Yates, almost a mirror image of Chambers on the right side, made 112 appearances over 6 seasons at Oakwell. Home-grown players solved only part of Barnsley's problem. With no money to spend, Steele found himself pushing the limits of creativity to find players for nothing, yet even he could never have imagined the most remarkable discovery of the era. When Mick Butler arrived in early 1973, it was as if the Gods had dropped Barnsley Football Club into a time warp. Before the Great War, it was said that all the Club had to do was call down a pitshaft and up would come a centre-forward. Suddenly, in the era of skimpy shorts, flowing hair and 'pop star' professionals, Barnsley's latest hero was a coalworker turning out in the Football League on his day off from the pit.

An electrician at Dodworth Colliery, 22-year-old Mick Butler's rise could have been the inspiration for a footballing comic. He worked five shifts at the pit while playing, at the weekend, for Worsboro' Bridge Miners' Welfare in the Yorkshire League, and Ward Green Working Men's Club. When Barnsley F.C. showed an interest in him, he added their midweek Reserve team games to his calender without dropping his other games, or his work.

Butler made his Football League debut against Bradford City in February 1973, still employed by the National Coal Board, and earning £5 per match expenses from Barnsley F.C. as an amateur footballer. He scored in his first game, and added eight more goals in Barnsley's remaining thirteen matches, including a first-half hat trick away at Hartlepool in April, before signing as a full-time professional.

At last, the Club had found a natural goalscorer. Butler's slim, waif-like build belied his liveliness in front of goal; like some of Barnsley's earlier strikers, he broke the mould of the giant centre-forward in favour of quick reflexes, enthusiastic running and sharp finishing. If the ball was loose in the box, up popped Butler ever ready to snap at a half chance. He was Player of the Year in 1973-74, his first full season, and top scorer two years in a row before a broken leg interrupted his career.

In the Boardroom, the Directors hoped for something equally miraculous to occur with the Club's finances. The money wasted on poor transfers, and the gloom that Fourth Division football cast over attendances, had come to roost with a vengeance. In 1972-73, when as few as 1,638 attended a Friday night game with Exeter City, the Club reported a loss of £33,000; its overdraft at the bank was like a ton weight tied to a man on a rock, just waiting for the tide to come in. Although not as well publicized as the 1966 crisis, the situation was rapidly becoming just as desperate. In the end, it was solved in much the same way, by the belief and generosity of a small group of loyal supporters at the heart of the Club.

The situation was so bad that on some Fridays, Norman Rimmington was despatched to Chairman Ernest Dennis's home with the request, *"Mr. Dennis, they've no money to make up the wages; can you send some?"* Others like Norman Moody, Arthur Raynor, Johnny Steele and Gordon Pallister dipped into their own pockets and helped the Club meet its bills. Unknown to the average fan turning over his coin at the turnstile, without them there may have been no business as usual on a Saturday afternoon.

In desperation, the Board considered selling off some of the property the Club had accumulated around Oakwell in order to cover its debts, and create the financing needed for another revival.

Negotiations took place with a developer to sell off the Grove Street car park, and plans were drawn up to create a giant Spar supermarket. Things went so far that the Club accepted a down payment of £40,000. When planning permission for the project was turned down, the developer withdrew, and the Club found itself in another crisis. The £40,000 which had been given to the Club was conditional to planning permission being granted, and had to be returned. As the due date for repayment arrived, there seemed little hope of the Board finding the money; the possibility of legal action and bankruptcy, on top of problems on the football field, closed like a roof over the Director's heads.

Around the same time, Ernest Dennis announced to his family that they were making a loan of about £40,000 to Barnsley Football Club. Sons Anthony and John, the present Chairman, looked at each other and shrugged. *"I don't think we'll ever see that again"*, they decided.

The down payment was returned to the Developer on time, and Barnsley Football Club narrowly escaped scandal and another financial crisis, enabling it to turn its full attention to the plight on the football field.

In April 1973, Jim Iley was appointed new Team Manager. The delay in making an appointment had been caused by finding a man to fit the Director's agenda. The Club was £100,000 in debt; a hasty choice, and a reckless and impatient Manager might have catapulted it over the edge. The Board wanted someone knowledgeable and patient, who could help them build their way out of the situation. Perhaps Iley turned out to be a little too cautious to inspire the best from his players, or to earn the confidence of the fans.

Born in South Kirkby, Iley had played First Division football with Sheffield United, Tottenham Hotspur, Nottingham Forest and Newcastle United, as well as being capped once at England U-23 level. If there is any doubt that a player's style is any indication of his temperament as a Manager, Iley dispelled it.

A guileful wing-half, the thinking player's position, Iley also brought a quiet, academic approach to management. He had once been Player-Manager with Peterborough United, but was developing what would perhaps be his best strength when Barnsley offered him his first fully fledged managerial opportunity; he was a Scout for Cambridge United. Ultimately, it was Iley's ability to identify and acquire bargain players, and price his own players for sale, which helped Barnsley not only prepare a team for promotion but also bring its books back into line.

Chairman Ernest Dennis knew from experience that attempting to go too far too fast was likely to end in disaster. In Jim Iley, he found a partner with the necessary patience to build up the Club slowly and effectively. The Iley years were spent taking Barnsley Football Club off the respirator and into convalescence, a process far too slow and painful for many fans. Iley, towards the end of his five years at Oakwell, was hated and despised. To supporters, his name suggested everything that was wrong with the Club, from their point of view - dull football, a lack of ambition and a Board which sold its best players and tried to run things 'on the cheap'. By April 1978, the terraces rang out with chants of *"Iley Out! Dennis Out! Iley Out! Dennis Out!"*

Iley's contributions, like Dennis', were made mostly behind the scenes, and their importance was recognized only in private by a few; in actual fact, without Iley's work at the Club, Barnsley F.C. may never have made another successful recovery. In the overall scheme of things, his Managership turned out to be, not only the right thing at the right time, but a valuable building block towards the Club's success in the future.

One of the biggest causes of fans' dissatisfaction was Iley's turnover of players. Beginning in March 1976, the sales of Mick Butler, Bobby Doyle, Martin Gorry, Anton Otulakowski and Mike Pickering generated over £200,000 in a little over 12 months. (Ernest Dennis did finally get his £40,000 back). Each of the players sales upset fans in its own way, and viewed together, they helped tip supporters over the edge.

Bobby Doyle, an energetic and stylish Scottish midfielder, who was the supporters Player of the Year in 1976, was, two months later given away to Peterborough for £20,000; his true worth was reflected 3 years later when he was transferred again, from Peterborough to Blackpool, for £110,000. Mick Butler, the local hero, was shipped to rivals Huddersfield Town.

Gorry, Otulakowski and Pickering were all home produced youngsters at the outset of their careers; Otulakowski set a new record for the Club with a fee of £70,000 when he went to West Ham, and Gorry brought in £50,000 by leaving for Newcastle, but their departures set off the old argument on the terrace - *"What's the point in selling your best prospects if you want to have a decent team?"*

When Barrowclough had been sold a few years before, the incoming cash was immediately ploughed back into the transfer market for new players. Now, to further annoy frustrated fans, little was spent on replacements. Jim Iley's policy seemed to be to root around football's bargain basements, and come up with players which others had missed or discarded. It appeared to supporters, who realized neither the severity of the financial mess, nor the reasons behind the deliberately patient build-up, that the Board was sitting on the money the Club had made through the transfer market, and that failure to spend showed the old lack of ambition.

In replacing promising youngsters with low-priced veterans, Iley was playing a dangerous game. It was a policy which sat his future on a razor's edge. The 'more experienced' players could easily turn out to be deadbeats, and more than one manager had sliced himself this way. However, in the cut and thrust of the lower divisions, Iley preferred the proven tough, survivalist mentality of these players over the raw experience of naive youngsters, who he was happy to ship off to other clubs. When in doubt, he mitigated risk by taking players on loan before committing to them; popular strikers Peter Price and John Peachey, and full-back John Collins were all acquired this way.

Iley's legacy proved he made sound choices. By the time he quit in April 1978, Barnsley Football Club's finances were in good health again, and he had assembled the nucleus of a squad that would win promotion the next year. Despite all the criticism that Iley took, that was a notable achievement, but it was lost in the fan's impatience and the hullabaloo that surrounded the next two Managers, Allan Clarke and Norman Hunter. Johnny Steele reflected on that in an interview with the Sunday Express in 1981; *"...when Jim Iley was here, we had a good team but were not getting the support. Jim didn't have the charisma of Allan or Norman....and that was what we needed."*

Amongst the team which Jim Iley left behind were Brian Joicey and Peter Springett, signed on free transfers from Sheffield Wednesday. Joicey, once the darling of Hillsborough, had been put out to pasture in the Owls' reserves; in his first year at Oakwell in 1976-77, he was Player of the Year with 26 League goals, the most ever scored by a Red's player in the Fourth Division. Illness ended his career in 1978. Peter Springett, a former England U-23 goalkeeper, had also lost his way in Owls' reserves; after Iley brought him to Oakwell, he was voted a member of the PFA's 1977-78 Fourth Division team. In midfield, Alan Little was a bargain at £6,000 - he was later sold for £30,000 after helping Barnsley to promotion from the Fourth to Third Division.

Joe Joyce

Peter Springett

Journeymen professionals Neil Warnock and Graham Pugh had also been picked up for a song, and central defender John Saunders had been thrown into the deal for Butler by Huddersfield Town. Full-back John Collins had cost only £3,000.

This team, not the first nor last that Barnsley assembled on a shoestring, took the Club to the fringes of promotion in Iley's last two years; its failure to kick down the door is what finally led to his end. Performances early in Iley's reign had often been less than satisfactory. Arguably the worst performance in Barnsley FC's history was on 22nd November 1975, when the Reds crumbled to non-League Marine in the First Round of the FA Cup; a 3-1 humiliation left Chairman Ernest Dennis in tears, describing it as the worst day of his life, and caused the Board to seriously consider firing Iley there and then. However, by the time Iley eventually left for Blackburn Rovers, Barnsley's defence, featuring a promising youngster named Mick McCarthy, had become a little more watertight, and the road to goal a little less arduous. All the team needed to set it on fire, as Johnny Steele had noted, was the right kind of spark.

The McSeveney and Iley years were a time when lights dimmed both literally and figuratively at Oakwell. The team produced a low-watt glow on the field, and the floodlights were turned off by order. Barnsley had played their first game under floodlights in a friendly at Falkirk as early as 1953, but it was 23rd January, 1962, before Oakwell's floodlights were turned on for the first time, and night games became a regular occurrence. During the sixties, the Club used floodlit games as an experiment, switching some Saturday afternoon games to Friday nights to see if they could attract more people, but in 1972, the Club was forced into an unwanted experiment when floodlights were banned. Midweek games were played with an afternoon kick-off because a miner's strike had reduced the amount of coal available for power stations, and floodlights were forbidden, to conserve energy.

A midweek game against Wrexham on 8th March, 1972, drew less than half an already low average attendance, for only 2,185 showed up. When Chesterfield visited Oakwell the previous December for the replay of a Second Round F.A. Cup-tie, a 1.00 p.m. Wednesday afternoon kick-off had produced an amazing 13,954, but many of the unofficial absentees from work and school were making a special effort to see Eric Winstanley's first return to Oakwell in another club's colours.

Early in 1974, another power crisis set an historic precedent. Since the Football League began, most weekend games had kicked-off on Saturdays, close to 3.00 p.m., and had been played, more or less, simultaneously. Strict Sunday trading laws had always prevented paid admission to football games on Sundays.

Now, to ease demands on electricity at peak periods on Winter afternoons, the Football League re-arranged its calender to stagger kick-offs and include games on Sunday, for the first time. There was strong opposition, but the Football League found a loophole. Spectators were required to buy a team sheet outside the ground, priced at normal ground admission, and were then admitted by producing the team sheet at the turnstile.

The Government condoned the loophole and professional football on Sunday afternoons became a reality. The first Sunday game in Barnsley's history was played at home to Chester on 27th January 1974. Because of the trading laws, the Club were required to let in free anyone who asked, but a combination of loyal fans, and a cluster of Club Officials and bobbies on the only 'free' gate, kept Oakwell's paid attendance close to normal.

While Jim Iley edged the Club along with careful transfer dealings, Commercial Manager Brian Handley underpinned its financial recovery with the launch of the Reds' Golden Lottery. By the end of the seventies, it was difficult to go into a pub in the Barnsley area and not buy a fund-raising Barnsley Football Club lottery ticket; it became second nature to order a 'scratch-off' with almost every round of drinks. The extra revenue which came from sales of lottery tickets put an ace in the Club's hand to finance a push for promotion. Ernest Dennis, whose long term goals for the Club's upward climb had been forced to take second place while financial fires were fought and put out, decided the time was right to take a step forward again.

Billy Bremmer, the veteran captain of Scotland and Don Revie's Leeds United, was nearing the end of his playing career, and was a prime candidate to move into management. Towards the end of the 1977-78 season, Barnsley were one of several clubs enquiring about his availability. Bremmer told Barnsley that he wasn't in a position to consider a move to Oakwell, but did they know that his friend Allan Clarke had been thinking about going into management as a player-manager, and would they like to talk to him? The news was a surprise. Ernest Dennis contacted Allan Clarke and talked about Barnsley Football Club's prospects with the enthusiasm of an energetic salesman. In May 1978, the offer of the largest salary ever paid at Oakwell, and a fee of £55,000 raised by lottery money, brought the England international to Barnsley as player-manager.

The news was a football bombshell, shattering doubters complaints that the Club lacked ambition. Even regular supporters were dazed. The Club kept to its well beaten path in offering a novice his first chance of management, but it brought new ground in attracting a celebrity of Allan Clarke's stature to Oakwell. Here was the man who had twice been the most expensive player in England, was Man-of-the-Match in the 1969 Cup Final, a winner of

League Championship, Fairs Cup and FA Cup Final medals with Leeds United, who had scored 10 goals in 19 England appearances. At 31-years-old, there was still some life in his boots, and the town fizzed with excitement at the prospect of him leading Barnsley on the field.

Although Allan Clarke was previously untried as a manager, his arrival had a big effect on the team from the start. His celebrity aura swept away the dowdiness which had lingered after Iley, and gave an instant fillip to the players. Coming from Don Revie's legendary Elland Road academy, he brought the discipline and standards of a successful First Division background to Oakwell, and expectations that had not yet been poisoned by the futility of life at the lower ends of the Football League. He expected his players to play and behave in the fashion he had been used to, like successful footballers, and his higher expectations rubbed off.

New Manager Allan Clarke

and was struggling to return at Crystal Palace when he came to Oakwell on loan the same year, eventually becoming the Club's record purchase at £95,000. In June 1979, Clarke made one of Oakwell's best ever buys when he brought Ronnie Glavin from Celtic for £40,000.

There is a common thread running through most of Clarke's signings, besides the fact that their arrivals were courtesy of lottery income. They tended to be mostly out-of-favour players at the clubs from which they were signed, and it was unlikely to be Clarke's own eye that had first evaluated them. In fact, the longer he was at Oakwell, the greater the rumours became that he did not know as much about the game as people thought, but that he bluffed his way through on reputation.

His introduction was made easier by the Fourth Division squad he had inherited from Iley. It needed only a little tinkering to jump-start into life. Clarke's foot on the accelerator gained confidence with some excellent buys. Derek Bell arrived from Halifax for £30,000 in October 1978, when goals had dried up early in the first campaign. Bell was instantly the season's leading scorer with 19 goals in 35 games. When Brian Joicey collapsed on the field during a game at York City only a few weeks later, Clarke quickly added Tommy Graham, a striker who had been idling in Aston Villa's reserve team, for £30,000. Graham knocked in 12 goals in 27 games to help the Reds secure promotion at the end of the season.

Clarke was on a roll. The following year he replaced Bell and Graham Pugh with Trevor Aylott (£50,000) plus Derrick Parker (a Club record £55,000), the striking partnership that would eventually lead Barnsley back to Division Two. Neil Cooper, a former Scottish Youth international in Aberdeen's reserves, was signed for £35,000 in 1980.

Ian Evans had been out of the game with an injury for two years (his leg was broken in a tackle with George Best),

Some of Clarke's success in building a winning team might be traced to his key aides in the Oakwell camp. Martin Wilkinson had been an enthusiastic youth coach in amateur football with no professional soccer experience, and he earned a reputation by referring promising young players to clubs throughout the North of England. Wilkinson became Oakwell's Chief Scout. Former Club captain and veteran professional Barry Murphy was Clarke's first team Trainer at Oakwell. Clarke valued these two men so highly that when he quit Barnsley to join Leeds United as Manager in September 1980, he took both with him.

More than once Clarke had been accused of being a 'big-head' as a player; as the novelty wore off his management skills, that same arrogance at times seemed to take the place of genuine know-how. When David Speedie worked his way out of Barnsley Juniors to the fringes of the first team, it is said that Clarke told him he would never make a football player and ought to pack his bags.

Unwanted by Barnsley, Speedie was picked up by Darlington, where he excelled and attracted the attention of Chelsea. At Stamford Bridge, he became a successful First Division player and Scottish international, whilst Clarke the manager joined football's army of unemployed.

In fact, arrogance eventually proved to be Allan Clarke's downside. It allowed him to boost the Club (he once claimed that modest midfielder Alistair Millar had a stronger shot than Leeds Peter Lorimer, an international clocked as the hardest shooter in football), and gave him the gall to introduce his ideas without fear, but it also left him without a sense of how his brashness was working against him. After Barnsley slumped to a 7-0 defeat at Reading in December 1980, Clarke took his team down a coal mine so they could 'see what its like to do real work'. Instead of being motivated, some players resented Clarke for humiliating them. Despite the reviving sparkle that Clarke brought with him, when he left for Leeds in 1980 there were some not sorry to see him go.

David Speedie - not wanted!

The sparkle had become evident as soon as Barnsley took the field for the start of the 1979-80 season. With Allan Clarke in charge, Barnsley were for once taken seriously, winning the favours of media attention and national interest. When the season began with a record-tying five consecutive wins, three of them away from home, 13,088 supporters - Barnsley's largest League attendance for 8 years - joined Press and TV crew at Oakwell for what should have been the record breaking 6th win. Unfortunately, in the face of all the attention, Barnsley tripped and fell to Torquay United, 2-1.

Oakwell. Average home attendances almost doubled from the previous season, from almost 5,700 to just over 11,000, and a colourful, noisy travelling band of supporters (the first 'red and white army'), swelled into thousands to regularly boost the atmosphere at away games. The team was always up amongst the promotion contenders, and only a stutter in the spring months, when the team seemed to freeze in sight of the prize, prevented them taking the Championship outright.

But fans and players never swayed from their belief that this was going to be Barnsley's year. In the end, three clubs were tied on 61 points for second, third and fourth promotion places. Barnsley took the fourth spot on goal difference and went up to Division Three at Clarke's first attempt.

On the evening of 8th May 1979, the Reds drew 21,261 to Oakwell to celebrate promotion with a 2-1 win over second-placed Grimsby Town. Goals from Saunders and Bell brought the house down; the largest Fourth Division attendance of the season invaded the field and revelled in the rare sweet taste of success, calling players and Manager into the Directors' Box for encores, and singing raucously with delight in a great swaying sea of red and white that rolled and broke over the field around the players tunnel.

However, the fires of promotion had been lit by a wonderful start, and enthusiastic support continued to fan its flames for the rest of the campaign. No one could remember such refreshing season-long excitement at

Glyn Riley, over 130 League appearances for Barnsley, in action.

For Ernest Dennis, looking down from the West Stand, these emotional scenes were his last memories of Barnsley Football Club. In 20 years of service as a Director, the last 12 of them as Chairman, his hard work and inspiration had helped lead Barnsley F.C. through the first turn. The glamour of a club led to promotion from the Fourth Division by an England international surely left behind forever the glummest, most sterile period in its history. Less than two months later, Ernest Dennis passed away, aged 66. The baton was passed to his old colleague, Geoff Buckle.

In August, Barnsley's return to the Third Division gave Clarke's squad a rude awakening. Arriving on a train of high expectations, the dream of riding through like an express was derailed at the first set of points. In a much awaited kick-off, local rivals Sheffield Wednesday visited Oakwell for the opening day in front of 22,360 rabid supporters, and drubbed the home team 3-0. The rest of the season was spent rolling up shirt sleeves and getting back on track, as Clarke learned that his Fourth Division squad was not equipped to take the Club on to any further destination.

Clarke infused the team with his string of new signings in Aylott, Parker, Glavin, Cooper and Evans. Former Leeds United and England colleague Norman 'bite-your-legs' Hunter, signed during the close season on a free transfer from Bristol City, braced up the middle with reputation and experience as the season progressed, making his first appearance two days shy of his 36th birthday in October. Mike Lester, from Grimsby, added flair to midfield for £20,000, and local 18-year-old phenomenon Ian Banks added strength. Clarke's adjustments transformed the quality of play, and lifted Barnsley from the lower half of the table to an 11th place finish. By the end of the season, initial concern had been dispelled by a fresh brew of optimism that appeared to be just coming to the boil.

In 1980-81, the team that Clarke had built in his first season in Division Three, began to blend into one of the best footballing sides ever seen at Oakwell. Leader of the Borough Council and lifelong Barnsley fan, Councillor Fred Lunn, remarked in a 1981 speech that *"..........they have brought a great deal of pleasure to many people by playing a style of football we have not been privileged to see for many years. It's been wonderful.........even in Sheffield they are saying that Barnsley are one of the finest footballing teams in the Country".*

In fact, although most Barnsley fans agreed that the team was as good as any they had ever seen, its style was very different. Previously, successful Barnsley teams had followed rudimentary tactics, but the 1980-81 squad were more sophisticated. In full flow, its football was passionate and glorious, playing the ball sweetly along the ground and carving open opponents with rapid movement across the full width of the field. Players made runs from deep in all directions to add constantly changing dimensions in attack, and they drove for goal with urgency. When playing out of the back was not possible, the old fashioned 'gi' it some clog' ball matured into long probing passes that found forward target players with rapid support, giving the team the chance to build from a new field position. Driven by ambition, confidence and a sense of style, the team began to buzz in almost every department.

The team was so self-sufficient that when Allan Clarke quit as Manager to go to Leeds United after only seven League games into the new season, and took Wilkinson and Murphy with him, it caused barely a ripple on the field. Norman Hunter retired from playing and settled into the Manager's dug-out, holding the reins of Clarke's chargers as they led him to promotion at the end of the season. This was Hunter's only success in his brief career as a Manager, and the idea that the players achieved it for him, rather than Hunter helping himself, is suggested by the facts.

Norman Hunter

Hunter made only adjustments, not significant alterations, to the squad he inherited from Clarke during the seven months of the promotion season he was in charge. When Neil Cooper was suspended, Hunter had to find a replacement, and Joe Joyce came up from the Juniors and played well enough to keep his place.

During the last quarter of the season, Ray Mc-Hale (£60,000 from Brighton) took the place of Mike Lester in midfield, and Stewart Barrowclough (£50,000 from Bristol Rovers) returned to the Club to add width and pace going forward, the only role that had not been well filled on the left side of the field, by anyone amongst Clarke's pool. However, by then, the team's direction had already been displayed, and Hunter was merely topping up the oil of a hot and well-run machine.

When left to his own devices to rebuild the team after promotion, he effectively dismantled it and couldn't put it back together, leaving Barnsley's run of success in pieces all over the yard, instead of humming at the gates of Division One. Hunter also proved to be a poor communicator, except when roused to anger; his moody introversion at other times prevented him from gaining the trust of the players, and helped his downward slide. Even as Barnsley won promotion, Glavin, Cooper and Lester were all on the transfer list at their own request, and while each had his reasons, the situation was an ominous sign of Hunter's inability to keep players happy and together. Therefore, his best contribution to the team which won promotion from the Third Division was to leave it well alone.

Mick McCarthy - over 300 appearances
in his six years with Barnsley

Despite an infuriating loss at home to start the 1980-81 season, the team quickly looked unlikely to give much away. Mick McCarthy, still only 21-years-old but with three full seasons of experience behind him, had come to dominate the centre of defence. At six feet tall, McCarthy was slim but well-muscled, and gripped by a single-minded determination to stop every foreign attack. He was quick off the mark to cover, marked tightly, tackled strongly, kept the play in front of him and was good in the air. Barnsley born and bred, McCarthy fitted the bill of a traditional Oakwell hero hewn from the same stone that had produced generations of local hard men at the heart of the defence, from Frank Barson to 'Big Winnie'.

Jack Charlton described McCarthy as *"one of the most loyal, trustworthy players I have ever managed......(he was) strong, aggressive, exceptionally competitive........"*. The Barnsley Chronicle, reviewing Barnsley's 1980-81 promotion season, reported that *"His determination and dedication have shone like a beacon........he demonstrated supreme defensive qualities".*

Typically, McCarthy got no serious acclaim from other commentators whilst a player at unfashionable Oakwell. Eventually he would become one of the Club's most successful exports as captain of Jack Charlton's legendary Republic of Ireland, after first being transferred to Manchester City for a Club record £200,000, and later to Celtic for £500,000. 'Macker' is the only player to have won Barnsley's Player of the Year Trophy three times - in 1978, 1979 and 1981.

As the season wore on, not only did the team look solid at the back as McCarthy's partnership with a rejuvenated Ian Evans took effect, but its artistry began to flourish and produce goals. In midfield, Ronnie Glavin competed with McCarthy as Barnsley's most popular player, winning the fan's vote twice, in 1980 and 1983. Glavin was unique. He was a midfielder who could turn the play in all directions, shuffling the ball out of defence or playing long team-splitting passes with vision and accuracy. He would explode on the run from deep in midfield, either with or without the ball. His arrival from nowhere often made him the open man on the edge of the box, and the ball at his feet made him electrifyingly dangerous. He was top scorer in 1980, 1981 and 1983.

When Glavin was on form, Barnsley sang. Without Glavin, they could be ordinary. He was a virtuoso rather than a tireless worker; sometimes he could be invisible for almost the whole match, appearing suddenly and changing the course of the game with a single flash of magic. At other times, he could rise to the occasion, and carry the game single-handedly.

In the last match of the 1980-81 season, for example, Barnsley needed to score four goals to stand a chance of winning the Third Division Championship, depending on results elsewhere. After a slow-paced first-half against mid-table Newport County, the Reds went in just one goal ahead, looking unlikely to reach their target. In the 57th minute, Glavin broke out with a one man dash for goal; sixteen minutes later, he had his hat-trick, and Barnsley had the four goal lead they needed. It was as simple as that. Unfortunately results elsewhere took away Barnsley's chance of the title. Glavin was a footballer of true craft and apparently effortless skill. At the peak of his career, he played in four Scottish League Cup finals, one Scottish F.A. Cup Final and all three European competitions with Glasgow Celtic.

He was their leading scorer when they won the Scottish First Division in 1977 (with more goals than team-mate Kenny Dalglish), and was capped for Scotland the same year. Barnsley supporters could barely believe their luck that he was playing for them, and were able to forgive him for not always working as hard as they might have demanded of less gifted midfielders. It seemed such an oversight for Glavin to be at Oakwell that there was always a fear he was about to move somewhere else, but an off-the-field reputation, his age (thirty in 1981) and the £400,000 price tag that Barnsley put on him conspired to keep him a Barnsley player.

Another local lad added power to midfield. Ian 'Banger' Banks, with thighs the size of oak trees, earned his nickname from the wilting power of his shot, particularly from free kicks within 30 yards of goal. He was second highest scorer behind Glavin in the promotion season, with fourteen goals. Behind them came Aylott and Parker with eleven each. It was a testimony to Barnsley's more sophisticated style of play that midfielders, not the two 'up front' men came out as top scorers, Aylott and Parker, although capable finishers, were employed as work horses. Their job was to win and keep possession of the ball in the attacking third of the field, and lay it off to supporting players; for Aylott particularly, at over six feet tall, that meant winning everything in the air. With Barnsley in possession, they scurried and ran across the field, taking players with them, to open up space for marauders like Banks and Glavin to come crashing through the middle.

No game showed the mood of the team better than a visit to Fulham on the evening of 16th January, 1981. Twelve minutes into the game, 'keeper Gary Pierce was carried off injured. Teams only carried one substitute in those days, and Barnsley's was the diminutive midfielder Glynn Riley, who gamely pulled on the 'keeper's shirt. Six minutes later, Fulham were a goal ahead. To any normal team the circumstances would have looked bleak, but Barnsley took the game to Fulham and played inspired football, keeping the home team pressed into their own half for long periods.

It was an illustration that the best form of defence is attack, and showed beyond any doubt the belief the players had in themselves that they could sustain it for an entire game. At one time, the Reds were coasting at 3-1 up, although a late Fulham breakaway pulled the final score back to 3-2. The win made the Reds top of Division Three until Saturday afternoon's results came in, and convinced their supporters that they had what it took to go up.

It was not a formality however, and the team hit more than one bump that shook it to the bone. The F.A. Cup Fourth Round draw paired Barnsley with non-League Enfield, who almost snatched a win at Oakwell, and the Reds were labelled 'camels' by the Enfield Manager, whilst the nation pointed at Barnsley and rocked with laughter.

The replay was switched to White Hart Lane where, despite a huge Barnsley following, most of the 35,244 crowd were hostile 'neutrals' baying for an Enfield win. Against the grain, the Reds saved themselves from shame with three goals to none, in a win that was not as easy as the result suggested. Their victory earned them a Fifth Round tie away at First Division Middlesbrough, where they displayed their true colours. Playing beautiful football, they gave the team from the top flight a run for their money, and left the field to a standing ovation from both sets of supporters, but at the wrong end of a 2-1 scoreline.

In the League, a win at lowly Blackpool in April would have sealed promotion, but the Reds played as if they had a hangover and lost 1-0. Despite supporters confidence that promotion was inevitable, this result could have had a disastrous effect. Barnsley, with only two games left, were in third place, and only the top two clubs were promoted - there were no play-offs at this time.

The following Tuesday, they had to meet first place Rotherham United at Oakwell; Charlton Athletic separated the two clubs. It was not a 'shoo-in'. Rotherham were already promoted, and the game, stoked by a passionate rivalry at the time, had its passion cranked up yet another notch. It was a must-win situation for the Reds.

Barnsley's largest League attendance in over 20 years, almost 26,000 fans, drove the atmosphere inside Oakwell to steam pressure. In the 31st minute, Ronnie Glavin blew open the valves when he rifled the ball through a clutch of goal-line defenders and into the Rotherham net. One goal was enough not only to send Barnsley up, but to prove Glavin's ultimate worth. Keith Lodge wrote in the Barnsley Chronicle that Glavin proved *"there is no substitute for naturally-harnessed class"*.

Certainly, Glavin's class inspired the team, produced results when they were needed, and ultimately won the prize for them. Barnsley beat out Charlton Athletic for the second promotion spot by goal difference, a margin which could be attributed not only to Glavin's match-winning goal against Rotherham, but to his effectiveness over an entire season as leading goalscorer and as leading goal-maker as well.

However, without the dreams, the sacrifices and the dedication of a whole generation of players, supporters and officials, Barnsley Football Club might never have been around to savour that wonderful moment on a cool spring evening when Glavin, like a knight turning over the grail to end an ancient quest, finally delivered the Club's long awaited return to the Second Division.

CHAPTER 14

HUNTER'S RED AND WHITE ARMY

For 22 seasons, Barnsley had languished in the lower divisions, and now they were back where the majority of supporters believe they belong, but a few clinging to the hope of even greater things. Those few had to wait another 16 years before their dreams were fulfilled. Thirteen long seasons of mid-table obscurity, and three 'nearly' seasons, one of which saw Barnsley cruelly denied a place in the play-offs by virtually the last kick of the season. Norman Hunter had started the charge, albeit with a squad built by his predecessor, Allan Clarke, and a succession of Managers came and went until a certain Mr.D.J. Wilson took the helm. It has been well documented, but who will forget that emotional Saturday in late April, 1997, when Danny's team achieved the impossible dream, and guaranteed a place in Barnsley folklore history for the talented manager.

However, the man who won the hearts of the townsfolk of Barnsley was in the Chesterfield squad during Barnsley's promotion campaign of 1980-81, although he didn't play in either of the games between the two clubs, and was unknown to the Red's fans as they looked forward to the

win instead of two was the main talking point, and Sunday soccer was to be introduced. So was the advent of the all-weather pitch, and QPR would be the guinea pigs, converting their Loftus Road pitch to a new synthetic grass surface, which would become unpopular with opposing teams, and which would eventually be discarded.

Barnsley started the new campaign with a back four of Chambers, Joyce, McCarthy and Evans. Mick McCarthy and Phil Chambers were local lads, and Joe Joyce arrived through the Oakwell scouting net, as did midfield player Ian Banks. It is interesting to note that McCarthy, Chambers and Banks were ever-presents in a season which gave their supporters renewed hope for the future.

Whilst the first team enjoyed a tremendous start to the new campaign with an emphatic 4-0 victory over Shrewsbury Town before a crowd of over 13,000, the reserves lost by the same scoreline at home against a 10 man Bradford City, Norman Hunter making a rare appearance and vowing to hang up his boots for ever.

Trevor Aylott scores the winner against Manchester City in the Milk Cup, to earn Barnsley a place in the Quarter-Finals.

challenge of 2nd Division soccer. To compete against the likes of Newcastle, Blackburn and Leicester and to renew local rivalry with Sheffield Wednesday was a treat to look forward to, and not seen since the days of Lol Chappell, Arthur Kaye and Johnny McCann. The fact that a national newspaper predicted Barnsley would finish bottom of the pile didn't deter the fans expectations for the coming season.

The club's promotion to the 2nd Division coincided with various changes in British football. Three points for a

The highlights of the season were the 1-0 victories over neighbours Sheffield Wednesday and the exciting Milk Cup exploits which took the Reds to the Quarter-Finals, only to be beaten by the eventual winners, Liverpool. The Oakwell crowd of nearly 29,000 for the visit of the Owls was the highest home attendance since the visit of Manchester United in the 1963-64 season.

The crowds flocked back to Oakwell, with average home gates of over 15,000, the highest since Cecil McCormack and Eddie McMorran plied their considerable skills 30

Action from the home match versus Derby County on the 10th April 1982.

years previously. In this, their first season back in the 2nd Division, Barnsley finished a creditable 6th, after being serious promotion contenders for most of the season.

The season also saw Oakwell staging an International soccer match for the first time, albeit at schoolboy level, when 7,000 turned up for the under-15 game between England and Northern Ireland. Johnny Steele retired as General Manager after 44 years association with the club, and was co-opted onto the board of Directors, and sadly, Brian Handley - the club's Commercial Manager - passed away at the age of 46.

The reserve side were elected to the Central League after an absence of 14 years, and transfer dealings were brisk, including the signing of Alan Birch from Wolves for a £95,000 fee and the departure of Trevor Aylott to Millwall for a tribunal fixed fee of £150,000.

The love affair between Barnsley Football Club and Norman Hunter ended in February 1984, a few days after a defeat at Oakwell at the hands of Cardiff City left the club 5th from bottom of the Second Division. So, the man who had led Barnsley out of the wilderness, was swiftly and unceremoniously sent to pastures new. The club said the parting was amicable, yet Mr. Hunter, in press reports, said his sacking was *"a bit sneaky",* and that the Board had over-reacted to a couple of bad results. Ironically, Hunter was the 13th Manager to lose his job in this particular season, but was soon back in business when he joined his former team-mate Johnny Giles at West Bromwich Albion.

The fans had been baying for Hunter's blood all season, and they stayed away from Oakwell in their thousands, which was a far cry from not so long before, when 17,000 members of Hunter's red and white army converged on Liverpool for that epic League Cup encounter. Or when Barnsley attained the dizzy heights of 5th in the table after a Ronnie Glavin special had earned them a memorable victory over Sheffield Wednesday at Hillsborough; this gave the team the honour of being the highest placed Yorkshire club for the first time in their

history. Sadly, the last 8 games of that season produced just five points, and the 5-0 humiliation by Newcastle at Oakwell was the team's biggest home defeat for 17 years.

The club were finding it difficult to break even, and it was no surprise when star players Ian Banks and Mick McCarthy were sold, the latter for a club record fee of £200,000. Ground improvements were still being held back due to lack of finance, but the stand for the disabled, the only one of it's kind in the Football League, was opened by MP Roy Mason prior to the Blackburn game in April, 1984, the £30,000 cost of which was raised by the good folk of the town. Added to this, the club's earlier offer to make the facilities at Oakwell available to the unemployed people of the town showed the Board's continued interest in the Community.

Controversies in the game which are in evidence to-day, are not new, and Barnsley can point to a reserve game at Wigan early in the 1982-83 season when the debate concerning the referee blowing for full time reared it's head. Wigan scored the first goal of the game in the 90th minute, but the Reds attacked straight from the kick-off, and Colin Walker, currently Youth Team coach at Oakwell, fired in a goal-bound shot. The referee signalled the end of the game a split second before the ball crossed the line. Sixteen years on, and the debate continues.

The juniors had a tremendous season, and reached the Semi-Finals of the F.A. Youth Cup for the first time when they defeated Sunderland before a near 3,000 crowd at Oakwell. An even larger crowd, just over 5,000, turned up at Oakwell to watch the 2nd leg of the Semi-Final against Everton, who ran out 2-1 winners overall. In the Barnsley squad were David Hirst and Steve Agnew, who were to make their names away from Oakwell. The latter made his first team debut at the age of 18 when he came on as substitute in the home game against Charlton Athletic. Steve's debut lasted just 15 seconds, when the referee blew for full time. John Dennis, the current Chairman, joined the Board of Directors, and sadly Eddie McMorran, the affable, former Irish International, died at the age of 60.

## CHAPTER 15

THE WEE SCOTSMAN

Bobby Collins, the Youth Team coach, took over from Norman Hunter in a caretaker capacity, and his first game in charge saw the Reds go down 2-1 at Middlesbrough. However, he didn't have to wait long to savour the sweet taste of victory with a superb 2-1 win at Elland Road.

A few days after, Bobby was asked to take charge until the end of the season. But he started his reign with two 1-0 defeats, the first against arch-rivals Sheffield Wednesday before a bumper Oakwell crowd of more than 20,000, the highest gate of the season. The team was strengthened by the signings of Paul Futcher and Calvin Plummer, and any relegation worries were soon dismissed.

New Manager Bobby Collins

including one that he wanted 'full control', which the Board were not prepared to give. To avoid further speculations, Bobby Collins was finally confirmed as Barnsley's 8th Manager since the War.

The short reign of Bobby Collins was dominated by three events, the Miners' strike, the Heysel tragedy, and the blazing inferno at Valley Parade, all of which have been well documented. The Bradford tragedy had officials of football clubs throughout the land vigorously doing safety checks on their grounds and Barnsley was no exception. After consultations with fire, police and building authorities, Oakwell was deemed to be as safe as it could be.

The Reds finished the season in 14th position, but only 4,672 turned up for the last game, surely a reminder to the club what the supporters thought about a disappointing season.

In the close season, Keith Burkinshaw, who had resigned from his Manager's post at 'Spurs, after a successful time with the London club, was offered the 'hot seat' at Barnsley. The Barnsley Board were confident of getting their man as Keith was born at Higham and had supported the team as a youngster, later playing for Barnsley Boys. The town was excited at the prospect of getting a 'top' manager, but Mr. Burkinshaw, for reasons only known to himself, turned down the offer. Various rumours regarding his declining the post spread through the town,

Johnny Steele - a very long association with the Club.

The 1984-85 campaign started with three defeats, two at home, and the poor attendances could have been attributable to the general despondency of the fans, or more realistically, to the Miners' strike. This was born out in early December when less than 7,000 turned up to see the Reds beat Fulham 1-0 to record their 14th game without defeat, and go 4th in the table, just two points behind the leaders, Blackburn.

The financial plight of the striking miners, who were the backbone of the club's supporters, was evident throughout the town, and Eric Winstanley - who was later to form an ex-Barnsley Players Association - joined other former Barnsley players in a match against striking miners at Darfield WMC in aid of the Houghton Main Hardship fund.

94

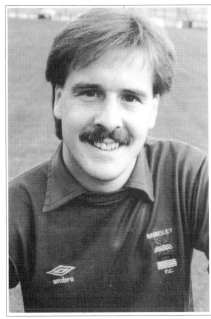

Amongst the newcomers, were: Clive Baker (who went on to make over 300 appearances for Barnsley), Gordon Owen, and Roger Wylde.

During the season, transfer activities were brisk, and Bobby Collins brought in Clive Baker, Ian Walsh, Roger Wylde, Ron Futcher - to join his brother Paul - plus local boy Gordon Owen from Cardiff. Oakwell favourite Ronnie Glavin left the club to seek his fortune in Portugal, and David Geddis was transferred to Birmingham for a reported £80,000 fee. Four Directors, Norman Moody, Gordon Pallister, Charlie Williams and Johnny Steele quit the board, paving the way for younger blood.

The Juniors reached the semi-final of the F.A. Youth Cup for the second year running, bowing out to Watford on a 4-3 aggregate after 2 legs. The reserves just managed to hold on to their 1st Division (Central League) status, and whilst the 1st team were playing to Oakwell gates of less than 5,000, the reserves visit to Old Trafford attracted a Central League gate of 7,271, where a certain Arnold Muhren was in the opposition.

A mid-season drop in form dispelled any promotion aspirations, although a good run in the F.A. Cup saw the Reds reach the 6th round and a home tie with Liverpool.

The Miners' strike was over, and a good crowd of almost 20,000 were hoping to celebrate with a place in the Quarter-Finals. However, it was not to be, and on the day Liverpool were too good, running out 4-0 winners.

Nevertheless, Bobby Collins could feel fairly happy with his 1st season in charge, after a good cup run and a respectable mid-table position. It came as a shock to most people in the town when Mr. Collins was sacked in June 1985. He was offered a coaching job, but declined. Rumours were circulating that Collins had been sacked to make way for the return of Allan Clarke, and supporters didn't have to wait long for the expected appointment.

Billy Ronson, with Barnsley from 1982 to 1985.

CHAPTER 16

MANAGERS COME AND GO

Allan Clarke, who the local press had dubbed 'The People's Choice', but who had recently been sacked as Manager of 4th Division Scunthorpe, was duly appointed Club Manager, as opposed to Team Manager which, according to the Club, meant greater responsibilities for the new man.

Mr. Clarke's first move was to switch groundsman Norman Rimmington back to his previous role as physio, and during the close season Phil Chambers left the club after 16 loyal years. Clarke brought Ronnie Glavin back to Oakwell as Player/Youth Team coach, and Kenny Burns - a former Scottish international - joined the club. Both players were released at the end of the season for 'economic reasons', and so was Billy Ronson.

Former Scottish International Kenny Burns....
A short term acquisition.

The Club were so hard up, that Mr. Clarke invited fans to spend a match day with him at £100 a go, to raise money. He fielded most of the first team in a reserve game against Manchester United, and 1,775 turned up at Oakwell (5 times more than the average), which brought in some more badly needed cash.

The Directors of the Club sent out an open letter to the fans expressing their fear that the Club, who were losing £4,000 per week, would fold unless extra revenue was forthcoming. They launched the Oakwell Centenary Society, and a target figure of 1,500 members would earn £80,000 income. The initial response was poor, and just 300 fans subscribed, but another plea brought an immediate response, and the limited membership figure of 1,500 was soon reached.

David Hirst, just one first team season,
but a Club record transfer fee received.

Along with 13 other clubs, Barnsley declined an invitation to enter the new knockout competition, The Full Members Cup, and the decision may have been regretted in the light of future financial problems. Allan Clarke's first season back at Oakwell was a disappointing one for him and for the fans, who showed their displeasure by staying away. Attendances dropped again, and less than 4,000 turned up for the last home game of the season.

However, not all was doom and despondency. Barnsley Juniors under-16 squad won a prestigious international tournament in France, and the exciting youngster, David Hirst, made his 1st team debut in the opening match of the season. However, the reserve team lost it's place in the 1st Division of the Central League.

Prior to the start of the new season, the fans were in for another shock when David Hirst was transferred to Sheffield Wednesday for a reported fee of £250,000, a record for the Club. So, another top class player left Oakwell, although the Club were quick to point out that most of the fee would be spent on new players. Hirst joined Gordon Owen and Ian Walsh in the exodus from Oakwell; Owen went to Bristol City for £40,000, and Walsh, the previous season's top scorer, was snapped up by Grimsby Town on a free transfer. However, on the plus side Clarke had strengthened his squad with the signings of Hedworth, Beresford and Lowndes, plus Paul Malcolm as an understudy to goalkeeper Clive Baker. Clive, as well as being a top class goalie, was no mean cricketer, and could boast taking 10 for 28 playing for Kexborough against Denby Dale.

Barnsley made a disastrous start to the 1986-87 season with 6 successive defeats, their worst start ever, and were left stranded at the foot of the 2nd Division. The only plus was a remarkable achievement by 17 years-old Carl Bradshaw, on loan from Sheffield Wednesday, who scored the quickest goal of the season against Palace when he netted after just 38 seconds.

The team recovered to finish the season in mid-table, but apart from a spirited display at Highbury in the 5th Round of the FA Cup, the supporters had little to cheer about, and yet again a top player left Oakwell when Larry May joined his former team-mate David Hirst at Sheffield Wednesday for £200,000.

Perhaps the most entertaining game of the season was at Roker Park in the Full Members Cup, which Barnsley decided to enter the second season, when Sunderland won 8-7 on penalties. But perhaps the most controversial issue was the Manager's decision to terminate the club's association with the nursery team Oakwell Juniors. The Juniors had supplied the entire squad, with the exception of one player, which reached the Semi-Final of the F.A. Youth Cup a few seasons before, and a number of players, including David Hirst, Steve Agnew and Simon Jeffels, came through their ranks.

Mr. Clarke was later to appoint Frank Barlow, the former Scunthorpe and Chesterfield Manager, as Youth Team coach, in an effort to improve the recruitment and coaching of young players.

The next campaign started well for the team and the Club. Early season results saw the Reds sitting proudly on top of the 2nd Division for the first time in 41 years, and the Club reported its best financial year since it was formed 100 years before. The Chairman was quoted as saying they would break the Club's transfer record if the right player came along, although a potential transfer fell through when the player concerned asked for an extra £50 per week. However, the first major transfer news was the departure of Stuart Gray to Aston Villa for £175,000, and the appointment of Mark Nile as the new physio to replace Norman Rimmington, who returned to his old duties as groundsman before his impending retiring the following season.

Larry May - another big money mover.

David Currie - a big money signing.

However, Norman, affectionately known as 'Mr. Barnsley' by many fans, is still involved with the Club as Kit Manager.

Nevertheless, the Club were as good as their word when David Currie joined the Oakwell staff at a Club record fee of £150,000. Even the acquisition of such a talented player, who scored twice on his debut against Ipswich, couldn't help Barnsley from sliding down the table, and they won just one of their last eight games to finish a disappointing 14th.

When Allan Clarke joined Barnsley for his 2nd spell as Manager, his ambition was to take the Club to Wembley and to the 1st Division. The latter was almost achieved in the 1988-89 season, when the team finished just two points away from a play-off place, and a good run in the FA Cup ended when Barnsley were unlucky to lose 1-0 to Everton in the 5th round before a bumper Oakwell crowd of more than 32,000.

But these deeds were overshadowed by another football disaster when 95 people were killed at Hillsborough on that fateful day in April. The Oakwell ground was again deemed to be safe, although two earlier incidents of crowd trouble caused concern - the cup matches against Stoke City and Everton, which attracted the two highest attendances of the season.

On the transfer front, Barnsley again smashed the Club record when John Beresford joined Portsmouth for £300,000, although the Reds managed to keep hold of their £1,000,000 rated player David Currie. In the close season, Ian Banks returned to Oakwell for a £100,000 fee, and Owen Archdeacon joined the club from Glasgow Celtic. On a sad note, George Robledo, the Oakwell hero of the forties, died at the age of 62.

John Beresford another big money departure

Many fans thought Mr. Clarke's dismissal was unfair, and others held the opinion that there was unrest in the boardroom and the real reasons behind the sacking had been kept under lock and key. The fact that Chairman Mr. Buckle resigned shortly afterwards added fuel to the latter argument.

However, a Manager is only as good as the results of his team, and after the home defeat by Portsmouth in early November, the Reds occupied 17th place in the 2nd Division. So Clarke was sacked, which was the second body blow to the man who had so nearly taken his team into the play-offs the previous season. Earlier in the current campaign, Mr. Clarke had been fined £3,000 by the FA Disciplinary Committee for remarks he had made about Mr. Vinny Jones.

The retiring Chairman, who had been made Vice-President of the club, was succeeded by John Dennis, the son of former Chairman Ernest Dennis, and Eric Winstanley took over from the retiring Manager, in a caretaker capacity. Eric's first foray in football management saw his team beaten 7-0 at West Brom to record their worst defeat in 10 years.

Not to be deterred, the local lad, who made over 400 1st team appearances in the famous red and white, made his intentions known that he wanted the job on a permanent basis. No doubt Mr. Winstanley was one of the 100 applications received for the vacant job, but the Board chose to appoint Mel Machin, who had earlier been released by Manchester City. Mr. Machin's first signings were to recruit John Deehan and Gerry Taggart from his old club, Deehan being given the added responsibility of Player/coach.

However, the new Manager's biggest coup was transferring David Currie to Nottingham Forest for a reported £700,000. Whilst the departure of Currie fell in line with the Club's policy to sell their best players, the sale was a good business transaction and represented a profit of £550,000 on the player.

When Johnny Steele vacated the Barnsley hot seat in 1971, he had been just the 3rd Manager of the club in 34 years. When Allan Clarke was sacked in 1989, he became the 6th casualty in 18 years, such is the changing face of football management.

Machen's first task was to steer Barnsley clear of the relegation zone, and transfer activities were brisk with many changes in the playing staff, the most notable signings being Gary Fleming and Brendan O'Connell. Even so, relegation was still a possibility, until away victories at Leeds and Middlesbrough and a home draw against West Brom assured survival.

However, the highlight of the Manager's first four months in charge was the epic FA Cup encounter with near neighbours Sheffield United. Barnsley had reached the 5th round of the FA Cup for the 2nd successive season, and the visit to Bramall Lane was the first FA Cup visit to the ground since the team won the trophy in that memorable 1911-12 campaign. The Reds were not to repeat their success of that distant season, but it took two replays to decide this particular tie, and although Barnsley generally had the better of the three matches, Sheffield United sneaked it in the end by a solitary goal. Consolation in defeat was much needed revenue when a massive 87,345 spectators were attracted to the three games.

As Barnsley FC were fighting for their 2nd Division lives, school soccer in the town had never had it so good. Nicky Eaden, who was later to join the club as a trainee, was a member of the successful 6th Form college team which won the English Schools under-19 Championship Trophy for the first time, and the under 14's won the Yorkshire Trophy. The under 11's made it a hat-trick of cup successes when they lifted the Green 'Un Cup.

Paul Futcher made over 250 appearances for Barnsley before moving to Halifax in 1989

Carl Tiler - yet another big transfer fee.

were required to deny a Brighton victory at the Goldstone Ground, and Barnsley would be just three games away from the top flight. A Carl Tiler goal secured the victory at Oakwell, and a loudspeaker announcement that Brighton had only drawn led to hundreds of fans invading the pitch to salute their heroes. However, the joy was soon turned to despair as the news filtered through that Brighton had scored an injury time winner to take Barnsley's place in the play-offs.

Nevertheless, Barnsley had only themselves to blame as they were clear favourites to clinch the last play-off place in the final run-in, but three defeats in the space of five days at the end of April let the pack close in, which culminated in such a disappointing finale.

Yet again, the seniors were upstaged by their younger counterparts. Barnsley Boys won the English Schools Trophy for the first time since 1961, and Barnsley Juniors won the Northern Intermediate League title which included a 12-0 thrashing of Halifax Juniors. In the junior squad were David Watson, Nicky Eaden and Andy Liddell, who were later to make their mark in the Premiership. The reserves continued their yo-yo life in the newly named Pontins League, by winning promotion to the 1st Division.

This era would not be complete without giving a mention to the loyal and long-serving Joe Joyce, who joined Scunthorpe on a free transfer, or to the enigmatic Norman Smith, a classy midfielder of the fifties side, who died at the age of 65.

Mel Machin's pledge that he would take Barnsley into the play-offs within three years almost came true in his first full season. A win against Middlesbrough in the last game of the season plus a helping hand from Ipswich who

In the close season, the Oakwell coffers were increased by more than £2 million when Carl Tiler was transferred to Nottingham Forest for £1.5 million, and Steve Agnew went to Blackburn for a reported £750,000 fee. With money burning a hole in his pocket, Mel Machin went on a summer spending spree and forked out £800,000 or so on six new players, including John Pearson from Leeds United and Steve Davis from Burnley, which still left the Oakwell fund with a tidy profit on the transfer activities. Mr. Machin reduced that profit early in the new season when David Currie rejoined Barnsley from Oldham at a Club record fee of £250,000, and Neil Redfearn arrived from the same club on a loan period, later to be signed on a permanent basis.

After the 'nearly' season of the previous year, the fans were hopeful of going one step further, but the team made a wretched start to the new campaign by gaining just one point from the first six games, and halfway through the season, relegation threatened. A late rally, losing only four of the last 17 games, dismissed the threat of demotion, but a final position of 16th was disappointing for the Club's supporters. Mr. Machin was now unpopular with the majority of fans, although the Manager was still confident he could achieve his ambitions with the Club.

On the other hand, the Youth Team coach, Eric Winstanley, was having another successful year with the Juniors, who retained the Northern Intermediate League title, and Barnsley Boys won the Yorkshire Trophy.

The main talking point in the summer of 1992 was the news that the Club would commence it's first structural improvement to Oakwell for 38 years, when extensions were made to the cover of the Brewery stand at a cost of £6,000. This figure was a drop in the ocean compared to the estimated cost of £2.25 million for the new project. The Taylor Report which followed the Hillsborough tragedy recommended all-seater stadiums, and Barnsley FC made their first step towards implementing the recommendation when the old Brewery Stand was demolished to make way for a new stand which would accommodate 7,400 spectators, and would include hospitality rooms, sponsors' lounges and executive boxes. The Club received a grant of £1 million from the Football Trust, with the balance to be met from Club funds.

Barnsley started the new season in the 1st Division for the first time in the Club's history when the introduction of the new 'Premiership' involved re-structuring of the other divisions, and if the Manager's earlier promise of top flight soccer in 3 years was to be achieved, then this was his last chance.

The fact that the team Machin built were never in the hunt for a play-off place, and were described in some quarters as the worst Barnsley side for 25 years, may have been a contributory factor towards the Manager's resignation just prior to the penultimate game of the season.

It was reported that Mr. Machin was shaken and visibly upset by verbal abuse from a section of the home supporters, but whatever the reason Barnsley were yet again without a manager.

However, the season was not without its high points, notably a 5-1 victory at Bristol Rovers and an excellent 1-0 win over runaway leaders Newcastle United in front of Oakwell's highest League gate of the season. There were also exciting FA Cup exploits and the 3rd round tie against Leicester City was decided on penalties, Mark Robinson netting the all important winner. Mark, Barnsley's longest serving player, was later to join Newcastle United for a reported £450,000 fee.

Mark Robinson

Leicester City were also Barnsley's opponents on the 6th March when the new stand was opened. A good crowd of over 9,000 turned up on this special occasion, but the away team ruined the day when they got their revenge over the earlier Cup defeat.

This was also the season when five Barnsley players were called up for international duty. Gerry Taggart and Gary Fleming were named in the Northern Ireland World Cup squad, Dave Watson - who had already played for the under-19 team - was called up for the England under 21's, and Chris Jackson and Troy Bennett enjoyed a 3 day training session with the England under-17 squad.

The Juniors had another excellent season, winning the Northern Intermediate League for the third year running, only the second team to do so in the 44 year history of the league, and Barnsley Boys retained the Yorkshire Trophy.

Two legends of the past, Gavin Smith and Tim Ward, passed away. Gavin was Johnny Kelly's wing partner in those heady days just after the war, and his son Bobby played a few games for the Reds in the 1962-63 campaign. Tim Ward had a couple of years on the playing staff in the early fifties followed by 7 years as Manager.

The Barnsley Board were quick to advertise for a new Manager, and in the interim period, Club coach Mick Wadsworth, who was later to join Carlisle United as Director of Coaching, took over team affairs. It was reported that Gordon Strachan turned down the job, but an appointment was soon made, and the Board's decision to appoint Viv Anderson as Player/Manager was a popular choice with the Barnsley fans.

The Club also acquired the services of Danny Wilson, who worked with Mr. Anderson at Sheffield Wednesday, as Player/Coach. Danny cost £200,000, and future events would dictate that this would be the Club's shrewdest investment in its entire history.

The management team was complete when Eric Winstanley, the highly successful Youth coach, was promoted to 1st team coach, and Colin Walker took over the coaching of the youngsters.

Viv's first move into the transfer market was to sign Darren Sheridan from non-League Winsford United, and a near 13,000 crowd turned up for the first match of the new campaign, surely an indication that the fans were behind the management's new appointments. However, the Reds made a poor start to the season winning just five of the first 23 games, and

the home defeat at the hands of Derby County, in the last game of the year, left the Reds third from bottom, just four points better off than basement club Peterborough. During this period, Mr. Anderson gave free transfers to a number of players and, once again, dipped into non-League football to sign Martin Bullock from Eastwood Town. He also went north of the border to recruit Andy Payton from Glasgow Celtic.

The new year started well with a home victory against Portsmouth, and a good performance at Sunderland, who were fortunate to scrape home by the only goal of the match. The supporters then were optimistic as they travelled to Vauxhall Conference side Bromsgrove Rovers in the 3rd round of the FA Cup. It is history now, but the non-Leaguers were two minutes away from a memorable victory, until late goals from Rammell and Archdeacon gave Barnsley a lucky passage into the next round.

The second-half of the season was a mixture of good performances - notably the 4-0 victory over Sunderland - and indifferent performances, which included the 5-0 defeat at Middlesbrough. Relegation threatened, until the 2-0 home win against Wolves, in late April, ensured another season in the 1st Division.

The Juniors again stole the limelight when coach Colin Walker kept up the good work of his predecessors by leading the boys to their 4th successive triumph in the Northern Intermediate League Cup.

Nevertheless, it was overall a disappointing season for the new management team and the fans, who perhaps had mixed feelings when they heard the news of Mr. Anderson's departure to Middlesbrough. Danny Wilson was immediately appointed Caretaker/Manager, swiftly followed by the offer of Player/Manager, which he accepted.

## CHAPTER 17

DANNY BOY

Danny soon acquired the services of ex-player Malcolm Shotton, to take charge of the reserve team, and the 37 year-old made a number of appearances for the 1st team in a season which saw a serious challenge for promotion after a slow start.

1994-95 was also a season which saw further changes to the Oakwell ground, thus reducing the capacity from 27,398 to 11,666, which would eventually lead to an all-seater stadium as required by the Taylor Report. In fact Barnsley FC, along with other clubs, had asked for more time to complete the project, but this was denied them by the Heritage Minister. Work started in mid-July to put just over 2,000 seats on the Kop, which would accommodate away supporters, as would the old West Stand and initially home fans would be restricted to the new East Stand.

For the opening game of the season, Oakwell would have looked a strange place for any fans who hadn't been for a while. It was virtually a three-sided stadium, the Ponty End being closed to supporters in readiness for demolition, and this was blamed for the lack of atmosphere and poor home support during the season.

Nevertheless, the new season started, and the fact that Mr. Wilson had virtually the same squad as the previous campaign, with no new acquisitions, spoke volumes for the ability of the new man, and the fans who stayed away missed some exciting and attractive football.

There was to be no decent FA Cup run as in the previous two seasons, but youngster Adie Moses had an excellent debut in the 3rd round defeat at the hands of Premier side Aston Villa. Although the record books show this game as Adie's debut, he in fact played in the abandoned game at Middlesbrough a few days earlier, thus becoming possibly the first football player to make 'two' debuts.

In the League, the Reds enjoyed their best form against the two promoted teams Middlesbrough and Bolton Wanderers. Bolton, who won through via the play-offs, were comprehensively beaten 3-0 at Oakwell, and Barnsley were unfortunate to go down 2-1 in the return. Champions Middlesbrough had to settle for a share of the spoils when both fixtures ended all square.

It was still mathematically possible for Barnsley to nick the last play-off spot when they travelled to Southend for the last match of the season, and 1,500 Reds fans converged on the seaside town. However, the game turned out to be an anti-climax, and Southend ran out easy 3-1 winners, leaving Barnsley, yet again, missing out on that elusive play-off position.

In the close season, it was rumoured that Mr. Wilson was to join Sheffield Wednesday, but to the relief of the Club and fans, Danny signed a new contract which would keep him at Oakwell for at least another two years.

The transformation of Oakwell was apparent to supporters who turned up for the first home game of the season, a new, impressive, cantilever stand at the Ponty End, and seats to replace the terracing below the old West stand, meant that Oakwell had now joined the ever-growing list of all-seater stadia. The immortal Skinner Normanton would have been gobsmacked at the imposing site, but sadly he died earlier in the year aged 68.

The new stand was named after the Club sponsors ORA, and apart from housing 4,500 spectators, it would provide facilities for the disabled, a walk-in Club shop, plus new administration offices, and the capacity of Oakwell was now just under 19,000. ORA Electronics were also responsible for kitting out the Juniors who were to field teams at under 16, 15, 14 and 13; the latter group for the first time.

Gerry Taggart, a £1.5m. move

However, even before a ball had been kicked, the main talking point was the departure of Club captain Gerry Taggart to Bolton for a club record £1.5 million. Taggart was out of contract, and it was obvious he wanted to go, so it was a good deal for Barnsley who were by now on a good financial footing.

The opening of the ORA Stand on the 19th August 1995.

Danny's first signing was to recruit local lad Peter Shirtliff from Wolves for an undisclosed fee. The player was to make 32 appearances in a season that promised so much, and in the end delivered very little, even though more signings were made, notably the acquisition of Dutch defender Arjan de Zeeuw for a six figure fee from 1st Division side Telstar. Arjan scored his first goal for the team in the 2-2 draw against Ipswich Town, and was perhaps Danny's most significant signing.

After a bright start to the season, winning three of the first four games, Barnsley then suffered a humiliating home defeat at the hands of Birmingham City. Dave Watson had the unenviable honour of being sent off, and although Birmingham didn't score their first goal until the resultant penalty, the Manager went on record saying it was the worst performance he had seen since arriving at the Club.

Charlie Bishop, one of five departures in the Summer of 1996.

Nevertheless, Barnsley recovered their form, and when they beat Millwall 3-1 on 27th February, before a poor Oakwell crowd of 6,366, they were 6th in the table, just six points behind 2nd placed club Charlton, and on course for a play-off place.

There were the unfortunate defeats in the two cup competitions, the most disappointing being the 2-1 reversal in the FA Cup 3rd round replay at Boundary Park. Week after week, season after season, controversial refereeing decisions are in evidence throughout the soccer world, and Barnsley have had their fare share of bad decisions. The penalty awarded to Oldham, when Gunnar Halle was allegedly tripped by Owen Archdeacon, changed the whole course of the game, and video evidence later showed that Archdeacon was nowhere near the Oldham player at the time.

The same old excuse is used every time that referees have only a split second to make a decision, and they don't have immediate access to slow motion replays etc. etc. However, on this particular occasion, the referee was just a few feet away from the incident, and his decision to award a penalty kick was inexcusable. Perhaps this particular debate will go on well into the next century before a remedy is found.

The defeat by Arsenal in the 3rd round of the Coca Cola Cup was not totally unexpected, but it drew an almost capacity crowd which approached 19,000, and the Barnsley players did themselves justice even in defeat by putting on a spirited display.

The fact that Barnsley slipped away to finish a disappointing 10th in the final analysis, could be attributed to a few factors. Some supporters still believed that the club did not want top flight football, but ambitious chairman Mr. Dennis, quite rightly, refuted this allegation. Others blamed former player Andy Rammell, who was earlier transferred to Southend United, but who came back to haunt his old club. Andy scored the goal in the 1-1 Oakwell draw between the two sides, which denied Barnsley two precious points. More realistically though, perhaps the players never recovered from the astonishing fight-back by Ipswich when they scored three goals in the last seven minutes of the match, to turn a 3-0 deficit into a 3-3 draw.

Nonetheless, another season, another disappointment, although there were some good things to report. Colin Walker guided Barnsley Juniors to a close season international Youth tournament trophy in Holland, when the boys won all of their seven fixtures, scoring 12 goals and conceding none. The Barnsley Schools under 15's won the Yorkshire Trophy, and former Oakwell favourite Stewart Barrowclough led Grimethorpe MW to a Wembley final in the Carlsberg Cup, although they finally lost out 4-2 on penalties to Dawlish Town.

Local lad, and former player Mick McCarthy, was appointed Team Manager of the Republic of Ireland, but on a sad note Barnsley 1st team squad member Chris Jackson was seriously injured in a car crash. Everyone connected with the club was devastated by the news, none more so than Danny Wilson who said he would gladly accept relegation to bring 'Jacko' back to full fitness.

During the 1996 close season, there were many comings and goings. Andy Payton, the previous season's top scorer - although never a favourite with the fans - joined Huddersfield Town for £350,000, and Charlie Bishop and Owen Archdeacon left for pastures new, as did goalkeeper Lee Butler and Brendan O'Connell. The latter joined Charlton Athletic for a £125,000 fee, which represented a £75,000 profit for the shrewd Manager.

In came Paul Wilkinson from Middlesbrough and Neil Thompson from Ipswich Town. Danny also acquired the services of Matt Appleby from Darlington when he had to pay £250,000 for the 24 year-old defender. The transfer merry go round was completed with the addition of Clint Marcelle, a Trinidadian international, and the Yugoslavian

Lee Butler
120 League games between 'the posts'.

Brendan O'Connell, sold for a good profit.

under-21 midfielder Jovo Bosancic. But perhaps Danny's most significant coup was to persuade club captain, Neal Redfearn, to sign a new three year contract.

The Reds had a dream start to the season, winning 2-1 at West Brom. All five summer signing were included in a much changed Barnsley side, and goals from Marcelle and Liddell gave the Club their first opening day win away from home for the first time in 20 years. Barnsley's first visit to Spotland for 17 years for the Coca Cola Cup 1st round 1st leg encounter held no fears for the confident team, and first-half superiority confirmed their beliefs, although their efforts were rewarded by just a solitary goal scored by Paul Wilkinson.

However, in the second-half, complacency took over from skill and endeavour, and Rochdale's 2-1 win would have been greater but for the work of David Watson in goal.

The Reds were then faced with two home League games within the space of four days, the first, against local rivals Huddersfield, was captured by Sky TV cameras. Barnsley ran out comfortable winners with goals from Wilkinson, Redfearn and Marcelle, but the main talking point was referee Singh's decision to award Huddersfield a goal direct from Tom Cowan's long throw-in. Town's defender Morrison claimed the goal, although the referee, when questioned, said that Steve Davis had headed it past his own goalkeeper. Video evidence proved that neither Morrison, Davis or Watson touched the ball, so clearly the goal should not have been allowed to stand.

Reading were the next team to concede three goals at Oakwell, a brace from Andy Liddell and a rare Sheridan goal giving the Reds a comfortable victory and top spot in the 1st Division. A trip to Maine Road was next on the League agenda, but first there was the little matter of 3rd Division Rochdale to contend with in the Coca Cola Cup, and although goals from Redfearn and Wilkinson gave Barnsley a 3-2 aggregate victory, the team's performance didn't match the League form.

Manchester City are one of the teams with the label 'sleeping giant', and attract large crowds irrespective of their status. Such a crowd gathered at their impressive stadium to welcome the undefeated table-toppers from South Yorkshire, and as it turned out, the gate of 26,464 was the highest in the Division for this particular season.

Influential signing - John Hendrie.

The poor form continued in the 2nd round of the Coca Cola Cup, and only a last minute own goal deprived Gillingham of a deserved victory at Oakwell, but the Reds were not so lucky in the 2nd leg at Priestfield Stadium. Although Barnsley enjoyed the lions share of the game and created 26 goal attempts, Gillingham scored an extra time winner, which signalled an early exit for Barnsley from the competition.

Sandwiched between the two cup games with Gillingham was a battling display at Boundary Park when Neil Redfearn scored the only goal of this League encounter, with a disputed penalty, against his former club. Barnsley then welcomed 2nd from bottom Grimsby Town to Oakwell, and League placings suggested a comfortable win for the home side. But the Mariners, who defended in depth and relied on breakaways, scored the only goal in an eventful first half. When Andy Liddell equalized midway through the 2nd half, a victory looked on the cards until the away side plundered two late goals to inflict a second successive home defeat on the highly placed Reds. This surprising reversal was followed by five draws on the trot, the first at Ipswich when Neil Redfearn's penalty gave Barnsley only their second point in nine visits to Portman Road.

City were in some turmoil following the departure of Manager Alan Ball, and Danny's team were determined to take advantage of this dilemma. Cheered on by 2,000 noisy supporters, they took the lead midway through the second-half with a goal by Clint Marcelle, who was rapidly becoming a favourite with the fans, but when Nigel Clough equalized, it looked like Barnsley would have to settle for a point. However, the tricky Trinidadian was not to be outdone, and he popped up in injury time to maintain his team's 100% record.

A large crowd was expected for the mid-week clash with Stoke City, and perhaps the gate of 11,696 was a trifle disappointing in view of the tremendous start to the season. The fans who stayed away missed some exhilarating soccer from the Tykes, who swept away the team from the Potteries with goals from Davis, Thompson and Liddell.

Queens Park Rangers were the next visitors to Oakwell, and Barnsley were not in the mood to surrender their 100% record as they did way back in the 1978-79 Fourth Division Promotion campaign. On that occasion the Reds had also won their first five games, and Torquay United spoiled the party with a 2-1 victory at Oakwell. Like the Devon team before them, the team from Loftus Road had not read the script, and shortly after the break, the homesters found themselves three goals down. A goal from Paul Wilkinson mid way through the 2nd half gave the supporters some hope, but despite one or two near misses, it was not to be, and the London side came away worthy winners.

Prior to high-flying Crystal Palace's visit to Oakwell, Mr. Wilson, who had allowed Dave Regis a loan period with Peterborough United, dipped into the transfer market and bought John Hendrie to join his former team-mate Paul Wilkinson on the Oakwell staff. Hendrie, who was soon to earn the title 'Super John', cost £250,000 and was to prove to be yet another shrewd signing by the Barnsley manager.

Hendrie made his debut against Palace, but had little chance to shine in a disappointing game where both teams cancelled themselves out with similar formations. The two main talking points were the rare penalty miss by Neil Redfearn, and the disallowed Palace 'goal'.

The mid-week visit of Oxford United to Oakwell attracted just 6,337 fans, the lowest crowd of the season, and some spectators resorted to heckling and booing, as efforts to breach the Oxford defence failed. The meagre attendance was disappointing, and the booing was a little harsh bearing in mind that, despite a barren period, the team still enjoyed third spot in the table.

Andy Liddell's 6th goal of the season, and Steve Davis's late headed goal, kept Barnsley's unbeaten away record intact in an exciting Yorkshire Derby at Bradford City's Pulse stadium, which put the team in good spirits for the top of the table match with Bolton Wanderers. This eagerly awaited Oakwell clash of the titans was the town's second Sky TV extravaganza, and the near 10,000 crowd, and millions of TV viewers, saw a pulsating see-saw game.

The match saw the return of former player Gerry Taggart, and his team took a shock lead in the 1st minute, when Steve Davis was adjudged to have fouled John McGinlay in the penalty box, although a re-run of the incident showed that the incident occurred outside the area. Despite protests from the Barnsley players, the referee upheld his decision and McGinlay planted his spot kick past the diving Dave Watson. The Reds misfortune continued early in the second-half when a shot from Alan Thompson was deflected by Arjan de Zeeuw past the wrong-footed Watson. Captain Redfearn saved the day with two goals, one from the penalty spot, to salvage a point against a side who Manager Wilson described as the best team in the Division.

The point against Bolton kept Barnsley in the top three, and coincided with the Club's announcement of a healthy £185,116 profit for the year ending the 31st May 1997. Football is big business these days, and the Club could point to extra revenue in areas away from team affairs i.e. club shop, programmes, TV and broadcasting, ground advertising and sponsorship. But these sort of profits are a drop in the ocean compared to what the top Premiership sides achieve, and only time would tell if Barnsley could join this elite band.

Barnsley maintained their impressive away form with a well merited 3-1 victory over Port Vale. John Hendrie scored his first goal for the club and further strikes from de Zeeuw and Marcelle confirmed the Reds superiority. However, the players knew they were in for a sterner test as they travelled to Molineux to take on the ambitious Wolves, who were breathing down their necks in the scramble for glory. though Barnsley achieved a draw, thereby creating a club record of seven unbeaten away matches at the start of a season, the players and supporters were disappointed not to take all three points. Wolves took the lead, but goals from de Zeeuw, Eaden and another Redfearn penalty gave Barnsley a deserved 3-1 interval lead. The home side pulled one back 15 minutes into the second-half, and a late equalizer denied the Reds victory, and pushed them out of the top three.

Norwich City, who were one place ahead of Barnsley, were the next visitors to Oakwell, and the home side gave a scintillating performance to triumph by three goals to one. Adie Moses scored only his second 1st team goal to give his team the lead, and further goals from Wilkinson and Hendrie sealed the victory.

The County Ground, Swindon is never an easy place to get a result, and they are one of the few so called 'smaller' clubs who have enjoyed Premiership soccer, albeit for just one season. When Barnsley made the trip to Swindon, the Wiltshire club who had made an indifferent start to the season, and had progressed to 8th in the table.

In a 15 minute second-half spell, the team with the only unbeaten away record in the country, were torn apart, and poor defending allowed the home side to score 3 times, thereby inflicting on the Reds their biggest defeat, with perhaps their worst display of the season to date. Barnsley had a chance to redeem themselves in the eyes of their Manager and fans when Portsmouth, who were showing inconsistent form, visited the 'well.

Danny Wilson recalled Steve Davis and Neil Thompson, both fit again after injury, at the expense of Moses and Jones, and the changes paid off as goals from Wilkinson and Hendrie gave the home side a comfortable lead, and but for another missed penalty by Redfearn, the game would surely have been over. As it was, the visitors were given a lifeline when Appleby made a rash challenge in the area, and Durnin made no mistake from the resultant spot kick. Worse was to come when Pompey equalized with a scrambled goal, and the Reds were now under pressure, with the away side looking the more likely to snatch the winner. Cometh the hour, cometh the hero, in the form of Steve Davis, who's late goal gave his team-mates their first Saturday home victory for nine months.

The victory over Portsmouth put Barnsley back into 3rd place, and in confident mood as they travelled to Burnden Park to take on table-toppers Bolton Wanderers, who had just thrashed Premiership team 'Spurs 6-1 in the Coca Cola Cup. Despite conceding an early goal, the Reds fought back with grit, determination, and no little skill, and it was no surprise when they equalized through a Neil Redfearn penalty after John Hendrie had been upended in the box. It was Redfearn again who scored with just 10 minutes to go, with what looked like the winner, with a thunderbolt from 20 yards out.

But, with only a couple of minutes remaining, Steve Davis, the hero against Pompey, turned villain when he mishit a clearance and Alan Thompson spared the home side's blushes - and their undefeated home record - at the same time denying Barnsley what would have been a crucial victory.

David Watson made a number of outstanding saves including a spot kick taken by former Manchester United stalwart Steve Bruce, which helped his team gain a good point at St. Andrews, and then followed two comfortable home victories against Southend United and Tranmere Rovers. The Shrimpers frustrated Barnsley for 70 minutes, but when 'Super John' opened the scoring with a delicate chip, the final result was never in doubt, and Paul Wilkinson added two more to make it a memorable day for the two ex-Middlesbrough colleagues.

The Reds Premiership challenge gathered momentum with another three goal blitz against Tranmere, with goals from Hendrie, Wilkinson and Redfearn (penalty). The team played exciting one touch football which prompted the ORA stand supporters to break into 'It's just like watching Brazil', which would be the Reds anthem for the rest of the season.

The attendance against Tranmere was up by over 1,000 on the Southend game, and the Reds were well supported for the next match, at Bramall Lane, with 5,000 supporters making the short trip to Sheffield. John Hendrie gave his fans an early Christmas present when he poached the only goal of an entertaining game five minutes from time. It was enough to secure a hard fought victory, which took Barnsley - once again - to the top of the table. These dizzy heights were to be shortlived, and the team were knocked off their perch on a cold Boxing Day afternoon in the Potteries. Another good contingent of Barnsley fans swelled the crowd to over 19,000, but they knew the writing was on the wall when Darren Sheridan was controversially sent off for a second bookable offence at the start of the second-half. Up to that point, the Reds had held their own and looked well worthy of at least a point. Even with 10 men they battled on and held out until 20 minutes from time, when Sheron scored to give Stoke a rather fortunate victory.

The Oakwell authorities were expecting a near capacity crowd for the visit of Manchester City in the final fixture of the year. In fact, the attendance of 17,159 was the biggest gate for over five years, and Barnsley turned on the style as they bounced back from that disappointing reversal at Stoke. Jovo Bosancic scored his first goal for the Club when, in the absence of injured skipper Redfearn, he stepped up to bury a penalty awarded for hand ball. Just before half-time, the recalled Moses added a second to give the Tykes a comfortable half-time lead. Despite having the extraordinary skills of Georgi Kinkladze, Manchester City never really threatened, and his team's defeat could have been more severe.

The FA Cup 3rd round tie against Oldham Athletic was postponed due to inclement weather, and a freezing Oakwell pitch, but it was a blessing in disguise for Neil Redfearn who was recovering from a hamstring injury, and who was now hopeful of playing against his former club. In fact 'Captain Courageous' was back in the line-up for the next League fixture at QPR. Peter Shirtliff made only his 3rd start of the season in place of the injured Appleby, and Sheridan was absent due to suspension.

Redfearn celebrated his return by scoring direct from a free kick, and if Barnsley could have maintained this lead

going into the interval, the final outcome might have been different. As it was, Spencer equalized with almost the last kick of the half, which was a blow the Reds never really recovered from, and the QPR hit man completed his hat-trick in a second-half dominated by the home side. To make matters worse, Steve Davis, who was the king-pin of Barnsley's defence, suffered a broken leg after a challenge from the Rangers three goal hero, and would not take any further part in the season's activities.

Neil Thompson was recalled for the re-arranged cup match with Oldham, and a crowd approaching 10,000 saw a scintillating first-half display from the rampaging Reds, the only sour note being the sight of Jovo Bosancic being stretchered off after a nasty challenge. Even though a Redfearn penalty kick was saved by the overworked Kelly, goals from Bullock and Marcelle were scant reward for 45 minutes of dominance. Even though the second-half was goalless, a Red's victory, and a quick return to Loftus Road, was never in doubt.

Before the eagerly awaited 4th round clash with QPR, Barnsley had another severe test when Ipswich Town were the visitors to what had become an invincible Oakwell, the fans having witnessed six successive home wins. However, the team from Suffolk were to spoil the party, and despite a late goal from Liddell, it wasn't enough to avert a 2-1 defeat. The home side's performance was described as their worst for some time, but every team has an off day, and for Barnsley, this was one of those days.

Barnsley had good support for their third meeting with QPR, and they saw an exciting, blood and guts cup-tie. As in the last meeting a couple of weeks earlier, Redfearn scored an early opening goal direct from a free kick, and it was certainly a case of 'deja vu'. If Paul Wilkinson's headed 'goal' had been allowed to stand, it is doubtful whether the home side could have come back from a two goal deficit. However, Rangers took advantage of their good fortune and scored a brace of goals in the space of six minutes to gain a 2-1 advantage at the interval. The game had another dramatic twist early in the 2nd half, when Impey was sent off for punching Nicky Eaden. If Barnsley thought their superiority in numbers would turn the tie their way, they were in for a shock. The ten men defended in depth, relying on breakaways, and from such a move came the killer goal, a spectacular bicycle kick from Sinclair. Hendrie gave the dejected fans some hope when he reduced the arrears near the end, but the damage had been done, and there was no way back.

Nevertheless, John Hendrie made a more significant contribution in the 3-2 victory at Blundell Park. His hat-trick was sufficient to give his team maximum points in a below par performance against relegation candidates Grimsby Town who were reduced to ten men early in the 2nd half.

To win when not playing well is the hallmark of a successful team, and Barnsley could take consolation from this proven theory.

A visit to promotion rivals Norwich City was never going to be easy, but the Reds re-found their form and an early goal by Nicky Eaden should have resulted in three precious points. In fact, for the 3rd match running, their opponents had been reduced to 10 men when Fleck was sent off seconds before half-time. As in the previous two games, Barnsley found it difficult to play against 10 men, and their lacklustre second-half performance was in stark contrast to their first-half superiority. It was no surprise then when Norwich equalized, albeit with just a couple of minutes left, leaving the huge army of Barnsley fans stunned and silent.

So, was the promotion push taking it's toll? Were Barnsley going to fall by the wayside as they had done in previous seasons? Not so, said the Board when they appointed Graham Barlow, a life-long fan, as the Sales and Marketing Manager. The new man's brief was to increase the profile of the club and generate extra income in readiness for life in the top flight.

The attendance for the next Oakwell game against Port Vale was boosted by 2,500 children from local schools, who had eagerly accepted the Club's invitation to cheer on the Reds, and they saw a dour struggle against a well organized side. John Hendrie's first-half strike was enough to secure three vital points to maintain the town's bid for promotion.

The team then travelled to the Valley in the knowledge that Barnsley had not won there in 18 previous visits. When Charlton took the lead with barely a minute gone, things were looking bleak, but the boys in red are made of sterner stuff these days. They got the break they deserved early in the second-half when Hendrie continued his goal scoring form by netting from an acute angle.

After that, the game ebbed and flowed with neither side prepared to give way, until the last couple of minutes. A Lee header was clawed out of the air by the agility of Watson, but the referee deemed it had crossed the line, and, with seconds remaining, in a goalmouth melee, Super John scrambled the ball over the line to earn a deserved draw. Three Charlton defenders were booked as they protested the ball had never crossed the line, but perhaps justice was seen to be done as this cancelled out the home team's controversial effort a couple of minutes earlier.

The side were in good spirits as they prepared to entertain Wolves before a near capacity Oakwell crowd. The team from the Black Country were Barnsley's main rivals for that 2nd place and automatic promotion, which was now the target for Danny and his boys, the Championship already conceded to runaway leaders Bolton.

A win and the Reds would be three points clear of McGee's men with a game in hand, so an expectant home crowd settled down to see the Wolves devoured. Within two minutes, expectancy turned to despair as Bull latched onto a long clearance and rifled in his 18th goal of the season. Despair turned to disbelief when Roberts made it 2-0 halfway through the 1st half, sending the 4,500 travelling fans into wild hysteria. The Barnsley players never matched the appetite of their opponents, even though a Sheridan goal gave them a glimmer of hope. It was no surprise then, when the away side added a third to complete a convincing victory.

Like all good teams, the Reds bounced straight back with a comfortable 2-1 victory at Roots Hall against 3rd from bottom Southend United, Neil Redfearn being the two goal hero. 'Redders' scored again against Swindon Town at fog-shrouded Oakwell, but his team-mates had to thank David Watson, who had already been beaten, for some outstanding saves to protect a valuable point. A few boos were heard during the Swindon game, and Danny Wilson called on the supporters to cheer the team on as they prepared for another crucial game against fellow promotion contenders and South Yorkshire rivals Sheffield United, a game which would be Barnsley's third in front of the SKY cameras.

"It's just like watching Brazil" echoed round the stadium as the Tykes rediscovered their earlier season form which prompted the samba-like adulation from their adoring fans. Their big spending neighbours were swept aside and a brilliant backheel by John Hendrie gave his team a deserved lead. It was a moment of magic from Super John, and if the cheeky - almost impudent backheel - had been performed by Pele or Maradona, it would have been acclaimed across the world's soccer media. Nicky Eaden added a second late in the game to seal a comfortable and vital victory.

Barnsley then had to negotiate two successive away games at Tranmere and Huddersfield. A goal by Paul Wilkinson earned a point at Prenton Park, and a tough game at the McAlpine Stadium ended all square and goalless. Two points out of six was perhaps disappointing, but other results went Barnsley's way and they were still favourites to take the second automatic promotion place, being just one point behind Wolves with two games in hand.

Things were looking good for the so called 'unfashionable' team from South Yorkshire, and the fans had more to cheer about when the news filtered through that Danny Wilson had signed a new three and a half year contract, pledging his future to the club into the next millennium.

Maximum points from the two Easter fixtures put the Reds firmly into the driving seat, four points clear of third placed Wolves with a game in hand. The town was getting used to media coverage, and SKY cameras were again at Oakwell to see a confident display against West Brom, a goal from Redfearn and a Neil Thompson penalty securing the points. It was a tougher game at Elm Park, and although an own goal and an Andy Liddell strike gave Barnsley a two goal lead, Reading pulled one back before half-time and dominated much of the 2nd half. The Reds defence, however, held firm and another three points were in the bag.

With three successive home games next on the agenda, a lot of fans were already counting their chickens, but Danny Wilson was quick to point out the dangers of over confidence and said that he was looking no further forward than the next match. That next match was against mid-table side Birmingham City, and the team managed by Trevor Francis took an early, bizarre lead. A speculative free kick from fully 40 yards got caught in the gusty wind and the ball sailed over Watson and into the net. Barnsley tried hard to get back into the game, but their style of play was not conducive to the windy conditions, and the Blues held out for an unexpected win.

After losing their 5th home game of the season, the promotion hopefuls had two home games to get back on the winning track, the first against Charlton Athletic. Two first-half goals from Marcelle and Thompson set the tempo for what turned out to be their biggest victory of the season, although it wasn't until the final 10 minutes that the fans could rest easy. The team from the Valley had enjoyed much of the play without creating too many chances, but they capitulated when Neil Thompson hammered in his second goal, and a classy strike from John Hendrie completed the rout.

The fans were buzzing with excitement, and many stayed behind to hear the news that their rivals, Wolves, had been beaten at Reading, thereby putting the Reds firmly in the driving seat. The equation was now quite clear. A victory against Oldham Athletic, and Barnsley would be seven points clear of Wolves with just 4 games to play.

The club's decision to reduce the admission charge to £5 across the board paid off handsomely as over 17,000 packed the ground in eager anticipation of another giant step towards their goal. Even though Barnsley were without the services of suspended players Neil Redfearn and Darren Sheridan, the team played with skill and determination with no sign of nerves.

The importance of the game was motivation enough, but remarks made by Wolves boss McGee made the players even more determined. Nevertheless, the supporters had one or two tension packed moments as Oldham fought for their First Division survival, and their battling play held out until the 44th minute, when 'Super' John Hendrie latched on to a Watson clearance to score the vital first goal. When Clint Marcelle fired in a 30 yard scorcher with half an hour to go, the result was never in doubt, and Premiership football was just around the corner.

Two thousand fans made the journey to South London, and they were hopeful of a victory against play-off contenders Crystal Palace to edge even closer to that elusive 2nd place. The supporters were also well aware that a Barnsley victory plus a Wolves defeat at home to lowly Southend United, and the champagne bottles could be opened.

Palace opened brightly, dominating the early play, and but for some outstanding saves from David Watson, the half-time deficit would have been greater than a solitary goal. However, the Reds started the second period with all guns blazing, and when Wilkinson was sent sprawling in the box the referee had no hesitation in awarding a penalty. Neil Thompson, who had taken over from Neil Redfearn as the penalty taker, lashed the ball home to the delight of the red and white army of fans. The game was now on a knife edge, and it could have gone either way, but Watson again distinguished himself with some fine saves. A draw was perhaps a fair result, and when news filtered through that Wolves had won 4-1 to edge a little closer, the champagne was put on ice, at least for the time being.

Another away game beckoned, this time at Fratton Park for a Tuesday night clash with Portsmouth, who still had play-off aspirations. A large contingent of Barnsley fans gathered in the away enclosure to cheer their heroes to victory, but were stunned into silence when the home side were awarded a dubious penalty, which was converted. A second goal after 35 minutes and a third just 5 minutes into the second-half, and the Reds looked dead and buried. There seemed no way back and the sound of the Pompey Chimes echoed around the stadium.

Neil Redfearn then turned the game upside down when he rifled in 2 goals in 10 minutes, and the fans now sensed that a game that seemed lost was there for the taking. The Reds threw caution to the wind as they charged forward in search of the equalizer, but it was not to be, and with their defence exposed, Portsmouth broke quickly and killed the game with a fourth goal.

It had been a valiant fight back but to no avail, and it now looked likely that Barnsley had to win their last two remaining games to clinch automatic promotion. However, fate took a hand, and the following evening, a 19 year-old lad named John Oster became an unlikely hero in the eyes of the townsfolk of Barnsley when he scored for Grimsby Town to deny Wolves a victory.

A win in the last home game of the season against relegation strugglers Bradford City, and Barnsley would land the ultimate prize, a place in the top flight for the first time in their history.

CHAPTER 18

WE ARE PREMIERSHIP

Grown men cried.   **Strangers hugged each other.**

Oakwell had never seen scenes like it as uncontrollable emotion engulfed the ecstatic crowd.

Yet 90 minutes or so earlier, there were different emotions as the home supporters waited patiently for battle to commence. Of course, there was expectation, but this was tinged with nervous tension, so important was the conflict ahead. Fortunately, the tension didn't spill onto the field of play as the promotion hopefuls laid siege on Davison's goal, and during the first 45 minutes chance after chance was created with football skills of the highest order.

The crowd soon sensed the tide was going their way, and they roared their players on with ear shattering vocal support, but when the whistle blew for half-time, a Paul Wilkinson goal was the only reward.

The mood of the crowd changed again in the 2nd half as Bradford City threw caution to the wind and mounted a spirited fight back. For the first time in the game, the Reds were under threat as they were pushed back deeper and deeper into their own half.

The supporters were now a little subdued, the tension also spreading to the players, and the away team sensed they could deny Barnsley the victory and gain for themselves valuable points in their fight against relegation.

The visitors best chance fell to Norwegian international Sundgot who could only hit the post from six yards as a cut-back from Brazilian Edinho fell at his feet.

The home fans sighed with relief, but there was still twenty minutes remaining of this nerve tingling, heart stopping drama.

Could there still be a twist to the story?

Danny Wilson, the shrewd manager that he is, could see the danger, and immediately after Sundgot's miss, he reverted to the sweeper formation by bringing on Shirtliff for Liddell. This substitution stemmed the tide, and then Danny went for the kill, by replacing the tiring Bullock for the fresh legs of Marcelle. However, the minutes ticked away, with no further addition to the score, and a one goal margin is never enough. The home fans started whistling for time with still 3 or 4 minutes to go, so eager were they for the game to end, but they needn't have worried.

The referee had already taken a quick glance at his watch when captain Neil Redfearn threaded a through ball to the feet of Marcelle, and the fresh legs of the tricky Trinidadian weaved into a shooting position before rifling the ball past a bewildered Davison.

The fans went wild with delight, and a couple of minutes later this turned into hysteria as the referee signalled the end of the contest.

They had done it.........

...........They had achieved the impossible dream.

The team that Danny built for less than a million pounds had defied all the odds and a place in top flight football had been achieved for the first time in the Club's history.

The smiling players did a lap of honour.

The delirious crowd submerged the pitch, with no fear of recrimination.

Oakwell was a mass of red and white as, *"There's only one Danny Wilson"* and *"Wilson's Wonderland"* echoed round the stadium.

The fans raised their scarves and to a man sang an emotional rendition of the song made famous on Liverpool's Kop, *"You'll Never Walk Alone"*.

Grown men cried................Strangers hugged each other.

The people of Barnsley could now proudly boast:
"WE ARE PREMIERSHIP"

The party and carnival atmosphere lasted all weekend and culminated in a Bank Holiday Monday civic reception for the victorious team. They travelled to the Town Hall in an open-topped double decker bus round the streets of Barnsley, and the pouring rain didn't dampen the spirits of the players, nor the supporters who turned up in their thousands to celebrate the most successful season in the history of the club.

Danny, his management team and players appeared on the Town Hall balcony to salute their supporters, and the scenes were reminiscent of the 1911-12 season when those heroes of yesteryear paraded the FA Cup in front of their fans, such was the importance of the occasion.

The fact that Barnsley lost to Oxford in the last game of the season didn't really matter. Even a 5-1 drubbing at the Manor Ground didn't dampen the enthusiasm of two and half thousand supporters who gave their team a standing ovation as they left the field.

This historic season would not be complete without giving a mention to the stars of the future, to Barnsley Boys under-15's and 13's, who completed a memorable double when both teams won their respective Yorkshire Cup finals, the two games being played as a double-header at Oakwell. The under-15's won the trophy for the fourth time in six years, and the under-13's for the first time in their history.

Barnsley fans were also given the opportunity to say their farewells to Gary Fleming, and 5,841 turned up at Oakwell for a testimonial match for the popular player who was forced into retirement through injury.

Danny Wilson's achievement in taking his team to the top flight for the first time in their history was honoured by his fellow managers, when they named him Manager of the Year.

John Hendrie became Barnsley's 24th Manager when he succeeded Danny Wilson in July 1998.

REVIEW OF 1997/98 SEASON

BY KEITH LODGE

Stern defending by Arjan De Zeeuw, Nicky Eaden and Neil Redfearn, in the home game versus Chelsea.

When Neil Redfearn headed home after only nine minutes of Barnsley's first history-making Premiership appearance on a hot summer's day in August, Oakwell was ecstatic. The celebrations of the previous April, when the Reds clinched their place in the top flight with a famous victory over Bradford City, were again mirrored in that magic moment, and the future looked brighter than ever.

However, visitors West Ham United proved spoilsport party-poopers as they hit back with two second-half goals from John Hartson and Frank Lampard which provided a foretaste of punishments to come for defensive frailties. At the same time, playing against a team who had finished the previous season as strongly as anyone, following the double signings of Hartson and Paul Kitson to eventually take 14th place, Barnsley had been the better side in the first-half and, despite a sticky spell in the second, still deserved a draw overall, and they provided a perfect response to the doubters on their trip to Selhurst Park three days later.

They emphasized the character of the side by bouncing back from the hammer blow of an opening day defeat to beat Crystal Palace, who had kicked off their campaign on returning to the Premiership with a shock success at Everton, courtesy of a Redfearn rocket in the 57th minute. Having notched the Reds' first Premiership goal against West Ham, the skipper thus assured himself of a double place in Oakwell history by also scoring the one which clinched their first win in the top flight.

It was the next home game against Chelsea which brought home to the Club and its supporters the size of the task facing them if they were to survive at the top level. For 25 minutes, the Reds were the better side, but then they were ripped apart by a rampant Chelsea, for whom Gianluca Vialli scored four times, including a second-half hat-trick in the space of 25 minutes. Dan Petrescu and Gustavo Poyet notched the other two goals as Ruud Gullit's side triumphed 6-0.

IT WAS JUST LIKE WATCHING BRAZIL

April 26 1997

Promotion Clinching Day

(Left) Captain, Neil Redfearn (Centre) and Dave Watson (left) lead the team out for the crucial match.

(Above) Late substitute, Clint Marcelle, on the ball. Peter Shirtliff, the other sub, also on hand (to the right).

(Right) Paul Wilkinson scores the all important first goal against Bradford City, and Martin Bullock joins in the celebrations.

Manager Danny Wilson
in profile during the match
(left) Pensive....
(Right) Encouraging
(along with Eric Winstanley)....
(Below) It's all over....Joy!

The final whistle has gone,
and the celebrations start....
Nickie Eaden, Mattie Appleby and
Martin Bullock show their feelings.

115

1997/98 Season: The Premier League comes to Oakwell

(Top) Goalscorer Neil Redfearn in the first match (v. West Ham), Martin Bullock looks on.

(Above) Scott Jones – goalscorer – turns away, Jan-Aage Fjortoft and Ashley Ward are on hand. (Home match v Southampton).

(Right) Defending in numbers – Barnsley players include Bosancic Moses and Jones – during the epic F.A.Cup win over Manchester United.

It was a stunning defeat for the Reds, but at least the fans retained their sense of humour, chanting *"we're going to win 7-6"* as Vialli pounced for Chelsea's sixth goal eight minutes from the end.

Having beaten one of the teams promoted with them - Crystal Palace - Barnsley did it again in the following mid-week game, the previous season's First Division champions, Bolton Wanderers, going down 2-1 at Oakwell, with the Reds' record signing, the £1.5 million Macedonian striker Georgi Hristov, scoring the goal which gave his side their first home win in the Premiership. Looking far more at ease with the return of Mattie Appleby and the sweeper system, the Reds took the game to the visitors from the start, and South African Eric Tinkler, another summer signing, made the breakthrough after only 12 minutes. Former Liverpool, Newcastle and England star Peter Beardsley, who was starting a game for Bolton for the first time, equalized on the half-hour mark, but Hristov restored the Reds' lead with a fine header from Darren Barnard's cross two minutes after half-time.

Barnsley's performance at Derby County's impressive new Pride Park Stadium the following Saturday suggested that there was not a lot wrong with the team. Unfortunately, although creating enough chances to have won the game twice over against Jim Smith's side, they did not take one of them, and the Rams snatched a 1-0 victory with a twice-taken penalty conversion from Stefano Eranio a minute before the break. The penalty was conceded by goalkeeper Lars Leese, a £250,000 summer signing from Bayer Leverkusen, who otherwise had a splendid first full game for the Club in place of the injured David Watson.

Despite the narrow defeats by West Ham and Derby, and the crushing reverse at the hands of Chelsea, there was still a mood of optimism around Oakwell, but a 3-0 home defeat at the hands of Aston Villa on 13th September sowed the first real seeds of doubt about Barnsley's ability to retain Premiership status. The Reds' naivety and frailty at that level were again cruelly exposed by a Villa side who were themselves still searching for a rhythm after a surprisingly poor start to the season. Ashley Ward had been signed for £1.3 million from Derby County in a bid to remedy the goalscoring problem, but it was the generosity of the defence in giving goals away at the other end that led to their downfall against Brian Little's side.

Midfielders Mark Draper and Ian Taylor netted after 50 and 71 minutes respectively, defender Ugo Ehiogu having got them off the mark with a miscue off his shin in the 26th minute.

Goals from Redfearn and Ward gave the Reds a 2-1 away victory over Chesterfield in the Coca Cola Cup second round, first leg, Tony Lormor replying for the Second Division side. The Oakwell team clinched their passage to the third round on a 6-2 aggregate after a 4-2 second leg success at home, Andy Liddell, Redfearn, Darren Sheridan and Hristov being the marksmen. Lormor was again on target for the Spireites.

In the League, however, four successive defeats, during which the Reds conceded 15 goals, stoked up fears of an immediate return to the Nationwide.

Everton were struggling when they entertained Danny Wilson's side in late September, and they were clearly there for the taking, but again poor defending cost Barnsley dearly. Gary Speed (two, including a penalty) and 17-year-old Danny Cadamarteri gave the Toffees a 3-1 lead - Redfearn equalized in the 33rd minute - and after Darren Barnard's excellent first goal for the Oakwell Club had given his side a glimmer of hope, Everton substitute John Oster set the seal on a 4-2 home victory.

Three days later, the Reds leaked another four goals as they slumped 4-1 away to Wimbledon, after Tinkler had given them the lead with the only goal of the first-half. They did not, however, make full use of a long period of first-half supremacy, and more dreadful defending after the break saw teenage prodigy Carl Cort, Robbie Earl, Ceri Hughes and Efan Ekoku turn the tables in devastating fashion.

The Reds then suffered their worst defeat of the season at home to Leicester City the following Saturday. In terms of goals conceded, the 2-0 reverse may have been an improvement on the three previous fixtures, and a good deal better than the 6-0 hiding at the hands of Chelsea, but the standard of the overall performance was extremely poor.

They failed to conjure up one shot on target throughout the 90 minutes, and ultimately succumbed to second-half goals from Ian Marshall and Graham Fenton, the latter ramming home the rebound after his initial spot-kick attempt had been blocked by Leese.

Wilson shuffled his defensive pack yet again for the visit to Highbury, but the result was very much the same, as Arsenal coasted to a 5-0 victory with goals from Dennis Bergkamp (2), Ray Parlour, David Platt and Ian Wright.

For 25 minutes the Reds were a better side than the League leaders, who appeared to be suffering from a hangover following their elimination from the UEFA Cup at the hands of PAOK Salonica in midweek, but once Bergkamp had produced a world-class goal out of nothing, it was not so much a case of whether the Gunners would win, but by how many.

This time, the Coca Cola Cup brought no respite. The third round home tie with Southampton brought the best football of the season from the Reds, but a brilliant goal by Matt Le Tissier in celebration of his 29th birthday, and a breakaway winner two minutes from time added to the Oakwell Club's continuing tale of woe. Liddell was Barnsley's marksman, netting the equalizer after 26 minutes.

The next League game, at home to Coventry City, brought a glimmer of hope. The Reds rolled up their sleeves to record a vital 2-0 victory which lifted them off the bottom of the table, and injected much needed confidence into the players. Right from the first whistle, there was a bristling aggression about Barnsley's play, which had not previously been in evidence. They were first to the ball; determined in the tackle; eager to attack; and much more solid in defence.

It was essentially an excellent team effort, but there were also outstanding individual contributions from goalkeeper David Watson, who was named as Sky TV's man of the match, striker Ashley Ward, the central defensive pairing of Arjan de Zeeuw and Ales Krizan, and Martin Bullock, who had Coventry in a dither every time he had the ball at his feet.

Ward notched his first Premiership goal for the Reds in the 11th minute and Redfearn clinched the victory with a 66th minute penalty, which was won by Bullock, who lured David Burrows into a late challenge.

Sadly, however, five days later the Reds meekly surrendered to champions Manchester United at Old Trafford as the Theatre of Dreams became, for them, the nightmare many people had predicted.

It was unbelievable that it was the same team that had performed so well against Coventry. It was, instead, a re-run of Chelsea and Arsenal as the Reds crashed 7-0 to a brilliant United side who were given far too much time and space to perform their party pieces.

They were doomed from the moment they presented Andy Cole with the first of his hat-trick of goals in the 18th minute. Ryan Giggs added two more, with Paul Scholes and substitute Karel Porborsky completing the rout.

If players heads were suitably bowed, however, the 3,000 plus fans in the corner of the magnificent stadium remained defiant to the end. At 7-0, they were still chanting *"We are going to win 8-7!"*

In what was a typical reaction through the season, the Reds bounced back immediately from the crushing defeat to produce a fired-up second-half performance which saw them gain a creditable draw at home to third-from-top Blackburn Rovers in the next game at Oakwell. the first half, Barnsley's apprehension at facing a side so high in the table and unbeaten away from home was all too obvious, but all the spirit, aggression, responsibility and belief which was so glaringly lacking before the interval suddenly re-appeared after it, following a half-time roasting from the Manager. Blackburn, who should have had a maximum three points in the bag at half-time, were relieved, in the end, to escape with just one point from a 1-1 draw.

Tim Sherwood stole in to give Rovers the lead on the half-hour, and it was Jovo Bosancic, revelling in his first full Premiership game after an early-season dogged with injury, who scored the equalizer in the 79th minute. For 45 minutes, Danny Wilson's side had outplayed one of the top teams in the Premiership, and the draw felt more like a win.

However, the roller-coaster season continued on its heart-stopping way down at the Dell as the Reds turned in a rock-bottom display against a Southampton side, whose victory was worth six points in the struggle to avoid the big drop.

Barnsley's inexperience at Premiership level was brought home again in the 4-1 defeat at the hands of a Saints' team full of experience - Francis Benali and Ken Monkou in defence; Kevin Richardson and Carlton Palmer in midfield; Barnsley born David Hirst, who started his career with his home-town team, up front, and the enigmatic Matthew Le Tissier.

A Le Tissier penalty opened the home team's account after only three minutes; Palmer made it 2-0 with only six minutes gone, and after Bosancic had pulled one back with a 29th minute penalty, Kevin Davies, continuing to show exciting potential following his summer recruitment from Chesterfield, made it 3-1 after 36 minutes. It was as good as over then, but more woeful defending in the 54th minute gifted Saints a fourth goal, Hirst delightedly scoring against his former club.

In the words of skipper Redfearn, manager Wilson 'went ballistic' after that performance, and his untypical tirade struck home. In the next match at Anfield, the players responded with such pride and passion that they brought off one of the shock results of the season, beating Liverpool 1-0 in front of their own supporters.

Every Barnsley player raised his game to an unprecedented Premiership pitch, with four in particular deserving special mention.

Wilson's latest signing, 25-year-old Peter Markstedt, took the massive leap from the Swedish Second Division to a Premier League match at Anfield in his stride; defensive colleague Arjan de Zeeuw had by far his best game in the top flight; Lars Leese, preferred in goal to David Watson, justified his selection with a string of good saves; and Ashley Ward defied the effects of a meningitis virus to crown a tireless display by scoring the winning goal in the 36th minute.

In the face of unrelenting chasing and terrier-like tackling, Liverpool were made to look anything but championship material. They eventually ran out not only of ideas, but also belief, with Karlheinz Reidle missing a trio of gilt-edged chances. The Reds had some luck, but no one begrudged them that.

Buoyed by that shock win, Barnsley ran fifth-from-top Leeds United ragged for the first half-an-hour of the next home game, but, after building up a 2-0 lead with goals from Liddell and Ward in that time, they faded badly, and United hit back to win 3-2, Alf Inge Haaland (36 mins.), Rod Wallace (79 mins.) and substitute Derek Lilley (81 mins.) being the marksmen.

It was a devastating result for the Reds after producing their best football of the season for the opening 30 minutes, and there were fears that it could undermine much of the confidence which had built up as a result of the triumph at Merseyside.

A controversial last-minute defeat at the hands of Sheffield Wednesday, in the first top-flight meeting between the South Yorkshire rivals, did not help matters.

That it was Paulo Di Canio who scored the last-ditch decider when he took advantage of a cruel rebound off Mattie Appleby's attempted clearance, was even more upsetting for the Reds, because they were convinced that the Italian should not even have been on the field at that stage, having constantly disputed the decisions of Worthing referee Gary Willard and his assistant, even after being booked.

Despite the defeat, however, Barnsley looked far more self-assured and confident than in the early part of the season, and they deserved a point for their efforts, although they contributed to their own downfall by failing to take advantage of a stream of corners, and managing only three shots on target. The lack of concentration which allowed Dejan Stefanovic to give the Owls a 19th minute lead also played its part.

It took the Reds just 10 minutes to equalize, Redfearn sending the ball looping over the defensive wall from a free-kick, and into the net at the far post.

The improvement in the Reds' standard of performance continued when they held European campaigners Newcastle United to a 2-2 draw at Oakwell.

United had been decimated by injuries, not least the one which had sidelined England striker Alan Shearer since the start of the season, but they still included seven full internationals in their starting line-up.

It is to Barnsley's credit that they outplayed the visitors for nearly the entire first-half of a vastly entertaining encounter, after Redfearn had given them the lead with a brilliant curler in the seventh minute.

Keith Gillespie, who had a superb game, scored twice for United in the 43rd and 50th minutes, but the Reds rallied for substitute John Hendrie to equalize with his first goal in an injury-plagued return to the Premiership, thus securing a share of the spoils against one of his former clubs.

Sadly, however, the Reds fell back on old habits in a crucial relegation tussle at White Hart Lane, Tottenham Hotspur scoring three times in the first 18 minutes through Allan Nielsen and David Ginola (2), to virtually end the game as a contest.

The first 20 minutes contained so many elementary errors, both collectively and individually, that it was difficult to believe that it was more or less the same team that had kept a clean sheet in that famous victory at Anfield.

Just as they had begun to convince more than their own partisan supporters that they were capable of overcoming all the odds by staying up, the Reds had surrendered in such a way as to bring all the doubts flooding back.

The exasperation of watching Barnsley in their first Premiership campaign was encapsulated in a bottom-of-the-table Boxing Day clash at Bolton Wanderers' futuristic Reebok Stadium. Superb in the first-half, the Reds should have had all three points parcelled up by the interval, but they faded so badly on the resumption that they might so easily have ended up with no points at all; but they eventually returned over the Pennines with a 1-1 draw.

During the first-half, when they were so dominant that they could have gone in with a 4-0 lead, they had only a Georgi Hristov goal to show for their superiority, and they paid the penalty when Gudni Bergsson equalized with a speculative strike from 35 yards with his team's first shot on target, after 37 minutes.

It was fitting that Ashley Ward should score the winning goal against his former club when Derby County visited Oakwell two days later, as the Reds completed an unbeaten Christmas programme. His totally committed performance, so characteristic of him all through the campaign, deserved nothing less than a match-winners accolade.

Equally pleasing, however, was that the team kept a rare clean sheet, with Adie Moses, Arjan de Zeeuw and David Watson in particular, performing heroics to keep at bay a formidable County attack comprising the pace of Dean Sturridge, the gangling threat of Paulo Wanchope and the goal-poaching flair of Italian Francesco Baiano.

The third round of the F.A. Cup brought a welcome diversion from the relegation battle as the New Year dawned, and the ever-improving Reds made it three games without defeat as they put paid to Bolton Wanderers' hopes in the competition, courtesy of a Darren Barnard free-kick in a hard-fought tie at Oakwell.

It was tough on the Reds that de Zeeuw and Moses were both suspended for the League visit to Upton Park the following Saturday, but no-one could have imagined that the absence of these two would bring a return of the bad old days as West Ham hit their visitors for six. The scoreline was no reflection on 20-year-old home-grown debutant defender Chris Morgan, who did better than most, but overall, the Barnsley side showed little heart for the fight.

It was in midfield where the game was won and lost. Israeli Eyal Berkovic and coach's son Frank Lampard ran the show from there, and it was the latter who sparked off the rout in the fifth minute. Samassi Abou hit the second and third goals, John Moncur the fourth, John Hartson the fifth, and Stan Lazaridis wrapped it up with the sixth.

The emphasis in the following match at Oakwell had to be on winning. It was all about taking three points against relegation rivals Crystal Palace, and the Reds did just that, although it was a close run thing, an Ashley Ward goal being the difference between the teams.

Former Penistone Grammar School pupil Chris Morgan had an outstanding home debut after the trauma of the previous week's first appearance at Upton Park, and there was a promising debut for Norwegian international striker Jan Aage Fjortoft, signed for £850,000 from Sheffield United. It was Barnsley's first - and only - double of the season.

The fourth round of the FA Cup brought a return trip to White Hart Lane, but it was a far different story from the 3-0 drubbing the Reds had suffered in the League meeting the previous month. When Sol Campbell sneaked in to head home from a 29th minute corner, 'Spurs fans were no doubt expecting another easy ride, but this time the Reds showed far more doggedness and determination, and they thoroughly deserved the replay chance provided by Neil Redfearn's penalty equalizer in the 59th minute, after Ward had been brought down by Clive Wilson.

Another London visit, this time in the League, a week later, saw the Reds fail to bridge the gap in class as Chelsea coasted to a 2-0 victory, Gianluca Vialli adding to the four goals he scored at Oakwell in the first meeting. Mark Hughes was the other marksman.

Then came a memorable cup reply with 'Spurs when the Reds recorded a thrilling 3-1 victory to earn a plum fifth round tie against Manchester United at Old Trafford.

The result of a crackerjack of a contest hinged on two separate 60-second slices of cut-and-thrust action. The first came shortly after the interval when 'Spurs midfielder, Stephen Clemence, was sent off for a second bookable offence - he was adjudged by referee Gerald Ashby to have taken a dive in the penalty area. The Reds immediately counter-attacked for Ward to give his side the lead.

Shortly afterwards, Chris Morgan cleared off the line, and the Reds tore upfield for Redfearn to ram home his 10th goal of the season. It could, therefore, have been 1-1. Instead it was 2-0 to the Reds, and they were almost there. David Ginola raised Spurs' hopes with a typical free-kick goal in the 72nd minute after Ward had seen a goal ruled out for offside, but Darren Barnard, who had earlier rattled the post, put the result beyond the visitors' reach with a peach of a goal in the last minute.

Back in the League, another two points got away as the Reds drew 2-2 at home to fellow-strugglers Everton in a game they should have won. They failed to chalk up their fifth successive home win because they did not put away a good enough percentage of the chances they created, and there were continuing lapses of concentration at the other end.

Jan Aage Fjortoft made the breakthrough in the 25th minute with his first goal for the Club, but Duncan Ferguson equalized five minutes before the break, and Tony Grant gave the visitors the lead five minutes after the resumption. Darren Barnard made it 2-2 in the 63rd minute, but the Reds were denied the winner by impressive Everton goalkeeper Thomas Myhre.

After suffering the 7-0 massacre at Old Trafford in October, Barnsley could be forgiven for viewing their return February visit for the fifth round FA Cup-tie with more than a little trepidation.

However, not a bit of it. They looked upon it, instead, as an opportunity to prove they were nowhere near as bad a side as their previous surrender suggested, and they seized the chance with such glorious gusto that, but for a blatant refereeing error, they would have turned a comparatively minor Cup upset into a major one.

With the tie locked at 1-1 and both teams striving for the winner, Neil Redfearn stabbed the ball through to substitute Andy Liddell, and just as the latter was about to shoot, he went down under a desperate lunging tackle from Gary Neville. It seemed a clear penalty at the time, and Sky TV's action replays put the issue beyond doubt. Leeds' referee Mike Riley had got it wrong when he waved play on.

John Hendrie had given the Oakwell team the lead in the 37th minute when he pounced onto a sliced clearance from goalkeeper Peter Schmeichel as the Danish international attempted a first-time punt upfield from Gary Pallister's back pass. However, Teddy Sherringham equalized within four minutes to curb the ecstasy of the 8,500 Barnsley fans in the crowd of 54,700.

The Reds then found themselves on the receiving end of further spot-kick controversy on their visit to Coventry City; referee Alan Wilkie awarding a debatable penalty to the home team two minutes from time as Dion Dublin went down in the box. The big striker picked himself up to net the only goal of the game from the spot.

It was a devastating blow for the Reds who thought they were about to achieve a hard-earned point, despite the absence of defenders Chris Morgan and Darren Barnard through suspension. Scott Jones came in for the latter at left back and had an excellent Premier League debut. The match also marked John Hendrie's 600th career appearance.

The 22-year-old from Sheffield, who had turned down a new contract in the summer and almost signed for Third Division Mansfield Town, crowned his first start in an F.A. Cup game with the double salvo that sank the best team in the country, and created the biggest upset of the competition.

While it was true that United were without Ryan Giggs, Paul Scholes, Nicky Butt, Jordi Cruyff, Ronnie Johnsen, Ole Solksjaer, Henning Berg and long-time absentee Roy Keane, they were still able to field a starting line-up which included seven full internationals - and two more had joined the fray by the 48th minute.

It was still, therefore, a side capable of beating any team in the Premiership, and that is a measure of a Barnsley achievement which bordered on sheer fantasy. There was talk that United were so focused on Europe and the League title that they were not too bothered about the F.A. Cup, but they strained every nerve and sinew to try to peg Barnsley back.

There was controversy after only nine minutes when John Hendrie appeared to be just offside as he fired his side into the lead with a superb right foot shot, but there was no disputing the legality of Jones's opportunist effort which made it 2-0 following a free-kick four minutes after the break.

Teddy Sheringham reduced the arrears with the aid of a deflection off Adie Moses in the 57th minute, but Jones restored the Reds' two-goal cushion with a header from a Redfearn corner eight minutes later. That was the signal for a renewed

Goal!! Mattie Appleby, Jovo Bosancic, and Martin Bullock celebrate, United are stunned.

Wednesday, 25th February brought one of the most memorable matches in Barnsley's history, as the Premiership's bottom team bundled the top team out of the F.A. Cup in front of a disbelieving capacity crowd of 18,655 at Oakwell.

It was not only the typical Cup-tie tale of small-town club overcoming all the odds to beat big-city rivals, a barnstorming fifth round replay also threw up an unlikely folk hero in the shape of defender Scott Jones, who stepped out of obscurity to play a key two-goal role in the Reds 3-2 victory over Manchester United.

United onslaught, and a fabulous Cup-tie was put back in the melting pot nine minutes from time when Andy Cole pounced to make it 3-2. However, the Reds held out, despite six nerve-wrecking minutes of stoppage time.

The Barnsley players had given so much in that game that there were doubts as to whether they would have sufficient left in the locker to cope with the demands of a gruelling battle with uncompromising Wimbledon three days later, but they overcame the formidable hurdle, despite suffering a further handicap during the course of the game.

A shot on the United goal by Neil Redfearn is unsuccessful.

Central defender Peter Markstedt suffered a blow to the head and failed to re-appear for the second-half, thus stretching the home team's capabilities of dealing with the Dons' aerial bombardment.

However, South African international Eric Tinkler, normally a midfield player, stepped into the breach as the Reds not only held on to the 1-0 lead given them by Fjortoft in the first-half, but also increased it through the same player with 62 minutes gone.

Jason Euell pulled a goal back in the 71st minute but, despite further pressure, the Reds held firm to record a vital victory which took them off the bottom of the table for the first time since Saturday, 29th November.

The Reds' Wembley dream finally died at St. James' Park on Sunday 7th March, when they were beaten 3-1 by Newcastle United in a Quarter-final tie which again was bathed in controversy, the result hinging on two debatable decisions which both went Newcastle's way to scupper the Oakwell Club's hopes of a 1912 trophy-winning repeat.

First of all, Temuri Ketsbaia was given the benefit of a very close offside call when he gave his side the lead in the 16th minute, and then, after 74 minutes, came the incident which was even more crucial at a time when the Reds, having shown great character and resolve to peg United back from 2-0 to 2-1, were pressing for the equalizer.

Adie Moses went to challenge Alan Shearer, missed his first tackle and clipped the England captain with an attempted second. Scunthorpe referee Neale Barry immediately pulled out a yellow card, which was harsh enough in itself, the young defender having made a legitimate attempt to win the ball. However, to make matters worse, the yellow card was followed by a red one because Moses had already been booked for another comparatively innocuous challenge 11 minutes earlier.

It was the first time that Moses had ever been sent off, and Barnsley's hopes went with him, although it was rubbing salt into the wound when David Batty made it 3-1 for United in the fifth minute of stoppage time. Gary Speed scored Newcastle's second, with Andy Liddell pulling one back for the Reds in the 56th minute.

Typically, Barnsley followed up that disappointment with a shock win over Aston Villa at Villa Park three days later. Ashley Ward, scorer of the goal when Barnsley recorded their last away victory of the season at Liverpool, was again the match-winner with a 17th minute strike.

There were other similarities to the game at Anfield as the Reds recorded their first League win at Villa Park, with Villa missing a host of second-half chances, and the Oakwell team riding their luck.

However, the visitors stuck to their task admirably, always putting the opposition players under pressure, and the way they ground out a result over a Villa side rejuvenated since the arrival of new manager John Gregory, suggested that they could yet cling on to their Premiership place.

Clint Marcelle makes a determined run on the Liverpool goal, with Neil Redfearn in support.

The revival continued with a 4-3 home victory over Southampton in a roller-coaster of a contest. Although the standard of football often left a good deal to be desired, the entertainment value of the game was first class. It was a thrill a minute from first whistle to last.

Ward gave the Reds the lead in the 16th minute; Egil Ostenstad pounced for an equalizer eight minutes later; but the home team were back in front within seven minutes, Scott Jones headed in a corner from Darren Sheridan. Then, injuries began to pile up. Jones had to leave the field for stitches in a cut under his left eye; Ward limped off with a hamstring injury to be replaced by Andy Liddell, who had himself to be substituted by Georgi Hristov after suffering a broken nose.

It was during Jones's absence for treatment that Matt Le Tissier scored a second Southampton equalizer, but two minutes later the Reds were back in front, Jan Aage Fjortoft whipping in a superb shot. When Neil Redfearn notched his 11th goal of the season from the penalty spot after referee Gerald Ashby had controversially decided that Fjortoft had been pulled back by Claus Lundekvam, it looked all over.

However, there was more hard work to do after Le Tissier had curled in his second and the Saints' third with 20 minutes still remaining, but the Reds held out to take another important step along the survival way.

Oakwell had never witnessed a match quite like the one when Liverpool were the visitors on Saturday, 28th March. There were five goals, including a last-minute winner; three sendings off; five bookings; a so-called pitch 'invasion'; and a walk-out by Worthing referee Gary Willard.

The first dismissal came in the 53rd minute when Darren Barnard, who had made an impressive debut for Wales in a goalless draw with Jamaica in mid-week, was adjudged to have clipped the heels of Liverpool striker Michael Owen. Twelve minutes later, Chris Morgan followed his colleague for an early bath when he stretched out an arm to try to hold Owen off as the two chased for the ball - and caught him in the face. Mr. Willard deemed it to be more malicious than accidental, and flourished another red card.

That prompted one irate fan to race on to the pitch, but he was well tackled by Fjortoft, and marched away by stewards.

It was then that, acting on the advice of the supervising steward, Mr. Willard allowed himself to be escorted from the pitch for his own safety. Unfortunately, no-one knew what was happening until the official returned to re-start the game four minutes later.

When Steve McManaman stole in to make it 3-2 for Liverpool in the last minute of normal time, and Darren Sheridan was sent off a minute later after an altercation with Paul Ince, who was very fortunate not to be dismissed as well, it was the last straw for six more fans, who brought about a further stoppage by running on to the pitch.

It was all so cruel on the Reds. Their nine men had performed heroics to battle their way back after Karlheinz Reidle had added to his 44th minute equalizer - Neil Redfearn had given the home team the lead eight minutes before half-time - with a superb 30 yard strike in the 59th minute.

Redfearn's penalty equalizer was no more than Barnsley deserved, and McManaman's winner five minutes later served only to add to the feeling that a great injustice had been done.

The local papers were inundated with letters protesting about Mr. Willard's handling of the game, and hundreds of supporters also wrote to the Football Association. It did not prevent the latter from holding an inquiry and charging the Oakwell Club with failure to control their fans, although Barnsley were subsequently exonerated.

It is, perhaps, significant, that the Reds won only one of their remaining eight matches after that.

Their unfortunate habit of conceding a late goal cost them another precious point at Ewood Park three days later, Kevin Gallacher climbing off the substitute's bench to give Blackburn Rovers a 2-1 victory with only four minutes remaining. Barnsley did enough to deserve a draw, but that was scant consolation as they surveyed a relegation scene that had suddenly taken a turn for the worse after the encouragement of three successive wins.

Martin Dahlin gave Rovers the lead with a classic goal in the eighth minute, but Georgi Hristov, given a rare place in the starting line-up alongside Ashley Ward, crowned his best performance for the Club with a 67th minute equalizer that held the promise of a point. However, Rovers re-doubled their efforts and, just when it seemed that the Reds were going to survive, Gallacher pounced.

Yet another odd-goal defeat away to Leeds United in the next game reflected the vast improvement made by the team since the thrashings of early-season, but on this occasion the Reds deserved nothing. Leeds were much the better side and had they taken even half their chances, they would have won by a much more comfortable margin than 2-1.

Even so, it took a spectacular own goal from Adie Moses 11 minutes from time to clinch maximum points for the home team. Jimmy Hasselbank scored their first after 19 minutes, Hristov equalising with an excellent right-foot volley two minutes before the break.

It was obvious in the Easter Saturday game that Barnsley not only needed, but wanted, to win more than derby visitors Sheffield Wednesday, who played as if they were safe from relegation.

Ashley Ward seized on to a long throw from Ales Krizan, deputising for the suspended Darren Barnard, in the 64th minute and Jan Aage Fjortoft, who had replaced John Hendrie in the 52nd minute, fired in a second with 19 minutes remaining. A goal by Dejan Stefanovic five minutes from the end sent a few tremors running through the stands, but this time, the Reds held on.

Easter Monday, however, brought a further set-back. In a tense relegation tussle at St. James's Park, England skipper Alan Shearer netted the winner for Newcastle United five minutes from time, just when it seemed that the Reds had done enough to hang on for a hard-earned point from a 1-1 draw.

Shearer also played a key part in Newcastle's 40th minute opener, thudding a shot against the bar, and Swede Andreas Anderson following up to head his first goal since his £3.5 million signing from AC Milan.

Barnsley's equalizer came five minutes after half-time when Shay Given failed to hold a shot from Ashley Ward, and Fjortoft again displayed his goal-poaching instincts to slide in his sixth goal in only nine starts since his move from Sheffield United. Unfortunately, he collided with the goalpost as he did so, and had to be substituted by John Hendrie.

Rarely can a draw have felt more like a defeat than it did when relegation rivals Tottenham Hotspur visited Oakwell the following Saturday. So much had been made of the fact that the crucial relegation scrap was one that the Reds had to win and 'Spurs could not afford to lose, that the eventual sharing of the spoils from a 1-1 result seemed anything but equally beneficial.

With three games remaining, the Reds knew they had lost a glorious chance to leapfrog over 'Spurs and out of the bottom three, particularly as the visitors had been reduced to ten men following the sending-off of Ramon Vega for man-handling Ashley Ward 25 minutes from time.

The score was already 1-1 by then, Redfearn having given the Reds the lead with his 14th goal of the season in the 19th minute, and Colin Calderwood having levelled matters two minutes after the break. The red card inspired Spurs rather than the home team, whose lack of penetration persisted, and it was the ten-men who looked the more likely victors.

The difference between the top and bottom of the Premier League was clearly demonstrated when Arsenal paid a visit to Oakwell. On the one hand there was the spirit and commitment of relegation strugglers, epitomized by Ashley Ward, who defied a kidney infection - and Doctor's orders - to clamber from the substitute's bench in a desperate effort to salvage a point.

On the other hand, there was the class and composure oozing from a team of internationals of past, present and future, typified by the £7 million talent of Dutch master Dennis Bergkamp, who scored the brilliant 23rd minute goal which, in effect, ended Barnsley's hopes of a shock result.

Arsenal coasted through the rest of the game and only some wayward finishing, desperately heroic defending, good goalkeeping and the woodwork, prevented the champions elect from adding more than a second goal scored by another Dutch international, Marc Overmars, in the 76th minute. The Reds gave of their best, but it was not good enough.

It was all or nothing for Barnsley at Filbert Street in the penultimate game of the season. They had to beat Leicester City to have any hope at all of retaining their hard-earned Premiership status - and even that might not be enough. It had reached the stage where Danny Wilson's side had to rely on any two of Everton, Tottenham and Bolton losing their last two games if they were to avoid an instant return to the Nationwide League.

Sadly, there was an air of resignation about the way the Barnsley players went about their business. Gone was the fire, the passion, the never-say-die spirit, that had characterized so many of their performances in the second-half of the campaign. There was hardly a spark left.

The inevitability of relegation had probably hit them after their failure to beat Tottenham two weeks earlier, and they never looked like taking even one point from a game in which they had to take all three. In the end, the 1-0 defeat - Theo Zagorakis netted the only goal in the 57th minute - did not matter. Results elsewhere confirmed the Reds' relegation.

To add to the disappointment of the day, Jovo Bosancic, who did not go on as substitute until ten minutes after half-time, was sent off five minutes from the end for a second bookable offence.

Barnsley failed to ring down the curtain on their maiden Premier League campaign with the desired flourish in the final fixture against deposed champions Manchester United at Oakwell on Sunday, 10th May.

Already doomed to a swift return to Division One, they were always second best to a United side which featured four emerging Old Trafford starlets, with five more sitting on the substitute's bench, thus emphasising the huge gap in terms of playing resources between the two clubs.

Yet, it hardly mattered. Such was the marvellous atmosphere created by the supporters, treating the Reds' hopefully temporary exit from the top flight as a carnival rather than a wake, that the football was relegated to a mere sideshow.

In many ways, the 2-0 defeat - Andy Cole and Teddy Sheringham were the United marksmen - summed up the season-long story of defensive frailties, a lack of midfield support for the admirable Neil Redfearn, and a shortage of finishing flair.

However, the superb backing from the fans never flagged. Five minutes from the end they reminded their team that they would 'Never Walk Alone' and after the game they remained to give their heroes an emotional send-off when the players returned to the pitch to fittingly acknowledge what Danny Wilson described as 'the fantastic' support the Reds had received throughout a truly memorable campaign.

A placard paraded by Ashley Ward and Darren Sheridan summed up the feeling of all concerned.

It said simply *"We'll be back."*

BARNSLEY F.C. ACADEMY.

The appointment of Howard Wilkinson as the F.A. Technical Director of Football signalled the F.A's determination to completely restructure Youth Development in this country. With this in mind, we began to examine what we were doing here at Oakwell. It was obvious that facilities were inadequate, the time given over to coaching needed extending and the quality of the players coming into the Youth Development Department needed improving. This was partially resolved last season with the hiring of the Dorothy Hyman Stadium, the doubling of coaching time and the formation of coaching and assessment centres. Nevertheless, both Ian Potter, the Director responsible for Youth Development, and myself both felt that we could not possibly afford to have an Academy here at Barnsley, as we journeyed to the first meeting called by Howard Wilkinson at Leicester. The rest is history. We both came out of the meeting, looked at each other and agreed that we could not possibly afford to miss out.

In many ways, events were working in our favour. We were now Premier League, the former Co-operative Ground had at last been purchased and City Challenge Funding was made available to finance any developments. The result is there for all to see. Our facilities are magnificent with a full sized astro turf, four full sized grass pitches, one small sized pitch, all floodlit to a very high standard, a small astro turf and five temporary changing rooms. The plans for the new North Stand are ready which will incorporate the permanent changing rooms, offices, gymnasium, physiotherapy room, classrooms, parents' lounge and catering facilities. Plans are also well advanced for an indoor playing area which must be in place by the year 2001. When all this is completed, the facilities will be second to none!

The Academy criteria also insist upon certain staffing levels and a management structure. Colin Walker is responsible for the 16 to 21 age group and Maurice Firth for the 9 to 16 age group, both with the title of Assistant Director.

Barrie Wagstaff is the Academy Coach, Bob Widdowson the Academy Goalkeeper Coach and Dave Hancock the Junior School and Community Coach. The Education/Welfare Officer is Tony Warden, the Physiotherapist is Paul Smith and his assistant will be appointed shortly. All the part-time coaches are in post, many of them having professional links with the Club.

The Academy will run teams in every age group from Under 9 to Under 16 plus an Under 17 and an Under 19 team. Academies are only allowed to play against other Academies and the number of games is limited. We already have a wealth of young players coming through but the search for better players will be relentless. At the age of 16, scholarships will be awarded to those who merit them and this will guarantee them an opportunity to become a professional footballer besides an education to suit their capabilities. In fact, the Academy guarantees a quality experience for all its young players but their commitment has to be total.

Besides the development of young players, the Academy has two other important functions. It has a vital role to play in the community in conjunction with the Football in the Community Scheme and support will be given where possible both with regard to facilities and coaching to schools, local clubs and associations. Secondly, the Academy is committed to develop girls' football and the aim is to place Barnsley Ladies alongside the best clubs in the country. But above all, the Academy has to produce a steady stream of young players capable of stepping into the first team as early as possible in order to justify the huge investment in Youth by the Board of Directors and in particular by the Chairman, Mr John Dennis.

✦ ✦ ✦ ✦ ✦ ✦ ✦ ✦ ✦ ✦ ✦ ✦

Peter Casken. (Academy Director)

★ POINTS OF VIEW (1) ★

THE PERSONALITIES:

JOHN A DENNIS
CHAIRMAN, BARNSLEY FOOTBALL CLUB

The 26th April, 1997 was an emotional day for all associated with Barnsley Football Club, and I was a proud man as I witnessed the never to be forgotten scenes that heralded the rise into the Premiership. Top flight football had been achieved for the first time in the Club's history, and the man responsible, Danny Wilson, richly deserved the award of Managers' Manager of the Year for his outstanding achievement.

The 1997/98 season is now over, and although it ended in disappointment and relegation, we have proved we can compete against the likes of Man U. and Liverpool, and myself and the Board of Directors have every confidence in securing a quick return to the Premier League.

Visiting Anfield, Old Trafford and Highbury was only a distant thought when I first started watching Barnsley as an 8-year-old, but one of my earliest memory is the exciting FA Cup run in 1960/61 when we reached the 6th round, only to be beaten by Leicester City in a replay at Oakwell. I suppose that was when the 'bug' really got hold of me, and I have been a fan ever since.

The 60's and 70's were a torrid time for the club, and apart from the cup run mentioned, there was little to cheer as we languished in the 3rd and 4th Divisions, but my support never waned as I followed the team home and away.

When my late Father took office as Chairman in 1967, I was fortunate enough to become a 'privileged' fan, although I didn't take advantage of this privilege except for Reserve matches when I would sit in the Directors Box. For first team games, I was happy to occupy one of three seats in the Centre stand Row E 77, 78 and 79.

Allan Clarke and Norman Hunter were instrumental in guiding Barnsley from the wilderness into the old 2nd Division, and optimism was high.

On a personal note, I was honoured to be appointed a Director of the Club in January 1984, and thoroughly enjoyed working with Chairman Geoff Buckle and my fellow Directors. A few years later, in November, 1989, I was appointed Chairman to succeed Geoff Buckle, and my first task was to find a Manager to replace the deposed Allan Clarke who had ended his second spell with the Club. I approached Mel Machin, who had just been released by Manchester City, and was delighted when Mr. Machin accepted the post.

Subsequent events have been well documented, and it only remains for me to look to the future, and to say that the Manager and his staff have got the Board's full backing, and with a little luck and the continued support of the fans, I am confident that Premiership football will return to the town.

JOHN G HENDRIE
MANAGER, BARNSLEY FOOTBALL CLUB (July 1998 to date)

I was born in Lennoxtown on the 24h October, 1963, and from an early age my ambition was to become a professional footballer. My ambition was about to be fulfilled, when I was recommended to Coventry City by a local Scottish scout, and joined the 'Sky Blues' as an apprentice in 1980. My first team appearances at Highfield Road were restricted, although I did play in the last two games of the 1982/83 season, scoring in each game, which helped the team avoid relegation from the old 1st Division at the expense of Manchester City.

After a brief loan spell with Hereford United, I joined Bradford City and was an ever-present in the 3rd Division

Championship side of 84/85. I was the club's leading goalscorer in 86/87, and spent 4 happy years at Valley Parade, although this happiness was tinged with great sadness as the horrific blazing inferno on the 11th May 1985 claimed so many lives. To this day, I find it difficult to come to terms with this tragedy, but life goes on although, perhaps, in a different perspective.

After short spells with Newcastle and Leeds, I joined Middlesbrough in 1990, and in my second season with the club, we secured promotion to the newly named Premier League under the guidance of Lennie Lawrence. I recall playing against Barnsley in that 91/92 season in the 3rd round of the Rumbelows Cup, and my mate Paul Wilkinson scored the only goal in a hard fought game. It's ironic that both of us would later join Barnsley for that memorable 96/97 campaign.

'The Boro' found life in the top flight tough and although Paul and I were the club's leading goalscorers, our first season in the Premier League ended in relegation. A new management beam of Bryan Robson and Viv Anderson were appointed, and the 94/95 season culminated in the 1st Division Championship, and a return to the Premier League which coincided with a move to the new Riverside Stadium. I like to think I played a small part in that promotion season as I was the club's leading goalscorer with 15 goals.

My appearances in the following season were limited, and it was obvious to me that, with the acquisition of foreign players such as Ravanelli and Juninho, my future lay elsewhere. When Danny Wilson approached me in October 1996, I was impressed by the man and had no hesitation in joining him at Barnsley, where I would team up with Paul Wilkinson who had joined the club prior to the start of this monumental season.

Helping Barnsley win promotion to the top flight for the first time in the club's history was an exciting time, and it was a twist of fate that my old club Bradford City would be our opponents on that never to be forgotten day. Whilst I was elated that promotion had been secured, I was a little sad for my old club as they were fighting for their 1st Division lives, and I was pleased when they won their last two games of the season to safeguard their status.

Like Middlesbrough before us, we found life in the Premier League tough, but we battled on and defied the critics who had forecast that we would be relegated before Christmas. That we were in with a chance of survival right up to the penultimate match of the season is down to Danny's motivation and the players never say die attitude. So, it's back to the Nationwide, but we are confident that with the continued fantastic support of the fans, we will, like Middlesbrough, make a hasty return to the top flight.

On a personal note, I hope to play a part in Barnsley's future success story for a few years yet, now having turned my attentions to the coaching/management side of the game. I am a fully qualified coach, and it would be nice to give something back to a sport that has been so good to me over the years

John's League Career:

Season	Club	Apps	Goals		Season	Club	Apps	Goals
1981/82	Coventry City	6	0		1989/90	Leeds United	27	5
1982/83	Coventry City	12	2		1990/91	Middlesbrough	41	3
1983/84	Coventry City	3	0		1991/92	Middlesbrough	38	3
1983/84	Hereford United (loan)	6	0		1992/93	Middlesbrough	32	9
1984/85	Bradford City	46	9		1993/94	Middlesbrough	29	13
1985/86	Bradford City	42	10		1994/95	Middlesbrough	39	15
1986/87	Bradford City	42	14		1995/96	Middlesbrough	13	1
1987/88	Bradford City	43	13		1996/97	Barnsley	36	15
1988/89	Newcastle United	34	4		1997/98	Barnsley	20	1

Total: 509 Apps 117 Goals
John is a Scotland Youth International, and author of *'Don't Call me Happy'*.

NORMAN RIMMINGTON

I suppose I've done just about every job going at Oakwell - player, coach, Assistant Manager, groundsman, physiotherapist and now kit man. That covers 55 years, and I've seen good and bad times, although in the last 20 years there have been many more of the former than the latter.

As a goalkeeper playing for Barnsley and Hartlepools United, I had my finger and thumb broken, injured my leg and dislocated my shoulder. You could really get walloped and hammered in those days, and if I had my time again, I wouldn't choose to be a goalkeeper.

When I returned to my home town, and the pits, on hanging up my boots, I was invited to become Barnsley's coach for the 'A' team and Reserves, and I worked my way up to be first team coach under Johnny Steele when we won promotion from the Fourth Division in 1967-68. However, we did not stay up long, and there were some dark days in the early 1970's when we were in the bottom half of the Fourth Division and desperate for cash. Gates were down, and we were having to perform miracles with players we'd got on free transfers.

the end, I packed in the coaching, and decided to have a
ash at being groundsman. I liked the fresh air and it took
lot of the pressure away. However, when former Leeds
nited and England striker Allan Clarke arrived as Player-
anager in 1978, I swapped jobs again. He offered to
uble my wages to be the physio., and it didn't take long for
e to decide.

e never looked back as Clarke got the place buzzing. The
g revival had begun as we won promotion twice in three
asons, once with Clarke and then with Norman Hunter,
hich took us to the old Second Division. We gradually
nsolidated, getting closer and closer to the play-offs, until
e finally made it to the top flight by the direct route, with
anny Wilson in charge. That was my fourth promotion
ith the club, and I was certain by Christmas that we were
ing to be promoted. So was the gaffer, but he told me to
ep my mouth shut because he knew that so much could go
rong.

he standard of football the team consistently produced that
ason was way above anything I had previously
xperienced at the club. When we made it, I was
articularly pleased for our coach, Eric Winstanley, who I
membered as a kid in the juniors. Later on, he was captain
f the 1967-68 promotion team when I was coach. Then, he
pped it all by helping the club into the Premiership for the
rst time in its history, as coach himself. It was his ultimate
mbition, and he deserved it. It gave me a lot of pleasure to
e someone I have known from his teenage days achieve
mething like that.

here have, of course, been many players I have known at
akwell, but somehow, it is the home-town Barnsley lads
ke Eric who bring back the fondest memories; Mick
cCarthy and Pat Howard are two others that spring to
ind.

ick was one of the best centre-halves I have seen, and he
now, of course, doing a very good job as manager of the

Republic of Ireland team, having had the difficult task of
taking over from the highly successful and popular 'adopted'
Irishman, Jack Charlton.

I recall Barrie Thomas and Johnny Evans being brought to
the club when we were rooted to the bottom of the Fourth
Division., and in dire financial straits. They helped us avoid
relegation and we somehow survived. but it was touch and
go. Nevertheless, things were so bad that the club was on
the brink of going out of existence and we were grateful that
Ernest Dennis and Geoff Buckle had stepped in, paid off the
debts and put some of their own money into the club to make
sure we survived. However, during the next few years, we
still had to keep a tight rein on the purse-strings.

There were no overnight stays in those days, and on one long
haul down to Colchester, the players ended up getting
changed in taxis on the way to the ground from the railway
station, after the train had been delayed. We still won 2-1!
On another journey to Chester, the coach driver got lost and
the team arrived 15 minutes late, trying to explain that fog
had held them up. Whereupon they were asked "How is it,
then, that the supporter's bus arrived in plenty of time?" I
was physio at the time and because of the rush I didn't have
the chance to change, so when one of our players was
injured, I dashed on to treat him wearing a suit and tie. The
referee was staggered. *"Good grief,"* he said, *"You're the
best-dressed trainer l have ever clapped eyes on."*

There was another occasion up at Hartlepool when an irate
crowd started throwing coins onto the pitch. One of our
players, Graham Pugh, collected a couple of handfuls and I
told him to give them to me. He replied, *"Not likely, thee go
and find thee oarn."* There have been characters like Pugh;
players who worked their socks off because they were
Barnsley born and bred and proud of it; players who have
had a lot of ability but not quite the bottle to go with it, and
players who have managed to combine both. It has been a
joy and a pleasure working with them all.

Norman's League Career:

Season	Club	Apps		Also played for:
944/45	Barnsley (War time)	3		Mapplewell Town (Pre-war)
946/47	Barnsley	27		Wisbech Town (Post-war)
947/48	Hartlepools United	24		Buxton (Post-war)
948/49	Hartlepools United	42		Denaby United (Post-war)
949/50	Hartlepools United	19		
950/51	Hartlepools United	*25*		
951/52	Hartlepools United	14		

Total App: 151

DANNY WILSON
MANAGER, BARNSLEY FOOTBALL CLUB (June 1994 - July1998)

I was born in Wigan on New Year's day 1960, and from an early age I wanted to play football for my home town club. I achieved this ambition in 1976 when I joined the 'Latics', who at the time were playing in the Northern Premier League.

I enjoyed my early days at Wigan, but I was anxious to ply my trade in the Football League, and I will always be indebted to Bobby Smith who signed me to play for Bury in the old 3rd Division. In that 1977/78 season, I made 9 appearances and came on as substitute on 3 occasions. I vividly recall scoring my first League goal at London Road in my 3rd appearance for my new club, but it was only scant consolation as Peterborough won 2-1.

After leaving Bury I had spells with Chesterfield, Nottingham Forest, Scunthorpe United (loan), Brighton & Hove Albion and Luton Town before joining Sheffield Wednesday in 1990, and I have worked with some great managers and coaches, including the enigmatic Brian Clough, albeit for just 10 games, Ray Harford and Trevor Francis.

I have been fortunate enough to play at Wembley on a number of occasions, including a League Cup Final with Luton Town, scoring one of the goals in the 3-2 defeat of Arsenal, and, together with Peter Shirtliff, helping Sheffield Wednesday beat Man. United 1-0, again in the final of the same competition.

When the offer came to join Barnsley, to work with my Wednesday colleague Viv Anderson, I jumped at the chance. Although I have always enjoyed playing football, I was now ready for a step up the ladder and I was impressed with the set-up at Oakwell, and the ambitions of Chairman, Jo Dennis. It was a different ball game, but I relished t challenge, and although the season was a disappointing or I knew in my heart that better things lay ahead.

When Viv left to join Bryan Robson at Middlesbrough was offered the job as Player/Manager, and I had hesitation in accepting the post. My first season in charg was an exciting time for me, the Club, the players and t fans, and although playing and managing is not the easie job in the world, I managed to put in 39 League and c appearances, and the team were in with a chance of a pla off place right down to the last match of the season. T fact that we just missed out didn't detract from a satisfyi first season in club management. Before the start of t 1995/96 season, I decided to hang up my boots and put a my efforts into getting Barnsley into the Premiershi although, due to some indifferent performances, o challenge petered out, and we finished a disappointing 10t

The promotion season of 1996/97 has been we documented, and so has our efforts in the top flight. Ev though our first season in the Premiership ended relegation, I have thoroughly enjoyed pitting my wits agair some of the top Managers in the game. It was a learni process for me and the players, and now all possible effo will be made for a quick return. I am confident th Barnsley can survive amongst the 'big' boys, and next tin the Club will be prepared to do just that.

In conclusion, may I thank all the fans for their outstandi support and impeccable behaviour throughout this pa remarkable season.

Danny's League Career:

Season	Club	Apps.	Goals	Season	Club	Apps.	Goa
1977/78	Bury	12	1	1985/86	Brighton & Hove Albion	33	11
1978/79	Bury	46	7	1986/87	Brighton & Hove Albion	38	7
1979/80	Bury	32	0	1987/88	Luton Town	38	8
1980/81	Chesterfield	33	3	1988/89	Luton Town	37	9
1981/82	Chesterfield	43	3	1989/90	Luton Town	35	7
1982/83	Chesterfield	24	7	1990/91	Sheffield Wednesday	36	6
1982183	Nottingham Forest	10	1	1991/92	Sheffield Wednesday	36	3
1983/84	Scunthorpe United (loan)	6	3	1992/93	Sheffield Wednesday	26	2
1983/84	Brighton & Hove Albion	26	10	1993/94	Barnsley	43	0
1984/85	Brighton & Hove Albion	38	5	1994/95	Barnsley	34	2

Total: 626 App   95 Goals

Danny was capped by Northern Ireland on 24 occasions, and scored 1 goal.

THE OFFICIAL BARNSLEY FC SUPPORTERS CLUB

The Official Supporters Club came into being following a letter from long-time supporter Alan Bloore to Barnsley FC Chairman John Dennis in May 1993 expressing his concerns at the public image and commercial direction of the club, as well as it's 'distance' from its supporters. It was seen by the founder-members that a club with the obvious potential and ambitions of Barnsley should have a body to allow input from, and represent the interests of supporters, which was officially recognised by the club. Following various meetings between supporters and Football Club officials, the Official Barnsley FC Supporters club was launched on the 8th October 1994.

In setting up the club, existing unofficial supporters clubs as well as the South Riding fanzine were approached, their views sought and they were offered an involvement in the new official body. A committee and officials were elected, and an inaugural meeting was held, with Barnsley FC Chairman John Dennis and Director Chris Harrison accepting posts as President and Vice-President respectively. The committee also has posts specifically representing the interests of both Ladies and disabled supporters. The supporters club officials hold regular meetings at a forum consisting of Chris Harrison and the Marketing Manager of the Football Club.

From the outset and as reflected in their constitution, the aims of the Supporters Club were to bring together all interested parties in Barnsley Football Club in helping to promote and support the good name and reputation of the Football Club, and to assist in helping them achieve success:
To give financial support to the Football Club in that any surplus generated would benefit Barnsley F.C. ....
To arrange social activities on behalf of members and friends of the club. ....
To encourage members to participate in social and fundraising activities. ....
To arrange trips to away games for supporters using both coach and private car travel. ....
To make and maintain contacts with other supporters clubs.

The Club started out with a modest table under the East Stand as a congregation point before matches and at half-time. Lengthy negotiations with the Football Club led to them securing the use of an unused area beneath the recently opened ORA Stand. A frantic weekend of painting, carpet fitting and joinery, by four enthusiastic Supporters Club members led to the new Supporters Club office being opened live on Sky television by Sky commentator Rob Hawthorne, prior to Barnsley's first home game of the 1995/96 season against Huddersfield Town.

The Supporters Club are active members of The National Federation of Football Supporters Clubs, a body who seek to bring together supporters associations from all football clubs at all levels and represent their interests with bodies such as the police and the football authorities.

Membership of the Federation helped the Supporters Club in securing a dictate from the FA as to how supporters should be compensated, following the abandoned game at Middlesbrough in the 1994/95 season. They are also assisting a campaign to have a permanent memorial sighted at Hillsborough to commemorate the disaster of 1989. A number of initiatives have been championed by the Supporters Club including the Family Area in the East Stand and the 'Quid a Kid' scheme used, albeit just once, in the 1994/95 season.

A major feature of the Supporters Club is its monthly meetings to which different guest speakers are invited each month. Meetings were initially held in the Oakwell Executive Suite but limited space and the predictable growth in membership of the supporters club led to a later move to the Ardsley House Hotel. To date, the Supporters Club has played host to, amongst others, Barnsley FC Manager Danny Wilson and Coach Eric Winstanley, Chairman John Dennis, former Reserve Team Coach Malcolm Shotton, Premiership Referee Steve Lodge, the Chairman of Club sponsor, ORA Electronics, Malcolm Hanson, Club general manager, Michael Spinks, local radio and press reporters, Steve Banyard, Keith Lodge and Simon Clark, not to mention a host of first team players.

Promotion to the Premiership at the end of the 1996/97 campaign obviously brought a huge increase in interest in Barnsley FC, and with it the Supporters Club. Various groups of supporters got together at pubs and clubs, and one such group at the 'Beggar and Gentleman' public house in Hoyland became affiliated to the Official club. The old London Supporters Club reformed and became known as 'The Official Supporters Club, Southern Branch', and has a healthy membership of exiled Barnsley fans.

Another supporters club worthy of note, unofficial but recognised by the Supporters Club and Football Club alike, is 'The Star Supporters Club', based at the pub of the same name at Hoyland Common. Formed more than twenty years ago, and existing primarily to provide coach transport from Hoyland Common, Hemingfield, Birdwell and the surrounding area to Oakwell for home games, they are unique in the fact that they are the only unofficial supporters club to give an annual player of the year award. Traditionally, the winning player visits 'The Star' for an informal presentation evening. Recent winners having visited 'The Star' include Gary Fleming, Danny Wilson (ably assisted by Eric Winstanley), Arjan De Zeeuw and John Hendrie.

Currently, membership of the Official Supporters Club offers the following benefits: 10% discount on purchases from the Oakwell Club Shop (excluding Matchday programmes and match videos); priority ticket sales for all-ticket games (priority is behind Season Ticket Holders,

Oakwell Centenary Society Members and Lottery Agents, but before tickets go on general sale); free, monthly members draw for a £10.00 voucher to spend in the club shop; travel arrangements to away games for supporters wishing to use either coach or car travel; 10% discount on all full price purchases from Barnsley Outdoor Centre, 35 Peel Parade, Barnsley.

Three categories of membership are offered, namely Adult - £5.00 per year, Joint (Family) - £7.50 per year and Concessionary (Junior/OAP/Student) - £3.00 per year.

Contact:
The Official Barnsley FC Supporters Club.
c/o Barnsley FC, Oakwell Ground, Grove Street Barnsley, S71 1ET.

BARNSLEY FC SUPPORTERS CLUB, JERSEY BRANCH

Most people have heard of Jersey but are not quite sure where it is. Likewise, most people in Jersey have heard of Barnsley but not quite sure where that is either! For those that don't know, Jersey, the largest of the Channel Islands, is a pretty little island, about nine miles across and five north to south, sitting a mere 12 miles from the Normandy coast of France. With the exception of the south coast where most of the 85,000 population live, the island is very rural. Why then should such a small and remote place have a Barnsley FC Supporters Club?

The answer lies in the enthusiasm of one man, founder Dave Moore. Barnsley born and bred, and a product of Broadway Grammar School, he came to Jersey in 1986. Unhappy with the walk from Park Road to Oakwell, he thought he'd make his matchdays more interesting by starting his journey 100 miles south of Southampton. In order to meet like minded-people, an advertisement was placed in the Jersey Evening Post and the respondents became members of the "Barnsley FC Supporters Club, Jersey Branch" - free of charge! Well over 50 people expressed an interest, but the hard core members number about a dozen. The membership consists largely of Barnsley ex-pats., living and working in Jersey, together with a small number of locals. Some of the local people have links with Barnsley from the Second World War when many Jersey families were evacuated from the island during the German occupation and spent the war years in Barnsley.

Given the remote location, it's not easy to take advantage of the privileges of being a member of the official Supporters Club, and therefore the Jersey club is an unofficial branch. That said, members do have links with the Club and it's possible to get tickets for most away matches. It also helps that five season tickets are held by members in Jersey.

The overwhelming success of the season ticket sales for this, the first Premiership year, has been a limiting factor in the 'Jersey Reds' visiting Oakwell. Planning a visit to Barnsley to coincide with a home fixture is no longer a matter of glancing at the fixture list before booking a flight and then arranging to meet in 'The Outpost' at 12.30pm, before turning up at the ground at 2.45pm.

It's now having to beg, steal or borrow, or - equally inconvenient - the offer of a ticket on a Friday with no chance of making it in time for the match the following afternoon!

Despite all the problems, there have been a number of enjoyable, if not victorious, outings. Most of these courtesy of Sky television. The first was the dismal defeat by Chelsea, 6-0. About 20 Jersey Reds arrived with much enthusiasm and great anticipation at Tam's Bar in St. Brelades Bay. It was a hot Sunday afternoon and being surrounded by so many ORA shirts in a beachside bar seemed surreal. For twenty-five minutes Barnsley's free-flowing football showed no signs of the disaster which was to follow. It wasn't until the first goal went in that those Reds fans present realised they were surrounded by Chelsea fans who made the embarrassing defeat much worse. The planned celebration binge was abandoned and the departure was as though from a funeral.

The second live match, this time against Coventry was a night of great celebration, not only due to the 2-0 win, but this ended a run of six consecutive League defeats. The next live match was a joint event with the Jersey Owls, and despite being the better team on the night (an observation made by both sets of fans), Di Canio scored a well taken but undeserved goal in the last minute denying the Reds a point.

Although some people travel to the mainland on a regular basis, the only trip managed as a group was to the Dell to see the 4-1 defeat by Southampton. Nine members braved the turbulent winds gusting through the channel to spend a day in Southampton. It was a great day out and one of many meetings, particularly with members of the Barnsley Internet supporters. The match itself is best forgotten, going two goals behind within five minutes and never really showing signs of competing against a team that should have been beaten.

The Club members continue to meet for televised matches and further trips are likely. New members are always welcome, and notices for meetings are placed in the Jersey Evening Post 3-4 days before the event.

★ POINTS OF VIEW (2) ★
FANS - AT HOME

Bob Davies

I was born and went to school in the West Midlands. As a youngster, I supported Coventry City but then during the '70s did not pay too much attention to the game. In 1980 I became interested in greyhound racing and regularly 'went to the dogs'. My partner in crime came from Wakefield and used to talk on a Saturday night about his team - Barnsley. I started to take an interest myself in the results, read newspaper reports, etc and that's how it all started.

I went to my first game, at Wolves, in 1982 and then got totally hooked. I spent the rest of the '80s travelling the length and breadth of the country. Supporting Barnsley has given me many happy memories - like the time I won the programme competition and had to go onto the pitch at the Newcastle game to get my prize - and not so happy - the 7-0 defeat at West Brom! In recent years family circumstances (children!) mean that it is more difficult for me to get to games, however there is the television and the Internet supporters list which is an invaluable way of keeping up to date with what is happening at the Club.

During the period of my regular attendance at games in the '80s, the Club achieved little real success - my only real memory was of the time we almost made the play-offs and due to a mis-announcement at the ground, champagne corks popped in the Directors Box only for everything to go 'flat' when the real situation emerged.

At the time of writing, we are undergoing a titanic struggle to avoid the drop. The spirit being shown by everyone involved with the Club is first class and I hope that by all pulling together we can make it, and if not, I look forward to future seasons and major successes in the top flight - Europe, here we come!

Miriam Harper

I was born in Barnsley in 1963, and my first visit to Oakwell was with my Dad in the late sixties, although I don't remember too much about it. My Father and brother are Barnsley fanatics, although my Mum hasn't quite got the hang of it all yet. My first recollections are watching players like Mike Lester, Alistair Millar, Alan Little, Barry Murphy, Phil Chambers and Kenny Brown, and the following are just some of the highlights:

The day we signed Allan Clarke. It was very big at the time. Was that the start of it all?...... The away victory at Portsmouth in 1978-79 which secured promotion to the 3rd Division. I didn't go, because I couldn't stand the tension. I went shopping with Mum instead......Promotion to the 2nd Division in 1980/81..... The trip to Rotherham in the 1981-82 season to see Barnsley win 4-2. My parents thought I was at a friends doing homework...... The League Cup run in the same season, and in particular, the away match at Liverpool.

During the 1996-97 season, there were so many wonderful moments, including: Wednesday night, when Wolves drew with Grimsby. I went to the pub at half-time as my nerves couldn't take anymore. At full-time I rang Dad for the final score, but my mum answered. SHE KNEW THE SCORE. This is not normal. The next day, the feeling that we were actually going to do it hit me. I was a complete mess, and they nearly sent me home from work.

Bradford City- I'm not sure I can add anything that hasn't already been said except that I had bought the tickets months in advance for my Dad's birthday. In the 'We'll never Walk Alone' chorus at the beginning of the match, my Dad turned to me and said it was the best birthday present he had ever had. I was nearly in tears and we hadn't even kicked-off. When I got back to Brighton still wearing my Barnsley shirt, people were congratulating me as though I had personally done it all by myself. I didn't buy a drink for at least a week. 'Phone calls and email from people I hadn't seen or even thought of for years... "I thought of you on Saturday"......The promotion run-in, with so much goodwill from other football fans......The 1997-98 season, obviously:..... The West Ham match at home: I had never had a season ticket before. I had always dreamt of having one, but I hadn't really needed one before. This is the prize for last season, and I was going to enjoy every minute of the season...... Liverpool away...... My Dad's face when I saw him the day after the home Cup replay against Manchester United. He was grinning from ear to ear, proudly wearing his Barnsley tie, as I gave him my ticket for the Newcastle match because I couldn't make it.

Not too many lows, and my Dad thinks I am very fortunate because in his time there were many, including the day we sold Eddie McMorran and Tommy Taylor, and the 6th round Oakwell Cup defeat by Leicester in 1960-61.

My personal lows: The day we sold Carl Tiler. It seemed very bad news at the time, and I remember thinking, *"We are never going to get anywhere if we sell our best players"*......The day we didn't get into the play-offs in 1990-91 because Brighton scored in injury time and took our place. Ironically, I moved to Brighton in 1983. How fortunes change...... I felt ill after the Newcastle Cup match. It still feels bad.

Footnote: I asked a Brighton fan how long the promotion high lasts for. His answer: 19 years and still going. He went to watch Brighton get promotion in 1979 away at Newcastle.

DAMIAN GREEN

The first game I ever went to watch was Barnsley v Leeds at Oakwell which we won 3-0 and from that point on I've been hooked. That was almost 15 years ago and is just a distant memory that has stuck in my mind and like many other good moments, one that I will never forget.

However, like every football club, there have been bad times along the way as well. The ones that stick in my mind are the days when the Club was dicing with relegation and the threat of the old Third Division was upon us. Luckily, we always escaped the drop but due to limited financial resources it seemed to happen year after year. However, no matter how bad things got, come the end of the season Barnsley Football Club would be sitting around 12th place in the old Second Division.

Something else I distinctly remember was how most supporters used to share the feeling of "the Board don't want to go up", and I myself had doubts about the Club's ambitions. However, over the years I began to realise we were slowly but surely moving forward. The initial signs were the erection of the East Stand in replacement of the old Brewery Stand. This was the first major development work to take place at Oakwell for decades and previously a new lick of paint on the walls was a talking point.

In my time supporting Barnsley I've seen a few managers come and go, including the likes of Alan Clarke, Mel Machin and Viv Anderson, but none in my mind come close to Danny Wilson, also known in Barnsley as 'God'! When he took over from Viv Anderson I was one of those people rather dubious about the appointment but I am glad to say I've been proved well and truly wrong. My personal feeling is we have the best manager in the Premiership, and every Barnsley fan will rue the day he decides to move on, which I'm hoping will be many years in coming around.

My first major disappointment whilst supporting Barnsley occurred when we lost out making the play-offs by goal difference. This however was also my first major high point because for half-an-hour after the final whistle was blown, several thousand others, and I, thought we had made it. There were jubilant scenes starting with a mass pitch invasion to the foot of the Directors' Box where all the players came out to the celebrations. Champagne flowed and tears of happiness were shed, but as news came though that Brighton had scored a goal deep in injury time, they turned to tears of sadness.

Several years passed before we had something else to cheer about and this came in the form of the finest season the club has ever seen. The kick-off to the 1996-97 season was no different to all those past years but no one knew what was in store. The pre-season games suggested we had signed some decent, yet unknown players, and after the first couple of games everyone thought we were

playing some excellent football. After five games of the season we were top of the League with a 100 percent record but still, going previous form, most people expected us to dwindle away and once again finish mid-table. Personally, I felt we were good enough for a play-off place but not for automatic promotion. Part way through the season our form dipped slightly, yet we didn't drop out of the top four. Then came Super Johnny Hendrie, and no matter what happens to him from now on, he will always be remembered for his contribution to our promotion.

We went from strength to strength, and by Christmas we were top of the tree after beating Sheffield United at Bramall Lane. The feeling around Barnsley was tremendous and everyone was pondering the fact of whether we were going to do it. The crowds were swelling week by week and the chant *"Its Just Like Watching Brazil"* was now a household phrase. The well-publicised ranting of Wolves manager Mark McGhee had promoted him to public enemy number one around Barnsley, and this made our promotion even sweeter, knowing we had defied his remarks.

It all came down to the last home game of the season and our destiny was in our own hands. If we beat Bradford City, we would gain automatic promotion to the Premier League for the first time in the Club's history. No one could wait for the game to come around but once it had, it was well worth the wait. We got a dream start with an early Paul Wilkinson goal, and when Clint Marcelle notched the second late in the second-half, the whole place erupted. Everyone went crazy and knew that we were almost there. It was nail-biting stuff right to the end, and when the final whistle went I have never witnessed scenes like it in my life.

The most moving part of the celebration was when the whole ground sang their hearts out to 'You'll Never Walk Alone' with their arms and scarves held high. I've never had a feeling like that before and I was welling up inside like most other people in the ground. People were crying, singing, dancing, cheering and basically just going mad. No one could contain themselves any longer and a mass pitch invasion was imminent. It brought back memories of the time we thought we were in the play-offs, but this time everyone knew it was real and no-one could take anything away from us.

After everyone left the ground, the party moved into the town centre, where there were more amazing scenes. Everyone was in party mood and the celebrations had begun. The champagne corks were popping and practically everyone, including myself, ended up absolutely soaked through to the skin with the stuff. People were driving around with flags and scarves flapping in the wind and tooting their horns. Even the police turned a blind eye to most things.

The singing and dancing went on all through the night in the pubs and clubs, and then carried on for several days afterwards. All in all it was a day I will remember for the rest of my life. The feeling was indescribable and amazing doesn't even come close. It was something many others and I, thought we would never see, and no matter what happened in the Premier League, it was going to be a year long party.

We knew it would be hard in the top flight but the adjustment took a lot longer than everyone thought. We all had high ambitions and dreams of thrashing the likes of Manchester United and Liverpool, but after the first few games we all came down to Earth with a thud. We didn't seem to be playing too badly but were being punished for silly mistakes and gradually we slipped down the League until we hit rock bottom. We stayed there all through the Christmas period and into the New Year. In comparison to last season, this was a sharp contrast, but no one really got depressed about it, we just hoped Danny would turn things around and get us out of trouble.

He didn't make any rash signings in an attempt to buy our way out of trouble, but instead, concentrated on making the players we had believe in themselves. From day one of the season, Danny has always maintained the players have what it takes to keep Barnsley Football Club in the Premiership.

Once they started to believe him and stopped being frightened of the big boys, the results started to go our way a little more. We enjoyed a tremendous cup run which came to what most people thought was an unfair end at Newcastle, after removing the likes of Manchester United and Tottenham. The confidence rubbed off into the League games and instead of being relegated by Christmas, which most people outside of Barnsley predicted, we still had a fighting chance of staying in the Premier League.

Barnsley Football Club has given its supporters, and also the rest of the country a season to remember. I just hope there will be a chapter in a future book about how Barnsley managed to get back into the Premier League.

FANS FROM AFAR

ANDY RAMSDEN - GERMANY

During the Spring of 1995, when Barnsley were just about to miss out once again on the play-offs from Division 1, my family and I decided to move to Munich, Germany, where I had been offered a two year secondment with my emplyer. We fancied the challenge of living and working abroad but, with two young children both under 3 years old, we knew it wouldn't be easy. There would be things we would miss, notably friends and family, the comfortable lifestyle in the UK, familiar surroundings, and for me at least, following Barnsley FC. Although I moved away from Barnsley some years ago, I still followed the team, timing matches with visits back home to see family, and watching occasional away games in the south.

We were settled into our new home in Munich around the time the 1995/96 season started. I followed this particular season through day-old English newspapers which I bought from Munich Train Station (at hugely inflated prices), and picked up nuggets of team information through telephone conversations with my Dad, who still went along to watch The Reds whenever he could. Nevertheless, I felt very much out of touch with the side of 95/96.

When I read match reports, they listed players I didn't recognise - the line-up was becoming unfamiliar to me, and I was more out of touch than I had been in the last 20 years. What made it worse, was that I heard they were playing attractive, stylish, football under Danny Wilson. Danny was proving to be a popular manager, and there

was a buzz of excitement and expectation amongst the fans that something good was about to happen. I wasn't part of this, this was second-hand news.

The following season I was determined not to let distance stop me from following The Reds. After all I worked in telecommunications, an industry that was, and still is, undergoing massive changes. Technological advances were presenting ordinary folk with new and exciting opportunities in all aspects of life - the Internet enabled people across the world to chat together for the price of a local phone call, satellites enabled people to receive news and entertainment from all over the world, and mobile telephony meant people could stay in touch wherever they went, 24 hours a day. I decided that living abroad needn't be a barrier and I vowed it wouldn't prevent me from following The Reds any more than it did when I lived in England.

By the start of the 96/97 season, we had a Sky dish installed on our house in Munich. Not only did this give us access to 30 or so German channels, but also access to the Sky channels normally viewed in the UK. Sky were transmitting Nationwide matches live on Friday evenings and Sunday afternoons and, on the 25th August 1996, I watched a stylish Barnsley side thrash Huddersfield 3-1 in front of a 9,000 plus crowd. It felt a little strange watching the lads "*laking down the 'Well*" whilst I was sitting in Munich drinking wheat beer. Watching The Reds live on UK terrestrial TV didn't happen too often, so to be watching them live in Munich felt odd, especially when I thought I was probably the only person in Germany watching the game! More ironically, my Dad, who lives in Barnsley but couldn't make that particular game, phoned me up during the match for a progress report - I was 1000 miles away, he was five miles away in Darfield!

As everyone reading this knows, the season just got better. I followed progress on matchdays by listening to Radio 5 on Sky, and watching the goals on Sky Sports 2. Detailed team information could be gleaned from Sky Teletext where Nationwide Division 1 teams had their own text pages showing team news, match statistics and latest transfer rumours. If I was desperate, I could even follow progress on matchdays by watching Teletext, waiting for the score to automatically update throughout the game. However, this particularly unsociable activity didn't - quite understandably - go down too well with the rest of the family; cries of "*Quiet kids, I'm watching Teletext*", fell on deaf, unsympathetic ears.

It was around this time that my Dad got himself a mobile phone, and it wasn't long before we discovered we could send short text messages between his phone in England, and mine in Germany. This technological breakthrough opened up a whole new avenue of information retrieval for me on matchdays. I remember one Saturday in December when my family and I were walking round the Christmas markets in Munich. My parents were at the match with their phone, and at 15:17hrs, 14/12/96, my mobile phone beeped at me and told me, "*You have a message.*" I pressed a couple of buttons and retrieved a message which read "Reds 1 Tranmere 0; Hendrie - Dad." This was followed several minutes later by more messages "*Wilko makes it two*", and finally "*Redders pen, 3-0 , Dad.*" I could now follow The Reds in real time whilst out and about, not just in front of the TV.

The next televised match was the last Friday in October when Barnsley, again at home, played Bolton. Given the hour's difference, it was 9pm as I settled down in front of the TV to watch the game. Bolton were already established as firm favourites to win the League, and this was certainly the biggest test Barnsley were to face. With only two defeats behind them, Barnsley were in 3rd spot going into the game and points were crucial if they were to stay in contention with the top teams. I remember watching that game, frequently shouting at the TV, screaming at the referee, momentarily forgetting I was 1000 miles away and he wouldn't be able to hear me too well. Two goals from Redfearn earned The Reds a well deserved point, and for me a few local wheat beers toasted The Reds that night many times. I taped the match as well and decided to watch it once more before bedtime, just to check I hadn't missed anything. I'm glad I did because we played even better second time around.

Four days before Christmas, Barnsley beat old rivals Sheffield United 1-0 at Bramall Lane to lift them to top spot.

My family and I flew home for Christmas and I managed to watch The Reds defeat Manchester City at Oakwell. I must admit it was great to be at the ground, in what was one of the biggest crowds I had seen at Oakwell in many a long time, over 17,000. This was my first "*live*" live match of the season and although it was great to be at the ground, I must admit I missed the wheat beer and not seeing the replay of Adie Moses goal. My family and I returned to Germany early in the New Year to complete the last five months of our secondment, and I remember sitting on the plane wondering if I would be coming home to Premiership football.

1997, and the team remained in the top three. Once again, Sky provided most of the information, but I now had Internet access at work which opened up a whole new area of information retrieval for me. The first thing I did was subscribe to The Electronic Telegraph which provided me with match reviews, reports and season statistics.

I also discovered the unofficial Barnsley F.C. web sites, which were a fantastic revelation. Through mailing lists I discovered like-minded exiles all over the world - Reds fans could be found in the USA, Canada, Australia, Japan, Scandinavia, and all corners of Europe. Mailing lists and Internet web pages meant I could converse with other remote fans, similarly stranded in some distant land. Here, in cyberspace, people would mail Yorkshire Post and Barnsley Chronicle match reports, tell stories of their favourite players from the past, and swap rumours on the latest transfer happenings.

I also discovered other football sites such as the one run by Nationwide, the League sponsors. Here you could find pages dedicated solely to Barnsley FC. Detailed match reports were available, latest transfer news and team statistics were only the click of a button away.

Suddenly I was telling my dad what the latest transfer rumours were, and he was asking me what the team would be on Saturday. March 6th was his birthday, so I sent him the 2-0 victory video of Barnsley against Sheffield United, televised live on 7th March, 1996. He works in Sheffield and keeps the video in his office with an 'available for loan' sticker on it. I don't think anyone has ever borrowed it, they're a funny lot in Sheffield!

April was our last month in Germany. The secondment was drawing to a close and we had a lot of things to arrange. My wife and children travelled back to the UK in the last week of April, whilst I stayed behind to tidy up the loose ends in Germany. On Saturday 26th April, Barnsley played Bradford City in their penultimate game of the season. This was the biggest match Barnsley had ever faced - victory and they were assured of promotion. I vividly remember that Saturday afternoon as I sat alone in Munich, listening to Radio 5 who were broadcasting the match live. Everyone knows what happened that day, and when Clint Marcelle scored in the 87th minute, I could scarcely believe what had happened.

Shortly after the final whistle, I received a call from the Oakwell car park, it was my Mum on the mobile. I could hear the singing and celebrations in the background and I suddenly felt very much alone. I looked out of the window and saw Herr and Frau Schmidt cutting the grass - why weren't they celebrating? Suddenly, someone grabbed the phone from my mum, it was a Bradford fan. He shouted down the phone "*Congratulations pal, Barnsley are in the Prem!*", before handing it back. It was only then that it really sank in - Barnsley really were in The Premier League.

I don't know if it was the beer I was drinking, or if it was just relief, or maybe excitement, but I became very emotional at that moment. A lifelong dream had just come true, one which I thought would never be realised. I hadn't been at the game, nay, I hadn't been at the season! However, I shared the emotions of those nine months with the rest of the Barnsley fans.

I could tell you the best players, the fans' favourites and the best team performances of the season. I could have walked into any pub in Barnsley and joined straight in with the team talk, holding my own with those lads who religiously went to the 'well', week in, week out.

Don't get me wrong, modern technology, no matter how advanced, couldn't give me the matchday atmosphere, the banter on the terraces and the barracking of the away teams. I couldn't hug the bloke next to me when Wilkinson scored against Bradford, and I couldn't discuss the finer points of team selection after the match over a pint of John Smiths. You can't ever beat being there, nothing will ever beat being at Oakwell seeing the team coming out of the tunnel and step onto the pitch, but, given the circumstances, I made the best of what was available, and I will cherish that season along with the rest of the town, until the day I die.

BRIAN MARCH - CANADA

Having lived in Canada for the past twenty-five years, I have to admit to a degree of surprise in myself that I am still a Barnsley fan and that I care as much as I do about the fortunes of the club. But then again I was born in Barnsley, and as a ten-year-old I walked along Grove Street past the school that my Mother and her sisters attended twenty years earlier, down the hill to Oakwell, where I handed over my pocket money for the first time to see the lads in red.

That was in 1957 when Harry Hough, who also had a sports shop in town, kept goal and Duncan Sharp who, in his own inimitable style, was in charge of the defence, a style which today would bring a fine collection of yellow cards. It was also before floodlights, and when, a few years later, the first set was constructed I went at every opportunity to watch the building. I was also at the first match that Eric Winstanley played in at Oakwell, when he took over from Duncan Sharp.

Eric has become something of a legend at Oakwell and to this day he is still a member of the staff.

Since moving to Canada in 1974 I have followed the fortunes of the club through English newspapers, particularly the Barnsley Chronicle supplied by family, albeit a week old when it reaches me. Recently access to the Internet has given me up to the minute contact and I am a regular visitor to the web sites and the subscribers list. When visiting England a priority is a visit to "The Well" of course.

Barnsley being promoted to the Premier Division has proved to be somewhat traumatic for me. After forty years of modest expectations from the club I find myself caught up in the drama of life in the Premier. Wishing sometimes, as the team struggles to find its feet in the first-half of this historic season, that it had never left the lower divisions. But it's better as it is, our day has come and whatever happens we can always say we made the big time and we were there.

DAVID WAKE - HONG KONG

I suppose one thing about being a long term expat and not being able to get back to watch them very often is that the Barnsley you supported tends to be fossilized in the team you used to watch. In my case it was the dark days of the 1960's when the club nearly went under, but then Allan Clarke came along and we started the long climb back that has led us to the Premier League.

My earliest memories go back to the 50's though, when my Dad first took me to Oakwell and we sat in the main stand. Sharp, Swift and Swallow - magic names of my childhood and as Parky said in most of his articles about Barnsley as well as his book; *"The scent of Woodbines and beer wafted up from the stand!"*

As a teenager - I stood with my mates in the East Stand and watched Eric Winstanley and Pat Howard provide steel in the defence, as the flying winger Bob Earnshaw sped towards goal and usually couldn't stop in time! The "enigmatic" Norman Dean would pop up with the occasional goal and provide five minutes of class and vanish for the rest of the game.

It was always the case that the fans appreciated good football - and the nickname 'battling Barnsley' was one that belonged to an earlier era. But one frustrating fact is the fickle nature of the Barnsley public - ready to support the team when it is doing well, but vanishing in tough times. I think we are seeing it now. The start of the season saw me watching Barnsley versus Chelsea on satellite TV in the Hong Kong Football club, with my mate who is a Northampton Town supporter, and the local branch of the Hong Kong Chelsea Supporters Club. There I was wearing my Barnsley shirt which I had bought on a visit home that summer - and by the end of the match my face was probably as red as my shirt! Still the local Chelsea fans were generous in victory (that's pretty easy!), and I was left wondering where the Hong Kong branch of B.F.C. supporters were. There isn't one. There is a Hong Kong Fulham Supporters Association so why can't we have one? So if any Barnsley supporters in Hong Kong are reading this - please get in touch.

Last season I managed to get to Oakwell over Christmas to see them beat Man City. Next week I shall be in UK for just a week and will be able to go to Chelsea, hopefully to see them avenge the 6-0 defeat. If they don't - well I will have been there.

And now the final results on World Service. Bolton have lost. 'Spurs have won. Barnsley have won! Wednesday won. So I can go to bed happy - even if we are still at the bottom - at least we are Premier League - say we are Premier League (this season anyway!)

IAN ROBERTS - USA

Barnsley in Columbus. 1st March 1998: It's been a mild winter in Columbus; a couple of days of snow, a bare handful of what we could call cold days, and a great fear from the locals that we're going to have a bloody hot summer. Outside today it was miserable and grey. Inside, we got a roaring log fire going and we settled down to watch a surprise airing from Fox TV of the Barnsley v Man Utd. F.A. Cup replay. Watching the game, and looking at the close-up's of some of the faces of the Barnsley fans, it really made me think how vital the world of football needs Barnsley and similarly passionately supported teams. I am not a Barnsley fan to any great degree......I've been a (long-suffering) fan of Fulham for many years, and when my family moved to Gloucestershire I also followed Cheltenham Town.

However, Barnsley have always been part of my football consciousness. When Michael Parkinson mentioned Barnsley I paid attention. When cricket umpire Dickie Bird mentioned Barnsley, I paid attention. When the so-called comedians of the 1970's would joke *"....it was worse than watching Barnsley v Grimsby on a Wednesday night with the fish and chip shops closed "*, I listened. Fulham have had their share of celebrity fans, and jokes against the team. Years before George Best actually signed for Fulham, the common joke was, *" George Best has given up football......he's signed for Fulham!"* It was once said, that in London, everybody's second favourite team was Fulham. That seems to be true in the north of England. Football is about passion, romance, sweat, tears and joy. And in the last couple of years our eyes have seen all this in the form of Barnsley Football Club. It's been a tough game to follow in the United States, but following the success of World Cup 1994, TV coverage of English football has intensified.

Thankfully, having a computer at home has meant instant football access via the Internet. I remember how excited we were when we heard ESPN were going to cover Barnsley in their football TV schedule. Who cares about Man Utd., Liverpool, Arsenal etc. when you can watch a real team (not made up of millions of pounds) of guts and courage. Am I a Barnsley fan ? Looking back at these words.....YES !! I don't know half the players' names, but I've eagerly, unofficially, followed the team for years. Does this all make sense? I couldn't tell you, I'm still in the afterglow of watching the F.A Cup replay! Commentator Martin Tyler said during the game that a nationwide poll was taken, with the result that Barnsley was voted the happiest place to live in England....I'm still paying attention !

The first programme illustrated cost twopence (just over 1p), and consisted of 8 pages - representing good value for money. Thirteen years later, and a F.A.Cup one sheet programme was halved in price to a penny, the same cost as a similar programme for a War Cup game in 1944.

1921/22
Season

1934/35
Season

The glossy 40 plus page matchday magazine for the 1997/98 Premiership campaign set the buyer back to the tune of £1-80, which many consider still represents a good buy.

PROGRAMME PARADE

The following illustrations cover the changing face of Barnsley programmes over a time span of nearly 80 years, and highlights the change from black and white to colour, and changes in size from the small compact programme in 1961/62, to today's glossy magazine.

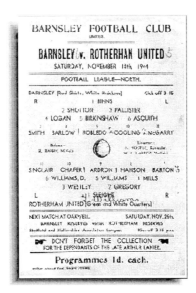

1944/45
Season

1945/46
Season

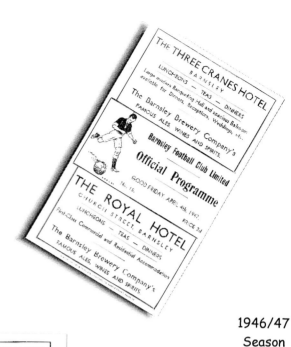

1946/47
Season

1947/48
Season

954/55
Season

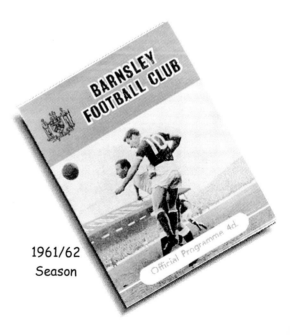

1961/62
Season

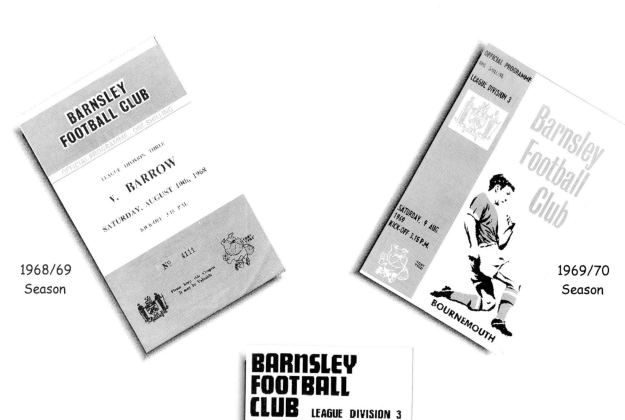

1968/69
Season

1969/70
Season

1970/71
Season

1972/73
Season

1973/74
Season

1975/76
Season

1977/78
Season

1978/79
Season

1979/80
Season

1981/82
Season

1982/83
Season

1983/84
Season

1984/85
Season

1985/86
Season

1986/87
Season

1987/88
Season

1988/89
Season

BARNSLEY V
BRIGHTON & HOVE ALBION
Saturday, August 26, 1989.
Kick-off 3.00p.m.

1989/90
Season

1990/91
Season

1991/92
Season

1992/93
Season

1993/94
Season

1995/96
Season

1996/97
Season

1997/98
Season

RECORDS & ACHIEVEMENTS

ATTENDANCES

From 1925 onwards, clubs were required to submit attendance figures to the Football League. Prior to this date, figures were obtained from contemporary press reports. Source of information *'Through the Turnstiles'* by Brian Tabner.

Season	Div.	Home League Gates Total	Ave.	Season	Div.	Home League Gates Total	Ave.	Season	Div.	Home League Gates Total	Ave.
1898/99	2	45050	2650	1931/32	2	131394	6257	1968/69	3	217563	9459
1899/00	2	42500	2500	1932/33	3N	107408	5115	1969/70	3	235384	10234
1900/01	2	52275	3075	1933/34	3N	204981	9761	1970/71	3	151582	6590
1901/02	2	39100	2300	1934/35	2	186249	8869	1971/72	3	122854	5341
1902/03	2	62050	3650	1935/36	2	207719	9891	1972/73	4	65816	2862
1903/04	2	69700	4100	1936/37	2	252821	12039	1973/74	4	97838	4254
1904/05	2	70550	4150	1937/38	2	247888	11804	1974/75	4	106851	4646
1905/06	2	93100	4900	1938/39	3N	289309	13777	1975/76	4	85280	3708
1906/07	2	90250	4750		(World War 2)			1976/77	4	127166	5529
1907/08	2	93575	4925	1946/47	2	403335	19206	1977/78	4	130148	5659
1908/09	2	107350	5650	1947/48	2	446502	21262	1978/79	4	254102	11048
1909/10	2	101175	5325	1948/49	2	405389	19304	1979/80	3	273472	11890
1910/11	2	88920	4680	1949/50	2	389004	18524	1980/81	3	294407	12800
1911/12	2	119035	6265	1950/51	2	402340	19159	1981/82	2	317050	15098
1912/13	2	127110	6690	1951/52	2	333214	15867	1982/83	2	259161	12341
1913/14	2	148200	7800	1952/53	2	238526	11358	1983/84	2	204498	9738
1914/15	2	106875	5625	1953/54	3N	218781	9512	1984/85	2	151725	7225
	(World War 1)			1954/55	3N	279679	12160	1985/86	2	127407	6067
1919/20	2	184590	8790	1955/56	2	309145	14721	1986/87	2	123270	5870
1920/21	2	238770	11370	1956/57	2	271209	12915	1987/88	2	169004	7682
1921/22	2	246960	11760	1957/58	2	293349	13969	1988/89	2	165945	7215
1922/23	2	223440	10640	1958/59	2	235444	11212	1989/90	2	207759	9033
1923/24	2	208845	9945	1959/60	3	145156	6311	1990/91	2	205551	8937
1924/25	2	187425	8925	1960/61	3	146257	6359	1991/92	2	172684	7508
1925/26	2	168916	8044	1961/62	3	140295	6100	1992/93	1	147545	6415
1926/27	2	178580	8504	1962/63	3	161488	7021	1993/94	1	175030	7610
1927/28	2	175393	8352	1963/64	3	149008	6479	1994/95	1	149707	6509
1928/29	2	164776	7846	1964/65	3	98297	4274	1995/96	1	185978	8086
1929/30	2	145346	6921	1965/66	4	103727	4510	1996/97	1	261188	11356
1930/31	2	144060	6860	1966/67	4	126983	5521	1997/98	P	350526	18449
				1967/68	4	248804	10818				

Highest ever attendance:	77747	-	23/4/1910 v Newcastle United (at Crystal Palace - FA Cup Final)
Highest ever League attendance:	64757	-	26/3/1948 away v Newcastle United (Division 2)
Highest ever League Cup attendance:	33707	-	12/1/1982 away v Liverpool (5th round)
Lowest home attendance:	500 (est)	-	23/4/1899 v Woolwich Arsenal (Division 2)
	1451	-	12/12/1932 v Crewe Alexandra (Division 3 N)
Lowest home FA Cup attendance:	2000 (est)	-	10/12/1904 v Burslem Port Vale (6th Q round)
	2876	-	4/11/1961 v West Auckland Town (2nd round)
Lowest home League Cup attendance:	1977	-	9/10/1961 v Workington (2nd round)
Highest home attendance:	40255	-	15/2/1936 v Stoke City (FA Cup 5th round)
Highest home League attendance:	35308	-	9/10/1948 v Sheffield Wednesday (Division 2)
Highest home League Cup attendance:	33792	-	2/12/1981 v Manchester City (4th round)

Highest home attendances by progression:

League				FA Cup				FL Cup			
1500 (est)	Gainsborough Trin.	22/10/1898		4000 (est)	Doncaster Rovers	3/11/00		4489	Southport	13/9/61	
4000 (est)	Manchester City	5/11/1898		7000 (est)	Lincoln City	7/2/03		5130	Hartlepools United	13/9/62	
5000 (est)	Sheffield Wednesday	24/3/00		10000 (est)	Nottingham Forest	17/1/06		5408	Grimsby Town	25/9/62	
5500 (est)	Manchester City	14/4/03		10266	Portsmouth	2/2/07		10335	Luton Town	16/10/62	
6000 (est)	Woolwich Arsenal	31/10/03		13077	Bury	23/2/07		11946	Doncaster Rovers	7/9/65	
8000 (est)	Bolton Wanderers	24/4/05		13781	Woolwich Arsenal	9/3/07		15898	West Ham United	4/9/79	
9000 (est)	Oldham Athletic	9/4/09		13939	Blackpool	20/1/10		19534	Brighton & Hove Alb.	10/11/81	
10000 (est)	Derby County	28/12/09		18636	West Bromwich Alb.	19/2/10		33792	Manchester City	2/12/81	
12000 (est)	Bristol City	25/12/11		23574	Queen's Park Rangers	5/3/10					
13000 (est)	Notts County	4/4/14		24987	Bradford City	9/3/12					
21000 (est)	Huddersfield Town	3/4/20		30800	Blackburn Rovers	1/2/13					
28124	Sheffield Wednesday	13/3/26		36881	Preston North End	18/2/22		(est) = estimated attendance			
28219	Birmingham City	14/9/46		40255	Stoke City	15/2/36					
34262	Newcastle United	28/9/46									
35308	Sheffield Wednesday	9/10/48									

HIGHEST/LOWEST LEAGUE ATTENDANCES
PER SEASON

Season	Highest		Lowest	Season	Highest		Lowest
1925/26	28124	Sheffield Wed.	1916	Stoke City	1965/66	13358	Doncaster Rovers 1577 Wrexham
1926/27	23599	Middlesbrough	2290	South Shields	1966/67	11192	Bradford City 2188 Luton Town
1927/28	17252	Manchester City	4516	Grimsby Town	1967/68	15913	Port Vale 4663 Rochdale
1928/29	11793	Stoke City	3688	Nottingham F.	1968/69	14160	Swindon Town 5631 Torquay Utd.
1929/30	15001	Oldham Athletic	2303	Stoke City	1969/70	17395	Doncaster Rovers 5842 Torquay Utd.
1930/31	16039	Everton	3657	Preston N. E.	1970/71	14563	Rotherham Utd. 2975 Reading
1931/32	9556	Bradford City	4015	Bristol City	1971/72	8632	Aston Villa 2185 Wrexham
1932/33	9138	Hartlepools Utd.	**1451**	**Crewe Alex.**	1972/73	5900	Mansfield Town 1638 Exeter City
1933/34	26366	Stockport County	4111	New Brighton	1973/74	8511	Chester 2274 Newport C.
1934/35	14511	Newcastle United	2992	Fulham	1974/75	7810	Rotherham Utd. 2666 Northampton T.
1935/36	20957	Manchester Utd.	4846	Bury	1975/76	8697	Lincoln City 2353 Torquay Utd.
1936/37	22760	Newcastle United	7086	Burnley	1976/77	10180	Doncaster Rovers 2531 Rochdale
1937/38	16820	Sheffield United	5817	Plymouth Arg.	1977/78	8797	Swansea City 2642 Wimbledon
1938/39	21569	Southport	5234	Lincoln City	1978/79	21261	Grimsby Town 5828 Halifax Town
1946/47	34262	Newcastle United 11109		West Ham Utd.	1979/80	22360	Sheffield Wed. 8567 Blackpool
1947/48	33131	Sheffield Wed.	14979	Cardiff City	1980/81	25935	Rotherham Utd. 8693 Millwall
1948/49	**35308**	**Sheffield Wed.**	12068	Leicester City	1981/82	28870	Sheffield Wed. 9287 Charlton Ath.
1949/50	27017	Leeds United	4438	Plymouth Arg.	1982/83	23275	Sheffield Wed. 6457 Charlton Ath.
1950/51	33867	Doncaster Rovers	8371	Swansea T.	1983/84	20322	Sheffield Wed. 4672 Carlisle Utd.
1951/52	29795	Sheffield Wed.	8003	Everton	1984/85	16199	Leeds United 3053 Wimbledon
1952/53	28789	Huddersfield T.	3204	Fulham	1985/86	9410	Sunderland 3827 Middlesbrough
1953/54	12960	Gateshead	5860	Tranmere R.	1986/87	8564	Huddersfield T. 4163 Plymouth Arg.
1954/55	18929	Bradford City	6192	Workington	1987/88	13240	Middlesbrough 4396 Reading
1955/56	22067	Port Vale	8432	West Ham Utd.	1988/89	12498	Brighton & H.A. 4937 Bournemouth
1956/57	21189	Sheffield United	7652	Notts County	1989/90	16629	Sheffield United 5524 Portsmouth
1957/58	21787	Derby County	8801	Leyton Orient	1990/91	23079	Sheffield Wed. 4921 Portsmouth
1958/59	23184	Sheffield Wed.	4976	Swansea T.	1991/92	13337	Blackburn R. 5328 Southend Utd.
1959/60	13677	Halifax Town	3583	Bury	1992/93	13263	Newcastle Utd. 3855 Southend Utd.
1960/61	15461	Bradford City	3210	Colchester Utd.	1993/94	13270	Nottingham F. 4380 Watford
1961/62	10818	Bournemouth	2371	Northampton T.	1994/95	11782	Middlesbrough 3659 Southend Utd.
1962/63	9645	Peterborough Utd. 3807		Crystal Palace	1995/96	13669	Leicester City 5440 Reading
1963/64	17186	Wrexham	3655	Shrewsbury T.	1996/97	18605	Bradford City 6337 Oxford United
1964/65	6940	Hull City	2297	Workington	1997/98	18694	Manchester Utd. 17172 Wimbledon

Note: Two attendances shown in bold type are records (highest and lowest authenticated)

CHAIRMEN

Fred Senior	1898 - 1901
John Charlesworth	1901 - 1903
Tom Fisher	1903 - 1908
John Rose	July 1908 - July 1933
Walter Donald	July 1933 - December 1933
Joe Richards	January 1934 - July 1936
George Tomlinson	July 1936 to August 1948
Joe Richards	August 1948 - November 1966
Sid Edmundson	November 1966 to December 1966 (5 days - died whilst in office)
Arthur Raynor	December 1966 to September 1967
Ernest Dennis	September 1967 to July 1979 (died whilst in office)
Arthur Raynor	July 1979 to September 1979
Geoff Buckle	September 1979 - November 1989
John Dennis	November 1989 to date

EVERPRESENTS.

Joe Greaves	1899/00	Gordon Pallister	1949/50	Bobby Doyle	1975/76
Don Lees	1899/00	Harry Hough	1953/54	Peter Springett	1976/77
Arthur Seymour	1901/02	Joe Thomas	1953/54	Barry Murphy	1976/77
Arnold Oxspring	1902/03	Bobby Brown	1953/54	Brian Joicey	1976/77
Bob Hewitson	1903/04	Harry Hough	1954/55	Kenny Brown	1976/77
Arnold Oxspring	1904/05	Harry May	1954/55	John Saunders	1977/78
Arnold Oxspring	1905/06	Harry Hough	1955/56	Mick McCarthy	1977/78
Dickie Downs	1908/09	Don Leeson	1959/60	John Collins	1978/79
Dickie Downs	1910/11	Frank Beaumont	1959/60	John Saunders	1978/79
George Utley	1910/11	Billy Houghton	1961/62	Mick McCarthy	1978/79
Jack Cooper	1912/13	Alan Hopper	1963/64	Bobby Horn	1981/82
George Lillycrop	1912/13	Eric Winstanley	1963/64	Phil Chambers	1981/82
Jack Cooper	1913/14	Billy Houghton	1963/64	Ian Banks	1981/82*
Jack Bethune	1913/14	Dick Hewitt	1965/66	Mick McCarthy	1981/82
Frank Barson	1913/14	Bob Parker	1966/67	Clive Baker	1985/86
Jack Cooper	1914/15	Barry Murphy	1967/68	Clive Baker	1987/88
George Donkin	1920/21	Pat Howard	1967/68	Steve Lowndes	1987/88*
Charlie Baines	1922/23	Barry Murphy	1968/69	Clive Baker	1988/89
Ernie Hine	1922/23	Barry Murphy	1969/70	Steve Agnew	1989/90
Ernie Hine	1924/25	Brian Arblaster	1970/71	Clive Baker	1990/91
Eric Brook	1926/27	Pat Howard	1970/71	Gary Fleming	1992/93
Cyril Dixon	1927/28	David Booth	1970/71*	Neil Redfearn	1992/93
Cyril Dixon	1930/31	Barry Murphy	1971/72	Gary Fleming	1993/94
Tom Ellis	1933/34	Phil Chambers	1972/73	Neil Redfearn	1993/94
Bob Shotton	1933/34	Paddy Greenwood	1972/73	Gary Fleming	1994/95
Ernie Whitworth	1933/34	Phil Chambers	1973/74	Nicky Eaden	1995/96
Harold Andrews	1933/34	Ally Millar	1973/74	David Watson	1996/97
Gavin Smith	1946/47	Phil Chambers	1974/75	Nicky Eaden	1996/97
George Robledo	1946/47	Peter Springett	1975/76	* includes substitute appearances

GOALSCORERS
LEADING GOALSCORERS - SEASON BY SEASON

Season	Leading scorer	Lge.	FAC	L.Cup	Total
1898/99	Davis H	15	3		18
1899/00	Jones R	8			8
1900/01	Swann A	18	1		19
1901/02	Lees W	10			10
	McCairns T	9	1		10
1902/03	Green B.H.	16			16
1903/04	Hellewell Alec	7			7
1904/05	Jones A	11	1		12
1905/06	Wall G	14	1		15
1906/07	Reeves G	13			13
	Hellewell Alec	11	2		13
1907/08	Reeves G	14			14
1908/09	Lillycrop G.B.	18	1		19
1909/10	Lillycrop G.B.	23	2		25
1910/11	Tufnell H	14			14
1911/12	Lillycrop G.B.	9	6		15
1912/13	Lillycrop G.B.	22	2		24
1913/14	Moore J	13			13
1914/15	Tufnell H	9			9
1919/20	Halliwell J.A.	20			20
1920/21	Wainscoat W.R.	13			13
1921/22	Fletcher B	17	4		21
1922/23	Hine E.W.	24	1		25
1923/24	Hine E.W.	19			19
1924/25	Hine E.W.	15			15
1925/26	Hine E.W.	12			12
1926/27	Eaton F	21	2		23
1927/28	Eaton F	15			15
1928/29	Eaton F	15			15
1929/30	Wallbanks John	12			12
1930/31	Wallbanks John	11			11
	Curran J	10	1		11
	Harvey W.A.	9	2		11
1931/32	Wallbanks John	22			22
1932/33	Wallbanks John	20			20
1933/34	Blight A.B.	31			31
1934/35	Chivers F.C.	12			12
1935/36	Hine E.W.	14	5		19
1936/37	Hine E.W.	13			13
1937/38	Hunt D.A.	14	1		15
1938/39	Asquith B	28			28
1946/47	Robledo G.O.	23			23
1947/48	Griffiths J.S.	9			9
	Smith G	9			9
	Robledo G.O.	9			9
1948/49	Baxter J.C.	15			15
1949/50	Wright A.M.	17	1		18
1950/51	McCormack J.C.	33	1		34
1951/52	McMorran E.J.	15	1		16
1952/53	Taylor T	19	2		21

Season	Leading scorer	Lge.	FAC	L.Cup	Total
1953/54	Brown R	24	1		25
1954/55	Chappell L	21			21
1955/56	Brown R	11	2		13
1956/57	Kaye A	15	3		18
1957/58	Chappell L	19			19
1958/59	Chappell L	17			17
1959/60	Lunn J	13			13
1960/61	Bartlett F	17	4	1	22
1961/62	Oliver K	14	2	4	20
1962/63	Leighton A	22	1	1	24
1963/64	Leighton A	24	1	2	27
1964/65	Leighton A	13			13
1965/66	Kerr G.A.M.	17	2	2	21
1966/67	Thomas B.E.	10	3		13
1967/68	Evans J.D.	14			14
1968/69	Winstanley E	12	1	1	14
1969/70	Evans J.D.	15	1		16
1970/71	Lea L	9	1		10
1971/72	Seal J	12	1		13
1972/73	Lea L	12	1		13
1973/74	Butler M.A.	21	1		22
1974/75	Butler M.A.	19			19
1975/76	Peachy J.M.	10			10
	Butler M.A.	8	1	1	10
1976/77	Joicey B	26	3		29
1977/78	Joicey B	14			14
1978/79	Bell D.M.	18	1		19
1979/80	Glavin R.M.	20	2	1	23
1980/81	Glavin R.M.	18	1	5	24
1981/82	Banks I.F.	15			15
	Aylott T.K.C.	11		4	15
1982/83	Glavin R.M.	17	1	3	21
1983/84	Geddis D	14			14
1984/85	Owen G	14	4		18
1985/86	Walsh I.P.	15			15
1986/87	Gray S	11		2	13
1987/88	Lowndes S.R.	9		1	10
1988/89	Currie D.N.	16	3	1	20
1989/90	Agnew S.M.	8			8
	Currie D.N.	7	1		8
1990/91	Rammell A.V.	12			12
	Saville A.V.	12			12
1991/92	Rammell A.V.	8			8
1992/93	Biggins W	14			14
1993/94	Payton A.P.	12	1		13
1994/95	Liddell A.M.	13			13
	Redfearn N.D.	11		2	13
1995/96	Payton A.P.	17		3	20
1996/97	Redfearn N.D.	17	1	1	19
1997/98	Redfearn N.D.	10	2	2	14

HAT TRICKS..... AND MORE

Football League

Dick Jones	3	14/1/1899	H	Small Heath		Tommy Lumley	3	05/09/53	H	Chesterfield
Harry Davis	4	28/1/1899	H	Loughborough		Bobby Brown	4	23/01/54	H	Darlington
Don Lees	3	24/02/00	H	Gainsborough Trin.		Lol Chappell	3	06/03/54	A	Carlisle United
Benny Green	3	01/01/03	H	Burnley		Lol Chappell	3	16/10/54	H	Tranmere Rovers
Aaron Jones	4	28/01/05	H	Burton United		Frank Bartlett	3	06/11/54	A	Gateshead
George Reeves	3	28/09/07	H	Fulham		Lol Chappell	3	13/11/54	H	Darlington
George Reeves	3	16/11/07	H	Wolverhampton W.		Lol Chappell	3	27/11/54	H	Crewe Alexandra
Harry Kay	3	04/01/08	H	Hull City		Frank Bartlett	3	12/02/55	H	Workington
George Lillycrop	3	03/10/08	H	Blackpool		Bobby Brown	3	04/05/55	H	Chester
George Lillycrop	3	13/02/09	H	Chesterfield		Lol Chappell	3	31/08/57	A	Derby County
Ernie Gadsby	3	30/10/09	H	Wolverhampton W.		Arthur Kaye	3	04/09/57	H	Ipswich Town
George Lillycrop	3	25/03/11	H	Bradford Park Ave.		Lol Chappell	4	27/08/58	H	Bristol City
George Lillycrop	3	15/02/13	H	Blackpool		Malcolm Graham	4	10/09/58	H	Charlton Athletic
Jimmy Moore	3	07/02/14	H	Grimsby Town		Frank Bartlett	3	21/01/61	H	Notts County
Joe Halliwell	3	01/09/19	H	West Ham United		Ollie Hopkins	3	13/03/61	A	Newport County
Joe Halliwell	3	18/10/19	H	Lincoln City		Ken Oliver	3	11/11/61	H	Bristol City
Joe Halliwell	3	22/11/19	H	Wolverhampton W.		Eddie O'Hara	3	27/11/62	H	Bristol Rovers
Russell Wainscoat	3	06/03/20	H	Fulham		Johnny Byrne	3	31/03/64	H	Peterborough United
Jimmy Spoors	3	26/03/21	A	Birmingham		Eric Winstanley	3	22/04/69	H	Watford
Joe Halliwell	3	10/03/23	H	South Shields		Johnny Evans	3	21/02/70	H	Fulham
Ernie Hine	3	31/03/23	H	Coventry City		Mick Butler	3	14/04/73	A	Hartlepool
Joe Halliwell	3	27/10/23	H	Leicester City		Mick Butler	3	01/01/74	H	Scunthorpe United
Ernie Hine	3	02/02/24	H	Port Vale		Peter Price	3	04/01/75	H	Southport
Ernie Hine	3	26/04/24	H	Crystal Palace		Mick Butler	3	15/03/75	A	Newport County
Sam Kennedy	3	30/10/26	H	Notts County		Mick Butler	3	22/03/75	H	Rochdale
Jimmy Curran	3	28/12/26	H	Fulham		John Peachey	3	07/04/76	A	Workington
Jimmy Curran	3	22/01/27	H	Blackpool		John Peachey	3	06/11/76	H	Scunthorpe United
Frank Eaton	3	19/02/27	H	Clapton Orient		Brian Joicey	3	19/08/78	H	Halifax Town
Frank Eaton	5	09/04/27	H	South Shields		Allan Clarke	3	26/12/78	H	Port Vale
Brough Fletcher	3	07/05/27	H	Southampton		Tommy Graham	3	13/03/79	H	Scunthorpe United
Frank Eaton	4	28/01/28	H	Fulham		Trevor Aylott	3	11/11/80	H	Hull City
John Wallbanks	3	26/09/31	A	Notts County		Ronnie Glavin	3	02/05/81	H	Newport County
John Wallbanks	3	15/10/32	H	Mansfield Town		Ian Banks	3	14/11/81	A	Rotherham United
Harold Andrews	3	12/12/32	H	Crewe Alexandra		David Geddis	3	29/09/84	H	Wolverhampton W.
John Wallbanks	3	12/12/32	H	Crewe Alexandra		Ron Futcher	3	02/03/85	A	Charlton Athletic
Peter Cunningham	5	04/02/33	H	Darlington		Gordon Owen	3	02/04/85	H	Oxford United
Teddy Ashton	3	01/01/34	H	Rotherham United		Ian Chandler	3	01/01/87	A	Hull City
Abe Blight	4	03/02/34	A	Accrington Stanley		David Currie	4	26/11/88	H	Bournemouth
Abe Blight	3	10/02/34	H	Chesterfield		Gareth Williams	3	17/04/93	H	Southend United
Teddy Ashton	3	02/04/34	H	Mansfield Town		Andy Payton	3	26/12/94	H	Grimsby Town
Harold Andrews	3	07/04/34	A	Carlisle United		John Hendrie	3	28/01/97	A	Grimsby Town
Ernie Hine	3	14/12/35	H	Leicester City		**F.A.Cup**				
Fred Fisher	4	04/03/36	H	Bradford Park Ave.		Harry Davis	3	3/11/1898	H	Gainsborough Trin.
Beaumont Asquith	5	12/11/38	H	Darlington		Brough Fletcher	3	08/01/27	H	Crewe Alexandra
Johnny Lang	3	11/02/39	H	Hull City		Brian Joicey	3	20/11/76	H	Boston United
George Robledo	3	31/08/46	H	Nottingham Forest		Andy Rammell	3	24/01/93	H	West Ham United
Walter Bennett	3	27/09/47	A	Brentford		**F.L.Cup**				
Steve Griffiths	3	14/01/50	H	Grimsby Town		Ken Oliver	3	13/09/61	H	Southport
Alex Wright	3	25/02/50	A	Bradford Park Ave.		Ronnie Glavin	3	02/09/80	H	Mansfield Town
Jimmy Baxter	3	29/04/50	H	Plymouth Argyle		Andy Payton	3	03/10/95	H	Huddersfield Town
Cecil McCormack	5	09/09/50	H	Luton Town		**Full Members Cup**				
Cecil McCormack	3	07/10/50	H	Grimsby Town		Ian Banks	3	21/11/90	A	West Bromwich Alb.
Tommy Taylor	3	04/11/50	H	Queen's Park Rangers						

INTERNATIONAL REPRESENTATIVE APPEARANCES (Whilst with Barnsley)

FULL:

Darren Barnard	Wales	Steve Lowndes	Wales
Danny Blanchflower	Northern Ireland	Clint Marcelle	Trinidad & Tobago
Charlie Dowdall	Republic of Ireland	Eddie McMorran	Northern Ireland
Gary Fleming	Northern Ireland	Nai Richards	Wales
Georgi Hristov	Macedonia	Gerry Taggart	Northern Ireland
Johnny Kelly	Scotland	Eric Tinkler	South Africa
Pat Kelly	Northern Ireland	George Utley	England
Ales Krizan	Slovenia		

'B' INTERNATIONAL:

Johnny McCann   Scotland

FOOTBALL LEAGUE:

Martin Bullock   Arthur Kaye   Gordon Pallister
Dickie Downs   Adie Moses   George Utley

Martin Bullock	England	Adie Moses	England	Carl Tiler	England
Andy Liddell	Scotland			David Watson	England

UNDER 23 INTERNATIONAL:

Arthur Kaye	England	Gerry Taggart	Northern Ireland

WARTIME INTERNATIONAL:

Bernard Harper   England

REPRESENTATIVE PLAYERS WHO NEVER MADE A COMPETITIVE FIRST TEAM APPEARANCE FOR BARNSLEY

Terry Connelly   England Youth   M. Fidler   England Youth

ADDITIONAL REPRESENTATIVE HONOURS

Tommy Gale   FA tour to Canada 1926

YOUTH INTERNATIONALS:

David Barber	England	Billy Houghton	England
Frank Beaumont	England	Simon Jeffels	England
Eric Brookes	England	Andy Kiwomya	England
Terry Craven	England	David Watson	England
David Hirst	England	Eric Winstaniey	England

MANAGERS

Arthur Fairclough	1899 (close season) - April 1901	John McSeveney	September 1971 - October 1972
John McCartney	April 1901 - 1904 (close season)	Johnny Steele (Caretaker)	Oct. 1972 - April 1973
Arthur Fairclough	1904 (close season) -1912 (close season)	Jim Iley	April 1973 - April 1978
John Hastie	1912 (close season) - April 1914	Allan Clarke	May 1978 - September 1980
Harry 'Percy' Lewis	April 1914 - April 1919	Norman Hunter	September 1980 - February 1984
Peter Sant	April 1919 - 1926 (close season)	Bobby Collins	February 1984 - June 1985
John Commins	1926 (close season) - May 1928	Allan Clarke	June 1985 - November 1989
Arthur Fairclough	May 1928 - May 1930	Eric Winstanley (Caretaker)	Nov. 1989 - Dec. 1989
Brough Fletcher	May 1930 - February 1937	Mel Machin	December 1989 - May 1993
Angus Seed	Feb.1937-Feb.1953 (died whilst in office)	Viv Anderson	June 1993 - June1994
Tim Ward	March 1953 - February 1960	Danny Wilson	June 1994 - July 1998
Johnny Steele	March 1960 - September 1971	John Hendrie	July 1998 to date

PLAYERS RECORDS - GAMES PLAYED

MOST LEAGUE GAMES

Barry Murphy	512	Harry Hough	346	Charlie Baines	322
Phil Chambers	442	Bobby Wood	338	Joe Halliwell	312
Eric Winstanley	410	Joe Joyce	334	Brough Fletcher	311
		Eric Brookes	326		

MOST LEAGUE & CUP GAMES

Barry Murphy	567	Charlie Baines	339	Mick McCarthy	314
Phil Chambers	494	Neil Redfearn	338	Tommy Gale	308
Eric Winstanley	461	Clive Baker	337	Ian Banks	307
Joe Joyce	388	Brough Fletcher	332	Ernie Hine	307
Eric Brookes	378	Joe Halliwell	328	Dickie Downs	306
Bobby Wood	373	Frank Bartlett	325	Teddy Ashton	303
Harry Hough	364	Ally Millar	324	Kenny Brown	303

MOST FA CUP GAMES

Eric Brookes	34	Joe Greaves	28	Wilf Bartrop	26
Eric Winstanley	33	George Lillycrop	28	Barry Murphy	26
Dickie Downs	32	Bobby Wood	28	George Utley	26
Harry Tufnell	29	Bob Glendenning	27		

MOST LEAGUE CUP GAMES

Phil Chambers	29	Joe Joyce	27	Ian Banks	25
Barry Murphy	29	Mick McCarthy	26	Ronnie Glavin	23

PLAYERS RECORDS - GOALS SCORED

MOST LEAGUE GOALS

Ernie Hine	124	Neil Redfearn	71	Tony Leighton	59
Lol Chappell	94	Teddy Ashton	70	Jimmy Baxter	57
George Lillycrop	92	Frank Bartlett	68	Mick Butler	57
Joe Halliwell	83	John Wallbanks	65	Bobby Brown	55
Ronnie Glavin	73	Harry Tufnell	60	Johnny Evans	54
Brough Fletcher	72	Frank Eaton	59	Arthur Kaye	54
Jimmy Curran	71			Russell Wainscoat	54

Ernie Hine	131	Neil Redfearn	83	Tony Leighton	64	Bobby Brown	58
George Lillycrop	104	Frank Bartlett	80	Frank Eaton	61	Russell Wainscoat	56
Lol Chappell	95	Teddy Ashton	73	Mick Butler	60	Ken Oliver	54
Ronnie Glavin	92	Jimmy Curran	73	Arthur Kaye	60	George Kerr	52
Brough Fletcher	83	Harry Tufnell	70	Jimmy Baxter	59	Ian Banks	51
Joe Halliwell	83	John Wallbanks	65	Johnny Evans	59	Don Lees	50
						Andy Rammell	50

MOST FA CUP GOALS

George Lillycrop	12	Brough Fletcher	11	George Kerr	8	Ernie Hine	7
Frank Bartlett	11	Harry Tufnell	10	Don Lees	8	Ken Oliver	7

MOST LEAGUE CUP GOALS

Ronnie Glavin	15	Neil Redfearn	6	George Kerr	4
Ken Oliver	9	Trevor Aylott	4	Derrick Parker	4

RECORDS - GENERAL
PLAYERS
Most Appearances

1. Barry Murphy 567 (512 League, 26 FA Cup, 29 FL Cup)   2. Phil Chambers 494 (442+23+29)   3.Eric Winstanley 461 (410+33+18)

Most consecutive FA Cup appearances	Dickie Downs 32 - 16/1/1909 to 31/1/1920
Most consecutive League Cup appearances	Barry Murphy 23 - 22/8/1967 to 23/8/1977
Most consecutive League appearances	Barry Murphy 165 - 18/3/1967 to 24/10/1970
Most consecutive League and Cup appearances	Barry Murphy 182 - 18/3/1967 to 24/10/1970
Most consecutive games goals scored	Abe Blight 7 - 10/3/1934 to 7/4/1934
Most Goals	Ernie Hine 131 (124 League, 7 FA Cup) George Lillycrop 104 (92+12)
Most League Goals in a Season	Cecil McCormack 33 (1950/51)
Most International Appearances	Gerry Taggart (Northern Ireland) 35
Youngest player	Alan Ogley - 16 years 226 days away v Bristol R. (Division 3) 18/9/1962
Oldest player	Tommy Thorpe - 40 years 310 days away v Stoke (Division 2) 25/3/1922

THE CLUB

FA Cup Winners: 1911/12   Champions Division 3 (North) 1933/34, 1938/39, 1954/55

Best League performance: 2nd in Division 1, 1996/97   Best League Cup performance: 5th Round, 1981/82

Most League points in a season: 67, Division 3(N), 1938/39 (win 2 pts.) 80; Division 1, 1996/97 (win 3 pts.)

Least League points in a season: 18, Division 2, 1952/53

Most League goals in a season: 118, Division 3 (N), 1933/34   Least League goals in a season 32, Division 3, 1971/72

Most League goals conceded in a season   108, Division 2, 1952/53   Least League goals conceded in a season 34, Division 3(N), 1938/39

Most League wins in a season 30, Division 3(N), 1938/39, Division 3(N), 1954/55   Least League wins in a season 5, Division 2, 1952/53

Most League draws in a season   18, Division 3, 1971/72, Division 1, 1995/96   Least League draws in a season 3, Division 2, 1914/15

Most League losses in a season   29, Division 2, 1952/53   Least League losses in a season 5, Division 3(N), 1938/39

Best League run undefeated	21, from 1/1/1934 to 5/5/1934
Undefeated League games - home	36, from 4/2/1933 to 24/11/1934
Undefeated League games - away	15, from 27/12/1938 to 5/10/1946
Best run of League wins	10, from 5/3/1955 to 23/4/1955
Best run of home League wins	12, from 3/10/1914 to 8/3/1915
Longest run of League draws	7, from 28/3/1911 to 22/4/1911
Longest run without a League win	26, from 13/12/1952 to 26/8/1953
Most consecutive League defeats	9, from 14/3/1953 to 25/4/1953
Best run of away League wins	5, from 27/12/1938 to 18/2/1939
Longest run without a home League win	11, from 6/12/1952 to 29/8/1953
Longest run without an away League win	29, from 14/3/1908 to 23/10/1909
Most consecutive League games, goals scored	44, from 2/10/1926 to 8/10/1927
Most consecutive League games, no goals scored	6, from 7/10/1899 to 2/12/1899
	6, from 27/11/1971 to 7/1/1972
Best start to a League season	5 wins: Division 4, 1978/79, Division 1, 1996/97
	10 matches without defeat (6 wins 4 draws) Division 2, 1946/47
Worst start to a League season	6 losses, Division 2, 1986/87
	9 matches without a win (3 losses 6 draws) Division 2, 1920/21

Best League home win	9-0 v. Loughborough 28/1/1899
Biggest League home defeat	0-6 v. Chelsea 24/8/1997
Best League away win	9-0 v. Accrington Stanley 3/2/1934
Biggest League away defeat	0-9 v. Notts County 19/11/1927
Best FA Cup win	8-0 v. Leeds AFC 3/11/1894
Biggest FA Cup defeat	1-8 v. Derby County 30/1/1897
Best League Cup win	6-0 v. Peterborough United 15/9/1981
Biggest League Cup defeat	1-4 v. Middlesbrough 22/8/1967.
	1-4 v. Chesterfield 13/8/1977

Most players used in one League season, 31: 1936/37 and 1951/52   Least players used in one League season 18: 1913/14

INTRODUCTION TO THE STATISTICS PAGES

The season by season grid shows the results of games in the Football League, the F.A. Cup, the Football League Cup (and subsequent Sponsors names), and other first team competitions. Some line-ups are known for the pre-League seasons (1894/95 season and earlier), but have been omitted due to space considerations.

'Home' games are identified by the opponents name in upper case, 'away' games by the use of lower case. Barnsley's score is always given first. Attendances for League games are taken from the official Football League records since 1925/26; estimated attendances based on newspaper reports have been used, where traced, for earlier seasons.

Substitutes are identified by the numbers 12, 13 and 14, 12 being the first or only substitute, 13 the second and 14 the third. Players that have been replaced are identified as follows:
 * substituted by No. 12...... " substituted by No. 13...... + substituted by No. 14.

✠✠✠✠✠✠✠✠✠✠✠✠✠✠✠✠✠✠✠✠✠✠✠✠✠✠✠✠✠✠✠✠✠✠✠

The main player database contains every player who made a League appearance: Date and place of birth are shown, where known, and the year of death, again, where known.

The next two columns 'seasons played', act as an index to the season by season grids. The years shown are the 'first year' of the season, i.e., 1981 refers to season 1981/82. The two columns show the season in which the player made his debut, and the final season he played. However, if only played in one season, the second column is blank. Note that some players also made F.A. Cup appearances before 1898 and in 1945/46. If a player also made a League appearance, his F.A. Cup appearances and goals from these seasons are included in the list, but the 'first/last League season' columns remain unchanged.

Previous and next clubs columns show where a player was transferred from, and the club moved to. Non-League club information is included where known.

Note that any changes i.e. transfers in/out after the 30th June, 1998, are not included.

The appearance columns have separate totals for the League, F.A. Cup, Football League Cup and the Full Members' Cup (the latter two played under a variety of sponsors' names). 'Goals scored' are also shown under the four headings.

If a player has had more than one spell at the Club, appearances and goals for each spell are shown separately.

Players who appeared in the F.A.Cup or League Cup only, can be found at the end of the 'Who's Who' section.

The World War I player database includes all League and Supplementary League matches.
The World War II player database includes all League and League Cup matches plus the three games played in the abandoned 1939/40 season. The 1945/46 F.A. Cup matches are not included, and will be found in the main player database.

In the 'Previous club' column, 'guest', following the club name, indicates the player was appearing as a guest for Barnsley (which was a common practice for all clubs during the two World Wars).

WHO'S WHO: FOOTBALL LEAGUE PLAYERS

Player			D.O.B	Place of Birth	Died	Season First	Season Last	Previous Club	Next Club	Appearances Lge	FAC	FLC	Oth	Goals Lge	FAC	FLC	Oth
Adamson	KB	Keith	03/07/45	Houghton-le-Spring		1965	1966	Tow Low Town	Scarborough	7	0	0	0	0	0	0	0
Adcock	W			Cudworth		1900		Ecclesfield	Grimsby Town	2	0	0	0	0	0	0	0
Addy	GW	George	27/04/1891	Carlton, Yorkshire	1971	1919		Carlton Victoria	Norwich City	1	0	0	0	0	0	0	0
Addy	M	Mike	20/02/43	Knottingley		1964	1966	Leeds United	Corby Town	51	2	1	0	5	0	0	0
Adey	W	Wilf	6/07/09	Featherstone	1975	1934	1936	Sheffield Utd.	Carlisle Utd.	66	2	0	0	0	0	0	0
Agnew	SM	Steve	09/11/65	Shipley		1983	1990	Apprentice	Blackburn Rovers	194	20	13	7	29	4	3	0
Ainscow	A	Alan	15/07/53	Bolton		1982		Everton (loan)	Everton	2	0	0	0	0	0	0	0
Airey	C	Carl	06/02/65	Wakefield		1982	1983	Apprentice	Darlington	38	1	1	0	5	0	0	0
Allan	J	John	26/09/31	Amble		1951	1952	Amble		11	0	0	0	0	0	0	0
Allen	F	Frank	05/05/01	Altofts	1989	1925	1927	Castleford Town	Bangor City	68	3	0	0	2	0	0	0
Anderson	E	Eric	12/07/31	Manchester		1957		Liverpool	Bournemouth	9	0	0	0	1	0	0	0
Anderson	VA	Viv	29/08/56	Nottingham		1993		Sheffield Wed.	Middlesbrough	20	0	2	0	3	0	0	0
Anderson	W	Bill	12/01/13	High Westwood	1986	1935		Sheffield Utd.		14	0	0	0	0	0	0	0
Anderson	WB	Bill	28/03/35	Sunderland		1955		Silksworth Juniors	Hartlepools Utd.	6	0	0	0	0	0	0	0
Andrews	H	Harold	13/08/03	Lincoln	1988	1932	1934	Notts County	Luton Town	110	5	0	1	42	2	0	0
Appleby	MW	Mattie	16/04/72	Middlesbrough		1996	to date	Darlington		50	3	5	0	0	0	0	0
Appleyard	GE	George	16/03/05	Rawmarsh		1923		Rawmarsh	Exeter City	4	0	0	0	2	0	0	0
Arblaster	BM	Brian	06/06/43	Kensington		1967	1973	Scunthorpe Utd.	Boston Utd	111	10	4	0	0	0	0	0
Archdeacon	OD	Owen	04/03/66	Greenock		1989	1995	Glasgow Celtic	Carlisle Utd.	233	15	16	10	22	2	2	4
Archer	R	Ron	03/09/33	Barnsley		1951	1955	Juniors	Worcester City	29	2	0	0	0	0	0	0
Archibald	RF	Bobby	06/11/1894	Strathaven	1966	1932		Stoke City		6	2	0	0	1	0	0	0
Armson	H	Herbert				1899		Ogden's F.C.(Liverpool)		13	2	0	0	2	0	0	0
Armstrong	JD	Jimmy	12/06/1899	Chester-le-Street		1921	1924	Chester-Le-Street	Bournemouth	59	6	0	0	0	0	0	0
Arthurs	G	George		Sheffield		1909	1910	Worksop Town	Rotherham County	19	0	0	0	2	0	0	0
Ashmore	RA	Dick	28/11/1892	Rotherham		1920		Bristol Rovers	Nottm. Forest	12	1	0	0	0	0	0	0
Ashton	E	Teddy	19/01/06	Kilnhurst	1978	1927	1936	Mexborough Town	Sheffield Utd.	289	13	0	1	70	3	0	0
Asquith	B	Beaumont	16/09/10	Painthorpe	1977	1934	1938	Painthorpe Albion	Manchester Utd.	105	5	0	0	40	1	0	0
						1946	1947	Manchester Utd.	Bradford City	40	3	0	0	5	1	0	0
Atkinson	JW	Josh	28/03/02	Blackpool	1983	1928	1929	Leeds United	Chester	61	2	0	0	2	0	0	0
Atterbury	S	Sep	18/10/1880	Allestree	1964	1899	1900	Loughborough Town	Wellingborough	34	3	0	0	1	0	0	0
Aylott	TKC	Trevor	26/11/57	Bermondsey		1979	1981	Chelsea	Millwall	96	9	10	0	26	4	4	0
						1985		Crystal Palace (loan)	Crystal Palace	9	0	0	0	0	0	0	0
Baines	CE	Charlie	09/02/1896	Ardsley	1954	1920	1930	Ardsley Athletic		322	17	0	0	5	1	0	0
Baines	RE	Reg	03/06/07	York	1974	1938		York City	Halifax Town	1	0	0	0	0	0	0	0
Baker	C	Chris	02/02/52	Maltby		1971				1	0	0	0	0	0	0	0
Baker	CE	Clive	14/03/59	North Walsham		1984	1990	Norwich City	Coventry City	291	23	15	8	0	0	0	0
Baker	LH	Len	18/11/1897	Sheffield	1979	1924	1928	Leeds United	Rochdale	78	1	0	0	1	0	0	0
Banks	IF	Ian	09/01/61	Mexborough		1978	1982	Apprentice	Leicester City	164	11	19	0	37	1	3	0
						1989	1991	West Bromwich Albion	Rotherham Utd	96	6	6	5	7	0	0	3
Bannister	E	Eddie	02/06/20	Leyland		1950		Leeds United		32	1	0	0	0	0	0	0
Barber	DE	David	06/12/39	Wombwell		1957	1960	Juniors	Preston NE	83	7	2	0	4	1	0	0
Barker	K	Keith	22/02/49	Stoke-on-Trent		1971		Cambridge United	Cambridge City	9	0	3	0	0	0	0	0
Barlow	H	Bert	22/07/16	Kilnhurst		1935	1937	Silverwood Colliery	Wolves	58	4	0	0	12	2	0	0
Barnard	D	Darren	30/11/71	Rinteln (Germany)		1997		Bristol City		35	5	3	0	2	2	0	0
Barnett	LH	Laurie	08/05/03	Bramley	1982	1924	1925	Gainsborough Trinity	Blackpool	28	2	0	0	0	0	0	0
Barnfather	P	Percy	17/12/1879	Newcastle	1951	1903		Wallsend Park Villa	New Brompton	27	1	0	0	3	0	0	0
Barrowclough	SJ	Stewart	29/10/51	Barnsley		1969		Apprentice	Newcastle United	9	1	0	0	0	0	0	0
						1980	1982	Bristol Rovers	Mansfield Town	52	2	8	0	1	0	1	0
Barson	F	Frank	10/04/1891	Grimesthorpe	1968	1911	1919	Cammell Laird FC	Aston Villa	91	3	0	0	0	0	0	0
Bartlett	F	Frank	08/11/30	Chester-le-Street		1952	1962	Blackhall Coll. Welfare	Halifax Town	297	23	5	0	68	11	1	0
Barton	DR	Roger	25/09/46	Jump		1966	1968	Lincoln City	Worcester City	54	6	2	0	3	0	0	0
Bartrop	W	Wilf	1889	Worksop	1918	1909	1913	Worksop Town	Liverpool	160	26	0	0	15	2	0	0
Bates	FG	Francis		Eckington	1947	1920		Beighton Rec.	Scunthorpe Utd.	7	1	0	0	0	0	0	0
Batty	W	Bill	04/06/05	South Bank	1974	1926	1928	Willington	Swindon Town	39	1	0	0	5	0	0	0
Batty	W	Billy	13/07/1886	Killamarsh		1922		Swindon Town		1	0	0	0	0	0	0	0
Baxter	AG	Arthur		Dundee	1944	1938		Dundee		6	0	0	0	2	0	0	0
Baxter	JC	Jimmy	08/11/25	Hill o' Beath	1994	1948	1951	Dunfermline Ath	Preston NE	222	13	0	0	54	2	0	0
						1959		Preston NE	Morecambe	26	2	0	0	3	0	0	0
Beaumont	F	Frank	22/12/39	Hoyland		1957	1961	Juniors	Bury	107	8	2	0	37	3	1	0
Beaumont	P	Percy	03/09/1897	Mexborough		1921	1924	Sheffield Utd.	Southend Utd.	138	12	0	0	7	0	0	0
Bedford	F	Fred	25/06/02	Blackburn	1972	1925		Accrington Stanley	Lancaster Town	9	0	0	0	0	0	0	0
Beech	GC	Jack		Sheffield		1904	1905	Sheffield Wed.		62	7	0	0	9	2	0	0
Beedles	N	Norman	13/06/07	Ardwick	1972	1934		Stockport County	New Brighton	1	0	0	0	0	0	0	0
Bell	DM	Derek	30/10/56	Wyberton		1978	1979	Halifax Town	Lincoln City	46	3	4	0	20	1	1	0
Bell	H	Harry	1898	Sheffield		1919		Craven Sports	Bristol Rovers	15	1	0	0	6	0	0	0
Bell	J	Jack	1884	Ryhope		1905	1906	Ryhope Villa		23	0	0	0	6	0	0	0
Bennett	GF	George	16/03/38	South Shields		1959	1960	Burnley	Morecambe	24	0	0	0	2	0	0	0
Bennett	GJ	George	1882	Mexborough		1901		Mexborough Thursday		9	3	0	0	3	2	0	0
Bennett	HE	Tip	1873	Mexborough	1905	1899	1904	Mexborough Town		115	14	0	0	4	1	0	0
Bennett	T	Troy	25/12/75	Barnsley		1992		Trainee	Scarborough	2	0	0	0	0	0	0	0
Bennett	WH	Walter	15/12/18	Mexborough		1946	1947	Mexborough Olympia	Doncaster Rovers	38	2	0	0	23	1	0	0
Beresford	J	John	04/09/66	Sheffield		1986	1988	Manchester City	Portsmouth	88	5	7	0	5	1	2	0
Bethune	J	Jack	19/10/1888	Milngavie	1955	1912	1919	Darlington	Bristol Rovers	103	4	0	0	1	0	0	0
Bettany	JW	John	16/12/37	Laughton		1964	1969	Huddersfield Town	Rotherham Utd.	198	17	7	0	25	2	0	0

Player			D.O.B	Place of Birth	Died	Season		Previous Club	Next Club	Appearances				Goals			
						First	Last			Lge.	FAC	FLC	Oth.	Lge.	FAC	FLC	Oth.
Betts	JB	Barry	18/09/32	Barnsley		1952	1956	Juniors	Stockport County	55	2	0	0	0	0	0	0
Biggins	FJ	Fred		South Kirkby		1908	1910	South Kirkby		29	1	0	0	2	0	0	0
Biggins	W	Wayne	20/11/61	Sheffield		1992	1993	Stoke City	Glasgow Celtic	47	4	0	0	16	0	0	0
Binns	CH	Cliff	09/03/07	Cowling	1977	1936	1938	Blackburn Rovers	Gainsborough Trinity	95	6	0	0	0	0	0	0
Birch	A	Alan	12/08/56	West Bromwich		1981	1982	Wolves	Chesterfield	44	2	3	0	10	0	1	0
Birtles	TJ	Tommy	26/10/1885	Higham, Yorkshire	1971	1903	1905	Higham	Swindon Town	35	4	0	0	7	0	0	0
						1910		Portsmouth	Rotherham County	3	0	0	0	1	0	0	0
Bishop	CD	Charlie	16/02/68	Nottingham		1991	1995	Bury	Wigan Ath.	130	9	12	5	1	0	0	0
Black	A	Alec	1867	Edinburgh		1898		Edinburgh St.Bernards		4	15	0	0	0	1	0	0
Blair	A	Andy	18/12/59	Bedworth		1987		Aston Villa (loan)	Aston Villa	6	0	0	0	0	0	0	0
Blanchflower	RD	Danny	10/02/26	Belfast	1993	1948	1950	Glentoran, Belfast	Aston Villa	68	2	0	0	2	0	0	0
Blenkinsopp	TW	Tom	13/05/20	Blyth		1952		Middlesbrough	Blyth Spartans	8	2	0	0	0	0	0	0
Blight	AB	Abe	1912	Blackhill		1933	1934	Blackhill	Annfield Plain	45	0	0	1	36	0	0	0
Boardman	G	George	14/08/43	Glasgow		1969	1972	Shrewsbury Town	St. Johnstone	126	8	7	0	14	0	0	0
Bochenski	S	Simon	06/12/75	Worksop		1995		Trainee	Scarborough	1	1	0	0	0	0	0	0
Boden	CD	Chris	13/10/73	Wolverhampton		1993		Aston Villa (loan)	Aston Villa	4	0	0	0	0	0	0	0
Bokas	F	Frank	13/05/14	Bellshill	1996	1936	1938	Blackpool	Gainsborough Trinity	88	5	0	0	4	1	0	0
Bonnar	P	Paddy	27/11/20	Ballymena		1949		Belfast Celtic	Aldershot	5	0	0	0	1	0	0	0
Bonnell	A	Arnold	23/03/21	Barnsley		1946	1947	Juniors	Rochdale	7	0	0	0	0	0	0	0
Booker	M	Mike	22/10/47	Barnsley		1966		Apprentice	Bradford PA	2	0	0	0	0	0	0	0
Booth	D	David	02/10/48	Kexborough		1968	1971	Higham Rovers	Grimsby Town	164	14	8	0	8	0	0	0
Bosancic	J	Jovo	07/08/70	Novi Sad (Yug)		1996	1997	CF Uniao Madeira (Port)	Guingamp (France)	42	6	4	0	3	0	0	0
Boughen	P	Paul	17/09/49	South Kirkby		1970		Apprentice		41	6	4	0	3	0	0	0
Bourne	RA	Dickie	1881	Roundle	1944	1902		Sheffield Utd.	Preston NE	19	6	0	0	0	1	0	0
Bowie	A	Alex		Canbloe		1923	1924	Rosehill Villa	Aberdeen	5	0	0	0	0	0	0	0
Boyd	G	Gordon	27/03/58	Glasgow		1980		Glasgow Rangers	Scunthorpe Utd.	2	0	1	0	0	0	0	0
Boyle	IR	Ian	07/12/53	Barnsley		1972	1973	Apprentice	Frickley Athletic	21	0	1	0	0	0	0	0
Boyle	TW	Tommy	29/01/1888	Hoyland	1940	1906	1911	Elsecar Athletic	Burnley	160	18	0	0	17	2	0	0
Bradbury	A	Allen	23/01/47	Barnsley		1964	1969	Apprentice	Hartlepool	69	5	5	0	9	0	1	0
Bradbury	JJL	John	1878	South Bank		1900		Derby County	Bristol City	16	3	0	0	2	1	0	0
Bradshaw	C	Carl	02/10/68	Sheffield		1986		Sheffield Wed. (loan)	Sheffield Wed.	6	0	0	0	1	0	0	0
Brannan	MH	Mike		Wombwell		1934	1935	Hull City	Notts County	5	0	0	0	0	0	0	0
Bratley	PW	Phil	26/12/1880	Rawmarsh	1962	1910	1913	Rotherham County	Liverpool	107	17	0	0	7	1	0	0
Bray	E	Eric				1935	1938	Barugh Green		37	3	0	0	12	0	0	0
Breedon	JN	Jack	29/12/07	South Hiendley		1928	1930	South Hiendley	Sheffield Wed.	8	0	0	0	0	0	0	0
Brindle	W	Billy	29/01/50	Liverpool		1970		Everton	Runcorn	1	0	0	0	0	0	0	0
Briscoe	J	John	31/05/47	Huddersfield		1966	1967	Juniors	LA Wolves (USA)	11	0	0	0	5	0	0	0
Broddle	JR	Julian	01/11/64	Laughton		1987	1989	Scunthorpe Utd.	Plymouth Argyle	77	3	5	2	4	2	0	1
Brodie	D	Duncan		Cumnock		1904		Cumnock		1	0	0	0	0	0	0	0
Broley	JF			Liverpool		1900		Tranmere Rovers		3	0	0	0	0	0	0	0
Brook	EF	Eric	27/11/07	Mexborough	1965	1925	1927	Wath Athletic	Manchester City	78	3	0	0	18	0	0	0
Brookes	C	Colin	02/01/42	Barnsley		1959	1960	Juniors	West Bromwich Albion	47	4	2	0	5	0	0	0
Brookes	E	Eric	03/02/44	Mapplewell		1960	1968	Juniors	Northampton Town	326	34	18	0	1	0	0	0
Brooks	J	Joe	1886	Stairfoot	1955	1904	1906	Ardsley Nelson F.C.	West Bromwich Albion	49	7	0	0	7	0	0	0
						1908		West Bromwich Albion	Rotherham County	4	1	0	0	0	0	0	0
Brown	A	Alfred		Sheffield		1923	1925	Blackpool	Swindon Town	12	0	0	0	0	0	0	0
Brown	KG	Kenny	21/03/52	Barnsley		1969	1977	Apprentice	Bournemouth	277	16	10	0	24	2	0	0
Brown	R	Bobby	09/08/24	Glasgow		1953	1956	Shrewsbury Town	Rotherham Utd.	120	4	0	0	55	3	0	0
Brunskill	NH	Norman	12/06/12	Dipton	1988	1938		Birmingham		28	1	0	0	2	0	0	0
Bryson	JIC	Ian	26/11/62	Kilmarnock		1993		Sheffield Utd.	Preston NE	16	0	2	2	3	0	1	0
Bullimore	WA	Wayne	12/09/70	Sutton-in-Ashfield		1991	1992	Manchester Utd.	Stockport County	35	2	3	0	1	0	0	0
Bullock	GF	George	1916	Wolverhampton	1943	1936	1938	Stafford Rangers		68	1	0	0	12	0	0	0
Bullock	MJ	Martin	05/03/75	Derby		1994	to date	Eastwood Town		131	10	8	1	1	1	0	0
Burke	P	Peter	26/04/57	Rotherham		1974	1977	Apprentice	Halifax Town	36	1	7	0	1	0	0	0
Burke	T	Tommy	18/10/39	Greenock		1962		Clyde		1	0	0	0	0	0	0	0
Burkinshaw	A	Abe	1886	Mexborough		1908		Mexborough Town	Mexborough Town	9	0	0	0	5	0	0	0
Burleigh	J					1898		Glossop North End	Scarborough	25	6	0	0	0	0	0	0
Burns	EO	Eric	08/03/45	Newton Stewart		1966		Bradford PA	Scarborough	3	0	0	0	0	0	0	0
Burns	K	Kenny	23/09/53	Glasgow		1985		Derby County	IF.Elfsborg (Sweden)	22	1	2	0	0	0	0	0
Burton	MA	Mark	07/05/73	Barnsley		1992		Trainee		5	0	0	2	0	0	0	0
Butler	I	Ian	01/02/44	Darton		1975		York City (loan)	York City	5	0	0	0	0	0	0	0
Butler	LS	Lee	30/05/66	Sheffield		1991	1995	Aston Villa	Wigan Ath.	120	9	5	4	0	0	0	0
Butler	MA	Mick	27/01/51	Barnsley		1972	1975	Worsborough Br. MW	Huddersfield Town	120	6	5	0	57	2	1	0
Byrne	J	John	25/05/39	Cambuslang		1963	1964	Hibernian	Peterborough Utd.	68	8	2	0	13	6	2	0
Caddick	GFR	George	02/03/00	Liverpool		1925	1931	Stockport County	Llanelly	169	7	0	0	0	0	0	0
Calder	J	Jack	19/10/13	Glengarnock		1938		Bolton Wanderers	Greenock Morton	9	0	0	0	5	0	0	0
Callaghan	WA	Willie	09/12/41	Glasgow		1964		Dumbarton	Albion Rovers	15	0	0	0	0	0	0	0
Campbell	A			Perth		1899		Holyhead Swifts	Dearne	6	0	0	0	1	0	0	0
Campbell	WR	Winston	09/10/62	Sheffield		1979	1986	Apprentice	Rotherham Utd.	128	6	10	0	9	0	1	0
Capstick	W	William				1931		Frickley Colliery	Mexborough Athletic	6	0	0	0	0	0	0	0
Carlin	JC	Jack	1878	Waverley		1900	1901	Glossop		48	4	0	0	9	1	0	0
Carrigan	J	John				1926		Vale of Clyde		6	0	0	0	0	0	0	0
Carroll	J	James		Dumbarton		1901		Renton		13	0	0	0	1	0	0	0
Carthy	T			Liverpool		1898		Liverpool White Star		1	1	0	0	0	0	0	0
Chambers	PM	Phil	10/11/53	Barnsley		1970	1984	Apprentice	Rochdale	442	23	29	0	7	0	0	0

Player			D.O.B	Place of Birth	Died	Season First	Last	Previous Club	Next Club	Appearances Lge.	FAC	FLC	Oth.	Goals Lge.	FAC	FLC	Oth.
Chandler	I	Ian	20/03/68	Sunderland		1986		Juniors	Aldershot	12	1	2	1	4	0	1	0
Chappell	L	Lol	19/12/30	HighGreen Sheffield	1988	1952	1958	Birdwell Rovers	Doncaster Rovers	218	12	0	0	94	1	0	0
Charlesworth	SF	Stan	10/03/20	Conisbrough		1946		Grimsby Town	Gainsborough Trinity	7	0	0	0	0	0	0	0
Chivers	FC	Frank	1909	Drybrook	1942	1930	1935	Goldthorpe Utd	Huddersfield Town	79	2	0	0	16	0	0	0
Clark	J	James				1936		Margate	Belfast Distillery	11	0	0	0	0	0	0	0
Clarke	AJ	Allan	31/07/46	Willenhall		1978	1979	Leeds United		47	5	3	0	15	3	0	0
Clarke	MD	Mick	22/12/67	Birmingham		1986	1988	Birmingham City	Scarborough	40	6	1	0	3	0	0	0
Clayson	WJ	Billy	12/07/1897	Wellingborough	1973	1926		Crewe Alexandra	Chesterfield	10	0	0	0	2	0	0	0
Clayton	L	Lew	07/06/24	Royston, Yorkshire		1948	1949	Carlisle Utd.	QPR	15	0	0	0	0	0	0	0
Clegg	JA	John	1890	Sheffield		1910	1911	Bristol City	Sheffield Wed.	33	2	0	0	0	0	0	0
Cliffe	JW	John	1913	Lincoln		1934		Bradford City	Carlisle Utd.	3	0	0	0	0	0	0	0
Coatsworth	G	Gary	07/10/68	Sunderland		1987		Juniors	Darlington	6	0	0	0	0	0	0	0
Cochrane	H	Hugh	09/02/43	Glasgow		1963		Dundee Utd	Wimbledon	5	0	0	0	0	0	0	0
Cockburn	K	Keith	02/09/42	Barnsley		1966			Bradford PA	1	0	0	0	0	0	0	0
Cole	R	Roy	08/12/53	Barnsley		1971	1973	Apprentice	Worksop Town	6	0	1	0	0	0	0	0
Collier	GR	Graham	12/09/51	Nottingham		1977		Scunthorpe Utd.	Buxton	24	2	3	0	2	0	0	0
Collingwood	G	Graham	08/12/54	South Kirkby		1973	1974	Apprentice		14	1	0	0	0	0	0	0
Collins	JL	John	21/01/49	Bedwellty		1976	1979	Sheffield Wed.	Kidderminster Harriers	130	7	9	0	1	0	0	0
Collins	WE	Bill	1887	Mansfield		1907		Sutton Town		1	0	0	0	0	0	0	0
Connelly	D	Dino	06/01/70	St.Helier		1990	1992	Arsenal	Wigan Ath.	13	0	0	1	0	0	0	1
Cookson	S	Sam	22/11/1896	Manchester	1955	1933	1934	Bradford PA		30	1	0	1	0	0	0	0
Cooling	R	Roy	09/12/21	Barnsley		1946		Mitchell's Main Welfare	Mansfield Town	6	4	0	0	3	0	0	0
Cooper	A	Arthur	1895	Sheffield		1919	1921	Birmingham	Oldham Athletic	99	4	0	0	0	0	0	0
Cooper	JC	Jack	1889	Sneinton		1908	1914	Sutton Town	Newport County	172	20	0	0	0	0	0	0
Cooper	N	Neil	12/08/59	Aberdeen		1979	1981	Aberdeen	Grimsby Town	60	3	8	0	6	1	1	0
Cooper	SB	Steve	22/06/64	Birmingham		1988	1990	Plymouth Argyle	Tranmere Rovers	77	9	5	1	13	3	1	0
Cooper	W	William		Mexborough		1906		Denaby Utd	Portsmouth	2	0	0	0	0	0	0	0
Cope	H	Harold	09/02/02	Rawmarsh	1980	1922	1924	Mexborough	Mexborough	32	2	0	0	0	0	0	0
Copley	G	Gary	30/12/60	Rotherham		1977	1978	Apprentice	Gainsborough Trinity	1	1	0	0	0	0	0	0
Cornan	F	Frank	05/05/1880	Sunderland	1971	1902	1904	Willington	Birmingham	88	9	0	0	18	4	0	0
						1909		Spennymoor Utd	Nelson	0	0	0	0	0	0	0	0
						1912		Exeter City		7	0	0	0	0	0	0	0
Cornock	M	Matthew		Airdrie		1911		Darlington	Castleford Town	12	0	0	0	5	0	0	0
Couchlin	D	David		Renfrew		1901		Renfrew Victoria	Thornliebank	11	1	0	0	0	0	0	0
Coulthard	ET	Ernest		Hylton		1908	1909	Sunderland West End		31	1	0	0	2	0	0	0
Cowley	JS	John	1886	Mexborough		1907		Mexborough Town		1	0	0	0	0	0	0	0
Coxon	LW	Leybourne				1933		Burnhope Institute		1	0	0	0	0	0	0	0
Craven	JR	Roger		Barnsley		1898	1899		Monk Bretton	20	2	0	0	1	0	0	0
Craven	T	Terry	27/11/44	Barnsley		1964		Juniors		3	0	0	0	0	0	0	0
Crompton	L	Len	26/03/02	Tottington		1930		Rochdale	Norwich City	17	2	0	0	0	0	0	0
Cross	P	Paul	31/10/65	Barnsley		1982	1991	Apprentice	Hartlepool Utd.	119	12	8	4	0	0	0	0
Crump	JA					1906		Elsecar Main	Rotherham Town	1	0	0	0	0	0	0	0
Cunningham	AE	Tony	12/11/57	Kingston (Jamaica)		1982	1983	Lincoln City	Sheffield Wed.	42	1	2	0	11	0	0	0
Cunningham	L	Laurie	20/10/21	Consett		1946	1947	Consett Utd	Bournemouth	51	8	0	0	1	0	0	0
Cunningham	P	Peter	13/07/06	Glasgow	1934	1932		Cork	Port Vale	14	0	0	0	17	0	0	0
Cunningham	WL	Willie	11/07/38	Paisley		1964		Third Lanark	Stirling Albion	24	2	2	0	0	0	0	0
Curran	J	Jimmy	1902	Ryton-on-Tyne		1921	1931	Spen Black & White	Southend Utd.	244	12	0	0	71	2	0	0
Currie	DN	David	27/11/62	Stockton		1987	1989	Darlington	Nottm. Forest	80	5	3	1	30	4	1	0
						1991	1993	Oldham Athletic	Carlisle Utd.	75	5	3	2	12	0	0	1
Curry	T	Thomas		Newcastle		1919		Clarence Wesleyans	Scotswood	1	0	0	0	0	0	0	0
Dartnell	H	Herbert				1901		Manchester City	Wellingborough	18	0	0	0	6	0	0	0
Davie	J	Jock	19/02/13	Dunfermline		1946		Stockton	Kidderminster Harriers	6	0	0	0	0	0	0	0
Davies	SC	Stan	24/03/1898	Chirk	1972	1930		Rotherham Utd.	Manchester Central	1	0	0	0	0	0	0	0
Davis	H	Harry	1879	Wombwell	1962	1898	1899	Ardsley	Sheffield Wed.	49	7	0	0	21	4	0	0
Davis	SP	Steve	26/07/65	Birmingham		1991	1996	Burnley	Oxford United	107	3	9	0	10	0	0	0
Deakin	WE	Billy	19/01/25	Maltby		1949	1951	Sunnyside WMC	Chester	25	1	0	0	3	0	0	0
Dean	N	Norman	13/09/44	Corby		1968	1972	Cardiff City	Bedford Town	60	8	3	0	19	4	0	0
Deehan	JM	John	06/08/57	Solihull		1989	1990	Manchester City		11	3	0	0	2	1	0	0
Deere	SH	Steve	31/03/48	Burnham Market		1975		Hull City (loan)	Hull City	4	0	0	0	0	0	0	0
De Zeeuw	A	Arjan	16/04/70	Castricum(Holland)		1995	to date	Telstar (Holland)		100	9	6	0	3	0	0	0
Diamond	JJ	Jack	30/10/10	Middlesbrough	1961	1934		Southport	Cardiff City	4	2	0	0	1	0	0	0
Dixon	C	Cyril	01/02/01	Rawmarsh	1978	1924	1931	Rawmarsh Athletic	Reading	251	10	0	0	7	0	0	0
Dobbin	J	Jim	17/09/63	Dunfermline		1986	1990	Doncaster Rovers	Grimsby Town	129	11	4	4	12	0	0	1
Dobson	GW	George	07/10/1897	Rotherham	1957	1919		Kimberworth Old Boys	Norwich City	25	2	0	0	0	0	0	0
Docherty	A	Archie		Hebburn		1904		Hebburn Argyle	Denaby Utd	3	0	0	0	1	0	0	0
Donagher	M	Mick		Kilmarnock		1904	1905	Cronberry		66	7	0	0	1	0	0	0
Doncaster	T	Tommy	1888	Dinnington		1911		Dinnington Colliery	Cardiff City	4	0	0	0	0	0	0	0
Donkin	GWC	George	01/12/1892	Carlton, Yorkshire	1927	1913	1924	Monckton Athletic		231	13	0	0	20	0	0	0
Dougal	W	Willie	30/10/23	Falkirk		1952		Preston NE		21	0	0	0	0	0	0	0
Dowdall	C	Charlie		Dublin		1928		Fordsons (Cork)	Swindon Town	3	0	0	0	0	0	0	0
Downes	RD	Bobby	18/08/49	Bloxwich		1979	1980	Watford	Blackpool	43	6	6	0	1	0	0	0
Downing	J	John		Royston, Yorkshire		1919		Monckton Athletic	Hednesford Town	7	0	0	0	0	0	0	0
Downs	JT	Dickie	05/04/1886	Middridge	1949	1908	1919	Shildon Athletic	Everton	274	32	0	0	10	1	0	0
Doyle	R	Bobby	27/12/53	Dumbarton		1972	1975	Juniors	Peterborough Utd.	149	6	5	0	16	0	0	0
Duerden	H	Harry	05/03/48	Barnsley		1965	1966	Apprentice	Kidderminster Harriers	25	3	2	0	1	0	0	0

Player			D.O.B	Place of Birth	Died	Season		Previous Club	Next Club	Appearances				Goals			
						First	Last			Lge.	FAC	FLC	Oth.	Lge.	FAC	FLC	Oth.
Dugdale	A	Alan	11/09/52	Liverpool		1979		Charlton Athletic (loan)	Charlton Athletic	7	0	2	0	0	0	0	0
Duggan	AJ	Andy	19/09/67	Bradford		1986		Trainee	Huddersfield Town	2	0	0	0	1	0	0	0
Duggins	G	Gordon	08/12/32	Tamworth		1955	1957	Gresley Rovers	Buxton	17	1	0	0	6	0	0	0
Dungworth	JH	John	30/03/55	Rotherham		1974		Huddersfield Town (loa	Huddersfield Town	3	0	0	0	1	0	0	0
Dunphy	S	Sean	05/11/70	Maltby		1989		Trainee	Lincoln City	6	0	0	0	0	0	0	0
Dyer	JA	Jimmy	24/08/1883	Blacker Hill		1901		Wombwell Town	Doncaster Rovers	2	0	0	0	0	0	0	0
Eaden	NJ	Nicky	12/12/72	Sheffield		1992	to date	Trainee		211	14	13	2	8	0	0	0
Earnshaw	RI	Bob	15/03/43	Rotherham		1962	1972	Juniors		225	14	13	0	35	1	1	0
Eaton	F	Frank	12/11/02	Stockport	1979	1925	1929	New Mills (Derbyshire)	Reading	150	5	0	0	59	2	0	0
Edgar	J	Tich	09/04/36	Worsborough Dale		1955	1957	Juniors	Gillingham	22	3	0	0	6	0	0	0
Edgley	BK	Brian	26/08/37	Shrewsbury		1962		Brentford	Caernarfon Town	4	0	0	0	0	0	0	0
Edwards	M	Matt	1882	South Shields		1903	1904	Gateshead NER	Crystal Palace	65	4	0	0	3	0	0	0
Ellis	EE	Ernest	1888	Norwich		1909		Doncaster Rovers	Hartlepools Utd.	4	0	0	0	0	0	0	0
Ellis	T	Tom		Coxhoe		1932	1938	Wolves		169	10	0	1	0	0	0	0
Evans	IP	Ian	30/01/52	Egham		1979	1982	Crystal Palace		102	6	14	0	3	0	2	0
Evans	JD	Johnny	13/03/38	Liverpool		1966	1970	Exeter City		170	15	4	0	54	4	1	0
Everest	J	Jack	1907	Dunnington		1937	1938	Southend Utd.		37	0	0	0	0	0	0	0
Farnsworth	PA	Peter	17/05/46	Barnsley		1964		Apprentice		1	0	0	0	0	0	0	0
Farrell	A	Arthur	01/10/20	Huddersfield		1951		Bradford PA	Scarborough	18	0	0	0	0	0	0	0
Fawcett	T					1898		Blackburn Rovers		1	0	0	0	0	0	0	0
Feeney	MA	Mark	26/07/74	Derry		1992		Trainee		2	0	0	0	0	0	0	0
Fell	G	Gerry	03/12/1898	Barnsley	1977	1919	1921	Elsecar	Bradford PA	61	2	0	0	3	0	0	0
Felton	GM	Graham	01/03/49	Cambridge		1975		Northampton Town(loan	Northampton Town	12	0	0	0	2	0	0	0
						1976		Northampton Town	Kettering Town	24	1	4	0	3	0	0	0
Ferguson	M	Martin	21/12/42	Glasgow		1965		Greenock Morton	Doncaster Rovers	40	3	2	0	17	0	0	0
Ferry	W	Willie	21/11/66	Sunderland		1986		Scunthorpe Utd.	Easington Colliery	4	0	0	0	1	0	0	0
Findlay	JW	Jake	13/07/54	Blairgowrie		1983		Luton Town (loan)	Luton Town	6	0	0	0	0	0	0	0
Finnigan	T	Tommy	13/07/13	West Stanley	1937	1934		Middlesbrough	Southport	4	0	0	0	1	0	0	0
Fisher	FW	Fred	11/04/10	Barnsley	1944	1933	1937	Monckton Athletic	Chesterfield	66	11	0	1	16	2	0	0
Fisher	L	Lewis		Barnsley		1923		Worsborough Dale WMC	Wombwell Town	1	0	0	0	0	0	0	0
Fjortoft	JA	Jan-Aage	10/01/67	Aaesund(Norway)		1997		Sheffield United		15	0	0	0	6	0	0	0
Fisher	S	Stan	29/09/24	Barnsley		1946		Rockingham Colliery	Halifax Town	1	1	0	0	0	0	0	0
Flavell	RW	Bobby	07/03/56	Berwick-on-Tweed		1979		Chesterfield	Halifax Town	25	2	4	0	0	0	0	0
Fleetwood	ED	Eddie		Barnsley		1932	1934	Mexborough Athletic	Denaby Utd	14	0	0	0	8	0	0	0
Fleming	JG	Gary	17/02/67	Derry		1989	1995	Manchester City		239	12	14	6	0	0	0	0
Fletcher	B	Brough	09/03/1893	Mealsgate	1972	1914	1925	Shildon Athletic	Sheffield Wed.	249	17	0	0	51	8	0	0
						1926	1929	Sheffield Wed.		62	4	0	0	21	3	0	0
Fletcher	MRJ	Mark	01/04/65	Barnsley		1983		Apprentice	Bradford City	1	0	0	0	0	0	0	0
Foreman	D	Darren	12/02/68	Southampton		1986	1989	Fareham Town	Crewe Alexandra	47	5	3	1	8	0	0	0
Forman	T	Tom	26/10/1879	Basford		1907	1910	Sutton Town	Tottenham Hotspur	126	12	0	0	16	2	0	0
Foster	J	Jimmy		Wigan		1935		Crewe Alexandra		6	0	0	0	0	0	0	0
Foulds	J	Jack	1874	Glasgow		1899		Partick Thistle		5	0	0	0	1	0	0	0
Fox	PD	Peter	05/07/57	Scunthorpe		1977		Sheffield Wed (loan)	Sheffield Wed.	1	0	0	0	0	0	0	0
Francis	A	Albert		Barnsley		1907		Hickleton Main		1	0	0	0	0	0	0	0
Frost	H	Harry		King's Lynn		1919	1920	Wath Athletic	Bournemouth	4	0	0	0	0	0	0	0
Fryer	W	Bill		Burradon		1919	1920	Byker West End	Todd Shipyards(USA)	9	0	0	0	0	0	0	0
Futcher	P	Paul	25/09/56	Chester		1983	1989	Derby County	Halifax Town	230	20	13	4	0	0	0	0
Futcher	R	Ron	25/09/56	Chester		1984		NAC Breda (Holland)	Oldham Athletic	19	4	0	0	5	2	0	0
Gadsby	E	Ernie	1889	New Whittington		1909	1910	Mexborough Town	Bristol City	44	9	0	0	13	3	0	0
Gale	T	Tommy	12/10/1895	Castleford	1976	1922	1930	Harrogate Town	Stockport County	296	12	0	0	0	0	0	0
Gallacher	F	Frank	1913	Paisley		1935	1937	Hamilton Academicals	Bristol City	40	5	0	0	9	2	0	0
Geddis	D	David	12/03/58	Carlisle		1983	1984	Aston Villa	Birmingham City	45	1	4	0	24	0	0	0
Gedney	C	Charlie		Elsecar		1906		Hoyland Town	Castleford	1	0	0	0	0	0	0	0
Gibbs	GHW	George	1907	Chester-le-Street		1928		Leicester City	Scarborough	1	0	0	0	0	0	0	0
						1929	1930	Scarborough	Worcester City	36	3	0	0	5	2	0	0
Gill	JE	James	1884	Halesowen		1903	1904	Halesowen Town	Swindon Town	32	0	0	0	0	0	0	0
Gillatt	K	Ernie	1900	Wensley		1924	1925	Mansfield Town		13	0	0	0	1	0	0	0
Gillott	P	Peter	20/07/35	Barnsley		1955	1958	Worsborough C. Utd	Chelmsford City	5	0	0	0	0	0	0	0
Gittins	JH	Jack	11/11/1893	Stanton Hill	1956	1914	1926	Bentley Colliery	Chesterfield	261	12	0	0	7	0	0	0
Glavin	RM	Ronnie	27/03/51	Glasgow		1979	1983	Glasgow Celtic	Belenenses (Portugal)	176	10	22	0	73	4	15	0
						1985		Belenenses (Portugal)	Stockport County	6	0	1	0	0	0	0	0
Glendenning	R	Bob	1889	New Washington	1940	1908	1912	Washington Utd	Bolton Wanderers	141	27	0	0	1	0	0	0
Glover	A	Arthur	27/03/18	Barnsley		1937	1952	Regent Street Congs		186	7	0	0	5	0	0	0
Glover	EL	Lee	24/04/70	Kettering		1989		Nottm. Forest (loan)	Nottm. Forest	8	4	0	0	0	0	0	0
Godderidge	AE	Albert	29/05/02	Tamworth	1976	1927		Leicester City	Newark Town	16	1	0	0	0	0	0	0
Godfrey	W	Warren	31/03/73	Liverpool		1992		Liverpool	Witton Albion	8	0	0	1	0	0	0	0
Goodison	WC	Wayne	23/09/64	Wakefield		1982	1985	Apprentice	Crewe Alexandra	36	3	1	0	0	0	0	0
Goodwin	J	John		Hallside		1925		Wigan Borough	Wigan Borough	2	0	0	0	0	0	0	0
Gordon	A	Arthur	1880			1901		Wallsend Park Villa	Gainsborough Trinity	14	4	0	0	6	1	0	0
Gorry	MC	Martin	29/12/54	Derby		1975	1976	Apprentice	Newcastle Utd	34	0	4	0	1	0	0	0
Gosling	T	Thomas		Wombwell		1899		Wombwell Town		14	2	0	0	1	0	0	0
Graham	DWT	Deiniol	04/10/69	Cannock		1991	1993	Manchester Utd.	Stockport County	38	0	4	0	2	0	0	0
Graham	M	Malcolm	26/01/34	Crigglestone		1954	1958	Hall Green	Bristol City	109	4	0	0	35	0	0	0
						1964		QPR	Buxton	20	1	1	0	5	1	0	0

Player			D.O.B	Place of Birth	Died	Season		Previous Club	Next Club	Appearances				Goals			
						First	Last			Lge	FAC	FLC	Oth	Lge	FAC	FLC	Oth
Graham	P	Peter	19/04/47	Worsborough Com.		1966	1969	Worsborough Bridge	Darlington	19	2	1	0	1	1	2	0
Graham	T	Tommy	31/03/58	Glasgow		1978	1979	Aston Villa	Halifax Town	38	1	2	0	13	0	1	0
Graham	TH	Thomas	1888	South Shields		1909			Castleford Town	1	0	0	0	0	0	0	0
Grainger	J	Jack	17/07/12	Royston, Yorkshire	1976	1932		Royston Athletic	Southport	1	0	0	0	0	0	0	0
Gray	H	Harry	26/10/18	Hemsworth		1946		Grimethorpe Rovers	Bournemouth	7	0	0	0	1	0	0	0
Gray	P	Phil	02/10/68	Belfast		1989		Tottenham H'spur(loan)	Tottenham Hotspur	3	1	0	0	0	0	0	0
Gray	S	Stuart	19/04/60	Withernsea		1983	1987	Nottm. Forest	Aston Villa	120	6	7	2	23	0	3	1
Greaves	A	Arthur		Doncaster		1934		Crewe Alexandra	Watford	3	0	0	0	0	0	0	0
Greaves	J	Joe				1898	1902	Sheffield Wed.		104	28	0	0	0	0	0	0
Green	A	Alan	14/12/39	Darfield		1960	1961	Dodworth Colliery	York City	19	2	0	0	0	0	0	0
Green	BH	Benny	23/02/1883	Penistone	1945	1901	1903	Penistone Jnrs. FC	Small Heath	46	3	0	0	18	0	0	0
Green	F	Frank	1902	Ashington	1982	1931		Crewe Alexandra	Racing Club Paris(Fr.)	4	0	0	0	0	0	0	0
Greenwood	PG	Paddy	17/10/46	Hull		1971	1973	Hull City	Nottm. Forest	111	8	4	0	6	0	0	0
Gridelet	PR	Phil	30/04/67	Edgware		1990	1992	Barnet	Southend Utd.	6	1	0	1	0	0	0	0
Griffin	MR	Mick	1887	Middlesbrough		1912	1914	Hartlepools Utd.		69	5	0	0	7	0	0	0
Griffiths	JS	Steve	23/02/14	Stairfoot		1947	1950	Aldershot	York City	65	6	0	0	29	1	0	0
Griffiths	W	Walter	1886	Nottingham		1907	1908	Ilkeston		16	1	0	0	3	0	0	0
Griffiths	W	William		Wombwell		1906		Mitchell's Main		7	1	0	0	4	0	0	0
Gullen	G	George		Newcastle		1903			Newcastle Utd	16	0	0	0	3	0	0	0
Hall	JE	Jack	1885	Tyne Dock		1905	1907	Kingston Villa	Brighton & Hove Albion	74	6	0	0	14	1	0	0
Hall	JE	Jack	1890	Boldon		1911	1912	Jarrow Croft	Manchester City	5	0	0	0	0	0	0	0
Halliwell	JA	Joe	17/01/1894	Lostock Hall		1913	1926	Preston NE	Nelson	312	16	0	0	83	0	0	0
Hallows	JH	Jack	16/02/07	Chester	1963	1935	1936	Bradford City		13	1	0	0	4	0	0	0
Hamill	A	Alex	1912	Dumbarton		1936	1937	Blackburn Rovers	Carlisle Utd.	24	1	0	0	4	1	0	0
Hamilton	E	Eddie	17/01/27	Glasgow		1949		Dundalk	St. Patrick's Ath (Dublin)	1	0	0	0	0	0	0	0
Hammerton	JD	John	22/03/00	Sheffield	1968	1920	1922	Oughtibridge	Rotherham County	30	0	0	0	9	0	0	0
Hamstead	GW	George	24/01/46	Rotherham		1966	1970	York City	Bury	149	13	3	0	22	0	0	0
Hanlon	E	Edward		Darlington	1925	1911		Darlington		12	0	0	0	1	0	0	0
Happs	R	Roland				1931	1933	Denaby Utd	Mexborough Athletic	12	0	0	0	0	0	0	0
Harper	B	Bernard	23/11/12	Gawber		1932	1938	West Ward FC	Scunthorpe Utd.	217	12	0	1	2	0	0	0
Harris	A	Albert	16/09/12	Horden		1936		Newcastle Utd	Darlington	15	0	0	0	1	0	0	0
Harris	LH	Les	29/05/55	Stocksbridge		1975	1976	Juniors	Buxton	26	0	0	0	2	0	0	0
Harron	J	Joe	19/03/00	Langley Park	1961	1928	1929	Scarborough	Dartford	28	0	0	0	4	0	0	0
Harston	E	Ted	27/02/07	Monk Bretton		1930		Sheffield Wed.	Reading	12	0	0	0	4	0	0	0
Harston	JC	Jack	07/10/20	Barnsley		1946	1948	Wolves	Bradford City	20	2	0	0	1	0	0	0
Harvey	WA	Bill	1908	Chopwell		1929	1931	Eden Colliery	Eden Colliery	42	3	0	0	12	2	0	0
Hay	J	Jimmy	1876	Lanark	1940	1901	1907	Renfrew Victoria	Chesterfield Town	145	13	0	0	1	0	0	0
Hayes	J	Joe	20/01/36	Kearsley		1965		Manchester City	Wigan Athletic	26	2	2	0	3	0	0	0
Hedworth	C	Chris	05/01/64	Wallsend		1986	1987	Newcastle Utd	Halifax Town	25	3	1	1	0	0	0	0
Hellewell	A	Albert		Huddersfield		1899	1902			67	10	0	0	14	3	0	0
Hellewell	A	Alec		Sheffield		1902	1909	Mexborough Town		196	17	0	0	44	3	0	0
Hemstock	B	Brian	09/02/49	Goldthorpe		1966		Juniors	Bradford PA	1	0	0	0	0	0	0	0
Henderson	GB	George	09/01/02	Kelty		1928	1936	Sunderland		258	14	0	1	11	1	0	0
Hendon	IM	Ian	05/12/71	Ilford		1992		Tottenham H'spur (loan	Tottenham Hotspur	6	0	0	0	0	0	0	0
Hendrie	JG	John	24/10/63	Lennoxtown		1996	to date	Middlesbrough		56	6	0	0	16	3	0	0
Heppinstall	F	Frank	1885	South Hiendley		1904		Denaby Utd	Denaby Utd	8	1	0	0	1	0	0	0
Hepworth	W	Walter		Barnsley		1898	1899	Worsbro'Com'n St.Lukes		26	7	0	0	9	2	0	0
Hewitson	R	Bob	26/02/1884	Blyth	1957	1903	1904	Morpeth Harriers	Crystal Palace	62	4	0	0	0	0	0	0
Hewitt	R	Dick	25/05/43	Moorthorpe		1965	1968	Bradford City	York City	98	8	3	0	20	2	1	0
Higgs	FJ	Frank	1910	Willington Quay		1931		Linfield, Belfast	Manchester City	35	2	0	0	0	0	0	0
Hill	A	Alan	03/11/43	Barnsley		1960	1965	Juniors	Rotherham Utd.	133	12	7	0	0	0	0	0
Hill	J	Joe	1906	Sheffield		1931		Newark Town	QPR	8	0	0	0	3	0	0	0
Hinch	JA	Jimmy	08/11/47	Sheffield		1977		Sheffield Wed.	California Surf (USA)	12	0	0	0	4	0	0	0
Hind	A	Arthur		Sheffield		1898		Owlerton Swifts		1	0	0	0	0	0	0	0
Hine	EW	Ernie	09/04/01	Smithy Cross	1974	1921	1925	Staincross Station	Leicester City	161	13	0	0	82	2	0	0
						1934	1937	Manchester Utd.		127	6	0	0	42	5	0	0
Hinsley	G	George	19/07/14	Sheffield		1935	1938	Denaby Utd	Bradford City	9	1	0	0	0	0	0	0
Hirst	DE	David	07/12/67	Cudworth		1985		Apprentice	Sheffield Wed.	28	0	1	0	9	0	0	0
Hirst	G	George		Barnsley		1901				1	0	0	0	0	0	0	0
Hirst	MW	Malcolm	28/12/37	Cudworth		1956		Darfield Road Jnrs	Yeovil Town	1	0	0	0	0	0	0	0
Hobson	J	John	01/06/46	Barnsley		1965	1968	Blackpool	Notts County	36	0	0	0	7	0	0	0
Hodgkinson	H	Bert	26/12/03	Penistone	1974	1923	1929	Penistone Jnrs. FC	Tottenham Hotspur	200	7	0	0	0	0	0	0
Holley	T	Tom	15/11/12	Sunderland	1992	1933	1935	Sunderland	Leeds Utd	72	8	0	0	4	0	0	0
Holmes	T	Tommy	14/12/34	Hemsworth Y.C.		1954	1958	Hemsworth Y.C.	Halifax Town	35	2	0	0	7	0	0	0
Hooley	JW	Joe	26/12/38	Barnsley		1956		Juniors	Sheffield Utd.	1	0	0	0	0	0	0	0
Hopkins	OT	Ollie	15/11/35	South Kirkby		1957	1960	Burtonwood FC	Peterborough Utd.	50	2	0	0	10	0	0	0
Hopkinson	A	Alan	15/04/53	Chapeltown		1970	1973	Apprentice		27	0	0	0	5	0	0	0
Hopper	A	Alan	17/07/37	Newcastle		1961	1964	South Shields	Bradford City	135	14	7	0	4	0	0	0
Horn	RI	Bobby	15/12/61	Westminster		1981	1983	Crystal Palace	Crystal Palace	67	1	12	0	0	0	0	0
Hosie	JE	Jim	03/04/40	Aberdeen		1962		Aberdeen		37	3	4	0	0	0	0	0
Hough	H	Harry	26/09/24	Chapeltown		1947	1958	Thorncliffe Welfare	Bradford PA	346	18	0	0	0	0	0	0
Houghton	WG	Billy	20/02/39	Hemsworth		1957	1963	Juniors	Watford	206	21	8	0	10	0	1	0
Howard	F	Fred		Blacker Hill		1898	1899	Lincoln City		49	8	0	0	1	0	0	0
Howard	P	Pat	07/10/47	Dodworth		1965	1971	Juniors	Newcastle Utd	177	15	9	0	6	0	1	0
Hristov	G	Georgi	30/01/76	Bitola(Macedonia)		1997		Partizan Belgrade (Yug)		23	2	3	0	4	0	1	0
Hudson	M	Maurice	12/09/30	Barnsley		1950	1953	Worsborough Dale ST	Bradford City	36	2	0	0	0	0	0	0

Player			D.O.B	Place of Birth	Died	Season		Previous Club	Next Club	Appearances				Goals			
						First	Last			Lge.	FAC	FLC	Oth.	Lge.	FAC	FLC	Oth.
Humes	J	Jimmy	06/08/42	Carlisle		1967		Chester		7	1	0	0	1	0	0	0
Hunt	DA	Doug	19/05/14	Shipton Bellinger	1989	1936	1937	Tottenham Hotspur	Sheffield Wed.	36	4	0	0	18	1	0	0
Hunt	S	Sam	1866	Smithies		1899				1	0	0	0	0	0	0	0
Hunter	N	Norman	29/10/43	Eighton Banks		1979	1982	Bristol City		31	2	1	0	0	0	0	0
Hunter	W	William	1888	Sunderland		1912		South Shields	Manchester Utd.	2	0	0	0	1	0	0	0
Hurst	G	Glynn	17/01/76	Barnsley		1994	1996	Tottenham Hotspur	Emley	8	0	1	0	0	0	0	0
Ironside	R	Roy	28/05/35	Sheffield		1965	1968	Rotherham Utd.		113	9	6	0	0	0	0	0
Ives	AE	Albert	1914	Newcastle		1935	1937	Sunderland		9	0	0	0	0	0	0	0
Jackson	B	Brian	02/02/36	Maltby		1965		Rotherham Utd.		29	1	0	0	0	0	0	0
Jackson	CD	Chris	16/01/76	Barnsley		1992	1995	Trainee		23	0	3	1	2	0	0	0
Jackson	M	Maurice	06/11/28	Royston,Yorkshire	1971	1949	1955	Carlton Utd	Barrow	34	1	0	0	0	0	0	0
Jackson	S	Sam		Belfast		1922		Swansea Town	Barn (N.Ireland)	1	0	0	0	0	0	0	0
Jagger	GN	George	30/09/41	Great Houghton		1960	1962	Houghton Main Colliery	Corby Town	45	3	1	0	2	0	0	0
Jarman	JE	John	04/02/31	Rhymney		1951	1955	Wellington Town	Walsall	45	2	0	0	1	1	0	0
Jebb	A	Alfred	1888	Nottingham		1909	1911	Ilkeston Utd	Watford	9	0	0	0	0	0	0	0
Jeffels	S	Simon	18/01/66	Darton		1983	1987	Apprentice	Carlisle Utd.	42	2	1	0	0	0	0	0
Jeffs	AS	Arthur	01/10/1897	Liverpool		1923		Everton	Tranmere Rovers	5	0	0	0	0	0	0	0
Johnson	A	Albert	1885	Sheffield		1906	1907	Attercliffe		11	1	0	0	0	0	0	0
Johnson	A	Arthur	1904	Atherstone		1925		Huddersfield Town	Birmingham	21	1	0	0	4	0	0	0
Johnson	DE	David	23/10/51	Liverpool		1983		Everton (loan)	Everton	4	0	0	0	1	0	0	0
Johnson	JC	Jack	03/10/05	South Kirkby	1991	1933		Rotherham Utd.	Carlisle Utd.	9	0	0	0	0	0	0	0
Johnson	P	Patrick		Wingate		1910		Crook Town		1	0	0	0	0	0	0	0
Johnson	WJ	Joe		Wednesbury		1925		Crystal Palace	West Ham Utd.	17	0	0	0	2	0	0	0
Joicey	B	Brian	19/12/45	Winlaton		1976	1978	Sheffield Wed.	Frickley Athletic	93	4	6	0	43	3	0	0
Jones	A	Aaron	1884	Rotherham	1950	1903	1904	Royston United	Birmingham	32	3	0	0	16	1	0	0
Jones	B	Ben		Rotherham		1908		Doncaster Rovers	Denaby Utd	16	0	0	0	5	0	0	0
Jones	B	Bryn	15/09/38	Barnsley		1957	1958	Juniors	York City	14	1	0	0	0	0	0	0
Jones	GH	George	27/11/18	Sheffield	1995	1950	1951	Sheffield Utd.		22	0	0	0	6	0	0	0
Jones	L	Len	09/06/13	Barnsley		1934	1937	Huddersfield Town	Chelmsford City	57	1	0	0	0	0	0	0
Jones	R	Dick		Liverpool		1898		Liverpool White Star	Liverpool White Star	30	7	0	0	10	0	0	0
						1899	1900	Glossop		34	3	0	0	9	2	0	0
Jones	S	Scott	01/05/75	Sheffield		1995	to date	Trainee		34	3	0	0	1	2	0	0
Jones	WD	Dai	04/04/05	Hafod	1946	1927		Preston NE	Denaby Utd	12	1	0	0	0	0	0	0
Jonsson	S	Siggi	27/09/66	Akranes (Iceland)		1985		Sheffield Wed. (loan)	Sheffield Wed.	5	0	0	0	0	0	0	0
Joyce	JP	Joe	18/03/61	Consett		1979	1990	Juniors	Scunthorpe Utd.	334	24	27	3	4	1	1	0
Jukes	AB	Bernard				1923	1924	Chesterfield		16	0	0	0	1	0	0	0
Kane	PJ	Paul	20/06/65	Edinburgh		1995		Aberdeen (loan)	Aberdeen	4	0	0	0	0	0	0	0
Kay	H	Harold	24/04/00	Chapeltown		1920	1922	Army	Southend Utd.	14	1	0	0	0	0	0	0
Kay	H	Harry		Elsecar		1907	1909	Elsecar	Rotherham Town	14	1	0	0	5	0	0	0
Kaye	A	Arthur	09/05/33	Higham, Yorkshire		1950	1958	Juniors	Blackpool	265	15	0	0	54	6	0	0
Kear	MP	Mike	27/06/43	Coleford		1970		Middlesbrough (loan)	Middlesbrough	6	0	0	0	1	0	0	0
Kelly	DC	Doug	30/05/34	Worsborough		1952	1954	Juniors	Bradford City	18	1	0	0	7	0	0	0
Kelly	F	Frank	1883	Liverpool		1903		Chester	Chesterfield Town	10	1	0	0	3	0	0	0
Kelly	J	Mick	1913	Sandbach		1935		Leeds Utd	Bradford City	3	0	0	0	0	0	0	0
Kelly	JC	Johnny	21/02/21	Paisley		1946	1952	Greenock Morton	Falkirk	217	12	0	0	25	1	0	0
Kelly	PM	Pat	09/04/18	Jo'burg S.Africa	1985	1946	1950	Aberdeen	Crewe Alexandra	144	3	0	0	0	0	0	0
Kelly	T	Thomas	13/01/02	Manchester		1923	1924	Corpus Christi FC	Rhyl Athletic	15	2	0	0	5	1	0	0
Kennedy	S	Sam	1896	Platts Common	1963	1926		Fulham	Mexborough Athletic	9	0	0	0	5	0	0	0
Kerr	GAM	George	09/01/43	Alexandria		1961	1965	Renton Select	Bury	166	14	10	0	40	8	4	0
Kerry	E	Ned	16/06/05	Creswell	1978	1929	1931	Mansfield Town	Llanelly	48	2	0	0	6	0	0	0
Kilner	A					1899			Penistone	2	0	0	0	1	0	0	0
King	S					1920				1	0	0	0	0	0	0	0
King	T					1898		Burton Wanderers		3	0	0	0	0	0	0	0
Kirsop	WS	William	1892	Wallsend		1914		Gateshead Athletic		3	0	0	0	0	0	0	0
Kitchen	J	Jack	28/02/25	Whitehaven	1992	1946	1951	Kells Athletic		53	2	0	0	0	0	0	0
Kiwomya	AD	Andy	01/10/67	Huddersfield		1985		Trainee	Sheffield Wed.	1	0	0	0	0	0	0	0
Krizan	A	Ales	25/07/71	Maribor(Slovenia)		1997		Maribor Branik(Slovenia)		12	1	3	0	0	0	0	0
Lake	CE	Ned		Penistone		1899	1900	Thurlstone	Thurlstone	29	2	0	0	8	0	0	0
						1903		Thurlstone	Rotherham Town	8	0	0	0	2	0	0	0
Lakin	W	William		Sheffield		1919		Woodhouse	Exeter City	5	0	0	0	0	0	0	0
Lambert	K	Ken	07/06/28	Sheffield		1950	1951	Ecclesfield Coll. Rovers	Gillingham	11	0	0	0	2	0	0	0
Lambert	R	Roy	16/07/33	Chapeltown		1965		Rotherham Utd.	Witton Albion	3	1	0	0	0	0	0	0
Lampard	AJ	Alfred		Nailsworth		1930	1931	Bournemouth		2	0	0	0	0	0	0	0
Lang	J	Johnny	16/08/1882	Kilbirnie		1902		Govan	Sheffield Utd.	13	4	0	0	2	3	0	0
Lang	J	Johnny	1908	Dumbarton		1937	1938	Aberdeen		43	2	0	0	10	0	0	0
Lathan	JG	John	12/04/52	Sunderland		1976		Carlisle Utd (loan)	Carlisle Utd.	7	0	0	0	0	0	0	0
Lavery	J	Jack	1884			1903		Jarrow	Denaby Utd	3	0	0	0	2	0	0	0
Law	N	Nicky	08/09/61	Greenwich		1981	1985	Arsenal	Blackpool	114	6	5	0	1	0	0	0
Lawton	P	Peter	25/02/44	Barnsley		1962	1963	Juniors	Rugby Town	2	0	0	0	0	0	0	0
Lawton	R	Robert		Barnsley		1899		Monk Bretton		2	0	0	0	0	0	0	0
Lax	G	George	1905	Pontefract		1931	1932	Wolves	Bournemouth	48	2	0	0	1	0	0	0
Lea	L	Les	05/10/42	Manchester		1970	1975	Cardiff City	Redfearns Sports	205	14	8	0	32	2	0	0
Leavey	HJ	Bert	1886	Guildford		1911		Liverpool	Bradford PA	28	7	0	0	2	1	0	0
Ledger	R	Roy	09/12/30	Barnsley		1950		Smithies Utd	Rotherham Utd	1	0	0	0	0	0	0	0
Ledingham	WD	William	1891	Newtongrange	1960	1913		Tranent Juniors		1	0	0	0	0	0	0	0

Player			D.O.B	Place of Birth	Died	Season		Previous Club	Next Club	Appearances				Goals			
						First	Last			Lge	FAC	FLC	Oth	Lge	FAC	FLC	Oth
Lees	JWD	Joe	1892	Coalville	1933	1914		Whitwick Imperial	Rotherham County	10	1	0	0	2	0	0	0
Lees	W	Don	1873	Cronberry		1898	1903	Darwen	Watford	187	24	0	0	42	8	0	0
						1904		Watford	Denaby Utd	1	0	0	0	0	0	0	0
Leese	L	Lars	18/08/69	Cologne(Germany)		1997		Bayer Leverkusen(Ger)		9	0	2	0	0	0	0	0
Leeson	D	Don	25/08/35	Askern		1956	1960	Askern Main Colliery		97	10	2	0	0	0	0	0
Leigh	WH	Harry	1888	Lymm		1908		Aston Villa	Stoke	1	0	0	0	0	0	0	0
Leighton	A	Tony	27/11/39	Leeds	1978	1962	1964	Doncaster Rovers	Huddersfield Town	107	10	9	0	59	2	3	0
Lester	MJ	Mike	04/08/54	Manchester		1979	1980	Grimsby Town	Exeter City	64	8	5	0	11	2	0	0
Liddell	AM	Andy	28/06/73	Leeds		1991	to date	Trainee		190	12	13	3	34	1	3	0
Lillycrop	GB	George	07/12/1886	Gosport	1962	1907	1912	North Shields Adelaide	Bolton Wanderers	195	28	0	0	92	12	0	0
Lindsay	D	David	23/09/19	Dumbarton	1992	1948	1951	Luton Town	Wisbech Town	78	3	0	0	3	0	0	0
Little	A	Alan	05/02/55	Horden		1977	1979	Southend Utd.	Doncaster Rovers	91	4	9	0	14	0	1	0
Little	J	Jack	1888	Seaton Delaval	1965	1908	1910	Scotswood	Crystal Palace	47	1	0	0	0	0	0	0
Little	T	Tommy	1872	Dumfries		1899		Swindon Town	Dumfries	14	2	0	0	2	1	0	0
Lockie	T	Tom	13/01/06	Duns	1977	1932		Leith Athletic	York City	14	1	0	0	1	0	0	0
Logan	JW	John	16/08/12	Horden	1980	1936	1946	Darlington	Sheffield Wed.	99	11	0	0	5	0	0	0
Longden	DP	Paul	28/09/62	Wakefield		1981	1982	Apprentice	Scunthorpe Utd.	5	0	0	0	0	0	0	0
Low	WR	Willie		Aberdeen		1920	1921	Gainsborough Trinity		41	1	0	0	0	0	0	0
Lowe	SJ	Simon	26/12/62	Westminster		1983		Ossett Town	Halifax Town	2	0	0	0	0	0	0	0
Lowndes	SR	Steve	17/06/60	Cwmbran		1986	1989	Millwall	Hereford Utd.	116	10	7	3	20	1	1	0
Loyden	E	Eddie	22/12/45	Liverpool		1968	1970	Shrewsbury Town	Chester	65	5	1	0	23	3	0	0
Lumley	IT	Tommy	09/01/24	Leadgate		1951	1955	Charlton Athletic	Darlington	146	7	0	0	36	3	0	0
Lunn	J	Jackie	14/10/37	Barnsley	1989	1956	1960	Juniors	Chesterfield	56	8	0	0	19	1	0	0
Lydon	T	Thomas				1901		Glasgow Celtic		1	0	0	0	0	0	0	0
Lynch	TJ	Paddy	31/08/07	Tredegar	1976	1932		Colwyn Bay Utd	Barrow	19	0	0	0	0	0	0	0
Lyon	S	Sam	20/01/1890	Prescot	1977	1914		Hull City		8	0	0	0	3	0	0	0
MacDonald	J	John	15/04/61	Glasgow		1986	1989	Glasgow Rangers	Scarborough	94	9	4	2	20	2	1	1
Mackay	DM	Morgan		Invergordon		1935		Dundee	Queen of the South	1	0	0	0	0	0	0	0
Mahoney	B	Brian	12/05/52	Tantobie		1971	1974	Huddersfield Town		90	4	2	0	16	0	1	0
Malcolm	AM	Alex	15/12/21	Alloa		1946	1947	Alloa Athletic	Scarborough	5	0	0	0	0	0	0	0
Malcolm	PA	Paul	11/12/64	Felling		1986		Shrewsbury Town	Doncaster Rovers	3	0	0	0	0	0	0	0
Mallender	GS	Gary	12/03/59	Barnsley		1976	1978	Apprentice	Boston Utd	2	0	0	0	0	0	0	0
Mann	JA	Jimmy	15/12/52	Goole		1981	1982	Bristol City	Scunthorpe Utd.	15	0	0	0	0	0	0	0
Manning	JJ	John	11/12/40	Liverpool		1973	1974	Crewe Alexandra	Crewe Alexandra	45	4	1	0	7	2	0	0
Mansley	VC	Cliff	05/04/21	Skipton		1946	1947	Preston NE	Chester	30	6	0	0	0	0	0	0
Marcelle	CS	Clint	09/11/68	Port of Spain (Trin)		1996	to date	Felgueiras (Portugal)		60	6	6	0	8	1	0	0
March	W	Billy	28/02/25	Chester-le-Street		1951		Ferryhill Athletic	Gateshead	2	0	0	0	0	0	0	0
Markstedt	P	Peter	11/01/72	Vasteras(Sweden)		1997		Vasteras SK (Sweden)		7	1	0	0	0	0	0	0
Marshall	C	Colin	01/11/69	Glasgow		1988	1990	Trainee		4	0	0	1	0	0	0	0
Marshall	J	John	1892	Stenhousemuir		1913	1914	Preston NE	Clyde	14	0	0	0	1	0	0	0
Martin	F	Fred	1889	Clay Cross	1932	1909	1911	South Kirkby	Sunderland	10	0	0	0	2	0	0	0
Martin	P	Peter	29/12/50	South Shields		1971	1972	Darlington	Cambridge City	26	2	0	0	6	0	0	0
Maskill	T	Tom	02/05/03	York	1956	1931		Carlisle Utd.	York City	17	2	0	0	3	0	0	0
Matthews	CM	Charles				1919		Leeds City	Scunthorpe Utd	2	0	0	0	0	0	0	0
Matthews	F	Frank	26/12/02	Wallsend	1981	1923	1924	Blackpool	Southampton	34	1	0	0	5	0	0	0
Mawson	F	Frank	1878	Ecclesfield	1938	1900	1902	Doncaster Rovers	Ecclesfield Church	61	5	0	0	8	1	0	0
May	H	Harry	15/10/28	Glasgow		1952	1954	Swindon Town	Southend Utd.	105	5	0	0	0	0	0	0
May	LC	Larry	26/12/58	Sutton Coldfield		1983	1986	Leicester City	Sheffield Wed.	122	10	6	1	3	2	1	0
McArdle	P	Peter	08/04/11	Lanchester	1979	1936	1937	Carlisle Utd.	Stockport County	16	0	0	0	3	0	0	0
McCairns	T	Tommy	22/12/1873	Dinsdale	1932	1901		Lincoln City	Wellingborough	23	4	0	0	9	1	0	0
McCann	H	Henry	1888	Falkirk		1912		Birtley	Exeter City	1	0	0	0	0	0	0	0
McCann	J	Johnny	23/07/34	Govan		1955	1958	Bridgeton Waverley	Bristol City	118	7	0	0	17	0	0	0
McCarthy	MJ	Mick	07/02/59	Barnsley		1977		Worsborough Br.M.W.	Manchester City	272	16	26	0	7	0	3	0
McCarthy	RS	Roy	17/01/45	Barugh Green		1961	1962	Barugh Green Sports	Barrow	3	0	0	0	0	0	0	0
McCartney	WJ	John	1866	Glasgow	1933	1898	1900	Luton Town		63	7	0	0	3	1	0	0
McCartney	WJ					1904		Cronberry		1	0	0	0	0	0	0	0
McCartney	WJ	Willie				1901	1903	Lugar Boswell		7	3	0	0	0	0	0	0
McColl	D	Duncan	28/12/45	Glasgow		1965		Partick Thistle	Ballymena Utd	5	0	0	0	0	0	0	0
McCord	BJ	Brian	24/08/68	Derby		1989		Derby County (loan)	Derby County	5	0	0	0	0	0	0	0
						1989	1991	Derby County	Stockport County	38	0	4	2	2	0	0	0
McCormack	JC	Cec	15/02/22	Newcastle	1995	1950	1951	Chelmsford City	Notts County	50	1	0	0	42	1	0	0
McCullough	F	Fred		Liverpool		1898		Liverpool White Star	Liverpool White Star	32	7	0	0	5	1	0	0
McDonagh	P	Patrick		Glasgow		1927		St. Anthony's	Nelson	9	0	0	0	2	0	0	0
McDonald	J					1900				1	0	0	0	0	0	0	0
McDonald	RR	Rikki	18/12/33	Paisley		1958		Saltcoats Victoria		1	0	0	0	0	0	0	0
McGarry	D	Danny	1911	Howwood		1938		Greenock Morton	Greenock Morton	41	1	0	0	12	1	0	0
McGee	J					1898		Stalybridge Rovers		3	0	0	0	0	0	0	0
McGowan	D	Duncan	1880	Renton		1901		Renton	Clyde	3	0	0	0	0	0	0	0
McGran	W	Willie		Beith	1922	1902		Lochwinnoch NB	Glasgow Rangers	7	0	0	0	0	0	0	0
McGugan	PJ	Paul	17/07/64	Glasgow		1987	1988	Glasgow Celtic	Chesterfield	49	6	3	2	2	0	0	0
McGuinness	W	Billy	30/11/13	Workington	1978	1936		Blackpool		1	0	0	0	0	0	0	0
McGuire	J	James	10/12/1883	Wallsend		1903	1904	North Shields Athletic	North Shields Athletic	34	1	0	0	0	0	0	0
McGuire	MJ	Mick	04/09/52	Blackpool		1982	1984	Norwich City	Oldham Athletic	47	1	2	0	6	0	0	0
McHale	R	Ray	12/08/50	Sheffield		1980	1981	Brighton & Hove Albion	Sheffield Utd.	53	1	8	0	1	0	0	0
McKenzie	IE	Ian	22/08/66	Wallsend		1985		Newcastle Utd	Stockport County	1	0	0	0	0	0	0	0
McLauchlan	R	Bob		Whitburn		1934		Gateshead	Wigan Athletic	3	0	0	0	0	0	0	0

Player			D.O.B	Place of Birth	Died	Season		Previous Club	Next Club	Appearances				Goals			
						First	Last			Lge.	FAC	FLC	Oth.	Lge.	FAC	FLC	Oth.
McMahon	K	Kevin	01/03/46	Tantobie		1972		York City	Hartlepool	5	0	2	0	0	0	0	0
McMorran	EJ	Eddie	02/09/23	Larne	1984	1950	1952	Leeds Utd	Doncaster Rovers	104	5	0	0	32	2	0	0
McNeil	MA	Matt	28/07/27	Glasgow	1977	1951	1952	Newcastle Utd	Brighton & Hove Albion	68	2	0	0	1	0	0	0
McPhee	J	John	21/11/37	Motherwell		1970		Blackpool	Southport	26	4	1	0	3	0	0	0
McPherson	PC	Peter	19/03/12	Livingston Station	1993	1933		Hibernian	Southport	1	0	0	0	0	0	0	0
McShea	E	Ernie		Glasgow		1907		Port Glasgow Athletic	Clyde	20	0	0	0	8	0	0	0
Mearns	FC	Fred	31/03/1879	Sunderland	1931	1909	1910	Hartlepools Utd.	Leicester Fosse	26	7	0	0	0	0	0	0
Mears	F	Frank	1899	Chorlton		1928	1929	Leeds Utd		42	0	0	0	13	0	0	0
Millar	A	Ally	15/01/52	Benburb, Glasgow		1970	1979	Benburb	York City	289	16	19	0	17	0	0	0
Millar	JM	Jock	31/12/06	Coatbridge		1928		Kilmarnock	Hartlepools Utd.	17	1	0	0	5	0	0	0
Millership	H	Harry	1889	Chirk	1959	1922		Rotherham County	Castleford Town	5	0	0	0	0	0	0	0
Milton	A	Albert		Sheffield	1917	1907		South Kirkby	Sunderland	15	0	0	0	0	0	0	0
Mitchell	R	Bob	1889	Paisley		1911	1912	Cliftonville, Belfast		4	0	0	0	0	0	0	0
Molby	J	Jan	04/07/63	Kolding (Denmark)		1995		Liverpool (loan)	Liverpool	5	0	0	0	0	0	0	0
Moore	J	Jimmy	01/09/1891	Felling	1972	1911	1914	Boldon Colliery	Southampton	101	8	0	0	23	1	0	0
Moores	IR	Ian	05/10/54	Chesterton	1998	1982		Bolton Wanderers (loan	Bolton Wanderers	3	0	0	0	0	0	0	0
Moran	BJ	Brian	03/06/47	Hemsworth		1966		Juniors	Goole Town	1	0	0	0	0	0	0	0
Mordue	J	Jackie	13/12/1886	Edmondsley	1957	1906		Spennymoor Utd	Arsenal	25	0	0	0	12	0	0	0
Morgan	C	Chris	09/11/77	Barnsley		1997		Trainee		11	3	0	0	0	0	0	0
Morris	FA	Freddie	11/03/20	Sheffield	1973	1946	1948		Southend Utd.	23	2	0	0	9	0	0	0
Morris	GR	George	1879	Manchester		1900		Glossop	Millwall Athletic	23	1	0	0	1	0	0	0
Morris	H	Harold	02/09/02	Bolsover	1976	1929		Mansfield Town	Shirebrook	1	0	0	0	0	0	0	0
Morris	R	Bob		Coppull		1920		Fleetwood	Accrington Stanley	13	0	0	0	3	0	0	0
Morrison	FR	Frank	1874	Falkirk		1899	1901	Luton Town		48	3	0	0	0	0	0	0
Morton	J	James		Leith		1913		Edinburgh St.Bernard's	Bristol City	18	0	0	0	3	0	0	0
Morton	R	Bobby	03/03/06	Widdrington	1990	1927		Bedlington Utd	Nottm. Forest	1	0	0	0	1	0	0	0
Moses	AP	Adie	04/05/75	Doncaster		1994	to date	Trainee		91	10	5	0	3	0	0	0
Mulligan	PG	Peter	17/07/42	Barnsley		1959	1963	Juniors		9	2	0	0	0	0	0	0
Murfin	C	Clarrie	02/04/09	Barnsley		1930	1931	Barnsley West Ward	Scunthorpe Utd.	22	0	0	0	1	0	0	0
Murphy	BL	Barry	10/02/40	Consett		1962	1977	South Shields		512	26	29	0	3	0	0	0
Murphy	E	Eddie	13/05/24	Hamilton		1950	1951	Northampton Town	Exeter City	18	1	0	0	2	0	0	0
Murray	A	Ally	22/12/43	Longtown		1963		Sunderland	Carlisle Utd.	21	0	3	0	1	0	2	0
Murray	J					1898		Wellingborough		4	0	0	0	0	0	0	0
Musgrove	R	Robert		Ryhope		1912	1914	Saltworth Colliery		12	0	0	0	2	0	0	0
Myers	J	Joseph		Sheffield		1925		Heeley Friends		3	0	0	0	2	0	0	0
Naylor	H	Harry				1898		Rotherwood Rovers		1	0	0	0	0	0	0	0
Ness	HM	Harry	1885	Scarborough	1957	1908	1910	Parkgate	Sunderland	70	11	0	0	6	0	0	0
New	MP	Martin	11/05/59	Swindon		1980		Mansfield Town		24	4	6	0	0	0	0	0
Newton	A	Albert	13/03/1894	Barnsley	1975	1919	1925	Barnsley St. George's	Bradford City	222	15	0	0	21	0	0	0
Nicholson	S	Sidney	1912	Shildon		1935	1937	Scunthorpe Utd.	Aberdeen	7	0	0	0	0	0	0	0
Nicol	RBM	Bobby	11/05/36	Edinburgh		1962	1963	Hibernian	Berwick Rangers	37	3	5	0	1	0	0	0
Nimrod	J	Joseph	1881	Jarrow		1901	1902	Jarrow	Denaby Utd	12	0	0	0	0	0	0	0
Nixon	JC	Jon	20/01/48	Ilkeston		1977		Shrewsbury Town	Halifax Town	10	0	0	0	0	0	0	0
Nixon	T	Tom	21/09/1867	Wombwell		1898	1899	Darwen		40	17	0	0	0	0	0	0
Noble	WD	Bill	1883	Wellingborough	1947	1905	1906	Wellingborough	Northampton Town	11	0	0	0	1	0	0	0
Normanton	SA	Skinner	20/08/26	Barnsley	1995	1947	1953	Barnsley Main Colliery	Halifax Town	123	7	0	0	2	0	0	0
Norton	P	Percy	1884	Wellingborough		1906		Wellingborough		1	0	0	0	0	0	0	0
O'Connell	BJ	Brendan	12/11/66	Waterloo, London		1989	1995	Burnley	Charlton Athletic	240	14	11	8	35	1	1	3
O'Connor	D	Doug	29/04/54	Barnsley		1970	1973	Apprentice	Mansfield Town	36	0	1	0	7	0	0	0
O'Donnell	M	Magnus	1882	Willington Quay		1906		Lincoln City	Newark Town	19	5	0	0	4	2	0	0
Ogle	R	Roger	15/09/04	Bedlington		1929	1930	Shildon Athletic	Norwich City	11	0	0	0	0	0	0	0
Ogley	A	Alan	04/02/46	Barnsley		1962		Apprentice	Manchester City	9	0	0	0	0	0	0	0
Ogley	MA	Mark	10/03/67	Barnsley		1985	1986	Apprentice	Carlisle Utd.	19	1	1	0	0	0	0	0
O'Hara	EA	Eddie	28/10/35	Glasgow		1962	1964	Greenock Morton	Bloemfontein (SA)	127	11	9	0	36	3	1	0
Oliver	K	Ken	26/11/38	Pelton		1959	1962	South Shields	Watford	94	13	6	0	38	7	9	0
Oram	DC	David		Ruabon		1936		Blackpool	Burton Town	10	1	0	0	1	0	0	0
O'Riley	PJ	Paul	17/10/50	Prescot		1974		Hull City	Goole Town	14	0	1	0	2	0	0	0
Ormond	JL	Ian	10/08/47	Larkhall		1968				1	0	0	0	1	0	0	0
Otulakowski	A	Anton	29/01/56	Dewsbury		1974	1976	Ossett Town	West Ham Utd.	42	1	4	0	2	0	0	0
Owen	G	Gordon	14/06/59	Barnsley		1984	1985	Cardiff City	Bristol City	68	5	2	0	25	4	0	0
Owen	JR	Jackie	1883	Busby	1924	1903		Hibernian	Greenock Morton	1	0	0	0	0	0	0	0
						1905	1906	Greenock Morton	Bolton Wanderers	33	3	0	0	13	0	0	0
Owencroft	GE	George	30/04/11	Prestwich	1986	1932		Reading	Southport	5	0	0	0	2	0	0	0
Oxspring	A	Arnold		Ecclesfield		1901	1909	Doncaster Rovers		271	21	0	0	4	0	0	0
Padgett	D	Daniel				1898		Ward Green		1	1	0	0	0	0	0	0
Page	G	George	30/11/1898	Darlington		1921		Doncaster Rovers	Accrington Stanley	1	0	0	0	0	0	0	0
Pallister	G	Gordon	02/04/17	Howden-le-Wear		1938	1951	Bradford City		220	12	0	0	3	2	0	0
Parker	D	Derrick	07/02/57	Wallsend		1979	1982	Southend Utd.	Oldham Athletic	107	6	14	0	32	3	4	0
Parker	RW	Bob	26/11/35	Seaham		1965	1968	Huddersfield Town		108	8	1	0	0	1	0	0
Parry	S	Steve	11/12/56	Upton		1973	1974	Apprentice		5	0	0	0	0	0	0	0
Patterson	MT	Michael	24/03/00	South Shields	1995	1930		Doncaster Rovers	Southport	5	0	0	0	0	0	0	0
Pattison	FM	Frank	23/12/30	Barrhead		1951	1954	Alloa Athletic	Stirling Albion	29	2	0	0	5	0	0	0
Payton	AP	Andy	23/10/67	Burnley		1993	1995	Glasgow Celtic	Huddersfield Town	108	7	7	0	41	1	3	0
Peachey	JM	John	21/07/52	Cambridge		1974	1978	York City	Darlington	127	5	9	0	31	0	2	0
Pearson	JS	John	01/09/63	Sheffield		1991	1992	Leeds Utd	Carlisle Utd.	32	3	3	2	4	0	1	0
Pedwell	R	Ralph		Durham		1934		Hartlepools Utd.	Frickley Colliery	10	2	0	0	2	0	0	0

Player			D.O.B	Place of Birth	Died	Season		Previous Club	Next Club	Appearances				Goals			
						First	Last			Lge.	FAC	FLC	Oth.	Lge.	FAC	FLC	Oth.
Pegg	E	Dick	1878	Leicester	1916	1905		Fulham		8	1	0	0	2	0	0	0
Pepper	F	Frank	1875	Sheffield		1899	1901	Newton Heath	Doncaster Rovers	58	2	0	0	0	0	0	0
Pettit	RJ	Ray	11/12/46	Hull		1972	1973	Hull City	Scarborough	51	6	1	0	1	0	0	0
Phoenix	AF	Ginger	1902	Manchester		1925		Aston Villa	Exeter City	4	0	0	0	0	0	0	0
Pickering	J	John	07/11/44	Stockton		1974		Halifax Town		43	1	1	0	2	0	0	0
Pickering	MJ	Mike	29/09/56	Heckmondwike		1974	1976	Juniors	Southampton	100	3	6	0	1	0	0	0
						1983		Sheffield Wed (loan)	Sheffield Wed.	3	0	0	0	0	0	0	0
Pierce	G	Gary	02/03/51	Bury		1979	1982	Wolves	Blackpool	81	4	4	0	0	0	0	0
Pigg	A	Albert		Durham		1929		Raith Rovers	Consett	5	0	0	0	1	0	0	0
Plummer	CA	Calvin	14/02/63	Nottingham		1983	1985	Derby County	Nottm. Forest	54	1	2	1	7	0	0	0
Porteous	D	Dave				1898		Darwen	Monckton Athletic	31	7	0	0	0	0	0	0
Powell	H	Bert	1880	Maidstone		1906		Chesterfield Town	Carlisle Utd.	6	2	0	0	2	1	0	0
Prendergast	MJ	Mick	24/11/50	Denaby		1977	1978	Sheffield Wed.	Mexborough Town	20	0	1	0	2	0	0	0
Price	B	Bryn	15/11/36	Treorchy		1956	1957	Treorchy Boys Club	Buxton	2	0	0	0	0	0	0	0
Price	PW	Peter	17/08/49	Wrexham		1974	1978	Portsmouth		79	4	7	0	28	0	2	0
Priestley	RM	Roy	26/11/48	Barnsley		1967		Juniors		1	0	0	0	0	0	0	0
Proudfoot		Jimmy	31/01/06	Usworth Colliery	1963	1927	1931	Usworth Colliery	Notts County	143	4	0	0	28	1	0	0
Provan	AMH	Andy	01/01/41	Greenock		1963		St Mirren	York City	3	0	0	0	0	0	0	0
Pugh	JG	Graham	12/02/48	Hoole		1976	1979	Chester	Scunthorpe Utd.	130	5	8	0	8	0	1	0
Raggett	BC	Brian	11/01/49	Barnsley		1966	1971	Apprentice		64	2	1	0	0	0	0	0
Rammell	AV	Andy	10/02/67	Nuneaton		1990	1995	Manchester Utd.	Southend Utd.	185	13	14	8	44	4	1	1
Rawson	AN	Albert	1900	West Melton	1980	1924		Birmingham		15	1	0	0	6	0	0	0
Redfearn	ND	Neil	20/06/65	Dewsbury		1991	1997	Oldham Athletic	Charlton Athletic	292	20	21	5	71	6	6	0
Redford	J	Jack				1921		Aberdeen Mugiemoss	Scunthorpe Utd.	3	1	0	0	2	0	0	0
Reed	C	Charles	1885	Sunderland		1905		Sunderland West End	Sunderland West End	11	1	0	0	0	0	0	0
						1907		Sunderland West End		16	1	0	0	0	0	0	0
Reed	G	Graham	24/06/61	Doncaster		1978	1979	Apprentice	Frickley Athletic	3	1	0	0	2	0	0	0
Rees	AA	Tony	01/08/64	Merthyr Tydfil		1987	1988	Birmingham City	Grimsby Town	31	1	2	1	3	0	0	0
Reeves	G	George	1884	Hucknall	1954	1906	1907	Sutton Town	Aston Villa	30	0	0	0	27	0	0	0
Regis	D	Dave	03/03/64	Paddington		1995	1996	Southend Utd.	Leyton Orient	16	0	3	0	1	0	0	0
Reid	W	Billy		Rotherham		1899		Attercliffe		6	0	0	0	0	0	0	0
Rhodes	AC	Andy	23/08/64	Askern		1983	1984	Apprentice	Doncaster Rovers	36	1	2	0	0	0	0	0
Richards	AG	Nai	28/04/02	Mardy	1976	1927	1933	Bridgend	Southport	123	8	0	0	0	0	0	0
Richardson	F	Fred	18/08/25	Middlestone Moor		1948	1949	Hartlepools Utd.	West Bromwich Albion	41	1	0	0	12	0	0	0
Richardson	GC	George		Newcastle		1902		Willington Athletic		5	0	0	0	1	0	0	0
Richmond	J	Joe	1897	Leasingthorpe	1953	1925		Leeds Utd	Norwich City	13	0	0	0	5	0	0	0
Ridyard	A	Alf	05/03/08	Cudworth	1981	1930	1931	Shafton	West Bromwich Albion	21	0	0	0	3	0	0	0
Riley	G	Glyn	24/07/58	Barnsley		1974	1981	Apprentice	Bristol City	131	8	11	0	16	1	3	0
Rimmer	SA	Stuart	12/10/64	Southport		1990		Walsall	Chester City	15	0	1	1	1	0	0	0
Rimmington	N	Norman	29/11/23	Staincross		1946		Mapplewell Town	Hartlepools Utd.	27	2	0	0	0	0	0	0
Ring	T	Tommy	08/08/30	Glasgow	1997	1961	1962	Everton	Aberdeen	21	0	0	0	1	0	0	0
Ritchie	R	Robert				1898		Stockton	Middlesbrough	3	0	0	0	0	0	0	0
Roberts	NE	Neville	15/06/02	Penmachno		1936		Wolves	Carlisle Utd.	7	0	0	0	0	0	0	0
Robertson	SP	Sam	1887	Hebburn		1904	1905	Hebburn Argyle		22	1	0	0	1	0	0	0
Robinson	EG	Ernie	21/01/10	Shiney Row	1990	1932		Tunbridge Wells Ranger	Sheffield Utd.	23	0	0	0	0	0	0	0
Robinson	J	Jamie	22/02/72	Liverpool		1992	1993	Liverpool	Carlisle Utd.	9	0	0	3	0	0	0	0
Robinson	MJ	Mark	21/11/68	Manchester		1987	1992	West Bromwich Albion	Newcastle Utd	137	8	9	5	6	0	0	1
Robledo	EO	Ted	26/07/28	Iquique (Chile)	1970	1947	1948	Notts County	Newcastle Utd	5	0	0	0	0	0	0	0
Robledo	GO	George	14/04/26	Iquique (Chile)	1989	1946	1948	Huddersfield Town	Newcastle Utd	105	9	0	0	45	2	0	0
Robson	J	Jimmy	23/01/39	Pelton		1967	1969	Blackpool	Bury	87	7	4	0	15	1	1	0
Rolph	DG	Darren	19/11/68	Romford		1987		King's Lynn	King's Lynn	2	0	0	0	0	0	0	0
Ronson	W	Billy	22/01/57	Fleetwood		1982	1985	Wrexham	Blackpool	113	7	7	0	3	0	0	0
Rooney	T	Thomas		Felling	1936	1914		Gateshead	Durham City	25	1	0	0	0	0	0	0
Round	E	Elijah	1882	Stoke-on-Trent		1904	1907	Mexborough West End	Oldham Athletic	45	1	0	0	0	0	0	0
Roystone	A	Albert		Barnsley		1911	1913	Redfearns	Doncaster Rovers	1	1	0	0	0	0	0	0
Ruddlesdin	A	Arthur	07/02/1899	Hoyland	1972	1920	1922	Tankersley Utd	Swindon Town	4	0	0	0	1	0	0	0
Ruddlesdin	W	William	1884	Birdwell		1906		Birdwell	Birdwell	14	0	0	0	0	0	0	0
Rushton	R	Richard	18/09/02	Willenhall	1981	1926		Sheffield Wed.	Wombwell Town	6	0	0	0	0	0	0	0
Russell	HG	Harry		Burton-on-Trent		1923		Burton All Saints	Burton All Saints	2	0	0	0	0	0	0	0
Rutherford	C	Colin	11/07/44	Rowlands Gill		1963		Sunderland		1	1	0	0	0	0	0	0
Rutter	A	Arthur	1887	South Shields		1910		South Shields	Exeter City	16	0	0	0	5	0	0	0
Ryalls	J	Joe	1881	Sheffield		1905		Sheffield Wed.	Fulham	17	0	0	0	0	0	0	0
Rymer	GH	George	06/10/23	Barnsley		1946		Ardsley Victoria	Accrington Stanley	3	0	0	0	0	0	0	0
Sampy	T	Tom	14/03/1899	Shiremoor	1978	1934		Sheffield Utd.		1	0	0	0	0	0	0	0
Sanderson	CA	Charles		Wombwell		1923	1925	Wombwell	Mexborough Athletic	24	2	0	0	0	0	0	0
Sanderson	P	Phil	01/11/53	Barnsley		1974		Worsborough Bridge		2	0	0	0	1	0	0	0
Sanderson	R	Robert		Barnsley		1907		Sunderland Royal Rov.		5	0	0	0	0	0	0	0
Saunders	JG	John	01/12/50	Worksop	1998	1975		Huddersfield Town (loa	Huddersfield Town	9	0	0	0	0	0	0	0
						1975	1978	Huddersfield Town	Lincoln City	140	7	4	0	7	0	0	0
Saville	AV	Andy	12/12/64	Hull		1989	1991	Walsall	Hartlepool Utd.	82	3	6	4	21	0	0	1
Sawyer	R	Roy	29/03/40	Barnsley		1960	1961	Worsborough Bridge		2	0	0	0	0	0	0	0
Saxton	E	Edgar	1896	Carlton, Yorkshire		1919	1920	Carlton Victoria	Bournemouth	3	0	0	0	0	0	0	0
Sayles	T	Tommy	1892	Worksop		1921	1922	Cardiff City	Southend Utd.	20	4	0	0	0	0	0	0
Scattergood	E	Eric	09/09/29	Barnsley		1949	1951	Worsborough Dale ST	Wisbech Town	12	0	0	0	0	0	0	0
Scott	JW	Joe	06/07/00	Lye	1962	1927		Rotherham Utd.	Tottenham Hotspur	10	0	0	0	3	0	0	0

Player			D.O.B	Place of Birth	Died	Season		Previous Club	Next Club	Appearances				Goals			
						First	Last			Lge.	FAC	FLC	Oth.	Lge.	FAC	FLC	Oth.
Seal	J	Jimmy	09/12/50	Walton, Wakefield		1971		Wolves	York City	43	3	3	0	12	1	0	0
Semley	A	Alan	21/02/66	Barnsley		1983		Apprentice	Matlock Town	4	1	0	0	0	0	0	0
Senior	RV	Roy	21/06/40	Barnsley		1964		Millwall	Rugby Town	21	1	0	0	4	1	0	0
Senior	S	Stuart	26/10/53	Barnsley		1972		Apprentice	Frickley Colliery	2	0	0	0	0	0	0	0
Seymour	A	Arthur		South Shields	1931	1901	1902	Hebburn Argyle	Bradford City	61	8	0	0	0	0	0	0
Sharp	D	Duncan	16/03/33	Barnsley		1953	1961	Woolley Colliery	Bedford Town	213	21	4	0	0	0	0	0
Sharp	F	Frank	28/05/47	Edinburgh		1970	1972	Cardiff City	Grimsby Town	125	9	4	0	7	0	0	0
Shaw	EL	Eric	12/02/47	Barnsley		1964		Apprentice		2	0	0	0	0	0	0	0
Shaw	MV	Michael		Stockport		1925		Cheshire Regiment	Crewe Alexandra	5	0	0	0	1	0	0	0
Sheavills	JE	Jimmy	28/07/40	Aylesham		1963	1964	Peterborough Utd.		65	6	5	0	6	0	1	0
Sheridan	DSD	Darren	08/12/67	Manchester		1993	to date	Winsford Utd		146	9	8	2	4	0	1	0
Sherman	E	Ernest				1903		Chester	Rotherham Town	3	0	0	0	1	0	0	0
Sherratt	B	Brian	29/03/44	Stoke-on-Trent		1969		Oxford Utd	Gainsborough Trinity	15	0	0	0	0	0	0	0
Sherwin	H	Harry	1893	Walsall	1953	1924	1925	Leeds Utd		14	0	0	0	0	0	0	0
Shirtliff	PA	Peter	06/04/61	Hoyland		1995	to date	Wolves		49	1	1	0	0	0	0	0
Short	J	Jack	18/02/28	Barnsley	1976	1956	1959	Stoke City	Houghton Main Colliery	109	7	0	0	0	0	0	0
Shotton	M	Mal	16/02/57	Newcastle		1988	1989	Huddersfield Town	Hull City	66	4	2	2	6	0	0	0
						1994	1995	Ayr Utd		10	0	1	0	1	0	0	0
Shotton	R	Bob	27/10/10	Bearpark		1932	1938	Hartlepools Utd.		221	15	0	1	8	0	0	1
Shutt	SJ	Steve	29/11/64	Barnsley		1982	1983	Apprentice	Goole Town	1	0	1	0	0	0	0	0
Silto	WA	Billy	1883	Washington		1904	1908	Hebburn Argyle	Swindon Town	92	6	0	0	3	0	0	0
Simmons	W	William	1879	Sheffield	1911	1899		Sheffield Wed.	Sheffield Wed.	15	0	0	0	6	0	0	0
Smart	E	Ernest		Kinsley		1923	1924	Frickley Colliery		3	0	0	0	0	0	0	0
Smillie	RD	Ron	27/09/33	Grimethorpe		1951	1955	Juniors	Lincoln City	29	1	0	0	1	0	0	0
						1960	1961	Lincoln City	Chelmsford City	85	13	3	0	16	1	0	0
Smith	F	Frank	22/11/1889	Darnall	1982	1914	1919	Sheffield Club	Swansea Town	26	0	0	0	0	0	0	0
Smith	G	Gavin	25/09/17	Cambuslang	1992	1946	1953	Dumbarton	Stocksbridge Works	257	14	0	0	35	3	0	0
Smith	J	Jackie		Littletown		1932	1934	West Stanley	Plymouth Argyle	104	3	0	0	26	0	0	0
Smith	JW	Jack		Halesowen		1928	1931	Halesowen Town	Notts County	118	6	0	0	1	0	0	0
Smith	MC	Mark	21/03/60	Sheffield		1989	1992	Plymouth Argyle	Notts County	104	6	6	5	10	1	0	1
Smith	N	Norman	02/01/25	Darwen	1990	1952	1958	Arsenal	Shrewsbury Town	156	9	0	0	14	1	0	0
Smith	R	Bobby	20/06/41	Barnsley		1961	1962	Juniors	Chelmsford City	3	0	1	0	0	0	0	0
Smith	T	Tom	1869	Ecclesfield		1898	1899	Sheffield Strollers		11	9	0	0	3	0	0	0
Snodin	G	Glynn	14/02/60	Rotherham		1993	1994	Heart of Midlothian	Carlisle Utd.	25	0	3	0	0	0	0	0
Souter	DD	Don	01/12/61	Hammersmith		1982		Ipswich Town	Aldershot	21	0	4	0	0	0	0	0
Speedie	DR	David	20/02/60	Glenrothes		1978	1979	Juniors	Darlington	23	0	0	0	0	0	0	0
Spence	R	Dickie	18/07/08	Platts Common	1983	1932	1934	Platts Common WMC	Chelsea	64	1	0	1	25	0	0	0
Spoors	J	Jimmy		Jarrow		1920	1921	Sheffield Wed.		23	2	0	0	10	1	0	0
Springett	PJ	Peter	08/05/46	Fulham	1997	1975	1979	Sheffield Wed.	Scarborough	191	9	11	0	0	0	0	0
Sproates	J	John	11/04/43	Houghton-le-Spring		1963		West Auckland Town	Gateshead	2	0	0	0	0	0	0	0
Spruce	GD	George	03/04/23	Chester		1952	1956	Wrexham	Chester	149	5	0	0	0	0	0	0
Stacey	GW	George	1887	Thorpe Hesley		1905	1906	Thornhill Utd	Manchester Utd.	64	8	0	0	6	2	0	0
Stainsby	J	John	25/09/37	Stairfoot		1959	1960	Wath Wanderers	York City	34	0	2	0	12	0	0	0
Stark	J	James		Glasgow		1926	1927	St. Roch's	Bradford City	8	0	0	0	2	0	0	0
Steele	J	Johnny	24/11/16	Glasgow		1938	1948	Ayr Utd		49	1	0	0	21	0	0	0
Stevenson	GW	General	1877	Hapton		1900	1901	Liverpool	Wellingborough	54	7	0	0	0	0	0	0
Stewart	G	Gerry	02/09/46	Dundee		1971	1974	Preston NE	Boston Utd	138	8	3	0	0	0	0	0
Storer	JA	Jackie	03/02/08	Swinton, Yorkshire		1928	1930	Mexborough Athletic	Bristol Rovers	22	1	0	0	6	0	0	0
Storey	S	Sid	25/12/19	Darfield		1956		York City	Accrington Stanley	29	2	0	0	0	0	0	0
Stott	GRB	George	31/01/06	North Shields	1963	1926		Monckton Athletic	Bedlington Utd	2	0	0	0	0	0	0	0
Suddick	G					1931				1	0	0	0	0	0	0	0
Surtees	E	Ernie	1886	Rotherham		1907		Parkgate		10	0	0	0	3	0	0	0
Swaby	HN	Harry	22/01/06	Grimsby	1982	1932		Grimsby Town	Scarborough	18	0	0	0	0	0	0	0
Swallow	BE	Barry	02/07/42	Arksey		1964	1966	Crewe Alexandra	Bradford City	96	5	3	0	1	0	0	0
Swallow	E	Ernie	09/07/19	Wheatley Hill	1962	1947	1949	Doncaster Rovers	Oldham Athletic	36	1	0	0	0	0	0	0
Swan	E	Eddie		Glasgow		1924		Aberdeen	Dumbarton	2	0	0	0	0	0	0	0
Swann	A	Andrew	1878	Dalbeattie		1900		New Brompton	Arsenal	29	3	0	0	18	1	0	0
Swann	G	Gordon	07/12/37	Maltby		1961		Rotherham Utd.	Heanor Town	2	0	0	0	0	0	0	0
Swift	C	Colin	23/12/33	Barnsley		1955	1961	Juniors		241	18	4	0	0	0	0	0
Swindells	J	Jackie	12/04/37	Manchester		1961		Accrington Stanley	Workington	14	3	0	0	8	3	0	0
Sylph	J	James				1903		Jarrow		1	0	0	0	0	0	0	0
Taggart	GP	Gerry	18/10/70	Belfast		1989	1994	Manchester City	Bolton Wanderers	212	14	15	6	16	2	1	1
Taylor	A	Archie	1882	Dundee		1911	1912	Huddersfield Town	York City	57	15	0	0	0	0	0	0
Taylor	AM	Archie	07/11/39	Dunscroft		1961		Bristol City	Mansfield Town	2	0	0	0	0	0	0	0
Taylor	BJ	Brian	24/03/37	Walsall		1967		Port Vale	Kidderminster Harriers	23	1	1	0	2	0	1	0
Taylor	JH	Harry	1888	Sutton-in-Ashfield		1909	1910	Sutton Town	Portsmouth	16	1	0	0	7	0	0	0
Taylor	T	Tommy	29/01/32	Barnsley	1958	1950	1952	Smithies Utd	Manchester Utd.	44	2	0	0	26	2	0	0
Ten Heuvel	L	Laurens	06/06/76	Duivendrecht (Hol)		1995	to date	FC Den Bosch (Hol)		7	0	1	0	0	0	0	0
Thomas	BE	Barrie	19/05/37	Measham		1966	1967	Scunthorpe Utd.		43	6	1	0	19	3	0	0
Thomas	DG	Gwyn	26/09/57	Swansea		1983	1989	Leeds Utd	Hull City	201	13	11	3	17	2	0	0
Thomas	JC	Joe	22/09/32	Westhoughton		1952	1957	Wolves	Mansfield Town	134	5	0	0	0	0	0	0
Thomas	RS	Bob	1911	Durham		1934	1935	Blackpool	Millwall	39	3	0	0	2	0	0	0
Thomas	W	William	1885	Liverpool		1908		Leeds City	Huddersfield Town	3	0	0	0	0	0	0	0
Thompson	L	Len	18/02/01	Sheffield		1919		Hallam FC	Hallam FC	2	0	0	0	0	0	0	0
Thompson	N	Neil	02/10/63	Beverley		1996	1997	Ipswich Town	York City	27	1	4	0	5	0	0	0

Player			D.O.B	Place of Birth	Died	Season First	Season Last	Previous Club	Next Club	Appearances Lge.	FAC	FLC	Oth.	Goals Lge.	FAC	FLC	Oth.
Thompson	N	Norman	05/09/00	Forest Hall		1926		Middlesbrough	Chilton Colliery	4	0	0	0	0	0	0	0
Thorpe	T	Tommy	19/05/1881	Kilnhurst	1953	1905	1908	Doncaster Rovers	Northampton Town	105	10	0	0	1	0	0	0
						1921		Northampton Town		13	3	0	0	0	0	0	0
Tiler	C	Carl	11/02/70	Sheffield		1987	1990	Trainee	Nottm. Forest	71	5	4	4	3	0	0	0
Tilson	SF	Fred	19/04/04	Barnsley	1972	1926	1927	Regent St. Congs	Manchester City	61	3	0	0	23	1	0	0
Tindall	TJ	Jack	12/05/1891	Barnsley	1971	1913	1922	St.Barnabas FC	Accrington Stanley	140	8	0	0	0	0	0	0
Tindill	H	Bert	31/12/26	South Hiendley	1973	1959	1961	Bristol City	Frickley Colliery	98	15	1	0	29	2	0	0
Tingay	P	Phil	02/05/50	Chesterfield		1972		Chesterfield (loan)	Chesterfield	8	0	0	0	0	0	0	0
Tinkler	E	Eric	30/07/70	Roodeport(S.Afr.)		1997		Cagliari (Italy)		25	2	2	0	2	0	0	0
Tomlinson	F	Fred	1886	South Shields		1907	1908	West Stanley	Stoke	16	4	0	0	1	0	0	0
Topping	H	Harry	1908	Manchester	1935				Macclesfield Town	14	5	0	0	2	0	0	0
Travers	JE	George	04/11/1888	Birmingham	1946	1910	1913	Leicester Fosse	Manchester Utd.	84	17	0	0	23	2	0	0
Travers	P	Paddy	28/05/1883	Renfrew	1962	1901		Renfrew Victoria	Thornliebank	13	0	0	0	4	0	0	0
						1903		Thornliebank	Thornliebank	9	0	0	0	0	0	0	0
Troops	H	Harry	10/02/26	Sheffield	1963	1948		Hadfield Works	Lincoln City	3	0	0	0	1	0	0	0
Tufnell	H	Harry	02/03/1886	Burton-on-Trent	1959	1909	1919	Bury	Wakefield City	200	29	0	0	60	10	0	0
Tummon	O	Oliver	03/03/1884	Sheffield	1955	1920		Sheffield Utd.		1	0	0	0	0	0	0	0
Turnbull	JM	Jimmy		Ashington		1932		Hakoah (USA)	Tunbridge Wells Rangers	1	0	0	0	0	0	0	0
Turner	J	Joe	21/03/31	Barnsley		1961		Scunthorpe Utd.	Goole Town	7	0	0	0	0	0	0	0
Turner	JH	Joe		Sheffield		1920	1921	Rotherham Town	Worksop Town	12	0	0	0	0	0	0	0
Turner	P	Paul	08/07/53	Barnsley		1970	1974	Apprentice	Frickley Athletic	35	3	0	0	1	0	0	0
Turner	PJ	Percy	1880			1900		Swindon Town	Chesterfield Town	5	0	0	0	1	0	0	0
Underwood	A	Albert		Glencartra		1902		Rutherglen Glencairn	Airdrieonians	14	4	0	0	3	0	0	0
Utley	G	George	1887	Elsecar	1966	1908	1913	Elsecar	Sheffield Utd.	170	26	0	0	8	1	0	0
VanDerVelden	C	Carel	03/08/72	Arnhem(Holland)		1995	1996	FC Den Bosch (Hol)	Scarborough	9	0	1	0	0	0	0	0
Vaughan	H	Harry				1919		Wath Athletic		5	0	0	0	1	0	0	0
Viveash	AL	Adrian	30/09/69	Swindon		1995		Swindon Town (loan)	Swindon Town	2	0	0	0	1	0	0	0
Waddell	W	Willie	16/04/50	Denny		1971		Kilmarnock	Hartlepool	18	3	2	0	4	0	0	0
Wadsworth	W	Wilf		Kilnhurst		1932		Doncaster Rovers		17	0	0	0	4	0	0	0
Wainscoat	WR	Russell	28/07/1898	Maltby	1967	1919	1923	Maltby Main	Middlesbrough	144	9	0	0	54	2	0	0
Waldron	H	Harry		Sheffield		1899		Attercliffe		14	0	0	0	1	0	0	0
Walker	C	Colin	01/05/58	Rotherham		1980	1982	Gisborne City (NZ)	Gisborne City (NZ)	24	1	3	0	12	0	1	0
Walker	PG	Paul	03/04/49	Bradford		1975		Peterborough Utd.	Ottawa Tigers (Can)	13	1	2	0	0	0	0	0
Wall	G	George	20/02/1885	Boldon Colliery	1962	1903	1905	Jarrow	Manchester Utd.	75	5	0	0	24	1	0	0
Wallbanks	J	Jimmy	12/09/09	Platt Bridge	1979	1930		Annfield Plain	Norwich City	9	0	0	0	0	0	0	0
Wallbanks	J	John		Hindley, Lancashire		1929	1932	Crook Town	Portsmouth	118	8	0	0	65	0	0	0
Walls	J	Jack	08/05/32	Seaham		1952		Juniors	Peterborough Utd.	7	1	0	0	0	0	0	0
Walsh	C	Charlie		Glossop		1926		Preston NE		6	0	0	0	0	0	0	0
Walsh	IP	Ian	04/09/58	St Davids		1984	1985	Swansea City	Grimsby Town	49	1	3	0	15	0	0	0
Walters	H	Henry	15/03/25	Wath-on-Dearne		1953	1959	Walsall	Wombwell	160	12	0	0	4	0	0	0
Ward	A	Ashley	24/11/70	Manchester		1997		Derby County		29	6	3	0	8	1	1	0
Ward	J	John				1903		Wallsend Park Villa		8	0	0	0	0	0	0	0
Ward	TV	Tim	17/10/18	Cheltenham	1993	1950	1952	Derby County		33	0	0	0	0	0	0	0
Wardle	IS	Ian	27/03/70	Doncaster		1989		Juniors	Maltby Miners Welfare	9	0	2	0	0	0	0	0
Wardle	W	Billy	20/01/18	Houghton-le-Spring	1989	1953	1954	Birmingham City	Skegness Town	28	1	0	0	1	0	0	0
Waring	T	Pongo	12/10/06	High Tranmere	1980	1935		Aston Villa	Wolves	18	4	0	0	7	2	0	0
Warner	P	Percy		Birdwell		1905		Birdwell		3	0	0	0	2	0	0	0
Warnock	N	Neil	01/12/48	Sheffield		1976	1977	Aldershot	York City	57	3	3	0	10	1	1	0
Warrilow	F	Frank				1935		Wellington Town	Dudley Town	13	0	0	0	4	0	0	0
Watson	D	Don	27/08/32	Barnsley		1961		Bury	Rochdale	8	0	0	0	1	0	0	0
Watson	DN	David	10/11/73	Barnsley		1992	to date	Trainee		172	11	14	1	0	0	0	0
Watson	PR	Phil	23/02/07	Dykehead		1937		Blackpool	Queen of the South	4	0	0	0	0	0	0	0
Welch	C	Chris	1878	Hebburn	1922	1901	1903	Hebburn Argyle	Denaby Utd	57	10	0	0	0	1	0	0
West	A	Alf	15/12/1881	Nottingham		1902	1903	Ilkeston Town	Liverpool	42	6	0	0	0	1	0	0
White	ET	Earl		Barnsley		1919		Dearne Athletic	Wakefield City	1	0	0	0	0	0	0	0
Whitehead	PM	Phil	17/12/69	Halifax		1991	1992	Halifax Town	Oxford Utd	16	0	0	0	0	0	0	0
Whitehouse	D	Dean	03/10/63	Mexborough		1983		Apprentice	Torquay Utd	2	0	1	0	0	0	0	0
Whitham	V	Vic	1894	Burnley	1962	1919		Kimberworth Old Boys	Norwich City	3	0	0	0	0	0	0	0
Whitworth	E	Ernie		Treeton		1932	1934	Rotherham Utd.	Aldershot	78	5	0	1	4	0	0	0
Whitworth	NA	Neil	12/04/72	Wigan		1991		Manchester Utd (loan)	Manchester Utd.	11	0	0	0	0	0	0	0
Whyke	P	Peter	07/09/39	Barnsley		1957	1960	Smithies FC	Rochdale	26	0	1	0	1	0	0	0
Whyte	JA	Archie	17/07/19	Redding	1973	1946	1949	Armadale Thistle	Oldham Athletic	91	1	0	0	2	0	0	0
Wigg	RG	Ron	18/05/49	Great Dunmow		1976	1977	Grimsby Town	Scunthorpe Utd.	18	0	2	0	5	0	0	0
Wigmore	C	Clive	1892	Kiveton Park		1911	1914	Dinnington	Aston Villa	61	2	0	0	5	0	0	0
Wilcock	GH	George	24/01/1890	Edinburgh		1911		Bradford PA	Goole Town	4	0	0	0	0	0	0	0
Wilcox	A	Tony	13/06/44	Rotherham		1964		Rotherham Utd.	Kidderminster Harriers	6	0	0	0	0	0	0	0
Wilkes	DA	David	10/03/64	Barnsley		1981	1983	Apprentice	Harps (Hong Kong)	17	0	2	0	2	0	0	0
Wilkinson	F	Fred		Durham		1908		Shildon Athletic	Darlington	15	0	0	0	0	0	0	0
Wilkinson	J	Jack		Ilkeston		1905	1907	Hickleton Main		24	3	0	0	2	1	0	0
Wilkinson	P	Paul	30/10/64	Grimoldby		1996	1997	Middlesbrough	Millwall	49	2	4	0	9	0	2	0
Williams	C	Clarrie	13/01/33	Wardley		1960	1961	Grimsby Town		24	2	0	0	0	0	0	0
Williams	E	Emlyn	15/01/12	Maesteg	1989	1936	1938	Buxton Town	Preston NE	88	5	0	0	0	0	0	0
						1947	1948	Preston NE	Accrington Stanley	17	0	0	0	0	0	0	0
Williams	GJ	Gareth	12/03/67	Cowes		1991	1993	Aston Villa	Bournemouth	34	2	1	2	6	0	0	0
Williams	JH	John		Staincross		1919	1920	Staincross	Doncaster Rovers	39	2	0	0	0	0	0	0

Player			D.O.B	Place of Birth	Died	Season		Previous Club	Next Club	Appearances				Goals			
						First	Last			Lge.	FAC	FLC	Oth.	Lge.	FAC	FLC	Oth.
Williamson	R	Bob	06/12/33	Edinburgh		1963	1964	St. Mirren	Leeds Utd	46	4	4	0	0	0	0	0
Wilshaw	J	John		Ashington		1927		Bedlington Utd	Wath Athletic	2	0	0	0	0	0	0	0
Wilson	DJ	Danny	01/01/60	Wigan		1993	1994	Sheffield Wed.		77	5	6	1	2	0	0	0
Wilson	JB	John				1935		Blackhall Coll. Welfare	Margate	3	0	0	0	0	0	0	0
Wilson	JW	Joe	29/09/10	West Butsfield	1996	1946		Reading	Blyth Spartans	20	8	0	0	0	1	0	0
Winstanley	E	Eric	15/11/44	Barnsley		1961	1972	Juniors	Chesterfield	410	33	18	0	35	3	1	0
Woffinden	RS	Richard	20/02/17	Rotherham	1987	1938		Winterwell Athletic	Hartlepools Utd.	2	0	0	0	0	0	0	0
Wood	BW	Barrie	05/12/36	Doncaster		1960	1961	South Shields	Grantham	4	0	1	0	2	0	0	0
Wood	CC	Chris	18/05/55	Penistone		1972		Huddersfield Town (loa	Huddersfield Town	1	0	0	0	0	0	0	0
Wood	R	Bobby	15/02/30	Elphinstone		1951	1964	Hibernian		338	28	7	0	41	3	0	0
Wood	RE	Ray	11/06/31	Hebburn		1966	1967	Bradford City		30	4	1	0	0	0	0	0
Wormley	P	Paul	16/09/61	Leeds		1979		Yorkshire Amateurs	Huddersfield Town	1	0	0	0	0	0	0	0
Worrall	A	Arthur				1898		Crewe Alexandra	Belfast Distillery	7	0	0	0	0	0	0	0
Wren	C	Cecil		Hemsworth		1909		South Kirkby		2	0	0	0	0	0	0	0
Wright	AM	Alex	18/10/25	Kirkcaldy		1947	1950	Hibernian	Tottenham Hotspur	84	2	0	0	31	2	0	0
Wright	P	Peter	1882	Hebburn		1904		Hebburn Argyle		2	0	0	0	0	0	0	0
Wroe	H	Harold	1906	Birdwell		1925		Birdwell	Wombwell Town	1	0	0	0	0	0	0	0
Wylde	RJ	Rodger	08/03/54	Sheffield		1984	1987	Sunderland	Stockport County	52	5	2	1	19	1	0	0
Yates	D	Sammy	18/03/53	Barnsley		1972	1977	Apprentice	Frickley Athletic	104	7	1	0	2	0	0	0
Youell	JH	Jasper	23/03/25	Bilston		1952		Portsmouth	Weymouth	19	1	0	0	0	0	0	0
Young	NJ	Norman	1907	Birmingham		1936		Aston Villa	Brierley Hill Alliance	22	1	0	0	0	0	0	0

Appeared in FA Cup only

Cotton	J					1899		Burton Wanderers		0	1	0	0	0	1	0	0
Ferrier	HR	Harry	20/05/20	Ratho		1945		Ratho Amateurs	Portsmouth	0	1	0	0	0	0	0	0
Holdcroft	GH	Harry	23/01/09	Burslem	1983	1945		Preston NE	Morecambe	0	6	0	0	0	0	0	0
Scott	J	Joe				1906				0	2	0	0	0	0	0	0
Shears	AE	Bert	12/05/00	Newcastle	1954	1931		Wigan Borough	Aldershot	0	1	0	0	0	0	0	0

Appeared in League Cup only

Markham	D	Eric	1959			1978		Apprentice	Rotherham Utd	0	0	1	0	0	0	0	0
Mokone	SV	Steve	23/03/32	Pretoria (SA)		1961		Benfica(Portugal)		0	0	1	0	0	0	0	0

SPANNING THE YEARS
1887 - 1997

PLAYERS OF THE FIRST WORLD WAR (1915-1918)

Player			D.O.B	Place of Birth	Died	Season First	Last	Previous Club	Next Club	Apps	Goal
Allen						1918				1	0
Allott						1915				1	0
Anderson						1918				1	0
Armstrong						1915				1	0
Atkinson						1917				2	0
Barnes						1917				1	0
Barrowclough						1917		Bradford Park Avenue (Guest)		1	0
Barson	F	Frank	10/04/1891	Grimesthorpe	1968	1915	1918	Played for Barnsley 1914/15	Played for Barnsley 1919/20	91	14
Bates						1918				4	0
Batty	W	Billy	13/07/1886	Killamarsh		1915		Swindon Town (Guest)		21	3
Bethune	J	Jack	19/10/1888	Milngavie	1955	1916	1918	Played for Barnsley 1914/15	Played for Barnsley 1919/20	3	0
Birtles	TJ	Tommy	26/10/1885	Higham, Yorkshire	1971	1915	1918	Doncaster Rovers (Guest)		58	18
Black						1917				1	0
Box	H					1915				3	0
Bradley	P					1917				1	0
Bratley	PW	Phil	26/12/1880	Rawmarsh	1962	1915	1918	Liverpool (Guest)		70	8
Brelsford	C			Sheffield		1918		Sheffield Wednesday (Guest)		1	0
Briscoe						1918				5	1
Broomhead						1918				2	0
Brown						1917				2	0
Brown						1916				2	0
Buddery	H	Harold	1889	Sheffield		1917		Portsmouth (Guest)		2	0
Burkinshaw	JDL	Jack	12/05/1890	Kilnhurst	1947	1917		Sheffield Wednesday (Guest)		1	1
Burkinshaw	L	Laurence	02/12/1893	Kilnhurst	1969	1915	1916	Rotherham Town (Guest)		41	1
						1918		Kilnhurst FC (Guest)		1	0
Burkinshaw	R	Ralph	26/03/1898	Mexborough	1951	1915	1917			60	25
Burrows						1917				1	0
Caffrey						1915				1	0
Campey						1915				1	0
Carpenter						1915				2	0
Carr						1918				1	1
Chapman	G					1917				29	14
Chard						1917				7	0
Clarke						1916				1	0
Clarkson						1918				2	0
Cockerill						1917	1918			4	1
Cooper	JC	Jack	1889	Sneinton		1915		Played for Barnsley 1914/15	Newport County	15	0
Cooper	W					1915				3	0
Corner						1918				1	0
Crabtree						1918				1	0
Crummond						1918				2	0
Dawson						1918				1	0
Day						1917				1	0
Dennis	H					1915	1916			2	0
Dickenson						1918				6	0
Dobson	GW	George	07/10/1897	Rotherham	1957	1918		Kimberworth Old Boys	Played for Barnsley 1919/20	12	1
Donkin	GWC	George	01/12/1892	Carlton, Yorkshire	1927	1915	1918	Played for Barnsley 1914/15	Played for Barnsley 1919/20	115	19
Downing	J	John		Royston, Yorkshire		1918		Monckton Athletic	Played for Barnsley 1919/20	3	0
Downs	JT	Dickie	05/04/1886	Middridge	1949	1915	1918	Played for Barnsley 1914/15	Played for Barnsley 1919/20	31	3
Elshaw						1918				1	0
Fagan	S					1916				4	0
Fearnley	E					1916	1917	Bradford Park Avenue (Guest)		2	0
Fell	G	Gerry	03/12/1898	Barnsley	1977	1918		Elsecar	Played for Barnsley 1919/20	1	0
Fletcher	B	Brough	09/03/1893	Mealsgate	1972	1918		Played for Barnsley 1914/15	Played for Barnsley 1919/20	2	0
Gittins	JH	Jack	11/11/1893	Stanton Hill	1956	1915	1918	Played for Barnsley 1914/15	Played for Barnsley 1919/20	48	0
Glendenning	R	Bob	1889	New Washington	1940	1916		Bolton Wanderers (Guest)		1	0
Goddard						1918				5	3
Green						1916				1	0
Griffin	MR	Mick	1887	Middlesbrough		1915		Played for Barnsley 1914/15		2	0
Hakin	JT	Tom	1882	Mexborough	1950	1916		Rotherham County (Guest)		1	0
Hall	J					1915	1917			4	0
Halliwell	JA	Joe	17/01/1894	Lostock Hall		1918		Played for Barnsley 1914/15	Played for Barnsley 1919/20	3	1
Hargreaves						1915				2	0
Harrison	J					1918				2	0
Hollyoak	E					1918				16	0
Holman						1917				1	0
Holman						1917				2	0

Player			D.O.B	Place of Birth	Died	Season First	Last	Previous Club	Next Club	Apps	Goal
Holt						1918				1	0
Horsfield	S					1916				1	0
Hoult						1916		Rotherham County (Guest)		1	0
Howarth						1918				1	0
Johnson						1915				1	0
Kay	H	Harry		Elsecar		1916	1917	Rotherham County (Guest)		49	8
Keenlyside	G	George		Jarrow		1915	1918	Jarrow (Guest)		44	11
Kilner						1918				1	0
Layton	A					1915	1916			50	2
Leavey	HJ	Bert	1886	Guildford		1918				1	0
Ledingham	WD	William	1891	Newtongrange	1960	1918				1	0
Lees	JWD	Joe	1892	Coalville	1933	1915	1918	Played for Barnsley 1914/15	Rotherham County	22	10
Lester						1918				2	0
Livingstone						1918				1	0
Longlands	J					1917		Leicester Fosse (Guest)		1	0
Lydon						1918				2	0
Marshall	J	John	1892	Stenhousemuir		1916	1918	Played for Barnsley 1914/15	Clyde	12	3
Maw	JW					1918		Sheffield Wednesday (Guest)		1	0
Milton	E	Ernest	07/08/1897	Kimberworth	1984	1918		Sheffield United (Guest)		9	0
Mitchell	JT	Joe	01/01/1886	Darnall	1964	1918		Luton Town (Guest)		11	0
Moore	J	Jimmy	01/09/1891	Felling	1972	1915	1918	Played for Barnsley 1914/15	Southampton	42	22
Musgrove	R	Robert		Ryhope		1915		Played for Barnsley 1914/15		2	0
Newton	A	Albert	13/03/1894	Barnsley	1975	1915	1918	Barnsley St. George's	Played for Barnsley	21	15
Osborne						1918				1	0
Palmer	W	Billy	1888	Barnsley		1915	1916	Everton (Guest)		43	7
Peart	JG	Jack	03/10/1889	South Shields	1948	1917		Notts County (Guest)		1	1
Plowman						1915				1	0
Pointon						1917				1	0
Pratt						1917				1	0
Race	E					1915				5	1
Raybourne						1916				1	0
Roberts						1917				2	0
Roe	A	Archie	09/12/1893	Hull	1947	1917	1918	Sheffield Wednesday (Guest)		14	4
Ross	JE					1918		Sheffield Wednesday (Guest)		2	0
Round	E	Elijah	1882	Stoke-on-Trent		1915	1918	Manchester United (Guest)		98	0
Salt	H	Harold		Sheffield		1918		Sheffield Wednesday (Guest)		1	0
Saxton	E	Edgar	1896	Carlton, Yorkshire		1917	1918	Carlton Victoria	Played for Barnsley	39	0
Sherwin	H	Harry	1893	Walsall	1953	1917		Sunderland (Guest)		1	0
Shorte						1917				1	0
Simmonite						1918				1	0
Smelt						1917				1	1
Smith	F	Frank	22/11/1889	Darnall	1982	1917	1918	Played for Barnsley 1914/15	Played for Barnsley	37	4
Smith	G					1917				3	0
Stevenson						1916				1	0
Storey						1918				1	0
Swift						1918				1	0
Sykes	H	Herbert				1917	1918	Houghton Main Colliery (Guest)		10	1
Tebbett						1918				3	0
Thompson	L	Len	2/18/01	Sheffield		1918		Hallam FC	Played for Barnsley	14	2
Thompson	R					1916	1917			18	10
Thorpe	T	Tommy	19/05/1881	Kilnhurst	1953	1915		Northampton Town (Guest)		2	0
Tindall	TJ	Jack	12/05/1891	Barnsley	1971	1915	1918	Played for Barnsley 1914/15	Played for Barnsley	54	0
Tindall	C					1915				1	0
Tingle						1918				3	0
Tiplady						1917				1	0
Tufnell	H	Harry	02/03/1886	Burton-on-Trent	1959	1915	1917	Played for Barnsley 1914/15	Played for Barnsley	43	20
Turner						1917				2	0
Wainwright						1918				3	0
Ward						1917				1	0
Whitehead						1917				21	0
Whiteman						1917	1918			9	0
Whitham	V	Vic	1894	Burnley	1962	1918		Kimberworth Old Boys	Played for Barnsley	12	1
Wigmore	C	Clive	1892	Kiveton Park		1915	1918	Played for Barnsley 1914/15	Aston Villa	22	0
Williams	JH	John		Staincross		1915	1918	Staincross	Played for Barnsley	84	2
Winship						1918				1	0
Wooding						1917		Huddersfield Town (Guest)		1	0

Players Of The Second World War (1939 -1945)

Player			D.O.B.	Place of Birth	Died	Season		Previous Club	Next Club	App	Goal
						First	Last				
Adey	W	Wilf	06/07/09	Featherstone	197	1939		Aberdeen (Guest)		1	0
Allison	JJ	John	17/11/13	Consett	197	1939		Workington	Hartlepools United	5	2
Allott	JV					1941		Barnsley Main Colliery (Guest)		1	0
Arran	F					1941		South Bank (Guest)		1	0
Armeson	LR	Lawrence		Rotherham		1943		Coventry City (Guest)		6	0
Asquith	B	Beaumont	16/09/10	Painthorpe	197	1939	194	Manchester United (Guest)		201	52
Barclay	R	Bobby	27/10/06	Scotswood	196	1941		Huddersfield Town (Guest)		1	0
Barlow	H	Bert	22/07/16	Kilnhurst		1942	194	Portsmouth (Guest)		25	9
Baxter	AG	Arthur		Dundee	194	1939		Played for Barnsley 1938/39		1	0
Baxter	JC	Jimmy	08/11/25	Hill O'Beath	199	1945		Dunfermline Athletic	Played for Barnsley 1946/47	25	6
Bennett	B					1939				1	0
Bennett	WH	Walter	15/12/18	Mexborough		1939	194	Mexborough Olympia	Played for Barnsley 1946/47	10	3
Binns	CH	Cliff	09/03/07	Cowling	197	1940	194	Played for Barnsley 1938/39	Gainsborough Trinity	189	0
Bokas	F	Frank	13/05/14	Bellshill	199	1939	194	Played for Barnsley 1938/39	Gainsborough Trinity	138	1
Boocock						1943		Wombwell Town		1	0
Bramham	A	Arnold		West Melton		1939		Rotherham United (Guest)		1	0
Bray	E	Eric		Barnsley		1939	194	Played for Barnsley 1938/39		12	5
Brown	AW	Alan	26/08/14	Consett	199	1943		Huddersfield Town (Guest)		5	0
Brunskill	NH	Norman	26/06/12	Dipton	198	1939	194	Played for Barnsley 1938/39		13	0
Bullock	GF	George	1916	Wolverhampton	194	1939	194	Played for Barnsley 1938/39		59	24
Burkinshaw	GA	George	01/10/22	Barnsley	198	1943	194	Woolley Colliery	Carlisle United	50	0
Burton	S	Stan	03/12/12	Wombwell	197	1941	194	West Ham United (Guest)		4	0
Calder	J	Jack	19/10/13	Glengarnock		1939		Greenock Morton (Guest)		1	2
Clayton	L	Lew	07/06/24	Royston, Yorkshire		1945		Monckton Athletic	Carlisle United	2	0
Clegg	H					1940	194			8	2
Cooling	R	Roy	09/12/21	Barnsley		1942	194	Mitchell's Main Welfare	Played for Barnsley 1946/47	59	22
Coulston	WB	Walter		Warwell		1942		Notts County (Guest)		1	0
Cox	AEH	Albert	24/06/17	Treeton		1945		Sheffield United (Guest)		1	0
Cunningham	L	Laurie	20/10/21	Consett		1945		Consett United	Played for Barnsley 1946/47	25	0
Davis	H	Bert	11/08/06	Bradford		1941		Crystal Palace (Guest)		1	1
Dawson	WR					1942		Jump (Guest)		1	0
Deakin	J	John	27/09/12	Altofts		1939		Bradford City (Guest)		2	2
Dodd	RI	Ronnie				1939		Shrewsbury Town (Guest)		1	0
England	AA	Alf				1939				8	3
Everest	J	Jack	1907	Dunnington		1939		Played for Barnsley 1938/39		3	0
Fenton	R					1942		Wombwell Town (Guest)		2	0
Fenton	WH	Billy	23/06/26	Hartlepool	197	1945			Horden Colliery Welfare	1	1
Ferrier	HR	Harry	20/05/20	Ratho		1945		Ratho Amateurs	Portsmouth	3	0
Fisher	FW	Fred	11/04/10	Barnsley	194	1940	194	Millwall (Guest)		3	1
Fisher	S	Stan	27/09/24	Barnsley		1943	194	Rockingham Colliery	Played for Barnsley 1946/47	16	11
Fleetwood	ED	Eddie		Barnsley		1941	194			95	33
Flood	T					1944				1	1
Forster	JW					1942				1	0
Gallacher	F	Frank	1913	Paisley		1939		Bristol City (Guest)		1	1
Gibson	FW	Fred	18/06/02	Summerscoat		1941		Boston United (Guest)		1	0
Gladwin	GWE	George	28/03/07	Worksop		1939		Manchester United (Guest)		2	0
Glover	A	Arthur	27/03/18	Barnsley		1939	194	Played for Barnsley 1938/39	Played for Barnsley 1946/47	11	0
Gray	H	Harry	26/10/18	Hemsworth		1945		Grimethorpe Rovers	Played for Barnsley 1946/47	14	4
Greaves	G	George		Darfield		1940		Aldershot (Guest)		2	0
Gregory	CF	Fred	24/10/11	Doncaster		1940	194	Crystal Palace (Guest)		9	6
Griffiths	JS	Steve	23/02/14	Stairfoot		1942		Portsmouth (Guest)		2	2
Harper	B	Bernard	23/11/12	Gawber		1939	194	Played for Barnsley 1938/39	Scunthorpe United	107	0
Harper	K	Ken	15/04/07	Barnsley		1939	194	Walsall (Guest)		100	1
Harper	R					1944				2	0
Harston	JC	Jack	07/10/20	Barnsley		1939	194	Wolverhampton Wanderers	Played for Barnsley 1946/47	116	6
Henry	GR	Gerry	05/10/20	Hemsworth		1941	194	Leeds United (Guest)		3	1
Hold	O	Oscar	19/10/18	Carlton, Yorkshire		1940	194	Aldershot (Guest)		4	1
Holdcroft	GH	Harry	23/01/09	Burslem	198	1945		Preston North End	Morecambe	14	0
Horbury	K					1944				1	0
Hubbard	C	Cliff	1911	Worksop	196	1939	194	West Ham United (Guest)		10	4

Player			D.O.B	Place of Birth	Died	Season First	Last	Previous Club	Next Club	App	Goal
Hullett	WA	Bill	19/11/15	Liverpool	1982	1941		Manchester United (Guest)		2	3
Hydes	AJE	Arthur	24/11/10	Barnsley		1939		Newport County (Guest)		3	1
Jackson	E	Ernie	11/06/14	Sheffield	1996	1945		Sheffield United (Guest)		1	0
Jones	W					1939	1942			23	0
Kelly	JC	Johnny	21/02/21	Paisley		1945		Greenock Morton	Played for Barnsley 1946/47	24	3
Kilpatrick	W					1941				4	0
King	J	John				1940		Sheffield United (Guest)		1	0
Kitchen	J	Jack	28/02/25	Whitehaven	1992	1944	1945	Kells Athletic	Played for Barnsley 1946/47	5	0
Lacey	E					1941	1942			5	2
Lang	J	Johnny	1908	Dumbarton		1939		Played for Barnsley 1938/39		6	1
Logan	JW	John	16/08/12	Horden	1980	1939	1945	Played for Barnsley 1938/39	Played for Barnsley 1946/47	234	8
Makepeace						1943				1	0
Mansley	VC	Cliff	05/04/21	Skipton		1945		Preston North End	Played for Barnsley 1946/47	23	0
Marsh	R					1942				2	0
Maxwell	JM	Buddy	15/01/13	Kilmarnock	1990	1939		Preston North End	Shrewsbury Town	3	4
Morgan						1945				1	0
Mount	G					1945				1	0
Myers	JH	Jimmy	05/03/20	Barnsley		1942		Cardiff City (Guest)		2	1
McGarry	D	Danny	1911	Howwood		1939	1945	Played for Barnsley 1938/39	Greenock Morton	80	29
Nicholls	JH	James	27/11/19	Coseley		1941		Bradford Park Avenue (Guest)		4	0
Nicholson	L					1944	1945			5	0
Oldroyd	K					1942		Woolley Colliery (Guest)		1	0
Pallister	G	Gordon	02/04/17	Howden-le-Wear		1939	1945	Played for Barnsley 1938/39	Played for Barnsley 1946/47	101	4
Pond	H	Harold	19/04/17	Kilnhurst		1943		Carlisle United (Guest)		1	0
Richardson	G					1940				1	0
Rimmington	N	Norman	29/11/23	Staincross		1944		Mapplewell Town	Played for Barnsley 1946/47	3	0
Robinson	TW					1939	1941			4	0
Robinson	W	Bill	04/04/19	Whitburn	1992	1939		Sunderland (Guest)		2	1
Robledo	GO	George	14/04/26	Iquique (Chile)	1989	1941		Brampton Welfare	Huddersfield Town	1	0
						1943	1945	Huddersfield Town	Played for Barnsley 1946/47	96	46
Rogers	W	Billy	03/07/19	Pennington, Cumberland		1943		Blackburn Rovers		2	1
Rymer	GH	George	06/10/23	Barnsley		1943	1945	Ardsley Victoria	Played for Barnsley 1946/47	27	0
Sagar	E	Ted	07/02/10	Moorends	1986	1940		Everton (Guest)		2	0
Settle	A	Alf	17/09/12	Barugh Green	1988	1941		Sheffield United (Guest)		1	0
Shanks	R	Robert				1945		Crystal Palace (Guest)		1	0
Shotton	R	Bob	27/10/10	Bearpark		1939	1945	Played for Barnsley 1938/39		169	12
Sinclair	T					1943		Doncaster Rovers (Guest)		11	2
Sloan	J					1943				18	2
Smith	G	Gavin	25/09/17	Cambuslang	1992	1939	1945	Dumbarton	Played for Barnsley 1946/47	237	102
Smith	J	Jackie		Littletown		1944		Plymouth Argyle (Guest)		1	0
Spence	A					1941		Barnsley Main Colliery (Guest)		1	0
Spence	R	Dickie	18/07/08	Platts Common	1983	1943		Chelsea (Guest)		2	0
Stabb	GH	George	26/09/12	Paignton	1994	1943		Bradford Park Avenue (Guest)		1	1
Steele	J	Johnny	24/11/16	Glasgow		1939	1944	Played for Barnsley 1938/39	Played for Barnsley 1946/47	106	61
Stevens	W					1943				1	0
Stubbs						1939				1	0
Styles	W					1941		Rotherham United (Guest)		1	0
Taylor	J	Jack	15/02/14	Barnsley	1978	1944		Norwich City (Guest)		3	0
Thorogood	J	Jack	04/04/11	Dinnington	1970	1939	1945	Millwall (Guest)		101	32
Walker	RG	Geoff	29/09/26	Bradford		1943		Bradford Park Avenue (Guest)		1	2
Wesley	JC	Jack	19/01/08	Cheltenham		1941		Bradford Park Avenue (Guest)		1	0
Whitelum	C	Cliff	02/12/19	Farnworth		1940		Sunderland (Guest)		1	0
Wilkinson	C	Cyril				1940		Rotherham United (Guest)		2	0
Williams	R					1943				1	0
Willingham	CK	Ken	01/12/12	Sheffield	1975	1943		Huddersfield Town (Guest)		5	0
Wilson	JW	Joe	29/09/10	West Butsfield	1996	1945		Reading	Played for Barnsley 1946/47	15	1
Wipfler	CJ	Charlie	15/07/15	Trowbridge	1983	1941		Frickley Colliery (Guest)		1	1
Woffinden	RS	Richard	20/02/17	Rotherham	1987	1939	1943	Hartlepools United		21	3
Wright	T					1939				2	0

1887/88 Friendlies

1	Sep	17	Manor House, Ward Green	4-1	Denton 2, Thompson A, Chappell
2		24	Honeywell	0-4	
3	Oct	15	GAWBER RANGERS	0-0	
4		15	Gawber 2nd	1-2	
5		22	Barnsley White Lily	1-4	Denton
6		22	HONEYWELL	0-1	
7		29	Monk Bretton	0-2	
8	Nov	5	Birdwell Rangers	0-2	
9		12	Worsborough Bridge United	1-1	Denton
10		19	Gawber Rangers	2-0	Denton 2
11	Dec	3	NEXT SIXTEEN	0-2	
12		17	Barnsley Standard	2-0	Denton 2
13		24	SILKSTONE COMMON	1-0	Wike
14		31	BARNSLEY STANDARD	5-0	Wike 2, Nixon, Midgley, Needham
15	Jan	6	Shepherd Rest	0-1	
16		13	CARLTON	0-1	
17		20	Broomhill	5-0	Hirst 2, Denton 2, Macey
18	Feb	11	ARDSLEY WANDERERS	1-0	
19		11	ROYSTON JUBILEE	4-1	Denton 2, Hirst, Wike
20		18	ARDSLEY NELSON	4-2	Wike, Midgley 2, Preedy
21	Mar	3	Ardsley Old	0-0	
22		10	ARDSLEY OLD	0-0	
23		17	Silkstone Common	4-0	
24		24	Ardsley Wanderers	0-2	

Note: The above results include 1st and 2nd team matches.

1888/89 Sheffield & Hallamshire Challenge Cup

R1	Oct	13	Heeley Olympic	3-3	Berry
rep		27	HEELEY OLYMPIC	3-1	Wike, R Taylor, G Taylor
R2	Nov	3	Staveley	0-12	

Friendlies

1	Sep	8	BARNSLEY FITZWILLIAM	1-0	Guest
2		15	Sheffield Ellesmere	4-1	Wike, Midgley
3		29	Park Grange, Sheffield	3-2	R Taylor, Wike 2
4	Oct	6	MEXBOROUGH	4-2	R Taylor 2, Walker 2
5		20	TANKERSLEY UNITED	8-0	
6	Nov	10	WOMBWELL TOWN	5-0	G Taylor 2, Midgley 2, Hirst
7		17	ARDSLEY WOODMAN	3-2	R Taylor, G Taylor, Wike
8		24	CARLTON	3-0	
9		24	Worsborough Dale	4-2	
10	Dec	1	Doncaster Rovers	0-6	
11		8	Mexborough	0-2	
12		15	SHEFFIELD ELLESMERE	3-0	
13		26	BULWELL (Notts)	0-0	
14		29	STAINCROSS	4-2	
15	Jan	1	Sheffield Clinton	1-4	
16		12	Leeds Association	1-3	og
17		19	Thurlstone	2-1	
18		26	Springfield Star	3-3	
19		26	WORSBOROUGH DALE	3-1	
20	Feb	2	Wombwell Town	1-1	Raley
21		9	Spring Victoria	2-3	
22		23	PARK GRANGE, SHEFFIELD	2-1	Nixon, Raley
23	Mar	2	SHEFFIELD CLUB	4-2	Raley
24		23	THURLSTONE	3-5	
25		30	LEEDS ASSOCIATION	2-1	
26	Apr	6	Staincross	7-3	
27		13	BARNSLEY & DISTRICT	4-0	
28		22	ARDSLEY OLD	1-3	

Note: The above results include 1st and 2nd team matches.

Tournament for eleven Gladstone Bags (at Queens Ground)

	May	6	Low Valley	4-0	
		11	Snape Hill	7-0	
Final		25	Ardsley Woodman	7-1	

1889/90 Sheffield & Hallamshire Challenge Cup

R1	Oct	19	Sheffield Clinton	1-5	Beevers

Friendlies

1	Sep	14	SHEFFIELD CLUB	8-0	
2		21	WATH	2-1	
3		21	Low Valley Wanderers	0-1	
4		28	HEXTHORPE WANDERERS	1-1	Raley
5		28	Wombwell Main	0-4	
6	Oct	5	Huddersfield	8-1	Raley 3, Needham, Beevers 3, Hirst
7		12	Stocksbridge Foresters	4-2	
8		12	HOYLE MILL	4-1	
9		19	Greasborough	0-11	
10*		26	Greasborough	2-1	Beevers, Hirst
11	Nov	2	Hexthorpe Wanderers	1-0	
12		16	Wath	3-0	Hunt, Hirst, Haigh
13		23	Mexborough	5-1	
14		30	LEEDS STEELWORKERS	13-0	
15**	Dec	14	Sheffield Clinton	0-2	
16		21	WENTWORTH	4-6	
17		28	MEADOW HALL	3-1	
18	Jan	4	STOCKSBRIDGE FORESTERS	6-3	
19		11	THURLSTONE	2-0	
20		25	WAKEFIELD	2-1	
21	Feb	1	Kilnhurst	2-2	Hunt, Roebuck
22		8	GREASBROUGH	4-1	
23		22	Wakefield	0-0	
24	Mar	1	STAINCROSS	5-2	
25		8	Thurlstone	3-3	
26		15	MEXBOROUGH	3-1	Hunt 2, Hirst
27		22	Meadow Hall	4-0	
28		29	SNAPE HILL	3-0	
29	Apr	5	Wentworth	0-0	
30		7	SHEFFIELD CLINTON	6-1	
31		8	CARBROOK CHURCH	8-0	

* Match 10 - Barnsley only played with 7 men.
** Match 15 - Only played 15 minutes each way, Barnsley arrived late.
The above results include 1st and 2nd team matches.

1890/91 Sheffield & District League

1*	Sep	27	Kilnhurst	1-4	Hunt
2	Oct	11	Sheffield Montrose	3-7	Payman, Hunt, Raley
3		25	CARBROOK CHURCH	1-0	Hunt
4	Nov	22	Carbrook Church	1-1	Needham
5	Dec	6	Ecclesfield	0-3	
6	Jan	3	Mexborough	1-1	Payman
7		24	ECCLESFIELD	1-2	Hirst
8	Feb	14	KILNHURST	2-2	Raley, Hirst
9		28	ECKINGTON WORKS	3-3	
10	Mar	14	OWLERTON	3-1	Raley, Jones, Hunt
11		28	Owlerton	2-5	Raley
12	Apr	4	SHEFFIELD MONTROSE	3-2	Beevers 2, Hellewell
13		11	Eckington Works	1-3	
14		25	MEXBOROUGH	0-4	

* Match 1 - Barnsley arrived late and only 50 minutes play was possible.

Sheffield & Hallamshire Challenge Cup

R1	Oct	18	Attercliffe	0-2	

Friendlies

1	Sep	6	BIRDWELL	1-0	
2		13	WALKLEY	3-2	Hunt, Roebuck, Hirst
3	Oct	4	HEMSWORTH	9-1	
4	Nov	1	Wakefield	3-3	
5		15	THURLSTONE	5-0	Hunt 2, Hirst, Roebuck, Payman
6	Dec	13	LEEDS ALBION	2-2	
7		27	SHEFFIELD CLINTON	13-0	
8	Jan	2	STAINCROSS	6-0	
9*		31	Hexthorpe Wanderers	3-1	
10	Feb	7	WAKEFIELD	2-1	Raley, Hirst
11		21	Sheffield Clinton	2-2	
12	Mar	7	Kilnhurst	3-6	
13		21	Thurlstone	3-1	
14		30	BIRDWELL	4-2	
15		31	SHEFFIELD CLUB	3-2	
16	Apr	18	HEXTHORPE WANDERERS	2-2	

* Match 9 - Barnsley only played with 7 men.

1887
Unnamed Team group

Season 1891/92
Team photo v. Carbrook Church 23.1.1892: Back row: Nixon, Nicholson, Needham
Centre row:Cartwright (trainer), Wagstaffe (Linesman), Longworth H, Hirst, Longworth A, Rushworth (Secretary)
Front row: Seal (Landlord), Beevers, Hellewell, Hunt, Haigh, Roebuck

1891/92 Sheffield & District League

#		Date	Opponent	Score	Scorers
1	Sep	12	MEXBOROUGH	3-4	Hunt 2, Beavers
2		26	Melville	2-2	Needham, og
3	Oct	3	KIVETON PARK	3-0	
4		10	Eckington Works	2-1	Hunt 2
5		17	ECCLESFIELD	6-3	Walker, Hunt 2, Hellewell 2, Roebuck
6		24	CHESTERFIELD	4-2	Longworth 2, Roebuck 2
#7	Dec	5	Ecclesfield	4-6	
8		26	MELVILLE	6-0	Hunt 4, Roebuck, Hellewell
9	Jan	30	KILNHURST	1-1	Roebuck
10	Feb	6	Mexborough	0-5	
11		27	CARBROOK CHURCH	7-1	Raley, Beevers, Roebuck, Hunt 2, Hellewell 2
12	Mar	1	Kilnhurst	3-1	Hellewell, Roebuck, Hunt
13		12	Kiveton Park	1-5	Hunt (pen)
14		26	Chesterfield	1-5	
15	Apr	2	ECKINGTON WORKS	4-0	Hellewell, Hunt 3
16		9	Carbrook Church	2-1	Barton 2
17			Owlerton	won	(No further details known)
18			OWLERTON	won	(No further details known)

Barnsley Charity Cup

	Date	Opponent	Score	Scorers
R1 Oct	31	Wombwell Main	4-2	Hunt 2, Raley, Roebuck
R2 Nov	21	KILNHURST	3-2	Hellewell, Hunt 2
R3 Jan	9	HOYLAND TOWN	1-1	Raley
rep	16	Hoyland Town	7-3	Hellewell 2, Hunt 3, Roebuck 2
SF Mar	5	Parkgate & Rawmarsh*	1-1	Hellewell
rep	10	Parkgate & Rawmarsh+	2-0	Raley, Hellewell
Final	19	Ecclesfield^	2-3	Hunt 2

Note: * at Shaw Lane. + at Queen's Ground. ^ at Shaw Lane.

Sheffield & Hallamshire Challenge Cup

	Date	Opponent	Score	Scorers	
R1 Nov	7	ARDSLEY	3-2	Hellewell 2, Raley	
R2	28	Mexborough	2-2	Hellewell, Hunt	Att.360
rep Dec	12	MEXBOROUGH	2-1	Hellewell 2	
R3 Jan	23	CARBROOK CHURCH	4-2	Hunt 2, Beevers, Hellewell	
SF Feb	20	Wednesday Wanderers*	1-6	Hunt	Att. 1000

Note: * at Carbrook

1892/93 Sheffield & District League

#		Date	Opponent	Score	Scorers
1	Sep	10	Sheepbridge Works	3-2	F Woolhouse, T Smith 2
2		17	ECKINGTON WORKS	3-4	F Woolhouse, Hunt 2
3		24	Kiveton Park	4-1	Stringer, T Smith 2, Hunt
4	Oct	1	ATTERCLIFFE	4-0	T Smith 3, Hellewell
5		15	Mexborough	3-6	F Woolhouse, Stringer, Ward
6		22	WEDNESDAY WANDERERS	0-0	
7		29	Wath	1-2	F Woolhouse (pen)
8	Nov	5	CHESTERFIELD	2-1	T Smith, F Woolhouse
9		26	Worksop Town	3-4	Hellewell, F Woolhouse, Hunt
10	Dec	10	Attercliffe	0-3	
11		17	Penistone Athletic	2-1	Hunt, Greaves
12		24	KIVETON PARK	5-0	T Smith, Hirst 3, F Woolhouse
13		26	WATH	3-2	Needham, T Smith, Fitzpatrick
14	Jan	14	MEXBOROUGH	3-3	F Woolhouse (pen), Hunt, S Smith
15		21	Ecclesfield	5-0	Fitzpatrick, Black, Hellewell, Hunt 2
16		28	ECCLESFIELD	4-2	Shaw 2, F Woolhouse, Black
17	Feb	11	Wednesday Wanderers	3-6	T Smith, F Woolhouse, og
18		25	KILNHURST	1-1	Hunt
19	Mar	4	SHEEPBRIDGE WORKS	4-1	T Smith, Hunt, Black, Shaw
20		11	Rotherham United	4-3	Hellewell 2, Hunt, Tie
21		25	WORKSOP TOWN	5-0	Vickers 2, T Smith, Hunt, og
22	Apr	1	Kilnhurst	4-0	Vickers, Hunt, Hellewell, F Woolhouse
23		3	PENISTONE ATHLETIC	6-0	Hunt 2, F Woolhouse 2, Greaves, Vickers
24		4	ROTHERHAM UNITED	12-1	Hunt 4, S Smith 3, Vickers 3, F Woolhouse 2
25		5	Chesterfield	0-1	
26		8	Eckington Works	0-1	

Barnsley Charity Cup

	Date	Opponent	Score	Scorers	
R3 Jan	23	Kilnhurst	2-1	Hellewell, Fitzpatrick	
SF Feb	4	WOMBWELL TOWN	5-2	F Woolhouse 2, Fitzpatrick 2, Hirst	
Rep. Mar	2	Wombwell Town *	2-1	Replay due Wombwell's objections.	
Final	18	Mexborough *	1-1	Hellewell	Att. 6000
Fin. Rep	23	Mexborough *	4-1	Hunt, Vickers, F Woolhouse (pen), T Smith	Att. 7000

(* At Queen's Ground)

Sheffield & Hallamshire Challenge Cup

	Date	Opponent	Score	Scorers
R1 Oct	8	ARDSLEY	1-0	Hellewell
R2 Dec	3	Rotherham United	3-6	Fairclough, F Woolhouse, Hellewell

1893/94 F.A. Cup

	Date	Opponent	Score	Scorers
Q1 Oct	14	GAINSBOROUGH TRINITY	4-5	Stringer 2, Hirst, Smith

Sheffield Challenge Cup League

#		Date	Opponent	Score	Scorers
1	Sep	9	ROTHERHAM UNITED	5-1	Taylor, Black 2, Smith, Hirst2
		16	SHEEPBRIDGE WORKS	3-1	Bairstow 2, Stringer
3		23	Eckington Works	2-0	Bairstow, Black
4		30	WATH	4-0	Stringer, Smith 2, Bairstow
5	Oct	7	Ardsley	2-0	Black, Bairstow
6		21	SHEFFIELD CLUB	5-3	Black 2, Merriless, Nixon, Bairstow7
		28	Attercliffe	2-1	Baxter, Black
8	Nov	11	CHESTERFIELD	3-1	Black, Bairstow, Wright
9		18	Rotherham United	1-0	Bairstow
10		25	Wednesday Wanderers	2-2	Black 2
11	Dec	2	WORKSOP TOWN	2-3	Black 2
12		9	SHEFFIELD STROLLERS	1-3	Black
13		16	Kilnhurst	3-3	Black 2, Baxter
14	Jan	2	Sheffield Club	11-1	Taylor 4, Hirst, Bairstow 3, Smith, Baxter, Woolhouse
15		13	ECKINGTON WORKS	4-1	Bairstow, Taylor 2, Black
16		20	Sheffield Strollers	0-11	
17	Feb	3	Worksop Town	4-1	Black 2, Smith 2
18		10	WEDNESDAY WANDERERS	0-1	
19		17	Chesterfield	3-3	Bairstow 2, Smith
20	Mar	3	KILNHURST	2-0	Bairstow, Black
21		10	Sheepbridge Works	1-4	Higgins
22		15	Mexborough	1-7	Smith
23		24	ATTERCLIFFE	2-1	Black, Wright
24		26	ARDSLEY	2-0	Wright, Taylor
25		27	MEXBOROUGH	0-0	
26		31	Wath	2-2	Wright 2

Barnsley Charity Cup

	Date	Opponent	Score	Scorers
R2 Jan	6	Wombwell Main	6-0	
SF Feb	24	DARFIELD MAIN	7-1	Bairstow 4, Hunt 2, White
Final Mar	17	Wombwell Town (at Dearne)	6-3	Black 2, Hunt 2, Taylor, Smith

1894/95 F.A. Cup

	Date	Opponent	Score	Scorers	
Q1 Oct	13	GRANTHAM ROVERS	3-1	Partridge 2, Bairstow	
Q2 Nov	3	LEEDS AFC	8-0	Keech 2, Partridge 2, Vost 2, Bairstow 2	
Q3	24	Mexborough	1-1	Smith	
rep	28	MEXBOROUGH	1-0	Black	
Q4 Dec	15	WORKSOP TOWN	3-1	Keech 2, og	
R1 Feb	2	LIVERPOOL* (aet)	1-2	Cutts	Att: 5000
rep	11	Liverpool	0-4		Att: 3600

* Note: Barnsley objected - extra time should not have been played; a replay was ordered.

Sheffield Challenge Cup League

#		Date	Opponent	Score	Scorers
1	Sep	1	Wath	1-1	Partridge
2		15	Mexborough	3-1	Black, Partridge 2
3		29	Eckington Works	0-2	
4	Oct	6	Ecclesfield	2-0	Bairstow, Smith
5		20	Worksop Town	5-2	Bairstow, Partridge 2, Smith, og
6		27	CHESTERFIELD	2-1	Bairstow, Keech
7	Nov	10	MEXBOROUGH	4-3	Smith, Partridge 2, Bairstow
8	Dec	8	SHEEPBRIDGE WORKS	3-1	Mouel, Black, Bairstow
9		25	Wednesday Wanderers	2-5	Vost, Bairstow
10		26	ATTERCLIFFE	6-1	Mouel 2, Vost 2, Keech, Smith
11		27	ARDSLEY	2-1	Partridge, Cutts
12	Jan	5	Attercliffe	1-0	Partridge
13		19	SHEFFIELD STROLLERS	1-0	Hey
14		26	Sheepbridge Works	1-1	Rawson
15		28	Sheffield Strollers	1-2	Mouel
16	Feb	16	Rotherham United	2-3	Calder, Bairstow
17		23	SHEFFIELD CLUB	3-4	Keech 3
18	Mar	2	WORKSOP TOWN	1-1	Thompson
19		16	Chesterfield	0-2	
20		18	Sheffield Club	4-0	Black 3, Rawson
21		23	WATH	1-2	Hirst
22		28	KILNHURST	3-1	Rawson 2, Calder
23	Apr	6	ECCLESFIELD	2-0	Rawson, Smith
24		8	Kilnhurst	2-1	Smith, Calder
25	Apr	12	Ardsley	3-2	Bairstow, Calder, Rawson
26		15	WEDNESDAY WANDERERS	1-3	Bairstow
27		16	ROTHERHAM UNITED	6-1	Black 3, Bairstow, Cutts, Keech
28		20	ECKINGTON WORKS	5-1	Keech 2, Cutts, Black, Bairstow

Sheffield & District League (Central Division) Wharncliffe Charity Cup

#		Date	Opponent	Score	Scorers
1	Oct	22	Wednesday Wanderers	1-3	Vost
2	Dec	24	Chesterfield	5-0	Partridge 2, Calder 2, Cutts
3		29	Doncaster Rovers	1-5	Nixon
4		31	Sheffield Strollers	1-2	Vost
5	Jan	2	MEXBOROUGH	0-4	
6		12	WEDNESDAY WANDERERS	4-3	Cutts 2, Bairstow, Smith
7	Feb	9	DONCASTER ROVERS	1-1	Vost
8		26	SHEFFIELD STROLLERS	4-0	Vost 2, Bairstow 2
9	Mar	2	Mexborough	0-3	
10	Apr	27	CHESTERFIELD	2-0	Rawson, Bairstow

1895/96 8th in Midland League

No.	Date	Opponent	Score	Scorers	Greaves	Nixon	Bird B	Widdowson	Hey	Lingard	Bairstow	Rodgers	Lees	Woolhouse H	Cronshaw	Drummond	Smith T	Rawson	Tyas	Black	Woolhouse F	Torr	Collier	Taylor	Hirst
1	Sep 7	WELLINGBOROUGH	4-0	Lees, Hey, Rodgers 2	1	2	3	4	5	6	7	8	9	10	11							8			
2	14	GAINSBOROUGH T	1-1	og	1	2	3	6	4	5		11	10	9		7									
3	21	Wellingborough	0-1		1	2	3	4	6	5		11	8	9	10	7									
4	28	KETTERING	1-2	Lees	1	2	3	6	4	5		8	9	10	11			7							
5	Oct 5	Matlock	2-1	Widdowson, Drummond	1	2		6	4	5		8	9	10	7	11			3						
6	19	Mansfield FC	3-5	Drummond, Cronshaw, Lees	1	3	2	5	6	4		11	9		7	10		8							
7	26	DONCASTER R	3-1	Woolhouse H, Smith, Cronshaw	1	2	3	6	4	5		8		9	7	11	10								
8	Nov 9	MATLOCK	6-0	Rawson, Smith, Lees, Drummond 2, og	1	3		6	4	2			5	9	7	11	10	8							
9	16	Walsall	0-5		1	3		6	4			8	5	9	7	11	10		2						
10	Dec 7	GRANTHAM R	5-4	Drummond, Lingard, Smith 2, og	1	3		6	4	5		8		9	7	11	10		2						
11	14	NEWARK	4-1	Woolhouse H 3, Cronshaw	1	3		6	4			8	5	9	7	11	10		2						
12	21	Grantham Rovers	2-2	Drummond 2	1	3		6	2			8	5	9	7	11	10						4		
13	28	Gainsborough Trinity	0-0		1	3			6			8	5	9	7	11	10		2	4					
14	Jan 1	WALSALL	5-1	See below	1	3				6		8	5	9	7	11	10		2	4					
15	4	Rushden Town	1-4	Woolhouse H	1	3			4			8	5	9	7	11	10		2	6					
16	11	HEANOR TOWN	0-1		1	3				6		8	5	9	7		10		2	4	11				
17	18	Newark	3-0	Rodgers, Taylor, Woolhouse H	1	3			4			8	5	9	7				2	6	11			10	
18	25	MANSFIELD FC	3-1	Smith, Cronshaw 2	1	3			4			8	5	9	7		10		2	6	11				
19	Feb 1	ILKESTON TOWN	0-1		1	3			4	10		8	5	9	7				2	6	11				
20	8	Long Eaton Rangers	1-2	Tyas	1	3			4			8	5	9	7		10		2	6	11				
21	Mar 7	Dresden United	2-4	Cronshaw, Rodgers	1	3			4			8	5	9	7		10		2	6	11				
22	14	RUSHDEN TOWN	3-1	Lees, Smith, Rawson	1	3			4			8	5	9	7		10	11	2	6					
23	21	Heanor Town	4-5	Rodgers, Drummond, Cronshaw, Smith	1	3			4			8	5	9	7	11	10		2	6					
24	28	Kettering	1-3	AN Other	1	3			5	6		10	9	8	7			11	2	4					
25	Apr 3	Doncaster Rovers	0-4		1		3	6	4			8	5	9	7	11	10		2						
26	4	DRESDEN UNITED	2-0	Rodgers, Rawson	1	3			5	6		10	9	8	7			11	2	4					
27	9	LONG EATON RANGERS	3-0	Drummond 2, Rodgers	1	3			4			8		9	7	11	10		2	6					5
28	11	Ilkeston Town	4-2	Rodgers 2, Smith, Woolhouse H	1	3			4			8		9	7	11	10		2	6					5
				Apps	28	27	8	12	26	14	3	27	23	25	28	17	19	5	20	15	6	1	1	1	2
				Goals				1	1	1		10	6	8	8	10	9	3	1						

Scorers in game 14: Rodgers, Smith, Lees, Woolhouse H. Cronshaw

F.A. CUP

	Date	Opponent	Score	Scorers	Greaves	Nixon	Bird B	Widdowson	Hey	Lingard	Bairstow	Rodgers	Lees	Woolhouse H	Cronshaw	Drummond	Smith T	Rawson	Tyas	Black	Woolhouse F	Torr	Collier	Taylor	Hirst
Q1	Oct 12	Rotherham Town	1-1	Hey	1	2		6	4	5		8	9	10	7	11			3						
ep	16	ROTHERHAM TOWN	3-7	Rawson, Lees, Drummond	1	2		6	4	5		8	9	10		11		7	3						

		P	W	D	L	F	A	Pts
1	Kettering	28	20	5	3	74	28	45
2	Gainsborough Trinity	28	17	6	5	59	26	40
3	Walsall	28	17	6	5	91	47	40
4	Long Eaton Rangers	28	18	3	7	68	39	39
5	Rushden Town	28	14	4	10	61	46	32
6	Heanor Town	28	12	7	9	70	45	31
7	Ilkeston Town	28	14	2	12	62	41	30
8	Barnsley St. Peter's	28	13	3	12	63	52	29
9	Grantham Rovers	28	11	5	12	64	47	27
10	Doncaster Rovers	28	10	6	12	44	56	26
11	Dresden United	28	9	6	13	44	49	24
12	Wellingborough	28	10	4	14	44	71	24
13	Mansfield FC	28	9	2	17	35	68	20
14	Newark	28	6	1	21	36	78	13
15	Matlock	28	0	0	28	9	130	0

1896/97   11th in Midland League

#	Date	Opponent	Result	Scorers	Thompson	Bowram	Hutchinson	Hey	Shepherd	Lingard	Cronshaw	Field	Woolhouse F	Black	Smith W	Greaves	Taylor M	Drummond	Ritchie	Padgett	Hepworth	Smith T	Booth	Burridge	Bird J	Hanson	Webster	Walker	Hill	Evans
1	Sep 5	LONG EATON RANG.	3-4	Shepherd, Cronshaw, Woolhouse	1	2	3	4	5	6	7	8	9	10	11															
2	12	KETTERING	4-0	Black, Cronshaw, M Taylor, Field		2	3	4		5	7	8	9	6		1	10	11												
3	19	WELLINGBOROUGH	2-3	Drummond, Field		2	3	5		6	7	8	9	4		1	10	11												
4	26	Chesterfield	3-3	Cronshaw, Drummond 2			3	5	2	6	7	8	9	4		1	10	11												
5	Oct 3	WORKSOP TOWN	3-0	M Taylor 3			3			5	7		9	6		1	10	11	2	4	8									
6	12	GLOSSOP N. E.	1-3	Hepworth			3		5	4	7		9	6		1	10	11	2		8									
7	17	DRESDEN UNITED	3-1	Woolhouse 3			3	5		4	7		9	6		1	10	11	2			8								
8	Nov 7	Burslem Port Vale	1-3	Black			3	5		4		8	9	11		1	10		2	6	7									
9	14	HEANOR TOWN	4-1	Woolh'se, Cron'w, Black, M.Taylor			3	5		10	7		9	4		1	8	11	2				6							
10	28	Dresden United	2-4	W Smith, AN Other			3	5					9	4	7	1	10	11	2				6	8						
11	Dec 5	Long Eaton Ranger	0-2					6		5	7		9	4		1	10	11	3				8	2						
12	19	Ilkeston Town	0-2				3	5		4	7		10	6		1		11	2			8		9						
13	26	Mexborough T.	1-1	Cronshaw				6		5	7			4		1	9	11	3			10			2					
14	Jan 1	DONCASTER R.	0-3	Att: 3000	1		3			6	7		9	4			10	11	2			8			5					
15	2	Glossop N. E.	1-7	M Taylor	1		3							4			10								5					
16	14	RUSHDEN TOWN	3-1	Hepworth 2, T Smith			3			4			9	5		1	10	11	2		7	8			6					
17	16	Heanor Town	0-3				3	5			7		9	6		1	10	11	2			8	4							
18	23	BURSLEM P. VALE	7-2	T Smith 2, Han'n 3, Woolh'se, og			3	5		4	11		9	6		1			2		7	8				10				
19	Feb 20	Rushden Town	3-1	Cronshaw, Woolhouse, T Smith			3	5		4	11		9	6		1			2		7	8				10				
20	Mar 6	Worksop Town	1-1	T Smith				5		4	11		9	6		1	10		2		7	8					3			
21	13	Grantham Rovers	0-2				10	5		8	11		9	4	7				1		2	6					3			
22	Apr 3	Kettering	1-6	og				5					9						1		2	7	8							
23	10	GRANTHAM R.	6-1	See below			10	5		6			9	4	7				2			8					3	11		
24	16	Doncaster R.	1-1	Walker (Only fielded 10 men)			10	5					6	7			1		2	4	8						3	11		
25	17	ILKESTON TOWN	5-2	T Smith, Hey, Ling'd, Black, Hep'th				5		4			6			1	8		3	2	11	10							9	
26	19	MEXBOROUGH T.	0-0					5					7	6	11		8		2		10						3		9	1
27	20	CHESTERFIELD	2-1	W Smith, M Taylor			11	5					9	4	7		10		2	6	8						3			1
28	24	Wellingborough	0-3										4						2										1
				Apps	3	3	21	22	3	20	17	5	23	27	7	18	22	14	23	6	12	12	3	3	5	2	6	2	2	3
				Goals			1	2	1	1	6	2	9	5	2		7	3			4	7				3			1	

Note: Players unknown where line-up is incomplete.
Scorers in game 23: Woolhouse 2, T Smith, Hey, Black, Hutchinson

Game 13: Johnson No. 8. Game 23: Dunk No. 1. Game 25: Wade No. 7. Game 26: Taylor No. 4.

F.A.Cup

Rnd	Date	Opponent	Result	Scorers	Hutchinson	Hey	Cronshaw	Field	Woolhouse F	Black	Smith W	Greaves	Taylor M	Drummond	Ritchie	Smith T	Booth
Q3	Nov 21	HUNSLET	3-2	Cronshaw, Woolh'se, Drummond	3	5	8	7	9	6		1	10	11			4
Q4	Dec 12	SHEFFIELD CLUB	2-1	Cronshaw, Woolhouse	3	5	4	7	9	6		1	10	11	2	8	
Q5	28	Lincoln City	2-1	Cronshaw, M Taylor	3	5	4	7	9	6		1	10	11	2	8	
R1	Jan 30	Derby County*	1-8	Smith T	Att: 8000	3	5	4	7	9	6	1	10	11	2	8	

Q3: Little No.2

*Note: Drawn at home but Barnsley sold ground advantage for £100 and 50% of gate receipts.

		P	W	D	L	F	A	Pts
1	Doncaster Rovers	28	17	5	6	77	40	39
2	Glossop North End*	27	15	4	8	67	39	36
3	Long Eaton Ranger	28	15	2	11	55	39	32
4	Chesterfield	28	13	6	9	74	53	32
5	Kettering	28	13	5	10	51	40	31
6	Wellingborough	28	12	7	9	52	46	31
7	Burslem Port Vale	28	14	3	11	62	56	31
8	Heanor Town	28	12	6	10	55	47	30
9	Ilkeston Town	28	11	7	10	60	57	29
10	Dresden United	28	12	5	11	48	63	29
11	Barnsley St. Peter'	28	10	4	14	57	71	24
12	Rushden Town	28	9	5	14	43	53	23
13	Mexborough Town	28	7	7	14	39	50	21
14	Worksop Town	28	6	5	17	27	63	17
15	Grantham Rovers*	27	6	3	18	26	76	15
16	* Not played. Glossop NE awarded 2 points							

1897/98 — 2nd in Midland League

#	Date	Opponent	Score	Scorers	Greaves	Nixon	Stothert	Hey	Porteous	Black	Parkinson	Lees	Platt	McCullough	Jones	Webster	Hepworth	Daw	Farmer	Davis	Howard	Smith T	Royston	Hunt	Padgett	Smith W	Dawson
1	Sep 11	BURSLEM PORT VALE	4-2	McCullough, Lees 2, Jones	1	2	3	4	5	6	7	8	9	10	11												
2	18	Chesterfield	1-2	Parkinson	1	2	3	4	5	6	7	8	9	10	11												
3	25	ILKESTON TOWN	1-3	McCullough	1	2	3		5	6				10	11	4	8						7				
4	Oct 9	Burslem Port Vale	1-0	Hepworth	1	2	3	4	5	6		8	9	10	11		7										
5	16	Ilkeston Town	3-2	Platt 2, Jones	1	2	3	4	5	6		8	9	10	11		7										
6	23	WELLINGBOROUGH	2-1	Hunt, Lees	1	2	3	4	5	6		8		10	11		7							9			
7	Nov 13	Doncaster Rovers	3-1	Farmer, Lees (pen), Jones		2		4		6		5	8	10	11	3	7	1	9								
8	Dec 4	LONG EATON RANGERS	2-3	Platt, Davis		2				6	4	5	9	8	11	3		1	10	7							
9	18	MEXBOROUGH TOWN*	2-2	Davis, McCullough										10	11					7							
10	25	Glossop North End	2-2	Platt, Jones									9		11												
11	Jan 8	Long Eaton Rangers	0-0							6		5		10			8	1		7							
12	15	RUSHDEN TOWN	5-1	Jones, Lees, Davis, McCullough 2		2		5	3	4		8	6	10	11		7	1		9							
13	22	DONCASTER ROVERS	2-0	Davis, Jones		2		5	3	6		8	4	10	11			1		9	7						
14	Feb 19	Kettering	1-0	Jones	1	2		5	3	6		8		10	11	4	7			9							
15	Mar 12	Burton Wanderers	2-0	T Smith 2	1				2				9							7		8			3		
16	19	Wellingborough	3-0	T Smith 2, Hepworth	1	2											7			9		8					
17	26	KETTERING	2-0	Black, Lees	1	2		5	3	6		9		10	11		7				4	8					
18	Apr 2	Mexborough Town	2-4	Lees, Davis Att: 5000	1	2		5	3			9	6	10	11					8	4					7	
19	9	BURTON WANDERERS	3-1	T Smith, Jones, Lees	1	2		5	3	6		9		10	11					7	4	8					
20	11	GLOSSOP NORTH END	2-1	Lees, T Smith	1	2		5	3	6		9		10	11					7	4	8					
21	12	CHESTERFIELD	3-0	Black, Platt, Davis	1	2		5	3	4		9	6	10	11					7		8					
22	16	Rushden Town	1-4	McCullough	1	2			3	6		9		10	11					7	4	8					5
		Apps			15	18	6	15	17	16	2	18	12	19	19	4	10	5	2	13	6	7	1	1	1	1	1
		Goals								2	1	9	5	6	8		2		1	6		6					

*Note: Abandoned after 80 minutes due to fog with the score at 2-2.   Note: Players unknown where line-up is incomplete.

The remaining 10 minutes were played before the Yorkshire League game on 3rd February, with no addition to the score.

F.A. CUP

#	Date	Opponent	Score	Scorers	Greaves	Nixon	Stothert	Hey	Porteous	Black	Lees	Platt	McCullough	Jones	Hepworth
23	Oct 30	Mexborough Town	1-2	Lees Att: 3000	1	2	3	4	5	6	8	9	10	11	7

		P	W	D	L	F	A	Pts
1	Mexborough Town	22	15	3	4	53	30	33
2	Barnsley	22	14	3	5	47	29	31
3	Chesterfield	22	11	7	4	54	23	29
4	Ilkeston Town	22	9	6	7	37	39	24
5	Burslem Port Vale	22	10	3	9	46	32	23
6	Rushden Town	22	9	5	8	35	44	23
7	Kettering	22	7	5	10	19	28	19
8	Long Eaton Rangers	22	7	5	10	26	44	19
9	Glossop North End	22	8	2	12	41	47	18
10	Doncaster Rovers	22	5	6	11	33	35	16
11	Burton Wanderers	22	5	6	11	31	44	16
12	Wellingborough	22	5	3	14	21	48	13

1898/99 11th in Division 2

League — Division 2

#	Date		Opponent	Score	Scorers	Att	Fawcett T	Nixon T	McCartney J	King T	Burleigh J	Porteous D	Davis H	Lees W	Murray J	McCullough F	McGee J	Black A	Carthy T	Craven JR	Greaves J	Hepworth W	Hind A	Howard F	Jones R	Naylor H	Padgett D	Ritchie R	Smith T	Worrall AJ
1	Sep	1	Lincoln City	0-1			1	3	2	4	5	6	7	8	9	10	11													
2		3	Burslem Port Vale	0-2		4000		3	2	4	5	6	7	8	9	10	11				1									
3		10	LUTON TOWN	2-1	McCartney (pen), Davis			3	2		5	6	7		9	10	11				1							4	8	
4		17	Small Heath	1-3	Davis	5000		3	2		5	6	7					11			1			8				4		
5		24	LEICESTER FOSSE	3-4	Hepworth, Lees, Davis			3	2		5	6	7		9	10					1	8			11			4		
6	Oct	8	DARWEN	6-0	Hepworth 2, McCullough 2, Howard, Davis			3			5	2	7			10			6	11	1	8		4		9				
7		22	GAINSBOROUGH TRIN.	1-0	Davis	1500		3	2		5	6	7		9	10					1	8		4	11					
8	Nov	5	MANCHESTER CITY	1-1	Lees	4000		3	2		5	6	7		9	10					1	8		4	11					
9		12	Newton Heath	0-0		4000		3	2		5	6	7		9	10					1	8		4	11					
10		26	New Brighton Tower	1-2	Hepworth			3			5	2	7		9	10					1	8		4	11		6			
11	Dec	3	WALSALL	1-1	Hepworth	2500		3			5	2	7		9	10					1	8	6	4	11					
12		17	Burton Swifts	0-5				3			5	2	7		9	10		6			1	8		4	11					
13		24	WOOLWICH ARSENAL	2-1	Lees, Davis	3000			2		5	3	7		9	10				4	1	8		6	11					
14		26	Grimsby Town	1-0	Jones	4500			2		5	3	7		9	10				4	1	8		6	11					
15		27	GLOSSOP NORTH END	1-1	Davis				2		5	3	7		9	10				4	1	8		6	11					
16		31	BURSLEM PORT VALE	2-1	Hepworth, Lees (pen)	1000			2		5	3	7		9	10				4	1	8		6	11					
17	Jan	7	Luton Town	1-4	Jones				2		5	3	7		9	10				4	1	8		6	11					
18		14	SMALL HEATH	7-2	Jones 3, Hepworth, Lees 2, Davis	2000		3	2		5	4	7		9	10					1	8		6	11					
19		21	Leicester Fosse	1-3	Lees (pen)			3	2		5	4	7		9	10					1	8		6	11					
20		28	LOUGHBOROUGH	9-0	*see below	2000		3	2		5	4	7		9	10					1	8		6	11					
21	Feb	11	BLACKPOOL	2-1	Hepworth, McCullough			3	2		5	6	7		9	10					1	8		4	11					
22		18	Gainsborough Trinity	0-2				3	2		5	6	7		9	10					1	8		4	11					
23		25	GRIMSBY TOWN	2-2	Davis, Jones	2000		3	2		5	6	7		9	10					1			4	11	8				
24	Mar	4	Manchester City	0-5		12000		3	2		5		7		9	10				6	1	8		4	11					
25		11	Loughborough	0-2		1200		3	2		5		7		9	10				6	1			4	11				8	
26		15	Blackpool	1-3	McCartney	600		3	2	4			7	5		10		6		9	1				11				8	
27		21	Darwen	1-1	Davis			3	2	4			7	5		10					1			6	11				8	9
28		25	NEW BRIGHTON TOWER	2-1	Jones, Craven			3	2	4			7	5		10				8	1			6	11					9
29		31	Glossop North End	0-1				3	2	4			7	5		10				8	1			6	11					9
30	Apr	1	Walsall	1-1	Davis	2000		3	2	4			7	5						8	1			10	6					9
31		3	LINCOLN CITY	1-0	Lees			3	2	4			7	5		10				8	1			11	6					9
32		4	Newton Heath	0-2		4000		3	2	4				5		10				11	1			9	6					
33		15	BURTON SWIFTS	2-0	Jones, McCullough			3	2	4			7	5		10				11	1			9	6				8	
34		22	Woolwich Arsenal	0-3		4000		3	2	4			7	5		10				11	1			8	6					9
			Apps				1	27	32	3	25	31	33	31	4	32	3	4	1	14	33	24	1	28	30	1	1	3	5	7
			Goals					2					15	9		5				1		9		1	10					

Scorers in game 20: Davis 4, Jones 2, Hepworth, McCullough, Lees

F.A. Cup

Rd	Date		Opponent	Score	Scorers	Att	Nixon T	McCartney J	Burleigh J	Porteous D	Davis H	Murray J	McCullough F	Black A	Carthy T	Craven JR	Greaves J	Hepworth W	Howard F	Jones R	Padgett D
Q2	Oct	15	Wombwell Town	1-0	Hepworth			2	5	3	7		10	6		11	1	8	4	9	
Q3		29	Gainsborough Trinity	2-2	McCartney (pen), McCullough		3	2	5	6	7	9	10				1	8	4	11	
rep	Nov	3	GAINSBOROUGH TRIN.	4-0	Lees, Davis 3		3	2	5	6	7	9	10				1	8	4	11	
Q4		19	Doncaster Rovers	2-1	Hepworth, Lees	3000	3		5	2	7	9	10				1	8	4	11	6
Q5	Dec	10	GRIMSBY TOWN	0-0			3	2	5	6	7	9	10				1	8	4	11	
rep		14	Grimsby Town	1-2	Lees	2000		2	5	6	7	9	10	3			1	8	4	11	

Division 2 Final Table

		P	W	D	L	F	A	W	D	L	F	A	Pts
1	Manchester City	34	15	1	1	64	10	8	5	4	28	25	52
2	Glossop N.E.	34	12	1	4	48	13	8	5	4	28	25	46
3	Leicester Fosse	34	12	5	0	35	12	6	4	7	29	30	45
4	Newton Heath	34	12	4	1	51	14	7	1	9	16	29	43
5	New Brighton Tower	34	13	2	2	48	13	5	5	7	23	39	43
6	Walsall	34	12	5	0	64	11	3	7	7	15	25	42
7	Woolwich Arsenal	34	14	2	1	55	10	4	3	10	17	31	41
8	Small Heath	34	14	1	2	66	17	3	6	8	19	33	41
9	Burslem Port Vale	34	12	2	3	35	12	5	3	9	21	22	39
10	Grimsby Town	34	10	3	4	39	17	5	2	10	32	43	35
11	BARNSLEY	34	11	4	2	44	18	1	3	13	8	38	31
12	Lincoln City	34	10	5	2	31	16	2	2	13	20	40	31
13	Burton Swifts	34	7	5	5	35	25	3	3	11	16	45	28
14	Gainsborough Trinity	34	8	4	5	40	22	2	1	14	16	50	25
15	Luton Town	34	8	1	8	37	31	2	2	13	14	64	23
16	Blackpool	34	6	3	8	35	30	2	1	14	14	60	20
17	Loughborough	34	5	4	8	31	26	1	2	14	7	66	18
18	Darwen	34	2	4	11	16	32	0	1	16	6	109	9

1899/1900 — 16th in Division 2

Match results

#	Month	Date	Opponent	Result	Scorers	Att
1	Sep	2	BURTON SWIFTS	4-1	Armson, Foulds, Little, Gosling	3000
2		9	Leicester Fosse	0-1		8000
3		16	LUTON TOWN	2-1	Davis 2	2500
4		23	Burslem Port Vale	1-3	Davis	2000
5		30	WALSALL	2-2	Davis, Armson	2000
6	Oct	7	Middlesbrough	0-3		
7		21	Gainsborough Trinity	0-1		
8	Nov	4	Loughborough	0-0		500
9		11	NEWTON HEATH	0-0		3000
10		25	LINCOLN CITY	0-4		1000
11	Dec	2	Small Heath	0-5		4000
12		9	NEW BRIGHTON TOWER	1-1	Little	
13		16	Grimsby Town	1-8	Lake	2500
14		25	Walsall	2-4	Lake, Kilner	3500
15		26	BOLTON WANDERERS	1-6	Davis	
16		30	Burton Swifts	0-4		
17	Jan	6	LEICESTER FOSSE	1-2	Campbell	
18		13	Luton Town	0-3		
19		20	BURSLEM PORT VALE	3-0	Davis, Waldron, Lees	2000
20	Feb	10	MIDDLESBROUGH	5-2	Lake 2, Simmons 2, Lees	
21		17	Chesterfield	1-2	Jones	1000
22		24	GAINSBOROUGH TRIN.	5-0	Lees 3, Simmons, Jones	
23		27	Sheffield Wednesday	1-5	Simmons	
24	Mar	10	LOUGHBOROUGH	7-0	Simmons 2, Jones 2, Lees 2, McCartney	
25		17	Newton Heath	0-3		3000
26		24	SHEFFIELD WEDNESDAY	1-0	Jones	5000
27		31	Lincoln City	1-1	Lake	
28	Apr	7	SMALL HEATH	1-1	Jones	2000
29		13	Bolton Wanderers	0-2		
30		17	CHESTERFIELD	0-0		3000
31		21	GRIMSBY TOWN	0-1		
32		23	WOOLWICH ARSENAL	3-2	Jones, Lake, (og)	500
33		25	New Brighton Tower	2-6	Helliwell, Jones	1000
34		28	Woolwich Arsenal	1-5	Lake	3000

Appearances (shirt numbers)

Column key: Gr = Greaves J, Nx = Nixon T, Mc = McCartney J, Pp = Pepper F, Le = Lees W, Fo = Foulds J, Da = Davis H, Go = Gosling T, Ar = Armson H, Li = Little T, Cr = Craven JR, At = Atterbury S, Be = Bennett HE, Ca = Campbell A, He = Helliwell Alb., Hp = Hepworth W, Ho = Howard F, Hu = Hunt S, Jo = Jones R, Lk = Lake CE, Lw = Lawton R, Mo = Morrison FR, Re = Reid W, Si = Simmons W, Sm = Smith T, Wa = Waldron H, Ki = Kilner A

#	Gr	Nx	Mc	Pp	Le	Fo	Da	Go	Ar	Li	Cr	At	Be	Ca	He	Hp	Ho	Hu	Jo	Lk	Lw	Mo	Re	Si	Sm	Wa	Ki
1	1	2	3	4	5	6	7	8	9	10	11																
2	1	2	3	4	5	6	7		9	10	11						8										
3	1	2	3	4	5	6	7		9	10	11						8										
4	1	2		5	10		7		9		11						4				3	6			8		
5	1	2	3	5	9	6	7			10	11						4								8		
6	1	2	3	5	9	6	7			10	11						4								8		
7	1	2	3	6	5		7			10	11						4								8		9
8	1	2	3	6	5			8	10	9	11						4								7		
9	1	2	3	6	5		7	8	10	9	11						4										
10	1	2	3	6	5			8	10								4	9		11					7		
11	1	2	3	6	5		7		10	9						8	4			11							
12	1	2	3	5			7		10	9				6		8	4			11							
13	1		2	6	5		7		10	9		3	8				4			11							
14	1			4	5		7		9			3	8				2			11		6					10
15	1		2	5			7	4	9			3	8	6						11		10					
16	1		2	5	10		7	4	9			3	8							11		6					
17	1	3	2	5	9		7						8	6			4			11				10			
18	1		2	5	9							3	7				4			10	11			8			
19	1		3	5	8		7					2	4						6	11		10				9	
20	1		2	5	8							3	4						10	11		6		7		9	
21	1		2	5	8							3	4						10	11		6		7		9	
22	1		2	5	8							3	4						10	11		6		7		9	
23	1		2	5	8							3	4						10	11		6		7		9	
24	1		2	5	8							3	4						10	11		6		7		9	
25	1		2	5	11			8				3	4						10			6		7		9	
26	1		2	5	8							3	4						10	11		6		7		9	
27	1		2	5	8							3	4						10	11		6		7		9	
28	1		2	5	8							3	4						10	11		6		7		9	
29	1			5	8							3	4				2		10	11		6		7		9	
30	1			5	8							3	2				4		10	11		6		7		9	
31	1			5	8			4				3	2						10	11		6		7		9	
32	1			5	9			4				3	2						10	11		6		7		8	
33	1			5	9			4				3	2		8				10	11		6		7			
34	1			5	9							3	2		8		4		10	11		6		7			
Apps	34	13	26	31	34	5	16	14	13	14	6	21	15	6	2	2	21	1	17	23	2	15	6	15	6	14	2
Goals			1		7	1	6	1	2	2				1	1				8	7				6		1	1

One own goal

F.A. Cup

Rd	Month	Date	Opponent	Result	Scorers	Att	Gr	Nx	Mc	Pp	Le	Da	Go	Ar	Li	Cr	Ho
Q3	Oct	28	Lincoln City	1-0	Davis		1	2	3	4	5	7	8	10	9	11	6
Q4	Nov	21	Grimsby Town	2-3	Cotton, Little	3000	1	2	3	4	5		8	10	9	11	6

Played in Q4: J Cotton (at 7)

Division 2 table

Pos	Team	P	W	D	L	F	A	W	D	L	F	A	Pts
1	Sheffield Wed.	34	17	0	0	61	7	8	4	5	23	15	54
2	Bolton Wanderers	34	14	2	1	47	7	8	6	3	32	18	52
3	Small Heath	34	15	1	1	58	12	5	5	7	20	26	46
4	Newton Heath	34	15	1	1	44	11	5	3	9	19	16	44
5	Leicester Fosse	34	11	5	1	34	8	6	4	7	19	28	43
6	Grimsby Town	34	10	3	4	46	24	7	3	7	21	22	40
7	Chesterfield	34	10	4	3	35	24	6	2	9	30	36	38
8	Woolwich Arsenal	34	13	1	3	47	12	3	3	11	14	31	36
9	Lincoln City	34	11	5	1	31	9	3	3	11	15	34	36
10	New Brighton Tower	34	9	4	4	44	22	4	5	8	22	36	35
11	Burslem Port Vale	34	11	2	4	26	16	3	4	10	13	33	34
12	Walsall	34	10	5	2	35	18	2	3	12	15	37	32
13	Gainsborough Trin.	34	8	4	5	37	24	1	3	13	10	51	25
14	Middlesbrough	34	8	4	5	28	15	0	4	13	11	54	24
15	Burton Swifts	34	8	5	4	31	24	1	1	15	12	60	24
16	BARNSLEY	34	8	5	4	36	23	0	2	15	10	56	23
17	Luton Town	34	5	3	9	25	25	0	5	12	15	50	18
18	Loughborough	34	1	6	10	12	26	0	0	17	6	74	8

1900/01 — 15th in Division 2

#		Date	Opponent	Score	Scorers	Att	Greaves J	McCartney J	Stevenson GW	Bennett HE	Lees W	Morrison FR	Bradbury JH	Turner PJ	Swann A	Jones R	Mawson F	Atterbury S	Broley JF	Carlin JC	Hellewell Alb.	Lake CE	Morris GR	Pepper F	Adcock W	McDonald J
1	Sep	1	Walsall	0-3		3000	1	3	2	4	5	6	7	8	9	10	11									
2		8	BURTON SWIFTS	3-2	Swann 2, Turner	2500	1		2	4	10	6	7	8	9	11		3						5		
3		15	CHESTERFIELD	4-1	Hellewell 2, Bradbury, Swann	3000	1	3	2	4	5	6	7		10	9					8	11				
4		22	Woolwich Arsenal	2-1	Swann 2	7000	1	3	2	4	5	6	7		10	9					8	11				
5		29	BLACKPOOL	0-1		4000	1	3	2	4	5	6	7		10	9					8	11				
6	Oct	6	Stockport County	1-2	Swann		1		2	4	5	6	7		9			3			8	11			10	
7		13	SMALL HEATH	1-2	Lake	4000			2	4	10	6	7		9			3	1		8	11		5		
8		20	Grimsby Town	0-1					2	4		6	7		9	10		3	1		8	11		5		
9		24	Gainsborough Trinity	2-4	Swann, Hellewell				2	4		6	7		9	10		3	1		8			5	11	
10		27	LINCOLN CITY	0-0			1		2	4		6	7		9	10	11	3			8			5		
11	Dec	1	Burslem Port Vale	2-3	Bradbury, Swann		1		2	4	5	6	7		9	11		3		10	8					
12		15	New Brighton Tower	0-2		2000	1		2	3	5	6	7		9	11	10				8		4			
13		22	GAINSBOROUGH TRIN.	1-3	Swann	2000	1		2		5	6	7		9	11	10	3			8		4			
14		25	Leicester Fosse	0-2			1		2	6	8				9	11	10	3			7		4	5		
15		26	Middlesbrough	0-3		8000	1	3	2			8	6		9	11	10				7		4	5		
16		29	WALSALL	2-1	Hellewell, Swann	2000	1		2	4	8				9	11	10	3			7		6	5		
17	Jan	1	LEICESTER FOSSE	1-0	Mawson		1		2	4			3	7	9	11					8		6	5		
18		5	Burton Swifts	1-1	Mawson		1		2	4			3	7	9	11	10				8		6	5		
19		12	Chesterfield	2-1	Hellewell, Swann		1		2	4			3	7	9	11				10	8		6	5		
20		19	WOOLWICH ARSENAL	3-0	Swann 2, Lees	3000	1		2	4	8		3		9	11				10	7		6	5		
21	Feb	9	STOCKPORT COUNTY	2-0	Swann 2		1		2	4			3		9	11				10	7		6	5		8
22		16	Small Heath	1-3	Carlin	8000	1		2	4			3		9	11				10	7		6	5		
23		23	GRIMSBY TOWN	2-3	Carlin, Mawson	2000	1		2	4			3		9	11				10	7		6	5		
24	Mar	2	Lincoln City	0-3		1500	1		2	4	8		3			10	11			9	7		6	5		
25		13	Newton Heath	0-1		6000	1		2	4	8		3			10	11			9	7		6	5		
26		14	MIDDLESBROUGH	3-1	Jones, Lees, Carlin		1		2	4	8		3			10	11			9	7		6	5		
27		16	Glossop	1-2	Morris	2000	1		2	4	8		3			10	11			9	7		6	5		
28		20	Blackpool	1-1	Atterbury	500	1			4	8		3			10	11	2		9	7		6	5		
29		30	Burnley	0-4			1				8		3		9		11	2		10	7		6	5		
30	Apr	5	BURNLEY	2-1	Swann, Lees		1		2	4	8		3		9	11				10	7		6	5		
31		6	BURSLEM PORT VALE	1-3	Bennett		1			4	8		3		9	10	11	2			7		6	5		
32		8	GLOSSOP	2-2	Bennett 2		1		2	4	8		3		9	11				10	7		6	5		
33		9	NEWTON HEATH	6-2	Hellewell 2, Carlin, Mawson, Swann, Lees	3000	1		2	4	8		3		9	11				10	7		6	5		
34		20	NEW BRIGHTON TOWER	1-1	Swann	3000	1		2	4	8		3		9	11				10	7		6	5		
					Apps		30	5	32	31	28	32	16	5	29	17	27	13	3	16	32	6	23	26	2	1
					Goals					3	4		2	1	18	1	4	1		4	7	1	1			

F.A. Cup

		Date	Opponent	Score	Scorers	Att	Greaves J	McCartney J	Stevenson GW	Bennett HE	Lees W	Morrison FR	Bradbury JH	Turner PJ	Swann A	Jones R	Mawson F	Atterbury S	Broley JF	Carlin JC	Hellewell Alb.	Lake CE	Morris GR	Pepper F	Adcock W	McDonald J
Q3	Nov	3	DONCASTER ROVERS	2-1	Bradbury, Jones	4000	1		2	4	5	6	7		9	10		3			8	11				
Q4		17	LINCOLN CITY	1-0	Jones		1		2	4	5	6	7		9	10		3			8	11				
Q5	Dec	8	CHESTERFIELD	1-5	Swann	3000	1		2		5	6	7		9	10	11	3			8		4			

Division 2 Final Table

	Team	P	W	D	L	F	A	W	D	L	F	A	Pts
1	Grimsby Town	34	14	3	0	46	11	6	6	5	14	22	49
2	Small Heath	34	14	2	1	41	8	5	8	4	16	16	48
3	Burnley	34	15	2	0	39	6	5	2	10	14	23	44
4	New Brighton Tower	34	12	5	0	34	8	5	3	9	23	30	42
5	Glossop	34	11	2	4	34	9	4	6	7	17	24	38
6	Middlesbrough	34	11	4	2	38	13	4	3	10	12	27	37
7	Woolwich Arsenal	34	13	3	1	30	11	2	3	12	9	24	36
8	Lincoln City	34	12	3	2	39	11	1	4	12	4	28	33
9	Burslem Port Vale	34	8	6	3	28	14	3	5	9	17	33	33
10	Newton Heath	34	11	3	3	31	9	3	1	13	11	29	32
11	Leicester Fosse	34	9	5	3	30	15	2	5	10	9	22	32
12	Blackpool	34	7	6	4	20	11	5	1	11	13	47	31
13	Gainsborough Trin.	34	8	4	5	26	18	2	6	9	19	42	30
14	Chesterfield	34	6	5	6	25	22	3	5	9	21	36	28
15	BARNSLEY	34	9	3	5	34	23	2	2	13	13	37	27
16	Walsall	34	7	7	3	29	23	0	6	11	11	33	27
17	Stockport County	34	9	2	6	25	21	2	1	14	13	47	25
18	Burton Swifts	34	7	3	7	16	21	1	1	15	18	45	20

1901/02 — 11th in Division 2

#		Date	Opponent	Score	Scorers	Att	Seymour A	Hay J	Stevenson GW	Bennett HE	Carroll J	Couchlin D	McGowan D	Lees W	McCairns T	Carlin JC	Mawson F	Bennett GJ	Dartnell H	Gordon A	Green BH	Hellewell Alb.	Lydon T	McCartney WJ	Nimrod J	Oxspring A	Pepper F	Travers P	Welch C	Dyer JA	Hirst G	Morrison FR
1	Sep	2	Woolwich Arsenal	1-2	McCairns	4000	1	2	3	4	5	6	7	8	9	10	11															
2		7	BURTON UNITED	3-2	Mawson, Gordon, Carlin	3000	1	2	3	4		6	7	8		10	11			9			5									
3		14	Leicester Fosse	0-2			1	2	3	4		6	8			10	11		7	9							5					
4		21	PRESTON NORTH END	0-4		2000	1	2	3			6		5		10	11		7	9					4	8						
5		28	Burnley	0-2		3000	1	2				6		5		10	11		7	9					4	8			3			
6	Oct	5	BURSLEM PORT VALE	4-0	Gordon 2, Hellewell, Carlin		1	2				6		5		10	11			9		7			4	8			3			
7		12	Chesterfield	2-1	Lees 2	3000	1	2				6		5	9	10	11					7			4	8			3			
8		19	GAINSBOROUGH TRIN.	2-0	Mawson, Gordon	2000	1	2		4		6		5		10	11			9		7				8			3			
9		26	Middlesbrough	1-2	Gordon	5000	1	2		4		6		5	9	10	11			8		7							3			
10	Nov	9	Blackpool	1-2	Mawson	2000	1			2	4	6			9	10	11			8		7			5				3			
11		23	Newton Heath	0-1		4000	1			2	4			5	9	10	11		7	8			6						3			
12	Dec	7	Doncaster Rovers	1-0	Carlin	3000	1	3	2	4					11	10			7	9	8					6				5		
13		14	Preston North End	0-4		2000	1	3	2	4					11	10			7	9	8					6				5		
14		21	West Bromwich Albion	1-3	GJ Bennett	6000	1	3	2	4	5				11	9		10	7							6		8				
15		25	BRISTOL CITY	2-2	McCairns 2		1			2	4			5	8	9	7	11								6		10	3			
16		26	GLOSSOP	1-4	Lees		1			2	4			5	8	9	7	11								6		10	3			
17		28	WOOLWICH ARSENAL	2-0	GJ Bennett 2	3000	1			2	4			5	8	9			7	11						6		10	3			
18	Jan	1	BURNLEY	2-2	Lees (2 pens)		1			2	4			5	8	9			7	11						6		10	3			
19		4	Burton United	1-2	Lees (pen)		1			2	4			5	8	9	7			11						6		10	3			
20		11	LEICESTER FOSSE	2-3	Travers 2		1			2	7		5	4	11	9	10									6		8	3			
21	Feb	1	Burslem Port Vale	1-2	Lees	1500	1			2				5	9		7		11	10					4	6		8	3			
22		8	CHESTERFIELD	3-2	McCairns 2, Lees (pen)		1			2	4			5	8		7		11	10	9					6			3			
23		15	Gainsborough Trinity	0-0			1			2				5	8		7		11	10	9				4	6			3			
24		22	MIDDLESBROUGH	2-7	Travers, Dartnell	2000	1			2	9			5			7		11	10					4	6		8	3			
25	Mar	1	Bristol City	1-3	Gordon	4000	1			2	4			5	8		7		11	10	9					6			3			
26		8	BLACKPOOL	2-0	Dartnell, Carlin	2000	1			2	4			5	8		7		11	9						6		10	3			
27		15	Stockport County	3-2	McCairns 2, Green		1			2	4			5	9		7		11	10	8					6			3			
28		22	NEWTON HEATH	3-2	Green, Carroll, Dartnell	2500	1	2			4	9		5					11	10	8					6			3		7	
29		28	Lincoln City	1-1	Lees		1	2			4			5	9		7		11		8					6		10	3			
30		29	Glossop	1-1		2000	1	2			4			5	9		7		11		8					6		10	3			
31		31	STOCKPORT COUNTY	3-1	Travers, Carlin, Lees (pen)		1	2			4			5	9		7		11		8					6		10	3			
32	Apr	5	DONCASTER ROVERS	3-0	Dartnell 2, McCairns	1000	1	2			4			5	9		7			10	8			11		6						3
33		12	LINCOLN CITY	2-2	Mawson, McCairns	1000	1	2			4			5	9		7		11	10	8					6			3			
34		19	WEST BROMWICH ALB.	0-2		4000	1	2			4			5	9		7		11	10	8					6			3			
				Apps			34	19	22	25	13	11	3	32	23	32	21	9	18	14	10	6	1	4	8	25	1	13	26	2	1	1
				Goals							1			10	9	5	4	3	6	6	2	1						4				

F.A. Cup

		Date	Opponent	Score	Scorers	Seymour A	Hay J	Stevenson GW	Bennett HE	Carroll J	Couchlin D	McGowan D	Lees W	McCairns T	Carlin JC	Mawson F	Bennett GJ	Dartnell H	Gordon A	Green BH	Hellewell Alb.	Lydon T	McCartney WJ	Nimrod J	Oxspring A	Pepper F	Travers P	Welch C
Q3	Nov	2	GAINSBOROUGH TRIN.	1-0	McCairns	1			2	4	6		5	9	10	11			8		7							3
Q4		16	Ilkeston Town	4-2	GJ Bennett 2, Gordon, Mawson	1			2	4			5	9	10	11			8						6			3
Q5		30	LINCOLN CITY	0-0		1			2	4			5	9	10	11		7	8						6			3
rep	Dec	4	Lincoln City	1-3	Carlin	1			2	4			5	9	10	11		7	8						6			3

Q5 replay a.e.t.

Division 2 Final Table

		P	W	D	L	F	A	W	D	L	F	A	Pts
1	West Bromwich Alb.	34	14	2	1	52	13	11	3	3	30	16	55
2	Middlesbrough	34	15	1	1	58	7	8	4	5	32	17	51
3	Preston North End	34	12	3	2	50	11	6	3	8	21	21	42
4	Woolwich Arsenal	34	13	2	2	35	9	5	4	8	15	17	42
5	Lincoln City	34	11	6	0	26	4	3	7	7	19	31	41
6	Bristol City	34	13	1	3	39	12	4	5	8	13	23	40
7	Doncaster Rovers	34	12	3	2	39	12	1	5	11	10	46	34
8	Glossop	34	7	6	4	22	15	3	6	8	14	25	32
9	Burnley	34	9	6	2	30	8	1	4	12	11	37	30
10	Burton United	34	8	6	3	32	23	3	2	12	14	31	30
11	BARNSLEY	34	9	3	5	36	33	3	3	11	15	30	30
12	Burslem Port Vale	34	7	7	3	26	17	3	2	12	17	42	29
13	Blackpool	34	9	3	5	27	21	2	4	11	13	35	29
14	Leicester Fosse	34	11	2	4	26	14	1	3	13	12	42	29
15	Newton Heath	34	10	2	5	27	12	1	4	12	11	41	28
16	Chesterfield	34	10	3	4	35	18	1	3	13	12	50	28
17	Stockport County	34	8	3	6	25	20	0	4	13	11	52	23
18	Gainsborough Trin.	34	4	9	4	26	25	0	2	15	4	55	19

Season 1901/02

Back row: Stevenson, Seymoor, Welch.

Centre row: McCartney (Manager), Bennett, Lees, Couchlin, Hunt (Coach)

Front row: Hellewell, Gordon, McCairns, Carlin

1902/03 — 8th in Division 2

							Seymour A	Hay J	West A	Bennett HE	McGran W	Oxspring A	Lang J	Green BH	Richardson GC	Lees W	Bourne RA	Cornan F	Greaves J	Hellewell, Alb.	Hellewell, Alec	McCartney WJ	Mawson F	Nimrod J	Underwood A	Welch C
1	Sep	6	STOCKPORT COUNTY	2-1	Green 2	3000	1	2	3	4	5	6	7	8	9	10	11									
2		13	Blackpool	3-3	Lees (pen), Green 2	2000	1	2	3	4	5	6	7	8	9	11									10	
3		20	WOOLWICH ARSENAL	1-1	Underwood	5000	1	2	3	4	5	6	7	8		9							11		10	
4		27	Doncaster Rovers	0-2		3000	1		2	4	5	6	7	9		8	11								10	3
5	Oct	4	LINCOLN CITY	0-0		3000	1		2	4	5	6	7	8	9		11								10	3
6		11	Small Heath	1-2	Richardson	7000	1		2	4	5	6	7	8	9		11								10	3
7		18	LEICESTER FOSSE	1-2	Bennett		1		2	4	5	6	7	8	9		11								10	3
8	Nov	8	Preston North End	0-3		1500	1		2	4		6	7			5	11	8		9					10	3
9		22	Chesterfield	0-3		3000	1		2	4		6	7			5	11	8		9					10	3
10		24	Manchester City	2-3	Underwood, Orr (og)	8000	1		2	4		6	7			5	11	8		9					10	3
11	Dec	6	BURTON UNITED	4-0	Lang 2, Underwood, Cornan				2	4		6	7	8			11	10	1	9		5				3
12		20	GLOSSOP	0-1		2000		2	3	4		6	7			5	11	8	1	9					10	
13		25	Bristol City	3-3	Davis (og), Green, Cornan	6000	1		2			4		8		5	11	10		9	7				6	3
14		27	Manchester United	1-2	Lees	9000	1		2			4		8		5	11	10		9	7				6	3
15	Jan	1	BURNLEY	3-0	Green 3		1		2			6		8		5				9	7		11	4	10	3
16		3	Stockport County	1-4	Lees		1		2			6	7	8		5		10		9	11			4		3
17		10	BLACKPOOL	6-0	Alec Hellewell 2, Alb. Hellewell 2, Green 2		1		2	4		6		8		5		10		9	7		11			3
18		17	Woolwich Arsenal	0-4		10000	1		2	4		6		8		5		10		9	7		11			3
19		21	Lincoln City	3-1	Alec Hellewell 2, Green		1		2	4		6		8		5		10		9	7		11			3
20		24	DONCASTER ROVERS	2-0	Lees, Alb Hellewell	4000	1		2	4		6		8		5		10		9	7		11			3
21	Feb	14	Leicester Fosse	2-1	Lees, Alb Hellewell		1		2	4		6		8		5	11	10		9	7					3
22		28	Burnley	2-1	Cornan, Green		1		2	4		6		8		5	11	10		9	7					3
23	Mar	7	PRESTON NORTH END	3-0	Green 2, Cornan	3000	1		2	4		6		8		5	11	10		9	7					3
24		21	CHESTERFIELD	2-2	Alec Hellewell, Cornan	3000	1		2	4		6		8		5	11	10		9	7					3
25		25	Gainsborough Trinity	2-1	Cornan, Green		1		2	4		6		8		5	11	10		9	7					3
26		28	GAINSBOROUGH TRIN.	2-3	Cornan 2		1		2	4		6		8		5	11	10		9	7					3
27	Apr	4	Burton United	1-1	Cornan		1		2	4		6		8		5	11	10		9	7					3
28		10	BURSLEM PORT VALE	1-0	Green	4000			2	4		6		8		5		10	1	9	7		11			3
29		11	BRISTOL CITY	2-0	Lewis (og), Lees (pen)	4000			2	4		6		8		5		10	1	9	7		11			3
30		13	SMALL HEATH	3-0	Alb Hellewell, Alec Hellewell, Cornan	5000		2	3	4		6		8		5		10	1	9	7		11			
31		14	MANCHESTER CITY	0-3		5500		2		4		6		8		5			1	9	7	3	11		10	
32		18	Glossop	2-2	Lees 2	1000		2	3	4		6		8		5		10	1	9	7		11			
33		20	Burslem Port Vale	0-2			1	2	3			6		8		5		10		9	7		11	4		
34		25	MANCHESTER UNITED	0-0		2000	1		2			6		8		5		10		9	7		11	4		3
						Apps	27	8	33	28	7	34	13	30	5	30	19	25	7	27	22	2	13	4	14	26
						Goals				1			2	16	1	8		10		5	6				3	

Three own goals

F.A. Cup

							Seymour A	Hay J	West A	Bennett HE	McGran W	Oxspring A	Lang J	Green BH	Richardson GC	Lees W	Bourne RA	Cornan F	Greaves J	Hellewell, Alb.	Hellewell, Alec	McCartney WJ	Mawson F	Nimrod J	Underwood A	Welch C
Q3	Nov	1	Belper Town	4-1	Lang 2, Cornan 2		1		2	4		6	7			5	11	8		9					10	3
Q4		15	CHESTERFIELD	3-2	Lees (pen), Bourne, Alb Hellewell	3000	1		2	4		6	7			5	11	8		9					10	3
Q5		29	GAINSBOROUGH TRIN.	3-2	Lang, Alb Hellewell 2				2	4		6	7	8		5	11		1	9					10	3
IR	Dec	13	SWINDON TOWN	4-0	Lees, Cornan, West, Hay			2	3	4		6	7			5	11	8	1	9					10	
R1	Feb	7	LINCOLN CITY	2-0	Bennett, Welch	7000	1		2	4		6		8		5	11	10		9	7					3
R2		21	Aston Villa	1-4	Lees	28000	1		2	4		6		8		5	11	10		9	7					3

R2. Drawn at home but agreed to play at Aston Villa for £250 and 50% of gate receipts

		P	W	D	L	F	A	W	D	L	F	A	Pts
1	Manchester City	34	15	1	1	64	15	10	3	4	31	14	54
2	Small Heath	34	17	0	0	57	11	7	3	7	17	25	51
3	Woolwich Arsenal	34	14	2	1	46	9	6	6	5	20	21	48
4	Bristol City	34	12	3	2	43	18	5	5	7	16	20	42
5	Manchester United	34	9	4	4	32	15	6	4	7	21	23	38
6	Chesterfield	34	11	4	2	43	10	3	5	9	24	30	37
7	Preston North End	34	10	5	2	39	12	3	5	9	17	28	36
8	BARNSLEY	34	9	4	4	32	13	4	4	9	23	38	34
9	Burslem Port Vale	34	11	5	1	36	16	2	3	12	21	46	34
10	Lincoln City	34	8	3	6	30	22	4	3	10	16	31	30
11	Glossop	34	9	1	7	26	19	2	6	9	17	38	29
12	Gainsborough Trin.	34	9	4	4	28	14	2	3	12	13	45	29
13	Burton United	34	9	4	4	26	20	2	3	12	13	39	29
14	Blackpool	34	7	5	5	32	24	2	5	10	12	35	28
15	Leicester Fosse	34	5	5	7	20	23	5	3	9	21	42	28
16	Doncaster Rovers	34	8	5	4	27	17	1	2	14	8	55	25
17	Stockport County	34	6	4	7	26	24	1	2	14	12	50	20
18	Burnley	34	6	7	4	25	25	0	1	16	5	52	20

1903/04 — 8th in Division 2

No		Date	Opponent	Score	Scorers	Att	Hewitson R	West A	Welch C	Bennett HE	Lees W	McCartney WJ	Hellewell, Alec	Green BH	Gullen G	Sherman E	Lake CE	Barnfather P	Birtles TJ	Cornan F	Edwards M	Gill JE	Jones A	Kelly F	Lavery J	McGuire J	Owen JR	Oxspring A	Sylph J	Travers P	Wall G	Ward J
1	Sep	5	LEICESTER FOSSE	1-1	Sherman		1	2	3	4	5	6	7	8	9	10	11															
2		12	Blackpool	2-0	Hellewell 2	3000	1	2		4	5		7	8	9	10	11				3							6				
3		19	GAINSBOROUGH TRIN.	2-0	Gullen, Hellewell	3000	1	2		4	5		7	8	9	10	11				3							6				
4		26	Burton United	1-1	Gullen	2000	1	2		4	5		7	8	9		11			10	3							6				
5	Oct	3	BRISTOL CITY	2-0	Lees (pen), Lake	4000	1	2		4	5		7	8	9		11			10	3							6				
6		10	Manchester United	0-4		18000	1	2		4	5		7	8	9		11			10	3							6				
7		17	GLOSSOP	4-0	Lake, Barnfather, Hellewell, Jones		1	2		4	5		8				11	7		10	3		9					6				
8		24	Bradford City	1-3	Jones	12000	1	2		4	5		8				11	7		10	3		9					6				
9		31	WOOLWICH ARSENAL	2-1	Kelly 2	6000	1	2		4	5		9					7		10	3		8	11				6				
10	Nov	7	Burslem Port Vale	0-3		2000	1		2	4	5		9					7		10	3		8	11				6				
11		21	STOCKPORT COUNTY	0-0			1		2	4	5		9					7		10	3		8	11				6				
12	Dec	19	PRESTON NORTH END	1-0	Kelly		1				5		9		8			7		10	3	2		11				6				4
13		25	Bolton Wanderers	1-5	Gullen	12000	1				5		9		8			7		10	3	2		11				6				4
14		26	Grimsby Town	1-5	Cornan	4000	1			4	5		9		8			7		10	3	2		11				6				
15		28	Lincoln City	0-0			1			4	5		9		8			7		10		2		11				6	3			
16	Jan	2	Leicester Fosse	0-2		5000	1			4	5		9		8			7		10	3	2		11				6				
17		9	BLACKPOOL	2-2	Barnfather, Lees (pen)	3000	1				5		9		8			7		10	3	2		11				6				4
18		16	Gainsborough Trinity	2-4	Cornan, Jones	2000	1				5				8			7		10	3	2	9	11				6				4
19		23	BURTON UNITED	2-1	Jones, Lees (pen)		1				5				8			7		10	3	2	9					6			11	4
20		30	Bristol City	0-2		2500	1		2		5							7		10	3		9			8		6			11	4
21	Feb	13	Glossop	0-7			1		2		5		9		8			7		10	3							6			11	4
22		20	BRADFORD CITY	1-2	Cornan	5000	1		2		5		9		8			7		10	3							6			11	4
23		27	Woolwich Arsenal	0-3		14000	1				5							7		10	3	2	9			8		6			11	4
24	Mar	5	BURSLEM PORT VALE	1-0	Wall		1											7		10	3	2	9			8	5	6			11	
25		12	LINCOLN CITY	2-1	Wall, Lavery		1				5		9					7		10	3	2			4	8		6			11	
26		19	Stockport County	2-2	Hellewell, Lavery		1				5		9					7		10	3	2			4			6		8	11	
27		26	CHESTERFIELD	0-0		3000	1				5		9					7		10	3	2				4		6		8	11	
28	Apr	1	Burnley	2-2	Hellewell, Cornan		1				5		9					7		10	3	2				4		6		8	11	
29		4	BOLTON WANDERERS	1-0	Lees (pen)		1				5		9					7		10	3	2				4		6		8	11	
30		5	MANCHESTER UNITED	0-2		5000	1				5		9					7		10	3	2				4		6		8	11	
31		9	BURNLEY	1-1	Barnfather		1				5							7		10	3	2	9			4		6		8	11	
32		16	Preston North End	1-1	Jones	6000	1				5		9					7			3	2	8			4		6		10	11	
33		23	GRIMSBY TOWN	3-1	Hellewell, Wall 2		1				5		9					7		10	3	2	8			4		6			11	
34		30	Chesterfield	0-1			1						9					7	5		3	2	8			4		6		10	11	
			Apps				34	9	5	15	32	1	29	6	16	3	8	27	1	30	32	20	13	10	3	12	1	33	1	9	16	8
			Goals								4		7		3	1	2	3		4			5	3	2						4	

F.A. Cup

		Date	Opponent	Score		Hewitson R	West A	Welch C	Bennett HE	Lees W	McCartney WJ	Hellewell, Alec	Green BH	Gullen G	Sherman E	Lake CE	Barnfather P	Birtles TJ	Cornan F	Edwards M	Gill JE	Jones A	Kelly F	Lavery J	McGuire J	Owen JR	Oxspring A	Sylph J	Travers P	Wall G	Ward J
IR	Dec	12	Grimsby Town	0-2		1		2	4	5		9					7		10	3		8	11				6				

		P	W	D	L	F	A	W	D	L	F	A	Pts
1	Preston North End	34	13	4	0	38	10	7	6	4	24	14	50
2	Woolwich Arsenal	34	15	2	0	67	5	6	5	6	24	17	49
3	Manchester United	34	14	2	1	42	14	6	6	5	23	19	48
4	Bristol City	34	14	2	1	53	12	4	4	9	20	29	42
5	Burnley	34	12	2	3	31	20	3	7	7	19	35	39
6	Grimsby Town	34	12	5	0	39	12	2	3	12	11	37	36
7	Bolton Wanderers	34	10	3	4	38	11	2	7	8	21	30	34
8	BARNSLEY	34	10	5	2	25	12	1	5	11	13	45	32
9	Gainsborough Trin.	34	10	2	5	34	17	4	1	12	19	43	31
10	Bradford City	34	8	5	4	30	25	4	2	11	15	34	31
11	Chesterfield	34	8	5	4	22	12	3	3	11	15	33	30
12	Lincoln City	34	9	4	4	25	18	2	4	11	16	40	30
13	Burslem Port Vale	34	10	3	4	44	20	0	6	11	10	32	29
14	Burton United	34	8	6	3	33	16	3	1	13	12	45	29
15	Blackpool	34	8	2	7	25	27	3	3	11	15	40	27
16	Stockport County	34	7	7	3	28	23	1	4	12	12	49	27
17	Glossop	34	7	4	6	42	25	3	2	12	15	39	26
18	Leicester Fosse	34	5	8	4	26	21	1	2	14	16	61	22

1904/05 7th in Division 2

No		Date	Opponent	Score	Scorers	Att	Hewitson R	Gill JE	Edwards M	McGuire J	Cornan F	Oxspring A	Birtles TJ	McCartney WJ	Hellewell Alec	Robertson SP	Wall G	Beech GC	Bennett HE	Brodie D	Brooks J	Docherty A	Donagher M	Hay J	Heppinstall F	Jones A	Lees W	Round E	Silto WA	Wright P
1	Sep	3	Grimsby Town	0-0			1	2	3	4	5	6	7	8	9	10	11													
2		10	BLACKPOOL	2-1	Beech, Wall	3000	1	2	3	4	5	6	7		8	10	11	9												
3		17	Doncaster Rovers	0-2		3500	1	2	3	4	5	6	7		8	10	11	9												
4		24	GAINSBOROUGH TRIN.	2-1	Heppinstall, Edwards (pen)		1	2	3		5	6	7		8	10	11	9							4					
5	Oct	1	Burton United	2-1	Hellewell, Beech		1	2	3		5	6	7		8		11	9						4	10					
6		8	LIVERPOOL	0-2		4000	1	2	3		5	6	7		8		11	9						4	10					
7		15	Burslem Port Vale	2-0	Cornan, Cotton (og)	3000	1	2	3		5	6	7		8		11	9						4	10					
8		22	BRISTOL CITY	1-0	Beech	6000	1	2	3		5	6	7		8		11	9						4	10					
9		29	Manchester United	0-4		16000	1	2	3		5	6	7		8		11	9						4	10					
10	Nov	5	GLOSSOP	0-0			1	2	3		5	6	7		8		11	9						4	10					
11		12	Chesterfield	0-2		3000	1	2	3		5	6	7		8		11	9						4	10					
12		19	BRADFORD CITY	1-0	Beech	4000	1		3		5	6	7		8		11	9						4	10					2
13		26	Lincoln City	0-2		3000	1		3	8	5	6	7			10	11	9						4						2
14	Dec	3	LEICESTER FOSSE	2-1	Edwards (pen), Silto	3000	1		3		8	6	7			10		9					11	5	2				4	
15		17	West Bromwich Albion	1-4	Cornan	1000	1		3		10	6			7		8		4				11	5	2	9				
16		24	BURNLEY	1-2	Oxspring	2000	1		3	4	10	6			7		8						11	5	2	9				
17		26	Liverpool	1-2	Beech	25000	1		3	4	10	6			7			8					11	5	2	9				
18		31	GRIMSBY TOWN	2-2	Beech, Jones	3000	1		3	4	10	6			7			8					11	5	2	9				
19	Jan	2	Bolton Wanderers	1-2	Cornan		1		3	4	10	6			7						8		11	5	2	9				
20		7	Blackpool	0-6			1		3	4	10	6			7		11	8						5	2	9				
21		21	Gainsborough Trinity	0-4		2000	1		3	4	10	6			7		11	9					8	5	2					
22		28	BURTON UNITED	7-0	Jones 4, Wall 2, Edwards		1		3	4	10	6	7				11	8						5	2	9				
23	Feb	11	BURSLEM PORT VALE	3-0	Jones, Wall, Cornan		1		3	4	10	6	7				11	8						5	2	9				
24		25	MANCHESTER UNITED	0-0		4000	1		3	4	10	6			7		11	8						5	2	9				
25	Mar	4	Glossop	0-5		1200	1	3		4	10	6			7		11	8						5	2	9				
26		11	CHESTERFIELD	1-0	Wall		1		3	4	10	6					11					7		5	2	9	8	1		
27		18	Bradford City	2-1	Jones, Brooks	11000	1		3	4	10	6					11	8				7		5	2	9		1		
28		25	LINCOLN CITY	2-1	Jones 2		1		3	4	10	6					11	8				7		5	2	9		1		
29		29	Bristol City	0-3		3000	1		3	4	10	6					11	8						5	2	9		1		
30	Apr	1	Leicester Fosse	0-2		6000	1		3	4	10	6					11	8				7		5	2	9		1		
31		15	WEST BROMWICH ALB.	1-1	Jones	6000	1		3	4	10	6			7		11	8						5	2	9		1		
32		22	Burnley	0-3		3000	1		3	4	10	6					11	8				7		5	2	9				
33		24	BOLTON WANDERERS	2-1	Wall, Jones	8000	1		3	4	10	6					11	8				7		5	2	9				
34		25	DONCASTER ROVERS	2-1	Hellewell, Docherty	2000	1		3		10	6			7		11	10				8		5	2	9			4	
			Apps				28	12	33	22	33	34	16	1	24	6	28	31	1	1	12	3	30	21	8	19	1	6	2	2
			Goals						3		4	1			2		6	6				1	1		1	11			1	

One own goal

F.A. Cup

		Date	Opponent	Score	Scorers	Att	Hewitson R	Gill JE	Edwards M	McGuire J	Cornan F	Oxspring A	Birtles TJ	McCartney WJ	Hellewell Alec	Robertson SP	Wall G	Beech GC	Bennett HE	Brodie D	Brooks J	Docherty A	Donagher M	Hay J	Heppinstall F	Jones A	Lees W	Round E	Silto WA	Wright P
Q6	Dec	10	BURSLEM PORT VALE	0-0		2000	1		3		5	6	7		8		9				11		4	2	10					
rep		15	Burslem Port Vale	2-1	Jones, Cornan		1		3		10	6			7		8	4			11		5	2		9				
Int	Jan	14	Plymouth Argyle	0-2		15000	1		3	4	10	6			7		11	8						5	2	9				

		P	W	D	L	F	A	W	D	L	F	A	Pts
1	Liverpool	34	14	3	0	60	12	13	1	3	33	13	58
2	Bolton Wanderers	34	15	0	2	53	16	12	2	3	34	16	56
3	Manchester United	34	16	0	1	60	10	8	5	4	21	20	53
4	Bristol City	34	12	3	2	40	12	7	1	9	26	33	42
5	Chesterfield	34	9	6	2	26	11	5	5	7	18	24	39
6	Gainsborough Trin.	34	11	4	2	32	15	4		10	29	43	36
7	BARNSLEY	34	11	4	2	29	13	3	1	13	9	43	33
8	Bradford City	34	8	5	4	31	20	4	3	10	14	29	32
9	Lincoln City	34	9	4	4	31	16	3	3	11	11	24	31
10	West Bromwich Alb.	34	8	2	7	28	20	5	2	10	28	28	30
11	Burnley	34	10	1	6	31	21	2	5	10	12	31	30
12	Glossop	34	7	5	5	23	14	3	5	9	14	32	30
13	Grimsby Town	34	9	3	5	22	14	2	5	10	11	32	30
14	Leicester Fosse	34	8	3	6	30	25	3	4	10	10	30	29
15	Blackpool	34	8	5	4	26	15	1	5	11	10	33	28
16	Burslem Port Vale	34	7	4	6	28	25	3	3	11	19	47	27
17	Burton United	34	7	2	8	20	29	1	2	14	10	55	20
18	Doncaster Rovers	34	3	2	12	12	32	0	0	17	11	49	8

Season 1904/05
Back row: Wood (Director), Gill, Hewitson, Edwards.
Centre row: Bedford (Dir.), Norman, Donagher, Cornan, Oxspring, Fisher (Chair.), Fairclough (Sec.)
Front row: Birtles, Hellewell, Beech, Heppinstall, Wall.

Season 1905/06
Back row: Fairclough (Secretary) Fisher (Chairman) Hay, Bedford (Director) Rounds, Stacey, Pleasant
(Director) Bott (Director) Lodge (Director) Marston (Trainer) Centre row: Silto, Wilkinson, Robertson
Front row: Ryalls, Beech (Captain) Hellewell, Bell, Wall

1905/06 12th in Division 2

No	Month	Day	Opponent	Score	Scorers	Att	Thorpe T	Hay J	Stacey GW	Hellewell, Alec	Donagher M	Oxspring A	Ryalls J	Beech GC	Pegg E	Bell J	Wall G	Birtles TJ	Brooks J	Hall, John	Noble WD	Owen JR	Reed C	Robertson SP	Round E	Silto WA	Warner P	Wilkinson J
1	Sep	2	Hull City	1-4	Bell	8000	1	2	3	4	5	6	7	8	9	10	11											
2		9	LINCOLN CITY	4-2	Pegg 2, Wall 2		1	2	3		5	6	7	8	9	10	11							4				
3		16	Chesterfield	0-2			1	2	3		5	6	7	8	9	10	11							4				
4		23	BURSLEM PORT VALE	4-0	Oxspring, Hellewell, Bell, Beech	3000	1	2	3		5	6	7	8	9	10	11							4				
5		30	GRIMSBY TOWN	2-0	Wall, Donagher		1	2		9	5	6	7	8		10	11						3	4				
6	Oct	7	Clapton Orient	0-0			1	2		9	4	6	7	8		10	11						3					5
7		14	BURNLEY	1-2	Oxspring	3000	1	2		9	4	6	7	8		10	11						3					5
8		21	Leeds City	2-3	Bell, Hellewell	12000	1	2	3	9	5	6	7			10	11					8		4				
9		28	BURTON UNITED	3-0	Beech 2, Robertson		1	2	3	9	5	6	7	8		10	11							4				
10	Nov	4	Chelsea	0-6		10000	1		3	9	5	6	7	8		10	11				2			4				
11		11	GAINSBOROUGH TRIN.	2-1	Wall, Noble (pen)		1		3	9	5	6	7	8		10	11				2			4				
12		18	Bristol City	0-3		8000	1		3	9	5	6	7	8		10	11				2			4				
13		25	MANCHESTER UNITED	0-3		4000	1	2		9	5	6	7	8			11						3	10		4		
14	Dec	2	Glossop	2-2	Bell, Wall		1	2		7	5	6		8	9	10	11						3	4				
15		16	Blackpool	0-0		3000	1				5	6	7	8	9	10	11				2		3	4				
16		23	BRADFORD CITY	0-1		5000	1				5	6	7	8	9	10	11				2		3	4				
17		25	Leicester Fosse	0-1		10000	1	2			5	6	7	8	9	10	11						3	4				
18		26	West Bromwich Albion	3-5	Hellewell 2, Manners (og)	7000	1	2		9	5	6	7	8		10	11						3	4				
19	Jan	1	STOCKPORT COUNTY	4-0	Birtles 2, Bell, Wall	4000		2		9	5	6				10	11	7				8	3	4	1			
20		6	Lincoln City	1-4	Hellewell		1	2	3	9	4	6		10			11	7				8						5
21		20	CHESTERFIELD	8-1	*see below	3000	1	2	3	9	4	6		10			11	7				8						5
22		27	Burslem Port Vale	2-1	Hellewell, Wall			2	3	9	4	6		10			11	7				8			1			5
23	Feb	10	CLAPTON ORIENT	4-1	Hellewell, Wilkinson, Wall, Birtles		1	2	3	9	4	6		10			11	7				8						5
24		17	Burnley	1-2	Birtles	3000	1	2	3	9	4	6					11	7				8					10	5
25		24	LEEDS CITY	3-0	Warner, Wall 2	5000	1	2	3	9	4	6					11	7				8					10	5
26	Mar	3	Burton United	1-4	Warner		1	2	3	9	4	6		10			11	7				8						5
27		10	CHELSEA	1-2	Wall	8000	1	2	3	9	4	6		10			11	7				8						5
28		17	Gainsborough Trinity	0-1			1		3	9	4	6		10			11	7			2	8						5
29		24	BRISTOL CITY	2-2	Owen, Birtles	6000	1	2	3	9	4	6		10			11	7				8						5
30		31	Manchester United	1-5	Wall	11000	1			9	4	6		10			11	7			2	8	3					5
31	Apr	5	Grimsby Town	1-2	Owen	1500	1	2	3	9	4	6		10			11	7				8						5
32		7	GLOSSOP	1-1	Birtles		1	2	3	9	4	6		10				7	11			8				5		
33		13	WEST BROMWICH ALB.	3-0	Owen, Hellewell, Brooks	5000	1	2	3	9	4	6		10				7	11			8						5
34		14	Stockport County	0-0		4000	1	2	3	9	4	6		10				7	11			8				5		
35		16	LEICESTER FOSSE	0-0		6000	1	2	3	9	4	6				8		7	11							5	10	
36		17	HULL CITY	2-0	Bell, Owen	4000	1	2	3	9	4	6				10			11	7		8				5		
37		21	BLACKPOOL	1-1	Stacey		1	2	3	9		6				10			11	7		8				4		5
38		28	Bradford City	0-0		8000	1	4	3	9		6		8		10		7	11		2							5
						Apps	36	31	27	32	36	38	17	31	8	22	31	18	7	2	8	19	11	16	2	6	3	17
						Goals			3	9	1	2		3	2	6	14	7	1		1	6		1			2	1

Scorers in game 21: Owen 2, Stacey 2, Wall 2, Birtles, Hellewell

One own goal

F.A. Cup

Rd	Month	Day	Opponent	Score	Scorers	Att	Thorpe T	Hay J	Stacey GW	Hellewell, Alec	Donagher M	Oxspring A	Ryalls J	Beech GC	Pegg E	Bell J	Wall G	Birtles TJ	Brooks J	Hall, John	Noble WD	Owen JR	Reed C	Robertson SP	Round E	Silto WA	Warner P	Wilkinson J
Q4	Dec	9	Earlstown	2-0	Beech 2		1	2		7	5	6		8	9	10	11						3	4				
R1	Jan	13	Crewe Alexandra	1-1	Stacey (pen)		1	2	3	9	4	6		10			11	7				8						5
rep		18	CREWE ALEXANDRA	4-0	Hellewell, Wall, Stacey, Wilkinson		1	2	3	9	4	6		10			11	7				8						5
R2	Feb	3	Liverpool	0-1		10000	1	2	3	9	4	6		10			11	7				8						5

R2. Drawn at home, but agreed to play at Liverpool, for share of expected bigger match receipts.

		P	W	D	L	F	A	W	D	L	F	A	Pts
1	Bristol City	38	17	1	1	43	8	13	5	1	40	20	66
2	Manchester United	38	15	3	1	55	13	13	3	3	35	15	62
3	Chelsea	38	13	4	2	58	16	9	5	5	32	21	53
4	West Bromwich Alb.	38	13	4	2	53	16	9	4	6	26	20	52
5	Hull City	38	10	5	4	38	21	9	1	9	29	33	44
6	Leeds City	38	11	5	3	38	19	6	4	9	21	28	43
7	Leicester Fosse	38	10	3	6	30	21	5	9	5	23	27	42
8	Grimsby Town	38	11	7	1	33	13	4	3	12	13	33	40
9	Burnley	38	9	4	6	26	23	6	4	9	16	30	38
10	Stockport County	38	11	6	2	36	16	2	3	14	8	40	35
11	Bradford City	38	7	4	8	21	22	6	4	9	25	38	34
12	BARNSLEY	38	11	4	4	45	17	1	5	13	15	45	33
13	Lincoln City	38	10	1	8	46	29	2	5	12	23	43	30
14	Blackpool	38	8	3	8	22	21	2	6	11	15	41	29
15	Gainsborough Trin.	38	10	2	7	35	22	2	2	15	9	35	28
16	Glossop	38	9	4	6	36	28	1	4	14	13	43	28
17	Burslem Port Vale	38	10	4	5	34	25	2	0	17	15	57	28
18	Chesterfield	38	8	4	7	26	24	2	4	13	14	48	28
19	Burton United	38	9	4	6	26	20	1	2	16	8	47	26
20	Clapton Orient	38	6	4	9	19	22	1	3	15	16	56	21

1906/07   8th in Division 2

#	Mon	Date	Opponent	Res		Att	Thorpe T	Noble WD	Stacey GW	Hay J	Wilkinson J	Oxspring A	Hall John	Owen JR	Hellewell Alec	O'Donnell M	Brooks J	Bell I	Boyle TW	Cooper W	Crump JA	Gedney C	Griffiths Will	Johnson A	Mordue J	Norton P	Powell H	Reeves G	Round E	Ruddlesdin W	Silto WA
1	Sep	1	BLACKPOOL	3-2	Owen 2, O'Donnell		1	2	3	4	5	6	7	8	9	10	11														
2		8	Bradford City	0-2		13000	1	2	3	4	5	6	7	8	9	10	11														
3		15	WEST BROMWICH ALB.	0-1		3000	1	2	3		5	6	7	8	9	10	11													4	
4		22	Leicester Fosse	1-2	Griffiths		1		3	2	5	6	7	8		10	11						9							4	
5		29	NOTTM. FOREST	0-1			1		3	2		6	7	8	5	10	11						9							4	
6	Oct	6	Lincoln City	0-1					3	2	5	6	7		9	8	11									10			1	4	
7		13	BURTON UNITED	6-1	Griffiths 2, Hellewell, Owen, Hall, Wilkinson				3	2	5	6	7	10	8		11						9						1	4	
8		20	Grimsby Town	0-1					3	2		6	7	10	8		11						9						1	4	5
9		27	BURSLEM PORT VALE	3-2	Mordue 2, Owen	1000			3	2		6	7	10		8	11								9				1	4	5
10	Nov	3	Burnley	2-2	Hellewell, Hall				3	2		6	7		9	8	11	10											1	4	5
11		10	LEEDS CITY	3-0	Stacey (pen), Mordue, Owen	4000			3	2		6	7	8	9		11								10				1	4	5
12		17	Chesterfield	2-3	Owen, Oxspring	4000			3	2		6	7	8	9		11								10				1	4	5
13		24	Chelsea	1-2	Mordue	14000			3	2		6	7	9	8		11		4						10				1		5
14	Dec	1	WOLVERHAMPTON W.	0-1		4000	1		3	2		6	7	9	8		11		4						10						5
15		8	Hull City	0-2		7000	1		3	2		6	7	9	8		11		4						10						5
16		15	GAINSBOROUGH TRIN.	6-0	Griffiths, Hall 2, Owen, Brooks, Mordue		1		3	2		6	7	8			11		4				9		10						5
17		22	Stockport County	0-0			1		3	2		6	7	8			11		4				9		10						5
18		25	GLOSSOP	3-0	Reeves 2, Mordue	5000	1		3	2		6	7		9		11		4						10			8			5
19		26	HULL CITY	4-2	Hellewell 2, Mordue 2	4000	1		3	2		6	7	8	9		11		4						10						5
20		29	Blackpool	3-2	Hellewell 2, Brooks	2000	1		3	2		6	7		9		11		4						10			8			5
21	Jan	1	CLAPTON ORIENT	3-2	Mordue, Reeves 2	4000	1		3	2		6	7		9		11		4						10			8			5
22		5	BRADFORD CITY	3-1	Reeves 2, Mordue		1		3	2		6	7		9		11		4						10			8			5
23		26	LEICESTER FOSSE	2-2	Hellewell, Reeves		1		3	2		6	7		9		11		4						10			8			5
24	Feb	9	LINCOLN CITY	6-2	O'Donnell 2, Brooks, Stacey, Hall, Hellewell		1		3	2		6	7		9	8	11		4						10						5
25		16	Burton United	1-1	Hellewell	3000	1		3	2		6	7		9	10	11		4									8			5
26	Mar	2	Burslem Port Vale	2-2	Brooks 2	3000	1						7		9		11		4	6	2	3			10			8			5
27		16	Leeds City	1-2	Hellewell	14000			3	2		6		9	8	11		4						10			7	1		5
28		23	CHESTERFIELD	2-1	Stacey (pen), O'Donnell	3000	1		3	2		6			9		11		4						10		8	7			5
29		29	Glossop	1-2	Hall	4000			3	2		6	7		9		11		4						10			8	1		5
30		30	CHELSEA	3-1	Reeves 2, Silto	5000			3	2		6	7		9		11		4						10			8	1		5
31	Apr	1	STOCKPORT COUNTY	3-1	Mordue 2, Hall	5000			3	2		6	7		9		11		4						10			8	1		5
32		2	Nottingham Forest	0-0		15000			3			6	7		9	10			4			5		2	11			8	1		
33		6	Wolverhampton Wan.	1-5	Reeves	4000			3	2			7		9		11		4	6					10			8	1		5
34		11	GRIMSBY TOWN	1-1	Hall				3	2		6	7		9		11		4						10			8	1		5
35		13	Clapton Orient	0-1		6000			3			6	7		9		11		4					2			10	8	1	5	
36		18	BURNLEY	5-0	Reeves 2, Hellewell, Hall, Powell				3	2		6	7		9		11		4								10	8	1	5	
37		20	Gainsborough Trinity	1-1	Reeves				3	2		6	7		9		11		4								10	8	1	5	
38		25	West Bromwich Albion	1-3	Powell	5000			3	2		6	7		9		11		4								10	8	1	5	
			Apps				19	3	37	34	6	36	36	14	34	19	30	1	26	2	1	1	7	3	25	1	6	18	19	14	26
			Goals						3		1	1	9	7	11	4	5						4		12		2	13			1

F.A. Cup

Rnd	Mon	Date	Opponent	Res		Att	Thorpe T		Stacey GW	Hay J		Oxspring A	Hall John	Owen JR	Hellewell Alec	O'Donnell M	Brooks J		Boyle TW				Griffiths Will		Mordue J		Powell H	Reeves G			Silto WA
R1	Jan	12	Nottingham Forest	1-1	Hellewell	7000	1		3	2		6	7	8		10	11		4				9								5
rep		17	NOTTINGHAM FOREST	2-1	Hellewell, Hall	10000	1		3	2		6	7	8		10	11		4												5
R2	Feb	2	PORTSMOUTH	1-0	O'Donnell	10266	1		3	2		6	7	8		10	11		4												5
R3		23	BURY	1-0	Powell	13077	1		3			6	7		9	10	11		4						2		8				5
R4	Mar	9	WOOLWICH ARSENAL	1-2	O'Donnell	13781			3	2		6	7		9	10	11		4								8		1		5

Played in R1 replay and R2: J Scott (at 9)

		P	W	D	L	F	A	W	D	L	F	A	Pts
1	Nottingham Forest	38	16	2	1	43	13	12	2	5	31	23	60
2	Chelsea	38	18	0	1	55	10	8	5	6	25	24	57
3	Leicester Fosse	38	15	3	1	44	12	5	5	9	18	27	48
4	West Bromwich Alb.	38	15	2	2	62	15	6	3	10	21	30	47
5	Bradford City	38	14	2	3	46	21	7	3	9	24	32	47
6	Wolverhampton Wan.	38	13	4	2	49	16	4	3	12	17	37	41
7	Burnley	38	12	4	3	45	13	5	2	12	17	34	40
8	BARNSLEY	38	14	2	3	56	21	1	6	12	17	34	38
9	Hull City	38	11	2	6	41	20	4	5	10	24	37	37
10	Leeds City	38	10	5	4	38	26	3	5	11	17	37	36
11	Grimsby Town	38	13	2	4	34	16	3	1	15	23	46	35
12	Stockport County	38	8	8	3	26	12	4	3	12	16	40	35
13	Blackpool	38	9	4	6	25	19	2	7	10	8	32	33
14	Gainsborough Trin.	38	12	3	4	33	20	2	2	15	12	52	33
15	Glossop	38	10	4	5	32	21	3	2	14	21	58	32
16	Burslem Port Vale	38	11	5	3	45	26	1	2	16	15	57	31
17	Clapton Orient	38	9	7	3	25	13	2	1	16	20	54	30
18	Chesterfield	38	10	3	6	36	26	1	4	14	14	40	29
19	Lincoln City	38	10	2	7	29	24	2	2	15	17	49	28
20	Burton United	38	7	3	9	24	23	1	4	14	10	45	23

Season 1906/07
Back row: Fairclough (Secretary) Noble, Thorpe, Stacey, Bedford (Director) Marston (Trainer) Garner (Director)
Centre row: Hay, Wilkinson, Oxspring, Master Fairclough
Front row: Hall, Owen, Hellewell, O'Donnell, Brooks

BARNSLEY F.C. 1907-08

Season 1907/08
Back row: Marston (Trainer) Foundhere, Wood, Pleasant, Hay, Reed, Thorpe, Round, Johnson,
Lodge, Stringer, Wilkinson, Bott, Charlesworth, Bedford, Fairclough (Secretary)
Centre row: Walker, Gedney, Crump, Illingsworth, Boyle, Silto, Oxspring, Lillycrop, Tomlinson, Moran
Front row: Sanderson, Hall, Reeves, McShea, Hellewell, Kaye, Collins, Glendenning, Forman, Palmer

1907/08   16th in Division 2

Results

No	Month	Date	Opponent	Score	Scorers	Att
1	Sep	5	CLAPTON ORIENT	2-2	Reeves (2 pens)	3000
2		7	Hull City	0-2		9000
3		14	DERBY COUNTY	2-4	McShea 2	4000
4		21	Lincoln City	2-0	Reeves 2	
5		28	FULHAM	6-0	Reeves 3, McShea 2, Forman	7000
6	Oct	5	GRIMSBY TOWN	2-1	Reeves 2	4500
7		12	Chesterfield	3-1	Reeves 2 (1 pen), McShea	6000
8		19	BURNLEY	2-3	McShea, Boyle	
9		26	Oldham Athletic	0-1		9000
10	Nov	9	Leeds City	1-1	Hall	7000
11		16	WOLVERHAMPTON W.	5-0	Reeves 3, Silto, McShea	5000
12		23	Gainsborough Trinity	1-0	Forman	3000
13		30	STOCKPORT COUNTY	0-0		4000
14	Dec	14	LEICESTER FOSSE	1-3	Tomlinson	
15		21	Blackpool	1-1	Hellewell	3000
16		24	Derby County	0-3		6000
17		25	Bradford City	0-2		18000
18		26	WEST BROMWICH ALB.	1-3	Hellewell	6000
19		28	STOKE	0-1		3000
20	Jan	1	BRADFORD CITY	1-2	Hall	6000
21		4	HULL CITY	4-2	Kay 3, Lillycrop	4000
22		18	LINCOLN CITY	2-1	Lillycrop 2	
23		25	Fulham	0-2		12000
24	Feb	8	CHESTERFIELD	5-2	Surtees 2, Lillycrop 2, Hall	2500
25		15	Burnley	1-4	Hellewell	
26		29	Clapton Orient	0-2		7000
27	Mar	7	LEEDS CITY	1-3	Lillycrop	5000
28		14	Wolverhampton Wan.	1-0	Lillycrop	12500
29		19	OLDHAM ATHLETIC	2-1	McShea, Surtees	6000
30		21	GAINSBOROUGH TRIN.	1-2	Lillycrop	
31		28	Stockport County	0-2		5000
32	Apr	9	Grimsby Town	1-4	Griffiths	3000
33		11	Leicester Fosse	0-4		
34		17	Glossop	1-3	Hall	3000
35		18	BLACKPOOL	0-0		4000
36		20	West Bromwich Albion	1-1	Hall	5000
37		21	GLOSSOP	4-1	Hellewell 2, Griffiths, Lillycrop	5000
38		25	Stoke	0-4		2000

Appearances (shirt numbers)

No	Thorpe T	Hay J	Johnson A	Boyle TW	Silto WA	Oxspring A	Hall John	Reeves G	McShea E	Hellewell Alec	Forman T	Collins WE	Cowley JS	Francis A	Griffiths Walt	Kay H	Lillycrop GB	Milton A	Reed C	Round E	Sanderson R	Surtees E	Tomlinson F	Wilkinson J
1	1	2	3	4	5	6	7	8	9	10	11													
2	1	2	3	4	5	6	7	8		9	11	10												
3	1	2	3	4	5		7	8	9		11										10		6	
4		2	3	4	5	6	7	8	9	10	11								1					
5		2	3	4	5	6	7	8	9	10	11								1					
6		2	3	4	5	6	7	8	9	10	11								1					
7		2	3	4	5	6	7	8	9	10	11								1					
8		2		4	5	6	7	8	9	10	11													
9		2		4	5	6	7	8	9		11						10		3	1				
10		2		4	5	6	7	8	9		11						10		3	1				
11		2		4	5	6	7	8	9		11						10		3	1				
12		2		4	5	6	7	8	9		11						10		3	1				
13		2		4	5	6	7		9	8	11						10		3	1				
14		2			5	6	7		8		11					10	9		3	1			4	
15		2		4	5	6	7			10	11				8		9		3	1				
16	1	2		4	5	6	7			10	11				8		9		3					
17	1	2		4	5	6	7			10	11				8		9		3					
18	1	2		4	5	6	7		9	8	11				10				3					
19		2		8	5	6	7		9		11	1			10				3				4	
20	1	2		4	5	6	7		8		11						9		3			10		
21	1		2	4	5	6	7		8		11					10	9		3					
22		2		4		6	7		8		11					10	9		3	1			5	
23		2		4		6	7		8		11						9	3		1		10		5
24		2		4	5	6	7		8								9	3		1	11	10		
25		2		4	5	6	7		8								9	3		1	11	10		
26		2		4	5	6	7		8		11						9	3		1		10		
27		2		4	5	6	7		8		11						9	3		1		10		
28	1		2		5	6	7	8			11						9	3				10	4	
29	1		2		5	6	7		8								9	3			11	10	4	
30	1		2		5	6			8						7		9	3			11	10	4	
31	1		2		5	6			8		11			10	7		9	3					4	
32	1		2		5	6	7		8		11					10	9	3					4	
33	1	2			5	6	7		8		11					10	9			3			4	
34	1	2			5	6	7		9		11					10				3		8	4	
35	1	2			5	6	7		8							11	10	9		3			4	
36	1	2			5	6	7		8		11					10	9			3			4	
37	1	2		4	5	6	7		8							10	9			3				
38																								
Apps	19	32	8	32	36	37	36	12	20	26	33	1	1	1	12	6	27	15	16	18	5	10	14	1
Goals			1	1		5	14	8	5	2					2	3	9					3	1	

F.A. Cup

Round	Month	Date	Opponent	Score	Att	Thorpe T	Hay J	Boyle TW	Silto WA	Oxspring A	Hall John	McShea E	Forman T	Kay H	Lillycrop GB	Reed C
R1	Jan	11	Plymouth Argyle	0-1	17539	1	2	4	5	6	7	8	11	10	9	3

Division 2 table

	Team	P	W	D	L	F	A	W	D	L	F	A	Pts
1	Bradford City	38	15	2	2	58	16	9	4	6	32	26	54
2	Leicester Fosse	38	14	2	3	41	20	7	8	4	31	27	52
3	Oldham Athletic	38	15	4	0	53	14	7	2	10	23	28	50
4	Fulham	38	12	2	5	50	14	10	3	6	32	35	49
5	West Bromwich Alb.	38	13	3	3	38	13	6	6	7	23	26	47
6	Derby County	38	15	1	3	50	13	6	3	10	27	32	46
7	Burnley	38	14	3	2	44	14	6	3	10	23	36	46
8	Hull City	38	15	1	3	50	23	6	3	10	23	39	46
9	Wolverhampton Wan.	38	11	4	4	34	11	4	3	12	16	34	37
10	Stoke	38	11	5	3	43	13	5	0	14	14	39	37
11	Gainsborough Trin.	38	9	4	6	31	28	5	3	11	16	43	35
12	Leeds City	38	9	6	4	33	18	3	2	14	20	47	32
13	Stockport County	38	9	4	6	35	26	3	4	12	13	41	32
14	Clapton Orient	38	10	5	4	28	13	1	5	13	12	52	32
15	Blackpool	38	11	3	5	33	19	0	6	13	18	39	31
16	BARNSLEY	38	8	3	8	41	31	4	3	12	13	37	30
17	Glossop	38	9	5	5	36	26	2	3	14	18	48	30
18	Grimsby Town	38	8	5	6	27	24	3	3	13	16	47	30
19	Chesterfield	38	6	6	7	33	38	0	5	14	13	54	23
20	Lincoln City	38	7	2	10	27	28	2	1	16	19	55	21

1908/09   17th in Division 2

#	Date	Opponent	Score	Scorers	Att.	Thorpe T	Boyle TW	Downs JT	Tomlinson F	Silto WA	Oxspring A	Biggins FJ	Thomas W	Lillycrop GB	Wilkinson F	Brooks J	Burkinshaw A	Cooper JC	Coulthard ET	Forman T	Glendenning R	Griffiths, Walt	Hellewell, Alec	Jones B	Kay H	Leigh H	Little J	Ness HM	Utley G
1	Sep 2	Blackpool	1-1	Lillycrop	4000	1	2	3	4	5	6	7	8	9	10	11													
2	5	BOLTON WANDERERS	0-1		6000	1	2	3	4	5	6	7	8	9	10	11													
3	12	Tottenham Hotspur	0-4		20000	1	4	3		5	6	7			10				8	11				9			2		
4	14	Leeds City	0-2		7000	1	4	3		5	6	7			10				8	11				9			2		
5	19	HULL CITY	2-1	Lillycrop, Jones	7000	1	4	3		5	6	7		8	10					11				9			2		
6	26	Derby County	0-0		7000	1	4	3		5	6	7		8	10					11				9			2		
7	Oct 3	BLACKPOOL	4-0	Lillycrop 3, Jones (og)		1	4	3		5	6	7		8	10					11				9			2		
8	10	Chesterfield	0-1		6000	1	4	3		5	6	7		8	10					11				9			2		
9	17	GLOSSOP	1-3	Jones		1	4	3		5	6	7		8	10					11				9			2		
10	24	Stockport County	1-2	Jones		1	4	3		5		7		8	10					11				9			2		6
11	31	WEST BROMWICH ALB.	0-2		7000	1	4	3		5		7		8	10					11				9			2		6
12	Nov 7	Birmingham	1-2	Lillycrop	10000	1	4	3		5					10					11		7	8	9			2		6
13	14	GAINSBOROUGH TRIN.	2-2	Lillycrop 2		1	4	3		5		7		8	10					11				9			2		6
14	21	Grimsby Town	0-0		6000	1		3		5		7								11	4		8	9	10		2		6
15	28	FULHAM	1-2	Thorpe (pen)	6000	1		3		5	6								7	11			8	9	10		2		4
16	Dec 5	Burnley	2-3	Hellewell, Coulthard	5000	1	2				6		10	9					7	11	4		8					3	5
17	12	BRADFORD PARK AVE.	3-1	Forman, Lillycrop 2		1	2				6			9	10				7	11	4		8					3	5
18	19	Wolverhampton Wan.	0-2		6000	1		3		5	6			9	10				7	11	4		8				2		
19	25	Clapton Orient	1-1	Lillycrop	20000	1	4	3		5	6			9					7	11			10	8			2		
20	26	CLAPTON ORIENT	3-0	Forman, Hellewell, Griffiths			4	3		5	6			9				1		11		7	10	8			2		
21	Jan 1	LEEDS CITY	2-1	Jones 2	6000		4	3		5	6			8				1		11		7	10	9			2		
22	2	Bolton Wanderers	0-3		18000		4	3		5	6			8				1		11		7	10	9			2		
23	9	TOTTENHAM HOTSPUR	1-1	Hellewell	6000	1	4	3		5	6			8					7	11			10	9			2		
24	23	Hull City	0-4		7000	1	5	3			6			9			11		7		4	8	10				2		
25	30	DERBY COUNTY	1-0	Burkinshaw	3000	1	5	3			6			9			8		7	11	4		10				2		
26	Feb 13	CHESTERFIELD	4-0	Lillycrop 3, Boyle	5000	1	5	3			6			9			8			11	4		10			7	2		
27	27	STOCKPORT COUNTY	2-0	Lillycrop 2		1	5	3			6			9					7	11	4		10				2		8
28	Mar 13	BIRMINGHAM	3-1	Burkinshaw 2, Utley	4000	1	5	3			6		10				8		7	11	4						2		9
29	20	Gainsborough Trinity	1-4	Forman		1	5	3			6		10						7	11	4		8				2		9
30	24	West Bromwich Albion	1-1	Lillycrop	4000	1	5	3			6			9					7	11	4		8				2		9
31	27	GRIMSBY TOWN	3-1	Boyle 2 (1 pen), Lillycrop		1	5	3			6			9			8		7	11	4						2		
32	30	Glossop	0-3			1	5	3			6			9					7	11	4						2		8
33	Apr 3	Fulham	2-2	Boyle (pen), Burkinshaw	16000	1	5	3			6			9			8		7	11	4						2		
34	9	OLDHAM ATHLETIC	2-0	Fay (og), Boyle (pen)	9000	1	5	3			6			9			8		7	11	4						2		
35	12	Oldham Athletic	0-0		3000			3		5	6					11	8	1	7		4		10				2		9
36	13	BURNLEY	1-2	Burkinshaw			5	3			6						8	1	7	11	4		10				2		9
37	17	Bradford Park Avenue	2-3	Forman, Boyle	10000		5	3			6						8	1	7	11	4		9		10		2		
38	24	WOLVERHAMPTON W.	1-1	Kay	3000		5	2			6						8	1	7	11	4		9		10			3	
		Apps				31	32	38	2	22	33	13	3	29	15	4	9	7	26	34	19	4	25	16	4	1	33	3	15
		Goals				1	6							18			5		1	4		1	3	5	1				1

Two own goals

F.A. Cup

Round	Date	Opponent	Score	Scorers	Att.	Thorpe T	Boyle TW	Downs JT	Oxspring A	Lillycrop GB	Burkinshaw A	Coulthard ET	Glendenning R	Hellewell, Alec	Kay H	Little J
R1	Jan 16	Everton	1-3	Lillycrop		1	5	3	6	9	11	7	4	8	10	2

		P	W	D	L	F	A	W	D	L	F	A	Pts	
1	Bolton Wanderers	38	14	3	2	37	8	10	1	8	22	20	52	1
2	Tottenham Hotspur	38	12	5	2	42	13	8	6	5	25	20	51	2
3	West Bromwich Alb.	38	13	5	1	35	9	6	8	5	21	18	51	3
4	Hull City	38	14	2	3	44	15	5	4	10	19	24	44	4
5	Derby County	38	13	5	1	38	11	3	6	10	17	30	43	5
6	Oldham Athletic	38	14	4	1	39	9	3	2	14	16	34	40	6
7	Wolverhampton Wan.	38	10	6	3	32	12	4	5	10	24	36	39	7
8	Glossop	38	11	5	3	35	17	4	3	12	22	36	38	8
9	Gainsborough Trin.	38	12	3	4	30	20	3	5	11	19	50	38	9
10	Fulham	38	8	4	7	39	26	5	7	7	19	22	37	10
11	Birmingham	38	10	6	3	35	21	4	3	12	23	40	37	11
12	Leeds City	38	12	3	4	35	19	2	4	13	8	34	35	12
13	Grimsby Town	38	9	5	5	23	14	5	2	12	18	40	35	13
14	Burnley	38	8	4	7	33	28	5	3	11	18	30	33	14
15	Clapton Orient	38	7	7	5	25	19	5	2	12	12	30	33	15
16	Bradford Park Ave.	38	9	2	8	30	25	4	4	11	21	34	32	16
17	BARNSLEY	38	11	3	5	36	19	0	7	12	12	38	32	17
18	Stockport County	38	11	2	6	25	19	3	1	15	14	52	31	18
19	Chesterfield	38	10	3	6	30	28	1	5	13	7	39	30	19
20	Blackpool	38	9	6	4	30	22	0	5	14	16	46	29	20

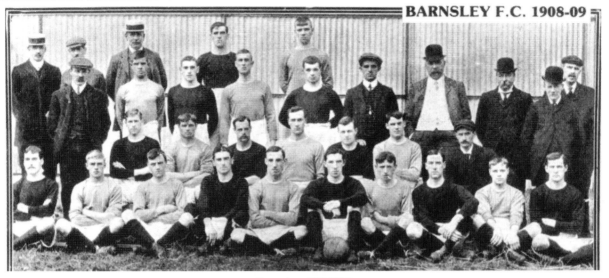

BARNSLEY F.C. 1908-09

Season 1908/09
Back row: Fairclough (Secretary) Smith (Referee) Gaunt (Director) Thorpe, Cooper
2nd back: Norman (Trainer) Little, Boyle, Ness, Downs, Glendenning, Fisher (Chairman) Hawke
(Director) Kenworthy (Director) Morton (Director)
2nd front: Tomlinson, Birkinshaw, Oxspring, Utley, Silto, Stringer, Moran (Assistant Trainer)
Front row: Biggins, Howard, Coulthard, Thomas, Lillycrop, Jones, Kaye, Wilkinson, Brooks, Forman

Season 1909/10 (English Cup Final Team)
Back row: Norman (Trainer) Rose (Cllr) Haigh (Cllr) Downs, Mearns, Ness, Gaunt, Bedford, Fairclough (Sec.)
Centre row: Glendenning, Boyle, Uttley   Front row: Bartrop, Gadsby, Lillycrop, Tufnell, Forman

1909/10   9th in Division 2

League – Division 2

No	Date		Opponent	Score	Scorers	Att
1	Sep	2	HULL CITY	1-2	Lillycrop	5000
2		4	Glossop	0-3		
3		11	BIRMINGHAM	5-1	Lillycrop 2, Tufnell, Gadsby, Forma	3000
4		18	West Bromwich Albion	3-4	Lillycrop 2, Boyle	10000
5		25	OLDHAM ATHLETIC	2-1	Gadsby, Taylor	4000
6	Oct	2	BRADFORD PARK AVE.	4-0	Tufnell 2, Forman, Lillycrop	6000
7		9	Fulham	0-3		20000
8		11	Hull City	0-1		8000
9		16	BURNLEY	0-0		4000
10		23	Leeds City	7-0	Gadsby 2, Lillycrop 2, Tufnell 2, Forman	8000
11		30	WOLVERHAMPTON W.	7-1	Gadsby 3, Boyle, Lillycrop, Forman, Bartr	5500
12	Nov	6	Gainsborough Trinity	0-0		
13		13	GRIMSBY TOWN	2-1	Lillycrop, Tufnell	5000
14		27	LEICESTER FOSSE	3-1	Gadsby, Tuffnell, Lillycrop	6000
15	Dec	11	CLAPTON ORIENT	2-1	Gadsby, Lillycrop	
16		18	Blackpool	0-0		
17		25	Derby County	1-2	Lillycrop	15000
18		27	STOCKPORT COUNTY	1-0	Lillycrop	
19		28	DERBY COUNTY	5-1	Lillycrop 2, Boyle 2, Gadsby	10000
20	Jan	1	Stockport County	0-5		5000
21		8	GLOSSOP	3-0	Lillycrop 2, Boyle	8000
22		22	Birmingham	1-2	Boyle	5000
23	Feb	12	Bradford Park Avenue	0-2		12000
24		24	FULHAM	2-1	Lillycrop, Forman	3000
25		26	Burnley	0-2		3000
26	Mar	9	Manchester City	0-0		15000
27		12	Wolverhampton Wan.	0-1		5000
28		14	Oldham Athletic	0-5		6000
29		17	LEEDS CITY	1-1	Gadsby	3000
30		19	GAINSBOROUGH TRIN.	4-1	Boyle (pen), Coulthard, Kay, Lillycr	3000
31		28	LINCOLN CITY	2-1	Taylor, Hellewell	3000
32	Apr	2	MANCHESTER CITY	1-1	Gadsby	10000
33		7	Clapton Orient	0-4		4000
34		9	Leicester Fosse	1-1	Lillycrop	
35		14	WEST BROMWICH ALB.	2-1	Forman, Bartrop	2500
36		16	Lincoln City	1-2	Lillycrop	6000
37		26	Grimsby Town	0-7		2000
38		30	BLACKPOOL	1-0	Lillycrop	3000

Appearances / shirt numbers

No	Cooper JC	Downs JT	Ness HM	Glendenning R	Boyle TW	Utley G	Coulthard ET	Gadsby E	Lillycrop GB	Tufnell H	Forman T	Arthurs G	Bartrop W	Ellis EE	Biggins FJ	Graham TH	Hellewell Alec	Jebb A	Kay H	Little J	Mearns FC	Martin F	Oxspring A	Taylor JH	Wren C
1	1	2	3	4	5	6	7	8	9	10	11														
2	1	2	3	4	5	6		8	9	10	11		7												
3	1	2	3	4	5	6		8	9	10	11		7												
4	1	2	3	4	5	6		8	9	10	11		7												
5	1	2	3	4	5	6		8	9		11		7											10	
6	1	2	3	4	5	6		8	9	10	11		7												
7	1	2	3	4	5	6		8	9	10	11		7												
8	1	2	3	4	5	6		8	9	10	11		7												
9	1	2	3	4	5	6	7		9		10	11												8	
10	1	2	3	4	5	6		8	9	10	11		7												
11	1	2	3	4	5	6		8	9	10	11		7												
12	1	2	3	4	5	6		8	9	10	11		7												
13	1	2	3	4	5	6		8	9	10	11		7												
14	1	2	3	4	5	6		8	9	10	11		7												
15	1	2	3	4	5	6		8	9	10	11		7												
16	1	2	3	4	5	6		8	9	10	11		7												
17	1	2	3	4	5	6		8	9	10	11		7												
18	1	2	3	4	5	6		8	9	10	11		7												
19	1	2	3	4	5	6		8	9	10	11		7												
20		2	3	4		5		8	9	10	11		7									1		6	
21		2	3	4	5	6		8	9	10	11		7								1				
22		2	3	4	5	6		8	9	10	11		7								1				
23	1	2	3	4		6		8	9	10	11		7			5									
24			3	4	5	6		8	9		11	10	7							2	1				
25			3	4	5	6		8	9		11	10	7							2	1				
26			3	4	5	6					11	10	7					9			2	1			
27	1	2	3	4	5	6		8	9		11	10	7									1			
28	1		3		5	6	10	8			11		7					9			2		4		
29	1	2	3	4	5	6		8	9	10	11		7												
30	1	2	3		5	6	8		9				7	11					4	10					
31	1		3		5						11						9			10	2		7	6	8
32		2	3	4	5	6		8	9	10	11		7									1			
33		2	3	4	5	6		8	9	10	11		7									1			
34			3		5	6			9	10	11		7		4						2	1		8	
35			3	4	5	6		8	9	10	11	2	7									1			
36			3	4	5			8	9	10	11	2	7					6				1			
37	1						7				11	2	4					9	5	10	3			8	6
38			3	4	5	6		8	9	10	11	2	7									1			
Apps	26	28	37	33	35	35	5	34	33	29	35	5	34	4	3	1	4	3	4	7	12	1	1	7	2
Goals					7		1	12	23	7	6		2				1		1					2	

F.A. Cup

Rnd	Date		Opponent	Score	Scorers	Att	Cooper	Downs	Ness	Glend.	Boyle	Utley	Coulthard	Gadsby	Lillycrop	Tufnell	Forman	Bartrop	Mearns
R1	Jan	15	Blackpool	1-1	Tufnell	8000		2	3	4	5	6		8	9	10	11	7	1
rep		20	BLACKPOOL	6-0	Lillycrop 2, Tufnell 2, Gadsby, Boyle (p)	13939		2	3	4	5	6		8	9	10	11	7	1
R2	Feb	5	BRISTOL R	4-0	Bartrop, Gadsby, Forman, Utley	10285	1	2	3	4	5	6		8	9	10	11	7	
R3		19	WEST BROMWICH A	1-0	Tufnell	18636	1	2	3	4	5	6		8	9	10	11	7	
R4	Mar	5	QUEENS PARK R	1-0	Bartrop	23574		2	3	4	5	6		8	9	10	11	7	1
SF		26	Everton	0-0		35000		2	3	4	5	6		8	9	10	11	7	1
rep		31	Everton	3-0	Gadsby, Forman, Tufnell	55000		2	3	4	5	6		8	9	10	11	7	1
F	Apr	23	Newcastle U	1-1	Tufnell	77747		2	3	4	5	6		8	9	10	11	7	1
rep		28	Newcastle U	0-2		65000		2	3	4	5	6		8	9	10	11	7	1

R2 Bristol Rovers drawn at home, but Barnsley paid £500 to switch tie to Oakwell
SF at Elland Road, replay at Old Trafford. Final at Crystal Palace, replay at Goodison Park.

Final table

		P	W	D	L	F	A	W	D	L	F	A	Pts
1	Manchester City	38	15	2	2	51	17	8	6	5	30	23	54
2	Oldham Athletic	38	15	2	2	47	9	8	5	6	32	30	53
3	Hull City	38	13	4	2	52	19	10	3	6	28	27	53
4	Derby County	38	15	2	2	46	15	7	7	5	26	32	53
5	Leicester Fosse	38	15	2	2	60	20	5	2	12	19	38	44
6	Glossop	38	14	1	4	42	18	4	6	9	22	39	43
7	Fulham	38	9	7	3	28	13	5	6	8	23	30	41
8	Wolverhampton Wan.	38	14	3	2	51	22	3	3	13	13	41	40
9	BARNSLEY	38	15	3	1	48	15	1	4	14	14	44	39
10	Bradford Park Ave.	38	12	1	6	47	28	5	3	11	17	31	38
11	West Bromwich Alb.	38	8	5	6	30	23	8	0	11	28	33	37
12	Blackpool	38	7	7	5	24	18	7	1	11	26	34	36
13	Stockport County	38	9	6	4	37	20	4	2	13	13	27	34
14	Burnley	38	12	2	5	43	21	2	4	13	19	40	34
15	Lincoln City	38	7	6	6	27	24	3	5	11	15	45	31
16	Clapton Orient	38	10	4	5	26	15	2	2	15	11	45	30
17	Leeds City	38	8	4	7	30	33	2	3	14	16	47	27
18	Gainsborough Trin.	38	8	3	8	22	21	2	3	14	11	54	26
19	Grimsby Town	38	8	3	8	31	19	1	3	15	19	58	24
20	Birmingham	38	7	4	8	28	26	1	3	15	14	52	23

1910/11 19th in Division 2

#		Date	Opponent	Score	Scorers	Att.	Mearns FC	Downs JT	Ness HM	Glendenning R	Utley G	Jebb A	Bartrop W	Gadsby E	Lillycrop GB	Tufnell H	Forman T	Arthurs G	Biggins FJ	Birtles TJ	Bratley PW	Boyle TW	Clegg JA	Johnson P	Little J	Martin F	Rutter A	Taylor JH	Travers JE
1	Sep	3	WOLVERHAMPTON W.	2-2	Lillycrop, Forman	5000	1	2	3	4	5	6	7	8	9	10	11												
2		10	Chelsea	1-3	Gadsby	21000	1	2	3	4	5	6	7	8	9	10	11												
3		17	CLAPTON ORIENT	1-2	Martin	5500	1	2	3	4	6		7	8		10	11				5					9			
4		24	Blackpool	0-1		7000	1	2	3	4	6			8	9	10	11			7	5								
5	Oct	1	GLOSSOP	4-0	Forman, Lillycrop 2, Birtles		1	2	3	4	6			8	9	10	11			7	5								
6		8	Lincoln City	0-1			1	2	3	4	6		7	8	9	10	11					5							
7		22	Birmingham	0-1		10000	1	2	3		6		7	10	9		11				4	5					8		
8		26	Gainsborough Trinity	1-1	Taylor		1	2	3		6		7	10	9		11				4	5					8		
9		29	WEST BROMWICH ALB.	1-1	Taylor	5000	1	2			6		7	10	9		11				4	5			3		8		
10	Nov	5	Hull City	1-5	Tufnell	7000	1	2	3		6		7		9	10	11				4	5					8		
11		12	FULHAM	4-2	Lillycrop, Taylor 2 (1 pen), Tufnel	5000	1	2	3		6		7		9	10	11		4			5					8		
12		17	HUDDERSFIELD T	1-2	Tufnell	2000	1	2	3		6				9	10	11		4	7		5					8		
13		19	Bradford Park Avenue	3-2	Rutter 2, Tufnell	12000	1	2	3		6			8		10	11			7	4	5					9		
14		26	BURNLEY	0-1		4000	1	2	3		6			8		10	11			7	4	5					9		
15	Dec	10	LEEDS CITY	4-0	Bartrop, Boyle, Lillycrop, Forman	4000		2	3		6		7		9	10	11				4	5	1				8		
16		17	Stockport County	2-2	Rutter, Lillycrop	2500		2	3		6		7		9	10	11		4			5	1				8		
17		24	DERBY COUNTY	0-2		5000		2	3		6		7		9	10	11		4			5	1				8		
18		27	Leicester Fosse	1-1	Forman (pen)	15000		2	3	4	6		7		9	10	11					5	1				8		
19		31	Wolverhampton Wan.	0-1		7000		2	3	4	6		7		9	10	11					5	1				8		
20	Jan	2	Bolton Wanderers	0-4				2	3	4	6		7		9	10	11					5	1					8	
21		7	CHELSEA	3-2	Boyle, Lillycrop, Tufnell	7000		2	3	4	6		7		9	10	11					5	1					8	
22		21	Clapton Orient	0-3		8000		2	3	4	6		7		9	10	11					5	1						8
23		28	BLACKPOOL	1-2	Tufnell	5000		2	3	4	6		7	8	9	10	11					5	1						
24	Feb	11	LINCOLN CITY	2-2	Tufnell, Rutter			2	3	4	6			8		10	11		7			5	1				9		
25		18	Huddersfield Town	0-2		8000		2	3	4	6			8		10	11		7			5	1				9		
26		25	BIRMINGHAM	2-3	Arthurs, Tufnell	2500		2	3	4	6					10	11	8	7			5	1				9		
27	Mar	4	West Bromwich Albion	3-3	Lillycrop, Rutter, Tufnell	8000		2		4	6		7			10	11	8				5	1	3			9		
28		11	HULL CITY	0-1		5000		2	3	4	6		7			10	11	8				5	1				9		
29		18	Fulham	2-0	Biggins, Bartrop	8000		2		4	6		7				11	8	10			5	1		3		9		
30		25	BRADFORD PARK AVE.	7-0	Lillycrop 3, Tufnell 2, Utley, Bartrop	4000		2		4	6		7		9	10	11	8				5	1		3				
31		28	Glossop	1-1	Arthurs			2		4	6		7		9	10	11	8				5	1		3				
32	Apr	1	Burnley	0-0		4000		2		4	6		7		9	10	11	8				5	1		3				
33		8	GAINSBOROUGH TRIN.	2-2	Tufnell, Biggins			2		4	6		7		9	10	11		8			5	1		3				
34		14	LEICESTER FOSSE	1-1	Tufnell	6000		2		4	6		7		9	10	11		8			5	1		3				
35		15	Leeds City	0-0		10000		2	3	4	6		7		9	10	11					5	1					8	
36		17	BOLTON WANDERERS	0-0				2	3	4	6		7		9	10	11					5	1					8	
37		22	STOCKPORT COUNTY	1-1	Tufnell	3000		2	3	4	6		7		9	10	11					5	1					8	
38		29	Derby County	1-5	Taylor	5000		2	3	4	6		7		9	10	11					5	1					8	
			Apps				14	38	30	27	38	2	30	10	35	33	24	14	13	3	13	30	24	1	7	1	16	9	6
			Goals								1		3	1	11	14	4	2	2	1		2				1	5	5	

F.A. Cup

#		Date	Opponent	Score	Scorers	Att.	Mearns FC	Downs JT	Ness HM	Glendenning R	Utley G	Jebb A	Bartrop W	Gadsby E	Lillycrop GB	Tufnell H	Forman T	Arthurs G	Biggins FJ	Birtles TJ	Bratley PW	Boyle TW	Clegg JA	Johnson P	Little J	Martin F	Rutter A	Taylor JH	Travers JE
R1	Jan	14	Watford	2-0	Lillycrop, Boyle	6000		2	3	4	6		7		9	10	11					5	1					8	
R2	Feb	4	Burnley	0-2				2	3	4	6		7		9	10	11		8			5	1						

		P	W	D	L	F	A	W	D	L	F	A	Pts
1	West Bromwich Alb.	38	14	2	3	40	18	8	7	4	27	23	53
2	Bolton Wanderers	38	17	2	0	53	12	4	7	8	16	28	51
3	Chelsea	38	17	2	0	48	7	3	7	9	23	28	49
4	Clapton Orient	38	14	4	1	28	7	5	3	11	16	28	45
5	Hull City	38	8	10	1	38	21	6	6	7	17	18	44
6	Derby County	38	11	5	3	48	24	6	3	10	25	28	42
7	Blackpool	38	10	5	4	29	15	6	5	8	20	23	42
8	Burnley	38	9	9	1	31	18	4	6	9	14	27	41
9	Wolverhampton Wan.	38	10	5	4	26	16	5	3	11	25	36	38
10	Fulham	38	12	3	4	35	15	3	4	12	17	33	37
11	Leeds City	38	11	4	4	35	18	4	3	12	23	38	37
12	Bradford Park Ave.	38	12	4	3	44	18	2	5	12	9	37	37
13	Huddersfield Town	38	10	4	5	35	21	3	4	12	22	37	34
14	Glossop	38	11	4	4	36	21	2	4	13	12	41	34
15	Leicester Fosse	38	12	3	4	37	19	2	2	15	15	43	33
16	Birmingham	38	10	4	5	23	18	2	4	13	19	46	32
17	Stockport County	38	10	4	5	27	26	1	4	14	20	53	30
18	Gainsborough Trin.	38	9	5	5	26	16	0	6	13	11	39	29
19	BARNSLEY	38	5	7	7	36	26	2	7	10	16	36	28
20	Lincoln City	38	5	7	7	16	23	2	3	14	12	49	24

Season 1910/11
Forman, Tufnell, Lillycrop, Gadsby, Bartrop, Utley, Boyle, Glendenning, Ness, Downs, Mearns, Cooper.

Season 1911/12 (with FA Cup) - players only named
Back row: Leavey (reserve) Cooper   Centre row: Glendenning, Downs, Taylor, Bratley, Utley
Front row: Bartrop, Tufnell, Lillycrop, Travers, Moore

1911/12 6th in Division 2

League — Division 2

No	Date	Opponent	Score	Scorers	Att	Clegg JA	Downs JT	Taylor A	Glendenning R	Boyle TW	Utley G	Bartrop W	Travers JE	Lillycrop GB	Tufnell H	Leavey HJ	Barson F	Bratley PW	Cooper JC	Cornock M	Doncaster T	Hall JE	Hanlon E	Jebb A	Martin F	Mitchell R	Moore J	Roystone A	Wilcock GH	Wigmore C
1	Sep 2	Huddersfield Town	1-2	Tufnell	12000	1	2	3	4	5	6	7	8	9	10	11														
2	Sep 9	BLACKPOOL	1-0	Boyle	7000	1	2	3	4	5	6	7	8	9	10	11														
3	Sep 11	Birmingham	3-1	Cornock 2, Tufnell	5000	1	2	3	4	5	6	7		8	10	11				9										
4	Sep 16	Glossop	2-0	Cornock, Tufnell	2000	1	2	3	4	5	6	7		8	10	11				9										
5	Sep 23	HULL CITY	1-2	Lillycrop	9000	1	2	3	4	5	6	7		8	10	11				9										
6	Sep 26	Grimsby Town	0-0		5000	1	2	3	4		6	7		8	10	11		5		9										
7	Sep 30	BURNLEY	1-1	Cornock	7000	1	2	3	4		6	7		8	10	11		5		9										
8	Oct 7	Bradford Park Avenue	0-1		20000	1	2	3	4		6			9	10	11		5						8	7					
9	Oct 14	FULHAM	2-2	Tufnell, Cornock	7000	1	2	3	4		6			8	10	11		5		9					7					
10	Oct 21	Derby County	0-0		8000		2	3	4		6			8	10	11		5		9					7	1				
11	Oct 28	STOCKPORT COUNTY	2-1	Lillycrop 2	6000		2	3	4		6			8	10	11		5		9					7	1				
12	Nov 4	Leeds City	2-3	Hanlon, Leavey	10000		2	3	4		6	7		8	10	11		5	1				9							
13	Nov 11	WOLVERHAMPTON W.	2-1	Martin, Utley	8000		2	3	4		6	7		8	10	11		5	1				9							
14	Nov 18	Leicester Fosse	0-0		6000		2	3	4		6	7		8	10	11		5	1	9										
15	Nov 25	GAINSBOROUGH TRIN.	4-0	Gunson (og), Bartrop 2, Utley	5000		2	3	4		6	7		8	10	11		5	1	9										
16	Dec 9	NOTTM. FOREST	1-0	Tufnell	5000		2	3	4		6	7		8	10	11		5	1	9										
17	Dec 16	Chelsea	1-2	Lillycrop	25000		2	3	4		6	7		8	10	11		5	1	9										
18	Dec 23	CLAPTON ORIENT	2-1	Lillycrop, Utley	6000		2	3	4		6	7	8	9	10	11		5	1											
19	Dec 25	BRISTOL CITY	4-1	Lillycrop, Utley, Travers, Tufnell	12000		2	3	4		6	7	8	9	10	11		5	1											
20	Dec 26	Bristol City	1-0	Tufnell	6000		2	3	4		6	7	8	9	10	11		5	1											
21	Jan 1	HUDDERSFIELD T	0-0		12000		2	3	4		6	7	8	9	10	11		5	1											
22	Jan 6	Blackpool	0-0		2000		2	3	4		6	7	8	9	10	11		5	1											
23	Jan 27	Hull City	0-0		10000		2	3	4		6	7	8	9	10	11		5	1											
24	Feb 10	BRADFORD PARK AVE.	1-0	Travers	5000			3	4		6	7	8	9	10	11		5	1		2									
25	Feb 12	Burnley	0-3				2	3	4		6		8	9	10	11		5	1						7					
26	Feb 17	Fulham	2-2	Leavey, Tufnell	20000		2	3	4		6		8	9	10	11		5	1											
27	Mar 2	Stockport County	1-1	Tufnell	7000		2	3	4		6	7	8		10	11		5	1				9							
28	Mar 16	Wolverhampton Wan.	0-5		6000		2	3	4		6	7	8	9		11		5	1				10							
29	Mar 23	LEICESTER FOSSE	0-0		4000		2					7	8	9			4		1		3		5	6			11	10		
30	Apr 6	GRIMSBY TOWN	2-2	Bartrop, Lillycrop	5000		2	3	4		6	7	8	9	10			5	1								11			
31	Apr 8	BIRMINGHAM	1-0	Lillycrop	5000		2	3	4		6	7	8	9	10			5	1								11			
32	Apr 10	Gainsborough Trinity	2-1	Floyd (og), Moore	5000		2		4			7	8				5		1		3	10		6	9		11			
33	Apr 11	LEEDS CITY	3-4	Tufnell, Travers 2	3000		2	3				7	8		10		4		1					6	9		11			
34	Apr 13	Nottingham Forest	2-0	Lillycrop, Tufnell	7000		2	3	4		6	7		9	8			5	1								11			10
35	Apr 22	DERBY COUNTY	0-2		5000		2	3	4		6	7	8	9	10			5	1								11			
36	Apr 25	CHELSEA	0-2		7000		2		4		6	7	8	9	10			5	1		3						11			
37	Apr 27	Clapton Orient	0-2				2	3			6	7	8			4		1				5	6	10		11			
38	Apr 29	GLOSSOP	1-0	Glendenning	2000		2		4		6	7	8		10			5	1		3						11			9
Apps						9	37	34	35	5	34	33	22	33	34	28	4	20	25	12	4	1	12	4	8	2	15	1	4	2
Goals									1	1	4	3	4	9	11	2				5			1		1		1			

Two own goals

F.A. Cup

Rd	Date	Opponent	Score	Scorers	Att	Downs JT	Taylor A	Glendenning R	Utley G	Bartrop W	Travers JE	Lillycrop GB	Tufnell H	Leavey HJ	Bratley PW	Cooper JC	Moore J
R1	Jan 13	Birmingham	0-0		18000	2	3	4	6	7	10	9	8	11	5	1	
rep	Jan 22	BIRMINGHAM	3-0	Lillycrop 2, Tufnell	12000	2	3	4	6	7	10	9	8	11	5	1	
R2	Feb 3	LEICESTER FOSSE	1-0	Lillycrop	15114	2	3	4	6	7	10	9	8	11	5	1	
R3	Feb 24	Bolton Wanderers	2-1	Lillycrop, Leavey	34598	2	3	4	6	7	10	9	8	11	5	1	
R4	Mar 9	BRADFORD CITY	0-0		24987	2	3	4	6	7	10	9	8	11	5	1	
rep	Mar 13	Bradford City	0-0		31910	2	3	4	6	7	10	9	8	11	5	1	
rep2	Mar 18	Bradford City	0-0		37000	2	3	4	6	7	10	9	8	11	5	1	
rep3	Mar 21	Bradford City	3-2	Lillycrop 2, Travers	38264	2	3	4	6	7	10	9	8		5	1	11
SF	Mar 30	Swindon Town	0-0		48057	2	3	4	6	7	10	9	8		5	1	11
rep	Apr 3	Swindon Town	1-0	Bratley	18000	2	3	4	6	7	10	9	8		5	1	11
F	Apr 20	West Bromwich Albion	0-0		54556	2	3	4	6	7	10	9	8		5	1	11
rep	Apr 24	West Bromwich Albion	1-0	Tufnell	38555	2	3	4	6	7	10	9	8		5	1	11

All R4 replays a.e.t. Final replay also a.e.t.
R4 replay 2 at Elland Road. R4 replay 3 at Bramall Lane. SF at Stamford Bridge, replay at Meadow Lane, Nottingham.
Final at Crystal Palace. Final replay at Bramall Lane.

Division 2 Final Table

		P	W	D	L	F	A	W	D	L	F	A	Pts
1	Derby County	38	15	2	2	55	13	8	6	5	19	15	54
2	Chelsea	38	15	2	2	36	13	9	4	6	28	21	54
3	Burnley	38	14	5	0	50	14	8	3	8	27	27	52
4	Clapton Orient	38	16	0	3	44	14	5	3	11	17	30	45
5	Wolverhampton Wan.	38	12	3	4	41	10	4	7	8	16	23	42
6	BARNSLEY	38	10	5	4	28	19	5	7	7	17	23	42
7	Hull City	38	12	3	4	36	13	5	5	9	18	38	42
8	Fulham	38	10	3	6	42	24	6	4	9	24	34	39
9	Grimsby Town	38	9	6	4	24	18	6	3	10	24	37	39
10	Leicester Fosse	38	11	4	4	34	18	4	3	12	15	48	37
11	Bradford Park Ave.	38	10	5	4	30	16	3	4	12	14	29	35
12	Birmingham	38	11	3	5	44	29	3	3	13	11	30	34
13	Bristol City	38	11	4	4	27	17	3	2	14	14	43	34
14	Blackpool	38	12	4	3	24	12	1	4	14	8	40	34
15	Nottingham Forest	38	9	3	7	26	18	4	4	11	20	30	33
16	Stockport County	38	8	5	6	31	22	3	6	10	16	32	33
17	Huddersfield Town	38	8	5	6	30	22	5	1	13	20	42	32
18	Glossop	38	6	8	5	33	23	2	4	13	9	33	28
19	Leeds City	38	7	6	6	21	22	3	2	14	29	56	28
20	Gainsborough Trin.	38	4	6	9	17	22	1	7	11	13	42	23

1912/13 4th in Division 2

No	Date	Opponent	Score	Scorers	Att	Cooper JC	Downs JT	Taylor A	Glendenning R	Bratley PW	Utley G	Bartrop W	Travers JE	Lillycrop GB	Tufnell H	Moore J	Barson F	Bethune J	Cornan F	Griffin M	Hall JE	Hunter W	Mitchell R	Musgrove R	McCann H
1	Sep 7	HUDDERSFIELD T	2-0	Bratley, Moore	10000	1	2	3	4	5	6	7	8	9	10	11									
2	14	Leeds City	0-2		15000	1	2	3	4	5	6	7	8	9	10	11									
3	21	GRIMSBY TOWN	3-0	Lillycrop, Travers, Bartrop	7000	1	2	3	4	5	6	7	8	9	10	11									
4	28	Bury	0-2		6000	1	2	3	4	5	6	7	8	9	10	11									
5	Oct 3	Nottingham Forest	0-2		10000	1	2		4	5	6	7	8	9	10	11					3				
6	5	FULHAM	2-1	Lillycrop 2	7000	1	2		4	5	6	7	8	9	10	11					3				
7	12	Blackpool	1-0	Bratley	8000	1	2			4	5	6		10	9	11				7	3		8		
8	19	Bradford Park Avenue	0-0		12000	1	2	3	4	5	6	7	8	9	10	11									
9	26	WOLVERHAMPTON W.	3-2	Lillycrop (pen), Tufnell, Travers	6000	1	2	3	4	5	6	7	8	9	10	11									
10	Nov 2	Leicester Fosse	0-1			1	2	3	4	5	6	7	8	9	10	11									
11	9	STOCKPORT COUNTY	1-1	Hunter		1	2	3	4	5	6	7	10	8		11						9			
12	16	Preston North End	0-4		6000	1	2	3	4	5	6	7		8		11				10		9			
13	23	BURNLEY	1-4	Lillycrop	7000	1	2			4	5	6		9	10	7		3		11			8		
14	Dec 7	GLOSSOP	2-1	Tufnell 2 (1 pen)		1	2	3	4	5	6	7	8	9	10	11									
15	14	Clapton Orient	2-2	Tufnell, Lillycrop		1	2	3	4	5	6		8	9	10	7				11					
16	19	Hull City	1-0	Travers	4000	1	2	3	4		6		8	9	10	7	5			11					
17	21	LINCOLN CITY	4-0	Lillycrop 2, Travers, Griffin		1	2	3	4	5	6	7	8	9	10					11					
18	25	Birmingham	1-3	Bratley	30000	1	2	3	4	5	6	7	8	9	10	11									
19	28	Huddersfield Town	0-2		11000	1	2	3	4	5	6	7	8	9	10					11					
20	Jan 1	NOTTM. FOREST	1-0	Lillycrop	9000	1	2	3	4	5	6	7	8	9	10					11					
21	4	LEEDS CITY	2-0	Tufnell, Bratley	5000	1	2	3	4	5	6	7		9	8					11					10
22	18	Grimsby Town	1-1	Moore		1	2	3	4	5	6		8	9	10	7				11					
23	25	BURY	4-3	Lillycrop, Moore 2 (1 pen), Bratley		1	2	3	4	5	6		8	9	10	7				11					
24	Feb 8	Fulham	1-1	Lillycrop	15000	1	2	3	4	5	6	7	8	9	10	11									
25	15	BLACKPOOL	5-3	Lillycrop 3, Travers 2		1	2	3	4	5		7	8	9	10	11								6	
26	Mar 1	Wolverhampton Wan.	0-3		7000	1		3	4	5		7	8	9	10	11						2		6	
27	8	LEICESTER FOSSE	1-0	Utley	4000	1	2	3	4	5	6	7	8	9	10	11									
28	15	Stockport County	3-0	Lillycrop 2 (1 pen), Travers	5000	1	2			5	6	7	8	9	10	11	4	3							
29	21	BRISTOL CITY	7-1	Lillycrop 2, Tufnell 2, Moore, Travers, Bartr	8000	1	2			5	6	7	8	9	10	11	4	3							
30	22	PRESTON NORTH END	1-1	Lillycrop		1	2			5	6	7	8	9	10	11	4	3							
31	24	Bristol City	0-3		15000	1	2			5	6	7	8	9	10	11	4	3							
32	25	BIRMINGHAM	1-0	Travers	10000	1	2			5	6	7	8	9	10	11		3	4						
33	Apr 3	BRADFORD PARK AVE.	4-0	Tufnell, Lillycrop 2, Travers	4000	1	2			5	6	7	8	9	10	11		3	4						
34	5	Hull City	2-1	Lillycrop, Tufnell	6000	1	2			5	6	7	8	9	10	11		3	4						
35	12	Glossop	0-1		3000	1	2			5	6	7	8	9	10	11		3	4						
36	19	CLAPTON ORIENT	0-0		4000	1	2			5	6	7	8	9	10	11		3	4						
37	23	Burnley	1-0	Bartrop	20000	1	2			5	6	7	8	9	10	11		3	4						
38	26	Lincoln City	0-2			1	2			5	6	7	8	9	10	11		3	4						
		Apps				38	37	23	27	37	36	32	35	38	35	34	5	12	7	11	4	2	2	2	1
		Goals								5	1	3	10	22	9	5				1		1			

F.A. Cup

Rd	Date	Opponent	Score	Scorers	Att	Cooper JC	Downs JT	Taylor A	Glendenning R	Bratley PW	Utley G	Bartrop W	Travers JE	Lillycrop GB	Tufnell H	Moore J	Griffin M
R1	Jan 11	Gillingham	0-0		11321	1	2	3	4	5	6	7	8	9	10		11
rep	16	GILLINGHAM	3-1	Tufnell, Lillycrop 2	9561	1	2	3	4	5	6		8	9	10	7	11
R2	Feb 1	BLACKBURN ROVERS	2-3	Tufnell, Moore	30800	1	2	3	4	5	6		8	9	10	7	11

		P	W	D	L	F	A	W	D	L	F	A	Pts
1	Preston North End	38	13	5	1	34	12	6	10	3	22	21	53
2	Burnley	38	13	4	2	58	23	8	4	7	30	30	50
3	Birmingham	38	11	6	2	39	18	7	4	8	20	26	46
4	BARNSLEY	38	15	3	1	46	18	4	4	11	11	29	45
5	Huddersfield Town	38	13	5	1	49	12	4	4	11	17	28	43
6	Leeds City	38	12	3	4	45	22	3	7	9	25	42	40
7	Grimsby Town	38	10	8	1	32	11	5	2	12	19	39	40
8	Lincoln City	38	10	6	3	31	16	5	4	10	19	36	40
9	Fulham	38	13	5	1	47	16	4	0	15	18	39	39
10	Wolverhampton Wan.	38	10	6	3	34	16	4	4	11	22	38	38
11	Bury	38	10	6	3	29	14	5	2	12	24	43	38
12	Hull City	38	12	2	5	42	18	3	4	12	18	37	36
13	Bradford Park Ave.	38	12	4	3	47	18	2	4	13	13	42	36
14	Clapton Orient	38	8	6	5	25	20	2	8	9	9	27	34
15	Leicester Fosse	38	12	2	5	34	20	1	5	13	15	45	33
16	Bristol City	38	7	9	3	32	25	2	6	11	14	47	33
17	Nottingham Forest	38	9	3	7	35	25	3	5	11	23	34	32
18	Glossop	38	11	2	6	34	26	1	6	12	15	42	32
19	Stockport County	38	8	4	7	32	23	0	6	13	24	55	26
20	Blackpool	38	8	4	7	22	22	1	4	14	17	47	26

1913/14 — 5th in Division 2

#	Mth	Dt	Opponent	Res	Scorers	Att	Cooper JC	Downs JT	Bethune J	Barson F	Bratley PW	Utley G	Bartrop W	Travers JE	Morton J	Tufnell H	Moore J	Donkin GWC	Griffin M	Halliwell JA	Ledingham WD	Marshall J	Tindall JT	Wigmore C
1	Sep	6	Lincoln City	2-2	Moore 2 (1 pen)	6000	1	2	3	4	5	6	7	8	9	10	11							
2		13	BLACKPOOL	2-1	Tufnell, Bartrop	8000	1	2	3	4	5	6	7	8	9	10	11							
3		20	Nottingham Forest	2-0	Morton, Travers	6000	1	2	3	4	5	6	7	8	9	10	11							
4		27	WOOLWICH ARSENAL	1-0	Travers	11000	1	2	3	4	5	6	7	8	9	10			11					
5	Oct	4	Grimsby Town	1-1	Travers	8000	1	2	3	4	5	6	7	8	9	10	11							
6		11	BIRMINGHAM	1-1	Utley	9000	1	2	3	4	5	6	7	8	9	10	11							
7		18	Bristol City	1-1	Griffin	15000	1		3	4	5	6		8	9	10	7		11				2	
8		25	LEEDS CITY	1-4	Moore	12000	1	2	3	4	5	6	7	8	9	10	11							
9	Nov	1	Clapton Orient	0-1			1		2	4	5	6		8	9	10	11		7				3	
10		8	GLOSSOP	2-0	Travers, Morton		1		2	4	5	6		8	9	10	11		7				3	
11		15	Stockport County	1-1	Tufnell	6000	1		2	4	5	6		8	9	10	11		7				3	
12		22	BRADFORD PARK AVE.	1-2	Wigmore	5000	1		2	4	5			8	9	10	11		7				3	6
13		29	Notts County	1-3	Moore	10000	1		2	4	5		7		9		10	8	11				3	6
14	Dec	6	LEICESTER FOSSE	3-0	Travers, Bratley, Moore		1		2	4	5	6		8	9	10	11		7				3	
15		13	Wolverhampton Wan.	1-0	Moore	10000	1	2	3	4	5		7	8	9		10		11					6
16		20	HULL CITY	0-2		4000	1	2	3	4	5		7	8	9		10		11					6
17		25	Bury	0-4		12000	1	2	3	4	5		7	8			10		11	9				6
18		26	BURY	2-0	Halliwell, Travers	7000	1	2	3	4	5		7	8			10		11	9				6
19		27	LINCOLN CITY	1-0	Travers		1	2	3	4	5		7	8			10		11	9				6
20	Jan	1	HUDDERSFIELD T	2-1	Moore, Halliwell	3000	1	2	3	4	5		7	8			10		11	9				6
21		3	Blackpool	1-3	Moore	10000	1	2	3	4	5		7	8			10		11	9				6
22		17	NOTTM. FOREST	5-0	Travers 2, Downs (p), Moore, Halliwell	5000	1	2	3	4	5		7	8			10		11	9				6
23		24	Woolwich Arsenal	0-1		25000	1	2	3	4	5		7			8	10		11	9				6
24	Feb	7	GRIMSBY TOWN	3-1	Moore 3		1	2	3	4	5		7			8	10		11	9				6
25		14	Birmingham	0-0		18000	1	2	3	4	5		7			8	10		11	9				6
26		21	BRISTOL CITY	3-0	Bartrop, Bratley, Halliwell	6000	1	2	3	4	5		7			8	10		11	9				6
27		28	Leeds City	0-3		20000	1	2	3	4	5		7			8	10		11	9				6
28	Mar	7	CLAPTON ORIENT	2-1	Halliwell, Bartrop		1	2	3	4	5		7			10	11			9		8		6
29		14	Glossop	1-5	Tufnell		1	2	3	4	5		7			10	11			9		8		6
30		21	STOCKPORT COUNTY	1-0	Halliwell		1	2	3	4			7			10			11	9	5	8		6
31		28	Bradford Park Avenue	1-1	Morton	18000	1	2	3	4	5		7		9				11	10		8		6
32	Apr	4	NOTTS COUNTY	0-1		13000	1	2	3	4	5		7		9				11	10		8		6
33		10	Fulham	2-1	Tufnell, Bartrop	25000	1	2	3	4	5		7			8	9		11	10				6
34		11	Leicester Fosse	2-0	Tufnell, Moore		1	2	3	4	5		7			8	9		11	10				6
35		13	FULHAM	1-0	Downs (pen)	10000	1	2	3	4	5		7			8	9		11	10				6
36		14	Huddersfield Town	1-3	Tufnell	10000	1	2	3	4	5		7			8	9		11	10				6
37		18	WOLVERHAMPTON W.	2-1	Donkin, Moore	11000	1	2	3	4	5					8	9	7	11	10				6
38		25	Hull City	1-0	Tufnell	5000	1	2	3	4	5		7			8	9		11	10				6
			Apps				38	31	38	38	37	12	31	21	18	27	34	7	25	22	1	5	7	26
			Goals					2			2	1	4	9	3	8	13	1	1	6				1

F.A. Cup

	Mth	Dt	Opponent	Res	Scorers	Att	Cooper JC	Downs JT	Bethune J	Barson F	Bratley PW	Utley G	Bartrop W	Travers JE	Morton J	Tufnell H	Moore J	Donkin GWC	Griffin M	Halliwell JA	Ledingham WD	Marshall J	Tindall JT	Wigmore C
R1	Jan	10	Liverpool	1-1	Travers	33000	1	2	3	4	5		7	8			10		11	9				6
rep		14	LIVERPOOL	0-1		23299	1	2	3	4	5		7	8		10				11	9			

Played in replay: A Roystone (at 6)

League Table

Pos	Team	P	W	D	L	F	A	W	D	L	F	A	Pts
1	Notts County	38	16	2	1	55	13	7	5	7	22	23	53
2	Bradford Park Ave.	38	15	1	3	44	20	8	2	9	27	27	49
3	Woolwich Arsenal	38	14	3	2	34	10	6	6	7	20	28	49
4	Leeds City	38	15	2	2	54	16	5	5	9	22	30	47
5	BARNSLEY	38	14	1	4	33	15	5	6	8	18	30	45
6	Clapton Orient	38	14	5	0	38	11	2	6	11	9	24	43
7	Hull City	38	9	5	5	29	13	7	4	8	24	24	41
8	Bristol City	38	12	5	2	32	10	4	4	11	20	40	41
9	Wolverhampton Wan.	38	14	1	4	33	16	4	4	11	18	36	41
10	Bury	38	12	6	1	30	14	3	4	12	9	26	40
11	Fulham	38	10	3	6	31	20	6	3	10	15	23	38
12	Stockport County	38	9	6	4	32	18	4	4	11	23	39	36
13	Huddersfield Town	38	8	4	7	28	22	5	4	10	19	31	34
14	Birmingham	38	10	4	5	31	18	2	6	11	17	42	34
15	Grimsby Town	38	10	4	5	24	15	3	4	12	18	43	34
16	Blackpool	38	6	10	3	24	19	3	4	12	9	25	32
17	Glossop	38	8	3	8	32	24	3	3	13	19	43	28
18	Leicester Fosse	38	7	2	10	29	28	4	2	13	16	33	26
19	Lincoln City	38	8	5	6	23	23	2	1	16	13	43	26
20	Nottingham Forest	38	7	7	5	27	23	0	2	17	10	53	23

1914/15   3rd in Division 2

#		Date	Opponent	Score	Scorers	Att	Cooper JC	Downs JT	Bethune J	Smith F	Barson F	Wigmore C	Griffin M	Halliwell JA	Lyon S	Tufnell H	Kirsop W	Donkin GWC	Fletcher B	Gittins JH	Lees JWD	Marshall J	Moore J	Musgrove R	Rooney T	Tindall JT
1	Sep	2	Derby County	0-7		2000	1	2	3	4	5	6	7	8	9	10	11									
2		5	LINCOLN CITY	3-1	Lyon 2, Tufnell		1	2	3	4	5	6	7	8	9	10	11									
3		12	Birmingham	0-2		10000	1	2	3	4	5	6	7	8	9	10	11									
4		19	GRIMSBY TOWN	0-0			1	2	3		4	6		10	9	5		7	8				11			
5		26	Huddersfield Town	0-1		7000	1	2	3		4	6	11		9	10		7	8						5	
6	Oct	3	BRISTOL CITY	2-1	Lyon, Tufnell	5000	1	2	3		4	6	11		9	10		7	8						5	
7		10	Bury	2-1	Fletcher, Downs (pen)	8000	1	2	3		4	6	11		9	10		7	8						5	
8		17	PRESTON NORTH END	2-1	Wigmore, Griffin	7000	1	2	3		4	6	11	9		10		7	8						5	
9		24	Nottingham Forest	1-2	Halliwell	6000	1	2	3		4	6	11	9		10		7	8						5	
10		31	LEICESTER FOSSE	1-0	Halliwell	5000	1	2	3		4	6	11	9		10		7	8						5	
11	Nov	7	Blackpool	1-1	Halliwell	4000	1	2	3		4	6	11	9		10		7	8						5	
12		14	Glossop	1-0	Fletcher	2000	1	2	3		4	6	11	9		10		7	8						5	
13		21	WOLVERHAMPTON W.	2-1	Donkin, Fletcher	5000	1	2	3		4	6	11	9		10		7	8						5	
14		28	Fulham	0-2		1000	1	2	3		4	6	11	9		10		7	8						5	
15	Dec	5	STOCKPORT COUNTY	2-0	Lees, Donkin	3000	1	2	3		4	6	11	9				7	8		10			5		
16		12	Hull City	1-2	Tufnell	3000	1	2	3		4	6	11	9		10		7	8						5	
17		19	LEEDS CITY	2-1	Musgrove, Lees	3000	1	2	3				11			10		7	8		6		9	4	5	
18		25	Clapton Orient	2-4	Halliwell, Moore	4000	1	2	3		4	6		9		10		7	8				11		5	
19		26	CLAPTON ORIENT	1-0	Downs (pen)	6000	1	2	3		4	6				10		7	8		9		11		5	
20	Jan	1	ARSENAL	1-0	Tufnell	5000	1	2	3		4	6		9		10		7	8				11		5	
21		2	Lincoln City	0-3			1	2	3		4	6				10		7	8		9		11		5	
22		23	Grimsby Town	3-2	Griffin 2, Downs (pen)	4000	1	2	3			6	11	9		10		7	8					4	5	
23		30	HUDDERSFIELD T	1-0	Donkin	6700	1	2	3	5		6	11			10		7	8				9	4		
24	Feb	6	Bristol City	1-3	Moore	4000	1		3				11			6		7		2	10	8	9	4	5	
25		13	BURY	2-0	Fletcher, Moore		1	2	3		4	6	11			10		7	8				9		5	
26		20	Preston North End	2-5	Marshall, Downs (pen)		1	2	3		4	6	11			10			8			9	7		5	
27		27	NOTTM. FOREST	3-0	Tufnell, Musgrove, Donkin	4000	1	2	3		4		11			10		7	8				9	6	5	
28	Mar	6	Leicester Fosse	1-0	Moore		1	2	3		4		11			10		7	8				9	6	5	
29		8	BIRMINGHAM	2-1	Tufnell 2	3000	1	2			4					10					7	8	9	6	5	3
30		13	BLACKPOOL	1-2	Tufnell	7000	1	2	3		4	5	11			10			8		7		9	6		
31		20	GLOSSOP	2-0	Wigmore 2		1	2	3		4	6	11			10		7	8				9		5	
32		27	Wolverhampton Wan.	1-4	Downs (pen)	6000	1	2	3		4	6	11			10		7	8				9		5	
33	Apr	2	DERBY COUNTY	1-0	Downs (pen)	10000	1	2	3	5		6	11			10		7	8				9	4		
34		3	FULHAM	2-2	Griffin 2	4600	1	2	3	5		6	11			10		7	8				9	4		
35		5	Arsenal	0-1		16000	1	2	3	5		6	11			10		7	8				9	4		
36		10	Stockport County	2-1	Wigmore, Fletcher		1	2	3	5		6	11			8		7	9		10	4				
37		17	HULL CITY	1-0	Fletcher	5000	1	2	3	5		6	11			8		7	9		10	4				
38		24	Leeds City	2-0	Green (og), Tufnell	5000	1	2	3		4	5	11			8		7	9		10				6	
			Apps				38	37	37	4	34	33	33	15	8	37	3	32	33	1	10	9	18	10	25	1
			Goals					6			4	5	4	3		9		4	6		2	1	4	2		

One own goal

F.A. Cup

		Date	Opponent	Score		Cooper JC	Downs JT	Bethune J	Smith F	Barson F	Wigmore C	Griffin M	Halliwell JA	Lyon S	Tufnell H	Kirsop W	Donkin GWC	Fletcher B	Gittins JH	Lees JWD	Marshall J	Moore J	Musgrove R	Rooney T	Tindall JT
R1	Jan	9	Everton	0-3		1	2	3		4	6	11			10		7	8		9				5	

		P	W	D	L	F	A	W	D	L	F	A	Pts
1	Derby County	38	14	3	2	40	11	9	4	6	31	22	53
2	Preston North End	38	14	4	1	41	16	6	6	7	20	26	50
3	BARNSLEY	38	16	2	1	31	10	6	1	12	20	41	47
4	Wolverhampton Wan.	38	12	4	3	47	13	7	3	9	30	39	45
5	Arsenal	38	15	1	3	52	13	4	4	11	17	28	43
6	Birmingham	38	13	3	3	44	13	4	6	9	18	26	43
7	Hull City	38	12	5	5	36	23	7	3	9	29	31	43
8	Huddersfield Town	38	12	4	3	36	13	5	4	10	25	29	42
9	Clapton Orient	38	12	5	2	36	17	4	4	11	14	31	41
10	Blackpool	38	11	3	5	40	22	6	2	11	18	35	39
11	Bury	38	11	5	3	39	19	4	3	12	22	37	38
12	Fulham	38	12	0	7	35	20	3	7	9	18	27	37
13	Bristol City	38	11	2	6	38	19	4	5	10	24	37	37
14	Stockport County	38	12	4	3	33	19	3	3	13	21	41	37
15	Leeds City	38	9	3	7	40	25	5	1	13	25	39	32
16	Lincoln City	38	9	4	6	29	23	2	5	12	17	42	31
17	Grimsby Town	38	10	4	5	36	24	1	5	13	12	52	31
18	Nottingham Forest	38	9	7	3	32	24	1	2	16	11	53	29
19	Leicester Fosse	38	6	4	9	31	41	4	0	15	16	47	24
20	Glossop	38	5	5	9	21	33	1	1	17	10	54	18

Season 1913/14
Back row: Hastie (Manager) Bethune, Cooper, Tindall, Norman (Trainer)
Centre row: Barson, Bratley, Utley. Front row: Donkin, Travers, Morton, Tufnell, Moore. Inset:Downs, Bartrop

Season 1920/21
Back row: Sant (Manager), Spoors, Cooper, Tindall, Woods (Trainer).
Centre row: Fell, Williams, Ashmore, Gittins, Halliwell.
Front row: Donkin, Fletcher, Newton, Wainscoat, Tummon.

1915/16 War League Midland Section

#	Date	Opponent	Result	Scorers	Att	1	2	3	4	5	6	7	8	9	10	11
1	Sep 4	Huddersfield Town	1-2	Lees	4000	Cooper JC	Downs	Tindall TJ	Cooper W	Bratley	Wigmore	Donkin	Tufnell	Moore	Lees	Palmer
2	11	GRIMSBY TOWN	3-2	Moore, Lees 2	3000	Cooper JC	Downs	Tindall TJ	Hall	Bratley	Tufnell	Donkin	Moore	Race	Lees	Palmer
3	18	Notts County	0-1		4000	Cooper JC	Downs	Tindall TJ	Cooper W	Bratley	Tufnell	Donkin	Moore	Race	Lees	Newton
4	25	DERBY COUNTY	1-1	Tufnell		Cooper JC	Layton	Tindall TJ	Hall	Bratley	Wigmore	Birtles	Tufnell	Race	Lees	Newton
5	Oct 2	Sheffield Wed	4-1	Lees, Palmer, Moore 2	6000	Cooper JC	Downs	Tindall TJ	Barson	Bratley	Wigmore	Birtles	Tufnell	Moore	Lees	Palmer
6	9	BRADFORD PA	5-2	Moore 3, Tufnell 2	1000	Cooper JC	Downs	Tindall TJ	Barson	Bratley	Layton	Birtles	Tufnell	Moore	Lees	Palmer
7	16	Leeds City	1-7	Lees	5000	Cooper JC	Downs	Tindall TJ	Carpenter	Bratley	Layton	Birtles	Tufnell	Moore	Lees	Palmer
8	23	HULL CITY	4-1	Downs, Tufnell 2, Moore		Cooper JC	Downs	Tindall TJ	Barson	Bratley	Layton	Birtles	Tufnell	Moore	Lees	Palmer
9	30	Nottm Forest	0-5			Cooper JC	Bratley	Tindall TJ	Cooper W	Caffrey	Tufnell	Armstrong	Batty	Race	Burkinshaw R	Moore
10	Nov 6	LINCOLN CITY	4-2	Bratley, Moore, Tufnell, og	6000	Thorpe	Layton	Tindall TJ	Williams	Bratley	Musgrove	Burkinshaw R	Batty	Moore	Tufnell	Palmer
11	13	LEICESTER FOSSE	3-2	Moore, Birtles, Bratley	2000	Thorpe	Layton	Tindall TJ	Tufnell	Bratley	Musgrove	Birtles	Batty	Moore	Burkinshaw R	Burkinshaw R
12	20	Sheffield United	0-1			Cooper JC	Downs	Tindall TJ	Williams	Bratley	Layton	Donkin	Batty	Box	Tufnell	Burkinshaw R
13	27	BRADFORD CITY	3-2	Race, Williams, Moore		Cooper JC	Bratley	Tindall TJ	Williams	Burkinshaw R	Tufnell	Donkin	Birtles	Race	Moore	Keenlyside
14	Dec 4	HUDDERSFIELD T	2-1	Palmer, Batty	200	Cooper JC	Downs	Tindall TJ	Burkinshaw R	Bratley	Layton	Donkin	Birtles	Batty	Moore	Keenlyside
15	11	Grimsby Town	1-4	Donkin		Cooper JC	Bratley	Tindall TJ	Williams	Johnson	Burkinshaw R	Donkin	Birtles	Moore	Batty	Plowman
16	18	NOTTS COUNTY	1-0	Donkin	3000	Cooper JC	Downs	Tindall TJ	Williams	Bratley	Layton	Donkin	Batty	Moore	Burkinshaw R	Palmer
17	25	Derby County	1-0	Palmer	2000	Cooper JC	Layton	Tindall TJ	Williams	Bratley	Burkinshaw R	Donkin	Batty	Box	Lees	Palmer
18	Jan 8	Bradford PA	0-6			Carpenter	Layton	Tindall TJ	Williams	Bratley	Tufnell	Donkin	Batty	Moore	Burkinshaw R	Palmer
19	15	LEEDS CITY	2-1	Burkinshaw R, Donkin	2000	Round	Layton	Tindall TJ	Williams	Bratley	Burkinshaw R	Donkin	Batty	Moore	Tufnell	Palmer
20	22	Hull City	0-1			Round	Layton	Tindall TJ	Williams	Bratley	Burkinshaw R	Donkin	Batty	Moore	Tufnell	Palmer
21	29	NOTTM FOREST	1-1	Downs	6000	Round	Gittins	Tindall TJ	Williams	Bratley	Layton	Birtles	Tufnell	Batty	Burkinshaw R	Palmer
22	Feb 5	Lincoln City	1-4	Donkin		Round	Gittins	Tindall TJ	Williams	Tufnell	Burkinshaw R	Birtles	Batty	Donkin	Tindall C	Palmer
23	12	Leicester Fosse	2-2	Burkinshaw R, Bratley		Round	Gittins	Tindall TJ	Williams	Bratley	Burkinshaw R	Birtles	Birtles	Moore	Tufnell	Palmer
24	19	SHEFFIELD U	0-0			Round	Downs	Tindall TJ	Williams	Bratley	Burkinshaw R	Donkin	Birtles	Moore	Tufnell	Palmer
25	Mar 21	Bradford City	2-6	Burkinshaw R, Bratley	3000	Round	Tufnell	Tindall TJ	Burkinshaw L	Williams	Layton	Donkin	Burkinshaw R	Birtles	Dennis	Palmer
26	25	SHEFFIELD WED	4-0	Burkinshaw R 3, Burkinshaw L	4432	Round	Downs	Tindall TJ	Williams	Bratley	Layton	Donkin	Burkinshaw R	Birtles	Burkinshaw L	Palmer

Supplementary Competition (Northern Division)

#	Date	Opponent	Result	Scorers	Att	1	2	3	4	5	6	7	8	9	10	11
1	Mar 4	Bradford PA	1-4	Batty		Round	Downs	Tindall TJ	Williams	Tufnell	Layton	Donkin	Birtles	Batty	Moore	Palmer
2	11	HUDDERSFIELD T	1-5	Batty		Round	Downs	Tindall TJ	Williams	Bratley	Layton	Donkin	Birtles	Batty	Burkinshaw R	Palmer
3	18	Bradford City	0-4			Round	Gittins	Tindall TJ	Burkinshaw R	Hargreaves	Layton	Keenlyside	Birtles	Batty	Tufnell	Palmer
4	25	ROCHDALE	0-1			Round	Gittins	Tindall TJ	Williams	Hargreaves	Layton	Allott	Birtles	Moore	Batty	Keenlyside
5	Apr 1	LEEDS CITY	4-6	Birtles, Palmer, Keenlyside, Tufnell		Round	Downs	Tindall TJ	Williams	Tufnell	Layton	Donkin	Birtles	Burkinshaw R	Palmer	Keenlyside
6	8	BRADFORD PA	3-0	Moore, Tufnell, Palmer		Round	Downs	Tindall TJ	Williams	Tufnell	Burkinshaw L	Donkin	Birtles	Moore	Palmer	Keenlyside
7	15	Huddersfield Town	1-4	Birtles		Round	Downs	Tindall TJ	Gittins	Tufnell	Williams	Donkin	Birtles	Box	Batty	Keenlyside
8	22	BRADFORD CITY	2-0	Birtles, Moore		Round	Downs	Tindall TJ	Williams	Tufnell	Layton	Burkinshaw L	Batty	Birtles	Moore	Griffin
9	24	Leeds City	0-1		6000	Round	Downs	Tindall TJ	Gittins	Tufnell	Williams	Burkinshaw L	Batty	Campey	Birtles	Palmer
10	29	Rochdale	1-2	Birtles		Round	Moore	Tindall TJ	Williams	Bratley	Burkinshaw L	Donkin	Burkinshaw R	Birtles	Palmer	Griffin

	P	W	D	L	F	A	Pts
Nottingham Forest	26	15	5	6	48	25	35
Sheffield United	26	12	7	7	51	36	31
Huddersfield Town	26	12	5	9	43	36	29
Bradford City	26	12	4	10	52	55	28
Barnsley	26	11	6	9	46	34	28
Leicester Fosse	26	11	5	10	42	43	27
Sheffield Wednesday	26	10	6	10	39	36	26
Notts County	26	12	2	12	54	54	26
Lincoln City	26	10	5	11	39	43	25
Leeds City	26	10	3	13	42	58	23
Hull City	26	9	4	13	46	46	22
Bradford PA	26	7	6	13	31	46	20
Grimsby Town	26	7	2	17	39	74	16

Supplementary Competition

	P	W	D	L	F	A	Pts
Leeds City	10	7	1	2	21	13	15
Bradford PA	10	6	3	1	27	17	15
Huddersfield Town	10	4	3	3	19	15	11
Bradford City	10	4	1	5	18	20	9
Rochdale	10	4	1	5	15	21	9
Barnsley	10	2	0	8	13	27	4

1916/17 War League Midland Section

#	Date	Match	Score & Scorers	1	2	3	4	5	6	7	8	9	10	11
1	Sep 2	GRIMSBY TOWN	2-2 Birtles, Moore	Round	Downs	Layton	Williams	Barson	Burkinshaw L	Donkin	Burkinshaw R	Birtles	Kay	Moore
2	9	Notts County	1-1 Kay	Round	Bratley	Layton	Tufnell	Barson	Burkinshaw L	Donkin	Burkinshaw R	Birtles	Kay	Palmer
3	16	ROTHERHAM COUNTY	1-1 Birtles	Round	Downs	Tindall	Glendenning	Barson	Burkinshaw L	Donkin	Burkinshaw R	Birtles	Kay	Palmer
4	23	Huddersfield Town	0-0	Round	Downs	Layton	Williams	Barson	Burkinshaw L	Donkin	Burkinshaw R	Birtles	Tufnell	Keenlyside
5	30	LINCOLN CITY	6-1 Downs, Tufnell 2, Birtles 2, og	Round	Downs	Layton	Williams	Barson	Burkinshaw L	Donkin	Burkinshaw R	Birtles	Tufnell	Keenlyside
6	Oct 7	Sheffield Wednesday	0-3	Round	Downs	Layton	Williams	Barson	Burkinshaw L	Donkin	Burkinshaw R	Birtles	Tufnell	Keenlyside
7	14	BRADFORD PA	3-0 Donkin, Birtles, og	Round	Downs	Bethune	Williams	Barson	Layton	Donkin	Tufnell	Birtles	Burkinshaw L	Keenlyside
8	21	Birmingham	0-2	Round	Layton	Tindall	Williams	Barson	Burkinshaw L	Donkin	Burkinshaw R	Birtles	Tufnell	Keenlyside
9	28	HULL CITY	8-2 Tufnell 5, Donkin, Palmer, og	Round	Downs	Layton	Williams	Barson	Burkinshaw L	Donkin	Tufnell	Burkinshaw R	Palmer	Kay
10	Nov 4	Nottingham Forest	0-3	Round	Layton	Tindall	Williams	Barson	Burkinshaw L	Donkin	Burkinshaw R	Birtles	Tufnell	Keenlyside
11	11	Chesterfield	1-1 Tufnell	Round	Bratley	Tindall	Williams	Barson	Burkinshaw L	Donkin	Tufnell	Burkinshaw R	Birtles	Palmer
12	18	LEEDS CITY	4-1 Tufnell,Layton,Burkinshaw R,Birtles	Round	Layton	Tindall	Williams	Barson	Burkinshaw L	Donkin	Tufnell	Burkinshaw R	Birtles	Keenlyside
13	25	Sheffield United	3-1 Burkinshaw R, Birtles, Keenlyside	Round	Layton	Tindall	Williams	Barson	Burkinshaw L	Donkin	Tufnell	Burkinshaw R	Birtles	Keenlyside
14	Dec 2	BRADFORD CITY	3-0 Tufnell 2, Burkinshaw R	Round	Downs	Bratley	Williams	Barson	Burkinshaw L	Donkin	Palmer	Burkinshaw R	Birtles	Keenlyside
15	9	Grimsby Town	2-2 Palmer, Birtles	Round	Bratley	Burkinshaw L	Williams	Barson	Kay	Donkin	Palmer	Burkinshaw R	Birtles	Keenlyside
16	16	NOTTS COUNTY	4-0 Barson, Birtles, Keenlyside, Donkin	Round	Layton	Tindall	Williams	Barson	Burkinshaw L	Donkin	Kay	Burkinshaw R	Birtles	Keenlyside
17	23	Rotherham County	3-9 Burkinshaw R 3	Round	Layton	Bratley	Hoult	Barson	Burkinshaw L	Donkin	Kay	Burkinshaw R	Hakin	Palmer
18	25	Leicester Fosse	2-1 Birtles 2	Round	Layton	Bratley	Williams	Barson	Burkinshaw L	Donkin	Kay	Burkinshaw R	Birtles	Palmer
19	26	LEICESTER FOSSE	5-0 Keenlyside, Bratley, Burkinshaw R	Round	Layton	Bratley	Williams	Barson	Burkinshaw L	Donkin	Kay	Burkinshaw R	Birtles	Keenlyside
20	30	HUDDERSFIELD T	1-1 Keenlyside	Round	Layton	Tindall	Williams	Barson	Burkinshaw L	Donkin	Kay	Burkinshaw R	Birtles	Keenlyside
21	Jan 6	Lincoln City	1-0 Donkin	Round	Layton	Bratley	Williams	Barson	Burkinshaw L	Donkin	Kay	Raybourne	Green	Palmer
22	13	SHEFFIELD WED	2-0 Burkinshaw R, Thompson	Round	Downs	Bratley	Williams	Barson	Layton	Donkin	Thompson	Burkinshaw R	Burkinshaw L	Keenlyside
23	20	Bradford PA	1-2 Burkinshaw R	Round	Layton	Bratley	Williams	Barson	Burkinshaw L	Donkin	Kay	Burkinshaw R	Birtles	Keenlyside
24	27	BIRMINGHAM	2-1 Layton, Burkinshaw R	Round	Layton	Bratley	Williams	Barson	Burkinshaw L	Donkin	Thompson	Burkinshaw R	Kay	Keenlyside
25	Feb 4	Hull City	1-0 Donkin	Round	Layton	Bratley	Williams	Barson	Burkinshaw L	Donkin	Kay	Burkinshaw R	Birtles	Keenlyside
26	10	NOTTM FOREST	0-1	Round	Layton	Bratley	Williams	Barson	Burkinshaw L	Donkin	Tufnell	Burkinshaw R	Birtles	Keenlyside
27	17	CHESTERFIELD	6-2 Thompson 4, Kay, Birtles	Round	Layton	Bratley	Williams	Barson	Burkinshaw L	Donkin	Thompson	Birtles	Kay	Keenlyside
28	24	Leeds City	0-3	Round	Layton	Bratley	Williams	Brown	Burkinshaw L	Donkin	Birtles	Thompson	Birtles	Keenlyside
29	Mar 3	SHEFFIELD UNITED	2-0 Thompson 2	Round	Bratley	Burkinshaw L	Williams	Barson	Kay	Donkin	Burkinshaw R	Thompson	Birtles	Keenlyside
30	10	Bradford City	1-1 Kay	Round	Layton	Bratley	Williams	Barson	Kay	Donkin	Fearnley	Burkinshaw R	Palmer	Keenlyside

Supplementary Competition (Midland Section)

#	Date	Match	Score & Scorers	1	2	3	4	5	6	7	8	9	10	11
1	Mar 17	SHEFFIELD UNITED	0-1	Round	Bratley	Burkinshaw L	Williams	Barson	Brown	Donkin	Kay	Burkinshaw R	Palmer	Keenlyside
2	24	Rotherham County	5-3 Burkinshaw R 3, Kay, Marshall	Round	Layton	Tindall	Williams	Bratley	Burkinshaw L	Donkin	Kay	Burkinshaw R	Marshall	Palmer
3	31	Sheffield Wednesday	2-2 Burkinshaw R 2	Round	Layton	Fagan	Williams	Bratley	Burkinshaw L	Donkin	Kay	Burkinshaw R	Dennis	Palmer
4	Apr 7	Sheffield United	0-2	Round	Layton	Fagan	Horsfield	Barson	Burkinshaw L	Donkin	Burkinshaw R	Thompson	Palmer	Keenlyside
5	14	ROTHERHAM COUNTY	0-0	Round	Clarke	Fagan	Stevenson	Barson	Burkinshaw L	Donkin	Kay	Thompson	Birtles	Palmer
6	21	SHEFFIELD WED	1-1 Thompson	Round	Bratley	Fagan	Kay	Barson	Burkinshaw L	Donkin	Birtles	Thompson	Burkinshaw R	Keenlyside

	P	W	D	L	F	A	Pts
Leeds City	30	18	10	2	68	29	46
Barnsley	30	15	8	7	65	41	38
Birmingham	30	14	9	7	56	38	37
Huddersfield Town	30	15	6	9	51	32	36
Bradford PA	30	14	6	10	57	39	34
Nottingham Forest	30	13	7	11	47	52	33
Notts County	30	12	8	11	41	41	32
Bradford City	30	11	9	12	53	52	30
Rotherham County	30	11	7	12	43	47	29
Sheffield United	30	10	7	13	36	57	27
Hull City	30	11	4	15	59	62	26
Chesterfield	30	9	6	15	36	48	24
Sheffield Wednesday	30	8	6	16	38	71	22
Grimsby Town	30	6	7	17	29	53	19
Leicester Fosse	30	5	9	16	38	65	19
Lincoln City	30	5	6	19	38	65	16

Supplementary Competition

	P	W	D	L	F	A	Pts
Sheffield United	6	4	0	2	12	7	8
Sheffield Wednesday	6	2	2	2	12	12	6
Barnsley	6	1	3	2	8	9	5
Rotherham County	6	2	1	3	9	13	5

1917/18 War League Midland Section

No	Date	Opponent	Result	1	2	3	4	5	6	7	8	9	10	11
1	Sep 1	Lincoln City	1-2 Barson	Round	Gittins	Bratley	Williams	Barson	Whitehead	Donkin	Burkinshaw R	Chapman	Thompson	Kay
2	8	LINCOLN CITY	1-0 Chapman	Round	Gittins	Lees	Williams	Barson	Whitehead	Donkin	Burkinshaw R	Chapman	Kay	Thompson
3	15	Grimsby Town	3-1 Burkinshaw R, Kay, Barson	Round	Gittins	Lees	Williams	Barson	Whitehead	Donkin	Burkinshaw R	Chapman	Kay	Thompson
4	22	GRIMSBY TOWN	4-0 Thompson,Chapman,Barson,Donkin	Round	Gittins	Lees	Williams	Barson	Bratley	Donkin	Thompson	Chapman	Burkinshaw R	Keenlyside
5	29	Birmingham	1-3 Kay	Round	Gittins	Bratley	Williams	Barson	Whitehead	Donkin	Roe	Chapman	Thompson	Pointon
6	Oct 6	BIRMINGHAM	3-3 Chapman, Barson, og	Round	Gittins	Lees	Williams	Barson	Kay	Donkin	Birtles	Chapman	Thompson	Keenlyside
7	13	NOTTS COUNTY	0-0	Round	Saxton	Bratley	Williams	Barson	Whitehead	Donkin	Roe	Chapman	Kay	Keenlyside
8	20	Notts County	2-4 Keenlyside 2	Round	Saxton	Day	Williams	Barson	Whitehead	Donkin	Roe	Ward	Thompson	Keenlyside
9	27	HUDDERSFIELD T	2-1 Burkinshaw J, Burkinshaw R	Round	Gittins	Saxton	Williams	Barson	Bratley	Donkin	Burkinshaw JDL	Burkinshaw R	Roe	Thompson
10	Nov 3	Huddersfield Town	0-5	Round	Gittins	Saxton	Williams	Barson	Black	Donkin	Roe	Burkinshaw R	Thompson	Keenlyside
11	10	SHEFFIELD WED	3-2 Tufnell, Donkin, Roe	Round	Saxton	Tindall	Kay	Barson	Whitehead	Donkin	Burkinshaw R	Chapman	Tufnell	AN Other
12	17	Sheffield Wednesday	2-4 Thompson, Kay	Round	Gittins	Saxton	Kay	Bratley	Whitehead	Donkin	Roe	Chapman	Thompson	Keenlyside
13	24	BRADFORD CITY	1-2 Bratley	Round	Roberts	Saxton	Kay	Bratley	Whitehead	Donkin	Roe	Chapman	Burkinshaw R	Keenlyside
14	Dec 1	Bradford City	1-5 Chapman	Round	Gittins	Gittins	Roberts	Pratt	Whitehead	Donkin	Roe	Chapman	Kay	Shorte
15	8	LEEDS CITY	3-4 Chapman 2, Keenlyside	Round	Smith G	Saxton	Gittins	Wigmore	Whitehead	Donkin	Roe	Chapman	Kay	Keenlyside
16	15	Leeds City	1-2 Roe	Round	Smith G	Saxton	Gittins	AN Other	Whitehead	Donkin	Roe	Chapman	Kay	AN Other
17	22	SHEFFIELD UNITED	3-6 Chapman, Roe, Peart	Williams	Smith G	Saxton	Gittins	Sherwin	Whitehead	Brown	Roe	Peart	Chapman	Keenlyside
18	25	Rotherham County	1-4 Chapman	Round	Saxton	Tindall	Gittins	Bratley	Whitehead	Donkin	Roe	Chapman	Kay	Chard
19	26	ROTHERHAM COUNT	1-2 Kay	Holman	Tindall	Bethune	Hall	Saxton	Whitehead	Donkin	Roe	Chapman	Kay	Chard
20	29	Sheffield United	0-3	Holman	Gittins	Bratley	Hall	Saxton	Whitehead	Donkin	Buddery	Chapman	Lees	Chard
21	Jan 5	Bradford PA	0-8	Round	Gittins	Saxton	Barrowclough	Wigmore	Whitehead	Donkin	Kay	Chapman	Feamley	Tiplady
22	12	BRADFORD PA	1-0 Keenlyside	Round	Gittins	Saxton	Wigmore	Bratley	Whitehead	Donkin	Chard	Chapman	Keenlyside	Atkinson
23	Feb 2	HULL CITY	1-3 Chapman	Bradley	Gittins	Saxton	Bratley	Barson	Whitehead	Donkin	Keenlyside	Chapman	Kay	Chard
24	9	Hull City	2-4 Chapman, Barson	Round	Gittins	Saxton	Williams	Barson	Bratley	Donkin	Kay	Chapman	Chard	Whitehead
25	16	LEICESTER FOSSE	1-0 Donkin	Bradley	Gittins	Saxton	Williams	Barson	Bratley	Donkin	Kay	Chapman	Chard	Brown
26	23	Leicester Fosse	1-5 Donkin	Chapman	Williams	Saxton	Holman	Barson	Whitehead	Donkin	Kay	Longlands	Smith F	Burrows
27	Mar 2	NOTTINGHAM FORES	1-0 Chapman	Round	Gittins	Saxton	Williams	Barson	Bratley	Donkin	Kay	Chapman	Smith F	Keenlyside
28	9	Nottingham Forest	0-1	Round	Gittins	Saxton	Williams	Barson	Bratley	Donkin	Kay	Chapman	Smith F	AN Other

Supplementary Competition (Midland Section)

No	Date	Opponent	Result	1	2	3	4	5	6	7	8	9	10	11
1	Jan 1	SHEFFIELD WED	4-1 Lees 3, Chapman	Round	Gittins	Saxton	Wigmore	Bratley	Barnes	Donkin	Buddery	Chapman	Lees	Kay
2	Mar16	ROTHERHAM COUNT	3-0 Bratley, Donkin, Keenlyside	Round	Gittins	Saxton	Williams	Barson	Bratley	Donkin	Kay	Chapman	Smith F	Keenlyside
3	23	Rotherham County	1-2 Smelt	Round	Bratley	Saxton	Turner	Barson	Whiteman	Donkin	Kay	Smelt	Smith F	Wooding
4	30	Sheffield United	3-2 Chapman 2, Barson	Round	Gittins	Saxton	Turner	Barson	Bratley	Donkin	Kay	Chapman	Smith F	Moore
5	Apr 1	Sheffield Wednesday	2-6 Smith, Williams	Chapman	Bratley	Williams	Whiteman	Barson	Atkinson	Donkin	Kay	Cockerill	Smith F	Sykes
6	6	SHEFFIELD UNITED	1-1 Cockerill	Round	Gittins	Saxton	Williams	Barson	Bratley	Donkin	Kay	Chapman	Smith F	Moore

Team	P	W	D	L	F	A	Pts
Leeds City	28	23	1	4	75	23	47
Sheffield United	28	20	1	7	66	27	41
Birmingham	28	14	6	8	59	38	34
Hull City	28	15	4	9	67	50	34
Nottingham Forest	28	13	4	11	41	28	30
Bradford PA	28	13	4	11	40	29	30
Leicester Fosse	28	13	3	12	52	43	29
Huddersfield Town	28	12	5	11	49	46	29
Rotherham County	28	8	9	11	42	52	25
Notts County	28	7	9	12	43	54	23
Sheffield Wednesday	28	9	5	14	45	59	23
Grimsby Town	28	5	11	12	24	62	21
Bradford City	28	8	4	16	34	55	20
Lincoln City	28	7	5	16	25	62	19
Barnsley	28	8	2	18	40	74	18

Supplementary Competition

Team	P	W	D	L	F	A	Pts
Sheffield Wednesday	6	3	2	1	15	8	8
Barnsley	6	3	1	2	14	12	7
Sheffield United	6	2	1	3	9	12	5
Rotherham County	6	1	2	3	4	10	4

1918/19 War League Midland Section

#	Date	Opponent	Score	Scorers	1	2	3	4	5	6	7	8	9	10	11
1	Sep 7	LINCOLN CITY	2-6	Smith, Thompson	Round	Anderson	Saxton	Williams	Barson	Dickenson	Donkin	Smith	Cockerill	Thompson	Sykes
2	14	Lincoln City	2-4	Smith, Barson	Round	Lester	Saxton	Williams	Barson	Dickenson	Donkin	Smith	Cockerill	Thompson	Sykes
3	21	GRIMSBY TOWN	2-4	Moore 2	Round	Lester	Saxton	Corner	Barson	Dickenson	Moore	Smith	Cockerill	Thompson	Sykes
4	28	Grimsby Town	0-0		Round	Hollyoak	Saxton	Williams	Barson	Dickenson	Donkin	Smith	Wainwright	Newton	Thompson
5	Oct 5	BRADFORD CITY	0-0		Tingle	Hollyoak	Tindall	Williams	Barson	Dickenson	Donkin	Smith	Briscoe	Thompson	Sykes
6	12	Bradford City	1-8	Briscoe	Tingle	Livingstone	Hollyoak	Howarth	Barson	Dickenson	Donkin	Smith	Salt	Briscoe	Thompson
7	19	Sheffield Wednesday	0-2		Round	Hollyoak	Brelsford	Williams	Clarkson	Wigmore	Sykes	Smith	Moore	Briscoe	Sykes
8	26	SHEFFIELD WED	0-1		Round	Hollyoak	Williams	Wigmore	Clarkson	Crummond	Moore	Smith	Wigmore	Lydon	Sykes
9	Nov 2	Huddersfield Town	1-2	Sykes	Round	Tindall	Hollyoak	Tingle	Barson	Crummond	Briscoe	Lydon	Wigmore	Harrison	Sykes
10	9	HUDDERSFIELD T	2-4	Donkin, Roe	Round	Hollyoak	Storey	Wigmore	Barson	Williams	Donkin	Roe	Harrison	Leavey	Sykes
11	16	Notts County	4-4	Carr, Keenlyside, Barson, Donkin	Round	Hollyoak	Williams	AN Other	Barson	Wigmore	Donkin	Carr	Keenlyside	Winship	Thompson
12	23	NOTTS COUNTY	1-0	Moore	Round	Bates	Saxton	Williams	Barson	Wigmore	Donkin	Birtles	Moore	Smith	Thompson
13	30	Birmingham	0-7		Tebbett	Williams	Saxton	Wigmore	Barson	Osborne	Birtles	Smith	Wainwright	Marshall	Thompson
14	Dec 7	BIRMINGHAM	2-1	Birtles, Barson	Tebbett	Hollyoak	Saxton	Williams	Barson	Smith	Donkin	Birtles	Moore	Marshall	Thompson
15	14	Leicester Fosse	1-2	Moore	Tebbett	Hollyoak	Saxton	Smith	Barson	Dawson	Donkin	Birtles	Moore	Marshall	Newton
16	21	LEICESTER FOSSE	3-2	Moore, Barson, Newton	Round	Hollyoak	Saxton	Smith	Barson	Wigmore	Donkin	Birtles	Moore	Marshall	Newton
17	25	Rotherham County	4-2	Moore 2, Marshall 2	Round	Hollyoak	Milton	Whiteman	Barson	Wigmore	Donkin	Smith	Moore	Marshall	Newton
18	26	ROTHERHAM COUNTY	1-0	Moore	Round	Hollyoak	Gittins	Whiteman	Barson	Wigmore	Donkin	Burkinshaw L	Newton	Marshall	Newton
19	28	Nottingham Forest	0-2		Round	Milton	Gittins	Whiteman	Barson	Wigmore	Donkin	Bates	Bates	Marshall	Thompson
20	Jan 11	Leeds City	0-4		Mitchell	Gittins	Hollyoak	Smith	Barson	Wigmore	Goddard	Birtles	Moore	Birtles	Moore
21	18	LEEDS CITY	0-1		Mitchell	Kilner	Gittins	Bratley	Barson	Wigmore	Goddard	Smith	Moore	Smith	Marshall
22	25	Sheffield United	0-8		Mitchell	Hollyoak	Saxton	Gittins	Barson	Wigmore	Donkin	Birtles	Moore	Smith	Elshaw
23	Feb 1	SHEFFIELD UNITED	2-0	Lees, Donkin	Mitchell	Gittins	Milton	Smith	Barson	Whiteman	Donkin	Lees	Newton	Whitham	Dobson
24	8	HULL CITY	3-4	Newton 2, Smith	Mitchell	Gittins	Milton	Smith	Barson	Wainwright	Wainwright	Lees	Newton	Whitham	Dobson
25	15	Hull City	3-1	Lees, Newton, Goddard	Mitchell	Saxton	Milton	Smith	Gittins	Whiteman	Goddard	Lees	Newton	Whitham	Dobson
26	22	COVENTRY CITY	6-2	Goddard2,Newton,Dobson,Barson	Mitchell	Gittins	Milton	Smith	Barson	Whiteman	Goddard	Lees	Newton	Whitham	Dobson
27	Mar 1	Coventry City	1-2	Whitham	Mitchell	Gittins	Milton	Smith	Barson	Whiteman	Goddard	Lees	Newton	Whitham	Dobson
28	8	Bradford PA	1-3	Newton	Mitchell	Gittins	Milton	Ross	Barson	Smith	Lees	Broomhead	Newton	Whitham	Dobson
29	15	BRADFORD PA	0-1		Mitchell	Tindall	Milton	Ross	Barson	Smith	Moore	Broomhead	Newton	Lees	Newton
30	Apr 22	NOTTM FOREST	3-2	Moore, Barson, Newton	Downing	Downs	Tindall	Smith	Barson	Gittins	Donkin	Moore	Newton	Whitham	Dobson

Supplementary Competition (Midland Section)

#	Date	Opponent	Score	Scorers	1	2	3	4	5	6	7	8	9	10	11
1	Jan 1	SHEFFIELD UNITED	2-2	Thompson, Donkin	Round	Hollyoak	Gittins	Smith	Barson	Wigmore	Donkin	Bates	Moore	Thompson	Maw
2	Mar 22	Rotherham County	2-5	Newton 2	Mitchell	Bratley	Tindall	Simmonite	Barson	Smith	Allen	Halliwell	Newton	Whitham	Dobson
3	29	ROTHERHAM COUNTY	4-3	Newton 3, Donkin	Round	Gittins	Bethune	Smith	Barson	AN Other	Donkin	Halliwell	Newton	Whitham	Dobson
4	Apr 19	SHEFFIELD WED	1-2	Newton	Downing	Tindall	Swift	Fletcher	Barson	Ledingham	Donkin	Marshall	Newton	Whitham	Dobson
5	21	Sheffield United	1-2	Halliwell	Holt	Saxton	Gittins	Fletcher	Barson	Smith	Donkin	Marshall	Halliwell	Lees	Newton
6	26	Sheffield Wednesday	3-4	Donkin, Newton 2	Downing	Downs	Crabtree	Fell	Barson	Gittins	Donkin	Moore	Newton	Whitham	Dobson

League Table

Team	P	W	D	L	F	A	Pts
Nottingham Forest	30	18	6	6	59	31	42
Birmingham	30	20	1	9	72	36	41
Notts County	30	16	9	5	65	38	41
Leeds City	30	17	4	9	53	41	38
Bradford PA	30	15	7	8	45	45	37
Huddersfield Town	30	13	8	9	48	42	34
Hull City	30	12	7	11	56	47	31
Sheffield United	30	12	6	12	55	59	30
Coventry City	30	13	4	13	53	53	30
Leicester Fosse	30	13	3	14	49	49	29
Sheffield Wednesday	30	11	6	13	38	59	28
Lincoln City	30	10	4	16	48	56	24
Bradford City	30	9	4	17	48	79	22
Barnsley	30	9	3	18	45	69	21
Grimsby Town	30	7	6	17	40	69	20
Rotherham County	30	2	8	20	23	60	12

Supplementary Competition

Team	P	W	D	L	F	A	Pts
Sheffield United	6	5	1	0	14	3	11
Sheffield Wesnesday	6	3	1	2	11	10	7
Barnsley	6	1	1	4	13	18	3
Rotherham County	6	1	1	4	11	18	3

1919/20 — 12th in Division 2

#	Date		Opponent	Score	Scorers	Att	Cooper A	Downs JT	Tindall JT	Fletcher B	Barson F	Gittins JH	Donkin GWC	Halliwell JA	Newton A	Whitham V	Dobson GW	Addy GW	Bell H	Bethune J	Curry T	Downing J	Fell G	Frost H	Fryer W	Lakin W	Matthews CM	Saxton E	Smith F	Thompson L	Tufnell H	Vaughan H	Wainscoat WR	Williams JH
1	Aug	30	Stoke	0-2		12000	1	2	3	4	5	6	7	8	9	10	11																	
2	Sep	1	WEST HAM UNITED	7-0	Hal'well 3,Don'n,Tuf'el,New'n,Flet'	6000	1	2	3	8	5	6	7		9		11												4		10			
3		6	STOKE	1-2	Downs (pen)	7000	1	2	3	8	5	6	7		9		11												4		10			
4		8	West Ham United	2-0	Newton 2	14000	1	2	3	8	5	6	7	10	9		11												4					
5		13	Nottingham Forest	1-0	Newton	10000	1	2	3	8	5	6	7	10	9		11												4					
6		20	NOTTM. FOREST	2-2	Fletcher, Newton	7000	1	2	3	8	5	6	7	10	9		11												4					
7		27	Rotherham County	0-1		10000	1	2	3	8	5	6	7	10	9		11												4					
8	Oct	4	ROTHERHAM COUNT	4-0	Newton 2, Halliwell, Fletcher		1	2	3	8	5	6	7		9		11		10										4					
9		11	Lincoln City	4-0	Halliwell 2, Fletcher, Newton	7000	1	2	3	8	5	6	7		9		11		10										4					
10		18	LINCOLN CITY	5-3	Halliwell 3, Bell 2	8000	1	2	3	8	5	6	7		9		11		10										4					
11		25	STOCKPORT COUNTY	0-0		7000	1	2	3	8		5	7		9		11	4	10															6
12	Nov	1	Stockport County	0-1		9000	1	2	3	4		5	7		9		11		10												8			6
13		6	HULL CITY	2-3	Fletcher, Halliwell	6000	1	2	3	8		5	7		9		11		10										4					6
14		15	Hull City	1-3	Halliwell	8000	1	2	3	8		5	7		9		11		10										4					6
15		22	WOLVERHAMPTON W	4-1	Halliwell 3, Fletcher	5000	1	2	3	8		5			9		11		10		7								4					6
16		29	Wolverhampton Wan.	4-2	Halliwell 2, Fletcher, Bethun	4000	1	2	3	8		5	7		9		11			10									4					6
17	Dec	6	SOUTH SHIELDS	0-1		6000	1	2	3	8		5	7		9		11			10	1								4					6
18		13	South Shields	0-0				2	3	8		5	7		9	10	11			4														6
19		20	TOTTENHAM HOT.	3-0	Fletcher, Bell, Halliwell	12000	1	2	3	8		5	7		9				10								4							6
20		25	Port Vale	2-0	Bell, Tufnell	14000	1	2	3	8		5	7		9				10								4							6
21		26	PORT VALE	2-0	Donkin	12000	1	2	3	8		5	7		10	9	11												4					6
22		27	Tottenham Hotspur	0-4		50000		2					7	8	9		11		10			1			5	3			4					6
23	Jan	1	Bury	0-2		16000	1						7	9			11		10	2					5					3	8			6
24		3	CLAPTON ORIENT	2-1	Downs, Bell	4500	1	2				5	7	9			11		10	3							4		8					6
25		17	Clapton Orient	0-2		13000	1	2	3			5	7				11		10								4		8					6
26		24	Grimsby Town	1-1	Bell	4000	1	2	3	8		5	7	10	9		11		4										6					
27	Feb	7	Birmingham	0-0		30000	1	2	3	4		5	7	10	9		11			2					6		8							
28		9	GRIMSBY TOWN	0-1		4000			3	4		5	7	9	10		11			2		1			6		8							
29		14	BIRMINGHAM	0-5		12000	1	2	3	4		5	7	9			11					10										8		6
30		28	LEICESTER CITY	0-1		7000		2	3	8		6	7	9			11		10			1			5				4					6
31	Mar	4	Leicester City	0-0		10000	1		3	4		5			9	10	11			2					8				7					6
32		6	FULHAM	4-1	Wainscoat 3, Gittins (pen)	6000	1		3	4		5	7		9		11			2									8				10	6
33		13	Fulham	1-1	Wainscoat	15000	1		3	4		5	7		9		11			2												8	10	6
34		20	COVENTRY CITY	1-0	Halliwell	11000	1		3	4		5	7		9		11			2												8	10	6
35		27	Coventry City	0-1		16000	1		3	4		5	7		9		11			2												8	10	6
36	Apr	2	BRISTOL CITY	0-0		13000	1		3	4		5	7			11				2										8		9	10	6
37		3	HUDDERSFIELD T	3-3	Fletcher, Newton, Halliwell	21000			3	8		5	7	9	11					2		1			4								10	6
38		5	BURY	1-3	Vaughan	13000			3			5	7	9	11					2		1			4							8	10	6
39		10	Huddersfield Town	1-4	Gittins (pen)	10000			3	4		5	8	9	11		7			2		1						2					10	6
40		17	BLACKPOOL	1-1	Newton	8000	1		3	4		2	8	9	11		7						5										10	6
41		24	Blackpool	2-0	Wainscoat, Gittins (pen)	5000	1		3	4		2	7	9			11						5						8				10	6
42	May	1	Bristol City	1-3	Halliwell	10000	1		3	4		2	7	9			11						5	8								10	6

Played in match 23: ET White (at 4)

		Cooper A	Downs JT	Tindall JT	Fletcher B	Barson F	Gittins JH	Donkin GWC	Halliwell JA	Newton A	Whitham V	Dobson GW	Addy GW	Bell H	Bethune J	Curry T	Downing J	Fell G	Frost H	Fryer W	Lakin W	Matthews CM	Saxton E	Smith F	Thompson L	Tufnell H	Vaughan H	Wainscoat WR	Williams JH
Apps		35	28	39	37	10	40	40	40	30	3	25	1	15	16	1	7	3	1	8	5	2	2	22	2	5	5	11	28
Goals			2		9		3	2	20	10				6	1											2	1	5	

F.A. Cup

	Date		Opponent	Score	Scorers	Att	Cooper A	Downs JT	Tindall JT	Fletcher B	Barson F	Gittins JH	Donkin GWC	Halliwell JA	Newton A	Whitham V	Dobson GW	Bell H	Bethune J	Matthews CM	Williams JH
R1	Jan	10	West Bromwich Albio	1-0	Fletcher	32327	1	2	3	8		5	7		9		11	10		4	6
R2		31	Plymouth Argyle	1-4	Downs	27000	1	2	3	8		5	7	10	9		11		4		6

		P	W	D	L	F	A	W	D	L	F	A	Pts
1	Tottenham Hotspur	42	19	2	0	60	11	13	4	4	42	21	70
2	Huddersfield Town	42	16	4	1	58	13	12	4	5	39	25	64
3	Birmingham	42	14	3	4	54	16	10	5	6	31	18	56
4	Blackpool	42	13	4	4	40	18	8	6	7	25	29	52
5	Bury	42	14	4	3	35	15	6	4	11	25	29	48
6	Fulham	42	11	6	4	36	18	8	3	10	25	32	47
7	West Ham United	42	14	3	4	34	14	5	6	10	13	26	47
8	Bristol City	42	9	9	3	30	18	4	8	9	16	25	43
9	South Shields	42	13	5	3	47	18	2	7	12	11	30	42
10	Stoke	42	13	3	5	37	15	5	3	13	23	39	42
11	Hull City	42	13	4	4	53	23	5	2	14	25	49	42
12	BARNSLEY	42	9	5	7	41	28	6	5	10	20	27	40
13	Port Vale	42	11	3	7	35	27	5	5	11	24	35	40
14	Leicester City	42	8	6	7	26	29	7	4	10	15	32	40
15	Clapton Orient	42	14	3	4	34	17	2	3	16	17	42	38
16	Stockport County	42	11	4	6	34	24	3	5	13	18	37	37
17	Rotherham County	42	10	4	7	32	27	3	4	14	19	56	34
18	Nottingham Forest	42	9	4	8	23	22	2	5	14	20	51	31
19	Wolverhampton Wan.	42	8	4	9	41	32	2	6	13	14	48	30
20	Coventry City	42	7	7	7	20	26	2	4	15	15	47	29
21	Lincoln City	42	8	6	7	27	30	1	3	17	17	71	27
22	Grimsby Town	42	8	4	9	23	24	2	1	18	11	51	25

1920/21 — 16th in Division 2

Date	Opponent	Score	Scorers	Att	Cooper A	Spoors J	Tindall JT	Williams JH	Ashmore RA	Gittins JH	Donkin GWC	Fletcher B	Newton A	Wainscoat WR	Tummon O	Baines CE	Bates FG	Fell G	Frost H	Fryer W	Halliwell JA	Hammerton JD	Kay Harold	King S	Low WR	Morris R	Ruddlesdin A	Saxton E	Turner JH
Aug 28	SHEFFIELD WEDNESDAY	0-0		15000	1	2	3	4	5	6	7	8	9	10	11														
Aug 30	Notts County	0-1		18000	1	2	3		5	6	7	8	9	10				4											11
Sep 4	Sheffield Wednesday	0-0		25000	1	2	3	6		5	7	8	11	10				4					9						
Sep 6	NOTTS COUNTY	2-2	Newton, Wainscoat	10000	1	2	3			5	7	6	11	10				4	8					9					
Sep 11	South Shields	2-3	Wainscoat, Halliwell	21000	1	2	3			6	7	5	8	10				4			9								11
Sep 18	SOUTH SHIELDS	1-1	Gittins (pen)	12000	1		3	4	6	2	7	8	11	10				5			9								
Sep 25	Hull City	0-3		15000	1	2	3	4		6	7	8	11					5			9						10		
Oct 2	HULL CITY	0-0		8000	1		3	4		2	7	8	11					5			10		9		6				
Oct 9	Wolverhampton Wan.	1-1	Gittins	20000	1	2	3			8	9	7		11				5	4		10				6				
Oct 16	WOLVERHAMPTON W.	3-2	Wainscoat 2, Halliwell	7000	1	2	3			6	7	4	11	10				5			8		9						
Oct 23	Stockport County	2-3	Wainscoat, Donkin	10000	1		3			2	7	4	11	10				5			8		9		6				
Oct 30	STOCKPORT COUNTY	2-0	Halliwell, Morris	12000	1		3			2	7	4	11	10				5			8				6	9			
Nov 13	CLAPTON ORIENT	1-0	Gittins (pen)	10000			3			2	7	4	11	10			1	5			8				6	9			
Nov 20	Bury	0-0		10000	1		3	6	4	2	7			10				5			8					9			11
Nov 25	Clapton Orient	2-3	Wainscoat, Gittins (pen)	10000	1		3			2	7	4		10				5			8				6	9			11
Nov 27	BURY	5-0	Halliwell 2, Morris 2, Fell	6000	1		3			2	7	4	10					5			8				6	9			11
Dec 4	Bristol City	0-1		18000	1		3			2	7	4	9	10				5			8				6				11
Dec 11	BRISTOL CITY	1-1	Donkin	10000	1		3			2	7	4	9	10				5			8				6				11
Dec 18	Nottingham Forest	0-0		8000	1		3				2	8	4	11				5			10				6	9			7
Dec 25	Blackpool	0-1		13000	1		3			2	7	4	11	10				5			8				6	9			
Dec 27	BLACKPOOL	0-1		10000	1		3				2	8	4	11				5			10				6	9			7
Jan 1	NOTTM. FOREST	0-0		13000			3			2	7	4	11	10		1		5			8				6	9			
Jan 15	LEICESTER CITY	2-1	Wainscoat 2	8000			3	4		2	7	8	11	10			1		5						6	9			
Jan 22	Leicester City	0-2		14000			3	4		2	7	8	11	10			1		5						6	9			
Jan 29	ROTHERHAM COUNTY	2-1	Fell 2	14000						2	7	4		10			1	5			8				6	9		3	11
Feb 5	Rotherham County	0-1		16000	1		3			2	7	4	11	10				5			8	9			6				
Feb 12	CARDIFF CITY	0-2		17000	1		3			2	7	8	11	10			4	5					9		6				
Feb 26	FULHAM	3-1	Halliwell, Donkin, Wainscoat	12000	1	2	3	4			7	8	11	10				5			9				6				
Mar 5	Fulham	0-1		20000	1	2	3	4			7	8	11	10				5			9				6				
Mar 9	Cardiff City	2-3	Newton, Wainscoat	25000	1	2	3				7	8	11	10				5			4				6	9			
Mar 12	WEST HAM UNITED	1-1	Spoors (pen)	13000	1	2	3				7	8	11					5			10		4		6	9			
Mar 19	West Ham United	1-2	Spoors	18000	1	9	3			2	7	8	11	10				5			4				6				
Mar 25	Port Vale	1-1	Spoors	13000	1	9	3			2	7	8	11	10				5			4				6				
Mar 26	Birmingham	3-1	Spoors 3	40000	1	9	3			2	7	8	11	10				5			4				6				
Mar 28	PORT VALE	3-0	Fletcher 2, Wainscoat	12000		9	3			2	7	8	11	10			1	5			4				6				
Apr 2	BIRMINGHAM	1-1	Donkin	19000		9	3			2	7	8	11	10			1	5			4				6				
Apr 9	Leeds United	0-0		13000	1	9	3			2	7	8	11	10				5			4				6				
Apr 16	LEEDS UNITED	1-1	Wainscoat	14000	1	9	3			2	7	8	11	10				5			4				6				
Apr 23	Coventry City	1-3	Halliwell	15000	1	9	3			2	7	8	11	10				5			4		6						
Apr 30	COVENTRY CITY	2-2	Spoors 2 (1 pen)	8000	1	9	3			2	7	8	11	10				5			4				6				
May 2	Stoke	2-3	Spoors, Wainscoat	5000	1	9	3			2	7	8	11	10				5			4				6				
May 7	STOKE	1-0	Spoors	6000	1	9	3			2	7	8	11	10				5			4				6				
Apps					35	23	35	11	12	40	42	39	38	36	1	1	7	37	3	1	35	1	7	1	33	13	1	1	9
Goals						10				4	4	2	2	13				3			7					3			

F.A. Cup

Date	Opponent	Score	Scorers	Att	Spoors J	Tindall JT	Williams JH	Gittins JH	Donkin GWC	Fletcher B	Newton A	Wainscoat WR	Bates FG	Fell G	Low WR
Jan 8	Bradford City	1-3	Fletcher	33256	9	3	4	2	7	8	11	10	1	5	6

TEAM GROUP - See page opposite 1914/15 season.

	P	W	D	L	F	A	W	D	L	F	A	Pts
1 Birmingham	42	16	4	1	55	13	8	6	7	24	25	58
2 Cardiff City	42	13	5	3	27	9	11	5	5	32	23	58
3 Bristol City	42	14	3	4	35	12	5	10	6	14	17	51
4 Blackpool	42	12	3	6	32	19	8	7	6	22	23	50
5 West Ham United	42	13	5	3	38	11	6	5	10	13	19	48
6 Notts County	42	12	5	4	36	17	6	6	9	19	23	47
7 Clapton Orient	42	13	6	2	31	9	3	7	11	12	33	45
8 South Shields	42	13	4	4	41	16	4	6	11	20	30	44
9 Fulham	42	14	4	3	33	12	2	6	13	10	35	42
10 Sheffield Wed.	42	9	7	5	31	14	6	4	11	17	34	41
11 Bury	42	10	8	3	29	13	5	2	14	16	36	40
12 Leicester City	42	10	8	3	26	11	2	8	11	13	35	40
13 Hull City	42	7	10	4	24	18	3	10	8	19	35	40
14 Leeds United	42	11	5	5	30	14	3	5	13	10	31	38
15 Wolverhampton Wan.	42	11	4	6	34	24	5	2	14	15	42	38
16 BARNSLEY	42	9	10	2	31	17	1	6	14	17	33	36
17 Port Vale	42	7	6	8	28	19	4	8	9	15	30	36
18 Nottingham Forest	42	9	6	6	37	26	3	6	12	11	29	36
19 Rotherham County	42	8	9	4	23	21	4	3	14	14	32	36
20 Stoke	42	9	5	7	26	16	3	6	12	20	40	35
21 Coventry City	42	8	6	7	24	25	4	5	12	15	45	35
22 Stockport County	42	8	6	7	30	24	1	6	14	12	51	30

1921/22 3rd in Division 2

#	Date	Opponent		Scorers	Att	Cooper A	Gittins JH	Tindall JT	Halliwell IA	Fell G	Low WR	Donkin GWC	Fletcher B	Hammerton JD	Wainscoat WR	Newton A	Armstrong JD	Baines CE	Beaumont P	Curran J	Hine EW	Kay Harold	Page G	Redford J	Ruddlesdin A	Sayles T	Thorpe T	Turner JH
1	Aug 27	Sheffield Wednesday	3-2	Hammerton, Fletcher, Newton	30000	1	2	3	4	5	6	7	8	9	10	11												
2	29	CRYSTAL PALACE	3-1	Hammerton 2, Fletcher	12000	1	2	3	4	5		7	8	9	10	11			6									
3	Sep 3	SHEFFIELD WEDNESDAY	2-0	Hammerton, Wainscoat	17000	1	2	3	4	5	6	7	8	9	10													11
4	7	Crystal Palace	1-0	Fletcher	12000	1	2	3	4	5		7	8	9	10				6									11
5	10	WOLVERHAMPTON W.	2-1	Hammerton, Fletcher	15000	1	2	3	4	5		7	8	9	10	11			6									
6	17	Wolverhampton Wan.	0-2		18000	1		3	4	5	6	7	8	9	10	11										2		
7	24	BURY	3-0	Newton, Fletcher 2 (1 pen)	10000	1		3	4	5	6	7	8	9	10	11										2		
8	Oct 1	Bury	2-1	Fletcher, Wainscoat	12000	1		3	4	5	6	7	8	9	10	11										2		
9	6	Notts County	4-1	*see below	12000	1		3	4	5	6	7	8	9	10	11										2		
10	8	COVENTRY CITY	0-1		12000	1		3	4	5		7	8	9	10	11		6								2		
11	15	Coventry City	1-0	Hammerton	25000	1	6	3	4	5		7	8	9	10	11										2		
12	22	DERBY COUNTY	2-1	Hammerton 2	10000	1	6	3	4	5		7	8	9	10	11										2		
13	29	Derby County	0-1		10000	1	6	3	4	5		7	8	9	10	11										2		
14	Nov 5	Leicester City	0-1		18000	1	2	3	4	5	6	7	8	9	10	11												
15	7	Rotherham County	0-0		20000	1	6	3				7	8	9	10	11		5								2		
16	12	LEICESTER CITY	0-0		11000		2	3	4	5	6	7	8	9	10	11											1	
17	19	West Ham United	0-4		18000	1	2	3	4	5		7	8	9	10							6						11
18	26	WEST HAM UNITED	1-1	Donkin (pen)	9000		5	3	4			7	8	9	10	11		6								2	1	
19	Dec 10	ROTHERHAM COUNTY	0-1		12000		5	3	4				8	9	10	11		6		7						2	1	
20	17	Port Vale	3-2	Retford, Fletcher, Ruddlesdin	6000		2	3	4	5		7	8			11		6						9	10		1	
21	24	PORT VALE	3-2	Fletcher 2 (1 pen), Retford	8000			3	4	5		7	8			11		6						9	10	2	1	
22	26	BRISTOL CITY	1-1	Wainscoat	11000		2	3	4	5		7	8	9	10	11		6									1	
23	27	Bristol City	0-3		20000		5	3	4			7	8	9	10	11		6								2	1	
24	31	South Shields	2-5	Wainscoat, Fletcher (pen)	10000	1	2	3	4	5		7	8		10	11		6						9				
25	Jan 21	Fulham	0-0		12000			3				7	9		10	11		6	5		8	4				2	1	
26	Feb 4	Blackpool	0-1		10000			3				7	9		10	11		6	5		8	4				2	1	
27	11	BLACKPOOL	3-2	Wainscoat, Hine, Donkin	10000			3				7	9		10	11		6	5		8	4				2	1	
28	25	BRADFORD PARK AVE.	2-0	Longran (og), Hine	10000			3	4	5			9		10	11	2	6		7	8						1	
29	27	SOUTH SHIELDS	2-1	Hine, Wainscoat	6000	1		3	4			7	9		10	11	2	6	5		8							
30	Mar 4	Clapton Orient	1-2	Wainscoat	10000	1		3	4				9		10	11	2	6	5	7	8							
31	6	FULHAM	2-1	Fletcher, Wainscoat	9000	1		3	4			7	9		10	11	2	6	5		8							
32	11	CLAPTON ORIENT	4-0	Donkin, Hine 2, Wainscoat	10000	1		3	4			7	9		10	11	2	6	5		8							
33	18	STOKE	2-2	Fletcher 2	16000	1	2	3	4			7	9		10	11		6	5		8							
34	22	Bradford Park Avenue	3-2	Newton, Hine, Wainscoat	7000		2	3	4			7	9		10	11		6	5		8						1	
35	25	Stoke	0-1		9000		2	3	4			7	9		10	11		6	5		8						1	
36	Apr 1	LEEDS UNITED	2-2	Hine, Fletcher	14000	1	2		4			7	9		10	11	3	6	5		8							
37	8	Leeds United	0-4		10000	1	2	3	4			7	9		10	11		6	5		8							
38	14	NOTTM. FOREST	2-0	Wainscoat, Newton	18000	1	2	3	4			7	8		10	11		6	5		9							
39	15	HULL CITY	4-1	Hine, Wainscoat 2, Fletcher	12000	1	2	3	4			7	8		10	11		6	5		9							
40	17	Nottingham Forest	1-1	Hine (pen)	28000	1	2	3	4			7	8		10	11		6	5		9							
41	22	Hull City	3-1	Hine 2, Wainscoat	10000	1	2	3	4			7	8		10	11		6	5		9							
42	29	NOTTS COUNTY	3-0	Wainscoat 2, Hine (pen)	13000	1	2	3	4			7	8		10	11		6	5		9							
		Apps				29	28	39	39	21	8	39	39	24	40	39	6	26	21	3	18	4	1	3	2	17	13	3
		Goals										3	17	9	17	4					12			2	1			

Scorers in game 9: Wainscoat, Fletcher (p), Ashurst (og), Hammerton

Two own goals

F.A. Cup

	Date	Opponent		Scorers	Att	Cooper A	Gittins JH	Tindall JT	Halliwell IA	Fell G	Low WR	Donkin GWC	Fletcher B	Hammerton JD	Wainscoat WR	Newton A	Armstrong JD	Baines CE	Beaumont P	Curran J	Hine EW	Kay Harold	Page G	Redford J	Ruddlesdin A	Sayles T	Thorpe T	Turner JH
R1	Jan 7	NORWICH CITY	1-1	Spoors	17000	1	6	3	4	5		7	8		10	11										2		
rep	12	Norwich City	2-1	Hine, Fletcher	13000	1		3				7	4		10	11		6	5		8			9		2		
R2	28	OLDHAM ATHLETIC	3-1	Wainscoat, Fletcher (2 pens)	26866			3				7	9		10	11		6	5		8	4				2	1	
R3	Feb 18	PRESTON NORTH END	1-1	Fletcher	36881			3	4			7	9		10	11		6	5		8					2	1	
rep	22	Preston North End	0-3		38000			3	4			7	9		10	11	2	6	5		8						1	

Played in R1: J Spoors (at 9)

		P	W	D	L	F	A	W	D	L	F	A	Pts
1	Nottingham Forest	42	13	7	1	29	9	9	5	7	22	21	56
2	Stoke	42	9	11	1	31	11	9	5	7	29	33	52
3	BARNSLEY	42	14	5	2	43	18	8	3	10	24	34	52
4	West Ham United	42	15	3	3	39	13	5	5	11	13	26	48
5	Hull City	42	13	5	3	36	13	6	5	10	15	28	48
6	South Shields	42	11	7	3	25	13	6	5	10	18	25	46
7	Fulham	42	14	5	2	41	8	4	4	13	16	30	45
8	Leeds United	42	10	8	3	31	12	6	5	10	17	26	45
9	Leicester City	42	11	6	4	30	16	3	11	7	9	18	45
10	Sheffield Wed.	42	12	4	5	31	24	3	10	8	16	26	44
11	Bury	42	11	3	7	35	19	4	7	10	19	36	40
12	Derby County	42	11	3	7	34	22	4	6	11	26	42	39
13	Notts County	42	10	7	4	34	18	2	8	11	13	33	39
14	Crystal Palace	42	9	6	6	28	20	4	7	10	17	31	39
15	Clapton Orient	42	12	4	5	33	18	3	5	13	10	32	39
16	Rotherham County	42	8	9	4	17	7	6	2	13	15	36	39
17	Wolverhampton Wan.	42	8	7	6	28	19	5	4	12	16	30	37
18	Port Vale	42	10	5	6	28	19	4	3	14	15	38	36
19	Blackpool	42	11	1	9	33	27	4	4	13	11	30	35
20	Coventry City	42	8	5	8	31	21	4	5	12	20	39	34
21	Bradford Park Ave.	42	10	5	6	32	22	2	4	15	14	40	33
22	Bristol City	42	10	3	8	25	18	2	6	13	12	40	33

Season 1921/22
Back row: Sant (Manager) Gittins, Cooper, Tindall, Wood (Trainer) Rose (Chairman)
Centre row: Halliwell, Fell, Low   Front row: Donkin, Fletcher, Hammerton, Wainscoat, Beaumont

Season 1922/23
Back row: Gittins, Gale, Tindall   Centre (3 figures sat) Halliwell, Beaumont, Baines
Front row: Donkin, Fletcher, Wainscoat, Hine, Newton

1922/23   9th in Division 2

#	Date	Opponent	Score	Scorers	Att	Gale T	Gittins JH	Tindall JT	Halliwell JA	Beaumont P	Baines CE	Donkin GWC	Fletcher B	Wainscoat WR	Hine EW	Newton A	Armstrong JD	Batty Billy	Cope H	Curran J	Hammerton JD	Jackson S	Kay Harold	Millership H	Ruddlesdin A	Sayles T
1	Aug 26	Clapton Orient	1-0	Wainscoat	16000	1	2	3	4	5	6	7	8	9	10	11										
2	" 28	BURY	2-1	Hine (pen), Potter (og)		1	2	3	4	5	6	7		9	10	11									8	
3	Sep 2	CLAPTON ORIENT	2-1	Wainscoat, Donkin	12000	1	2	3	4	5	6	7	8	9	10	11										
4	" 6	Bury	1-2	Hine (pen)	9000	1	2	3	4	5	6	7	8	9	10	11										
5	" 9	SOUTHAMPTON	3-0	Hine (pen), Wainscoat 2	11500	1	2	3	4	5	6	7	8	9	10	11										
6	" 16	Southampton	2-2	Hine 2	15000	1	2	3	4	5	6	7	8	9	10	11										
7	" 23	DERBY COUNTY	5-0	Wainscoat 2, Hine 2, Fletcher	12000	1	2	3	4	5	6	7	8	9	10	11										
8	" 30	Derby County	1-0	Wainscoat	13000	1	2	3	4	5	6	7	8	9	10	11										
9	Oct 7	NOTTS COUNTY	1-0	Fletcher	15000	1	2	3	4	5	6	7	8	9	10							11				
10	" 14	Notts County	0-1		15000	1	2	3	4		6	7	8	9	10	11							5			
11	" 21	Stockport County	1-3	Wainscoat	15000	1	2	3	4		6	7	8	9	10	11							5			
12	" 28	STOCKPORT COUNTY	1-1	Wainscoat	10000	1	2		4		6	7	8	9	10	11							5	3		
13	Nov 4	Fulham	1-0	Wainscoat	19000	1	2		4		6		8	9	10	11				7				3		
14	" 11	FULHAM	0-1		12000	1	2		4	5	6		8	9	10	11				7				3		
15	" 18	Crystal Palace	0-2		12000	1	2		4	5	6			9	10	11		8		7				3		
16	" 25	CRYSTAL PALACE	1-2	Hine (pen)	11000	1	2		4	5	6		8	9	10	11				7				3		
17	Dec 2	HULL CITY	1-0	Fletcher	9000	1	2	3	4	5	6	7	8	9	10	11										
18	" 9	Hull City	1-2	Wainscoat	7000	1	2	3	4	5	6	7	8	9	10	11										
19	" 16	SHEFFIELD WEDNESDAY	2-4	Hine, Wainscoat	8000	1	2	3	4	5	6	7	8	9	10	11										
20	" 23	Sheffield Wednesday	3-2	Hine 2 (1 pen), Fletcher	20000	1	2		10	5	6			4	8	11				7	9					3
21	" 25	Rotherham County	1-1	Hine	14500	1		3	10	5	6			4	8	11				7	9					2
22	" 26	ROTHERHAM COUNTY	2-2	Hine, Newton	16000	1	2	3	10	5	6			4	8	11				7	9					
23	" 30	LEICESTER CITY	0-1		10000	1	3		10	5	6			4	8	11	2			7	9					
24	Jan 1	Manchester United	0-1		25000	1	3		4	5	6			10	8	11	2			7	9					
25	" 6	Leicester City	2-2	Halliwell, Beaumont	17000	1	3		10	5	6		8	4	9	11	2			7						
26	" 20	BLACKPOOL	2-2	Hine, Newton	10000	1	3		10	5	6		8	4	9	11	2			7						
27	" 27	Blackpool	1-0	Halliwell	12000	1	3		10	5	6		8	4	9	11	2			7						
28	Feb 10	LEEDS UNITED	1-0	Halliwell	8000	1	3		10	5	6		8	4	9	11	2			7						
29	" 17	West Ham United	0-0		20000	1			10	5	6		8	4	9	11	2			7						3
30	" 24	Leeds United	1-1	Halliwell	10000	1	3		10	5	6		8	4	9	11	2			7						
31	Mar 3	South Shields	0-2		9000	1	3		10	5	6		8	4	9	11	2			7						
32	" 10	SOUTH SHIELDS	5-0	Halliwell 3, Wainscoat, Hine	9000	1	3		10	5	6		8	4	9	11	2			7						
33	" 17	WOLVERHAMPTON W.	1-0	Wainscoat	10000	1	3		10	5	6		8	4	9	11	2			7						
34	" 24	Wolverhampton Wan.	3-3	Halliwell, Curran, Hine	12000	1	3		10	5	6		8	4	9	11	2			7						
35	" 31	COVENTRY CITY	6-2	Hine 3(1 p), Halliwell 2, Wainscoat	8000	1	3		10	5	6		8	4	9	11	2			7						
36	Apr 2	BRADFORD CITY	3-1	Wainscoat, Hine (pen), Curran	15000	1	3	2	10	5	6		8	4	9	11				7						
37	" 3	Bradford City	0-2		24000	1	3	2	10	5	6		8	4	9	11				7						
38	" 7	Coventry City	0-3		12000	1	3		10	5	6		8	4	9	11	2			7						
39	" 14	PORT VALE	0-1		7000		3		10	5	6		8	4	9	11	2		1	7						
40	" 16	WEST HAM UNITED	2-0	Hine 2	10000		3		10	5	6		8	4	9	11	2		1	7						
41	" 21	Port Vale	1-1	Hine	8000	1	3	2	10	5	6		8	4	9	11				7						
42	" 28	MANCHESTER UNITED	2-2	Hine, Curran	10000	1	3		10	5	6		8	4	9	11	2			7						
		Apps				40	40	19	41	39	42	15	39	39	42	41	17	1	2	27	5	1	3	5	1	3
		Goals							10	1		1	4	16	24	2				3						

One own goal

F.A. Cup

#	Date	Opponent	Score	Scorers	Att	Gale T	Gittins JH	Halliwell JA	Beaumont P	Baines CE	Fletcher B	Wainscoat WR	Hine EW	Newton A	Armstrong JD	Curran J
R1	Jan 13	Swindon Town	0-0		20261	1	3	10	5	6	8	4	9	11	2	7
rep	" 18	SWINDON TOWN	2-0	Wainscoat, Hine	22951	1	3	10	5	6	8	4	9	11	2	7
R2	Feb 3	Sheffield Wednesday	1-2	Baines	66103	1	3	10	5	6	8	4	9	11	2	7

		P	W	D	L	F	A	W	D	L	F	A	Pts
1	Notts County	42	16	1	4	29	15	7	6	8	17	19	53
2	West Ham United	42	9	8	4	21	11	11	3	7	42	27	51
3	Leicester City	42	14	2	5	42	19	7	7	7	23	25	51
4	Manchester United	42	10	6	5	25	17	7	8	6	26	19	48
5	Blackpool	42	12	4	5	37	14	6	7	8	23	29	47
6	Bury	42	14	5	2	41	16	4	6	11	14	30	47
7	Leeds United	42	11	8	2	26	10	7	3	11	17	26	47
8	Sheffield Wed.	42	14	3	4	36	16	3	9	9	18	31	46
9	BARNSLEY	42	12	4	5	42	21	5	7	9	20	30	45
10	Fulham	42	10	7	4	29	12	6	5	10	14	20	44
11	Southampton	42	10	5	6	28	21	4	9	8	12	19	42
12	Hull City	42	9	8	4	29	22	5	6	10	14	23	42
13	South Shields	42	11	7	3	26	12	4	3	14	9	32	40
14	Derby County	42	9	5	7	25	16	5	6	10	21	34	39
15	Bradford City	42	8	7	6	27	18	4	6	11	14	27	37
16	Crystal Palace	42	10	7	4	33	16	3	4	14	21	46	37
17	Port Vale	42	8	6	7	23	18	6	3	12	16	33	37
18	Coventry City	42	12	2	7	35	21	3	5	13	11	42	37
19	Clapton Orient	42	9	6	6	26	17	3	6	12	14	33	36
20	Stockport County	42	10	6	5	32	24	4	2	15	11	34	36
21	Rotherham County	42	10	7	4	30	19	3	2	16	14	44	35
22	Wolverhampton Wan.	42	9	4	8	32	26	0	5	16	10	51	27

1923/24   11th in Division 2

#	Mon	Date	Opponent	Score	Scorers	Att	Gale T	Armstrong JD	Gittins JH	Fletcher B	Beaumont P	Baines CE	Curran J	Hine EW	Wainscoat WR	Halliwell JA	Newton A	Appleyard GE	Bowie A	Brown A	Cope H	Donkin GWC	Fisher L	Hodgkinson H	Jeffs AS	Jukes AB	Kelly T	Matthews F	Russell H	Sanderson CA	Smart E
1	Aug	25	Coventry City	3-2	Fletcher, Halliwell 2	20000	1	2	3	4	5	6	7	8	9	10	11														
2		27	BRISTOL CITY	3-1	Curran, Halliwell, Hine	12000	1	2	3	4	5	6	7	8	9	10	11														
3	Sep	1	COVENTRY CITY	1-1	Beaumont	12000	1	2	3	4	5	6	7	8	9	10	11														
4		3	Bristol City	1-1	Wainscoat	20000	1	2	3	4	5	6	7	8		10	11									9					
5		8	South Shields	0-2		12000		2	3	4	5	6	7	8		10	11				1					9					
6		15	SOUTH SHIELDS	1-0	Wainscoat	11000		2	3	4	5	6	7	8	10	9	11				1										
7		22	Oldham Athletic	1-1	Donkin	10000		2	3	4	5	6		8	10	9	11				1	7									
8		29	OLDHAM ATHLETIC	4-1	Hine 2, Halliwell, Donkin	12000		2	3	4	5	6		8	10	9	11				1	7									
9	Oct	6	Stockport County	1-1	Halliwell	10000		2	3	4	5	6		8	10	9	11				1	7									
10		13	STOCKPORT COUNTY	0-0		10000	1	2	3	4	5	6		8	10	9	11					7									
11		20	Leicester City	0-2		16000	1	2	3		5	6		8	10	9	11					7			4						
12		27	LEICESTER CITY	3-1	Halliwell 3	10000	1	2	3		5	6		8	10	9	11					7			4						
13	Nov	3	SHEFFIELD WEDNESDAY	0-0		16000	1	2	3	4	5	6		8	10	9	11											7			
14		10	Sheffield Wednesday	0-1		25000	1	2	3	4	5	6		8	10	9	11											7			
15		17	Leeds United	1-3	Appleyard	14000	1	2		4	5	6		8	10		11	9						3				7			
16		24	LEEDS UNITED	1-3	Hine (pen)	15000	1	2	5			6		8	10		11	9				7		3	4						
17	Dec	8	Port Vale	1-4	Hine (pen)	6000	1	2		4	5	6		8	10	9	11					7		3							
18		15	BRADFORD CITY	2-1	Hine, Wainscoat	8000	1	2	3		5	6		9	10	8	11					7								4	
19		22	Bradford City	2-3	Halliwell, Lloyd (og)	10000		2	3		5	6		8		9	11				1	7						10		4	
20		25	Manchester United	2-1	Halliwell, Matthews	40000		2	3		5	6		10		9					1	7				8		11		4	
21		26	MANCHESTER UNITED	1-0	Halliwell	14000		2	3		5	6		10		9					1	7				8		11		4	
22		29	CLAPTON ORIENT	1-0	Halliwell			2	3		5	6		8		9	11				1	7						10		4	
23	Jan	5	Clapton Orient	1-2	Baines	8000		2	3		5	6		8		9	11				1	7						10		4	
24		19	Southampton	0-6		7000		2	3		5	6				10					1					8		11	9	4	
25		26	SOUTHAMPTON	1-1	Hine (pen)	8000	1	2	3	4	5	6		8		9						7						10	11		
26	Feb	2	PORT VALE	3-0	Hine 3	7000	1	2	3	4		6		8		9						7					5	10	11		
27		9	FULHAM	2-1	Hine (pen), Jukes	6000		2	3	4	5	6		8		9					1	7						10	11		
28		16	Blackpool	2-0	Hine 2	8000		2	3	4	5	6		8		9					1	7						10	11		
29		23	BLACKPOOL	3-1	Halliwell, Donkin, Matthew	11000		2	3		5	6		8		9					1	7						10	11	4	
30	Mar	1	Derby County	1-2	Matthews	8000		2	3		5	6		8		9					1	7						10	11	4	
31		8	DERBY COUNTY	1-3	Halliwell	12000		2	3		5	6		8		9					1	7						10	11	4	
32		10	Fulham	0-3		7200		2	3		5	6		8					9		1	7				4		10			11
33		15	NELSON	0-0		8000		2	3		5	6		8		9	11			4	1	7						10			
34		22	Nelson	3-4	Matthews, Hine, Halliwell	7000		2	3	4	5	6		8		9	11				1	7						10			
35		29	HULL CITY	0-0		5000		2			5	6		8		10			9	4	1	7		3				11			
36	Apr	5	Hull City	2-1	Halliwell 2	8000		2			5	6		8		10			9	4	1	7		3				11			
37		12	Stoke	0-2		8000		2			5	6		8		10			9	4	1	7		3				11			
38		18	Bury	1-1	Appleyard	20000	1	2			5	6		8		10	11	9		4		7		3							
39		19	STOKE	0-0		12000	1	2			5	6		8		10	11	9		4		7		3							
40		21	BURY	2-0	Fletcher, Hine	12000	1	2		9	5			8		10	11			4		7								6	
41		26	CRYSTAL PALACE	5-2	Hine 3, Donkin, Kelly	4000		2	3		5			8		10	11			4	1	7					9			6	
42	May	3	Crystal Palace	1-3	Hine	8000	1	2			5	6		8			11			4		7		3			9	10			
			Apps				19	35	41	23	40	40	6	41	18	36	27	4	4	6	23	33	1	10	5	12	2	22	2	11	1
			Goals						2	1	1		1	19	3	17		2				4				1	1	4			

One own goal

F.A. Cup

Rnd	Mon	Date	Opponent	Score	Att	Gale T	Armstrong JD	Gittins JH	Fletcher B	Beaumont P	Baines CE	Curran J	Hine EW	Wainscoat WR	Halliwell JA	Newton A	Appleyard GE	Bowie A	Brown A	Cope H	Donkin GWC	Fisher L	Hodgkinson H	Jeffs AS	Jukes AB	Kelly T	Matthews F	Russell H	Sanderson CA	Smart E
R1	Jan	12	BRIGHTON & HOVE ALB.	0-0	18490		2	3	8	5	6		10	9		11				1	7								4	
rep		16	Brighton & Hove Albion	0-1	22086		2	3	8	5	6		10	9						1	7						11		4	

		P	W	D	L	F	A	W	D	L	F	A	Pts
1	Leeds United	42	14	5	2	41	10	7	7	7	20	25	54
2	Bury	42	15	5	1	42	7	6	4	11	21	28	51
3	Derby County	42	15	4	2	52	15	6	5	10	23	27	51
4	Blackpool	42	13	7	1	43	12	5	6	10	29	35	49
5	Southampton	42	13	5	3	36	9	4	9	8	16	22	48
6	Stoke	42	9	11	1	27	10	5	7	9	17	32	46
7	Oldham Athletic	42	10	10	1	24	12	4	7	10	21	40	45
8	Sheffield Wed.	42	15	5	1	42	9	1	7	13	12	42	44
9	South Shields	42	13	5	3	34	16	4	5	12	15	34	44
10	Clapton Orient	42	11	7	3	27	10	3	8	10	13	26	43
11	BARNSLEY	42	12	7	2	34	16	4	4	13	23	45	43
12	Leicester City	42	13	4	4	43	16	4	4	13	21	38	42
13	Stockport County	42	10	7	4	32	21	3	9	9	12	31	42
14	Manchester United	42	10	7	4	37	15	3	7	11	15	29	40
15	Crystal Palace	42	11	7	3	37	19	2	6	13	16	46	39
16	Port Vale	42	9	5	7	33	29	4	7	10	17	37	38
17	Hull City	42	8	7	6	32	23	2	10	9	14	28	37
18	Bradford City	42	8	7	6	24	21	3	8	10	11	27	37
19	Coventry City	42	9	6	6	34	23	2	7	12	18	45	35
20	Fulham	42	9	8	4	30	20	1	6	14	15	36	34
21	Nelson	42	8	8	5	32	31	2	5	14	8	43	33
22	Bristol City	42	5	8	8	19	26	2	7	12	13	39	29

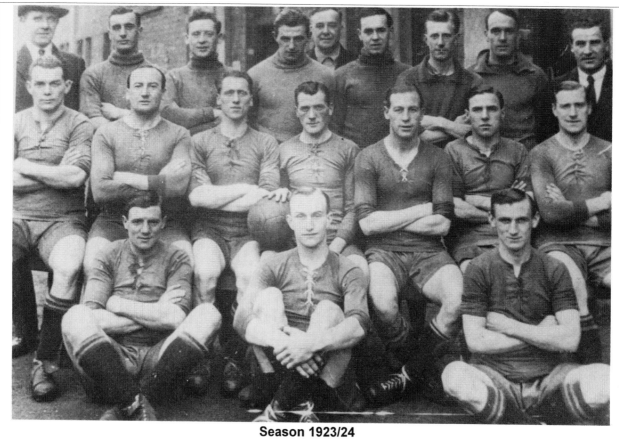

Season 1923/24
Back row: Sant (Manager) Brown, Matthews, Gale, Cooper (Trainer) Barnett, Jukes, Jeffs, Fletcher
Centre row: Armstrong, Tindall, Hine, Halliwell, Wainscoat, Curran, Gittins
Front row: Donkin, Beaumont, Baines

Season 1924/25
Back row: Halliwell, Kelly, Beaumont, Gale, Gittins, Newton
Front row: Donkin, Hine, Baines, Jukes, Hodgkinson

1924/25   15th in Division 2

#	Date	Opponent	Result	Scorers	Att	Cope H	Gittins JH	Hodgkinson H	Sanderson CA	Beaumont P	Baines CE	Donkin GWC	Hine EW	Halliwell JA	Matthews F	Smart E	Armstrong JD	Baker LH	Barnett LH	Bowie A	Brown A	Curran J	Dixon C	Fletcher B	Gale T	Gillatt K	Jukes AB	Kelly T	Newton A	Rawson AN	Sherwin H	Swan E
1	Aug 30	Middlesbrough	0-2		25000	1	2	3	4	5	6	7	8	9	10	11																
2	Sep 1	WOLVERHAMPTON W.	0-0		9000		2	3	4	5	6	7	8	9	10	11									1							
3	6	PORT VALE	1-3	Halliwell	8000		2	3		5	6	7	8	9	10				4						1				11			
4	8	Manchester United	0-1		16000		2	3		5	6	7	8	4	10					9					1				11			
5	13	Bradford City	0-1		12000		2	3		5	6	7	8	4											1		10	9	11			
6	20	SOUTH SHIELDS	1-0	Hine	8000		2	3		5	6	7	8	4											1		10		11	9		
7	27	Derby County	1-1	Rawson	18000		2	3		5	6	7	8	4											1		10		11	9		
8	Oct 4	BLACKPOOL	2-4	Rawson 2	10000		2	3		5	6	7	8	4											1		10		11	9		
9	11	Hull City	2-5	Hine 2	9000		2	3	4	5	6	7	8												1				11	9		10
10	18	PORTSMOUTH	1-4	Rawson	9000	1		3		5	6	7	8	4			2												11	9		10
11	25	LEICESTER CITY	1-1	Beaumont	7000	1		3		5	6	7		4	10								2	8				9	11			
12	Nov 1	Stoke	1-1	Fletcher	6000	1		3	4	5	6	7			10								2	8				9	11			
13	8	COVENTRY CITY	3-1	Hine, Fletcher, Rawson	7000	1		3		5	6	7		4	10								2	8					11	9		
14	15	Oldham Athletic	0-2		10000	1		3		5	6	7		4	10								2	8					11	9		
15	22	SHEFFIELD WEDNESDAY	3-0	Kelly, Newton, Hine	12000			3		5	6	7		4	10								2	8	1			9	11			
16	29	Clapton Orient	2-4		14000			3		5	6	7		4	10								2	8	1			9	11			
17	Dec 6	CRYSTAL PALACE	3-0	Donkin, Kelly 2	7000			3		5	6	7		4	10								2	8	1			9	11			
18	13	Southampton	1-3	Hine (pen)	9000			3			6	7	10	4		11			5				2	8	1			9				
19	20	CHELSEA	3-3	Hine 2 (1 pen), Kelly	10000			3		5	6		10	4		11						7	2	8	1			9				
20	25	Stockport County	0-1		15000			3		5	6		10	4		11						7	2	8	1			9				
21	26	STOCKPORT COUNTY	0-1		11000			3		5	6		10	4		11						7	2	8	1			9				
22	27	MIDDLESBROUGH	1-0	Matthews	7000			3		5	6		10	4		11						7	2		1			9			8	
23	Jan 3	Port Vale	0-2		7000		2	3		5	6		10	4		11						7			1			9			8	
24	17	BRADFORD CITY	3-1	Hine, Halliwell 2	10000	1	2	3		5	6	7	10	9					4										11		8	
25	24	South Shields	2-5	Halliwell, Rawson	7000		2	3		5	6	7	10	9					4						1				11		8	
26	Feb 7	Blackpool	2-1	Halliwell, Hine	8000		2	3		5		7	10	4							6				1	8			11		9	
27	14	HULL CITY	1-2	Beaumont	8000		2	3		5	6	7	10	4											1	8	9		11			
28	21	Portsmouth	0-0		15000		2			5	6	7	10	9					4				3		1	8			11			
29	28	Leicester City	0-6		20000		2			5	6		10	8					4				3		1	7		9	11			
30	Mar 7	STOKE	1-1	Hine	10000		2				6		8		10			5					3		1	7			11	9	4	
31	9	DERBY COUNTY	3-0	Beaumont 2, Curran	5000		2	3		9	6		8		10			5				7			1				11		4	
32	14	Coventry City	2-3	Beaumont, Hine	14000		2	3		9	6		8		10			5				7			1				11		4	
33	21	OLDHAM ATHLETIC	0-0		9000		2	3		9	6		8		10			5				7			1				11		4	
34	28	Sheffield Wednesday	0-1					2			9	6		8		10			5				7	3		1				11		4	
35	Apr 4	CLAPTON ORIENT	1-1	Hine	8000		2			9	6		8		10			5				7	3		1				11		4	
36	11	Crystal Palace	1-0	Baines	10000		2				6	7	8	9	10			5	4				3		1				11			
37	13	FULHAM	1-0	Hine (pen)	11000		2				6	7	8	9	10			5	4				3		1				11			
38	14	Fulham	2-1	Curran, Halliwell	6000		2				6	7	8	9	10			5	4				3		1				11			
39	18	SOUTHAMPTON	1-1	Newton	9000		2				6	7	8	9	10			5	4				3		1				11			
40	25	Chelsea	1-0	Halliwell	20000		2				6	7	8	9	10			5	4				3		1				11			
41	27	Wolverhampton Wan.	1-0	Hine	10000		2				6	7	10	9				5	4				3		1				11		8	
42	Ma 2	MANCHESTER UNITED	0-0		14000		2				6	7	10	9				5	4				3		1				11		8	
	Apps					7	30	29	4	33	41	23	42	35	12	2	1	13	12	1	1	17	24	19	35	9	4	13	32	15	6	2
	Goals									5	1	1	15	7	1							2		2				4	2	6		

F.A. Cup

	Date	Opponent	Result	Scorers	Att	Gittins JH	Hodgkinson H	Beaumont P	Baines CE	Donkin GWC	Hine EW	Halliwell JA	Matthews F	Barnett LH	Curran J	Dixon C	Fletcher B	Gale T	Gillatt K	Kelly T	Newton A	Sherwin H
R1	Jan 10	Millwall	0-0		31500	2	3	5	6		10	4			7		8	1		9	11	
rep	15	MILLWALL	2-1	Kelly, Fletcher	23300	2	3	5	6	7	10	4					8	1		9	11	
R2	31	BRADFORD CITY	0-3		22319	2	3	5	6	7	10	9		4				1			11	8

League Table

		P	W	D	L	F	A	W	D	L	F	A	Pts
1	Leicester City	42	15	4	2	58	9	9	7	5	32	23	59
2	Manchester United	42	17	3	1	40	6	6	8	7	17	17	57
3	Derby County	42	15	3	3	49	15	7	8	6	22	21	55
4	Portsmouth	42	7	13	1	28	14	8	5	8	30	36	48
5	Chelsea	42	11	8	2	31	12	5	7	9	20	25	47
6	Wolverhampton Wan.	42	14	1	6	29	19	6	5	10	26	32	46
7	Southampton	42	12	8	1	29	10	1	10	10	11	26	44
8	Port Vale	42	12	4	5	34	19	5	4	12	14	37	42
9	South Shields	42	9	6	6	33	21	3	11	7	9	17	41
10	Hull City	42	12	6	3	40	14	3	5	13	10	35	41
11	Clapton Orient	42	8	7	6	22	13	6	5	10	20	29	40
12	Fulham	42	11	6	4	26	15	4	4	13	15	41	40
13	Middlesbrough	42	6	10	5	22	21	4	9	8	14	23	39
14	Sheffield Wed.	42	12	3	6	36	23	3	5	13	14	33	38
15	BARNSLEY	42	8	8	5	30	23	5	4	12	16	36	38
16	Bradford City	42	11	6	4	26	13	2	6	13	11	37	38
17	Blackpool	42	8	5	8	37	26	6	4	11	28	35	37
18	Oldham Athletic	42	9	5	7	24	21	4	6	11	11	30	37
19	Stockport County	42	10	6	5	26	15	3	5	13	11	42	37
20	Stoke	42	7	8	6	22	17	5	3	13	12	29	35
21	Crystal Palace	42	8	4	9	23	19	4	6	11	15	35	34
22	Coventry City	42	10	6	5	32	26	1	3	17	13	58	31

1925/26 18th in Division 2

#	Mo	Date	Opponent	Score	Scorers	Att	Gale T	Gittins JH	Hodgkinson H	Barnett LH	Baker LH	Baines CE	Curran J	Hine EW	Halliwell IA	Johnson WJ	Newton A	Allen F	Beaumont P	Bedford F	Brook EF	Brown A	Caddick GFR	Eaton F	Fletcher B	Gillatt K	Goodwin J	Johnson AJ	Myers J	Phoenix AE	Richmond J	Sanderson CA	Shaw MV	Sherwin H
1	Au	29	Oldham Athletic	1-2	Halliwell	11731	1	2	3	4	5	6	7	8	9	10	11																	
2		31	BRADFORD CITY	0-0		8599	1	2	3	4	5	6		8	9	10	11			7														
3	Se	5	CLAPTON ORIENT	3-1	Hine 2, Fletcher	5657	1	2	3			5	6	10	9		11			7					8									4
4		7	Bradford City	1-4	Hine (pen)	9195	1	2		3	5	6	7	10	9		11													8				4
5		12	Chelsea	2-3	Hine, Halliwell	35161	1	2	3	4	5	6	7	10	9		11								8									
6		14	Port Vale	0-3		7277	1	2	3	4	5	6	7	10	9		11								8									
7		19	HULL CITY	2-1	Hine (pen), Halliwell	3314	1	2	3	4	5	6	7	10	9		11								8									
8		26	Darlington	2-2	Fletcher 2	8419	1	2	3	4	5	6	7	10	9		11								8									
9	Oc	3	BLACKPOOL	2-0	Hine, Halliwell	9119	1	2	3	4	5	6	7	10	9		11								8									
10		10	Southampton	0-0		10564	1	2	3	4	5	6	7	10	9		11								8									
11		17	Stockport County	1-1	Halliwell	5850	1	2	3	4	5	6	7	10	9		11								8									
12		24	FULHAM	2-2	Hine, Fletcher	8309	1	2	3	4	5	6	7	10	9		11								8									
13		31	Sheffield Wednesday	0-3		23920	1	2	3	4	5	6	7	8	9	10												11						
14	No	7	STOKE CITY	2-1	Baines, Hine	1916	1	2	3		5	6	7		9	10			4						8					11				
15		14	Middlesbrough	0-5		12760	1	2	3		5	6	7		9	10									8					11				4
16		21	PORTSMOUTH	2-2	Curran, Halliwell	4577			3	2	5	6	7		4	10	9								8	1		11						
17	De	5	SWANSEA TOWN	2-0	Fletcher, WJ Johnson	4786	1	2	3		5	6	7		8	10									9					11		4		
18		12	South Shields	0-3		6167	1	2	3		5	6	7		8	10									9					11		4		
19		19	PRESTON NORTH EN	2-0	Fletcher, A Johnson	3607	1	2	3		5			8	4	10				7					9			11				6		
20		25	Nottingham Forest	2-4	A Johnson, Hine	10537	1	2	3		5			8	4	10				7					9			11				6		
21		28	NOTTM. FOREST	4-1	Hine 2, Fletcher, A Johnson	6047	1	2	3		5	6		8		10				7					9			11				4		
22	Jan	1	PORT VALE	3-0	Fletcher 2, Hine	6804	1	2	3		5	6		8		10				7					9			11				4		
23		2	OLDHAM ATHLETIC	3-4	Bedford, Halliwell, WJ Johnson	10680	1	2	3		5	6		8	9	10				7								11				4		
24		16	Clapton Orient	0-4		8472	1	2	3		5	6		8						7						10	9	11				4		
25		23	CHELSEA	2-3	A Johnson, Bedford	7031	1	2	3		5	6		8						7						10	9	11				4		
26		30	Hull City	2-2	Shaw, Curran	8478	1	2	3				7						5				6	10	8			11					9	4
27	Fe	6	DARLINGTON	1-1	Richmond	8133	1	2	3				7						5				6	10				11			8		9	4
28		13	Blackpool	0-4		8620	1	2	3				7	4	8	10							6					11					9	5
29		20	SOUTHAMPTON	2-0	Gillatt, Richmond (pen)	8653	1	2	3	4			7										6			10		11			8		9	5
30		27	STOCKPORT COUNTY	1-1	Eaton	7663	1	2	3	4													6	10				11			8		9	5
31	Ma	6	WOLVERHAMPTON W.	1-1	Newton	5948	1	2	3			6	7		4		11	10	5						8								9	
32		13	SHEFFIELD WEDNESD	1-1	Richmond	28124	1	2	3				7		4	8		10	5				6								11		9	
33		20	Stoke City	2-1	Richmond, Allen	12977	1	2	3			6	7		4	10		8					5								11		9	
34		27	MIDDLESBROUGH	0-1		8361	1	2	3			6	7		4	10		8					5								11		9	
35	Ap	3	Portsmouth	2-1	Allen, Richmond	13724	1	2	3			6	7		4	10		8					5								11		9	
36		5	DERBY COUNTY	0-1		16687	1	2	3			6	7		4	10		8					5								11		9	
37		6	Derby County	0-4		17782	1	2	3		5	6	7		10			8		11			4										9	
38		17	Swansea Town	0-3		10343	1	2	3		5	6	7		10			8		11			4										9	
39		19	Fulham	2-2	Halliwell, Curran	7124	1	2	3		5	6	7		10					11			4						8				9	
40		24	SOUTH SHIELDS	3-1	Myers 2, Halliwell	4901	1	2	3		5	6	7		10			8		11									9					4
41		26	Wolverhampton Wan.	1-7	Curran	7135	1	2	3	4	5	6	7		10			8		11									9					
42	Ma	1	Preston North End	2-4	Halliwell 2	6997			3			6	7		10								5	8		1		11	9					4

Played in game 30: H Wroe (at 7). In game 42: C Dixon (at 2).

	Gale T	Gittins JH	Hodgkinson H	Barnett LH	Baker LH	Baines CE	Curran J	Hine EW	Halliwell IA	Johnson WJ	Newton A	Allen F	Beaumont P	Bedford F	Brook EF	Brown A	Caddick GFR	Eaton F	Fletcher B	Gillatt K	Goodwin J	Johnson AJ	Myers J	Phoenix AE	Richmond J	Sanderson CA	Shaw MV	Sherwin H
Apps	40	40	41	16	30	34	32	18	38	17	15	10	5	9	5	5	9	7	20	4	2	21	3	4	13	9	5	8
Goals						1	4	12	11	2	1	2		2				1	9	1		4	2		5		1	

F.A. Cup

#	Mo	Date	Opponent	Score	Scorers	Att	Gale T	Gittins JH	Hodgkinson H	Barnett LH	Baker LH	Baines CE	Curran J	Hine EW	Halliwell IA	Johnson WJ	Newton A	Allen F	Beaumont P	Bedford F	Brook EF	Brown A	Caddick GFR	Eaton F	Fletcher B	Gillatt K	Goodwin J	Johnson AJ	Myers J	Phoenix AE	Richmond J	Sanderson CA	Shaw MV	Sherwin H
R1	No	28	Northampton Town	1-3	Fletcher	14000	1		3	2	5	6	7	10	4		9								8			11						

		P	W	D	L	F	A	W	D	L	F	A	Pts
1	Sheffield Wed.	42	19	0	2	61	17	8	6	7	27	31	60
2	Derby County	42	17	2	2	57	17	8	5	8	20	25	57
3	Chelsea	42	10	7	4	42	22	9	7	5	34	27	52
4	Wolverhampton Wan.	42	15	4	2	55	15	6	3	12	29	45	49
5	Swansea Town	42	13	6	2	50	16	6	5	10	27	41	49
6	Blackpool	42	12	6	3	41	16	5	5	11	35	53	45
7	Oldham Athletic	42	14	4	3	52	24	4	4	13	22	38	44
8	Port Vale	42	15	3	3	53	18	4	3	14	26	51	44
9	South Shields	42	11	6	4	50	29	7	2	12	24	36	44
10	Middlesbrough	42	14	1	6	56	28	7	1	13	21	40	44
11	Portsmouth	42	12	4	5	48	27	5	6	10	31	47	44
12	Preston North End	42	17	2	2	54	28	1	5	15	17	56	43
13	Hull City	42	11	4	6	40	19	5	5	11	23	42	41
14	Southampton	42	11	2	8	39	25	4	6	11	24	38	38
15	Darlington	42	9	5	7	51	31	5	5	11	21	46	38
16	Bradford City	42	9	5	7	28	26	4	5	12	19	40	36
17	Nottingham Forest	42	11	4	6	38	25	3	4	14	13	48	36
18	BARNSLEY	42	10	7	4	38	22	2	5	14	20	62	36
19	Fulham	42	8	6	7	32	29	3	6	12	14	48	34
20	Clapton Orient	42	8	6	7	30	21	4	3	14	20	44	33
21	Stoke City	42	8	5	8	32	23	4	3	14	22	54	32
22	Stockport County	42	8	7	6	34	28	0	2	19	17	69	25

Season 1925/26
Back row: Caddick, Baker, Gale, Hodgkinson, Gittins, Sherwin, McMullan (Trainer)
Centre row: Curran, Eaton, Tilson, Halliwell, Baines   Front row: Myers, Brook

Season 1926/27
Back row: Commins (Manager) Dixon, Caddick, Hodgkinson, Gale, Baines, Allen, McMullan (Trainer).
Front row: Curran, Clayson, Fletcher, Eaton, Tilson, Brook

1926/27   11th in Division 2

							Gale T	Batty W	Hodgkinson H	Rushton R	Baker LH	Baines CE	Curran J	Halliwell JA	Stark J	Thompson N	Brook EF	Allen F	Caddick GFR	Carrigan J	Clayson WJ	Dixon C	Eaton F	Fletcher B	Gittins JH	Kennedy S	Stott GRB	Tilson SF	Walsh C
1	Aug	28	GRIMSBY TOWN	2-1	Stark, Curran	7004	1	2	3	4	5	6	7	8	9	10	11												
2		30	OLDHAM ATHLETIC	0-1		7213	1	2	3	4	5	6	7	8	9	10	11												
3	Sep	4	Blackpool	1-6	Stark	12673	1	2	3	4	5	6	7	8	9		11				10								
4		11	READING	2-2	Halliwell, Brook	5570	1	2	3	4		6	7	10			11		5		8		9						
5		13	Fulham	0-1		9857	1	2	3	4		6	7	10			11		5		8		9						
6		18	Swansea Town	2-5	Brook, Curran	15006	1	2	3		5	6	7	10			11		4		8		9						
7		25	NOTTM. FOREST	0-2		4829	1				5	6	7				11	4			8	3	10		2			9	
8	Oct	2	Clapton Orient	1-0	Tilson	13337	1		3		5	6	7				11	8			2					9		10	4
9		9	Manchester City	1-1	Kennedy	19430	1		3		5	6	7				11	8			2					9		10	4
10		16	PORT VALE	2-0	Tilson, Brook	5520	1		3		5	6	7				11	8			2					9		10	4
11		23	Middlesbrough	1-5	Curran	12740	1		3		5	6	7				11	8			2					9		10	4
12		30	NOTTS COUNTY	4-4	Kennedy 3, Tilson	4671	1	2			5	6	7				11				3		8			9		10	4
13	Nov	6	Wolverhampton Wan.	1-9	Kennedy	9528		2		10	5	6	7				11			1	3		8			9			4
14		13	HULL CITY	1-2	Curran	4159		2			6		7	4		10	11		5	1	3		8			9			
15		20	South Shields	1-7	Tilson	3754			3		6		7	4		10	11		5	1	2					9		8	
16	Dec	4	Chelsea	2-4	Ferguson (og), Fletcher	21904			3		6		7	4			11		5	1	2			8		9		10	
17		11	BRADFORD CITY	1-0	Tilson	5475	1		3		5	6	7	4			11				2		9	8				10	
18		18	Southampton	1-3	Eaton	8792	1		3			6	7				11	4	5		2		9	8				10	
19		25	Darlington	3-3	Brook 2, Curran	7455	1		3			6	7				11	4	5		2		9	8				10	
20		27	DARLINGTON	3-2	Brook, Tilson, Curran	11166	1		3			6	7				11	4	5		2		9	8				10	
21		28	FULHAM	5-0	Curran 3, Tilson 2	5472	1		3			6	7				11	4	5		2		9	8				10	
22	Jan	1	Oldham Athletic	4-0	Eaton 2, Tilson 2	13242	1		3			6	7				11	4	5		2		9	8				10	
23		15	Grimsby Town	3-1	Curran 2, Eaton	10596	1		3			6	7				11	4	5		2		9	8				10	
24		22	BLACKPOOL	6-1	Curran 3 (1 p),Eaton,Tilson,Brook	7533	1		3			6	7				11	4	5		2		9	8				10	
25	Feb	5	SWANSEA TOWN	1-1	Clayson	8308	1		3			6	7				11	4	5		10	2	9	8					
26		12	Nottingham Forest	1-3	Brook	11298	1		3			6					11	4	5		10	2	9	8			7		
27		19	CLAPTON ORIENT	4-2	Eaton 3, Fletcher	6812	1		3			6	7				11	4	5			2	9	8				10	
28		26	MANCHESTER CITY	1-1	Fletcher	16395	1		3			6	7				11	4	5			2	9	8				10	
29	Mar	5	Port Vale	2-3	Eaton, Maddock (og)	8462	1		3			6	7				11	4	5			2	9	8				10	
30		12	MIDDLESBROUGH	1-1	Curran	23599	1		3			6	7				11	4	5			2	9	8				10	
31		14	PRESTON NORTH EN	3-0	Curran, Fletcher, Eaton	11074	1		3			6	7				11	4	5		10	2	9	8				10	
32		19	Notts County	1-1	Clayson	15327	1		3			6	7				11	4	5		10	2	9	8				10	
33		26	WOLVERHAMPTON W.	4-1	Tilson, Curran, Eaton 2	8337	1	3				6	7				11	4	5			2	9	8				10	
34	Apr	2	Hull City	1-5	Eaton	8671	1	3				6	7				11	4	5			2	9	8				10	
35		6	Reading	2-3	Tilson, Curran	5894	1					6	7	3	9		11	4	5			2	8					10	
36		9	SOUTH SHIELDS	6-1	Eaton 5, Fletcher	2290	1		3			6	7				11	4	5			2	9	8				10	
37		15	Portsmouth	2-1	Baines, Curran	25306			3			6	7				11	4	5	1		2	9	8				10	
38		16	Preston North End	1-2	Eaton	15885			3			6	7				11	4	5	1	8	2	9					10	
39		18	PORTSMOUTH	2-0	Eaton 2	15948	1		3			6	7				11	4	5			2	9	8				10	
40		23	CHELSEA	3-0	Brook, Curran, Fletcher	9641	1		3			6	7				11	4	5			2	9	8				10	
41		30	Bradford City	1-1	Curran	7585	1		3			6	7				11	4	5			2	9	8				10	
42	May	7	SOUTHAMPTON	5-1	Fletcher 3, Brook 2	7592	1		3			6					11	4	5			2	9	8				7	10	

	Gale T	Batty W	Hodgkinson H	Rushton R	Baker LH	Baines CE	Curran J	Halliwell JA	Stark J	Thompson N	Brook EF	Allen F	Caddick GFR	Carrigan J	Clayson WJ	Dixon C	Eaton F	Fletcher B	Gittins JH	Kennedy S	Stott GRB	Tilson SF	Walsh C
Apps	36	11	35	6	15	39	40	11	4	4	42	30	31	6	10	36	33	25	1	9	2	30	6
Goals					1	21	1	2			11				2		21	9		5		13	

Two own goals

F.A. Cup

							Gale T		Hodgkinson H			Baines CE	Curran J				Brook EF	Allen F	Caddick GFR			Dixon C	Eaton F	Fletcher B				Tilson SF	
R3	Jan	8	CREWE ALEXANDRA	6-1	Fletcher 3, Tilson, Eaton, Curran	18598	1		3			6	7				11	4	5			2	9	8				10	
R4		29	Swansea Town	1-3	Eaton	27481	1		3			6	7				11	4	5			2	9	8				10	

		P	W	D	L	F	A	W	D	L	F	A	Pts
1	Middlesbrough	42	18	2	1	78	23	9	6	6	44	37	62
2	Portsmouth	42	14	4	3	58	17	9	4	8	29	32	54
3	Manchester City	42	15	3	3	65	23	7	7	7	43	38	54
4	Chelsea	42	13	7	1	40	17	7	5	9	22	35	52
5	Nottingham Forest	42	14	6	1	57	23	4	8	9	23	32	50
6	Preston North End	42	14	4	3	54	29	6	5	10	20	43	49
7	Hull City	42	13	4	4	43	19	7	3	11	20	33	47
8	Port Vale	42	11	6	4	50	26	5	7	9	38	52	45
9	Blackpool	42	13	5	3	65	26	5	3	13	30	54	44
10	Oldham Athletic	42	12	3	6	50	37	7	3	11	24	47	44
11	BARNSLEY	42	13	5	3	56	23	4	4	13	32	64	43
12	Swansea Town	42	13	5	3	44	21	3	6	12	24	51	43
13	Southampton	42	9	8	4	35	22	6	4	11	25	40	42
14	Reading	42	14	1	6	47	20	2	7	12	17	52	40
15	Wolverhampton Wan.	42	10	4	7	54	30	4	3	14	19	45	35
16	Notts County	42	11	4	6	45	24	4	1	16	25	72	35
17	Grimsby Town	42	6	7	8	39	39	5	5	11	35	52	34
18	Fulham	42	11	4	6	39	31	2	4	15	19	61	34
19	South Shields	42	10	8	3	49	25	1	3	17	22	71	33
20	Clapton Orient	42	9	3	9	37	35	3	4	14	23	61	31
21	Darlington	42	10	3	8	53	42	2	3	16	26	56	30
22	Bradford City	42	6	4	11	30	28	1	5	15	20	60	23

1927/28   13th in Division 2

No	Date	Opponent	Score	Scorers	Att	Gale T	Dixon C	Hodgkinson H	Allen F	Caddick GFR	Baines CE	Curran J	Fletcher B	Eaton F	Tilson SF	Brook EF	Ashton E	Baker LH	Batty W	Stark JW	Jones WD	Godderidge AE	McDonagh P	Morton R	Proudfoot J	Richards A	Scott JW	Wilshaw J
1	Aug 27	HULL CITY	1-1	Eaton	10830	1	2	3	4	5	6	7	8	9	10	11												
2	29	Leeds United	2-2	Tilson, Fletcher (pen)	21219	1	2	3	4	5	6	7	8	9	10	11												
3	Sep 3	Preston North End	2-1	Fletcher (pen), Curran	20431	1	2	3	4	5	6	7	8	9	10	11												
4	10	SWANSEA TOWN	3-3	Eaton 2, Curran	13643	1	2	3	4	5	6	7	8	9	10	11												
5	17	Fulham	1-3	Tilson	16924	1	2	3	4	5	6	7	8	9	10	11												
6	24	CLAPTON ORIENT	4-2	McDonagh 2, Fletcher, Curran	11951	1	2	3	4	5	6	7	8		9	11							10					
7	26	LEEDS UNITED	2-1	Tilson, Brook	13038	1	2	3	4	5	6	7	8		9	11							10					
8	Oct 1	WOLVERHAMPTON W.	2-2	Fletcher, Brook	9082	1	2	3	4	5	6	7	8		9	11							10					
9	8	Port Vale	1-2	Fletcher (pen)	10010	1	2	3	4	5	6	7	8		9	11							10					
10	15	SOUTH SHIELDS	0-0		10611	1	2	3	4	5	6	7	8		9	11							10					
11	22	Stoke City	0-0		8323	1	2	3	4	5	6	7	8		9	11							10					
12	29	BRISTOL CITY	2-3	Fletcher (pen), Baines	10079	1	2	3	4	5	6	7	8		9	11							10					
13	Nov 5	West Bromwich Albion	1-1	Fletcher	18129	1	2	3		8	5	6	7	10	9	11			4									
14	12	SOUTHAMPTON	0-1		7621	1	2	3		8	5	6	7	10	9	11			4									
15	19	Notts County	0-9		9382	1	2			8	6	7		10	9	11		5	3		4							
16	26	READING	2-0	Eaton, Tilson	7181	1	2	3	4	5	6	7		9	10	11					8							
17	Dec 3	Grimsby Town	1-3	Brook	10421	1	2	3	4	5	6	7		9	10	11					8							
18	10	OLDHAM ATHLETIC	0-1		4944	1	2	3	4	5	6	7	8		10	11				9								
19	17	Blackpool	3-1	Tilson 2, Curran	7629	1	2	3		5	6	7		9	10	11					4				8			
20	24	CHELSEA	3-1	Tilson, Curran (pen), Proudfoot	5634	1	2	3		5	6	7		9	10	11					4				8			
21	26	MANCHESTER CITY	0-3		17252	1	2			5		7		9	10	11		6	3		4				8			
22	31	Hull City	1-2	Eaton	9569	1	2			5		7		9	10	11		6			4				8		3	
23	Jan 2	Manchester City	3-7	Curran 2 (1 pen), Tilson	38226	1	2			5		7		9	10	11		6			4				8		3	
24	7	PRESTON NORTH END	2-1	Curran, Brook	7967		2		4	5	6	7		9	10	11						1			8		3	
25	21	Swansea Town	0-3		6420		2		4	5	6	7		9	10	11		3				1			8			
26	28	FULHAM	8-4	Eaton 4, Curran 2, Brook 2	4563		2	3	4	5	6	7	8	9	10	11						1						
27	Feb 4	Clapton Orient	0-2		8985		2	3	4	5	6	7	8	9	10	11						1						
28	11	Wolverhampton Wan.	1-2	Tilson	7151		2	3	4	5	6	7	8	9	10	11						1						
29	20	PORT VALE	4-2	Tilson, Eaton, Brook, Curran	5423		2	3	4	5	6	7		9	10	11						1			8			
30	25	South Shields	0-0		5513		2	3	4	5	6	7		9	10	11						1						8
31	Mar 10	Bristol City	0-2		12662		2	3		5	6	7		9	10	11		4	8			1						
32	17	WEST BROMWICH ALB.	2-4	Fletcher 2	8144		2	3	4		6	7	8	10				5				1				11		9
33	19	STOKE CITY	3-1	Scott 2, Eaton	4658		2	3		5	6	7	8	9				4				1			10		11	
34	24	Southampton	1-6	Fletcher	10528		2	3		5	6	7	8	9				4				1			10		11	
35	31	NOTTS COUNTY	0-0		5619		2	3		5	6	7	8	9				4				1			10		11	
36	Apr 7	Reading	1-1	Curran	10659		2	3		5	6	7		9				4			8	1			10		11	
37	9	Nottingham Forest	1-1	Morton	11640		2	3			6		8	9			7	5			4	1		11	10			
38	10	NOTTM. FOREST	2-1	Curran, Eaton	7688		2	3	4		6	7	8	9				5				1	10			11		
39	14	GRIMSBY TOWN	1-4	Fletcher	4516		2	3	4		6	7	8	9				5				1			10	11		
40	21	Oldham Athletic	1-0	Baker	7036	1	2	3		5		7	8	9				6			4				10		11	
41	28	BLACKPOOL	2-1	Eaton, Scott (pen)	4949	1	2	3		5	6	7	8	9							4				10		11	
42	May 5	Chelsea	2-1	Eaton 2	13707	1	2	3		5	6	7	8	9							4				10		11	
		Apps				26	42	36	28	37	37	40	29	31	31	31	2	14	4	4	12	16	9	1	17	3	10	2
		Goals									1	13	11	15	10	7		1					2	1	1		3	

F.A. Cup

Rd	Date	Opponent	Score		Att	Gale T	Dixon C	Hodgkinson H	Allen F	Caddick GFR	Baines CE	Curran J	Fletcher B	Eaton F	Tilson SF	Brook EF	Ashton E	Baker LH	Batty W	Stark JW	Jones WD	Godderidge AE	McDonagh P	Morton R	Proudfoot J	Richards A	Scott JW	Wilshaw J
R3	Jan 14	Port Vale	0-3		13162		2	8		5	6	7		9	10	11					4	1					3	

	P	W	D	L	F	A	W	D	L	F	A	Pts
1 Manchester City	42	18	2	1	70	27	7	7	7	30	32	59
2 Leeds United	42	16	2	3	63	15	9	5	7	35	34	57
3 Chelsea	42	15	2	4	46	15	8	6	7	29	30	54
4 Preston North End	42	15	3	3	62	24	7	6	8	38	42	53
5 Stoke City	42	14	5	2	44	17	8	3	10	34	42	52
6 Swansea Town	42	13	6	2	46	17	5	6	10	29	46	48
7 Oldham Athletic	42	15	3	3	55	18	4	5	12	20	33	46
8 West Bromwich Alb.	42	10	7	4	50	28	7	5	9	40	42	46
9 Port Vale	42	11	6	4	45	20	7	2	12	23	37	44
10 Nottingham Forest	42	10	6	5	54	37	5	4	12	29	47	40
11 Grimsby Town	42	8	6	7	41	41	6	6	9	28	42	40
12 Bristol City	42	11	5	5	42	18	4	4	13	34	61	39
13 BARNSLEY	42	10	5	6	43	36	4	6	11	22	49	39
14 Hull City	42	9	8	4	25	19	3	7	11	16	35	39
15 Notts County	42	10	4	7	47	26	3	8	10	21	48	38
16 Wolverhampton Wan.	42	11	5	5	43	31	2	5	14	20	60	36
17 Southampton	42	11	3	7	54	40	3	4	14	14	37	35
18 Reading	42	9	8	4	32	22	2	5	14	21	53	35
19 Blackpool	42	11	3	7	55	43	2	5	14	28	58	34
20 Clapton Orient	42	9	5	7	32	25	2	5	14	23	60	34
21 Fulham	42	12	7	2	46	22	1	0	20	20	67	33
22 South Shields	42	5	5	11	30	41	2	4	15	26	70	23

Season 1927/28
Back row: Allen, Dixon, Godderidge, Hodgkinson, Baines
Front row: Curran, Fletcher, Eaton, Tilson, Brook, Caddick

Season 1928/29
Back row: Richards, Smith, Batty, Gale, Dixon, Baines, McMullan (Trainer)
Front row: Ashton, Fletcher, Eaton, Proudfoot, Harron, Caddick

1928/29 16th in Division 2

	Date		Opponent	Score	Scorers	Att.	Gale T	Dixon C	Hodgkinson H	Baker LH	Caddick GFR	Atkinson JW	Ashton E	Fletcher B	Eaton F	Dowdall C	Millar JM	Baines CE	Batty W	Breedon JN	Curran J	Harron J	Henderson GB	Mears F	Proudfoot J	Richards A	Smith JW	Storer JA	Gibbs GWH
1	Aug	25	BRADFORD PARK AVE.	1-2	Millar	11072	1	2	3	4	5	6	7	8	9	10	11												
2		27	Grimsby Town	1-2	Ashton	12967	1	2	3	4	5	6	7		8		11							9	10				
3	Sep	1	Swansea Town	1-2	Ashton	12005	1	2	3	4	5	6	7		8		11							9	10				
4		8	BLACKPOOL	3-1	Mears 2, Eaton	7312	1	2	3		5	6	7		8		11							9	10		4		
5		15	Chelsea	0-1		34793	1	2	3		5	6	7		8		11							9	10		4		
6		22	OLDHAM ATHLETIC	2-1	Eaton, Fletcher	7421	1	2	3		5		7	8	9		11	6						10			4		
7		29	BRISTOL CITY	4-2	Eaton, Mears, Proudfoot, Ashton	6996	1	3			5		7		8		11	6	2					9	10		4		
8	Oct	6	Nottingham Forest	3-1	Batty, Millar, Mears	14785	1	3			5		7		8		11	6	2					9	10		4		
9		13	WEST BROMWICH ALB.	2-0	Proudfoot, Ashton	11072	1	3			5		7		8		11	6	2					9	10		4		
10		20	Southampton	2-1	Eaton, Millar	15175	1	3			5		7		8		11	6	2					9	10		4		
11		27	WOLVERHAMPTON W.	2-2	Mears, Millar	8444	1	3			5		7		8		11	6	2					9	10		4		
12	Nov	3	Notts County	1-4	Ashton	16917	1	3			5		7		8		11	6	2					9	10		4		
13		10	MIDDLESBROUGH	2-2	Eaton, Millar	9635	1	3			5		7		8		11	6	2					9	10		4		
14		17	Port Vale	0-3		7417	1	3			5		7		8		11	6	2					9	10		4		
15		24	HULL CITY	2-2	Eaton (pen), Mears	4693	1	3			5		7		8		11	6	2					9	10		4		
16	Dec	1	Tottenham Hotspur	0-2		18951	1	3				5	7		9	8	11	6	2						10		4		
17		8	READING	2-3	Proudfoot 2	5833	1	3			5		7		9	8	11	6	2						10		4		
18		15	Preston North End	1-2	Mears	12413	1	3				5	7		8			6	2					9	10		4		11
19		22	MILLWALL	2-2	Atkinson, Harron	5664	1	3				5	7		8			6	2			11		9	10		4		
20		25	Clapton Orient	1-3	Batty (pen)	9877	1	3				5	7		8			6	2			11		9	10		4		
21		26	CLAPTON ORIENT	2-0	Batty (pen), Harron	9910	1	3				5	7		8			6	2			11		9	10		4		
22		29	Bradford Park Avenue	1-2	Mears	17706	1	3			5		7		8			6	2			11		9	10		4		
23	Jan	1	GRIMSBY TOWN	0-2		9049	1	3			5		7		8			6	2			11		9	10		4		
24		5	SWANSEA TOWN	2-1	Eaton 2	3848	1	3		6	5	4	7	8	9				2			11			10				
25		19	Blackpool	1-0	Ashton	8937	1	3		5		4	7	8	9			6	2			11			10				
26		30	CHELSEA	0-1		7886	1	3			5	4	7	8	9			6	2			11			10				
27	Feb	2	Oldham Athletic	0-1		10803	1	3			5	4		8	9			6	2			11			10			7	
28		9	Bristol City	1-3	Proudfoot	11035	1		3	5		4	7	8				6	2			11		9	10				
29		16	NOTTM. FOREST	1-2	Batty (pen)	3688	1	3			5	4	7		8			6	2			11		9	10				
30		23	West Bromwich Albion	2-6	Eaton, Batty (pen)	13019	1	3			5		7	8	9			6	2			11			10		4		
31	Mar	2	SOUTHAMPTON	4-1	Eaton, Ashton 2, Harron	5223	1	3			5	4	7		9			6				11		10	8	2			
32		9	Wolverhampton Wan.	1-3	Curran	11289	1	3				4	11		9			6			7		5	10	8	2			
33		16	NOTTS COUNTY	2-0	Eaton, Curran	7518	1	2	3			4	11		9			6			7		5	10	8				
34		23	Middlesbrough	0-1		17050	1	2	3			4	11		9			6			7		5	10	8				
35		29	STOKE CITY	4-2	Ashton, Eaton, Proudfoot, Dixon	11793	1	2	3			4	10		9			6			7	11	5		8				
36		30	PORT VALE	6-0	Proudfoot 2, Curran 2, Dixon, Eato	9615	1	2	3			4	10		9			6			7	11	5		8				
37	Apr	1	Stoke City	0-0		13213	1	2	3			4	10		9			6			7	11	5		8				
38		6	Hull City	0-0		6977	1	2	3			4	10		9			6			7	11	5		8				
39		13	TOTTENHAM HOTSPUR	4-1	Ashton, Eaton 2, Curran	8449	1	2				4	11		9			6			7		5	10	8	3			
40		20	Reading	0-1		8404		2	3			4	11		9			6		1	7		5	10	8				
41		27	PRESTON NORTH END	4-1	Ashton, Proudfoot, Curran, Mears	9655	1	2	3			4	11		9			6			7		5	10	8				
42	May	4	Millwall	2-0	Curran, Mears	10952	1	2	3			4	11		9			6			7		5	10	8				
						Apps	41	41	16	6	24	28	41	8	41	3	17	36	24	1	11	17	11	30	40	3	21	1	1
						Goals		2				1	11	1	15		5		5		7	3		10	9				

F.A. Cup

	Date		Opponent	Score	Scorers	Att.	Gale T	Dixon C	Hodgkinson H	Baker LH	Caddick GFR	Atkinson JW	Ashton E	Fletcher B	Eaton F	Dowdall C	Millar JM	Baines CE	Batty W	Breedon JN	Curran J	Harron J	Henderson GB	Mears F	Proudfoot J	Richards A	Smith JW	Storer JA	Gibbs GWH
R3	Jan	12	Blackburn Rovers	0-1		31697	1	3			5	4	7	8	9		11	6	2						10				

		P	W	D	L	F	A	W	D	L	F	A	Pts
1	Middlesbrough	42	14	4	3	54	22	8	7	6	38	35	55
2	Grimsby Town	42	16	2	3	49	24	8	3	10	33	37	53
3	Bradford Park Ave.	42	18	2	1	62	22	4	2	15	26	48	48
4	Southampton	42	12	6	3	48	22	5	8	8	26	38	48
5	Notts County	42	13	4	4	51	24	6	5	10	27	41	47
6	Stoke City	42	12	7	2	46	16	5	5	11	28	35	46
7	West Bromwich Alb.	42	13	4	4	50	25	6	4	11	30	54	46
8	Blackpool	42	13	4	4	49	18	6	3	12	43	58	45
9	Chelsea	42	10	6	5	40	30	7	4	10	24	35	44
10	Tottenham Hotspur	42	16	3	2	50	26	1	6	14	25	55	43
11	Nottingham Forest	42	8	6	7	34	33	7	6	8	37	37	42
12	Hull City	42	8	8	5	38	24	5	6	10	20	39	40
13	Preston North End	42	12	6	3	58	27	3	3	15	20	52	39
14	Millwall	42	10	4	7	43	35	6	3	12	28	51	39
15	Reading	42	12	3	6	48	30	3	6	12	15	56	39
16	BARNSLEY	42	12	4	5	51	28	4	2	15	18	38	38
17	Wolverhampton Wan.	42	9	6	6	41	31	6	1	14	36	50	37
18	Oldham Athletic	42	15	2	4	37	24	1	3	17	17	51	37
19	Swansea Town	42	12	3	6	46	26	1	7	13	16	49	36
20	Bristol City	42	11	6	4	37	25	2	4	15	21	47	36
21	Port Vale	42	14	1	6	53	25	1	3	17	18	61	34
22	Clapton Orient	42	10	4	7	29	25	2	4	15	16	47	32

1929/30 — 17th in Division 2

#	Date	Opponent	Score	Scorers	Att	Gale T	Dixon C	Hodgkinson H	Atkinson JW	Henderson GB	Baines CE	Ashton E	Eaton F	Pigg A	Mears F	Harron J	Breedon JN	Caddick GFR	Curran J	Gibbs GWH	Harvey WA	Kerry E	Morris H	Ogle R	Proudfoot I	Richards A	Smith JW	Storer IA	Wallbanks John
1	Aug 31	SOUTHAMPTON	3-1	Ashton, Pigg, Henderson	7441	1	2	3	4	5	6	7	8	9	10	11													
2	Sep 7	Tottenham Hotspur	1-2	Mears	26056	1	2	3	4	5	6	7	8	9	10	11													
3	11	Chelsea	0-2		11353	1	2	3	4	5	6	11	8	9	10				7										
4	14	WEST BROMWICH ALB.	2-2	Ashton, Dixon (pen)	9705	1	2	3	4	5	6	11	9		10				7						8				
5	16	Oldham Athletic	2-3	Mears, Kerry	16635		2	3	4		6			9	11		1	5	7			10			8				
6	21	Bradford Park Avenue	4-4	Harron, Ashton, Proudfoot 2	14516	1	2	3	4	5	6	7	9		10	11									8				
7	28	SWANSEA TOWN	1-0	Ashton	7961	1	2	3	4	5	6	7	9		10	11									8				
8	Oct 5	BLACKPOOL	2-4	Henderson, Mears	8353	1	2	3		5	6	11	8		10			4	7				9						
9	12	Bury	1-2	Curran	10557	1	2	3	4	5	6	11			10				7						8				9
10	19	Cardiff City	0-1		12058	1	2	3	4	5	6	7	8	9		11									10				
11	26	PRESTON NORTH END	0-0		6076	1	2	3	4	5	6	7	8	9		11									10				
12	Nov 2	Bristol City	1-2	Wallbanks	8531	1	2	3	6	5			8			11						10					4	7	9
13	9	NOTTS COUNTY	2-2	Wallbanks 2	5116	1	2	3	6	5			8			11						10					4	7	9
14	16	Reading	0-1		4624	1	2	3	6	5		11	8									10					4	7	9
15	23	CHARLTON ATHLETIC	2-0	Wallbanks, Ashton	3142	1	2	3	6	5		11	8									10					4	7	9
16	30	Hull City	0-2		5706	1	2	3	6	5		11	8									10					4	7	9
17	Dec 7	STOKE CITY	3-1	Dixon (pen), Storer 2	2303	1	2	3	6	5		11	9							8		10					4	7	
18	14	Wolverhampton Wan.	0-3		13055	1	2	3	6	5		11	9							8		10					4	7	
19	21	BRADFORD CITY	2-1	Eaton, Storer	4791	1	2	3	6	5		11	9		10					8							4	7	
20	25	Nottingham Forest	0-4		16301	1	2	3		5	6	11	9		10					8							4	7	
21	26	NOTTM. FOREST	1-1	Eaton	9852	1	2	3	4		6	11	9					5		8		10						7	
22	28	Southampton	0-4		7832	1	2	3	4		6	11						5		8		10						7	9
23	Jan 1	CHELSEA	1-1	Storer	8773	1	2	3		5	6	11	8									10					4	7	9
24	4	TOTTENHAM HOTSPUR	2-0	Wallbanks, Ashton	5870	1	2	3	6	5		11	8									10					4	7	9
25	18	West Bromwich Albion	2-4	Wallbanks, Storer	11067	1	2		6	5		11	8									10		3			4	7	9
26	Feb 1	Swansea Town	2-0	Wallbanks, Ashton	9985	1	2	3	6	5		11	8									10					4	7	9
27	5	BRADFORD PARK AVE.	1-1	Atkinson	5932	1	2	3	6	5		11	8									10					4	7	9
28	8	Blackpool	1-2	Eaton (pen)	11785	1	2	3	6	5		11	8					7							10		4		9
29	15	BURY	2-1	Curran, Wallbanks	6032	1	2	3		5	6	11	8					7							10		4		9
30	22	CARDIFF CITY	2-2	Wallbanks, Harvey	7345	1	2	3		5	6	7	8						11		10						4		9
31	Mar 1	Preston North End	1-3	Wallbanks	9901	1		3	4	5	6	7	8						11		10					2			9
32	8	BRISTOL CITY	3-1	Harvey, Henderson 2	6656	1		3	4	5	6	11	8					7			10					2			9
33	15	Notts County	0-3		6006	1		3	4	5	6	11	8					7			10					2			9
34	22	READING	1-0	Wallbanks	5569	1		3	6	5		11	8					7			10					2	4		9
35	29	Charlton Athletic	0-2		11243	1			6	5		11	8					7			10			3		2	4		9
36	Apr 5	HULL CITY	3-0	Gibbs, Eaton (2 pens)	6243	1				5	6	11	8							7				3	10	2	4		9
37	12	Stoke City	0-3		9058	1				5	6	11	8							7				3	10	2	4		9
38	18	Millwall	1-2	Gibbs	18913				6	5		11	8				1			7				3	10	2	4		9
39	19	WOLVERHAMPTON W.	3-1	Eaton, Gibbs, Wallbanks	3642				6	5		11	8				1	5		7				3	10	2	4		9
40	21	MILLWALL	1-2	Eaton (pen)	9543				6			11	8				1	5		7				3	10	2	4		9
41	26	Bradford City	1-0	Curran	17197	1	2			5			8					6	7	11				3	10		4		9
42	May 3	OLDHAM ATHLETIC	2-1	Curran, Gibbs	15001	1	2			5			8					6	7	11				3	10		4		9
		Apps				38	32	33	33	36	23	37	38	5	12	11	4	8	9	11	10	17	1	8	16	11	26	16	27
		Goals					2		1	4		7	7	1	3	1			4	4	2	1			2			5	12

F.A. Cup

Rd	Date	Opponent	Score	Att	Gale T	Dixon C	Hodgkinson H	Atkinson JW	Henderson GB	Baines CE	Ashton E	Eaton F	Pigg A	Mears F	Harron J	Breedon JN	Caddick GFR	Curran J	Gibbs GWH	Harvey WA	Kerry E	Morris H	Ogle R	Proudfoot I	Richards A	Smith JW	Storer IA	Wallbanks John
R3	Jan 11	BRADFORD PARK AVE.	0-1	19700	1	2	3	6	5		11	8														4	7	9

Played at 10: B Fletcher

		P	W	D	L	F	A	W	D	L	F	A	Pts
1	Blackpool	42	17	1	3	63	22	10	3	8	35	45	58
2	Chelsea	42	17	3	1	49	14	5	8	8	25	32	55
3	Oldham Athletic	42	14	5	2	60	21	7	6	8	30	30	53
4	Bradford Park Ave.	42	14	5	2	65	28	5	7	9	26	42	50
5	Bury	42	14	2	5	45	27	8	3	10	33	40	49
6	West Bromwich Alb.	42	16	1	4	73	31	5	4	12	32	42	47
7	Southampton	42	14	6	1	46	22	3	5	13	31	54	45
8	Cardiff City	42	14	4	3	41	16	4	4	13	20	43	44
9	Wolverhampton Wan.	42	14	3	4	53	24	2	6	13	24	55	41
10	Nottingham Forest	42	9	6	6	36	28	4	9	8	19	41	41
11	Stoke City	42	12	4	5	41	20	4	4	13	33	52	40
12	Tottenham Hotspur	42	11	8	2	43	24	4	1	16	16	37	39
13	Charlton Athletic	42	10	6	5	39	23	4	5	12	20	40	39
14	Millwall	42	10	7	4	36	26	2	8	11	21	47	39
15	Swansea Town	42	11	5	5	42	23	3	4	14	15	38	37
16	Preston North End	42	7	7	7	42	36	6	4	11	23	44	37
17	BARNSLEY	42	12	7	2	39	22	2	1	18	17	49	36
18	Bradford City	42	7	7	7	33	30	5	5	11	27	47	36
19	Reading	42	10	7	4	31	20	2	4	15	23	47	35
20	Bristol City	42	11	4	6	36	30	2	5	14	25	53	35
21	Hull City	42	11	7	3	30	24	3	4	14	21	54	35
22	Notts County	42	8	7	6	33	26	1	8	12	21	44	33

Season 1929/30
Back row: Fletcher (Manager) Smith, Dixon, Gale, Hodgkinson, Atkinson, McMullan (Trainer)
Front row: Storer, Harvey, Eaton, Kerry, Ashton, Henderson

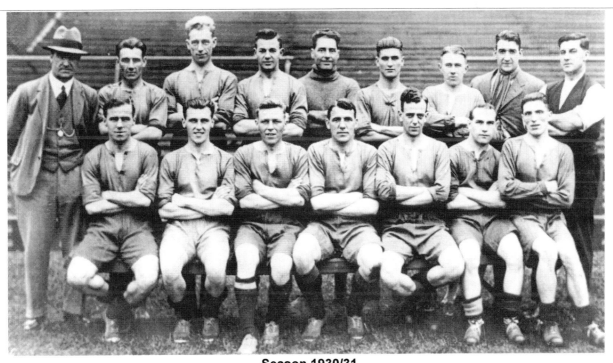

Season 1930/31
Back row: Fletcher (Manager) Dixon, Caddick, Smith, Gale, Stanyon, Storer, Ogle, Cooper (Trainer)
Front row: Curran, Proudfoot, Harston, Henderson, Kerry, Gibbs, Richards

1930/31   19th in Division 2

No		Date	Opponent	Score	Scorers	Att	Gale T	Dixon C	Ogle R	Smith JW	Henderson GB	Caddick GFR	Curran J	Proudfoot J	Harston E	Kerry E	Ashton E	Baines CE	Breedon JN	Chivers FC	Crompton L	Davies SC	Gibbs GWH	Harvey WA	Lampard AJ	Murfin C	Patterson MT	Richards A	Ridyard A	Storer JA	Wallbanks John	Wallbanks Jas
1	Aug	30	Port Vale	2-5	Ashton, Harston	9853	1	2	3	4	5	6	7	8	9	10	11															
2	Sep	1	SWANSEA TOWN	1-0	Curran	6721	1	2	3	4	5	6	7	8	9	10	11															
3		6	BRADFORD CITY	2-1	Harston, Proudfoot	8177	1	2	3	4	5	6	7	8	9	10	11															
4		10	Plymouth Argyle	0-4		18560	1	2		4	5	6	7		9		11					8		10				3				
5		13	Charlton Athletic	1-1	Harston	4642	1	2		4	5	6	7	8	9	10								11				3				
6		20	OLDHAM ATHLETIC	1-2	Kerry	8300	1	2		4	5	6	7	8	9	10								11				3				
7		27	BRISTOL CITY	1-0	Curran	6709	1	2		4	5	6	7	8	9	10								11				3				
8	Oct	4	Cardiff City	0-2		9884	1	2		4	5	6	7	8		10								11				3		9		
9		11	EVERTON	1-1	Curran	16039	1	2		4	5		7	8		10		6						11				3		9		
10		18	Stoke City	0-0		10356	1	2		4	5		7	8		10		6		9				11				3				
11		25	MILLWALL	2-3	Kerry, Dixon (pen)	7105	1	2		4	5		7	8		10		6		9				11				3				
12	Nov	1	Preston North End	1-1	Harvey	12726		2		4	5		7		9	10			1				8	11				3				6
13		8	BURNLEY	0-1		9427		2		4	5		7		9	10			1				8	11				3				6
14		15	Wolverhampton Wan.	0-2		9354		2		4	5			10		9	7		1				8	11				3				6
15		22	READING	3-2	Kerry, John Wallbanks, Henderson	4712	1	2		4	5	6	7			10	11						8					3			9	
16		29	Southampton	0-4		11613	1	2		4	5	6	7			10	11						8					3			9	
17	Dec	6	BRADFORD PARK AVE.	1-0	Dixon (pen)	8177	1	2		4	5	6	7			10							8	11				3	9			
18		13	Nottingham Forest	3-3	Harvey 2, Ridyard	7497	1	2		4	5	6	7			10							8	11				3	9			
19		20	TOTTENHAM HOTSPUR	0-1		7294	1	2		4	5	6	7			10							8	11				3	9			
20		25	WEST BROMWICH ALB.	0-0		10217	1	2		4	5	6	7	8	9								11	10				3				
21		26	West Bromwich Albion	0-5		22734	1	2		4	5	6			9								11	10			8	3	7			
22		27	PORT VALE	5-2	Storer, Harvey, Ridyard, Proudfoot 2	6469	1	2		4		6		8									11	10				3	5	7	9	
23	Jan	1	PLYMOUTH ARGYLE	0-4		8438	1	2		4		6		8									11	10				3	5	7	9	
24		3	Bradford City	0-1		13392	1	2		4		6		8									11	10				3		7	9	6
25		17	CHARLTON ATHLETIC	5-0	Harvey, Curran 2, John Wallbanks, Smith	4950		2		4	5	6	7	8							1		11	10				3			9	
26		26	Oldham Athletic	0-0		6706		2		4	5	6		8							1		11	10				3		7	9	
27		31	Bristol City	1-2	John Wallbanks	6222		2		4	5	6	7	8							1		11	10				3			9	
28	Feb	7	CARDIFF CITY	4-0	Harvey, John Wallbanks, Curran 2	5399		2		4	5	6	7	8							1		11	10				3			9	
29		18	Everton	2-5	Proudfoot 2	19042		2		4	5			8			7				1		11	10				3			9	6
30		21	STOKE CITY	4-2	John Wallbanks 2, Harvey, Gibbs	4526		2		4	5			8			7				1		11	10				3			9	6
31		28	Millwall	1-4	Harvey	12515		2		4	5			8			7				1		11	10				3			9	6
32	Mar	7	PRESTON NORTH END	1-1	Proudfoot	3657		2		4	5	6	7	8							1		11	10				3			9	
33		14	Burnley	2-2	Curran, Harvey	7877		2		4	5	6	7	8							1		11	10				3			9	
34		21	WOLVERHAMPTON W.	3-0	John Wallbanks 2, Ashton	5198		2		4	5	6	7	8			10				1			11				3			9	
35		28	Reading	1-6	Dixon (pen)	7320		2		4	5	6	7	8			10				1			11				3			9	
36	Apr	3	Bury	1-3	Harston	8195		2			5	6	7	8	9						1			11			10	3				4
37		4	SOUTHAMPTON	3-1	John Wallbanks 2, Curran	5307		2		4	5	6	7	8							1			11			10	3			9	
38		6	BURY	2-1	Proudfoot, Curran	6684		2		4	5	6	7	8							1			11			10	3			9	
39		11	Bradford Park Avenue	0-1		9124		2			5	6		8			7				1				11		10	3			9	4
40		18	NOTTM. FOREST	3-1	John Wallbanks, Proudfoot, Barrington (og)	3672		2		4	5	6	7	8		10	11				1							3			9	
41		25	Tottenham Hotspur	2-4	Henderson, Ashton	20762		2		4	5	6	7	8		10	11				1							3			9	
42	May	2	Swansea Town	0-1		5752		2		4	5	6	7	8									11	10		1		3			9	
			Apps				21	42	3	37	36	39	32	33	12	18	21	3	3	5	17	1	25	25	1	1	5	39	5	5	24	9
			Goals					3			1	2	10	8	4	3	3						1	9					2	1	11	

One own goal

F.A. Cup

Round		Date	Opponent	Score	Scorers	Att	Gale T	Dixon C	Smith JW	Henderson GB	Caddick GFR	Curran J	Proudfoot J	Ashton E	Crompton L	Gibbs GWH	Harvey WA	Richards A	Wallbanks John
R3	Jan	10	BRISTOL CITY	4-1	Proudfoot, Gibbs, Curran, Harvey	12903	1	2	4	5	6	7	8			11	10	3	9
R4		24	SHEFFIELD WEDNESDAY	2-1	Harvey, Gibbs	24032		2	4	5	6	7	8		1	11	10	3	9
R5	Feb	14	WOLVERHAMPTON WAN.	1-3	Henderson	33385		2	4	5	6		8	7	1	11	10	3	9

		P	W	D	L	F	A	W	D	L	F	A	Pts
1	Everton	42	18	1	2	76	31	10	4	7	45	35	61
2	West Bromwich Alb.	42	14	3	4	40	16	8	7	6	43	33	54
3	Tottenham Hotspur	42	15	5	1	64	20	7	2	12	24	35	51
4	Wolverhampton Wan.	42	15	2	4	56	25	6	3	12	28	42	47
5	Port Vale	42	15	3	3	39	16	6	2	13	28	45	47
6	Bradford Park Ave.	42	15	4	2	71	24	3	6	12	26	42	46
7	Preston North End	42	12	5	4	55	31	5	6	10	28	33	45
8	Burnley	42	13	5	3	55	30	4	6	11	26	47	45
9	Southampton	42	13	4	4	46	22	6	2	13	28	40	44
10	Bradford City	42	12	5	4	39	26	5	5	11	22	37	44
11	Stoke City	42	11	6	4	34	17	6	4	11	30	54	44
12	Oldham Athletic	42	13	5	3	45	28	3	5	13	16	44	42
13	Bury	42	14	3	4	44	20	5	0	16	31	62	41
14	Millwall	42	12	4	5	47	25	4	3	14	24	55	39
15	Charlton Athletic	42	11	4	6	35	33	4	5	12	24	53	39
16	Bristol City	42	11	5	5	29	23	4	3	14	25	59	38
17	Nottingham Forest	42	12	6	3	54	35	2	3	16	26	50	37
18	Plymouth Argyle	42	10	3	8	47	33	4	5	12	29	51	36
19	BARNSLEY	42	13	3	5	42	38	0	6	15	17	56	35
20	Swansea Town	42	11	5	5	40	29	1	5	15	11	45	34
21	Reading	42	11	2	8	47	33	1	4	16	25	63	30
22	Cardiff City	42	7	6	8	32	31	1	3	17	15	56	25

1931/32 — 21st in Division 2

#		Date	Match	Score	Scorers	Att	Higgs FJ	Dixon C	Richards A	Smith JW	Henderson GB	Caddick GFR	Curran J	Proudfoot J	Wallbanks John	Chivers FC	Ashton E	Capstick W	Green F	Happs R	Harvey WA	Hill J	Kerry E	Lampard AJ	Lax G	Maskill T	Murfin C	Ridyard A	Suddick G
1	Aug	29	BRADFORD CITY	1-2	Wallbanks	9556	1	2	3	4	5	6	7	8	9	10	11												
2		31	OLDHAM ATHLETIC	3-1	Proudfoot, Harvey, Ashton	5728	1		2	4	5	6		8	9		7				10							11	3
3	Sep	5	Leeds United	1-0	Wallbanks	13078	1	2	3	4	5	6		8	9		7						10				11		
4		7	BURY	0-1		7785	1	2	3	4	5	6		8	9		7						10				11		
5		12	SWANSEA TOWN	2-3	Kerry, Wallbanks	5213	1	2	3	4	5	6		8	9		7						10				11		
6		14	Bury	1-7	Curran	7366	1	2	3	4	5		7	8	9	10										6	11		
7		19	Tottenham Hotspur	2-4	Wallbanks 2	28585		2	3	4	5	6	7	8	9	10								1			11		
8		26	Notts County	3-2	Wallbanks 3	11700		2	3	4	5	6	7	8	9	10											11		
9	Oct	3	PLYMOUTH ARGYLE	0-0		6182	1	2	3	4		6	7	8	9	10											11	5	
10		10	Bristol City	0-4		8056	1	2	3	4	5	6	7	8	9	10											11		
11		17	MANCHESTER UNITED	0-0		4052	1	2	3	4	5	6	7	8	9				10								11		
12		24	Bradford Park Avenue	0-1		10857	1	2	3	4	5			8	9		7		10								11		
13		31	WOLVERHAMPTON W.	2-2	Wallbanks, Ashton	4986	1	2		4	5	6		8	9		7						10			3	11		
14	Nov	7	Nottingham Forest	2-1	Henderson, Ashton	8573	1	2	3	4	5	6		8	9		7						10				11		
15		14	STOKE CITY	1-0	Wallbanks	6839	1	2	3	4	5	6		8	9		7						10				11		
16		21	Southampton	0-2		11782	1	2	3	4	5	6		8	9		7						10				11		
17		28	PRESTON NORTH END	4-2	Wallbanks, Proudfoot, Murfin, Maskill	5549	1	2	3	4	5			8	9		7						10			6	11		
18	Dec	5	Burnley	3-5	Wallbanks, Proudfoot 2	5333	1	2	3	4	5	6		8	9		7						10				11		
19		12	CHESTERFIELD	3-1	Wallbanks, Kerry, Ashton	6455	1	2	3	4	5			8	9		7						10			6	11		
20		25	Millwall	0-2		18245	1	2	3	4	5			8	9		7						10			6	11		
21		26	MILLWALL	2-1	Wallbanks, Curran	11427	1	2	3	4	5		7	8	9		11						10			6			
22	Jan	2	Bradford City	1-9	Helsby (og)	12140	1	2	3	4	5		7	8	9		11						10			6			
23		16	LEEDS UNITED	0-2		9136	1	2	3	4	5		7	8	9	11									10	6			
24		23	Swansea Town	0-3		7998	1	2	3	4			7	8	9	11									10	6		5	
25		30	TOTTENHAM HOTSPUR	3-2	Wallbanks, Curran, Maskill (pen)	5852	1	2	3	4			7	8	9	11									10	6		5	
26	Feb	6	NOTTS COUNTY	1-1	Wallbanks	5188	1	2	3	4			7	8	9	11				10						6		5	
27		13	Plymouth Argyle	0-3		16251	1	2	3	4			7	8	9	11				10						6		5	
28		20	BRISTOL CITY	1-1	Proudfoot	4015	1	2	3	4			7	8	9	11				10						6		5	
29		27	Manchester United	0-3		18223	1	3	2	8	6		7	10	9		11										4	5	
30	Mar	5	BRADFORD PARK AVE.	2-2	Wallbanks, Curran	5727	1	3	2	8	6		7	10	9		11										4	5	
31		7	Charlton Athletic	1-3	Maskill	5183	1	3	2	4	5		7	8	9		11									6	10		
32		12	Wolverhampton Wan.	0-2		17641		2		4	5		7	8	9		11	1		3						6	10		
33		19	NOTTM. FOREST	3-1	Proudfoot 2, Wallbanks	4206		2		4	5		7	8	9		11	1		3						6	10		
34		25	Port Vale	0-3		9983		2		4	5		7	8	9		11	1	3							6	10		
35		26	Stoke City	0-2		9779		2				6	7		9		11	1	3			8	10		4			5	
36		28	PORT VALE	3-0	Wallbanks, Ashton, Henderson	5881		2			5		7	8	9		11	1		3			10		4		6		
37	Apr	2	SOUTHAMPTON	3-3	Wallbanks, Curran, Ridyard	5032		2	3		5		7	8	9		11	1					10		4		6		
38		9	Preston North End	2-1	Hill 2	7034	1		3		5		7	8	9		11					2	10		4		6		
39		16	BURNLEY	0-1		6991	1		3		5		7	8	9		11					2	10		4		6		
40		23	Chesterfield	2-2	Wallbanks, Proudfoot	8928	1		3		5			8	9		7					2	10		4		6	11	
41		30	CHARLTON ATHLETIC	1-4	Wallbanks	5594	1		3		5			8	9		7					2	10		4		6	11	
42	May	7	Oldham Athletic	2-2	Hill, Curran	6369	1		3		5		7	8	9		11					2	10		4		6		
			Apps				35	33	41	34	34	21	27	37	41	10	36	6	4	5	7	8	13	1	14	17	21	16	1
			Goals								2		6	8	22		5				1	3	2			3	1	1	

One own goal

F.A. Cup

		Date	Match	Score	Scorers	Att	Higgs FJ	Dixon C	Richards A	Smith JW	Henderson GB	Caddick GFR	Curran J	Proudfoot J	Wallbanks John	Chivers FC	Ashton E	Capstick W	Green F	Happs R	Harvey WA	Hill J	Kerry E	Lampard AJ	Lax G	Maskill T	Murfin C	Ridyard A	Suddick G
R3	Jan	9	SOUTHPORT	0-0		14850	1	2	3	4	5		7	8	9	11							10			6			
rep		12	Southport	1-4	Ashton	12500	1	2	3	4			7	8	9	11							10			6			

Played in replay: A Shears (at 5)

		P	W	D	L	F	A	W	D	L	F	A	Pts
1	Wolverhampton Wan.	42	17	3	1	71	11	7	5	9	44	38	56
2	Leeds United	42	12	5	4	36	22	10	5	6	42	32	54
3	Stoke City	42	14	6	1	47	19	5	8	8	22	29	52
4	Plymouth Argyle	42	14	4	3	69	29	6	5	10	31	37	49
5	Bury	42	13	4	4	44	21	8	3	10	26	37	49
6	Bradford Park Ave.	42	17	2	2	44	18	4	5	12	28	45	49
7	Bradford City	42	10	7	4	53	26	6	6	9	27	35	45
8	Tottenham Hotspur	42	11	6	4	58	37	5	5	11	29	41	43
9	Millwall	42	13	3	5	43	21	4	6	11	18	40	43
10	Charlton Athletic	42	11	5	5	38	28	6	4	11	23	38	43
11	Nottingham Forest	42	13	4	4	49	27	3	6	12	28	45	42
12	Manchester United	42	12	3	6	44	31	5	5	11	27	41	42
13	Preston North End	42	11	6	4	37	25	5	4	12	38	52	42
14	Southampton	42	10	5	6	39	30	7	2	12	27	47	41
15	Swansea Town	42	12	4	5	45	22	4	3	14	28	53	39
16	Notts County	42	10	4	7	43	30	3	8	10	32	45	38
17	Chesterfield	42	11	3	7	43	33	2	8	11	21	53	37
18	Oldham Athletic	42	10	4	7	41	34	3	6	12	21	50	36
19	Burnley	42	7	8	6	36	36	6	1	14	23	51	35
20	Port Vale	42	8	4	9	30	33	5	3	13	28	56	33
21	BARNSLEY	42	8	7	6	35	30	4	2	15	20	61	33
22	Bristol City	42	4	7	10	22	37	2	4	15	17	41	23

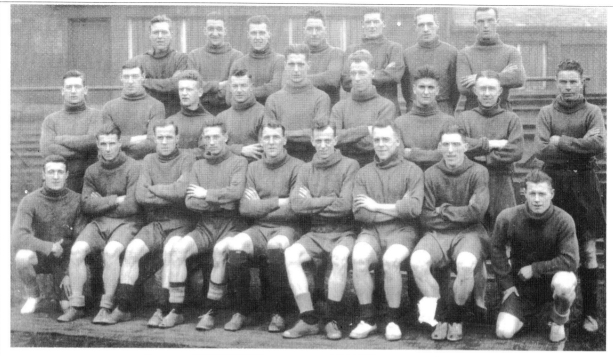

Season 1930/31 (Alternative) - 1931/32 Group not traced.
Back row: Harston, Ogle, Proudfoot, Gale, Crompton, Todd, Holmes
Centre row: John Wallbanks, Hayhurst, James Wallbanks, Smith, Ridyard, Caddick, Stanyon, Storer, Patterson
Front row: Chivers, Dixon, Curran, Harvey, Henderson, Kerry, Ashton, Richards, Murfin

Season 1932/33
Back row: Fletcher (Manager) Shotton, McPherson, Harper, Henderson, Andrews, Bollington, Tordoff,
Cooper (Ass Trainer) Holley (Trainer)   Centre row: Johnson, Chivers, Jones, Ellis, McPhail
Front row: Richards, Smith, Spence, Ashton, Cunningham, Asquith

1932/33 8th in Division 3(N)

#	Date	Opponent	Score	Scorers	Att	Lynch TJ	Happs R	Shotton R	Lax G	Henderson GB	Swaby HN	Wadsworth W	Cunningham P	Wallbanks John	Andrews H	Ashton E	Archibald RF	Chivers FC	Ellis T	Fleetwood ED	Grainger J	Harper B	Lockie T	Owencroft GE	Richards A	Robinson EG	Smith J	Spence R	Turnbull JM	Whitworth E
1	Aug 27	Wrexham	0-3		11013	1	2	3	4	5	6	7	8	9	10	11														
2	29	TRANMERE ROVERS	2-1	Ashton, Wadsworth	4608	1	2	3	4	5	6	7	8	9	10	11														
3	Sep 3	WALSALL	2-1	Wallbanks 2	5136	1		3	4	5	6	7		9	10	11		8									2			
4	5	Tranmere Rovers	0-3		4028	1		3	4	5		7		9	10	11		8									2			6
5	10	Gateshead	1-1	Fleetwood	7328	1		3	4	5	6	7		9	10	11				8							2			
6	17	STOCKPORT COUNTY	2-2	Andrews, Wadsworth	6662	1		3	4	5	6	7		9	10	11				8							2			
7	24	Darlington	1-1	Andrews	3447	1		3	4	5	6	7		9	10	11				8							2			
8	Oct 1	DONCASTER ROVERS	2-3	Ashton, Owencroft	6333	1		3	4	5	6			9	10	7								11	2		8			
9	8	Hull City	1-5	Andrews	7857	1		3	4	5	6	7			10	11		9							2		8			
10	15	MANSFIELD TOWN	6-2	Wallbanks 3, Ashton 2, Andrews	5145	1		3	4		6	7		9	10	11							5		2		8			
11	22	Rotherham United	0-0		7347	1		3	4		6	7		9	10	11							5		2		8			
12	29	ACCRINGTON STANLEY	4-0	Andrews 2, Smith 2	4023	1		3	4		6	7		9	10	11							5		2		8			
13	Nov 5	New Brighton	5-3	Wadsworth 2, Andrews 2, Wallbanks	3143	1		3	4		6	7		9	10	11					2		5				8			
14	12	CHESTER	0-3		6975	1		3	4		6	7		9	10	11							5		2		8			
15	19	Barrow	3-2	Smith, Wallbanks, Andrews	5445	1		3	4		6	7		9	10	11							5		2		8			
16	Dec 3	York City	2-3	Wallbanks, Johnson (og)	3480	1		3	4		6	7		9	10	11							5		2		8			
17	10	NEW BRIGHTON	1-2	Wallbanks	3353	1	4	3			6	7		9	10	11							5		2		8			
18	12	CREWE ALEXANDRA	7-1	Andrews 3, Wallbanks 3, Whitworth	1451	1		3	4	5				9	10	7								11	2		8			6
19	17	Rochdale	3-2	Andrews 2, Owencroft	4071	1		3	4	5				9	10	7								11	2		8			6
20	24	SOUTHPORT	2-0	Andrews, Wallbanks	5766			3	4	5				9	10	7			1					11	2		8			6
21	26	HARTLEPOOLS UNITED	3-2	Smith 2, Wallbanks	9138			3	4	5				9	10	7	11		1						2		8			6
22	27	Hartlepools United	4-6	Ashton, Andrews, Cunningham 2	4996			3	4	5			9		10	7	11		1						2		8			6
23	31	WREXHAM	5-3	Wallbanks, Andrews, Ashton 2, Archibald	5137			3	4	5				9	10	7	11		1						2		8			6
24	Jan 2	CARLISLE UNITED	4-1	Smith, Wallbanks, Andrews, Lockie	5663			3	4					9	10	7	11		1				5		2		8			6
25	7	Walsall	1-1	Cunningham	6393			3		4			9		10	7	11		1				5		2		8			6
26	21	GATESHEAD	2-4	Cunningham, Smith	4927			3	4				9		10	7	11		1				5		2		8			6
27	28	Stockport County	4-5	Cunningham 2, Smith, Ashton	3414			3	4				9		10	7			1				5	11		2	8			6
28	Feb 4	DARLINGTON	6-2	Cunningham 5, Spence	4714			3	4	5			9		10	11			1							2	8	7		6
29	11	Doncaster Rovers	1-3	Ashton	8247			3	4	5			9		10	11			1							2	8	7		6
30	18	HULL CITY	1-0	Cunningham	7360			3	4	5			9		10	11			1			6				2	8	7		
31	Mar 4	ROTHERHAM UNITED	3-1	Smith, Cunningham 2	6243			3	4	5			9		10	11			1			6				2	8	7		
32	11	Accrington Stanley	0-2		3122			3	4	5			9		10	11			1			6				2	8	7		
33	25	Chester	1-3	Cunningham	6508			3	4	5			9		10	11			1			6				2	8	7		
34	Apr 1	BARROW	3-0	Cunningham, Smith, Spence	3763			3	4	5			9		10	11			1			6				2	8	7		
35	8	Carlisle United	1-0	Smith	5145			3					9		10	11		6	1				4			2	8	7		6
36	14	Mansfield Town	1-0	Lax	5994			3	9	5					10	11		6	1				4			2	8	7		
37	15	YORK CITY	1-1	Cunningham	4667			3	8	5			9		10	11		6	1				4			2		7		
38	17	HALIFAX TOWN	1-1	Wallbanks	4413			3		5				9	10	11		4	1	8						2		7		6
39	18	Halifax Town	1-2	Fleetwood	5183			3		5					10	11		4	1	8						2		7	9	6
40	22	Crewe Alexandra	2-2	Wallbanks 2	3291			3						9	10	11		4	1	8			5			2		7		6
41	29	ROCHDALE	3-1	Fleetwood 2, Wallbanks	1931			3		5				9		11		4	1	10						2	8	7		6
42	May 6	Southport	0-2		1450			3		5				9		11		4	1	10			6			2	8	7		
			Apps			19	3	41	34	28	18	17	14	26	41	41	6	11	23	8	1	8	14	5	17	23	31	15	1	17
			Goals						1			4	17	20	18	9	1			4			1	2			11	2		1

One own goal

F.A. Cup

#	Date	Opponent	Score		Att			Shotton R	Lax G	Henderson GB				Wallbanks John	Andrews H	Ashton E	Archibald RF		Ellis T				Lockie T		Richards A		Smith J	Spence R		Whitworth E
R3	Jan 14	LUTON TOWN	0-0		15106			3	4	5				9	10	7	11		1						2		8			6
rep	18	Luton Town	0-2		10047			3	4					9	10	7	11		1				5		2		8			6

	P	W	D	L	F	A	W	D	L	F	A	Pts
1 Hull City	42	18	3	0	69	14	8	4	9	31	31	59
2 Wrexham	42	18	2	1	75	15	6	7	8	31	36	57
3 Stockport County	42	16	2	3	69	30	5	10	6	30	28	54
4 Chester	42	15	4	2	57	25	7	4	10	37	41	52
5 Walsall	42	16	4	1	53	15	3	6	12	22	43	48
6 Doncaster Rovers	42	13	8	0	52	26	4	6	11	25	53	48
7 Gateshead	42	12	5	4	45	25	7	4	10	33	42	47
8 BARNSLEY	42	14	3	4	60	31	5	5	11	32	49	46
9 Barrow	42	12	3	6	41	24	6	4	11	19	36	43
10 Crewe Alexandra	42	16	3	2	57	16	4	0	17	23	68	43
11 Tranmere Rovers	42	11	4	6	49	31	6	4	11	21	35	42
12 Southport	42	15	3	3	54	20	2	4	15	16	47	41
13 Accrington Stanley	42	12	4	5	55	29	3	6	12	23	47	40
14 Hartlepools United	42	15	3	3	56	29	1	4	16	31	87	39
15 Halifax Town	42	12	4	5	39	23	3	4	14	32	67	38
16 Mansfield Town	42	13	4	4	57	22	1	3	17	27	78	35
17 Rotherham United	42	14	3	4	42	21	0	3	18	18	63	34
18 Rochdale	42	9	4	8	32	33	4	3	14	26	47	33
19 Carlisle United	42	8	7	6	34	25	5	0	16	17	50	33
20 York City	42	10	4	7	51	38	3	2	16	21	54	32
21 New Brighton	42	8	6	7	42	36	3	4	14	21	52	32
22 Darlington	42	9	6	6	42	32	1	2	18	24	77	28

1933/34   1st in Division 3 (N)

#	Mon	Date	Opponent	Score	Scorers	Att	Ellis T	Richards A	Shotton R	Chivers FC	Henderson GB	Whitworth E	Spence R	Smith J	Blight AB	Andrews H	Ashton E	Cookson S	Coxon LW	Fisher FW	Fleetwood ED	Happs R	Harper B	Holley T	Johnson JC	McPherson PC
1	Aug	26	WREXHAM	3-0	Andrews, Spence 2	5444	1	2	3	4	5	6	7	8	9	10	11									
2		28	Rotherham United	2-0	Blight, Andrews	6691	1	2	3	4	5	6	7	8	9	10	11									
3	Sep	2	Southport	2-2	Blight, Henderson	3894	1	2	3	4	5	6	7	8	9	10	11									
4		9	DARLINGTON	4-0	Henderson, Smith, Blight, Spence	7163	1	2	3	4	5	6	7	8	9	10	11									
5		16	Gateshead	4-1	Ashton 2, Blight, Smith	5986	1	2	3	4	5	6	7	8	9	10	11									
6		23	ACCRINGTON STANLEY	6-0	Blight 2, Andrews, Ashton 2, Smith	9671	1	2	3	4	5	6	7	8	9	10	11									
7		30	Chesterfield	0-3		20592	1	2	3	4	5	6	7	8	9	10	11									
8	Oct	7	ROCHDALE	4-1	Andrews 2, Blight, Spence	8970	1	2	3	4	5	6	7	8	9	10	11									
9		14	Tranmere Rovers	2-5	Smith, Blight	5608	1	2	3	4	5	6	7	8	9	10	11									
10		21	Walsall	1-5	Spence	6108	1		3	4	5	6	7	8	9	10		2	11							
11		28	YORK CITY	1-0	Andrews	5300	1		3	4	5	6	7	8	9	10		2								11
12	Nov	4	Chester	2-4	Blight 2	6501	1		3	4	5	6	7	8	9	10	11	2								
13		11	DONCASTER ROVERS	2-2	Blight, Ashton	8642	1		3	4	5	6	7	8	9	10	11								2	
14		18	Barrow	4-3	Fleetwood 2, Andrews, Blight	4362	1		3			6	7		9	10	11	2			8		4	5		
15	Dec	2	Stockport County	1-1	Fleetwood	8359	1		3			6	7	8		10	11	2			9		4	5		
16		9	Rochdale	1-3	Ashton	2641	1		3			6	7	8	9	10	11	2					4	5		
17		16	Crewe Alexandra	2-4	Andrews, Shotton (pen)	2452	1		3	9		6	7	8		10	11	2					4	5		
18		23	NEW BRIGHTON	2-0	Fisher, Smith	4111	1		3			6	7	8		10	11	2		9			5		4	
19		25	Hartlepools United	2-5	Fisher, Spence	5461	1		3			6	7	8		10	11	2		9			5		4	
20		26	HARTLEPOOLS UNITED	5-4	Shotton (pen), Ashton 2, Fisher, Whitworth	8559	1		3			6	7	8		10	11	2		9			5		4	
21		30	Wrexham	2-4	Ashton 2	4183	1		3			6	7	8		10	11			9		2	5		4	
22	Jan	1	ROTHERHAM UNITED	5-1	Ashton 3, Blight, Whitworth	9036	1		3			6	7	8	9	10	11					2	5		4	
23		6	SOUTHPORT	3-2	Ashton, Spence, Blight	5893	1		3			6	7	8	9	10	11					2	5		4	
24		13	CARLISLE UNITED	1-0	Smith	7045	1		3			6	7	8	9	10	11					2	5		4	
25		20	Darlington	4-0	Andrews 2, Smith, Spence	4621	1		3			6	7	8		10	11	2		9			5		4	
26		27	GATESHEAD	0-0		7974	1		3			6	7	8		10	11	2		9			5		4	
27	Feb	3	Accrington Stanley	9-0	Blight 4, Spence 2, Andrews, Smith, Ashton	2814	1		3		5	6	7	8	9	10	11	2					4			
28		10	CHESTERFIELD	3-2	Blight 3	23960	1		3		5	6	7	8	9	10	11	2					4			
29		19	HALIFAX TOWN	1-0	Blight	7028	1		3		5	6	7	8	9	10	11	2					4			
30		24	TRANMERE ROVERS	5-1	Blight 2, Andrews, Shotton (pen), Spence	11108	1		3		5	6	7	8	9	10	11	2					4			
31	Mar	3	WALSALL	1-1	Smith	11819	1		3		5	6	7	8	9	10	11	2					4			
32		10	York City	1-1	Blight	2851	1		3		5	6	7	8	9	10	11	2					4			
33		17	CHESTER	2-0	Smith, Blight	8195	1		3		5	6	7	8	9	10	11	2					4			
34		24	Doncaster Rovers	4-4	Spence, Blight, Henderson, Smith	11231	1		3		5	6	7	8	9	10	11	2					4			
35		30	Mansfield Town	5-1	Spence 2, Andrews, Ashton, Blight	8422	1		3		5	6	7	8	9	10	11	2					4			
36		31	BARROW	3-1	Spence, Andrews, Blight	10081	1		3		5	6	7	8	9	10	11	2					4			
37	Apr	2	MANSFIELD TOWN	6-1	Ashton 3, Spence 2, Blight	10814	1		3		5	6	7	8	9	10	11	2					4			
38		7	Carlisle United	4-1	Andrews 3, Blight	4696	1		3		5	6	7	8	9	10	11	2					4			
39		14	STOCKPORT COUNTY	2-0	Spence, Shotton (pen)	26366	1		3		5	6	7	8	9	10	11	2					4			
40		21	Halifax Town	1-1	Smith	13880	1		3		5	6	7	8	9	10	11	2					4			
41		28	CREWE ALEXANDRA	5-2	Fleetwood, Shotton 2 (2p), Andrews, Whitworth	7797	1		3		5	6	7		9	10	11	2			8		4			
42	May	5	New Brighton	1-0	Spence	8508	1		3		5	6	7		9	10	11	2			8		4			
						Apps	42	9	42	15	29	42	41	39	34	42	40	28	1	6	5	4	29	4	9	1
						Goals			6		3	3	19	12	31	18	19			3	4					

F.A. Cup

| R1 | Nov | 25 | Halifax Town | 2-3 | Andrews 2 | | 1 | | 3 | | 5 | 6 | 7 | 8 | | 10 | 11 | 2 | | | | 9 | 4 | | | |

Third Division (North) Cup

| R1 | Jan | 29 | Rotherham United | 1-2 | Shotton (p) | 1845 | 1 | | 3 | | 5 | 6 | 7 | | 9 | 10 | 11 | 2 | | 8 | | | 4 | | | |

		P	W	D	L	F	A	W	D	L	F	A	Pts
1	BARNSLEY	42	18	3	0	64	18	9	5	7	54	43	62
2	Chesterfield	42	18	1	2	56	17	9	6	6	30	26	61
3	Stockport County	42	18	3	0	84	23	6	8	7	31	29	59
4	Walsall	42	18	2	1	66	18	5	5	11	31	42	53
5	Doncaster Rovers	42	17	1	3	58	24	5	8	8	25	37	53
6	Wrexham	42	14	1	6	68	35	9	4	8	34	38	51
7	Tranmere Rovers	42	16	2	3	57	21	4	5	12	27	42	47
8	Barrow	42	12	5	4	78	45	7	4	10	38	49	47
9	Halifax Town	42	15	2	4	57	30	5	2	14	23	61	44
10	Chester	42	11	6	4	59	26	6	0	15	30	60	40
11	Hartlepools United	42	14	3	4	54	24	2	4	15	35	69	39
12	York City	42	11	5	5	44	28	4	3	14	27	46	38
13	Carlisle United	42	11	6	4	43	23	4	2	15	23	58	38
14	Crewe Alexandra	42	12	3	6	54	38	3	3	15	27	59	36
15	New Brighton	42	13	3	5	41	25	1	5	15	21	62	36
16	Darlington	42	11	4	6	47	35	2	5	14	23	66	35
17	Mansfield Town	42	9	7	5	49	29	2	5	14	32	59	34
18	Southport	42	6	11	4	35	29	2	6	13	28	61	33
19	Gateshead	42	10	3	8	46	40	2	6	13	30	70	33
20	Accrington Stanley	42	10	6	5	44	38	3	1	17	21	63	33
21	Rotherham United	42	5	7	9	31	35	5	1	15	22	56	28
22	Rochdale	42	7	5	9	34	30	2	1	18	19	73	24

Season 1933/34
Back row: Andrews, Ellis, Shotton, Spence, Chivers, Fleetwood.
Front row: Whitworth, Blight, Smith, Cookson, Ashton, Henderson.

Season 1934/35
Back row: Harper, Adey, Ellis, Shotton, Henderson, Chivers
Front row: Fletcher (Manager) Spence, Smith, Blight, Andrews, Ashton, Holley (Trainer)

1934/35 16th in Division 2

#	Date		Opponent	Score	Scorers	Att.	Ellis T	Cookson S	Shotton R	Harper B	Henderson GB	Whitworth E	Spence R	Smith J	Blight AB	Andrews H	Ashton E	Asquith B	Adey W	Beedles N	Brannan MK	Chivers FC	Cliffe JW	Diamond JJ	Finnigan T	Fisher FW	Fleetwood ED	Greaves A	Hine EW	Holley T	Jones L	McLauchlan R	Pedwell R	Sampy T	Thomas RS
1	Aug	25	Bradford Park Ave.	2-3	Andrews, Shotton (pen)	14960	1	2	3	4	5	6	7	8	9	10	11																		
2		27	NOTTS COUNTY	1-1	Spence	10338	1		3	4	5	6	7	8	9	10	11		2																
3	Sep	1	PORT VALE	2-0	Blight 2	9370	1		3	4	5	6	7	8	9	10	11		2																
4		3	Notts County	4-1	Spence,Blight,Ashton,Andr	8662	1		3	4	5	6	7	8	9	10	11		2																
5		8	Manchester Utd.	1-4	Spence	22315	1		3	4		6	7	8	9		11	10	2											5					
6		15	SWANSEA TOWN	1-0	Blight	10186	1		3	4	5	6	7	8	9	10	11		2																
7		22	Burnley	1-4	Shotton (pen)	9424	1		3	4	5	6	7	8	9	10	11		2																
8		29	OLDHAM ATH.	4-0	Smith, Ashton 2, Spence	5600	1		3	4	5	6	7	8	9	10	11		2																
9	Oct	6	Bolton Wanderers	0-8		15009	1		3	4	5	6		8		10	7		2						9								11		
10		13	SOUTHAMPTON	1-1	Finnigan	7242	1		3	4		6		8		10	7		2						9					5			11		
11		20	Plymouth Argyle	1-3	Blight	7609	1		3	4					8	9	10	7	2											5			11		
12		27	NORWICH CITY	2-1	Andrews, Ashton	5674	1		3	4	5				8	9	10	11	2			6									7				
13	Nov	3	Newcastle United	1-4	Ashton	7959	1	2	3	4	5	6			8		10	11								9					7				
14		10	WEST HAM UTD.	1-1	Diamond	7878	1		3	4	5				8		10	11	2					9						6	7				
15		17	Blackpool	0-3		11428	1		3	4	5				8		10	11	2					7		9				6					
16		24	BURY	3-0	Ashton 2, Thomas	7048	1		3	4	5				8		10	11	2							9				6					7
17	Dec	1	Hull City	1-1	Andrews	10311	1		3	4	5				8	9	10	11	2											6					7
18		8	NOTTM. FOREST	1-2	Pedwell	9784	1		3	4	5					9	10		2										8	6			11		7
19		15	Brentford	1-8	Hine	11843	1		3	4	5			8			11										10		9	6		2			7
20		22	FULHAM	2-0	Ashton, Andrews	2992	1		3		5			8		10	11		2									4	9	6					7
21		26	Sheffield United	1-2	Hine	38860	1		3		5					10	11		2									4	8	9					7
22		29	BRADFORD P. A.	1-1	Pedwell	7783	1		3		5					10			2									4	8	9			11		7
23	Jan	1	SHEFFIELD UTD.	0-0		13263	1		3			6				10			2						9				8	5	4		11		7
24		5	Port Vale	0-4		6074	1		3			6							2						9				8	10	4		11		7
25		19	MANCHESTER U.	0-2		10177	1		3		5	6						10	2					7	9				8		4		11		
26		31	Swansea Town	1-1	Andrews	4295	1		3		5	6				10			2			9							8		4		11		7
27	Feb	2	BURNLEY	0-0		5924	1		3		5	6				10			2		7	9							8		4		11		
28		9	Oldham Athletic	4-1	Hine 2, Chivers 2	6257	1		3		5			7		10	11		2			9							8		4				
29		23	Southampton	1-0	Holley	5625	1		3		5	6		7		10	11		2			9							8		4				
30	Mar	2	PLYMOUTH ARG.	1-4	Holley	7609	1		3		5	6		7		10	11		2			9							8		4				
31		9	Norwich City	1-0	Smith	9128			3		5			8			11		2			9	1							6	4		10		7
32		16	NEWCASTLE UTD.	2-1	Ashton, Chivers	14511			3		5			8			11		2			9	1							6	4		10		7
33		23	West Ham United	3-4	Ashton, Hine, Chivers	27338			3		5			8			11		2			9	1							6	4		10		7
34		30	BLACKPOOL	2-2	Chivers, Hine (pen)	11369	1		3		5			8			11		2			9									4		10	6	7
35	Apr	6	Bury	1-4	Chivers	5383	1		3	6	5			8			11		2			9									4		10		7
36		10	BOLTON WANDS.	1-1	Ashton	13171	1		3	4	5			8			11		2			9									6		10		7
37		13	HULL CITY	2-2	Chivers 2	9120	1		3	4	5			8			11		2			9									6		10		7
38		20	Nottingham For.	1-4	Hine	5924	1		3	6	5			8			11		2			9									4		10		7
39		22	BRADFORD CITY	2-0	Chivers, Hine	10184	1		3	6	5			8			11		2			9									4		10		7
40		23	Bradford City	0-1		7009	1			6	5			8			11		2			9									4	3	10		7
41		27	BRENTFORD	3-3	Smith, Chivers, Thomas	7021	1		2	6	5			8			11					9									4	3	10		7
42	May	4	Fulham	3-1	Chivers 2, Hine	9624	1		3	6	5			8			11		2			9									4		10		7
					Apps		39	2	41	27	37	19	8	34	11	27	32	5	37	1	3	22	3	4	4	5	1	3	22	24	31	6	3	10	1	22
					Goals				2				4	3	5	6	11					12		1	1				9	2			2		2

F.A. Cup

	Date		Opponent	Score		Att.	Ellis T		Shotton R		Henderson GB	Whitworth E					Ashton E		Adey W			Chivers FC							Hine EW		Jones L		Pedwell R		Thomas RS
R3	Jan	12	PRESTON NORTH	0-0		21508	1		3		5	6					10		2			9							8		4		11		7
rep		16	Preston North End	0-1		22000	1		3		5	6					10		2			9							8		4		11		7

		P	W	D	L	F	A	W	D	L	F	A	Pts
1	Brentford	42	19	2	0	59	14	7	7	7	34	34	61
2	Bolton Wanderers	42	17	1	3	63	15	9	3	9	33	33	56
3	West Ham United	42	18	1	2	46	17	8	3	10	34	46	56
4	Blackpool	42	16	4	1	46	18	5	7	9	33	39	53
5	Manchester United	42	16	2	3	50	21	7	2	12	26	34	50
6	Newcastle United	42	14	2	5	55	25	8	2	11	34	43	48
7	Fulham	42	15	3	3	62	26	2	9	10	14	30	46
8	Plymouth Argyle	42	13	3	5	48	26	6	5	10	27	38	46
9	Nottingham Forest	42	12	5	4	46	23	5	3	13	30	47	42
10	Bury	42	14	1	6	38	26	5	3	13	24	47	42
11	Sheffield United	42	11	4	6	51	30	5	5	11	28	40	41
12	Burnley	42	11	2	8	43	32	5	7	9	20	41	41
13	Hull City	42	9	6	6	32	22	7	2	12	31	52	40
14	Norwich City	42	11	6	4	51	23	3	5	13	20	38	39
15	Bradford Park Ave.	42	7	8	6	32	28	4	8	9	23	35	38
16	BARNSLEY	42	8	10	3	32	22	5	2	14	28	61	38
17	Swansea Town	42	13	5	3	41	22	1	3	17	15	45	36
18	Port Vale	42	10	7	4	42	28	1	5	15	13	46	34
19	Southampton	42	9	8	4	28	19	2	4	15	18	56	34
20	Bradford City	42	10	7	4	34	20	2	1	18	16	48	32
21	Oldham Athletic	42	10	3	8	44	40	0	3	18	12	55	26
22	Notts County	42	8	3	10	29	33	1	4	16	17	64	25

1935/36 20th in Division 2

#	Date	Opponent	Res	Scorers	Att	Ellis T	Adey W	Anderson W	Holley T	Henderson GB	Harper B	Thomas RS	Hine EW	Chivers FC	Asquith B	Ashton E	Barlow H	Brannan MK	Bray E	Fisher FW	Foster J	Gallacher F	Hallows J	Hinsley G	Ives AE	Jones L	Kelly J	Nicholson S	Shotton R	Topping HW	Waring T	Warrilow F	Wilson J
1	Aug 31	PORT VALE	4-2	Asquith, Chivers 2, Hine	10145	1	2	3	4	5	6	7	8	9	10	11																	
2	Sep 4	Newcastle United	0-3		21150	1	2	3	4	5	6	7	10	9		11						8											
3	7	Fulham	1-1	Hine	22575	1	2	3	4	5	6	7	10	9								8										11	
4	9	NEWCASTLE UNITE	3-2	Hine (pen), Gallacher 2	12796	1	2	3	4	5	6	7	10	9					11			8											
5	14	BURNLEY	3-1	Hine, Holley, Bray	10921	1	2	3	4	5	6	7	10	9					11			8											
6	16	Tottenham Hotspu	0-3		14930	1	2	3	4	5	6	7	10	9					11			8											
7	21	Charlton Athletic	0-3		17635	1	2	3	4	5	6	7	10	9					11			8											
8	28	HULL CITY	5-1	Hol'y, Ash'n, Hine, Bray, Chiv'	9718	1	2	3	4	5	6		10	9		7			11			8											
9	Oct 5	West Ham United	0-2		21584	1	2	3	4	5	6		10	9		7			11			8											
10	12	Plymouth Argyle	1-7	Warrilow	16301	1	2	3	4	5	6		10			7						8										11	
11	19	BURY	1-1	Hine	4846	1	2	3		5	6		8	9	10	7													4			11	
12	26	Doncaster Rovers	1-1	Warrilow	19875	1		3	6	5		7	8		4	10								9				2				11	
13	Nov 2	BLACKPOOL	1-2	Warrilow	9075			3					8		4	10					1		6	9	5			2				11	
14	9	Nottingham Forest	0-6		8978			3					8		4	7				9	1		6		5			2				11	
15	16	NORWICH CITY	2-3	Chivers, Harper	6957		2			5	6		10	9		7					1	8								3			11	7
16	23	Swansea Town	0-0		8170		2		4	5	6		10	9							1	8								3			11	7
17	30	SHEFFIELD UNITED	3-2	Waring, Harper, Warrilow	13070		2		4	5	6		10								1	8								3	9		11	7
18	Dec 7	Bradford Park Ave.	0-3		9774		2		4	5	6		10								1	8								3	9		11	
19	14	LEICESTER CITY	3-3	Hine 3	9783		2		4	5	6	7	10								1	8								3	9		11	
20	21	Southampton	1-0	Gallacher	6622	1	2		4	5	6	7	10			11						8								3	9			
21	26	Manchester United	1-1	Waring	20993	1	2		4	5	6	7	10			11						8								3	9			
22	28	Port Vale	4-0	Hine, Waring 2, Ashton	7381	1	2		4	5		7	10	6		11						8								3	9			
23	Jan 1	MANCHESTER UTD.	0-3		20957	1	2		4	5	6	7	10			11						8								3	9			
24	4	FULHAM	2-0	Gallacher 2	8857	1	2		4	5	6	7	10			11						8								3	9			
25	18	Burnley	0-3		6757	1			4	5	6		10			11						8							2	3	9			
26	27	CHARLTON ATH.	1-2	Topping	7771	1			4	5	6		10			11				7		8							2	3	9			
27	Feb 1	Hull City	3-1	Waring 2, Ashton	4804	1			4	5	6		10			11				7		8							2	3	9			
28	8	WEST HAM UNITED	1-2	Hine (pen)	13458	1			4	5	6		10			11				7		8							2	3	9			
29	19	PLYMOUTH ARGYL	1-2	Gallacher	5849	1			4	5	6	7	10			11						8							2	3	9			
30	22	Bury	0-3		8589	1			4		6		10			11				7		8	9			5			2	3				
31	Mar 4	BRADFORD P. A.	5-1	Fisher 4, Hine	5929	1	2		4	5	6		10			11				7		8								3	9			
32	7	Norwich City	1-3	Topping	12652		2		4	5	6		10			11		1		7		8								3	9			
33	14	NOTTM. FOREST	0-2		8981	1	2		4	5	6		10			11						8								3	9			7
34	21	Blackpool	0-3		10123	1			4	5	6		10			11				7		8	9						2	3				
35	28	SWANSEA TOWN	0-0		8714	1			4	5	6		10							7		8	9						2	3	11			
36	Apr 4	Sheffield United	0-2		20591	1			4	5	6		10			11				7		8		3					2		9			
37	11	DONCASTER ROV.	2-1	Hine (pen), Waring	13323	1			4	5	6		10			11				7		8							2	3	9			
38	13	BRADFORD CITY	0-1		12196	1			4	5	6		10							7		8							2	3	9		11	
39	14	Bradford City	1-1	Barlow	9975				4	5	6	7	10			11	8	1											2	3	9			
40	18	Leicester City	0-2		11109	1			4	5	3	7	10	6		11	8												2					
41	25	SOUTHAMPTON	3-1	Barlow, Ashton, Hine	5102	1	2		6	5		7	10			11	8					9					4			3				
42	May 2	TOTTENHAM H.	0-0		9271	1	2			5	6	7	10			11	8					9					4			3				
		Apps				34	26	14	37	39	37	17	41	16	6	29	4	2	10	16	6	30	3	2	1	5	3	4	31	14	18	13	3
		Goals							2		2		14	4	1	4	2		2	4		6								2	7	4	

Played in game 10: Mackay DM (at 9)

F.A. Cup

Rd	Date	Opponent	Res	Scorers	Att	Ellis T	Holley T	Henderson GB	Harper B	Thomas RS	Hine EW	Ashton E	Fisher FW	Gallacher F	Hallows J	Shotton R	Topping HW	Waring T
R3	Jan 11	BIRMINGHAM	3-3	Hine 2, Ashton	29330	1	4	5	6	7	10	11		8		2	3	9
rep	15	Birmingham	2-0	Waring, Hine	34000	1	4	5	6		10	11	7	8		2	3	9
R4	25	Tranmere Rovers	4-2	Waring, Hine, Ashton, Fishe	22222	1	4	5	6		10	11	7	8		2	3	9
R5	Feb 15	STOKE CITY	2-1	Gallacher, Hine	40255	1	4	5	6		10	11	7	8		2	3	9
R6	29	Arsenal	1-4	Gallacher	60420	1	4	5	6		10	11	7	8	9	2	3	

Final Table — Division 2

		P	W	D	L	F	A	W	D	L	F	A	Pts
1	Manchester United	42	16	3	2	55	16	6	9	6	30	27	56
2	Charlton Athletic	42	15	6	0	53	17	7	5	9	32	41	55
3	Sheffield United	42	15	4	2	51	15	5	8	8	28	35	52
4	West Ham United	42	13	5	3	51	23	9	3	9	39	45	52
5	Tottenham Hotspur	42	12	6	3	60	25	6	7	8	31	30	49
6	Leicester City	42	14	5	2	53	19	5	5	11	26	38	48
7	Plymouth Argyle	42	15	2	4	50	20	5	6	10	21	37	48
8	Newcastle United	42	13	5	3	56	27	7	1	13	32	52	46
9	Fulham	42	11	6	4	58	24	4	8	9	18	28	44
10	Blackpool	42	14	3	4	64	34	4	4	13	29	38	43
11	Norwich City	42	14	2	5	47	24	3	7	11	25	41	43
12	Bradford City	42	12	7	2	32	18	3	6	12	23	47	43
13	Swansea Town	42	11	3	7	42	26	4	6	11	25	50	39
14	Bury	42	10	6	5	41	27	3	6	12	25	57	38
15	Burnley	42	9	8	4	35	21	3	5	13	15	38	37
16	Bradford Park Ave.	42	13	6	2	43	26	1	3	17	19	58	37
17	Southampton	42	11	3	7	32	24	3	6	12	15	41	37
18	Doncaster Rovers	42	10	7	4	28	17	4	2	15	23	54	37
19	Nottingham Forest	42	8	8	5	43	22	4	3	14	26	54	35
20	BARNSLEY	42	9	4	8	40	32	3	5	13	14	48	33
21	Port Vale	42	10	5	6	34	30	2	3	16	22	76	32
22	Hull City	42	4	7	10	33	45	1	3	17	14	66	20

Season 1935/36
Back row: Harper, Henderson, Nicholson, Thorpe (Groundsman) Holley, Hinsley, Topping
2nd back: Cooper (Trainer) McKay, Barlow, Ellis, Foster, unknown, Brannan, Asquith, Wheeler, Holley (Trainer)
2nd front: Chivers, Anderson, Adey, Fletcher (Manager) Fisher, Hine, Bray, Gallacher
Front row: unknown, Thomas, Shotton, Vicary (Secretary) Warrilow, Ashton, Sampy

Season 1936/37
Back row: Shotton, Ashton, Holley, Ellis, Harper, Henderson
Front row: Jones, Barlow, Fisher, Hine, Bray

1936/37 — 14th in Division 2

#	Date		Opponent	Score	Scorers	Att
1	Aug	29	Newcastle United	1-0	Hallows	30097
2		31	BURY	2-2	Barlow, Hallows	12990
3	Sep	5	BRADFORD PARK AV	2-1	Fisher, Barlow	10387
4		9	Bury	1-2	Gallacher	9814
5		12	Swansea Town	1-3	Fisher	8072
6		14	NORWICH CITY	2-1	Fisher, Hine	7388
7		19	Sheffield United	0-2		28793
8		26	TOTTENHAM HOTSPU	1-0	Hine	12024
9	Oct	3	Blackpool	1-1	Fisher	22839
10		10	BLACKBURN ROVERS	3-2	Fisher, Harris, Ashton	13826
11		17	BRADFORD CITY	1-1	Hine (pen)	10475
12		24	Aston Villa	2-4	Hine, Barlow	37951
13		31	CHESTERFIELD	1-1	Oram	14537
14	Nov	7	Nottingham Forest	1-4	Fisher	12669
15		14	PLYMOUTH ARGYLE	1-3	Hine (pen)	10555
16		21	Coventry City	0-3		25733
17		28	DONCASTER ROVERS	4-1	Hammill 2, Hine 2	11707
18	Dec	5	Fulham	0-1		11951
19		12	BURNLEY	1-1	Hamill	7086
20		19	Southampton	3-1	Hine, Bokas, Hallows	10675
21		25	Leicester City	1-5	Hallows	35610
22		26	NEWCASTLE UNITED	1-0	Hine	22760
23		28	LEICESTER CITY	1-2	Hine (pen)	10639
24	Jan	2	Bradford Park Avenu	1-2	Barlow	6636
25		9	SWANSEA TOWN	0-1		7690
26		23	SHEFFIELD UNITED	1-1	Bokas	7110
27	Feb	3	Tottenham Hotspur	0-3		11097
28		13	Blackburn Rovers	1-1	Hamill	14294
29		20	Bradford City	2-3	Clark (og), Asquith	10126
30		26	BLACKPOOL	2-1	Hine, Bokas	14013
31		27	ASTON VILLA	0-4		16485
32	Mar	6	Chesterfield	1-2	Asquith	10958
33		13	NOTTM. FOREST	1-0	Hunt	8199
34		20	Plymouth Argyle	2-1	Asquith, McArdle	15152
35		26	West Ham United	0-0		28967
36		27	COVENTRY CITY	3-0	Hunt 2, Hine (pen)	15921
37		29	WEST HAM UNITED	0-0		21718
38	Apr	3	Doncaster Rovers	1-0	McArdle	12716
39		10	FULHAM	1-0	Gallacher	9127
40		17	Burnley	0-3		4919
41		24	SOUTHAMPTON	2-1	McArdle, Hine	8184
42	May	1	Norwich City	1-0	Hunt	7305

Played in game 4: W McGuinness (at 10).

Appearances grid (shirt numbers by game)

#	Ellis T	Young NJ	Shotton R	Jones L	Harper B	Bokas F	Harris A	Barlow H	Hallows J	Hine EW	Roberts NE	Adey W	Ashton E	Asquith B	Binns CH	Bray E	Bullock GF	Clark J	Fisher FW	Gallacher F	Hamill A	Henderson GB	Hunt DA	Hinsley G	Ives AE	Logan IW	McArdle P	Nicholson S	Oram DG	Williams E
1	1	2	3	4	5	6	7	8	9	10	11																			
2	1		3	4		6	7	8	9	10	11	2													5					
3	1	2	3	4		6		8	9	10			11						7			5								
4	1	2		4		6							11				9		7	8		5			3					
5	1		2		4	6		8	9				11						7	10		5			3					
6	1			4		6	7	8		10		2	11						9			5			3					
7	1		3	4		6	7	8		10		2	11						9			5								
8	1	2	3	4	5	6		8		10			7					11	9											
9	1	2	3	4	5	6	7	8		10			11						9											
10	1	2	3	4	5	6	7	8		10			11						9											
11	1	2	3	4	5	6	7	8		10			11						9											
12	1	2	3	4	5	6	7	8		10			11						9											
13	1	2	3	4	5		7	8		10						6			9										11	
14	1	2	3	4	5			8		10						6		7	9										11	
15	1	2	3	4	5			8		10						6			7	9									11	
16	1	2	3	4		6				10					11		7		8	9	5									
17	1	2	3	4	5	6				10					11		7		8	9										
18	1	2	3	4	5	6				10									8	9									11	
19	1	2	3	4	5	6	7			10									8	9									11	
20	1	2	3	4	5	6	11	8	9	10									7											
21	1	2	3	4	5	6	11	8	9	10									7											
22			3	4	5	6	11	8	9	10				1					7										2	
23			3	4	5	6	11	8	9	10				1					7										2	
24			3	4	5	6		8	9	10				1					7										11	2
25		2	3	4	5	6		8	9	10				1					7											11
26			3	4	5	6		8		10				1					7	9									11	2
27			3	4	5	6		8		10				1					7	9									11	2
28		2	3	4		6		8			11		10	1					7	9		5								
29		2	3	4	5	6		8			11		10	1							7	9								
30		2	3	4	5	6		8			11		10	1							9									
31		2	3				4		8	10	11		6	1					9		7	5								
32			3		5	6		8			11		10	1					7				9			4				2
33			3		5	6		8					10	1					7				9			4			11	2
34			3		5	6		8					10	1							7		9			4	11			2
35			3		5	6		8					10	1							7		9			4	11			2
36			3		5	6		8					10	1							7		9			4	11			2
37			3		5	6		8					10	1							7		9			4	11			2
38			3		5	6		8					10	1							7		9			4	11			2
39			3		5	6							10	1						8	7		9			4	11			2
40			3		5	6		8					10	1					7				9			4	11			2
41			3		5	6		8					10	1					7				9			4	11			2
42			3	6	5			8					10	1					7				9			4	11			2
Apps	21	22	40	30	36	36	15	23	10	39	7	3	10	18	2	3	1	11	25	4	17	8	11	1	3	11	9	2	10	14
Goals						3	1	4	4	13			1	3					6	2	4		4				3		1	

One own goal

F.A. Cup

	Date		Opponent	Score	Scorer	Att	Young	Shotton	Jones	Harper	Bokas	Barlow	Hine	Asquith	Fisher	Gallacher	Williams
R3	Jan	16	Walsall	1-3	Hamill	13329	2	3	4	5	6	8	10	1	7	9	11

Division 2 — Final Table

		P	W	D	L	F	A	W	D	L	F	A	Pts
1	Leicester City	42	14	4	3	56	26	10	4	7	33	31	56
2	Blackpool	42	13	4	4	49	19	11	3	7	39	34	55
3	Bury	42	13	4	4	46	26	9	4	8	28	29	52
4	Newcastle United	42	11	3	7	45	23	11	2	8	35	33	49
5	Plymouth Argyle	42	11	6	4	42	22	7	7	7	29	31	49
6	West Ham United	42	14	5	2	47	18	5	6	10	26	37	49
7	Sheffield United	42	16	4	1	48	14	2	6	13	18	40	46
8	Coventry City	42	11	5	5	35	19	6	6	9	31	35	45
9	Aston Villa	42	10	6	5	47	30	6	6	9	35	40	44
10	Tottenham Hotspur	42	13	3	5	57	26	4	6	11	31	40	43
11	Fulham	42	11	5	5	43	24	4	8	9	28	37	43
12	Blackburn Rovers	42	11	3	7	49	32	5	7	9	21	30	42
13	Burnley	42	11	5	5	37	20	5	5	11	20	41	42
14	BARNSLEY	42	11	6	4	30	23	5	3	13	20	41	41
15	Chesterfield	42	12	3	6	54	34	4	5	12	30	55	40
16	Swansea Town	42	14	2	5	40	16	1	5	15	10	49	37
17	Norwich City	42	8	6	7	38	29	6	2	13	25	42	36
18	Nottingham Forest	42	10	6	5	42	30	2	4	15	26	60	34
19	Southampton	42	10	8	3	38	25	1	4	16	15	52	34
20	Bradford Park Ave.	42	10	4	7	33	33	2	5	14	19	55	33
21	Bradford City	42	8	8	5	36	31	1	4	16	18	63	30
22	Doncaster Rovers	42	6	6	9	18	29	1	4	16	12	55	24

1937/38 — 21st in Division 2

No	Date	Opponent	Res	Scorers	Att	Binns CH	Williams E	Bokas F	Logan JW	Harper B	Jones L	Fisher FW	Hine EW	Hunt DA	Asquith B	McArdle P	Barlow H	Bullock GF	Bray E	Ellis T	Gallacher F	Glover A	Everest J	Hamill A	Hinsley G	Ives AE	Lang J	Nicholson S	Watson PR	Shotton R
1	Aug 28	Bradford Park Avenue	3-4	Hunt, Asquith, Hine	12802	1	2	3	4	5	6	7	8	9	10	11														
2	Sep 1	Newcastle United	1-0	Bullock	19065	1	2	6	4	5		9	8		10	11		7											3	
3	" 4	STOCKPORT COUNTY	2-0	Fisher, Asquith	13408	1	2	6	4	5		9	8		10	11		7											3	
4	" 6	NEWCASTLE UNITED	3-0	Bullock, Richards (og), Hine (p)	13117	1	2	6	4	5			8	9	10	11		7											3	
5	" 11	Manchester United	1-4	Hine (pen)	22394	1	2	6	4	5			8	9		11		7			10								3	
6	" 15	Nottingham Forest	1-2	Hine	9218		2	6	4	5		11	8	9	10			7		1								3		
7	" 18	SHEFFIELD UNITED	1-1	Hunt	16820		2	6	4	5			8	9	10	11		7		1										3
8	" 25	Tottenham Hotspur	0-3		26417		2	6	4	5		9	8		10	11		7		1										3
9	Oct 2	BURNLEY	2-2	Hine, Logan	15358	1	2	6	4	5			8	9	10			7								11				3
10	" 9	Bury	2-0	Hunt, Asquith	9717	1	2	6	4	5			8	9	10			7								11				3
11	" 16	West Ham United	1-4	Hunt	27291	1	2	6	4	5			8	9	10			7								11				3
12	" 23	SOUTHAMPTON	0-2		8041	1	2	6	4	5			8	9	10			7								11				3
13	" 30	Blackburn Rovers	3-5	Hunt 2, Asquith	12353	1	2	6	4	5				9	10		8	7								11				3
14	Nov 6	SHEFFIELD WEDNESDA	4-1	Hunt 2, Bray 2	11709	1	2	6	4	5				9	10		8	7	11											3
15	" 13	Fulham	0-0		13207	1	2	6	4	5				9	10		8		11		7									3
16	" 20	SWANSEA TOWN	2-0	Barlow, Asquith	8836	1	2	6	4	5		7		9	10		8		11											3
17	" 27	Chesterfield	0-0		13753	1	2	6	4	5		7		9	10		8		11											3
18	Dec 4	PLYMOUTH ARGYLE	3-2	Hunt 2, Gallacher	5817	1	2	6	4	5		7		9			8		11		10									3
19	" 11	Norwich City	0-1		8243	1	2	6	4	5		7					8		11		10			9						3
20	" 18	ASTON VILLA	0-1		15500	1	2	6	4	5		7		10			8		11		9									3
21	" 25	Luton Town	0-4		15829	1	2	6	4	5		7		10			8		11		9									3
22	" 27	LUTON TOWN	3-1	Fisher 2, Barlow	8242	1	2	6	4	5		7		10			8		11		9									3
23	" 28	Aston Villa	0-3		40360	1	2	5	6		4	7		9	10		8		11											3
24	Jan 1	BRADFORD PARK AVE.	0-1		16654	1	2	6		5	4			9	10		8		11		7									3
25	" 15	Stockport County	2-1	Bray, Hunt	7772	1	2	6		5		7		9	10		8		11			4								3
26	" 29	Sheffield United	3-6	Bray 2, Asquith	20251	1	2	6		5		7		9	10		8		11					4						3
27	Feb 2	MANCHESTER UNITED	2-2	Hunt, Barlow	7859	1	2	3	6	5				9	10		8	7	11					4						
28	" 5	TOTTENHAM HOTSPUR	1-1	Barlow	13327	1	2	4		5				9	10		8	7	11				6		3					
29	" 12	Burnley	0-1		12178	1	2	6		5	4			9			8	7	11		10				3					
30	" 19	BURY	2-2	Hunt 2	9639	1		6		5	4			9			8	7	11		10				3		2			
31	" 26	WEST HAM UNITED	1-0	Barlow	10613	1	2	4	6	5				9	10		8	7	11						3					
32	Mar 5	Southampton	0-2		14769	1	2	4	6	5			10	9			8	7	11				3							
33	" 12	BLACKBURN ROVERS	0-0		11136	1	2	4	6	5					10		8	7	11			9	3							
34	" 19	Sheffield Wednesday	1-0	Asquith	24629		2	4	6	5					10		8	7	11	1		9	3							
35	" 26	FULHAM	0-0		9385		2	4	6	5					10		8	7	11	1			3		9					
36	Apr 2	Swansea Town	0-1		8733		2	4	6	5		7		9	10		8		11	1			3							
37	" 9	CHESTERFIELD	1-1	Bray	10310		2	4	6	5		7		9	10		8		11	1			3							
38	" 16	Plymouth Argyle	2-2	Hine, Bray	21406		2	4	6	5			9		10		8	7	11	1			3							
39	" 18	COVENTRY CITY	1-1	Bray	16228		2	4	6	5			9		10		8	7	11	1			3							
40	" 19	Coventry City	0-1		30104	1	3	4	6	5			9		10		8	7	11								2			
41	" 23	NORWICH CITY	0-0		9350	1	3	4	6	5			9		10		8	7	11								2			
42	May 7	NOTTM. FOREST	2-2	Asquith, Barlow	16539	1	3	4	6	5			9		10		8	7	11								2			
		Apps				35	33	38	38	39	16	14	23	25	35	7	31	28	21	7	6	2	11	7	5	5	12	1	4	19
		Goals						1				3	6	14	8		6	2	8		1									

One own goal

F.A. Cup

Rnd	Date	Opponent	Res	Scorers	Att	Binns CH	Williams E	Bokas F	Logan JW	Harper B	Jones L	Fisher FW	Hine EW	Hunt DA	Asquith B	McArdle P	Barlow H	Bullock GF	Bray E	Ellis T	Gallacher F	Glover A	Everest J	Hamill A	Hinsley G	Ives AE	Lang J	Nicholson S	Watson PR	Shotton R
R3	Jan 8	Southend United	2-2	Asquith, Barlow	15236	1	2	4	6	5		7		9	10		8		11											3
rep	" 11	SOUTHEND UNITED	2-1	Barlow, Hunt	18960	1	2	4	6	5		7		9	10		8	11												3
R4	" 22	MANCHESTER UTD.	2-2	Bokas, Fisher	35549	1	2	4	6	5		7		9	10		8	11												3
rep	" 26	Manchester United	0-1		33601	1	2	4	6	5		7		9	10		8	11												3

League Table

		P	W	D	L	F	A	W	D	L	F	A	Pts
1	Aston Villa	42	17	2	2	50	12	8	5	8	23	23	57
2	Manchester United	42	15	3	3	50	18	7	6	8	32	32	53
3	Sheffield United	42	15	4	2	46	19	7	5	9	27	37	53
4	Coventry City	42	12	5	4	31	15	8	7	6	35	30	52
5	Tottenham Hotspur	42	14	3	4	46	16	5	3	13	30	38	44
6	Burnley	42	15	4	2	35	11	2	6	13	19	43	44
7	Bradford Park Ave.	42	13	4	4	51	22	4	5	12	18	34	43
8	Fulham	42	10	7	4	44	23	6	4	11	17	34	43
9	West Ham United	42	13	5	3	34	16	1	9	11	19	36	42
10	Bury	42	12	3	6	43	26	6	2	13	20	34	41
11	Chesterfield	42	12	2	7	39	24	4	7	10	24	39	41
12	Luton Town	42	10	6	5	53	36	5	4	12	36	50	40
13	Plymouth Argyle	42	10	7	4	40	30	4	5	12	17	35	40
14	Norwich City	42	11	5	5	35	28	3	6	12	21	47	39
15	Southampton	42	12	6	3	42	26	3	3	15	13	51	39
16	Blackburn Rovers	42	13	6	2	51	30	1	4	16	20	50	38
17	Sheffield Wed.	42	10	5	6	27	21	4	5	12	22	35	38
18	Swansea Town	42	12	6	3	31	21	1	6	14	14	52	38
19	Newcastle United	42	12	4	5	38	18	2	4	15	13	40	36
20	Nottingham Forest	42	12	3	6	29	21	2	5	14	18	39	36
21	BARNSLEY	42	7	11	3	30	20	4	3	14	20	44	36
22	Stockport County	42	8	6	7	24	24	3	3	15	19	46	31

Season 1937/38
Back row: Ferrier, Gallacher, Wheat, Larkin, Ives, Woffinden, Robinson
2nd back: Holley (Trainer) Seed (Manager) Williams, Hinsley, Harper, Ellis, Binns, Bokas,
Nicholson, Cooper (Ass Trainer) Tomlinson (Chairman)
2nd front: Hamill, Fisher, Hine, Hunt, Asquith, McArdle, Bray
Front row: Logan, Bullock, Jones, Horner, Lacey, Trevitt, Barlow, Shotton

Season 1938/39 (Champions Div. 3 North - with Cup)
Back row: Seed (Manager) Asquith, Brunskill, Binns, Everest, Calder, Pallister, Ratcliffe (Trainer)
Centre row: Bokas, Shotton, Williams, Harper, Logan, Steele, Lang
Front row: Bullock, McGarry

1938/39 — Champions of Division 3(N)

No		Date	Opponent	Score	Scorers	Att	Binns CH	Williams E	Everest J	Hinsley G	Harper B	Bokas F	McGarry D	Steele J	Calder J	Asquith B	Bray E	Baxter AG	Baines RE	Brunskill NH	Bullock GF	Ellis T	Glover A	Lang J	Logan JW	Pallister G	Shotton R	Woffinden RS
1	Aug	27	Oldham Athletic	2-4	Asquith (pen), Steele	6802	1	2	3	4	5	6	7	8	9	10	11											
2		29	Lincoln City	4-2	Bray 2, Calder, Steele	8501	1	2	3		5	4	7	8	9	10	11								6			
3	Sep	3	HALIFAX TOWN	1-0	Bokas	8216	1	2	3		5	4	7	8	9	10	11								6			
4		5	ROTHERHAM UNITED	2-0	Lang, McGarry	17613	1	2	3		5	4	11	8		9					7			10	6			
5		10	New Brighton	2-1	McGarry, Steele	7574	1	2	3		5	4	11	8		9					7			10	6			
6		12	Rotherham United	1-0	Steele	20144	1	2			5	4	11	8		9					7			10	6			
7		17	BARROW	4-0	Asquith(pen), Steele, McGarry, Bullock	11682	1	2			5	4	11	8		9					7			10	6		3	
8		24	Chester	1-2	Steele	9479	1	2			5	4	11	8		9					7			10	6		3	
9	Oct	1	BRADFORD CITY	5-2	Asquith(pen), Steele 2, Lang, Bullock	12949	1	2			5	4	11	8		9					7			10	6		3	
10		8	Hull City	1-0	Asquith	10382	1	2	3		5	4	11	8		9					7			10	6			
11		15	DONCASTER ROVERS	1-1	Bullock	20253	1	2	3		5	4	11	8		9					7			10	6			
12		22	Southport	0-0		9399	1	2	3		5		11	8	9						7			10	6			4
13		29	CREWE ALEXANDRA	5-2	Asquith 2, Lang 2, Steele	17683		2			5	4	11	8		9					7			10	6	3		
14	Nov	5	Carlisle United	1-3	Asquith	6770	1	2	3		5		11	8		9					7			10	6			4
15		12	DARLINGTON	7-1	Asquith 5 (1 pen), Lang, Steele	11914	1	2	3		5		11	8		9				4	7			10	6			
16		19	Hartlepools United	1-0	Steele	8582	1	2			5		11	8		9				4	7			10	6	3		
17		26	YORK CITY	1-0	Asquith	10708	1	2			5		11	8		9				4	7			10	6	3		
18	Dec	3	Wrexham	1-1	Bullock	6268	1	2			5		11	8		9				4	7			10	6	3		
19		10	GATESHEAD	2-0	Asquith, McGarry	11423	1	2			5		11	8		9				4	7			10	6	3		
20		17	Rochdale	1-2	Asquith (pen)	5466	1	2			5		11	8		9				4	7			10	6	3		
21		24	OLDHAM ATHLETIC	3-0	Bullock, Asquith 2 (1 pen)	12409	1	2			5			8		9				4	7			10	6	3		
22		26	ACCRINGTON STANLEY	4-1	Bullock, McGarry, Asquith (2 pens)	19062	1	2			5		11	8		9		10		4	7				6	3		
23		27	Accrington Stanley	2-0	Steele, Bullock	5094	1	2			5			8		10			9	4	7			11	6	3		
24		31	Halifax Town	4-1	McGarry 2, Asquith 2	12636		2			5		11	8		9		10		4	7	1			6	3		
25	Jan	14	NEW BRIGHTON	1-1	Baxter	11342		2	3		5		11	8		9		10		4	7	1			6			
26		21	Barrow	2-1	Bullock, Steele	6593		2	3		5		11	8		9		10		4	7	1			6			
27		28	CHESTER	3-0	Logan, Bullock, Baxter	13161	1	2	3		5		11	8		9		10		4	7				6			
28	Feb	4	Bradford City	2-0	Lang, Asquith	22560	1	2	3		5		11	8		9				4	7			10	6			
29		11	HULL CITY	5-1	Lang 3, Asquith, Logan	16839	1	2	3		5		11	8		9				4	7			10	6			
30		18	Doncaster Rovers	3-1	Potts (og), Asquith 2 (1 pen)	34046	1	2	3		5		11	8		9				4	7			10	6			
31		25	SOUTHPORT	3-1	Logan, Asquith, McGarry	21569	1	2	3		5		11	8		9				4	7			10	6			
32	Mar	4	Crewe Alexandra	0-0		10036	1	2	3		5		11	8		9				4	7			10	6			
33		11	CARLISLE UNITED	3-0	Brunskill, McGarry, Logan	13104	1	2	3		5		11	8		9				4	7			10	6			
34		18	Darlington	1-0	Steele	6573	1	2	3		5		11	8		9				4	7			10	6			
35		25	HARTLEPOOLS UNITED	2-0	Steele, Brunskill	11611	1	2	3		5		11	8		9				4	7			10	6			
36	Apr	1	Gateshead	1-1	Calder	8701	1	2			5		11	8	9	10				4	7				6	3		
37		7	Stockport County	1-1	Asquith	17860	1	2	3		5		11		9	10				4	7			8	6			
38		8	WREXHAM	2-1	Calder, Asquith	14988	1	2			5		11		9	10				4	7				6	3		
39		10	STOCKPORT COUNTY	0-1		19146	1	2			5		11		9	10				4	7		6	8		3		
40		15	York City	3-2	Calder 2, McGarry	6454	1	2	3		5		11		9	10	8			4	7		6					
41		22	ROCHDALE	2-0	McGarry 2	8403	1	2	3		5	6	11	8		9				4	7			10				
42		29	LINCOLN CITY	4-0	Lang, Bullock, Steele 2	5234	1	2	3		5		11	8		9				4	7			10	6			
Apps							39	41	26	1	41	14	41	39	9	41	3	6	1	28	39	3	2	31	38	10	7	2
Goals											1		12	17	5	28	2	2		2	10			10	4			

One own goal

F.A. Cup

		Date	Opponent	Score	Scorers	Att	Binns	Williams			Harper		McGarry	Steele		Asquith				Brunskill	Bullock			Lang	Logan	Pallister		
R3	Jan	7	STOCKPORT COUNTY	1-2	McGarry	19281	1	2			5		11	8		9				4	7			10	6	3		

		P	W	D	L	F	A	W	D	L	F	A	Pts
1	BARNSLEY	42	18	2	1	60	12	12	5	4	34	22	67
2	Doncaster Rovers	42	12	5	4	47	21	9	9	3	40	26	56
3	Bradford City	42	16	2	3	59	21	6	6	9	30	35	52
4	Southport	42	14	5	2	47	16	6	5	10	28	38	50
5	Oldham Athletic	42	16	1	4	51	21	6	4	11	25	38	49
6	Chester	42	12	5	4	54	31	8	4	9	34	39	49
7	Hull City	42	13	5	3	57	25	5	5	11	26	49	46
8	Crewe Alexandra	42	12	5	4	54	23	7	1	13	28	47	44
9	Stockport County	42	13	6	2	57	24	4	3	14	34	53	43
10	Gateshead	42	11	6	4	45	24	3	8	10	29	43	42
11	Rotherham United	42	12	4	5	45	21	5	4	12	19	43	42
12	Halifax Town	42	9	10	2	33	22	4	6	11	19	32	42
13	Barrow	42	11	5	5	46	22	5	4	12	20	43	41
14	Wrexham	42	15	2	4	46	28	2	5	14	20	51	41
15	Rochdale	42	10	5	6	58	29	5	4	12	34	53	39
16	New Brighton	42	11	2	8	46	32	4	7	10	22	41	39
17	Lincoln City	42	9	6	6	40	33	3	3	15	26	59	33
18	Darlington	42	12	2	7	43	30	1	5	15	19	62	33
19	Carlisle United	42	10	5	6	44	33	3	2	16	22	78	33
20	York City	42	8	5	8	37	34	4	3	14	27	58	32
21	Hartlepools United	42	10	4	7	36	33	2	3	16	19	61	31
22	Accrington Stanley	42	6	5	10	30	39	1	1	19	19	64	20

			1	2	3	4	5	6	7	8	9	10	11
1	Aug 26 NOTTM FOREST	4-1 Maxwell 3, McGarry	11535	Binns	Bokas	Everest	Brunskill	B Harper	Logan	Bullock	Steele	Maxwell	Lang	McGarry
2	28 Sheffield Wed	1-3 Steele	23000	Binns	Pallister	Everest	Brunskill	B Harper	Logan	Bullock	Steele	Maxwell	Lang	McGarry
3	Sep 2 Coventry City	2-4 Steele, Maxwell	11611	Binns	Shotton	Everest	Brunskill	B Harper	Logan	Bullock	Steele	Maxwell	Lang	McGarry

Note: League Season abandoned due to outbreak of war.

East Midlands League

			1	2	3	4	5	6	7	8	9	10	11
1	Oct 28 Lincoln City	3-1 England 2, Shotton (pen)	1500	Binns	K Harper	Shotton	Wright	B Harper	Bokas	Smith	Steele	Dodd	Gladwin	England
2	Nov 4 MANSFIELD TOWN	2-1 Robinson, Steele	2500	Binns	K Harper	Shotton	Wright	B Harper	Bokas	Smith	Steele	W Robinson	Gladwin	England
3	11 ROTHERHAM UTD	2-2 Deakin, Shotton (pen)	2000	Binns	K Harper	Shotton	Bokas	B Harper	Logan	Smith	Steele	Deakin	W Robinson	England
4	18 Sheffield Wed	1-1 Deakin (pen)	4000	Binns	K Harper	Shotton	Bokas	B Harper	Logan	Smith	Steele	Deakin	B Bennett	England
5	25 NOTTS COUNTY	2-1 Steele, England	1500	Binns	K Harper	Shotton	Bokas	B Harper	Logan	Smith	Bullock	Steele	Allison	England
6	Dec 2 Chesterfield	2-5 og, Steele	3000	Binns	K Harper	Shotton	Harston	B Harper	Logan	Smith	Bullock	Steele	Allison	England
7	9 Doncaster Rovers	1-1 Smith	3866	Binns	K Harper	Shotton	Bokas	Bokas	Logan	Bullock	Steele	Smith	Allison	England
8	23 GRIMSBY TOWN	4-1 Allison 2, Smith, Thorogood	2000	Binns	K Harper	Shotton	Glover	B Harper	Logan	Smith	Bullock	Steele	Allison	Thorogood
9	Jan 6 Sheffield United	1-2 Smith	4000	Binns	K Harper	Shotton	Bokas	B Harper	Logan	Bullock	Steele	Smith	Allison	Thorogood
10	Feb 24 LINCOLN CITY	1-7 Gallacher	2000	Binns	K Harper	Shotton	Bokas	B Harper	Logan	Bullock	Steele	Bramham	Gallacher	Thorogood
11	Mar 9 Rotherham Utd	4-0 Smith 3, Hydes	3000	Binns	K Harper	Shotton	Bokas	B Harper	Logan	Bullock	Steele	Smith	Hydes	Thorogood
12	16 SHEFFIELD WED	2-0 Steele, Shotton	3000	Binns	K Harper	Shotton	Bokas	B Harper	Logan	Bullock	Steele	Smith	Hydes	Thorogood
13	22 NOTTM FOREST	3-0 Steele, Bullock, Thorogood	3000	Binns	K Harper	Shotton	Bokas	TW Robinson	Logan	Bullock	Steele	Asquith	Hydes	Thorogood
14	23 Notts County	6-0 Smith, Bullock, Steele, Thorogood, Asquith 2	3000	Binns	K Harper	Shotton	Bokas	TW Robinson	Logan	Smith	Steele	Smith	Asquith	Thorogood
15	25 Nottingham Forest	0-1	5000	Binns	K Harper	Shotton	Bokas	TW Robinson	Logan	Bullock	Steele	Asquith	Bullock	Thorogood
16	30 CHESTERFIELD	3-1 Smith 2, Steele	5000	Binns	K Harper	Shotton	Bokas	B Harper	Logan	Bullock	Steele	Smith	Asquith	England
17	Apr 6 DONCASTER ROVERS	1-1 Asquith	4000	Binns	Adey	Shotton	Woffinden	B Harper	Logan	Bullock	Steele	Smith	Asquith	Thorogood
18	13 Grimsby Town	0-0	3000	Binns	Bokas	Shotton	Bokas	B Harper	Logan	Bullock	Steele	Bray	Asquith	Thorogood
19	May 25 Mansfield Town	2-3 Thorogood, Shotton (pen)	2000	Binns	Jones	Shotton	Bokas	B Harper	Logan	Smith	Bullock	Bray	Steele	Thorogood
20	Jun 1 SHEFFIELD UNITED	3-1 Hubbard, Shotton (pen), Smith	1429	Binns	Bokas	Shotton	Steele	B Harper	Logan	Smith	Bullock	Hubbard	Asquith	Thorogood

League Cup

			1	2	3	4	5	6	7	8	9	10	11
R1/1	Apr 20 HARTLEPOOLS UTD	3-0 Lang, Calder 2	5755	Binns	K Harper	Shotton	Bokas	B Harper	Logan	Bullock	Steele	Calder	Lang	Thorogood
R1/2	27 Hartlepools Utd	1-1 Woffinden	2000	Binns	K Harper	Shotton	Bokas	B Harper	Logan	Bullock	Brunskill	Smith	Woffinden	Thorogood
R2/1	May 4 SHEFFIELD UNITED	3-0 Smith, Steele, Bullock	8529	Binns	K Harper	Shotton	Bokas	B Harper	Logan	Bullock	Steele	Smith	Woffinden	Thorogood
R2/2	11 Sheffield United	0-1	3770	Binns	K Harper	Shotton	Bokas	B Harper	Logan	Bullock	Steele	Smith	Baxter	Lang
R3	18 BLACKPOOL	0-1	10796	Binns	K Harper	Shotton	Bokas	B Harper	Logan	Bullock	Steele	Smith	Lang	Stubbs

	P	W	D	L	F	A	Pts
Chesterfield	20	14	2	4	69	23	30
Sheffield U	20	12	1	7	46	34	25
Barnsley	20	10	5	5	43	39	25
Grimsby	20	10	2	8	40	44	22
Mansfield	20	9	3	8	49	48	21
Doncaster	20	7	4	9	37	45	18
Lincoln	20	9	0	11	42	53	18
Rotherham	20	7	4	9	24	42	18
Sheffield W	20	5	5	10	33	42	15
Nottingham F	20	5	4	11	37	43	14
Notts Co	20	6	2	12	40	57	14

Season 1939/40
Back row: Clegg, Murphy, Humble, Harston, Bennett, Whyte, Hunt, Everest, Ferrier, Bray
2nd back: Hine (Coach) Gray, Brunskill, Steele, Hetherington, Robinson, Binns, Calder, Allison,
Woffinden, Jones, Bokas, Cooper (Ass Trainer)
2nd front: Bullock, Shotton, Baxter, Smith, Harper, Maxwell, Logan, Long, McGarry
Front row: Bonell, Hurrell, Vicary (Ass Secretary) England, Lacey

Season 1945/46
Back row: Mansley, Cunningham, Wilson, Rymer, Pallister, Logan
Front row: Smith, Cooling, Robledo G, Baxter, Kelly

LEAGUE TABLES 1940/41 TO 1945/46

1945/46 Season North League

	P	W	L	D	F	A	Pts
Sheffield U	42	27	9	6	112	62	60
Everton	42	23	10	9	88	54	55
Bolton	42	20	11	11	67	45	51
Manchester U	42	19	12	11	98	62	49
Sheffield W	42	20	14	8	67	60	48
Newcastle	42	21	16	5	106	70	47
Chesterfield	42	17	13	12	68	47	46
Barnsley	42	17	14	11	76	68	45
Blackpool	42	18	15	9	94	92	45
Manchester C	42	20	18	4	78	75	44
Liverpool	42	17	16	9	80	70	43
Middlesbrough	42	17	16	9	75	87	43
Stoke	42	18	18	6	88	79	42
Bradford PA	42	17	19	6	71	84	40
Huddersfield	42	17	21	4	90	89	38
Burnley	42	13	19	10	63	84	36
Grimsby	42	13	20	9	61	89	35
Sunderland	42	15	22	5	55	83	35
Preston	42	14	22	6	70	77	34
Bury	42	14	24	4	60	85	34
Blackburn	42	11	24	7	60	111	29
Leeds	42	9	26	7	66	118	25

Notes: The War seasons were generally run on the basis of clubs playing a limited number of games against relatively local opponents, i.e. each club did not play each other on a home and away basis as normal. Consequently composite league tables were composed. In addition some matches were 'double-headers' for other competitions. Such matches have been identified on the Barnsley appropriate seasonal record.

1945/46 was an interim season when each team played each other on a home and away basis, but the various leagues were regionalised.

1944/45 Season

North League 1st Championship

(Top 30 clubs shown only)

(2nd Championship)

(Top 30 clubs shown only)

League North Cup Qualifying Competition

(Top 25 clubs shown only — plus next seven)

1943/44 Season

North League 1st Championship

(2nd CHAMPIONSHIP)

(Top 30 clubs shown only)

League North Cup Qualifying Competition

(Top 15 clubs shown only)

1942/43 Season

North League 1st Championship

(top 25 clubs shown only)

(2nd CHAMPIONSHIP)

(Top 25 clubs shown only)

League North Cup Qualifying Competition

All above qualified (remainder not shown)

1940/41 Season (North League)

(Positions determined on goal average)

1941/42 Season (North League 1st Championship)

(2nd Championship)

Average points calculated on 23 matches. Only those playing 18 or more games qualified for the Championship. (Top 25 clubs shown only)

1940/41 North League

#	Date	Opponent	Score	Scorers	Att.	1	2	3	4	5	6	7	8	9	10	11
1	Aug 31	Doncaster Rovers	1-2	Bullock	3000	Binns	K Harper	Shotton	Bokas	B Harper	Logan	Smith	Bullock	Woffinden	Steele	Thorogood
2	Sep 7	CHESTERFIELD	2-0	Smith, Steele	2500	Binns	K Harper	Shotton	Woffinden	Bokas	Logan	Bullock	Steele	Smith	Asquith	Thorogood
3	14	Chesterfield	1-5	Clegg	3000	Binns	Bokas	Shotton	Woffinden	B Harper	Logan	Bullock	Steele	Clegg	Bray	Thorogood
4	21	DONCASTER ROVERS	6-2	Smith 2, Bullock 2, Asquith, Shotton	2000	Binns	K Harper	Shotton	Bokas	B Harper	Logan	Bullock	Steele	Smith	Asquith	Thorogood
5	28	Newcastle United	0-1		3500	Binns	K Harper	Shotton	Bokas	B Harper	Logan	Bullock	Steele	Smith	Pallister	Hold
6	Oct 5	NEWCASTLE UNITED	1-0	Bullock	2000	Binns	K Harper	Shotton	Bokas	B Harper	Logan	Bullock	Steele	Smith	Asquith	Thorogood
7	12	Sheffield Wednesday	2-2	Steele 2	3000	Binns	K Harper	Shotton	Bokas	B Harper	Logan	Bullock	Steele	Smith	Asquith	Thorogood
8	19	Huddersfield Town	2-1	Logan, Steele	2198	Binns	K Harper	Shotton	Bokas	B Harper	Logan	Bullock	Steele	Smith	Asquith	Thorogood
9	26	SHEFFIELD WEDNESDAY	5-0	Smith 2, Thorogood, Asquith, Steele	2000	Binns	K Harper	Shotton	Bokas	B Harper	Logan	Bullock	Steele	Smith	Asquith	Thorogood
10	Nov 2	LEEDS UNITED	3-0	Thorogood, Bullock, Steele	1000	Sagar	K Harper	Shotton	Bokas	B Harper	Logan	Bullock	Steele	Smith	Asquith	Thorogood
11	9	Sheffield United	1-3	Smith	2000	Sagar	K Harper	Shotton	Bokas	B Harper	Logan	Bullock	Steele	Smith	Asquith	Thorogood
12	16	Lincoln City	3-2	Smith 2, Steele	2000	Wilkinson	K Harper	Shotton	Bokas	B Harper	Logan	Bullock	Steele	Smith	Woffinden	Thorogood
13	23	HUDDERSFIELD TOWN	4-1	Steele 2, Bullock, Smith	2500	Wilkinson	K Harper	Shotton	Bokas	B Harper	Logan	Bullock	Steele	Smith	Asquith	Thorogood
14	30	SHEFFIELD UNITED	1-4	Steele	2500	King	K Harper	Shotton	Bokas	B Harper	Logan	Bullock	Steele	Smith	Richardson	Thorogood
15	Dec 7	Leeds United	1-1	Woffinden	3000	Binns	K Harper	Shotton	Bokas	B Harper	Logan	Bullock	Woffinden	Smith	Asquith	Thorogood
16	14	Hull City	2-1	og, Smith	500	Binns	K Harper	Shotton	Bokas	B Harper	Logan	Bullock	Woffinden	Smith	Asquith	Thorogood
17	21	HULL CITY	5-0	Bullock 2, Thorogood 2, Steele	4000	Binns	K Harper	Shotton	Bokas	B Harper	Logan	Bullock	Steele	Smith	Asquith	Thorogood
18	25	Rotherham United	3-0	Shotton (2 pens), Steele	2060	Binns	K Harper	Shotton	Bokas	B Harper	Logan	Bullock	Steele	Smith	Asquith	Thorogood
19	25	ROTHERHAM UNITED	3-3	Asquith, Bullock, Steele	2692	Binns	K Harper	Shotton	Woffinden	B Harper	Logan	Bullock	Steele	Smith	Asquith	Thorogood
20	28	LINCOLN CITY	6-0	Asquith 3, Fisher, Steele, og	2000	Binns	K Harper	Shotton	Woffinden	B Harper	Logan	Bullock	Steele	Fisher	Asquith	Smith
21	Jan 11	Rotherham United*	3-4	Smith, Steele, Asquith	1500	AN Other	AN Other	Shotton	AN Other	AN Other	Logan	AN Other	Steele	Smith	Asquith	AN Other
22	18	Bradford City	5-1	Steele, Bullock 3, Thorogood	400	AN Other	AN Other	Shotton	Bokas	AN Other	Logan	Bullock	Steele	Smith	AN Other	Thorogood
23	Feb 1	Everton	1-3	Bray	2000	AN Other	AN Other	Shotton	Bokas	AN Other	AN Other	AN Other	Steele	Smith	AN Other	Bray
24	Mar 1	SHEFFIELD WEDNESDAY	7-1	Gregory 3, Steele 2, Smith, Thorogood	2000	AN Other	AN Other	Shotton	Bokas	AN Other	Logan	AN Other	Steele	Smith	Gregory	Thorogood
25	Apr 5	ROTHERHAM UNITED	5-1	Smith 3, Steele, Bullock	1500	AN Other	AN Other	Shotton	Bokas	AN Other	Logan	Bullock	Steele	Smith	AN Other	AN Other
26	12	HUDDERSFIELD TOWN	4-3	Bullock 2, Smith 2	3000	AN Other	AN Other	Shotton	Bokas	AN Other	Logan	Bullock	Steele	Smith	AN Other	AN Other
27	14	YORK CITY	1-1	Asquith	2724	AN Other	AN Other	Shotton	Bokas	AN Other	Logan	AN Other	Steele	Smith	Asquith	AN Other
28	19	MIDDLESBROUGH	3-2	Smith, Gregory, og	3000	AN Other	AN Other	Shotton	Bokas	AN Other	Logan	AN Other	Steele	Smith	Gregory	AN Other
29	26	Middlesbrough	2-3	Steele, Bray	2000	AN Other	AN Other	Shotton	Bokas	AN Other	Logan	AN Other	Steele	Smith	AN Other	Bray
30	May 3	CHESTERFIELD	3-2	Steele 2, Gregory	1500	AN Other	AN Other	Shotton	Bokas	AN Other	Logan	AN Other	Steele	Smith	Gregory	AN Other

* Also counted as Sheffield County Cup Semi-Final

League Cup

Rd	Date	Opponent	Score	Scorers	Att.	1	2	3	4	5	6	7	8	9	10	11
R1/	Feb 15	Chesterfield	4-1	Thorogood 2, McGarry, Smith	5000	Binns	K Harper	Shotton	Bokas	B Harper	Harston	Bullock	Smith	McGarry	Steele	Thorogood
R1/	22	CHESTERFIELD	5-2	McGarry, Smith, Bullock 3	1000	Binns	K Harper	Shotton	Bokas	B Harper	Harston	Bullock	Smith	McGarry	Steele	Thorogood
R2/	Mar 8	GRIMSBY TOWN	1-1	McGarry	2500	Binns	K Harper	Shotton	Bokas	B Harper	Harston	Bullock	Smith	McGarry	Logan	Thorogood
R2/	15	Grimsby Town*	2-2	Steele, Woffinden	4000	Binns	Bokas	Gregory	Glover	B Harper	Logan	Bullock	Smith	Woffinden	AN Other	AN Other
R3/	22	Sheffield United	1-3	Bullock (pen)	7000	Binns	Bokas	Shotton	Glover	B Harper	Logan	Bullock	Smith	McGarry	Steele	Thorogood
R3/	29	SHEFFIELD UNITED	1-1	Smith	5000	Binns	Bokas	Shotton	Glover	B Harper	Logan	Bullock	Smith	Whitelum	Steele	Thorogood

*Note: With the scores level at the end of extra time, the game was to continue until one side scored i.e. sudden death. After a further 50 minutes with no further score, the Referee, Flying Officer McKenzie was called away for RAF duties and the game halted. The league awarded the tie to Barnsley, who had a higher league placing.

#	Date	Opponent	Score	Scorers	Att	1	2	3	4	5	6	7	8	9	10	11
1	Aug 30	GRIMSBY TOWN	2-1	Gregory, Steele	3000	Binns	K Harper	Shotton	Kilpatrick	B Harper	Logan	Smith	Steele	Gregory	Asquith	Thorogood
2	Sep 6	Grimsby Town	1-1	Thorogood	2500	Binns	Jones	Shotton	Kilpatrick	B Harper	Logan	Smith	Steele	Gregory	Asquith	Thorogood
3	13	Lincoln City	2-3	Smith 2	4000	Binns	K Harper	Gregory	Kilpatrick	B Harper	Logan	Smith	Steele	Hubbard	Asquith	Thorogood
4	20	LINCOLN CITY	1-2	Smith	3000	Binns	K Harper	Shotton	Kilpatrick	B Harper	Logan	Smith	Steele	Hubbard	Asquith	Thorogood
5	27	DONCASTER ROVERS	2-4	Asquith, Hubbard	3000	Binns	K Harper	Shotton	Bokas	B Harper	Logan	Smith	Steele	Hubbard	Asquith	Thorogood
6	Oct 4	Doncaster Rovers	1-1	Steele	3678	Binns	K Harper	Shotton	Bokas	B Harper	Logan	Smith	Steele	Hubbard	Asquith	Thorogood
7	11	Sheffield United	1-2	Hubbard	5000	Binns	K Harper	Shotton	Bokas	B Harper	Logan	Smith	Steele	Hubbard	Asquith	Thorogood
8	18	SHEFFIELD UNITED	2-1	Smith 2,	2000	Binns	K Harper	Shotton	Bokas	B Harper	Logan	Smith	Steele	Asquith	Settle	Thorogood
9	25	MANSFIELD TOWN	3-1	Smith, Hubbard, Wipfler	1500	Binns	K Harper	Shotton	Bokas	B Harper	Logan	Wipfler	Smith	Hubbard	Asquith	Thorogood
10	Nov 1	Mansfield Town	3-0	Steele 2, Smith	600	Binns	K Harper	Shotton	Bokas	B Harper	Logan	Smith	Steele	Hubbard	Asquith	Thorogood
11	8	Chesterfield	1-1	Smith	2000	Styles	K Harper	Shotton	Bokas	B Harper	Logan	Smith	Steele	Hubbard	Asquith	Asquith
12	15	CHESTERFIELD	1-0	Thorogood	2000	Binns	Jones	Shotton	Bokas	K Harper	Logan	Smith	Steele	Hubbard	Asquith	Thorogood
13	22	MIDDLESBOROUGH	3-1	Steele, Asquith 2	2000	Binns	Jones	Shotton	Bokas	K Harper	Logan	Smith	Harston	Asquith	Steele	Thorogood
14	29	Middlesborough	2-3	Harston, Steele	3000	Arran	Jones	Shotton	Harston	K Harper	Logan	Smith	Harston	Asquith	Steele	Thorogood
15	Dec 6	SHEFFIELD WEDNESDAY	4-3	Davis, Asquith, Steele 2	1000	Gibson	Jones	Shotton	Harston	Bokas	Logan	Davis	Steele	Smith	Wesley	Asquith
16	13	Sheffield Wednesday	0-3		2000	Nicholls	Jones	Shotton	Harston	Bokas	Logan	A Spence	Steele	Smith	Asquith	Thorogood
17	20	Rotherham United	3-3	Steele, Smith, Harston	2200	Nicholls	Allott	Shotton	Bokas	K Harper	Logan	Smith	Harston	Asquith	Steele	Lacey
18	25	ROTHERHAM UNITED	7-1	Smith 3, Lacey, Fleetwood, Asquith, Boka	4079	Nicholls	Harston	Shotton	Bokas	K Harper	Logan	Smith	Fleetwood	Asquith	Steele	Lacey

North League (2nd Championship)

#	Date	Opponent	Score	Scorers	Att	1	2	3	4	5	6	7	8	9	10	11
1	Dec 27	BRADFORD PA	5-2	Smith 2, Steele 2, og	5000	Nicholls	Harston	Shotton	Bokas	K Harper	Logan	Smith	Fleetwood	Asquith	Steele	Lacey
2	Jan 3	Bradford PA	1-1	Asquith	2500	Binns	K Harper	Shotton	Harston	TW Robinson	Bokas	Smith	Fleetwood	Asquith	Steele	Thorogood
3	10	GRIMSBY TOWN	0-0		3000	Binns	Harston	Shotton	Bokas	K Harper	Logan	Smith	Fleetwood	Asquith	Steele	Thorogood
4	17	Grimsby Town	0-2		1500	Binns	Harston	Shotton	Bokas	K Harper	Logan	Smith	Fleetwood	Asquith	Steele	Thorogood
5	Feb 14	Leeds United	2-3	Thorogood, Asquith	2500	Binns	Harston	Shotton	Bokas	K Harper	Logan	Smith	Fleetwood	Asquith	Steele	Thorogood
6	21	STOCKPORT COUNTY	6-1	Steele 4, Thorogood 2	1000	Binns	Harston	Shotton	Bokas	K Harper	Logan	Asquith	Fleetwood	Woffinden	Steele	Thorogood
7	28	Stockport County	6-3	Steele 3, Thorogood, Smith, Asquith	1000	Binns	Harston	Shotton	Bokas	K Harper	Logan	Smith	Fleetwood	Asquith	Steele	Thorogood
8	Mar 14	Halifax Town	4-2	Smith, Asquith (pen), Steele 2	3000	Binns	Harston	Shotton	Bokas	K Harper	Logan	Smith	Fleetwood	Asquith	Steele	Thorogood
9	21	LEEDS UNITED *	3-2	Fleetwood 3	4500	Binns	Harston	Shotton	Bokas	K Harper	Logan	Smith	Fleetwood	Woffinden	Asquith	Thorogood
10	28	HALIFAX TOWN	6-0	Asquith 2, Smith 2, Fleetwood, Lacey	2500	Binns	Harston	Shotton	Bokas	K Harper	Logan	Smith	Fleetwood	Asquith	Lacey	Thorogood
11	Apr 4	GRIMSBY TOWN	1-2	Henry	7550	Binns	Harston	Shotton	Bokas	K Harper	Logan	Smith	Fleetwood	Henry	McGarry	Thorogood
12	6	Grimsby Town	1-1	McGarry	3000	Binns	Harston	Shotton	Bokas	K Harper	Logan	Smith	Fleetwood	Henry	McGarry	Thorogood
13	May 9	SHEFFIELD UNITED	5-1	Hullett, Fleetwood 2, Asquith	3000	Binns	Harston	Shotton	Bokas	K Harper	Logan	Smith	Fleetwood	Hullett	Asquith	Thorogood
14	16	Rotherham United	5-1	Smith, Thorogood, Fleetwood, Hullett, og	3500	Binns	Harston	Shotton	Bokas	K Harper	Logan	Smith	Fleetwood	Hullett	Asquith	Thorogood
15	25	ROTHERHAM UNITED	3-2	Thorogood 3		Binns	Harston	Bokas	Barclay	K Harper	Logan	Burton	Steele	Smith	Robledo	Thorogood

Matches 11 and 12 also counted in League Cup knockout competition, match 11 1st round 1st leg, match 12 1st round 2nd leg.

Matches 11 and 14 also counted in League Cup competition, match 13 Semi-Final, match 14 Final 1st leg, match 15 Final 2nd leg.

Note: Matches 1 to 10 also counted in League Cup Qualifying competition.
Matches 13 to 15 also counted in Sheffield County Cup competition.

1942/43 North League (1st Championship)

					1	2	3	4	5	6	7	8	9	10	11
1	Aug 29	HUDDERSFIELD T	6-1	Fleetwood 3, Harston 2, Smith	4000	Binns	K Harper	Shotton	Bokas	B Harper	Logan	Smith	Fleetwood	Asquith	Harston	Thorogood
2	Sep 5	Huddersfield T	3-3	Fleetwood, Asquith, Smith	1513	Binns	K Harper	Shotton	Harston	B Harper	Logan	Smith	Fleetwood	Asquith	Steele	Thorogood
3	12	BRADFORD CITY	4-0	Steele 3 (1 pen), Harston	3631	Binns	Jones	Shotton	Bokas	B Harper	Logan	Smith	Fleetwood	Steele	Harston	Thorogood
4	19	Bradford City	3-2	Thorogood 2, Smith	4000	Binns	Jones	Shotton	Bokas	B Harper	Logan	Fleetwood	Harston	Smith	Asquith	Thorogood
5	26	GRIMSBY TOWN	1-3	Smith	4482	K Harper	Jones	Shotton	Bokas	B Harper	Logan	Fleetwood	Harston	Smith	Asquith	Thorogood
6	Oct 3	Grimsby Town	1-1	Thorogood	2500	Fenton	K Harper	Shotton	Bokas	B Harper	Logan	Burton	Fleetwood	Smith	Asquith	Thorogood
7	10	Sheffield United	1-3	Thorogood	8000	Fenton	K Harper	Shotton	Bokas	B Harper	Logan	Burton	Fleetwood	Smith	Asquith	Thorogood
8	17	SHEFFIELD UNITED	2-1	Fleetwood, K Harper	4000	Binns	K Harper	Shotton	Harston	B Harper	Woffinden	Burton	Fleetwood	Smith	Asquith	Thorogood
9	24	Sheffield Wed	1-5	Smith	7000	Binns	K Harper	Shotton	Bokas	Bokas	Logan	Smith	Fleetwood	Asquith	Harston	Thorogood
10	31	SHEFFIELD WED	0-3		4774	Binns	Harston	Shotton	Bokas	B Harper	Logan	Smith	Fleetwood	Asquith	Steele	Thorogood
11	Nov 7	ROTHERHAM UTD	2-3	Smith, Logan	3000	Binns	Harston	Shotton	Bokas	B Harper	Logan	Smith	Fleetwood	Asquith	Lacey	Thorogood
12	14	Rotherham Utd	5-1	Thorogood 2, Smith, Steele, og	3000	Binns	K Harper	Shotton	Bokas	B Harper	Logan	Smith	Fleetwood	Asquith	Steele	Thorogood
13	21	Bradford PA	1-1	Fleetwood	2500	Binns	K Harper	Shotton	Bokas	B Harper	Hold	Fisher	Fleetwood	Clegg	Asquith	Thorogood
14	28	BRADFORD PA	3-1	Griffiths, Smith, Thorogood (pen)	2820	Binns	K Harper	Shotton	Bokas	B Harper	Logan	Smith	Griffiths	Smith	Steele	Thorogood
15	Dec 5	DONCASTER R	1-1	Thorogood	1590	Binns	Jones	Shotton	Bokas	B Harper	Logan	Smith	Fleetwood	Henry	Asquith	Thorogood
16	12	Doncaster R	2-0	Thorogood, Smith	2996	Binns	Jones	Shotton	Bokas	B Harper	Logan	Smith	Fleetwood	Clegg	Asquith	Thorogood
17	19	CHESTERFIELD	3-1	Clegg, Smith, Myers	2000	Binns	Jones	Shotton	Bokas	B Harper	Logan	Smith	Fleetwood	Clegg	Asquith	Myers
18	25	Chesterfield	0-0				Jones	Shotton	Harston	Bokas	Woffinden	Smith	Cooling	Clegg	Fleetwood	Myers

North League (2nd Championship)

					1	2	3	4	5	6	7	8	9	10	11
1	Dec 26	LEEDS UNITED	2-1	Bullock (pen), Smith	6000	Binns	Jones	Shotton	Bokas	B Harper	Harston	Bullock	Barlow	Smith	Asquith	Clegg
2	Jan 2	Leeds United	3-1	Fleetwood 3	2000	Binns	Jones	Shotton	Bokas	B Harper	Logan	Smith	Fleetwood	Asquith	Steele	Clegg
3	9	Doncaster R	2-1	Griffiths, Asquith	2000	Binns	Jones	Shotton	Bokas	B Harper	Logan	Smith	Steele	Griffiths	Asquith	Bray
4	16	DONCASTER R	1-1	Fleetwood	4400	Binns	Jones	Shotton	Bokas	B Harper	Logan	Smith	Steele	Fleetwood	Asquith	Bray
5	23	HUDDERSFIELD T	3-2	Smith, McGarry, Fleetwood	5000	Binns	Bokas	Shotton	Brunskill	B Harper	Logan	Smith	Steele	Fleetwood	Asquith	McGarry
6	30	Huddersfield T	0-4		5000	Oldroyd	Jones	Bokas	Harston	Brunskill	Logan	Smith	Fleetwood	Dawson	Asquith	McGarry
7	Feb 6	BRADFORD CITY	1-2	Harston	5000	Binns	Jones	Shotton	Woffinden	Bokas	Logan	Smith	Harston	Clegg	Asquith	Forster
8	13	Bradford City	3-2	Bray, McGarry 2	3500	Binns	Harston	Shotton	Brunskill	Bokas	Logan	Coulston	Smith	McGarry	Asquith	Bray
9	20	SHEFFIELD UTD	2-4	Bray, Asquith	8116	Binns	Bokas	Shotton	Brunskill	B Harper	Logan	Smith	Fleetwood	McGarry	Asquith	Bray
10	27	Sheffield Utd	2-2	Smith, Fleetwood	15000	Binns	Shotton	Pallister	Brunskill	B Harper	Logan	Smith	Fleetwood	McGarry	Asquith	Thorogood
11	Mar 6	SHEFFIELD UTD	1-4	Smith	11680	Binns	Pallister	Shotton	Brunskill	B Harper	Logan	Smith	Fleetwood	McGarry	Asquith	Thorogood
12	13	Sheffield Utd	0-3		20000	Binns	Shotton	Pallister	Harston	B Harper	Logan	Bullock	Smith	McGarry	Asquith	Thorogood
13	20	HUDDERSFIELD T	2-1	Fleetwood, Thorogood	2000	Binns	AN Other	Shotton	Harston	B Harper	Logan	Smith	Fleetwood	AN Other	AN Other	Thorogood
14	27	Huddersfield T	0-5		2000	Binns	AN Other	Shotton	Harston	B Harper	Logan	Smith	Fleetwood	AN Other	AN Other	AN Other
15	Apr 17	SHEFFIELD UTD	4-1	Fleetwood, Asquith 2, Hold	2000	Binns	Harston	Shotton	Bokas	B Harper	Logan	Smith	Fleetwood	Asquith	Hold	AN Other
16	24	Sheffield Utd	1-2	Fleetwood	5000	Binns	Harston	Shotton	Bokas	B Harper	Logan	Smith	Fleetwood	Asquith	AN Other	AN Other
17	May 1	ROTHERHAM UTD	7-1	Asquith, Smith 2, Steele 3, Fleetwood	2000	Binns	Harston	Shotton	Harston	B Harper	Logan	Smith	Fleetwood	Asquith	Steele	AN Other

Note: matches 1 to 10 also counted in League North Cup qualifying competition.
Note: matches 11 and 12 also counted in League North Cup knockout competition, match 11 1st round 1st leg, match 12 1st round 2nd leg.
Note: matches 15 to 17 also counted in Sheffield County Cup competition, match 15 Semi-Final 1st leg, match 16 Semi-Final 2nd leg, match 17 Final 1st leg

Sheffield County Cup (Final 2nd Leg)

					1	2	3	4	5	6	7	8	9	10	11
	May 15	Rotherham Utd	3-5	Steele 2, Fleetwood	700	AN Other	AN Other	AN Other	AN Other	AN Other	AN Other	AN Other	Fleetwood	AN Other	Steele	AN Other

1943/44 North League (1st Championship)

#	Date	Opponent	Score	Scorers	Att	1	2	3	4	5	6	7	8	9	10	11
1	Aug 24	SHEFFIELD WED	3-1	Smith, Asquith (pen), Robledo	6000	Binns	Harston	Shotton	Bokas	B Harper	Logan	Smith	Steele	Robledo	Asquith	Fisher
2	Sep 4	Sheffield Wed	1-3	Asquith (pen)	7000	Binns	Harston	Shotton	Bokas	B Harper	Logan	Smith	Fleetwood	Robledo	Steele	Asquith
3	11	Huddersfield T	4-1	Fleetwood 2, Smith, og	2642	Binns	Harston	Pallister	Bokas	B Harper	Logan	Smith	Steele	Fleetwood	Asquith	Sloan
4	18	HUDDERSFIELD T	1-2	Steele	5264	Binns	Harston	Pallister	Bokas	B Harper	Logan	Smith	Steele	Fleetwood	Asquith	Boocock
5	25	Grimsby Town	0-1		2300	Binns	Harston	Pallister	Bokas	B Harper	Logan	Smith	Steele	Fleetwood	Asquith	Sloan
6	Oct 2	GRIMSBY TOWN	3-0	Smith 2 (1 pen), Fleetwood	4162	Binns	Harston	Pallister	Bokas	B Harper	Makepeace	Smith	Sloan	Fleetwood	Logan	Sinclair
7	9	Bradford City	1-2	Asquith (pen)	5000	Binns	Harston	Pallister	Logan	B Harper	Armeson	Smith	Fleetwood	Asquith	Sloan	Woffinden
8	16	BRADFORD CITY	3-0	Sinclair, Fleetwood, Sloan	4085	Binns	Harston	Pallister	Logan	Bokas	Armeson	Smith	Fleetwood	Asquith	Sloan	Sinclair
9	23	SHEFFIELD UNITED	3-2	Sloan, Smith, Logan	5000	Binns	Harston	Pallister	Bokas	B Harper	Logan	Smith	Sloan	Robledo	Asquith	Sinclair
10	30	Sheffield United	0-1		7000	Binns	Harston	Pallister	Bokas	B Harper	Logan	Smith	Sloan	Fleetwood	Asquith	Sinclair
11	Nov 6	Rotherham United	1-3	Asquith	4000	Binns	Harston	Pallister	Logan	B Harper	Armeson	Smith	Fleetwood	Williams	Sloan	Sinclair
12	13	ROTHERHAM UNITED	3-3	Fleetwood, Asquith 2	3200	Binns	Harston	Pallister	Logan	B Harper	Armeson	Smith	Fleetwood	Williams	Asquith	Sinclair
13	20	BRADFORD PA	1-5	Rogers	3764	Binns	Shotton	Pallister	Armeson	B Harper	Logan	Rogers	Fleetwood	Smith	Asquith	Sinclair
14	27	Bradford PA	3-5	Smith 2, og	2000	Binns	Shotton	Pallister	Bokas	B Harper	Logan	Smith	Fleetwood	Rogers	Asquith	Sinclair
15	Dec 4	Doncaster Rovers	3-3	Smith, Robledo, Sinclair	7446	Binns	Harston	Shotton	Bokas	B Harper	Logan	Smith	Cooling	Robledo	Asquith	Sinclair
16	11	DONCASTER ROVERS	0-4		3943	Binns	Harston	Pallister	Bokas	Burkinshaw	Logan	Smith	Cooling	Robledo	Asquith	Sinclair
17	18	Chesterfield	0-2		1500	Binns	Harston	Pallister	Bokas	Burkinshaw	Logan	Smith	Fleetwood	Robledo	Sloan	Asquith
18	25	CHESTERFIELD	2-4	Smith 2	5800	Binns	Harston	Pallister	Bokas	Burkinshaw	Logan	R Spence	Fleetwood	Robledo	Smith	McGarry

North League (2nd Championship)

#	Date	Opponent	Score	Scorers	Att	1	2	3	4	5	6	7	8	9	10	11
1	Dec 27	BRADFORD CITY	4-0	McGarry, Barlow, Asquith, Smith	6920	Binns	Harston	Shotton	Pond	Bokas	Logan	Smith	Barlow	McGarry	Asquith	R Spence
2	Jan 1	Bradford City	1-0	Fleetwood	2500	Binns	Harston	Shotton	Woffinden	Pallister	Logan	Robledo	Fleetwood	McGarry	Asquith	Sloan
3	8	Leeds United	0-2		7000	Binns	Harston	Shotton	Logan	Bokas	Sloan	Smith	Fleetwood	Steele	Asquith	McGarry
4	15	LEEDS UNITED	3-2	Smith 2, McGarry (pen)	4347	Binns	Harston	Shotton	Bokas	Pallister	Logan	Smith	Fleetwood	Steele	Asquith	McGarry
5	22	YORK CITY	2-1	Asquith 2	4363	Binns	Harston	Shotton	Logan	Pallister	Sloan	Smith	Fleetwood	Robledo	Asquith	McGarry
6	29	York City	0-2		5000	Binns	Harston	Shotton	Logan	Burkinshaw	Sloan	Smith	Fleetwood	Robledo	Asquith	McGarry
7	Feb 5	Huddersfield T	2-2	Robledo, McGarry	4872	Rymer	Harston	Shotton	Logan	Pallister	Sloan	Smith	Fleetwood	Robledo	Asquith	McGarry
8	12	HUDDERSFIELD T	4-1	Robledo, Fleetwood, Asquith, Smit	7652	Rymer	Harston	Shotton	Logan	Pallister	Hold	Smith	Fleetwood	Robledo	Asquith	McGarry
9	19	Bradford PA	3-3	Shotton, Asquith 2	5621	Rymer	Harston	Shotton	Bokas	Pallister	Logan	Smith	Fleetwood	Robledo	Asquith	McGarry
10	25	BRADFORD PA	3-3	Shotton, Asquith 2	8311	Rymer	Harston	Shotton	Bokas	Pallister	Logan	Smith	Fleetwood	Robledo	Asquith	McGarry
11	Mar 4	York City	1-4	McGarry	7563	Rymer	Shotton	Pallister	Willingham	Brown	Logan	Smith	Fleetwood	Robledo	Asquith	McGarry
12	11	YORK CITY	3-1	Smith, Fleetwood, Robledo	14001	Rymer	Shotton	Pallister	Willingham	Brown	Logan	Smith	Fleetwood	Robledo	Asquith	McGarry
13	18	Doncaster Rovers	1-1	Asquith	3866	AN Other	AN Other	Shotton	AN Other	AN Other	Logan	Smith	AN Other	Robledo	Asquith	AN Other
14	25	DONCASTER ROVERS	1-0	Smith	6359	AN Other	AN Other	Shotton	AN Other	AN Other	Logan	Smith	AN Other	Robledo	Asquith	AN Other
15	Apr 1	ROTHERHAM UNITED	1-4	Robledo	5000	AN Other	AN Other	Shotton	AN Other	AN Other	Logan	Smith	AN Other	Robledo	Asquith	AN Other
16	8	Rotherham United	0-3		9000	AN Other	AN Other	Shotton	AN Other	AN Other	Logan	Smith	AN Other	Robledo	Asquith	AN Other
17	10	SHEFFIELD UNITED	5-1	Robledo, Stabb, Walker 2, Asquith	6043	AN Other	AN Other	Shotton	AN Other	AN Other	Logan	Smith	Stabb	Robledo	Asquith	Walker

Note: Matches 1 to 10 also counted in League North Cup qualifying competition.
Matches 13 to 16 also counted in Sheffield County Cup. Match 13 QF 1st leg, Match 14 QF 2nd leg, Match 15 SF 1st leg, Match 16 SF 2nd leg.
Matches 11 and 12 also counted in League North Cup knockout competition, Match 11 1st round 1st leg, Match 12 1st round 2nd leg.

1944/45 North League (1st Championship)

#	Date		Score	Scorers	Att.	1	2	3	4	5	6	7	8	9	10	11
1	Aug 26	HUDDERSFIELD T	1-2	Robledo	7000	Binns	Shotton	Pallister	Harston	Burkinshaw	Logan	G Smith	Fisher	Robledo	Asquith	McGarry
2	Sep 2	Huddersfield T	1-2	G Smith	4049	Binns	Shotton	Pallister	Harston	Burkinshaw	Logan	G Smith	Fleetwood	Robledo	Asquith	McGarry
3	9	Derby County	2-1	McGarry, Logan	12000	Binns	Shotton	Pallister	Logan	Burkinshaw	Asquith	G Smith	Fleetwood	Robledo	Steele	McGarry
4	16	DERBY COUNTY	2-0	Robledo, G Smith	7000	Binns	Shotton	Pallister	Logan	Burkinshaw	Asquith	G Smith	Fleetwood	Robledo	Steele	McGarry
5	23	SHEFFIELD UTD	2-1	McGarry 2	7000	Binns	Shotton	Pallister	Logan	Burkinshaw	Asquith	G Smith	Fleetwood	Robledo	Fisher	McGarry
6	30	Sheffield Utd	0-1		10000	Binns	Shotton	Pallister	Logan	Burkinshaw	Glover	G Smith	Fleetwood	Robledo	Asquith	McGarry
7	Oct 7	Notts County	3-0	Robledo, McGarry 2	5000	Binns	Shotton	Pallister	Logan	Burkinshaw	Asquith	G Smith	Fleetwood	Robledo	Cooling	McGarry
8	14	NOTTS COUNTY	6-2	Robledo 3, Logan 2, Pallister (pen)	5000	Binns	Shotton	Pallister	Logan	Burkinshaw	Asquith	G Smith	Fleetwood	Robledo	Cooling	McGarry
9	21	CHESTERFIELD	3-1	Robledo 2, og	7313	Binns	Shotton	Pallister	Logan	Burkinshaw	Asquith	G Smith	J Smith	Robledo	Cooling	McGarry
10	28	Chesterfield	0-0		5000	Binns	Shotton	Pallister	Logan	Burkinshaw	Asquith	G Smith	Fleetwood	Robledo	Cooling	McGarry
11	Nov 4	Mansfield Town	1-1	Cooling	6000	Binns	Shotton	Pallister	Logan	Burkinshaw	Asquith	G Smith	Fleetwood	Robledo	Cooling	McGarry
12	11	MANSFIELD TOWN	3-2	McGarry, Fleetwood, Shotton (pen)	7666	Binns	Shotton	Pallister	Logan	Burkinshaw	Asquith	G Smith	Fleetwood	Robledo	Cooling	McGarry
13	18	ROTHERHAM UTD	6-5	Shotton (pen), Cooling 2, Robledo 2, Barlow	12187	Binns	Shotton	Pallister	Logan	Burkinshaw	Asquith	G Smith	Barlow	Robledo	Cooling	McGarry
14	25	Rotherham Utd	0-1		7000	Binns	Shotton	Pallister	Logan	Burkinshaw	Asquith	G Smith	Barlow	Robledo	Cooling	McGarry
15	Dec 2	Lincoln City	5-2	Robledo 2, Barlow, Smith, Cooling	2500	Binns	Nicholson	Pallister	Logan	Burkinshaw	Asquith	G Smith	Barlow	Robledo	Cooling	McGarry
16	9	LINCOLN CITY	5-3	Robledo 3, McGarry 2	7872	Binns	Nicholson	Pallister	Logan	Burkinshaw	Asquith	G Smith	Barlow	Robledo	Cooling	McGarry
17	16	SHEFFIELD WED	2-3	Barlow, Robledo	5811	Binns	Logan	Pallister	Barlow	Burkinshaw	Asquith	G Smith	Fleetwood	Robledo	Cooling	McGarry
18	23	Sheffield Wed	0-5		10000	Binns	Taylor	Pallister	Harston	Burkinshaw	Asquith	G Smith	Fleetwood	Robledo	Cooling	McGarry

North League (2nd Championship)

#	Date		Score	Scorers	Att.	1	2	3	4	5	6	7	8	9	10	11
1	Dec 25	Bradford PA	1-3	Asquith (pen)	11962	Binns	Taylor	Pallister	Logan	Burkinshaw	Asquith	G Smith	Fleetwood	Robledo	Barlow	McGarry
2	26	HUDDERSFIELD T	0-1		10933	AN Other	Taylor	AN Other	Logan	Burkinshaw	Asquith	G Smith	AN Other	AN Other	AN Other	McGarry
3	30	BRADFORD PA	2-1	McGarry 2	9300	Rymer	Harston	Pallister	Logan	Burkinshaw	Asquith	G Smith	Fleetwood	Robledo	Cooling	McGarry
4	Jan 6	Leeds United	1-0	McGarry	12000	Binns	Harston	Pallister	Logan	Burkinshaw	Asquith	G Smith	Cooling	Robledo	Barlow	McGarry
5	13	LEEDS UNITED	5-0	Barlow 2, Cooling 2, Robledo	7000	Binns	Harston	Pallister	Logan	Burkinshaw	Asquith	G Smith	Cooling	Robledo	Barlow	McGarry
6	20	Bradford City	1-0	Barlow	4000	Binns	Harston	Pallister	Logan	Burkinshaw	Asquith	G Smith	Cooling	Robledo	Barlow	McGarry
7	27	BRADFORD CITY	2-1	Smith, Cooling	7560	Binns	Harston	Pallister	Logan	Burkinshaw	Asquith	G Smith	Cooling	Robledo	Barlow	McGarry
8	Feb 3	YORK CITY	2-1	Cooling, Pallister	10232	Binns	Harston	Pallister	Bokas	Burkinshaw	Asquith	G Smith	Cooling	Fleetwood	Barlow	McGarry
9	10	York City	1-5	Cooling	5000	Binns	Shotton	Pallister	Harston	Burkinshaw	Asquith	G Smith	Cooling	Robledo	Barlow	McGarry
10	17	Hull City	0-3		4000	Binns	Harston	Pallister	Burkinshaw	Kitchen	Asquith	G Smith	Fleetwood	Robledo	Cooling	Horbury
11	24	HULL CITY	3-0	McGarry, Robledo, Cooling	7567	Binns	Harston	Pallister	Logan	Burkinshaw	Asquith	G Smith	Fleetwood	Robledo	Cooling	McGarry
12	Mar 3	Burnley	0-4		8000	AN Other	Harston	AN Other	Logan	Burkinshaw	Asquith	G Smith	AN Other	AN Other	AN Other	McGarry
13	10	BURNLEY	2-0	McGarry 2	8903	AN Other	Harston	AN Other	Logan	Burkinshaw	Asquith	G Smith	AN Other	AN Other	Cooling	McGarry
14	17	Blackpool	2-0	Asquith 2	6000	AN Other	Harston	AN Other	Logan	Burkinshaw	Asquith	G Smith	Barlow	Robledo	AN Other	McGarry
15	24	Rotherham Utd	1-2	McGarry	17530	Binns	Harston	Pallister	Logan	Burkinshaw	Asquith	G Smith	Cooling	Robledo	Barlow	McGarry
16	31	ROTHERHAM UTD	3-0	Robledo 2, Cooling	23326	Binns	Harston	Pallister	Logan	Burkinshaw	Asquith	G Smith	Cooling	Robledo	Barlow	McGarry
17	Apr 7	CHESTERFIELD	2-2	Smith, Cooling	17020	Binns	Harston	Pallister	Logan	Burkinshaw	Asquith	G Smith	Cooling	Fleetwood	Barlow	McGarry
18	14	Chesterfield	0-2		17000	Binns	Harston	Pallister	Logan	Burkinshaw	Asquith	G Smith	Cooling	Robledo	Barlow	McGarry
19	21	LEEDS UNITED	1-3	Fisher	3380	AN Other	Harston	AN Other	Logan	Burkinshaw	Asquith	G Smith	Fisher	Barlow	AN Other	McGarry
20	28	Leeds United	3-1	Flood, Robledo, Smith	4000	AN Other	Shotton	AN Other	Logan	Burkinshaw	Asquith	G Smith	Barlow	Robledo	Cooling	McGarry
21	May 5	SHEFFIELD WED	3-3	Robledo 2, Barlow	3624	AN Other	Shotton	AN Other	Logan	Burkinshaw	Asquith	G Smith	Barlow	Robledo	Flood	AN Other
22	8	HUDDERSFIELD T	2-4	Robledo, Barlow	527	AN Other	Shotton	AN Other	Logan	Burkinshaw	Asquith	G Smith	Barlow	Robledo	AN Other	Thorogood
23	9	Huddersfield T	1-2	Smith	4000	AN Other	Shotton	AN Other	Logan	Kitchen	Asquith	G Smith	Barlow	AN Other	AN Other	Thorogood
24	12	Sheffield Wed	1-4	Fisher	9000	AN Other	Shotton	AN Other	Logan	Kitchen	Asquith	AN Other	Barlow	AN Other	Fisher	Thorogood

Note: Matches 1 to 10 also counted in League North Cup qualifying competition.

Matches 15 to 18 also counted in League North Cup knockout competition, Match 15 1st round 1st leg, Match 16 1st round 2nd leg, Match 17 2nd round 1st leg, Match 18 2nd round 2nd leg

1945/46 North League

#	Date	Opponent	Score	Scorers	Att	1	2	3	4	5	6	7	8	9	10	11
1	Aug 25	PRESTON NORTH EN	1-5	Smith	10000	Binns	K Harper	Pallister	Logan	Burkinshaw	Asquith	Smith	Cooling	Robledo	Baxter	McGarry
2	Sep 1	Preston North End	3-2	Logan, McGarry, Robledo	11000	Binns	K Harper	Pallister	Harston	Kitchen	Logan	Smith	Cooling	Robledo	Asquith	McGarry
3	8	Leeds United	2-1	Cooling 2	8000	Binns	Nicholson	Pallister	Harston	Kitchen	Logan	Smith	Cooling	Robledo	Asquith	McGarry
4	12	Bury	1-1	Smith	4500	Binns	K Harper	Pallister	Harston	Burkinshaw	Logan	Smith	Cooling	Robledo	Asquith	McGarry
5	15	LEEDS UNITED	3-2	Robledo 2, Cooling	9900	Binns	Nicholson	K Harper	Harston	Burkinshaw	Logan	Smith	Cooling	Robledo	Asquith	Thorogood
6	22	MANCHESTER UNITED	2-2	Cooling, Asquith	11000	Binns	K Harper	Pallister	Harston	Burkinshaw	Logan	Smith	Cooling	Robledo	Baxter	McGarry
7	29	Manchester United	1-1	Cooling	20000	Binns	K Harper	Pallister	Harston	Asquith	Logan	Smith	Cooling	Robledo	Baxter	McGarry
8	Oct 6	Sunderland	0-1		18000	Binns	K Harper	Pallister	Logan	Shanks	Baxter	Smith	Cooling	Robledo	Bennett	Bennett
9	13	SUNDERLAND	4-2	Cooling 2, Pallister (pen), Baxte	14000	Binns	K Harper	Pallister	Logan	Glover	Asquith	Smith	Cooling	Robledo	Baxter	McGarry
10	20	SHEFFIELD UNITED	3-5	Fenton, Smith, Cooling	19700	Binns	K Harper	Pallister	Logan	Glover	Asquith	Smith	Cooling	Robledo	Baxter	Fenton
11	27	Sheffield United	1-1	McGarry	20000	Holdcroft	K Harper	Pallister	Baxter	Logan	Asquith	Smith	Cooling	Robledo	Fisher	McGarry
12	Nov 3	Middlesborough	5-2	Fisher 3, Pallister (pen), Baxter	12000	Holdcroft	K Harper	Pallister	Mansley	Logan	Asquith	Smith	Cooling	Fisher	Baxter	McGarry
13	10	MIDDLESBROUGH	2-2	Fisher 2	13000	Holdcroft	Nicholson	K Harper	Harston	Logan	Asquith	Smith	Cooling	Fisher	Baxter	McGarry
14	17	STOKE CITY	3-3	Smith 2, Asquith	25000	Holdcroft	Harston	Ferrier	Mansley	Logan	Asquith	Smith	Cooling	Fisher	Baxter	McGarry
15	24	Stoke City	0-4		20000	Holdcroft	Cunningham	Ferrier	Mansley	Logan	Asquith	Smith	Cooling	Fisher	Baxter	McGarry
16	Dec 1	Grimsby Town	0-0		11000	Holdcroft	Cunningham	Pallister	Mansley	Wilson	Logan	Smith	Cooling	Fisher	Baxter	McGarry
17	8	GRIMSBY TOWN	2-0	Fisher 2	11000	Holdcroft	Cunningham	Pallister	Mansley	Wilson	Logan	Smith	Cooling	Fisher	Baxter	McGarry
18	15	BLACKPOOL	1-1	Smith	22000	Holdcroft	Cunningham	Pallister	Mansley	Wilson	Logan	Smith	Robledo	Asquith	Baxter	Kelly
19	22	Blackpool	1-1	Smith	16000	Holdcroft	Cunningham	Pallister	Mansley	Wilson	Logan	Smith	Robledo	Asquith	Baxter	Kelly
20	Dec 25	Liverpool	2-5	Robledo, Fisher	30000	Holdcroft	Cunningham	Pallister	Baxter	Wilson	Logan	Fisher	Baxter	Robledo	Asquith	Kelly
21	26	LIVERPOOL	1-0	Smith	30000	Rymer	Cunningham	Pallister	Logan	Wilson	Logan	Smith	Robledo	Fisher	Baxter	Kelly
22	29	BURY	1-3	Smith	17600	Holdcroft	Cunningham	Pallister	Logan	Wilson	Asquith	Smith	Robledo	Robledo	Asquith	Kelly
23	Jan 1	Blackburn Rovers	1-3	Cooling	10400	Rymer	Harston	Shotton	Brunskill	Burkinshaw	Clayton	Smith	Cooling	Robledo	Asquith	Kelly
24	12	BRADFORD P.A.	3-0	Baxter, Wilson, Cooling	14000	Rymer	Cunningham	Pallister	Mansley	Wilson	Logan	Smith	Cooling	Robledo	Baxter	Kelly
25	19	Bradford PA	1-2	Baxter (pen)	8643	Holdcroft	Harston	Ferrier	Mansley	Glover	Morgan	Smith	Cooling	Bennett	Baxter	Kelly
26	Feb 2	MANCHESTER CITY	2-0	Bennett, Smith	20128	Holdcroft	Harston	Cunningham	Harston	Wilson	Logan	Smith	Robledo	Bennett	Baxter	Kelly
27	16	NEWCASTLE UNITED	1-3	Robledo	16900	Holdcroft	Harston	Cunningham	Logan	Wilson	Clayton	Smith	Robledo	Robledo	Asquith	Kelly
28	23	Sheffield Wed	3-0	Robledo 2, Kelly	20000	Rymer	Cunningham	Pallister	Mansley	Wilson	Logan	Smith	Cooling	Robledo	Asquith	Kelly
29	Mar 2	SHEFFIELD WED	4-0	Robledo, Gray, Fisher, og	16000	Rymer	Cunningham	Pallister	Mansley	Wilson	Logan	Fisher	Gray	Robledo	Asquith	Kelly
30	9	Huddersfield Town	1-2	Asquith	18161	Rymer	Cunningham	Pallister	Mansley	Wilson	Logan	Smith	Gray	Robledo	Asquith	Kelly
31	13	Manchester City	3-2	Robledo, Kelly, Asquith	6662	Rymer	Cox	Shotton	Jackson	Wilson	Logan	Smith	Gray	Robledo	Asquith	Kelly
32	16	HUDDERSFIELD TOW	1-0	Logan	18000	Rymer	Cunningham	Pallister	Mansley	Wilson	Logan	Smith	Gray	Robledo	Asquith	Kelly
33	23	Chesterfield	1-1	Robledo	12000	Rymer	Cunningham	Pallister	Mansley	Brunskill	Logan	Smith	Gray	Robledo	Asquith	Kelly
34	30	CHESTERFIELD	2-2	Smith, og	19000	Rymer	Cunningham	Pallister	Mansley	Brunskill	Logan	Smith	Gray	Robledo	Asquith	Kelly
35	Apr 6	BURNLEY	2-0	Robledo, Baxter	14500	Rymer	Cunningham	Pallister	Mansley	Logan	Asquith	Mount	Gray	Robledo	Baxter	Kelly
36	13	Burnley	2-3	Gray, Baxter	11000	Rymer	Cunningham	Pallister	Mansley	Logan	Logan	Smith	Gray	Robledo	Baxter	Kelly
37	19	EVERTON	2-0	Robledo 2	26000	Rymer	Cunningham	Pallister	Logan	Burkinshaw	Asquith	Smith	Gray	Robledo	Bennett	Kelly
38	20	Bolton Wanderers	0-2		10000	Rymer	Cunningham	Pallister	Mansley	Logan	Asquith	Smith	Gray	Robledo	Bennett	Kelly
39	22	Everton	4-0	Gray 2, Kelly, Robledo	45000	Rymer	Cunningham	Pallister	Mansley	Glover	Logan	Smith	Gray	Robledo	Bennett	Kelly
40	27	BOLTON WANDERERS	0-3		12000	Rymer	Cunningham	Pallister	Logan	Glover	Baxter	Smith	Gray	Robledo	Bennett	Asquith
41	May 1	Newcastle United	0-1		22000	Rymer	Cunningham	Pallister	Mansley	Logan	Asquith	Smith	Gray	Robledo	Bennett	Asquith
42	4	BLACKBURN ROVERS	4-0	Smith, Bennett 2, Robledo	12000	Rymer	Cunningham	Pallister	Mansley	Glover	Asquith	Smith	Bennett	Robledo	Baxter	Kelly

F.A.Cup

	Date	Opponent	Score	Scorers	Att	1	2	3	4	5	6	7	8	9	10	11
R3/1	Jan 5	Newcastle United	2-4	og, Pallister (pen)	60384	Holdcroft	Cunningham	Pallister	Mansley	Wilson	Logan	Smith	Cooling	Robledo	Baxter	Kelly
R3/2	9	NEWCASTLE UNITED	3-0	Smith, Wilson, Baxter	30000	Holdcroft	Cunningham	Pallister	Mansley	Wilson	Logan	Smith	Cooling	Robledo	Baxter	Kelly
R4/1	26	ROTHERHAM UNITED	3-0	Kelly, Smith, Robledo	37100	Holdcroft	Cunningham	Pallister	Mansley	Wilson	Logan	Smith	Cooling	Robledo	Baxter	Kelly
R4/2	31	Rotherham United	1-2	Pallister	19500	Holdcroft	Harston	Pallister	Mansley	Wilson	Logan	Smith	Cooling	Fisher	Fisher	Kelly
R5/1	Feb 9	BRADFORD PA	0-1		37770	Holdcroft	Cunningham	Ferrier	Mansley	Wilson	Logan	Smith	Robledo	Fisher	Bennett	Kelly
R5/2	13	Bradford PA	1-1	Robledo	29341	Holdcroft	Harston	Cunningham	Harston	Wilson	Logan	Smith	Robledo	Asquith	Baxter	Kelly

TEAM GROUP: See (earlier) page facing War-time League Tables.

1946/47 — 10th in Division 2

League (Division 2)

No	Date		Opponent	Score	Scorers	Att
1	Aug	31	NOTTM. FOREST	3-2	Robledo 3	17317
2	Sep	2	Sheffield Wednesday	4-2	Baxter, Robledo 2, Kelly	29745
3		7	Coventry City	1-1	Baxter	23409
4		9	SHEFFIELD WEDNESDAY	4-1	Baxter, Gray, Robledo, Smith	26726
5		14	BIRMINGHAM CITY	3-1	Baxter 2, Smith	28219
6		16	BURNLEY	1-0	Bennett	26247
7		21	West Bromwich Albion	5-2	Bennett 2, Baxter, Kelly, Robledo	38925
8		28	NEWCASTLE UNITED	1-1	Graham (og)	34262
9		30	Burnley	2-2	Robledo, Brown (og)	24959
10	Oct	5	Swansea Town	2-2	Kelly, Robledo	26217
11		12	TOTTENHAM HOTSPUR	1-3	Robledo	24494
12		19	Fulham	1-6	Robledo	37224
13		26	BURY	4-0	Asquith, Cunningham, Robledo, Smith	20827
14	Nov	2	Luton Town	1-3	Asquith	21723
15		9	PLYMOUTH ARGYLE	1-3	Robledo	18471
16		16	Leicester City	0-6		28524
17		23	CHESTERFIELD	1-2	Steele	16666
18		30	Millwall	1-3	Smith	19672
19	Dec	7	BRADFORD PARK AVE.	3-1	Bennett, Pallister (pen), Smith	13448
20		14	Manchester City	1-5	Bennett	24000
21		21	WEST HAM UNITED	1-2	Bennett	11109
22		25	SOUTHAMPTON	4-4	Bennett, Morris, Pallister, Robledo	16331
23		26	Southampton	1-1	Morris	21556
24		28	Nottingham Forest	1-2	Robledo	27239
25	Jan	4	COVENTRY CITY	0-2		16945
26		18	Birmingham City	2-1	Bennett, Trigg (og)	41409
27	Feb	1	Newcastle United	2-4	Asquith, Bennett	40182
28	Mar	1	Bury	4-4	Asquith, Bennett, Robledo, Smith	17571
29		15	Plymouth Argyle	2-3	Baxter (pen), Bennett	8249
30		22	LEICESTER CITY	1-0	Kelly	13936
31		29	Chesterfield	1-2	Bennett	10436
32	Apr	4	NEWPORT COUNTY	3-1	Asquith, Cooling, Robledo	14999
33		5	MILLWALL	4-1	Bennett 2, Glover, Kelly	13558
34		7	Newport County	1-2	Kelly	11013
35		12	Bradford Park Avenue	3-1	Bennett, Kelly, Robledo	18412
36		19	MANCHESTER CITY	0-2		26346
37		26	West Ham United	0-4		16275
38	May	3	FULHAM	4-1	Cooling, Kelly, Robledo, Smith	12327
39		10	Luton Town	4-0	Robledo 2, Cooling, Kelly	15264
40		17	SWANSEA TOWN	3-1	Bennett, Robledo, Smith	19417
41		26	WEST BROMWICH ALB.	2-1	Kelly, Vernon (og)	16426
42	Jun	7	Tottenham Hotspur	1-1	Robledo	17575

Appearances (shirt numbers by match)

No	Rymer GH	Cunningham L	Pallister G	Logan IW	Wilson JW	Asquith B	Smith G	Gray H	Robledo GO	Baxter JC	Kelly JC	Bennett WH	Bonnell A	Charlesworth SF	Cooling R	Davie J	Fisher S	Glover A	Harston JC	Kelly PM	Kitchen J	Malcolm AM	Mansley VC	Morris FA	Rimmington N	Steele J	Whyte JA
1	1	2	3	4	5	6	7	8	9	10	11																
2	1	2	3	4	5	6	7	8	9	10	11																
3		2	3		5	6	7	8	9	10	11												4		1		
4		2	3	4	5	6	7	8	9	10	11														1		
5		2	3	4	5	6	7	8	9	10	11														1		
6		2	3	4	5	6	7		9	10	11	8													1		
7		2	3	4	5	6	7		9	10	11	8													1		
8		2	3	4	5	6	7		9	10	11	8													1		
9		2	3		5	6	7		9	10	11	8											4		1		
10		2		4	5	6	7		9	10	11	8						3							1		
11		2	3	4	5	6	7	8	9	10	11														1		
12	1	2	3	4	5	6	7		9	10	11			8													
13		2	3		5	6	8		9	10	7												4	11	1		
14		2	3		5	6	8		9	10	7											11	4		1		
15		8	3	2	5				9	10	7							4				11			1		6
16			3	4		6	7	8	9									2	1	5							
17		2	3			6	7		9	10	11							5	1				4			8	
18		2	3			6	7		9	10	11							5	1				4			8	
19		2	3				7		9		11	10			5			6	1				4			8	
20		2	3				7		9		11	10			5			6	1				4			8	
21		2	3			6	7		8			10			5			9	4					11	1		
22		2	3			6	7		8			10			5	9		4						11	1		
23		2	3		5	6	7		8	10						9		4						11	1		
24		2	3		5	6	7		8			10				9		4						11	1		
25		2	3		5	6	7		8	10	11					9		4							1		
26		2	3		5	6	7		9	10		8						4						11	1		
27		2	3		5	6	7		9	10	11	8						4							1		
28			3			10	7		9	4	11	8			5			6					2		1		
29			3			10	7		9	4	11	8			5			6					2		1		
30			3			10	7		9	4	11	8			5			6					2		1		
31			3			10	7		9	4	11	8						6					2		1		5
32			3			10	7		9	4	11				8			6					2		1		5
33			3					7	9	4	11	10		8		9		6					2		1		5
34			3					7	9	4	11	10		8		9		6					2		1		5
35			3				7		9	4	11	10		8				6					2		1		5
36			3				7		9	4	11	10		8				6					2		1		5
37			3				7		9	4	11	8		2	10			6							1		5
38			3				7		9	10	11			2	8			6		1				4			5
39			3				6	7	9	8	11				10			2		1				4			5
40			3				6	7	9	10	11	8						2		1				4			5
41			3				6	7	9	10	11	8						2		1				4			5
42			3				6	7	9		11		10					2		1				4		8	5
Apps	3	26	41	12	20	36	42	7	42	35	37	24	4	7	6	6	1	27	8	12	1	2	13	5	27	5	13
Goals		1	2			5	8	1	23	7	10	16			3			1						2		1	

Four own goals

F.A. Cup

	Date		Opponent	Score	Scorers	Att
R3	Jan	11	Huddersfield Town	4-3	Asquith, Baxter, Bennett, Smith	39944
R4		25	Preston North End	0-6		39800

Rd	Cunningham L	Pallister G	Wilson JW	Asquith B	Smith G	Robledo GO	Baxter JC	Kelly JC	Bennett WH	Glover A	Morris FA	Rimmington N
R3	2	3	5	6	7	9	10	11	8	4		1
R4	2	3	5	6	7	9	10		8	4	11	1

Division 2 table

		P	W	D	L	F	A	W	D	L	F	A	Pts
1	Manchester City	42	17	3	1	49	14	9	7	5	29	21	62
2	Burnley	42	11	8	2	30	14	11	6	4	35	15	58
3	Birmingham City	42	17	2	2	51	11	8	3	10	23	22	55
4	Chesterfield	42	12	6	3	37	17	6	8	7	21	27	50
5	Newcastle United	42	11	4	6	60	32	8	6	7	35	30	48
6	Tottenham Hotspur	42	11	8	2	35	21	6	6	9	30	32	48
7	West Bromwich Alb.	42	12	4	5	53	37	8	4	9	35	38	48
8	Coventry City	42	12	8	1	40	17	4	5	12	26	42	45
9	Leicester City	42	11	4	6	42	25	7	3	11	27	39	43
10	BARNSLEY	42	13	2	6	48	29	4	6	11	36	57	42
11	Nottingham Forest	42	13	5	3	47	20	2	5	14	22	54	40
12	West Ham United	42	12	4	5	46	31	4	4	13	24	45	40
13	Luton Town	42	13	4	4	50	29	3	3	15	21	44	39
14	Southampton	42	11	5	5	45	24	4	4	13	24	52	39
15	Fulham	42	12	4	5	40	25	3	5	13	23	49	39
16	Bradford Park Ave.	42	7	6	8	29	28	7	5	9	36	49	39
17	Bury	42	11	6	4	62	34	1	6	14	18	44	36
18	Millwall	42	7	7	7	30	30	7	1	13	26	49	36
19	Plymouth Argyle	42	11	3	7	45	34	3	2	16	34	62	33
20	Sheffield Wed.	42	10	5	6	39	28	2	3	16	28	60	32
21	Swansea Town	42	9	1	11	36	40	2	6	13	19	43	29
22	Newport County	42	9	1	11	41	52	1	2	18	20	81	23

Season 1946/47
Back row: Logan, Cunningham, Rimmington, Wilson (Trainer) Pallister, Asquith
Front row: Smith, Bennett, Robledo G, Baxter, Kelly, Wilson (Capt)

Season 1947/48
Back row: Mansley, Asquith, Cunningham, Kelly P, Seed (Manager) Pallister, Wilson (Trainer) Glover
Front row: Smith, Bennett, Robledo G, Baxter, Kelly J, Whyte

1947/48   12th in Division 2

Match results

#	Date	Opponent	Score	Scorers	Att.
1	Aug 23	Birmingham City	3-2	Morris, Smith, Wright	37917
2	27	LEEDS UNITED	3-0	Morris 2, Smith	23440
3	30	WEST BROMWICH ALB.	0-1		23796
4	Sep 3	Leeds United	1-4	Kelly	36501
5	6	Sheffield Wednesday	2-5	Baxter (pen), Morris	33835
6	10	FULHAM	1-2	Wright	18016
7	13	Plymouth Argyle	0-1		19608
8	17	Fulham	1-0	Wright	18094
9	20	LUTON TOWN	3-0	Baxter, Kelly, Smith	17670
10	27	Brentford	3-3	Bennett 3	22137
11	Oct 4	LEICESTER CITY	2-0	Smith, Frame (og)	20765
12	11	TOTTENHAM HOTSPUR	2-1	Baxter, Bennett	24715
13	18	Millwall	3-3	Baxter (pen), Smith, Bennett	23627
14	25	CHESTERFIELD	0-3		22823
15	Nov 1	West Ham United	1-2	Smith	27877
16	8	BURY	2-1	Baxter, Glover	18874
17	15	Southampton	1-4	Robledo	21563
18	22	DONCASTER ROVERS	2-0	Bennett, Robledo	24017
19	29	Nottingham Forest	1-1	Robledo	18108
20	Dec 6	BRADFORD PARK AVE.	2-2	Bennett, Robledo	17327
21	13	Cardiff City	0-1		33538
22	20	BIRMINGHAM CITY	0-1		18880
23	25	Coventry City	2-3	Robledo, Smith	27600
24	26	COVENTRY CITY	0-1		19166
25	Jan 3	West Bromwich Albion	2-0	Griffiths, Wright	25045
26	17	SHEFFIELD WEDNESDA	3-1	Morris, Smith, Griffiths (pen)	33131
27	24	Bury	1-1	Glover	14960
28	31	PLYMOUTH ARGYLE	2-1	Griffiths, Wright	21317
29	Feb 14	BRENTFORD	1-1	Griffiths	21399
30	Mar 6	MILLWALL	1-0	Smith	17503
31	13	Chesterfield	1-1	Griffiths (pen)	13133
32	15	Tottenham Hotspur	3-0	Baxter, Griffiths, Robledo	31969
33	20	WEST HAM UNITED	1-1	Whyte	27877
34	26	Newcastle United	0-1		64757
35	29	NEWCASTLE UNITED	1-1	Griffiths	30702
36	Apr 3	SOUTHAMPTON	2-1	Griffiths, Harston	20126
37	5	Leicester City	1-4	Griffiths	21274
38	10	Doncaster Rovers	2-1	Baxter, Glover	24011
39	14	Luton Town	1-2	Robledo	13594
40	17	NOTTM. FOREST	2-2	Steele 2	18958
41	24	Bradford Park Avenue	2-3	Robledo, Steele	10440
42	May 1	CARDIFF CITY	1-2	Robledo	14979

Player appearances (shirt numbers)

#	Kelly PM	Glover A	Pallister G	Mansley VC	Whyte JA	Baxter JC	Smith G	Wright AM	Robledo GO	Morris FA	Kelly JC	Asquith B	Bennett WH	Bonnell A	Cunningham L	Griffiths JS	Harston JC	Hough H	Kitchen J	Malcolm AM	Normanton S	Robledo EO	Steele J	Swallow E	Williams E
1	1	2	3	4	5	6	7	8	9	10	11														
2	1	2	3	4	5	6	7	8	9	10	11														
3	1	2	3	4	5	6	7	8	9	10	11														
4	1	2	3	4	5	6	7	8	9	10	11														
5	1	2	3	4	5	6	7	8	9	10	11														
6	1		3	4	5	6	7	8	9	10	11		2												
7	1		3	4		6	7	8	9	10	11		2				5								
8	1	6	3	4		10	7	8	9		11		2				5								
9	1	6	3	4		10	7	8	9		11		2				5								
10	1	6	3	4	5	10	7			8	11	9			2										
11	1	6	3	4	5	10	7			8	11	9			2										
12	1	6	3	4	5	10	7			8	11	9			2										
13	1	6	3	4	5	10	7			8	11	9			2										
14	1	6		4	5	10	7			8	11	9			2	3									
15	1	2	3	4			7	8		10	11	9			5					6					
16	1	6	3	4	5	10	7	8			11	9			2										
17	1	6	3	4	5	10			9		7				2			8							
18	1	6	3		5	10	7		9				8		2				1						
19	1	6	3		5	10	7		9				8		2				1						
20	1	6	3		5	10	7		9				8		2	4									
21	1	4	3		5	10	7		9		11		8		2										
22	1	4	3		5	10	7		9		11		6	8	2										
23	1	5	3				4	7		10	11		9	6	2								8		
24	1	5	3				4	7		10	11		9	6	2								8		
25	1	6	3		5		7	8		10	11		2			9				4					
26	1	6			5		7	8		10	11		3			9				2			4		
27	1	6			5		7	8		10	11		3			9				2			4		
28	1	6			5		7	8		10	11		3			9				2			4		
29	1	6			5			7	9	10	11		2			8								3	
30	1	6	3		5			7	9				2			8							4		
31	1	6			5			7	9	10	11		2			8								3	
32	1	6	3		5	10	7		9		11					8								2	
33	1	6	3		5	10	7		9		11					8								2	
34	1	6	3		5		7		9		11		8		2										
35	1	6	3		5		7		9	10	11		8		2										
36	1	4	3		5	10	7		9				8		2		11			6					
37	1	6	3		5	10	7		9				8		2		11			4					
38	1	6	3		5	10	7		9				8				11			4		2			
39		6	3		5	10	7		9		11		8	2	1						4				
40		6	3		5	10	7		9		11			2	1						4		8		
41		6	3		5	10	7		9		11				1					4			8		2
42		6	3		5	10	7	8	9		11				1					4					2
Apps	36	40	36	17	36	32	40	20	36	14	40	4	14	3	25	16	8	6	4	3	19	2	4	5	2
Goals			3		1	7	9	5	9	5	2		7			9	1						3		

One own goal

F.A. Cup

Round	Date	Opponent	Score	Scorer	Att.	Kelly PM	Glover A	Pallister G	Whyte JA	Smith G	Robledo GO	Morris FA	Kelly JC	Bennett WH	Cunningham L	Griffiths JS
R3	Jan 10	Manchester City	1-2	Wright	54747	1	6	3	5	7	9	10	11	2	8	4

League table

		P	W	D	L	F	A	W	D	L	F	A	Pts
1	Birmingham City	42	12	7	2	34	13	10	8	3	21	11	59
2	Newcastle United	42	18	1	2	46	13	6	8	7	26	28	56
3	Southampton	42	15	3	3	53	23	6	7	8	18	30	52
4	Sheffield Wed.	42	13	6	2	39	21	7	5	9	27	32	51
5	Cardiff City	42	12	6	3	36	18	6	5	10	25	40	47
6	West Ham United	42	10	7	4	29	19	6	7	8	26	34	46
7	West Bromwich Alb.	42	11	4	6	37	29	7	5	9	26	29	45
8	Tottenham Hotspur	42	10	6	5	36	24	5	8	8	20	19	44
9	Leicester City	42	10	5	6	36	29	6	6	9	24	28	43
10	Coventry City	42	10	5	6	33	16	4	8	9	26	36	41
11	Fulham	42	6	9	6	24	19	9	1	11	23	27	40
12	BARNSLEY	42	10	5	6	31	22	5	5	11	31	42	40
13	Luton Town	42	8	8	5	31	25	6	4	11	25	34	40
14	Bradford Park Ave.	42	11	3	7	45	30	5	5	11	23	42	40
15	Brentford	42	10	6	5	31	26	3	8	10	13	35	40
16	Chesterfield	42	8	4	9	32	26	8	3	10	22	29	39
17	Plymouth Argyle	42	8	9	4	27	22	1	11	9	13	36	38
18	Leeds United	42	12	5	4	44	20	2	3	16	18	52	36
19	Nottingham Forest	42	10	5	6	32	23	2	6	13	22	37	35
20	Bury	42	6	8	7	27	28	3	8	10	31	40	34
21	Doncaster Rovers	42	7	8	6	23	20	2	3	16	17	46	29
22	Millwall	42	7	7	7	27	28	2	4	15	17	46	29

1948/49 — 9th in Division 2

Player columns (shirt numbers shown per match):
Kelly PM · Williams E · Pallister G · Normanton S · Whyte IA · Baxter JC · Smith G · Wright AM · Robledo GO · Steele J · Kelly JC · Bianchflower RD · Clayton L · Glover A · Griffiths JS · Harston JC · Hough H · Kitchen J · Lindsay D · Morris FA · Richardson F · Robledo EO · Swallow E · Troops H

#		Date	Opponent	Score	Scorers	Att	KllyPM	WillmsE	PallstrG	NrmntnS	WhyteIA	BxtrJC	SmithG	WrghtAM	RbldoGO	SteeleJ	KllyJC	BnchflwrRD	ClaytonL	GloverA	GrffthsJS	HarstnJC	HoughH	KitchenJ	LindsayD	MorrisFA	RchrdsnF	RbldoEO	SwallowE	TroopsH
1	Aug	21	PLYMOUTH ARGYLE	0-0		15593	1	2	3	4	5	6	7	8	9	10	11													
2		25	Fulham	1-1	Baxter (pen)	21005	1	2	3		5	6	7	8	9		11		4							10				
3		28	Blackburn Rovers	3-5	Morris, Smith, Robledo	24781	1	2	3		5	6	7	8	9		11		4							10				
4	Sep	1	FULHAM	1-1	Griffiths	17847	1	2	3			6	7		9		11		4		8				5	10				
5		4	CARDIFF CITY	1-1	Robledo	18527	1	2	3			10	7	8	9		11		4	6					5					
6		8	NOTTM. FOREST	4-0	Griffiths, Baxter 2, Robledo	14667	1			4	5	10	7		9		11			6	8	2							3	
7		11	Queen's Park Rangers	2-2	Robledo, Kelly	20791	1		3	4	5	10	7		9		11			6	8	2								
8		15	Nottingham Forest	1-0	Baxter	12988	1		3	4	5	10	7		9		11			6	8	2								
9		18	LUTON TOWN	1-2	Kelly	20922	1		3	4	5	10	7		9		11			6	8	2								
10		25	Bradford Park Avenue	2-0	Griffiths, Baxter	23145	1	2	3	4	5	10	7		9		11			6	8									
11	Oct	2	SOUTHAMPTON	3-0	Baxter, Webber (og), Robledo	23236	1	2	3	4	5	10	7		9		11			6	8									
12		9	SHEFFIELD WEDNESDAY	4-0	Baxter 2, Griffiths, Robledo	35308	1	2	3	4	5	10	7		9		11			6	8									
13		16	Coventry City	0-4		15710	1	2	3	4	5	10	7		9					6	8					11				
14		23	LEEDS UNITED	1-1	Morris	26010	1	2	3	4	5	10			9					6	8					11				7
15		30	Leicester City	1-1	Troops	29214	1	2	3	4	5	10			9		11			6	8									7
16	Nov	6	BRENTFORD	1-2	Robledo	20883	1	2	3	4	5	10			9		11			6	8									7
17		13	Tottenham Hotspur	1-4	Robledo	48989	1	2		4	5	10	7		9		11			6	8				3					
18		20	WEST HAM UNITED	2-3	Normanton, Baxter	20359	1	2		4	5	10	7	8			11			6					3		9			
19		27	Bury	2-4	Robledo, Richardson	13313	1	2		4	5	10	7		8		11			6					3		9			
20	Dec	4	WEST BROMWICH ALB.	2-0	Robledo, Richardson	20936					5	10	7	8			11			4			1	2			9	6	3	
21		11	Chesterfield	2-3	Richardson, Kelly	13318					5	10	7	8			11			4			1	2			9	6	3	
22		18	Plymouth Argyle	1-3	Baxter	21267				4	5	10	7	8			11			4			1	2			9	6	3	
23		25	Grimsby Town	0-3		18369	1		3	4	5	10	7	8			11			6							9		2	
24		27	GRIMSBY TOWN	2-1	Robledo, Richardson	19848	1		3	4	5	10	7		8		11			6							9		2	
25	Jan	1	BLACKBURN ROVERS	1-1	Richardson	18708	1		3	4		10	7	8			11			6				5			9		2	
26		15	Cardiff City	3-0	Richardson, Robledo, Kelly	29116	1		3	4		10	7		8		11			6				5			9		2	
27		22	QUEEN'S PARK RANGERS	4-0	Robledo, Kelly, Richardson, Baxter	20596	1		3	4		10	7		8		11			6				5			9		2	
28	Feb	5	Luton Town	0-1		16386	1		3	4	5	10	7	8			11			6							9		2	
29		19	BRADFORD PARK AVE.	0-0		21535	1		3		5	10	7	4			11			6	8				5		9		2	
30		26	Southampton	0-3		25892	1		3	4		10	7				11			6	8				5		9		2	
31	Mar	5	Sheffield Wednesday	1-1	Richardson	28085	1		3	4	5	10	7				11			6	8						9		2	
32		12	COVENTRY CITY	1-1	Simpson (og)	15269	1		3	4	5	10	7				11			6	8						9		2	
33		19	Leeds United	1-4	Wright	29701	1		3	4	5		7	10	8		11			6							9		2	
34	Apr	2	Brentford	0-0		18485	1		3	4		10	7	8			11			6				5			9		2	
35		6	LEICESTER CITY	3-1	Wright 2, Baxter (pen)	12068	1		3	4		10	7	8			11			6				5			9		2	
36		9	TOTTENHAM HOTSPUR	4-1	Kelly, Smith, Baxter 2	16796	1		3	4		10	7	8			11			6				5			9		2	
37		15	Lincoln City	1-0	Smith	15551	1		3	4	5	10	7				11			6	8						9		2	
38		16	West Ham United	0-2		20482	1		3	4		10	7		11					6	8			5			9		2	
39		18	LINCOLN CITY	2-0	Richardson 2	17346	1		3	4		10	7	8			11			6				5			9		2	
40		23	BURY	3-2	Wright 2, Baxter	15408	1		3	4	5	10	7	8			11			6							9		2	
41		30	West Bromwich Albion	0-2		31966	1		3	4	5	10	7	8			11			6							9		2	
42	Ma	7	CHESTERFIELD	0-1		13527	1		3		5	10	7	8			11	4		6							9		2	
			Apps				39	15	35	33	30	41	39	16	27	1	40	1	4	38	19	4	3	12	6	4	25	3	24	3
			Goals							1		15	3	5	13		6			4						2	10			1

Two own goals

F.A. Cup

	Date	Opponent	Score		Att	KllyPM	PallstrG	NrmntnS	BxtrJC	SmithG	WrghtAM	KllyJC	GloverA	KitchenJ	RchrdsnF	SwallowE
R3	Jan 8	BLACKPOOL	0-1		38000	1	3	4	10	7	8	11	6	5	9	2

League table (Division 2, 1948/49)

		P	W	D	L	F	A	W	D	L	F	A	Pts
1	Fulham	42	16	4	1	52	14	8	5	8	25	23	57
2	West Bromwich Alb.	42	16	3	2	47	16	8	5	8	22	23	56
3	Southampton	42	16	4	1	48	10	7	5	9	21	26	55
4	Cardiff City	42	14	4	3	45	21	5	9	7	17	26	51
5	Tottenham Hotspur	42	14	4	3	50	18	3	12	6	22	26	50
6	Chesterfield	42	9	7	5	24	18	6	10	5	27	27	47
7	West Ham United	42	13	5	3	38	23	5	5	11	18	35	46
8	Sheffield Wed.	42	12	6	3	36	17	3	7	11	27	39	43
9	BARNSLEY	42	10	7	4	40	18	4	5	12	22	43	40
10	Luton Town	42	11	6	4	32	16	3	6	12	23	41	40
11	Grimsby Town	42	10	5	6	44	28	5	5	11	28	48	40
12	Bury	42	12	5	4	41	23	5	1	15	26	53	40
13	Queen's Park Rgs.	42	11	4	6	31	26	3	7	11	13	36	39
14	Blackburn Rovers	42	12	5	4	41	23	3	3	15	12	40	38
15	Leeds United	42	11	6	4	36	21	1	7	13	19	42	37
16	Coventry City	42	12	3	6	35	20	3	4	14	20	44	37
17	Bradford Park Ave.	42	8	8	5	37	26	5	3	13	28	52	37
18	Brentford	42	7	10	4	28	21	4	4	13	14	32	36
19	Leicester City	42	6	10	5	41	38	4	6	11	21	41	36
20	Plymouth Argyle	42	11	4	6	33	25	1	8	12	16	39	36
21	Nottingham Forest	42	9	6	6	22	14	5	1	15	28	40	35
22	Lincoln City	42	6	7	8	31	35	2	5	14	22	56	28

Season 1948/49
Back row: Whyte, Glover, Williams, Kelly P, Pallister, Baxter
Front row: Smith, Wright, Robledo G, Morris, Kelly J

Season 1949/50
Back row: Swallow, Whyte, Blanchflower, Kelly P, Pallister, Glover
Front row: Smith, Griffiths, Wright, Baxter, Kelly J

1949/50 — 13th in Division 2

No		Date	Opponent	Res	Scorers	Att	Kelly PM	Swallow E	Pallister G	Blanchflower RD	Whyte JA	Glover A	Smith G	Griffiths JS	Wright AM	Baxter JC	Kelly JC	Bonnar P	Clayton L	Deakin WE	Hamilton E	Kitchen J	Lindsay D	Scattergood E	Hough H	Jackson M	Richardson F
1	Aug	20	CHESTERFIELD	1-2	Kelly	18428	1	2	3	4	5	6	7		8	10	11										9
2		24	SOUTHAMPTON	2-1	Griffiths, Baxter	17762	1	2	3	4	5	6	7	8	9	10	11										
3		27	West Ham United	1-2	Whyte	27541	1	2	3	4	5	6	7	8	9	10	11										
4		31	Southampton	0-0		22319	1	2	3	4	5	6	7	8	9	10	11										
5	Sep	3	SHEFFIELD UNITED	2-2	Griffiths 2	23287	1	2	3	4	5	6	7	8	9	10	11										
6		7	COVENTRY CITY	4-3	Griffiths 2 (1 pen), Baxter, Wright	15577	1	2	3	4	5	6	7	8	9	10	11										
7		10	Grimsby Town	2-2	Baxter, Wright	17523	1	2	3	4		6	7	8	9	10	11						5				
8		17	QUEEN'S PARK RANGERS	3-1	Wright 2, Griffiths	19787	1		3	4	5	6	7	8	9	10	11							2			
9		24	Preston North End	1-1	Baxter	31633	1		3	4		6	7	8	9	10	11						5	2			
10	Oct	1	SWANSEA TOWN	5-2	Smith,Wright,Baxter,Griffiths 2(1p)	19662			3			6	7	8	9	10	11			4			5	2	1		
11		8	BRADFORD PARK AVE.	3-2	Smith, Baxter, Griffiths	21642	1		3	4		6	7	8		10	11						5	2			9
12		15	Leicester City	2-2	Wright, Griffiths	27966	1		3	4		6	7	8	9	10	11						5	2			
13		22	BURY	1-0	Griffiths (pen)	20284	1		3			6	7	8	9	10	11			4			5	2			
14		29	Tottenham Hotspur	0-2		54856	1		3		5	6	7	8	9	10	11			4				2			
15	Nov	5	CARDIFF CITY	1-0	Wright	18564			3		5	6	7	8	9	10	11			4				2	1		
16		12	Blackburn Rovers	0-4		10948			3		5	6	7	8	9	10	11			4		2			1		
17		19	BRENTFORD	0-1		14942			3		5	6	7	8	9	10	11			4		2			1		
18		26	Hull City	0-2		31521			3	4		6	7	8	9		11	5			10	2			1		
19	Dec	3	SHEFFIELD WEDNESDAY	3-4	Richardson, Baxter, Wright	24995			3	4		6	7		8	10	11	5				2			1		9
20		10	Plymouth Argyle	2-2	Wright, Baxter	17001			3	4		6			8	10	11	7				2	5		1		9
21		17	Chesterfield	0-1		8968			3	4		6			8	10	11	7				2	5		1		9
22		24	WEST HAM UNITED	1-1	Bonner	17377			3	4		6			8	10	11	7				2	5		1		9
23		26	LEEDS UNITED	1-1	Lindsay (pen)	27017			3	4		6	7		8	10	11					2	5		1		9
24		27	Leeds United	0-1		47817			3	4			7		8	10	11					2	5	6	1		9
25		31	Sheffield United	1-1	Wright	35283			3	4			7		8	10	11					2	5	6	1		9
26	Jan	14	GRIMSBY TOWN	7-2	Griffiths 3(1p),Kelly 2,Smith,Baxter	13615	1		3	4		6	7	8	9	10	11					2	5				
27		21	Queen's Park Rangers	5-0	Smith 2, Baxter 2, Wright	16597	1		3	4			7	8	9	10	11					2	5	6			
28	Feb	4	PRESTON NORTH END	0-1		23800	1		3	4			7	8	9	10			11			2	5	6			
29		18	Swansea Town	0-4		20694	1		3	4			7	8	9	10				11		2	5	6			
30		25	Bradford Park Avenue	3-1	Wright 3	11134	1		3	4				8	9	10	11	7				2	5	6			
31	Mar	4	LEICESTER CITY	2-2	Wright 2	16637	1		3	4			7	8	9	10	11					2	5	6		1	
32		11	Bury	0-2		12729	1		3	4			7	8	9	10	11					2	5	6			
33		18	TOTTENHAM HOTSPUR	2-0	Richardson, Deakin	22346	1		3	4		6	7			10			8	11		2	5				9
34		25	Cardiff City	0-3		19987	1		3	4		6	7			10			8	11		2	5				9
35	Apr	1	HULL CITY	1-1	Blanchflower	22045	1		3	4		6	7			10			8	11		2	5				9
36		7	Luton Town	1-3	Wright	15149	1		3	4		6	7			10			8	11		2	5				9
37		8	Sheffield Wednesday	0-2		48119	1		3	4			7			10	8	11				6	5	2			9
38		10	LUTON TOWN	1-0	Smith	9476	1		3	4			7			10	8	11				6	5	2			9
39		15	BLACKBURN ROVERS	1-1	Baxter	12323	1		3	4			7			8	10	11				6	5	2			9
40		22	Brentford	0-3		16514	1		3	4			7		8	9	10	11				2	5			6	
41		29	PLYMOUTH ARGYLE	4-1	Baxter 3, Kelly	4438	1		3	4			7		8	9	10	11				2	5			6	
42	May	6	Coventry City	1-1	Griffiths (pen)	16121	1		3	4	5		7	8	9	10				11		2				6	
			Apps				29	7	42	36	12	28	38	27	41	40	37	5	11	5	1	28	35	8	13	3	16
			Goals							1	1		6	15	17	15	4	1		1			1				2

F.A. Cup

| R3 | Jan | 7 | Stockport County | 2-4 | Griffiths, Wright | 23800 | | | 3 | 4 | | 6 | 7 | 8 | 9 | 10 | 11 | | | | | | 5 | 2 | 1 | | |

		P	W	D	L	F	A	W	D	L	F	A	Pts
1	Tottenham Hotspur	42	15	3	3	51	15	12	4	5	30	20	61
2	Sheffield Wed.	42	12	7	2	46	23	6	9	6	21	25	52
3	Sheffield United	42	9	10	2	36	19	10	4	7	32	30	52
4	Southampton	42	13	4	4	44	25	6	10	5	20	23	52
5	Leeds United	42	11	8	2	33	16	6	5	10	21	29	47
6	Preston North End	42	12	5	4	37	21	6	4	11	23	28	45
7	Hull City	42	11	8	2	39	25	6	3	12	25	47	45
8	Swansea Town	42	11	3	7	34	18	6	6	9	19	31	43
9	Brentford	42	11	5	5	21	12	4	8	9	23	37	43
10	Cardiff City	42	13	3	5	28	14	3	7	11	13	30	42
11	Grimsby Town	42	13	5	3	53	25	3	3	15	21	48	40
12	Coventry City	42	8	6	7	32	24	5	7	9	23	31	39
13	BARNSLEY	42	11	6	4	45	28	2	7	12	19	39	39
14	Chesterfield	42	12	3	6	28	16	3	6	12	15	31	39
15	Leicester City	42	8	9	4	30	25	4	6	11	25	40	39
16	Blackburn Rovers	42	10	5	6	30	15	4	5	12	25	45	38
17	Luton Town	42	8	9	4	28	22	2	9	10	13	29	38
18	Bury	42	10	8	3	37	19	4	1	16	23	46	37
19	West Ham United	42	8	7	6	30	25	4	5	12	23	36	36
20	Queen's Park Rgs.	42	6	5	10	21	30	5	7	9	19	27	34
21	Plymouth Argyle	42	6	6	9	19	24	2	10	9	25	41	32
22	Bradford Park Ave.	42	7	6	8	34	34	3	5	13	17	43	31

1950/51 15th in Division 2

No	Date	Opponent	Score	Scorers	Att	Kelly PM	Lindsay D	Pallister G	Blanchflower RD	Kitchen J	Baxter JC	Smith G	McMorran EI	Wright AM	McCormack JC	Kelly JC	Bannister E	Deakin WE	Glover A	Griffiths JS	Hough H	Hudson M	Jones GH	Kaye A	Lambert K	Ledger R	Murphy E	Normanton S	Scattergood E	Taylor T	Ward TV
1	Aug 19	SOUTHAMPTON	1-2	Wright	19909	1	2	3	4	5	6	7	8	9	10	11															
2	24	Hull City	3-3	McCormack 2, Wright	41949	1		3	4	5	6	7	8	10	9	11	2														
3	26	Chesterfield	2-1	McCormack 2	14828	1		3	4	5	6	7	8	10	9	11	2														
4	30	HULL CITY	4-2	McCormack 2, Wright, McMorran	24583	1		3	4	5	6	7	8	10	9	11	2														
5	Sep 2	Sheffield United	2-0	McCormack, McMorran	41626	1		3	4	5	6	7	8	10	9	11	2														
6	6	BRENTFORD	2-3	Pallister, McCormack (pen)	15505	1		3	4	5	6	7	8	10	9	11	2														
7	9	LUTON TOWN	6-1	McCormack 5, Wright	22052	1		3	4		6	7	8	10	9	11	2		5												
8	13	Brentford	2-0	Griffiths, Baxter	18448	1	5	3	4			10	7		9	11	2		6	8											
9	16	Leeds United	2-2	Baxter, McCormack	37633	1	5	3	4			10	7	8	9	11	2		6												
10	23	WEST HAM UNITED	1-2	McCormack	25679	1		3	4	5		10	7	8	9	11	2		6												
11	30	Swansea Town	0-1		19091	1		3	4				7	8	9	11	2		5	10											
12	Oct 7	GRIMSBY TOWN	3-1	McCormack 3	18417	1		3	4			8	10	7	9	11	2		5									6			
13	14	Birmingham City	0-2		26617	1		3	4			8	10	7	9	11	2		5									6			
14	21	PRESTON N. END	4-1	McCormack, McMorran, Smith, Blanchflower	30081	1		3	4			8	10	7	9	11	2		5									6			
15	28	Notts County	1-2		39435	1		3	4			8	10	7	9	11	2		5									6			
16	Nov 4	QUEENS PARK RANG	7-0	Taylor 3, McCormack 2, Kelly, McMorran	17927	1		3	4				7	8	9	11	2		5									6		10	
17	11	Bury	3-0	McCormack 2, McMorran	17662	1		3	4				7	8	9	11	2		5											10	
18	18	CARDIFF CITY	0-0		21818	1		3	4		6		7	8	9	11	2		5						10						
19	25	Coventry City	3-3	Taylor, Kelly, McCormack	28680	1		3	4		6		7	8	9	11	2		5											10	
20	Dec 2	MANCHESTER CITY	1-1	McCormack (pen)	29681	1		3	4		6		7	8	9	11	2		5	10											
21	9	Leicester City	2-1	McMorran, Taylor	25869	1		3	4				7	8	9	11	2		5									6		10	
22	16	Southampton	0-1		17207	1		3	4				7	9		11	2		5					8				6		10	
23	23	CHESTERFIELD	0-0		16573	1		3	4				7	8	9		2	11	5									6		10	
24	25	Doncaster Rovers	2-3	McCormack (pen), McMorran	28995	1			4				7	8	9		2	11	5				3					6		10	
25	26	DONCASTER ROVER	0-1		33867	1			4				7	8	9	11	2		5				3					6		10	
26	Jan 13	Luton Town	1-1	Deakin	15032	1	2	3	4			10		8	9			11	5					7				6			
27	20	LEEDS UNITED	1-2	McCormack	21967	1		3	4			10		8	9		2	11	5					7				6			
28	Feb 3	West Ham United	2-4	Baxter, McCormack	16781	1	2	3	4		6			8	9			11	5					7	10						
29	17	SWANSEA TOWN	1-0	Smith	8371		2	3	4		6	7	8		9				5		1							10			
30	24	Grimsby Town	1-3	Jones	14862		2	3	4		6	7	8		9				5		1		11					10			
31	Mar 3	BIRMINGHAM CITY	0-2		15450		2	3	4		6	7	8		9				5		1		11					6			
32	10	Preston North End	0-7		31187		2	3	4		6	7	8		9				5		1									10	
33	17	NOTTS COUNTY	2-0	Lindsay, Deakin	12932		2	3			6	7	8		9				5		1						10				4
34	23	Blackburn Rovers	4-3	McCormack 2, McMorran, Jones	31060		2	3			6	7	8		9				5		1		11				10				4
35	24	Queen's Park Range	1-2	McCormack	15868		2	3			6	7	8		9				5		1		11				10				4
36	26	BLACKBURN ROVER	3-0	Murphy, Smith, McMorran	15125			3			6	7	8				2		5		1		11				9	10			4
37	31	BURY	2-3	McMorran, Baxter	11967			3			6	7	8				2		5		1		11				9	10			4
38	Apr 7	Cardiff City	1-1	Smith	27631			3			6	7	8				2		5		1							10		9	4
39	14	COVENTRY CITY	3-0	Taylor 2, Lindsay (pen)	12434			3			6	7	8				2		5		1							10		9	4
40	18	SHEFFIELD UNITED	1-1	McCormack (pen)	18120		5	3			6	7	8		9		2				1							10			4
41	21	Manchester City	0-6		39838		5	3			6	7	8		9		2				1		11					10			4
42	28	LEICESTER CITY	0-0		9882		5	3			6	7	8		9		2				1		11					10			4
		Apps				28	19	36	31	7	36	39	40	7	37	23	32	11	33	3	14	2	8	3	4	1	10	15	1	12	10
		Goals					2	1	1		4	4	10	4	33	2		2		1			2					1		7	

F.A. Cup

Rnd	Date	Opponent	Score	Scorers	Att	Kelly PM	Pallister G	Blanchflower RD	Smith G	McMorran EI	Wright AM	McCormack JC	Kelly JC	Bannister E	Glover A	Normanton S
R3	Jan 6	Northampton Town	1-3	McCormack	16818	1	3	4	10	7	8	9	11	2	5	6

		P	W	D	L	F	A	W	D	L	F	A	Pts
1	Preston North End	42	16	3	2	53	18	10	2	9	38	31	57
2	Manchester City	42	12	6	3	53	25	7	8	6	36	36	52
3	Cardiff City	42	13	7	1	36	20	4	9	8	17	25	50
4	Birmingham City	42	12	6	3	37	20	8	3	10	27	33	49
5	Leeds United	42	14	4	3	36	17	6	4	11	27	38	48
6	Blackburn Rovers	42	13	3	5	39	27	6	5	10	26	39	46
7	Coventry City	42	15	3	3	51	25	4	4	13	24	34	45
8	Sheffield United	42	11	4	6	44	27	5	8	8	28	35	44
9	Brentford	42	13	3	5	44	25	5	5	11	31	49	44
10	Hull City	42	12	5	4	47	28	4	6	11	27	42	43
11	Doncaster Rovers	42	9	6	6	37	32	6	7	8	27	36	43
12	Southampton	42	10	9	2	38	27	5	4	12	28	46	43
13	West Ham United	42	10	5	6	44	33	6	5	10	24	36	42
14	Leicester City	42	10	4	7	42	28	5	7	9	26	30	41
15	BARNSLEY	42	9	5	7	42	22	6	5	10	32	46	40
16	Queen's Park Rgs.	42	13	5	3	47	25	2	5	14	24	57	40
17	Notts County	42	7	7	7	37	34	6	6	9	24	26	39
18	Swansea Town	42	14	1	6	34	25	2	3	16	20	52	36
19	Luton Town	42	7	9	5	34	23	2	5	14	23	47	32
20	Bury	42	9	4	8	33	27	3	4	14	27	59	32
21	Chesterfield	42	7	7	7	30	28	2	5	14	14	41	30
22	Grimsby Town	42	6	8	7	37	38	2	4	15	24	57	28

Season 1950/51
Back row: Blanchflower, Glover, Bannister, Kelly P, Pallister, Baxter
Front row: Smith, McMorran, McCormack, Taylor, Kelly J

Season 1951/52
Back row: Semley (Masseur) Jarman, Lindsay, Wood, Hough, Hudson, Baxter, Shotton (Trainer)
Front row: Smith, McMorran, McCormack, Taylor, Jones, Glover

1951/52 20th in Division 2

#		Date	Opponent	Score	Scorers	Att	Ho	Li	Pa	Wa	McN	Ba	Sm	McM	McC	Wo	Jo	Al	De	Fa	Gl	Hu	Ja	Jar	Ka	Ke	La	Lu	Mar	No	Pat	Sm	Sc	Ta	Mu
1	Au	18	Hull City	0-0		37057	1	2	3	4	5	6	7			9	10	11																	8
2		25	SOUTHAMPTON	3-1	Jones, McCormack, McMorran	17274	1	2	3	4	5	6	7	8	9		11																		10
3		30	Notts County	0-4		15507	1	2	3	4	5	6	7	8			11																	9	10
4	Se	1	SHEFFIELD UNITE	3-4	McMorran, Jones, Murphy	25645	1	2	3	4	5	6	7	8	9		11																		10
5		5	LUTON TOWN	1-2	Jones	13109	1		3	4	5		7		9	8	11													2	6				10
6		8	West Ham United	1-2	Wood	20235	1	2	3	4	5		10	7	9	8	11			6															
7		12	NOTTS COUNTY	2-1	McMorran 2	16148	1	2			6	5	10	7	9		8			3			4												
8		15	COVENTRY CITY	1-0	McMorran	13451	1	2		4	5	6	7	8	9	10	11			3															
9		22	Swansea Town	1-2	McCormack	22335	1	2		4	5	6	7	8	9	10	11			3															
10		29	BURY	3-3	McCormack, McMorran 2	15531	1	2		4	5	6		8	9		11			3				7											10
11	Oct	6	Sheffield Wed.	1-2	Baxter (pen)	34191	1		3	4	5	10	7		9					6	2						11							8	
12		13	LEEDS UNITED	3-1	McCormack, McMorran, Smith	15565	1		3	4	5		7	8	9					2		6					11	10							
13		20	Rotherham United	0-4		22320	1		3	4	5	6	7	8	9					2							11	10							
14		27	CARDIFF CITY	2-0	McCormack, McMorran	11168	1	2				6	7	8	9		11			5	3			4										10	
15	No	3	Birmingham City	1-2	McCormack	19186	1	2				6	7	8	9		11			5	3			4										10	
16		10	LEICESTER CITY	3-3	Webb(og), McCormack, Baxter	11133	1	3			5	10	7	8	9				11					4						2	6				
17		17	Nottingham Forest	3-3	McCormack 2, Jones	23151	1	2	3		5	8	7		9		11							4							6				10
18		24	BRENTFORD	0-0		10149	1		3	8	5	10	7	9										4							6				11
19	De	1	Doncaster Rovers	2-1	McMorran, Wood	20902	1		3		5	10	7	9		8			11	2				4							6				
20		8	EVERTON	1-0	McMorran	8003	1		3		5	10	7	9		8			11	2				4							6				
21		15	HULL CITY	2-2	Smith, Baxter	12821	1		3		5	10	7	9		8			11	2				4							6				
22		22	Southampton	1-1	Smith	15735	1		3		5	10	7	9		8				2				4						6	11				
23		25	QUEEN'S PARK R.	3-1	Baxter, McMorran, Wood	15067	1		3	4	5	10	7	9		8				2				4						6	11				
24		26	Queen's Park R.	1-1	Pattison	13862	1	2		4	5	10	7	9		8					3			4						6	11				
25		29	Sheffield United	2-1	Pattison, McMorran	37237	1		3		5	10	7	9		8				2				4						6	11				
26	Jan	5	WEST HAM UNITED	1-1	Wood	16267	1	2			5	10	7	9		8				3				4						6	11				
27		19	Coventry City	0-0		17577	1	3			5	10	7	9		8				2				4						6	11				
28		26	SWANSEA TOWN	2-3	Smith, Glover	13870	1	3			5		7	8		9			10	2				4						6	11				
29	Fe	9	Bury	0-3		12585	1	9	3	8		10	7							2				6	4						11				
30		16	SHEFFIELD WED.	5-4	Lambert 2, Baxter 2, McNeil	29795	1		3	4	5	10	7	9						2							8				11		6		
31	Ma	1	Leeds United	0-1		32221			3	6		10	7	9				1		2				4							8			11	
32		8	ROTHERHAM UNIT	0-1		26922				4	5	10	7	9				1		2	3						11	8					6		
33		15	Cardiff City	0-3		24542				4	5		7	9				1		2	3						8	10			11		6		
34		22	BIRMINGHAM CITY	1-2	Ferris (og)	14377					5	6	7	9				1		2	3			4			8	10			11				
35		29	Leicester City	2-1	Lumley 2	17446					5	6		9				1	10	2	3			4	7			8			11				
36	Apr	5	NOTTM. FOREST	1-1	Lumley	11341					5	6		9				1	10	2	3			4	7			8			11				
37		11	Blackburn Rovers	1-2	Lumley	25183	1				5	6		9					10	2	3			7				8		4	11				
38		12	Brentford	1-1	Normanton	19912	1				5	6		9		10			11	2	3			7				8		4					
39		14	BLACKBURN ROVE	1-2	McMorran	18251	1				5	6		9		10				2	3			7				8		4	11				
40		19	DONCASTER ROVE	1-1	Lumley	17327	1				5	6		9		10				2	3			7				8		4		11			
41		26	Everton	1-1	Lumley	26566	1			6	5	10				9				2	3			7				8		4		11			
42	Ma	3	Luton Town	2-4	McMorran, Lumley	8789	1				5	6		9		10				3	2			7				8		4		11			

Played in game 29: J Kitchen (at 5). In game 31: R Archer (at 5).

	Ho	Li	Pa	Wa	McN	Ba	Sm	McM	McC	Wo	Jo	Al	De	Fa	Gl	Hu	Ja	Jar	Ka	Ke	La	Lu	Mar	No	Pat	Sm	Sc	Ta	Mu
Apps	36	18	20	22	38	38	33	37	13	20	14	6	9	18	15	15	3	19	9	4	7	10	2	20	16	3	3	4	8
Goals					1	6	4	15	9	4	4		1								2	7		1	2				1

Two own goals

F.A. Cup

		Date	Opponent	Score	Scorers	Att	Ho	Li	Pa	Wa	McN	Ba	Sm	McM	McC	Wo	Jo	Al	De	Fa	Gl	Hu	Ja	Jar	Ka	Ke	La	Lu	Mar	No	Pat	Sm	Sc	Ta	Mu
R3	Jan	12	COLCHESTER UTD.	3-0	Jarman, McMorran, Wood	24429	1		3		5	10	7	9		8				2				4						6	11				
R4	Fe	2	Arsenal	0-4		65000	1	2	3		5	10	7	9										4						6	11				8

		P	W	D	L	F	A	W	D	L	F	A	Pts
1	Sheffield Wed.	42	14	4	3	54	23	7	7	7	46	43	53
2	Cardiff City	42	18	2	1	52	15	2	9	10	20	39	51
3	Birmingham City	42	11	6	4	36	21	10	3	8	31	35	51
4	Nottingham Forest	42	12	6	3	41	22	6	7	8	36	40	49
5	Leicester City	42	12	6	3	48	24	7	3	11	30	40	47
6	Leeds United	42	13	7	1	35	15	5	4	12	24	42	47
7	Everton	42	12	5	4	42	25	5	5	11	22	33	44
8	Luton Town	42	9	7	5	46	35	7	5	9	31	43	44
9	Rotherham United	42	11	4	6	40	25	6	4	11	33	46	42
10	Brentford	42	11	7	3	34	20	4	5	12	20	35	42
11	Sheffield United	42	13	2	6	57	28	5	3	13	33	48	41
12	West Ham United	42	13	5	3	48	29	2	6	13	19	48	41
13	Southampton	42	11	6	4	40	25	4	5	12	21	48	41
14	Blackburn Rovers	42	11	3	7	35	30	6	3	12	19	33	40
15	Notts County	42	11	5	5	45	27	5	2	14	26	41	39
16	Doncaster Rovers	42	9	4	8	29	28	4	8	9	26	32	38
17	Bury	42	13	2	6	43	22	2	5	14	24	47	37
18	Hull City	42	11	5	5	44	23	2	6	13	16	47	37
19	Swansea Town	42	10	4	7	45	26	2	8	11	27	50	36
20	BARNSLEY	42	8	7	6	39	33	3	7	11	20	39	36
21	Coventry City	42	9	5	7	36	33	5	1	15	23	49	34
22	Queen's Park Rgs.	42	8	8	5	35	35	3	4	14	17	46	34

1952/53 22nd in Division 2

#		Date	Opponent	Score	Scorers	Att.
1	Aug	23	Doncaster Rovers	1-1		19662
2		27	NOTTM. FOREST	0-2		14186
3		30	SWANSEA TOWN	3-1	Lumley, Taylor, McMorran	11797
4	Sep	3	Nottingham Forest	0-3		19009
5		6	Huddersfield Town	0-6		33175
6		10	EVERTON	2-3	Taylor, D.Kelly	10835
7		13	SHEFFIELD UNITED	1-3	McMorran	16307
8		20	Rotherham United	1-3	Taylor	16327
9		27	Lincoln City	1-1	Taylor	15293
10	Oct	4	HULL CITY	5-1	Taylor 2(1p),Lumley,Kaye,D.Kelly	12347
11		11	PLYMOUTH ARGYLE	0-3		14855
12		18	Leeds United	1-4		22155
13		25	LUTON TOWN	2-3	D.Kelly, Taylor	11423
14	Nov	1	Birmingham City	1-3	Chappell	19927
15		8	BURY	3-2	Taylor 2, Lumley	11594
16		15	Southampton	2-1	Taylor, Lumley	10447
17		22	NOTTS COUNTY	1-2	McMorran	11626
18		29	Leicester City	2-2	Taylor, McMorran	20497
19	Dec	6	WEST HAM UNITED	2-0	Kaye, McMorran	8977
20		13	Fulham	1-3	Lumley	13651
21		20	DONCASTER ROVER	2-2	J.Kelly (pen), Taylor	9747
22		25	Brentford	0-4		15976
23		26	BRENTFORD	0-2		13725
24	Jan	1	Everton	1-2	Taylor	25485
25		3	Swansea Town	1-2		19607
26		17	HUDDERSFIELD T	2-4	Taylor (2 pens)	28789
27		24	Sheffield United	0-3		33495
28	Feb	7	ROTHERHAM UNITE	2-3	Taylor 2	16542
29		14	LINCOLN CITY	1-1	McMorran	7867
30		21	Hull City	2-2	Taylor, McMorran	25015
31		28	Plymouth Argyle	0-4		19005
32	Mar	7	LEEDS UNITED	2-2	Bartlett, Kaye	11536
33		14	Luton Town	1-1		15315
34		21	BIRMINGHAM CITY	1-3	Bartlett	7465
35		28	Bury	2-5	Chappell, N.Smith	7201
36	Apr	3	Blackburn Rovers	0-2		18467
37		4	SOUTHAMPTON	0-1		6524
38		6	BLACKBURN ROVER	1-4	Bartlett	4483
39		11	Notts County	0-1		13855
40		18	LEICESTER CITY	0-3		4697
41		25	West Ham United	1-3	Chappell	13038
42		29	FULHAM	1-1	Lumley	3204

Played in game 5: T Ward (at 4).

Player appearances grid

Column headers (left→right): Hough H, Youell JH, May H, Jarman JE, McNeil MA, Normanton S, Smith G, Lumley IT, McMorran EJ, Taylor T, Kelly JC, Allan J, Archer R, Bartlett F, Betts JB, Blenkinsop TW, Chappell L, Dougal W, Glover A, Hudson M, Jackson M, Kaye A, Kelly DC, Smillie RD, Smith N, Spruce GD, Thomas JC, Walls J, Wood R

#	Hou	You	May	Jar	McN	Nor	SmG	Lum	McM	Tay	KJC	All	Arc	Bar	Bet	Ble	Cha	Dou	Glo	Hud	Jac	Kay	KDC	Smi	SmN	Spr	Tho	Wal	Woo
1	1	2	3	4	5	6	7	8	9	10	11																		
2	1	2	3		5	6	7	10	9	8	11								4										
3	1	2	3		5	6	7	10	8	9	11										4								
4	1	2	3		5		7	10	8	9	11									6						4			
5	1	2			5		7	8	9		11									3									10
6	1				5			8		10	11	1	4		2				6				9	7			3		
7	1				5			8		10	11	1	4		2				6			7	9				3		
8	1		2		5			8	10	9	11	1	4						6				7			3			
9		2	3			4		8	9	11		1							6			7			5				10
10	1	2	3		4			8		10	11								6			7	9		5				
11		2	3		4	7	8			10	11	1							6				9		5				
12			3		4			9	8	11		1		2					6			7			5				10
13	1		2		5		7			8	10	11							6	3			9		4				
14	1		3		5					10	9	11		2		8	6				7		4						
15	1	2			5			8	9	10	11					3			6			7			4				
16	1	2			5			8	10	9	11					3			6			7			4				
17	1	2			5			8	9	10	11					3			6			7			4				
18	1	2			5			8	9	10	11					3			6			7			4				
19	1				5			8	9	10	11			2					6	3		7			4				
20	1				5			8		9	11			2					6	3		7			4				10
21	1				5			8	9	10	11			2					6	3		7			4				
22	1		2		5		11	10	9					8						3	6	7			4				
23	1				5	6	7		9		11			2				10		3		8			4				
24					5	6	7		10	9	11		2					8		3					4			1	
25					4	7		10			11		5	2				6		3		8	9					1	
26					5	4		8	10	9	11							6		3		7			2			1	
27	1	2				6			8	10	11			5						3		7	9		4				
28	1	2				6			8	10	11			5						3		7	9		4				
29	1	2				5	6	7	10	8	9									3				11	4				
30	1	2				5	6	7	10	8	9									3				11	4				
31	1	2				5	6	7	10	8	9													11	4	3			
32	1	2				5			10				6	8								7			11	4	3		9
33	1	2				5			10				6	8				9				7			11	4	3		
34	1				5	2					11		6	8				9				7			4	3			10
35					3	7	10				11		5	8				9						6	4	2	1		
36		3			4					10	11		5					9	6			7			8	2	1		
37		3			6					10	11			8				9				7			4	5	2		
38	1	3			6					10	11		5	8				9				7			4	2			
39		3			5	6					11			8				10				7	9		4	2			
40		3			5	6					11			8				10				7	9		4	2			
41		3			5	6		8			11			10				9						7	4	2			
42		3			6			8			11		5	10				9				7			4	2	1		
Apps	30	19	19	1	30	26	14	29	27	28	36	5	11	10	8	8	12	21	1	14	4	27	10	8	29	6	15	7	6
Goals							1	6	7	19	1			3			3					3	3		1				

F.A. Cup

	Date	Opponent	Score	Scorers	Att.	McN	Lum	McM	Tay	KJC	Arc	Cha	Glo	Kay	KDC	SmN	Woo
R3	Jan 10	BRIGHTON & HOVE	4-3	Taylor 2,Kaye,McMorran	17244	6	8	10	9	11	5	2	3	7		4	1
R4	31	Plymouth Argyle	0-1		27800	6	8	10	11		5	2	3	7	9	4	(1,2)

Division 2 final table

	Team	P	W	D	L	F	A	W	D	L	F	A	Pts
1	Sheffield United	42	15	3	3	60	27	10	7	4	37	28	60
2	Huddersfield Town	42	14	4	3	51	14	10	6	5	33	19	58
3	Luton Town	42	15	1	5	53	17	7	7	7	31	32	52
4	Plymouth Argyle	42	12	5	4	37	24	8	4	9	28	36	49
5	Leicester City	42	13	6	2	55	29	5	6	10	34	45	48
6	Birmingham City	42	11	3	7	44	38	8	7	6	27	28	48
7	Nottingham Forest	42	11	5	5	46	32	7	3	11	31	35	44
8	Fulham	42	14	1	6	52	28	3	9	9	29	43	44
9	Blackburn Rovers	42	12	4	5	40	20	6	4	11	28	45	44
10	Leeds United	42	13	4	4	42	24	1	11	9	29	39	43
11	Swansea Town	42	10	9	2	45	26	5	3	13	33	55	42
12	Rotherham United	42	9	7	5	41	30	7	2	12	34	44	41
13	Doncaster Rovers	42	9	9	3	26	17	3	7	11	32	47	40
14	West Ham United	42	9	5	7	38	28	4	8	9	20	32	39
15	Lincoln City	42	9	9	3	41	26	2	8	11	23	45	39
16	Everton	42	9	8	4	38	23	3	6	12	33	52	38
17	Brentford	42	8	8	5	38	29	5	3	13	21	47	37
18	Hull City	42	11	6	4	36	19	3	2	16	21	50	36
19	Notts County	42	11	5	5	41	31	3	3	15	19	57	36
20	Bury	42	10	6	5	33	30	3	3	15	20	51	35
21	Southampton	42	5	7	9	45	44	5	6	10	23	41	33
22	BARNSLEY	42	4	4	13	31	46	1	4	16	16	62	18

Season 1952/53
Back row: Shotton (Trainer) Normanton, Jackson, McNeill, Hough, Hudson, Baxter, Chappell
Front row: Kaye, Lumley, McMorran, Wood, Smillie

Season 1953/54
Back row: Smith, Spruce, Thomas, Hough, May, Walters
Front row: Kaye, Lumley, Chappell, Brown, Bartlett

1953/54   2nd in Division 3(N)

#		Date	Opponent	Score	Scorers	Att	Hough H	Thomas JC	May H	Smith N	Spruce GD	Normanton S	Kaye A	Lumley IT	Wood R	Brown R	Pattison FM	Kelly DC	Smith G	Hudson M	Walters H	Chappell L	Smillie RD	Archer R	Bartlett F	Wardle W	Jackson M	Sharp D
1	Aug	19	Bradford City	0-1		15630	1	2	3	4	5	6	7	8	9	10	11											
2		22	Port Vale	0-0		14223	1	2	3	4	5	6	7	8		10	11	9										
3		26	Chester	1-1	Brown	7117	1	2	3	4	5	6	7	8		10	11	9										
4		29	BRADFORD PARK AVE.	2-1	Smith N, Brown	7480	1	2	3	4	5	6		8		10	11	9	7									
5	Sep	2	CHESTER	3-0	Lumley, Kelly, Pattison	9969	1	2	3	4	5	6		8		10	11	9	7									
6		5	CHESTERFIELD	4-1	Lumley 3, Pattison	12640	1	2	3	4	5	6		8		10	11	9	7									
7		7	Crewe Alexandra	2-3	Lumley, Kelly	8895	1	2		4	5	6		8		10	11	9	7	3								
8		12	Darlington	1-1	Chappell	6912	1	2		4	5	6		8		10	11		7	3		9						
9		16	CREWE ALEXANDRA	1-1	Chappell	10866	1	2	3		5	6		8		10	11		7		4	9						
10		19	HARTLEPOOLS UNITED	3-2	Smillie, Chappell, Brown	10757	1	2	3		5	6		8		10			7		4	9	11					
11		23	SOUTHPORT	2-1	Brown, Lumley (pen)	9198	1	2	3		5			8		10			7		4	9	11	6				
12		26	Gateshead	0-0		10417	1	2	3		5			8		10			7		4	9	11	6				
13	Oct	3	WORKINGTON	4-2	Lumley 2, Chappell, Brown	10985	1	2	3	4	5			8		10			7		6	9	11					
14		10	Halifax Town	2-1	Lumley, Chappell	9354	1	2	3	4	5			8		10			7		6	9	11					
15		17	CARLISLE UNITED	1-1	Brown	11369	1	2	3	4	5			8		10			7		6	9	11					
16		24	Accrington Stanley	0-3		8891	1	2	3	4	5			8		10			7		6	9	11					
17		31	GRIMSBY TOWN	0-0		8438	1	2	3	4	5		7		8	10					6	9				11		
18	Nov	7	Stockport County	0-3		6530	1	2	3	4	5		7		8	10					6	9				11		
19		14	ROCHDALE	2-1	Kaye, Brown	8146	1	2	3	4	5		7	8		10					6	9				11		
20		28	MANSFIELD TOWN	2-1	Kaye, Brown	9241	1	2	3	4			7	8		10					6	9				11		5
21	Dec	5	Barrow	1-0	Brown	6311	1	2	3	4	5		7	8		10					6	9				11		
22		19	PORT VALE	0-1		11426	1	2	3	4	5		7	8		10						9				11	6	
23		25	York City	2-0	Chappell 2	5160	1	2	3	4	5		7	8		10					6	9				11		
24		26	YORK CITY	2-1	Chappell, Brown	9631	1	2	3	4	5		7		8	10					6	9				11		
25	Jan	1	Southport	2-5	Chappell 2	5483	1	2	3	4	5		7	8		10					6	9				11		
26		2	Bradford Park Avenue	2-0	Brown 2	11141	1	2	3	4	5		7	8		10					6	9				11		
27		9	BRADFORD CITY	4-2	Chappell 2, Brown, Wardle	8719	1	2	3	4	5		7	8		10					6	9				11		
28		16	Chesterfield	1-1	Walters	8399	1	2	3	4	5		7	8		10					6	9				11		
29		23	DARLINGTON	5-1	Kaye, Brown 4 (1 pen)	7956	1	2	3	4	5		7	8		10					6	9				11		
30	Feb	6	Hartlepools United	1-0	Chappell	7276	1	2	3	4			7	8		10					6	9				11		5
31		20	Workington	0-2		12172	1	2	3	4	5		7	8		10					6	9				11		
32		27	HALIFAX TOWN	1-2	Lumley	9123	1	2	3	4	5		7	8		10					6	9				11		
33	Mar	3	Tranmere Rovers	1-0	Lumley	3168	1	2	3	4	5		7	8		10					6	9				11		
34		6	Carlisle United	4-2	Chappell 3, Brown	4954	1	2	3	4	5		7	8		10					6	9				11		
35		13	ACCRINGTON STANLEY	5-0	Kaye 2, Chappell 2, Brown	8131	1	2	3	4	5		7	8		10					6	9				11		
36		20	Grimsby Town	1-0	Brown	6616	1	2	3	4	5		7	8		10					6	9				11		
37		27	STOCKPORT COUNTY	4-1	Walters, Chappell, Brown 2	9367	1	2	3	4	5		7	8		10					6	9				11		
38		31	GATESHEAD	0-2		12960	1	2	3	4	5		7	8		10					6	9				11		
39	Apr	3	Rochdale	1-1	Lumley	5785	1	2	3		5		7	8		10					6	9		4		11		
40		10	WREXHAM	3-0	Kelly 2, Brown	8763	1	2	3		5		7	8		10		9			6			4		11		
41		16	Scunthorpe United	0-6		10302	1	2	3		5		7	8		10					6	9		4		11		
42		17	Mansfield Town	0-2		10031	1	2			5		7	8		10			3		6	9				11	4	
43		19	SCUNTHORPE UNITED	0-1		10867	1	2			5		7	8		10			3		6	9				11	4	
44		21	TRANMERE ROVERS	3-0	Kaye, Chappell, Brown	5860	1	2			5		7	8		10			3		6	9				11	4	
45		24	BARROW	3-2	Lumley 2, Chappell	6889	1	2	3		5		7	8		10						9		6		11	4	
46		28	Wrexham	1-1	Chappell	6585	1	2	3		5		7	8		10					6	9				11	4	
			Apps				46	46	40	34	44	10	33	43	4	46	9	7	12	5	37	38	7	6	9	22	6	2
			Goals							1			6	14		24	2	4			2	22	1			1		

F.A. Cup

		Date	Opponent	Score	Scorers	Att	Hough H	Thomas JC	May H	Smith N	Spruce GD		Kaye A	Lumley IT	Wood R	Brown R					Walters H	Chappell L			Bartlett F	Wardle W		
R1	Nov	21	YORK CITY	5-2	Kaye, Lumley, Bartlett 2, Chappell	14755	1	2	3	4			7	8		10					6	9			5	11		
R2	Dec	12	Norwich City	1-2	Brown	20655	1	2	3	4	5		7	8		10					6	9				11		

		P	W	D	L	F	A	W	D	L	F	A	Pts
1	Port Vale	46	16	7	0	48	5	10	10	3	26	16	69
2	BARNSLEY	46	16	3	4	54	24	8	7	8	23	33	58
3	Scunthorpe United	46	14	7	2	49	24	7	8	8	28	32	57
4	Gateshead	46	15	4	4	49	22	6	9	8	25	33	55
5	Bradford City	46	15	6	2	40	14	7	3	13	20	41	53
6	Chesterfield	46	13	6	4	41	19	6	8	9	35	45	52
7	Mansfield Town	46	15	5	3	59	22	5	6	12	29	45	51
8	Wrexham	46	16	4	3	59	19	5	5	13	22	49	51
9	Bradford Park Ave.	46	13	6	4	57	31	5	8	10	20	37	50
10	Stockport County	46	14	6	3	57	20	4	5	14	20	47	47
11	Southport	46	12	5	6	41	26	5	7	11	22	34	46
12	Barrow	46	12	7	4	46	26	4	5	14	26	45	44
13	Carlisle United	46	10	8	5	53	27	4	7	12	30	44	43
14	Tranmere Rovers	46	11	4	8	40	34	7	3	13	19	36	43
15	Accrington Stanley	46	12	7	4	41	22	4	3	16	25	52	42
16	Crewe Alexandra	46	9	8	6	30	26	5	5	13	19	41	41
17	Grimsby Town	46	14	5	4	31	15	2	4	17	20	62	41
18	Hartlepools United	46	10	8	5	40	21	3	6	14	19	44	40
19	Rochdale	46	12	5	6	40	20	3	5	15	19	57	40
20	Workington	46	10	9	4	36	22	3	5	15	23	58	40
21	Darlington	46	11	3	9	31	27	1	11	11	19	44	38
22	York City	46	8	7	8	39	32	4	6	13	25	54	37
23	Halifax Town	46	9	6	8	26	21	3	4	16	18	52	34
24	Chester	46	10	7	6	39	22	1	3	19	9	45	32

1954/55 Champions of Division 3(N)

#	Date	Opponent	Score	Scorers	Att	Hough H	Thomas JC	May H	Smith N	Spruce GD	Walters H	Kaye A	Lumley IT	Chappell L	Brown R	Wardle W	Kelly DC	Betts JB	Wood R	Jackson M	Archer R	Jarman JE	Holmes T	Smillie RD	Graham M	Pattison FM	Bartlett F
1	Aug 21	OLDHAM ATHLETIC	2-2	Lumley, Brown	11386	1	2	3	4	5	6	7	8	9	10	11											
2	23	Bradford Park Avenue	0-1		12744	1	2	3	4	5	6	7	8		10	11	9										
3	28	Halifax Town	1-1	Brown	10247	1	2	3	4	5	6	7	8	9	10	11											
4	Sep 1	BRADFORD PARK AVE.	2-1	Brown, Pattison	12679	1	2	3	4	5	6	7		9	10				8							11	
5	4	York City	1-0	Smith	11446	1	2	3	4	5	6	7		9	10				8							11	
6	9	Scunthorpe United	0-1		12158	1	2	3		5	6	7	8	9	10	11			4								
7	11	Southport	2-0	Kaye, Brown	3996	1	2	3		5	6	7		9	10				8	4				11			
8	15	SCUNTHORPE UNITED	1-0	Brown	16431	1	2	3		5	6	7		9	10				8	4						11	
9	18	BARROW	3-0	Wood, Chappell 2	12175	1	2	3		5	6	7		9	10				8	4						11	
10	22	ACCRINGTON STANLEY	1-2	Chappell	14095	1	2	3		5	6	7		9	10	11			8		4						
11	25	Workington	0-1		7831	1	2	3		5	6	7		9	10				4	8				11			
12	27	Accrington Stanley	3-2	Lumley, Brown, Holliday (og)	12735	1	2	3		5	6	7	8	9	10				4								11
13	Oct 2	MANSFIELD TOWN	1-0	Bartlett	14234	1	2	3		5	6	7	8	9	10				4								11
14	9	Rochdale	0-3		11552	1	2	3		5	6	7	8	9	10				4								11
15	16	TRANMERE ROVERS	4-1	Lumley, Chappell 3	11001	1	2	3		5	6	7	8	9	10	11			4								
16	23	Stockport County	0-1		7325	1	2	3		5	6	7	8	9	10				4					11			
17	30	HARTLEPOOLS UNITED	0-0		10377	1	2	3		5	6		8	9	10				4				7				11
18	Nov 6	Gateshead	4-0	Wood, Bartlett 3	5290	1	2	3	4	5			8	9					10	6			7				11
19	13	Darlington	4-1	Chappell 3, Wood	8679	1	2	3	4	5		7	8	9					10	6							11
20	27	CREWE ALEXANDRA	3-1	Chappell 3	9102	1	2	3	4	5	6	7	8	9					10								11
21	Dec 4	Carlisle United	4-2	Lumley, Chappell, Wood, Bartlett	5153	1	2	3	4	5	6	7	8	9					10								11
22	18	Oldham Athletic	1-4	Chappell	8815	1	2	3	4	5	6	7	8	9					10					11			
23	25	Grimsby Town	3-1	Chappell, Bartlett 2	10400	1		3	4	5		7	8	9				2	10	6							11
24	27	GRIMSBY TOWN	1-3	Bartlett	16887	1		3	4	5	6	7	8	9				2	10								11
25	Jan 1	HALIFAX TOWN	3-0	Smith, Brown, Bartlett	13128	1	2	3	4	5		7	8		9				6						10		11
26	8	WREXHAM	4-2	Wood, Lumley, Brown, Graham	10694	1	2	3	4	5		7	8		9				6						10		11
27	15	York City	3-1	Chappell, Brown, Bartlett	7810	1	2	3	4	5		7	8	9	10				6								11
28	29	Wrexham	0-3		6675	1	2	3	4	5		7	8	9	10				6								11
29	Feb 5	Barrow	1-3	Brown	4809	1	2	3	4	5		7	8		9				6						10		11
30	12	WORKINGTON	3-1	Bartlett 3	6192	1	2	3	4	5		7	8	9					10			6					11
31	19	Mansfield Town	1-1	Brown	4020	1	2	3	4	5		7	8	9					10			6					11
32	Mar 5	Tranmere Rovers	1-0	Wood	5788	1	2	3	4	5			8	9					10			6	7				11
33	12	STOCKPORT COUNTY	2-0	Brown 2	9485	1	2	3	4	5			8	9					10			6					11
34	19	Hartlepools United	3-0	Kaye, Wood, Bartlett	8411	1	2	3	4	5		7	8	9					10			6					11
35	26	GATESHEAD	3-0	Kaye 2, Wood	6253	1	2	3	4	5		7	8	9					10			6					11
36	Apr 2	Darlington	1-0	Lumley	6760	1	2	3	4	5		7	8	9					10			6					11
37	9	CHESTERFIELD	3-0	Chappell 2, Wood	17248	1	2	3	4	5		7	8	9					10			6					11
38	11	BRADFORD CITY	1-0	Chappell	18929	1	2	3	4	5		7	8	9					10			6					11
39	12	Bradford City	2-0	Kaye, Wood	18514	1	2	3	4	5		7	8	9					10	6							11
40	16	Crewe Alexandra	2-1	Brown, Bartlett	5450	1	2	3	4	5		7	8	9	10							6					11
41	23	CARLISLE UNITED	3-1	Chappell 2, Mitton (og)	13581	1	2	3	4	5		7	8	9					10			6					11
42	25	Chesterfield	1-3	Jarman	13148	1	2	3	4	5		7	8	9					10			6					11
43	27	SOUTHPORT	0-0		13951	1	2	3	4	5		7	8	9					10			6					11
44	30	Chester	2-0	Lumley, Brown	6566	1	2	3	4	5	6	7	8		9				10								11
45	May 3	ROCHDALE	2-0	Wood 2	11682	1	2	3	4			5	7	8	9	11	6		10								
46	4	CHESTER	4-2	Lumley, Brown 3	10044	1	2	3	4				7	8	9	10	5							6	11		
				Apps		46	44	46	34	44	23	43	39	34	33	6	1	4	35	14	2	12	1	8	3	4	30
				Goals					2			5	8	21	18				12			1			1	1	15

Two own goals

F.A. Cup

	Date	Opponent	Score	Scorers	Att	Hough H	Thomas JC	May H	Smith N	Spruce GD	Walters H	Kaye A	Lumley IT	Chappell L	Brown R	Wardle W	Kelly DC	Betts JB	Wood R	Jackson M	Archer R	Jarman JE	Holmes T	Smillie RD	Graham M	Pattison FM	Bartlett F
R1	Nov 20	WIGAN ATHLETIC	3-2	Bartlett, Lumley 2	17767	1	2	3	4	5			8	9					10	6				7			11
R2	Dec 11	Gateshead	3-3	Wood, Kaye, Bartlett	11394	1	2	3	4	5	6	7	8	9					10								11
rep	16	GATESHEAD	0-1		13531	1	2	3	4	5	6	7	8	9					10								11

		P	W	D	L	F	A	W	D	L	F	A	Pts
1	BARNSLEY	46	18	3	2	51	17	12	2	9	35	29	65
2	Accrington Stanley	46	18	2	3	65	32	7	9	7	31	35	61
3	Scunthorpe United	46	14	6	3	45	18	9	6	8	36	35	58
4	York City	46	13	5	5	43	27	11	5	7	49	36	58
5	Hartlepools United	46	16	3	4	39	20	9	2	12	25	29	55
6	Chesterfield	46	17	1	5	54	33	7	5	11	27	37	54
7	Gateshead	46	11	7	5	38	26	9	5	9	27	43	52
8	Workington	46	11	7	5	39	23	7	7	9	29	32	50
9	Stockport County	46	13	4	6	50	27	5	8	10	34	43	48
10	Oldham Athletic	46	14	5	4	47	22	5	5	13	27	46	48
11	Southport	46	10	9	4	28	18	6	7	10	19	26	48
12	Rochdale	46	13	7	3	39	20	4	7	12	30	46	48
13	Mansfield Town	46	14	4	5	40	28	4	5	14	25	43	45
14	Halifax Town	46	9	9	5	41	27	6	4	13	22	40	43
15	Darlington	46	10	7	6	41	28	4	7	12	21	45	42
16	Bradford Park Ave.	46	11	7	5	29	21	4	4	15	27	49	41
17	Barrow	46	12	4	7	39	34	5	2	16	31	55	40
18	Wrexham	46	9	6	8	40	35	4	6	13	25	42	38
19	Tranmere Rovers	46	9	6	8	37	30	4	5	14	18	40	37
20	Carlisle United	46	12	1	10	53	39	3	5	15	25	50	36
21	Bradford City	46	9	5	9	30	26	4	5	14	17	29	36
22	Crewe Alexandra	46	8	10	5	45	35	2	4	17	23	56	34
23	Grimsby Town	46	10	4	9	28	32	3	4	16	19	46	34
24	Chester	46	10	3	10	23	25	2	6	15	21	52	33

Season 1954/55
Back row: Smith, Thomas, Spruce, Hough, May, Walters, Shotton (Trainer)
Front row: Kaye, Lumley, Chappell, Brown, Wardle

Season 1955/56
Back row: Smith, Archer, Jackson, Swift, Hough, Anderson, Betts, Chappell
Front row: Kaye, Lumley, Brown, Wood, Bartlett

1955/56 — 18th in Division 2

No	Date	Match	Score	Scorers	Att	Hough H	Thomas JC	Betts JB	Smith N	Spruce GD	Jarman IE	Kaye A	Wood R	Chappell L	Lumley IT	Brown R	Graham M	Swift C	Bartlett F	Jackson M	Walters H	Gillott P	Holmes T	Anderson WB	Sharp D	Archer R	Smillie RD	Duggins G	Edgar J	McCann J
1	Aug 20	LEEDS UNITED	2-1	Kaye, Wood	19341	1	2	3	4	5	6	7	10	9	8	11														
2	25	Notts County	2-2	Graham, Brown	15517	1	2	3		5	6	7	4	9	8	11	10													
3	27	Fulham	1-5	Graham	21645	1		3		5	6	7	4	9	8	11	10	2												
4	31	NOTTS COUNTY	3-1	Kaye, Graham 2	16636	1		3		5	6	7	4	9	8	11	10	2												
5	Sep 3	BURY	3-3	Brown, Graham 2	17149	1		3		5	6	7	4		8	9	10	2	11											
6	5	Rotherham United	0-0		18847	1		3		5	6	7	4		8	9	10	2	11											
7	10	Leicester City	0-0		22856	1		3		5	6	7	4		8	9	10	2	11											
8	14	ROTHERHAM UNITED	3-2	Brown, Graham, Bartlett	19446	1		3		5	6	7	4		8	9	10	2	11											
9	17	Middlesbrough	1-1	Brown	24960	1		3		5	6	7	4		8	9	10	2	11											
10	24	BRISTOL CITY	0-0		19545	1		3		5	6	7	10		8	9		2	11	4										
11	Oct 1	West Ham United	0-4		20863	1		3		5	6	7	10		8	9		2	11	4										
12	8	LINCOLN CITY	1-0	Lumley	14819	1		3				7	6	9	8	10		2	11	4	5									
13	15	Blackburn Rovers	1-5	Brown	22288	1		3				7	6	9		10		2	11	4	5		8							
14	22	PLYMOUTH ARGYLE	1-2	Wood	11306	1		3			6	7	10		8	9		2	11		5			4						
15	29	Nottingham Forest	0-1		11412	1					6	7	10		8	9		2	11		3			4	5					
16	Nov 5	SHEFFIELD WEDNESDAY	0-3		21669	1						7	6		8	9		2	11		3			4	5				10	
17	12	Doncaster Rovers	1-1	Brown	12517	1		3				7	10		8	9		2	11		6			4	5					
18	19	BRISTOL ROVERS	4-3	Brown 2, Wood, Bartlett	11707	1		3				7	10		8	9		2	11		6			4	5					
19	26	Stoke City	1-2	Wood	17729	1		3				7	10		8	9		2	11		6			4	5					
20	Dec 3	HULL CITY	2-1	Kaye, Brown	14050	1		3				7	4	9	8	10		2	11		6				5					
21	10	Liverpool	1-1	Brown	26241	1		3				7	4	9	8	10		2	11		6				5					
22	17	Leeds United	1-3	Bartlett	23493	1		3				7	4	9	8	10		2	11		6				5					
23	24	FULHAM	3-0	Chappell 2, Greenwood (og)	15018	1		3				7	4	9	8	10		2	11		6				5					
24	26	Port Vale	2-1	Wood, Bartlett	19130	1		3				7	4	9	8	10		2	11		6				5					
25	27	PORT VALE	1-2	Brown	22067	1		3				7	4	9	8	10		2	11		6				5					
26	31	Bury	0-3		12972	1		3				7	4	9	8	10		2	11		6				5					
27	Jan 14	LEICESTER CITY	0-1		13282	1		3				7	4		10	8		2	11		6				5			9		
28	21	MIDDLESBROUGH	0-4		15934	1		3				7	4	9	10	8		2	11		6				5					
29	Feb 4	Bristol City	0-2		19581	1		3				7			8	10		2	11		6				5	4		9		
30	11	WEST HAM UNITED	1-1	Graham	8432	1		3				7	10	9	8		11	2			6				5					
31	18	Bristol Rovers	1-1	Wood	20979	1		3				7	10	9			11	2			6		8		5					
32	25	BLACKBURN ROVERS	2-1	Chappell 2	11683	1		3				7	10	9			11	2			6		8		5					
33	Mar 3	Plymouth Argyle	0-3		12600	1		3				7	10	9			11	2			6		8		5					
34	10	LIVERPOOL	0-5		13778	1		3				7	10	9			11	2			6		8		5	4				
35	21	Sheffield Wednesday	0-3		30873	1	2	3				7	10	9			11		8		6				5	4				
36	24	DONCASTER ROVERS	2-2	Kaye 2	9892	1	2					7		9	10		11		8		6	3			5	4				
37	31	Lincoln City	0-4		11787	1	2	3		5		7			10	11			8		6					4		9		
38	Apr 2	SWANSEA TOWN	3-2	Wood, Chappell 2	12208	1	2	3		5			8	9	10	11					6					4	7			
39	7	STOKE CITY	1-0	Bartlett	9754	1	2	3		5			8	9	10	11					6					4	7			
40	14	Hull City	1-4	Kaye	8931	1	2	3		5			8	9	10	11					6					4	7			
41	21	NOTTM. FOREST	1-1	Wood	11429	1	2	3		5		7	8	9	10						6					4				11
42	28	Swansea Town	1-3	Kaye	11502	1	2	3	4	5		7		9	10				8		6									11
Apps						42	10	38	2	17	13	39	38	27	25	36	19	33	36	4	31	1	5	6	22	9	3	3	1	2
Goals												7	8	6	1	11	8		5											

One own goal

F.A. Cup

Round	Date	Match	Score	Scorers	Att	Hough H	Thomas JC	Betts JB	Smith N	Spruce GD	Jarman IE	Kaye A	Wood R	Chappell L	Lumley IT	Brown R	Graham M	Swift C	Bartlett F	Jackson M	Walters H	Gillott P	Holmes T	Anderson WB	Sharp D	Archer R
R3	Jan 7	Aldershot	2-1	Brown 2	12285	1		3				7	4	9		10	8	2	11		6				5	
R4	28	BLACKBURN ROVERS	0-1		38163	1		3				7	4		10	9	8	2	11		6				5	

Division 2 Final Table

		P	W	D	L	F	A	W	D	L	F	A	Pts
1	Sheffield Wed.	42	13	5	3	60	28	8	8	5	41	34	55
2	Leeds United	42	17	3	1	51	18	6	3	12	29	42	52
3	Liverpool	42	14	3	4	52	25	7	3	11	33	38	48
4	Blackburn Rovers	42	13	4	4	55	29	8	2	11	29	36	48
5	Leicester City	42	15	3	3	63	23	6	3	12	31	55	48
6	Bristol Rovers	42	13	3	5	53	33	8	3	10	31	37	48
7	Nottingham Forest	42	9	5	7	30	26	10	4	7	38	37	47
8	Lincoln City	42	14	5	2	49	17	4	5	12	30	48	46
9	Fulham	42	15	2	4	59	27	5	4	12	30	52	46
10	Swansea Town	42	14	4	3	49	23	6	2	13	34	58	46
11	Bristol City	42	14	4	3	49	20	5	3	13	31	44	45
12	Port Vale	42	12	4	5	38	21	4	9	8	22	37	45
13	Stoke City	42	13	2	6	47	27	7	2	12	24	35	44
14	Middlesbrough	42	11	4	6	46	31	5	4	12	30	47	40
15	Bury	42	9	5	7	44	39	7	3	11	42	51	40
16	West Ham United	42	12	4	5	52	27	2	7	12	22	42	39
17	Doncaster Rovers	42	11	5	5	45	30	1	6	14	24	66	35
18	BARNSLEY	42	10	5	6	33	35	1	7	13	14	49	34
19	Rotherham United	42	7	5	9	29	34	5	4	12	27	41	33
20	Notts County	42	8	5	8	39	37	3	4	14	16	45	31
21	Plymouth Argyle	42	7	6	8	33	25	3	2	16	21	62	28
22	Hull City	42	6	4	11	32	45	4	2	15	21	52	26

1956/57 19th in Division 2

#	Date	Opponent	Score	Scorers	Att	Hough H	Betts JB	Thomas JC	Smith N	Spruce GD	Walters H	Kaye A	Wood R	Chappell L	Graham M	Brown R	McCann J	Swift C	Bartlett F	Storey S	Short J	Holmes T	Duggins G	Edgar J	Sharp D	Hirst MW	Leeson D	Hooley JW	Price B	Gillott P	Lunn J
1	Aug 18	Port Vale	0-0		14336	1	2	3	4	5	6	7	8	9	10	11															
2	22	SWANSEA TOWN	2-3	Kaye, Brown	13610	1	2	3	4	5	6	7	8	9	10	11															
3	25	MIDDLESBROUGH	1-3	Chappell	11651	1	2	3	4	5	6	7	8	9	10	11															
4	30	Swansea Town	3-2	Walters 2, Kaye	19342	1	2	3	4	5	6	7	8	9	10				11												
5	Sep 1	SHEFFIELD UNITED	1-6	Kaye	21189	1	2	3	4	5	6	7	8	9	10				11												
6	5	LINCOLN CITY	5-2	Smith, Storey, Chappell, Graham, McCann	9377	1		2	4	5	6	7		9	10		11	3		8											
7	8	Bristol City	2-1	Brown, McCann	19863	1		2	4	5	6	7			10	9	11	3		8											
8	15	BLACKBURN ROVERS	3-3	Kaye 2, Graham	14605	1		2	4	5	6	7			10	9	11	3		8											
9	22	West Ham United	0-2		19412	1		2	4	5	6	7			10		11	3		8								9			
10	29	NOTTM. FOREST	1-1	McCann	15666	1		2		5	6	7			10		11	3	4	8			9								
11	Oct 6	Leicester City	2-5	Duggins, Kaye (pen)	27360	1		2		5	6	7			10		11	3	4	8			9								
12	13	BRISTOL ROVERS	0-2		15052	1		2		5	6	7			10		11	3	4	8			9								
13	20	Doncaster Rovers	2-5	Chappell, Graham	14971	1		2		5	6	7		9	10		11	3	4	8											
14	27	LIVERPOOL	4-1	Storey, McCann 2, Kaye (pen)	14035	1				5		7		9	10		11	3	4	8	2	6									
15	Nov 3	Leyton Orient	0-2		17441	1				5		7		9	10		11	3	4	8	2	6									
16	10	HUDDERSFIELD T	0-5		15234	1				5		7		9	10		11	3	4	8	2	6									
17	17	Bury	2-1	Duggins 2	9713	1				5	6	7			10		11	3	4	8	2		9								
18	24	GRIMSBY TOWN	2-0	Kaye 2	11371	1				5	6	7					11	3	4	8	2	10	9								
19	Dec 1	Notts County	2-3	Duggins 2	11133	1				5	6	7					11	3	4	8	2		9	10							
20	8	STOKE CITY	2-2	Kaye, McCann	11710	1				5	6	7					11	3	4	8	2		9	10							
21	15	PORT VALE	2-0	Kaye, Storey	9683	1				5	6	7					11	3	4	8	2		9	10							
22	22	Middlesbrough	2-1	Edgar, McCann	11147	1				5	6	7					11	3	4	8	2		9	10							
23	25	Rotherham United	0-0		14332	1				5	6	7					11	3	4	8	2		9	10							
24	26	ROTHERHAM UNITED	1-1	Duggins	11031					5	6	7	10				11	3	4	8	2		9				1				
25	29	Sheffield United	0-5		25893	1				5	6	7	10				11	3	4	8	2		9								
26	Jan 12	BRISTOL CITY	3-0	Bartlett, Kaye, Edgar	13517	1					6	7		9			11	3	4		2	8		10	5						
27	19	Blackburn Rovers	0-2		21075	1					6	7	8	9			11	3	4		2		10		5						
28	Feb 2	WEST HAM UNITED	1-2	Edgar	15931	1					6	7					11	3	4		2	8	9	10	5						
29	9	Nottingham Forest	1-7	Edgar	25994	1				5	6			9			11	3	4		2			10		8					7
30	23	Bristol Rovers	1-1	Holmes	13918	1					6	7		9			11	3	4	8	2	10			5						
31	27	LEICESTER CITY	2-0	Storey, Chappell	11240	1				5	6	7		9			11	3	4	8	2	10									
32	Mar 2	DONCASTER ROVERS	3-1	Graham 2, Kaye (pen)	16928	1				5	6	7		9	10		11	3	4		2		8								
33	9	Liverpool	1-2	McCann	30672	1				5	6	7		9			11	3	4	8	2	10									
34	16	LEYTON ORIENT	3-0	Holmes, Kaye (pen), Chappell	13000	1		3		5	6	7		9			11		4	8	2	10									
35	23	Huddersfield Town	0-2		16772	1				5	6	7		9			11	3	4	8	2	10									
36	30	BURY	1-1	Chappell	10196	1				5	6	7		9	10		11	3	4	8	2										
37	Apr 6	Grimsby Town	1-4	Kaye	10413	1				5	6	7	4	9	10		11	3			2			8							
38	13	NOTTS COUNTY	1-1	Graham	7652	1				5	6	7	4	9	10		11	3			2			8							
39	19	Fulham	0-2		16993	1		3		5	6	7	4	9			11			8	2	10									
40	20	Stoke City	0-3		11504	1		3		5	6	7	4	9	10		11			8	2										
41	22	FULHAM	1-1	Wood	8531	1		2		5	6	7	8	9			11						10						4	3	
42	27	Lincoln City	1-4	Holmes	7282	1		2		5	6	7	4	9			11	3		8		10									
		Apps				41	5	18	9	38	39	41	14	26	22	5	37	33	29	29	27	14	13	12	4	1	1	1	1	1	1
		Goals							1		2	15	1	6	6	2	8		1	4		3	6	4							

F.A. Cup

Round	Date	Opponent	Score	Scorers	Att	Hough H	Walters H	Kaye A	Wood R	Chappell L	McCann J	Swift C	Bartlett F	Storey S	Short J	Holmes T	Duggins G	Sharp D
R3	Jan 5	PORT VALE	3-3	Kaye 2, Bartlett	17951	1	6	7	10		11	3	4	8	2		9	
rep	7	Port Vale	1-0	Hayward og	15623	1	6	7		9	11	3	4		2	8	10	5
R4	26	Cardiff City	1-0	Bartlett	31919	1	6	7		9	11	3	4		2	8	10	5
R5	Feb 16	NOTTM. FOREST	1-2	Kaye	38598	1	6	7		9	11	3	4	8	2		10	5

Division 2 Final Table

		P	W	D	L	F	A	W	D	L	F	A	Pts
1	Leicester City	42	14	5	2	68	36	11	6	4	41	31	61
2	Nottingham Forest	42	13	4	4	50	29	9	6	6	44	26	54
3	Liverpool	42	16	1	4	53	26	5	10	6	29	28	53
4	Blackburn Rovers	42	12	6	3	49	32	9	4	8	34	43	52
5	Stoke City	42	16	2	3	64	18	4	6	11	19	40	48
6	Middlesbrough	42	12	5	4	51	29	7	5	9	33	31	48
7	Sheffield United	42	11	6	4	45	28	8	2	11	42	48	46
8	West Ham United	42	12	4	5	31	24	7	4	10	28	39	46
9	Bristol Rovers	42	12	5	4	47	19	6	4	11	34	48	45
10	Swansea Town	42	12	3	6	53	34	7	4	10	37	56	45
11	Fulham	42	13	1	7	53	32	6	3	12	31	44	42
12	Huddersfield Town	42	10	3	8	33	27	8	3	10	35	47	42
·	Bristol City	42	13	2	6	49	32	3	7	11	25	47	41
14	Doncaster Rovers	42	12	5	4	51	21	3	5	13	26	56	40
15	Leyton Orient	42	7	8	6	34	38	8	2	11	32	46	40
16	Grimsby Town	42	12	4	5	41	26	5	1	15	20	36	39
17	Rotherham United	42	9	7	5	37	26	4	4	13	37	49	37
18	Lincoln City	42	9	4	8	34	27	5	2	14	20	53	34
19	BARNSLEY	42	8	7	6	39	35	4	3	14	20	54	34
20	Notts County	42	7	6	8	34	32	2	6	13	24	54	30
21	Bury	42	5	3	13	37	47	3	6	12	23	49	25
22	Port Vale	42	7	4	10	31	42	1	2	18	26	59	22

Season 1956/57
Back row: Bartlett, Short, Hough, Spruce, Walters, Swift
Front row: Kaye, Storey, Duggins, Edgar, McCann

Season 1957/58
Back row: Wood, Bartlett, Hough, Short, Sharpe, Swift
Front row: Edgar, Anderson, Chappell, Beaumont, McCann

1957/58 14th in Division 2

#	Date	Opponent	Score	Scorers	Att	Hough H	Short J	Swift C	Bartlett F	Sharp D	Wood R	Kaye A	Anderson E	Chappell L	Beaumont F	McCann J	Smith N	Graham M	Edgar J	Houghton WG	Jones B	Barber DE	Lunn J	Gillott P	Whyke P	Duggins G	Hopkins OT	Thomas JC	Price B	Leeson D
1	Aug 24	BRISTOL ROVERS	2-2	Chappell, Beaumont	12725	1	2	3	4	5	6	7	8	9	10	11														
2	28	Ipswich Town	0-3		20468	1	2	3	4	5	6	7	8	9	10	11														
3	31	Derby County	4-1	Kaye, Chappell 3	22376	1	2	3	4	5	6	7	8	9		11	10													
4	Sep 4	IPSWICH TOWN	5-1	Kaye 3 (2 pens), Wood, Anderson	12272	1	2	3	4	5	6	7	8	9		11	10													
5	7	SWANSEA TOWN	1-0	Kaye (pen)	15844	1	2	3	4	5	6	7	8	9		11	10													
6	9	Blackburn Rovers	1-3	Smith	13006	1	2	3	4	5	6	7	8	9		11	10													
7	14	Fulham	1-1	Chappell	24440	1	2	3	4	5	6	7	8	9		11	10													
8	18	BLACKBURN ROVERS	0-2		12814	1	2	3	4	5	6	7	8	9		11	10													
9	21	MIDDLESBROUGH	1-1	Beaumont	11577	1	2	3	4	5		7			10		8	11			6					9				
10	28	WEST HAM UNITED	1-0	Smith	12182	1	2	3	4	5		7		9		11	8			10	6									
11	Oct 5	Sheffield United	0-0		25416	1	2	3	4	5		7		9		11	8			10	6									
12	12	Leyton Orient	1-2	Chappell	15149	1	2	3	4	5		7		9		11	8			10	6									
13	19	CHARLTON ATHLETIC	4-1	Bartlett, Wood, Smith, Graham	15124	1	2	3	4		6	7		9		11	8	10									5			
14	28	Doncaster Rovers	1-1	Graham	18971	1	2	3	4	5	6	7		9		11	8	10												
15	Nov 2	ROTHERHAM UNITED	3-0	Smith 2, Graham	18943	1	2	3	4	5	6	7		9		11	8	10												
16	9	Huddersfield Town	5-0	Wood, Smith, Graham 2, McCann	21662	1	2	3	4	5	6	7		9		11	8	10												
17	16	Grimsby Town	3-3	Chappell 2, Graham	16190	1	2	3	4	5	6	7		9		11	8	10												
18	23	Stoke City	1-3	Kaye (pen)	17555	1	2		4	5	6	7		9			8	10					11					3		
19	30	BRISTOL CITY	4-1	Graham 2, McCann, Kaye (pen)	13508	1	2		4	5	6	7		9		11	8	10							3					
20	Dec 7	Cardiff City	0-7		8941	1	2		4	5	6	7		9		11	8	10							3					
21	14	LIVERPOOL	2-1	Kaye, Chappell	15296	1	2	3	4	5	6	7		9		11	8	10												
22	21	Bristol Rovers	1-1	Kaye	13215	1	2	3	4	5	6	7		9		11	8	10												
23	25	Notts County	3-2	Wood, Kaye, Beaumont	11343	1	2	3	4	5	6	7		9	8	11		10												
24	26	NOTTS COUNTY	1-1	Smith	20307	1	2	3	4	5	6	7		9		11	8	10												
25	28	DERBY COUNTY	3-0	Wood, Chappell, Beaumont	21787	1	2	3	4	5	6	7		9	10	11	8													
26	Jan 11	Swansea Town	2-4	Chappell 2	9750	1	2	3	4	5	6			9		11	8	10							7					
27	18	FULHAM	1-0	Bartlett	14338	1	2	3	4	5	6		10	9		11	8								7					
28	Feb 1	Middlesbrough	1-3	Graham	19498	1	2	3	4	5	6			9		11	8	10	7											
29	8	West Ham United	1-1	McCann	27182	1	2	3	4	5	6			9		11	8	10	7											
30	22	STOKE CITY	1-2	Chappell	14270	1	2	3	4	5	6			9		11	8	10	7											
31	Mar 1	Charlton Athletic	2-4	Chappell, Graham	25760	1	2	3	4	5	6			9		11	8	10	7											
32	8	DONCASTER ROVERS	1-1	Chappell	11569	1		3	4	5	6	7		9		11	8	10				2								
33	15	Rotherham United	1-4	Bartlett	11572	1		3	4	5	6	7		9		11	8	10				2								
34	22	HUDDERSFIELD T	2-3	Kaye, Graham	16549	1		3	4	5	6	7		9		11	8	10				2								
35	29	Grimsby Town	1-2	Edgar	10103			3	4	5	6	7		9		11		10	8			2								1
36	Apr 5	LEYTON ORIENT	3-0	Smith, Chappell 2	8801	1	2	3	4	5	6	7		9		11	8	10												
37	7	Lincoln City	3-1	Edgar, Chappell 2	7004	1	2	3	4	5	6	7		9		11		10	8											
38	8	LINCOLN CITY	1-3	Smith	11501	1	2	3	4	5	6	7		9		11	8	10												
39	12	Bristol City	0-5		18249	1	2	3	4	5	6	7		9		11	8	10												
40	19	CARDIFF CITY	1-1	Wood	8948	1	2	3		5	6	7		9	8	11		10			4									
41	23	SHEFFIELD UNITED	0-2		8810	1	2	3	4	5				9		11	8	10						6	7					
42	26	Liverpool	1-1	McCann	26440	1	2	3	4	5				9		11	8	10						6	7					
		Apps				41	38	39	40	41	35	34	9	41	6	39	34	32	9	5	4	3	3	2	2	1	1	1	1	1
		Goals							3		6	11	1	19	4	4	9	11	2											

F.A. Cup

#	Date	Opponent	Score	Scorers	Att	Hough H	Short J	Swift C	Bartlett F	Sharp D	Wood R	Kaye A	Anderson E	Chappell L	Beaumont F	McCann J	Smith N	Graham M
R3	Jan 4	Hull City	1-1	Smith	21868	1	2	3	4	5	6	7		9		11	8	10
rep	8	HULL CITY	0-2		20890	1	2	3	4	5	6	7		9	10	11	8	

		P	W	D	L	F	A	W	D	L	F	A	Pts
1	West Ham United	42	12	8	1	56	25	11	3	7	45	29	57
2	Blackburn Rovers	42	13	7	1	50	18	9	5	7	43	39	56
3	Charlton Athletic	42	15	3	3	65	33	9	4	8	42	36	55
4	Liverpool	42	17	3	1	50	13	5	7	9	29	41	54
5	Fulham	42	13	5	3	53	24	7	7	7	44	35	52
6	Sheffield United	42	12	5	4	38	22	9	5	7	37	28	52
7	Middlesbrough	42	13	3	5	52	29	6	4	11	31	45	45
8	Ipswich Town	42	13	4	4	45	29	3	8	10	23	40	44
9	Huddersfield Town	42	9	8	4	28	24	5	8	8	35	42	44
10	Bristol Rovers	42	12	5	4	52	31	5	3	13	33	49	42
11	Stoke City	42	9	4	8	49	36	9	2	10	26	37	42
12	Leyton Orient	42	14	2	5	53	27	4	3	14	24	52	41
13	Grimsby Town	42	13	4	4	54	30	4	2	15	32	53	40
14	BARNSLEY	42	10	6	5	40	25	4	6	11	30	49	40
15	Cardiff City	42	10	5	6	44	31	4	4	13	19	46	37
16	Derby County	42	11	3	7	37	36	3	5	13	23	45	36
17	Bristol City	42	9	5	7	35	31	4	4	13	28	57	35
18	Rotherham United	42	8	3	10	38	44	6	2	13	27	57	33
19	Swansea Town	42	8	3	10	48	45	3	6	12	24	54	31
20	Lincoln City	42	6	6	9	33	35	5	3	13	22	47	31
21	Notts County	42	9	3	9	24	31	3	3	15	20	49	30
22	Doncaster Rovers	42	7	5	9	34	40	1	6	14	22	48	27

1958/59 22nd in Division 2

#		Date	Opponent	Score / Scorers	Att	Hough H	Short J	Swift C	Bartlett F	Sharp D	Wood R	Kaye A	Smith N	Chappell L	Graham M	McCann J	Houghton WG	Holmes T	Leeson D	Beaumont F	Jones B	Barber DE	Whyke P	Lunn J	Gillott P	Hopkins OT	McDonald RR	Walters H
1	Aug	23	Cardiff City	1-0 Graham	23731	1	2	3	4	5	6	7	8	9	10	11												
2		27	BRISTOL CITY	4-7 Chappell 4	14283	1	2	3	4	5		7	8	9	10	11					6							
3		30	HUDDERSFIELD T	1-0 Chappell	17684	1	2	3	4	5		7	8	9	10	11	6											
4	Sep	2	Bristol City	1-3 Holmes	28530	1	2	3	4	5				9	10	11	6	8					7					
5		6	Leyton Orient	1-5 Chappell	13288	1	2	3	4	5		7		9	10	11	6	8										
6		10	CHARLTON ATHLETIC	7-1 Graham 4, Lunn 2(2p), Chappell	11834	1	2	3	4	5	6		8	9	10	11								7				
7		13	Rotherham United	0-3	12747	1	2	3	4	5	6		8	9	10	11								7				
8		18	Charlton Athletic	1-0	10364	1	2		4	5	6	7		9	10	11				8					3			
9		20	SHEFFIELD UNITED	1-3 Wood	16881	1	2	3	4	5	10	7	8	9		11	6											
10		27	Brighton & Hove Albion	1-1 McCann	24566	1	2	3	4	5	10	7		9	8	11	6											
11	Oct	4	GRIMSBY TOWN	3-1 Kaye, Chappell 2	10267	1	2	3	4	5	10	7		9	8	11	6											
12		11	DERBY COUNTY	0-0	11971	1	2	3	4	5	10	7		9	8	11	6											
13		18	Bristol Rovers	2-0 Kaye, Wood	20186	1	2	3	4	5	10	7		9	8	11	6											
14		25	IPSWICH TOWN	3-0 Beaumont, Chappell, Kaye (pen)	11736	1	2	3	4	5	8	7		9	10		6			11								
15	Nov	1	Scunthorpe United	0-1	12956	1	2	3	4	5	10	7		9	8	11	6											
16		8	STOKE CITY	2-1 Kaye, Wood	12164	1	2	3	4	5	10	7		9	8	11	6											
17		15	Sunderland	2-2 Kaye, Graham	24390	1	2	3	4	5	10	7		9	8	11	6											
18		22	LINCOLN CITY	2-2 Graham, McCann	10277	1	2	3	4	5	10	7		9	8	11	6											
19		29	Fulham	2-5 Kaye, Graham	18523	1	2		4		10	7		9	8	11	6					3					5	
20	Dec	6	SHEFFIELD WEDNESDAY	0-1	23184	1	2		4	5	10	7		9	8	11	6					3						
21		13	Swansea Town	1-2 Wood	10238	1	2	3	4	5	10	7		9	8	11	6											
22		20	CARDIFF CITY	3-2 Graham, Chappell 2	7798	1	2	3	4	5	10	7		9	8	11	6											
23		26	Middlesbrough	1-3 Kaye	31720	1	2		4	5	10	7		9	8	11	6					3						
24		27	MIDDLESBROUGH	1-0 Chappell	14917	1	2		4	5	10			9	8	11	6					3	7					
25	Jan	3	Huddersfield Town	1-2 Wood	17933	1	2		4	5	10	7		9	8	11	6					3						
26		31	ROTHERHAM UNITED	1-1 Chappell	13475	1	2			5	10	7		9		11	6		4	8		3						
27	Feb	7	Sheffield United	0-5	17962	1	2		4	5		7		9	10	11	6			8		3						
28		14	BRIGHTON & HOVE ALB	0-2	8500		2		4	5	6	7	8		10	11			1			3					9	
29		21	Grimsby Town	3-3 Holmes, McCann 2	8616	1	2	3	4	5		7	8	9	10	11		6										
30		28	Stoke City	1-2 Chappell	13015			3	4	5		7	8	9	10	11		6	1	2								
31	Mar	7	BRISTOL ROVERS	0-0	5579		2	3	4	5		7	8	9	10	11		6	1									
32		14	Ipswich Town	1-3 Holmes	11122			3	4	5		7	8	9	10	11		6	1	2								
33		21	SCUNTHORPE UNITED	0-1	6082			3	4	5			8	9	10	11			1					6	7			2
34		27	Liverpool	2-3 Holmes, Beaumont	52546		2	3	4	5		7		9		11		8	1	10				6				
35		28	Derby County	0-3	18523		2	3	4	5		7	8	9		11	6	10	1									
36		30	LIVERPOOL	0-2	7611		2	3	4	5		7	11	9				8	1	10				6				
37	Apr	4	SUNDERLAND	0-2	10274		2	3	4	5		7		9				8	1	10				6				
38		11	Lincoln City	1-2 Beaumont	9394		2	3	4	5		7			10	11		8	1	9				6				
39		18	FULHAM	2-4 Beaumont, McCann	8068		2	3	4	5		7		9	10	11			1	8				6				
40		20	SWANSEA TOWN	3-1 Bartlett, Chappell 2	4976		2	3	4	5		7		9		11		10	1	8				6				
41		25	Sheffield Wednesday	0-5	17017		2	3	4	5		7		9		11		10	1	8				6				
42		29	LEYTON ORIENT	1-3 Bartlett	7883		2	3	4	5				9		11		10	1	8				6	7			
			Apps			28	39	33	41	41	23	36	14	40	33	40	23	15	14	12	10	10	3	3	1	1	1	1
			Goals						2		5	7		17	9	5		4		4				2				

F.A. Cup

		Date	Opponent	Score	Att	Hough H	Short J	Swift C	Bartlett F	Sharp D	Wood R	Kaye A	Smith N	Chappell L	Graham M	McCann J	Houghton WG	Holmes T	Leeson D	Beaumont F	Jones B	Barber DE	Whyke P	Lunn J	Gillott P	Hopkins OT	McDonald RR	Walters H
R3	Jan	10	Brentford	0-2	16890	1	2		4	5	10	7		9	8	11	6					3						

		P	W	D	L	F	A	W	D	L	F	A	Pts
1	Sheffield Wed.	42	18	2	1	68	13	10	4	7	38	35	62
2	Fulham	42	18	1	2	65	26	9	5	7	31	35	60
3	Sheffield United	42	16	2	3	54	15	7	5	9	28	33	53
4	Liverpool	42	15	3	3	57	25	9	2	10	30	37	53
5	Stoke City	42	16	2	3	48	19	5	5	11	24	39	49
6	Bristol Rovers	42	13	5	3	46	23	5	7	9	34	41	48
7	Derby County	42	15	1	5	46	29	5	7	9	28	42	48
8	Charlton Athletic	42	13	3	5	53	33	5	4	12	39	57	43
9	Cardiff City	42	12	2	7	37	26	6	5	10	28	39	43
10	Bristol City	42	11	3	7	43	27	6	4	11	31	43	41
11	Swansea Town	42	12	5	4	52	30	4	4	13	27	51	41
12	Brighton & Hove A.	42	10	9	2	46	29	5	2	14	28	61	41
13	Middlesbrough	42	9	7	5	51	26	6	3	12	36	45	40
14	Huddersfield Town	42	12	3	6	39	20	4	5	12	23	35	40
15	Sunderland	42	13	4	4	42	23	3	4	14	22	52	40
16	Ipswich Town	42	12	4	5	37	27	5	2	14	25	50	40
17	Leyton Orient	42	9	4	8	43	30	5	4	12	28	48	36
18	Scunthorpe United	42	7	6	8	32	37	5	3	13	23	47	33
19	Lincoln City	42	10	5	6	45	37	1	2	18	18	56	29
20	Rotherham United	42	9	5	7	32	28	1	4	16	10	54	29
21	Grimsby Town	42	7	7	7	41	36	2	3	16	21	54	28
22	BARNSLEY	42	8	4	9	34	34	2	3	16	21	57	27

Season 1958/59
Back row: Matthews, Barber, Bartlett, Hough, Wood, Swift, Short
Front row: Kaye, Smith, Chappell, Graham, McCann

Season 1959/60
Back row: Sawyer, Green, unknown, Short, Bartlett, Stainsby, Hopkins, Barber, unknown, unknown, unknown, Walters, Swift, Houghton
Front row: Mulligan, Jagger, Lunn, Baxter, Tindill, Beaumont, Brookes, Whyke

1959/60 — 17th in Division 3

No	Date	Opponent	Score	Scorers	Att	Leeson D	Short J	Swift C	Bartlett F	Hopkins OT	Barber DE	Lunn I	Baxter IC	Tindill H	Beaumont F	Brookes C	Walters H	Mulligan PG	Whyke P	Bennett GF	Houghton WG	Oliver K	Sharp D	Stainsby J	Wood R
1	Aug 22	BRENTFORD	1-2	Lunn	7553	1	2	3	4	5	6	7	8	9	10	11									
2	26	Swindon Town	1-1	Lunn	14144	1	2		4	5	6	9	8		10	11	3		7						
3	29	Colchester United	2-2	Lunn, Tindill	8246	1	2		4	5	6	7	8	9	10	11	3								
4	Sep 2	SWINDON TOWN	0-3		7088	1	2		4	5	6	7	8	9	10	11	3								
5	5	SOUTHEND UNITED	4-1	Beaumont 2, Lunn, Tindill	5457	1	2		4	5	6	7	8	9	10		3			11					
6	9	Norwich City	0-0		36479	1		3	4	5	6	7	8	9	10		2			11					
7	12	Mansfield Town	4-1	Beaumont, Lunn, Tindill, Whyke	8408	1		3	4	5	6	7	8	9	10		2			11					
8	16	NORWICH CITY	2-0	Lunn 2	9155	1		3	4	5	6	7	8	9	10		2			11					
9	19	HALIFAX TOWN	1-2	Tindill	13677	1		3	4	5	6	7	8	9	10		2			11					
10	21	Port Vale	0-1		10886	1		3	4	5	6	7	8	9	10		2			11					
11	26	Bury	2-0	Beaumont, Conroy (og)	10587	1		3	4	5	6	7	8	9	10		2			11					
12	30	PORT VALE	1-0	Tindill	7870	1		3	4	5	6	7	8	9	10		2			11					
13	Oct 3	Chesterfield	1-4	Beaumont	7976	1		3	4	5	6	7	8	9	10		2			11					
14	7	SOUTHAMPTON	1-0	Baxter	4638	1		3	4	5		7	8	9	10		2			11	6				
15	10	YORK CITY	1-1	Lunn	9411	1		3	4	5	6	11	8	9	10		2		7						
16	14	Southampton	1-2	Stainsby	16937	1		3	4	5	6	11	8		10		2		7					9	
17	17	Coventry City	1-2	Bartlett	17350	1		3	4	5	6	11	8		10		2		7					9	
18	24	BRADFORD CITY	2-0	Baxter, Stainsby	6371	1		3	4	5	6	11	8		10		2		7					9	
19	31	Newport County	0-4		7440	1		3	4	5	6	11	8		10		2		7					9	
20	Nov 7	GRIMSBY TOWN	3-3	Bartlett, Beaumont, Lunn	6627	1		3	4	5	6	11	8	9	10		2		7						
21	21	TRANMERE ROVERS	2-0	Lunn 2	5420	1		3	4	5	6	11	8	9	10		2		7						
22	28	Bournemouth	1-1	Stainsby	9709	1		3	4	5	6	11	8	7	10		2							9	
23	Dec 12	QUEEN'S PARK RANGERS	2-1	Barber, Stainsby	4450	1		3	4	5	6	11	8	7	10		2							9	
24	19	Brentford	0-3		6527	1		3		5	6	11	8	7	10		2					4		9	
25	26	READING	3-3	Bartlett, Lunn, Stainsby	5151	1		3	8	5	6	11		7	10		2					4		9	
26	30	Reading	2-3	Beaumont, Tindill	10702	1		3		5	6	11		7	10		2					4		9	8
27	Jan 2	COLCHESTER UNITED	2-1	Stainsby, Wood	5596	1		3		5	6	11		7	10		2					4		9	8
28	9	Accrington Stanley	1-2	Barber	4920	1		3		5	6	11		7	10		2					4		9	8
29	23	MANSFIELD TOWN	2-2	Bartlett, Wood	4989	1		3	10	5	6	11		7	9		2					4			8
30	Feb 6	Halifax Town	0-5		5157	1		3	4	5	6	7		9	10	11	2								8
31	13	BURY	2-2	Stainsby, Tindill	3583	1		2	4			7		8	10	11				3			5	9	6
32	20	CHESTERFIELD	3-1	Brookes, Lunn, Tindill	5200	1		2	4			7		8	10	11				3			5	9	6
33	27	York City	0-0		6920	1		2	4			7		8	10	11				3			5	9	6
34	29	Southend United	2-2	Stainsby, Tindill	10921	1		2	4			7		8	10	11				3			5	9	6
35	Mar 5	COVENTRY CITY	1-0	Beaumont	7301	1		2		4		7		8	10	11				3			5	9	6
36	9	Wrexham	0-1		4734	1		2		4		7		8	10	11				3			5	9	6
37	12	Bradford City	0-0		11329	1		2	4			7		8	10	11				3			5	9	6
38	19	BOURNEMOUTH	1-0	Stainsby	5621	1		2	4			7		8	10	11				3			5	9	6
39	26	Grimsby Town	0-2		4858	1		2	4				8		10	11		7		3	6		5	9	
40	Apr 2	WREXHAM	6-1	Bartlett, Beaumont, Stainsby 2, Tindill, Styles (og)	5027	1		2	4			7		8	10	11				3			5	9	6
41	9	Tranmere Rovers	0-2		6274	1		2	4						10	11		7		3	8		5	9	6
42	16	NEWPORT COUNTY	0-2		5671	1		2	4				8		10	11		7		3			5	9	6
43	18	Shrewsbury Town	2-2	Brookes, Oliver	8500	1		2	4						10	11		7		3	6	9	5		8
44	19	SHREWSBURY TOWN	0-0		5271	1		2	4						10	11		7		3	6	9	5		8
45	23	ACCRINGTON STANLEY	5-0	Hopkins 2, Brookes (p), Baxter, Beaumont	4129	1		2	4	9		7	8		10	11				3	6		5		
46	30	Queen's Park Rangers	0-1		5700	1		2	4	9		7	8		10	11				3	6		5		
Apps						46	5	42	40	32	31	38	26	36	46	21	29	7	17	16	12	2	16	24	20
Goals									5	2	2	13	3	10	10	3			1			1		11	2

Two own goals

F.A. Cup

	Date	Opponent	Score	Scorers	Att	Leeson D	Short J	Swift C	Bartlett F	Hopkins OT	Barber DE	Lunn I	Baxter IC	Tindill H	Beaumont F	Brookes C	Walters H	Mulligan PG	Whyke P	Bennett GF	Houghton WG	Oliver K	Sharp D	Stainsby J	Wood R
R1	Nov 14	BRADFORD CITY	3-3	Bartlett, Beaumont (pen), Barber	8397	1		3	4	5	6	11	8	9	10		2		7						
rep	18	Bradford City	1-2	Beaumont	13496	1		3	4	5	6	11	8	9	10		2		7						

		P	W	D	L	F	A	W	D	L	F	A	Pts
1	Southampton	46	19	3	1	68	30	7	6	10	38	45	61
2	Norwich City	46	16	4	3	53	24	8	7	8	29	30	59
3	Shrewsbury Town	46	12	7	4	58	34	6	9	8	39	41	52
4	Grimsby Town	46	12	7	4	48	27	6	9	8	39	43	52
5	Coventry City	46	14	6	3	44	22	7	4	12	34	41	52
6	Brentford	46	13	6	4	46	24	8	3	12	32	37	51
7	Bury	46	13	4	6	36	23	8	5	10	28	28	51
8	Queen's Park Rgs.	46	14	7	2	45	16	4	6	13	28	38	49
9	Colchester United	46	15	6	2	51	22	3	5	15	32	52	47
10	Bournemouth	46	12	8	3	47	27	5	5	13	25	45	47
11	Reading	46	13	3	7	49	34	5	7	11	35	43	46
12	Southend United	46	15	3	5	49	28	4	5	14	27	46	46
13	Newport County	46	15	2	6	59	36	5	4	14	21	43	46
14	Port Vale	46	16	4	3	51	19	3	4	16	29	60	46
15	Halifax Town	46	13	3	7	42	27	5	7	11	28	45	46
16	Swindon Town	46	12	6	5	39	30	7	2	14	30	48	46
17	BARNSLEY	46	13	6	4	45	25	2	8	13	20	41	44
18	Chesterfield	46	13	3	7	41	31	5	4	14	30	53	43
19	Bradford City	46	10	7	6	39	28	5	5	13	27	46	42
20	Tranmere Rovers	46	11	8	4	50	29	3	5	15	22	46	41
21	York City	46	11	5	7	38	26	2	7	14	19	47	38
22	Mansfield Town	46	11	4	8	55	48	4	2	17	26	64	36
23	Wrexham	46	12	5	6	39	30	2	3	18	29	71	36
24	Accrington Stanley	46	4	5	14	31	53	7	0	16	26	70	27

1960/61 8th in Division 3

#	Month	Date	Opponent	Score	Scorers	Att.
1	Aug	20	COVENTRY CITY	4-1	Hopkins, Tindill 2, Lunn	6109
2		24	Reading	1-0	Lunn (pen)	11286
3		27	Bristol City	0-4		8495
4		31	READING	1-1	Tindill	6640
5	Sep	3	QUEEN'S PARK RANGERS	3-3	Hopkins 2, Smillie	6162
6		5	Colchester United	2-4	Barber, Hopkins	6034
7		10	Notts County	1-5	Hopkins	13936
8		14	COLCHESTER UNITED	3-0	Barber, Houghton, Smillie	3210
9		17	BOURNEMOUTH	2-3	Bartlett, Brookes C (pen)	6004
10		19	Hull City	0-2		10527
11		24	Bradford City	4-1	Bartlett 2, Beaumont, Tindill	7146
12		28	HULL CITY	1-0	Stainsby	4840
13	Oct	1	Shrewsbury Town	2-1	Bartlett, Smillie	5574
14		8	TRANMERE ROVERS	2-1	Houghton, Harrop (og)	5152
15		15	Watford	2-1	Beaumont, Smillie	14045
16		22	BRENTFORD	1-1	Beaumont	7268
17	Nov	12	Port Vale	0-2		10760
18		19	SOUTHEND UNITED	2-1	Beaumont, Oliver	4597
19	Dec	3	BURY	3-1	Beaumont, Bartlett, Brookes C(p)	6870
20		10	Walsall	0-1		6707
21		17	Coventry City	2-5	Bartlett 2	10260
22		20	Grimsby Town	2-3	Bartlett, Tindill	5915
23		26	GRIMSBY TOWN	3-2	Oliver 2, Bartlett	10725
24		31	BRISTOL CITY	2-0	Houghton, Oliver	8043
25	Jan	14	Queen's Park Rangers	2-4	Oliver, Smillie	8859
26		21	NOTTS COUNTY	5-2	Bartlett 3, Lunn, Oliver	5522
27	Feb	4	Bournemouth	2-1	Beaumont, Lunn	6425
28		11	BRADFORD CITY	5-2	Oliver 2, Tindill 2, Beaumont	15461
29		25	Bury	1-2	Bartlett	9004
30	Mar	11	Brentford	0-0		7041
31		13	Newport County	3-2	Hopkins 3	6198
32		18	SWINDON TOWN	2-1	Beaumont, Oliver	7628
33		22	WATFORD	0-1		3691
34		25	Torquay United	1-1	Beaumont	5709
35		27	Chesterfield	1-5	Beaumont	6200
36	Apr	1	PORT VALE	5-1	Bartlett 2, Beaumont 2, Tindill	5680
37		3	HALIFAX TOWN	1-1	Bartlett	8995
38		8	Southend United	0-2		7167
39		10	Halifax Town	0-1	Bartlett	4683
40		12	TORQUAY UNITED	1-0	Tindill	5712
41		15	CHESTERFIELD	3-1	Beaumont, Smillie, Wood B	6493
42		19	Swindon Town	0-1		9776
43		22	Tranmere Rovers	1-2	Bartlett	9748
44		24	NEWPORT COUNTY	1-3	Wood B	4091
45		29	WALSALL	2-2	Oliver, Smillie	6977
46	May	3	SHREWSBURY TOWN	4-2	Beaumont 2, Oliver, Smillie	3378

Appearances and Goals

Player	Apps	Goals
Leeson D	35	
Swift C	45	
Bennett GF	8	
Barber DE	39	2
Sharp D	44	
Wood R	12	
Smillie RD	42	8
Tindill H	29	9
Hopkins OT	16	8
Beaumont F	37	15
Lunn J	11	4
Brookes E	25	
Houghton WG	40	3
Bartlett F	26	17
Stainsby J	10	1
Brookes C	26	2
Whyke P	4	
Oliver K	18	11
Green A	14	
Williams C	9	
Hill A	2	
Jagger GN	10	
Sawyer R	1	
Wood BW	3	2

One own goal

F.A. Cup

Round	Month	Date	Opponent	Score	Scorers	Att.
R1	Nov	5	Gateshead	0-0		5552
rep		9	GATESHEAD	2-0	Bartlett, Beaumont	5099
R2		26	Bradford City	2-1	Bartlett 2	6278
R3	Jan	7	Reading	1-1	Tindill	11426
rep		11	READING	3-1	Oliver, Tindill, Bartlett	11093
R4	Feb	1	Huddersfield Town	1-1	Oliver	44761
rep		6	HUDDERSFIELD T	1-0	Wood	29149
R5		18	Luton Town	1-0	Lunn	32923
R6	Mar	4	Leicester City	0-0		38744
rep		8	LEICESTER CITY	1-2	Oliver	39250

R3 and R6 replays - a.e.t.

F.L. Cup

Round	Month	Date	Opponent	Score	Scorers	Att.
R1	Oct	11	Ipswich Town	2-0	Beaumont, Bartlett	11175
R2		19	Derby County	0-3		11114

League Table

	Team	P	W	D	L	F	A	W	D	L	F	A	Pts
1	Bury	46	18	3	2	62	17	12	5	6	46	28	68
2	Walsall	46	19	4	0	62	20	9	2	12	36	40	62
3	Queen's Park Rgs.	46	18	4	1	58	23	7	6	10	35	37	60
4	Watford	46	12	7	4	52	27	8	5	10	33	45	52
5	Notts County	46	16	3	4	52	24	5	6	12	30	53	51
6	Grimsby Town	46	14	4	5	48	32	6	6	11	29	37	50
7	Port Vale	46	15	3	5	63	30	2	12	9	33	49	49
8	BARNSLEY	46	15	5	3	56	30	6	2	15	27	50	49
9	Halifax Town	46	14	7	2	42	22	2	10	11	29	56	49
10	Shrewsbury Town	46	13	7	3	54	26	2	9	12	29	49	46
11	Hull City	46	13	6	4	51	28	4	6	13	22	45	46
12	Torquay United	46	8	12	3	37	26	6	5	12	38	57	45
13	Newport County	46	12	7	4	51	30	5	4	14	30	60	45
14	Bristol City	46	15	4	4	50	19	2	6	15	20	49	44
15	Coventry City	46	14	6	3	54	25	2	6	15	26	58	44
16	Swindon Town	46	13	6	4	41	16	1	9	13	21	39	43
17	Brentford	46	10	9	4	41	28	3	8	12	15	42	43
18	Reading	46	13	5	5	48	29	1	7	15	24	54	40
19	Bournemouth	46	8	7	8	34	39	7	3	13	24	37	40
20	Southend United	46	10	8	5	38	26	4	3	16	22	50	39
21	Tranmere Rovers	46	11	5	7	53	50	4	3	16	26	65	38
22	Bradford City	46	8	8	7	37	36	3	6	14	28	51	36
23	Colchester United	46	8	5	10	40	44	3	6	14	28	57	33
24	Chesterfield	46	9	6	8	42	29	1	6	16	25	58	32

Season 1960/61
Back row: Swift, Wood, Sharp, Leeson, Houghton, Barber
Front row: Bartlett, Smillie, Beaumont, Tindill, Oliver, Lunn, Brookes

Season 1961/62
Back row: Jagger, Sawyer, Hill, Wood R, Wood B, Bartlett.   2nd back: Semley (Masseur) Vicary (Secretary)
Swann, Oliver, Houghton, Swift, Tindill, Brookes, Mulligan, Beaumont, Shotton (Trainer)
2nd front: Smillie, Sharp, Steele (Manager) Kerr, Swindells.   Front row: Taylor, Senior, Ogley, Hopper, Cartwright

Season 1961/62 — Division 3 (20th)

#		Date	Opponent	Score	Scorers	Att.	Wil C	Swi C	Bro E	Hou WG	Sha D	Woo R	Smi RD	Bar F	Swi J	Bea F	Jag GN	Gre A	Hil A	Hop A	Ker GAM	McC RS	Oli K	Rin T	Saw R	Swa G	Tay AM	Tin H	Tur J	Wat D	Win E	Woo BW
1	Au	19	Halifax Town	1-3	Bartlett	6114	1	2	3	6	5	6		7	4	8	9															
2		21	Newport County	2-0	Swindells, Jagger	8727	1	2	3	6	5		7	4	8	10	11										9					
3		26	QUEEN'S PARK RANGER	2-4	Beaumont, Tindill	7668	1	2	3	6	5		7	4	8	10	11										9					
4		30	NEWPORT COUNTY	1-1	Swindells	6998	1	2	3	6	5		7	4	8	10	11									9						
5	Se	2	READING	2-3	Swindells, Bartlett	6676	1	2	3	6	5	4	11	8	9					1		10					7					
6		7	Torquay United	2-6	Beaumont 2 (1 pen)	6571		2	3	6	5	4	11	8	9	10				1							7					
7		9	Portsmouth	2-3	Oliver, Beaumont	16014		2	3	6			11	4	7	10				1			8	5			9					
8		16	CRYSTAL PALACE	0-3		6699		2	3	6	5	4	7	8						1		10	9				11					
9		19	Swindon Town	1-1	Bartlett	9858		2	3	6	5	4	7	8			11			1			10				9					
10		23	Bournemouth	0-5		10441		2	3	6	5	4	7	8			11			1			10				9					
11		27	SWINDON TOWN	6-2	Bartlett 2, Oliver, Smillie, Tindill, Wood R	3551		2	3	6	5	4	7	8			11			1			10				9					
12		30	WATFORD	3-0	Oliver, Tindill, McNeice (og)	5678		2	3	6	5	4	7	8			11			1			10				9					
13	Oct	3	Northampton Town	1-3	Bartlett	11448		2	3	6	5	4	7	8			11			1			9								10
14		7	Southend United	2-1	Bartlett, Oliver	8892		2	3	6	5	4		8			11			1	7		9				10				
15		11	NORTHAMPTON T	3-2	Bartlett 2, Wood R	2371		2	3	6	5	4		8			11			1			10				9					
16		14	NOTTS COUNTY	2-0	Bartlett, Oliver	7100			3	6	5	4	7	8			11		1	2			10				9				
17		20	Coventry City	1-1	Smillie	8208			3	6	5	4	7	8			11		1	2			10				9				
18		28	BRENTFORD	2-2	Oliver, Swindells	6561			3	6	5	4	7		8		11		1	2			10				9				
19	No	11	BRISTOL CITY	7-3	Oliver 3, Swindells 2, Smillie, Connor (og)	5618			3	6	5	4	7		9		11			2			10				8	1			
20		18	Bradford Park Avenue	2-3	Houghton (pen), Swindells	12104			3	6	5	4	7		9		11			2			10				8	1			
21	De	2	Shrewsbury Town	1-4	Smillie	5635			3	6	5	4	7	8			10			2			9	11				1			
22		9	PETERBOROUGH UTD.	0-3		8104			3	6	5	4	7	8			10			2			9	11				1			
23		26	LINCOLN CITY	0-1		5572			3	6	5	4	7	8	9					2			10	11				1			
24	Jan	12	Reading	0-0		8542			3	6	5	4	7		9		10			2			8	11				1			
25		20	PORTSMOUTH	2-2	Swindells, Houghton (pen)	6054			3	6	5	4		9		10				2		7	8	11				1			
26		27	GRIMSBY TOWN	0-3		8161			3	6	5	4		9				1	2		7	8	11				10			
27		31	Lincoln City	2-2	Smillie, Watson	5317				6	5	4	7				11	3	1	2			10				9		8	
28	Fe	3	Crystal Palace	3-1	Tindill 2, Smillie	14095			3	6	5	4	7				11		1	2			10				9		8	
29		9	BOURNEMOUTH	2-2	Oliver, Smillie	10818			3	6	5	4	7				11		1	2			10				9		8	
30		17	Watford	1-0	Oliver	7826		2	3	6	5	4	7				11			2			10				9		8	
31		24	SOUTHEND UNITED	1-1	Jagger	4737	1		3	6	5	4	7				11			2			10				9			
32	Ma	3	Notts County	2-0	Oliver, Ring	7379	1		3	6	5	4	7	8						2			10	11			9			
33		5	Port Vale	0-2		4958	1		3	6	5	4	7	8						2			10	11			9			
34		9	COVENTRY CITY	2-1	Tindill 2	6083	1		3	6	5	4	7	8						2			10	11			9			
35		17	Brentford	1-1	Oliver	6096	1		3	6		4	7							2			10	11			9			8	5
36		19	Queen's Park Rangers	0-3		10310	1		3	6		4	7							2	8		10	11			9				5
37		24	PORT VALE	2-1	Bartlett, Oliver	4670	1		3	6	5	4	7	8						2			10	11			9			
38		27	HALIFAX TOWN	1-2	Bartlett	5080	1		3	6	5	4	7	8						2			10	11			9			
39		31	Bristol City	0-0		8506	1			6	5	4	7	8				3		2			10	11			9			
40	Apr	7	BRADFORD PARK AVE.	1-2	Wood R	5367	1			6	5	4	7	8				3		2			10	11			9			
41		14	Grimsby Town	0-4		11262				6	5		7	8			11	3	1	2	10		4						9	
42		20	Hull City	0-4		6296				4	5	10	7				6	3	1	2	8				11		9			
43		21	SHREWSBURY TOWN	1-1	Houghton (pen)	3404			3	4	5		7	8			6		1	2			10	11			9			
44		23	HULL CITY	1-0	Tindill	4781			3	4	5		7	8			6		1	2			10	11			9			
45		28	Peterborough United	2-4	Bartlett 2	8210			3	4	5		7	8			6		1	2			10	11			9			
46	Ma	2	TORQUAY UNITED	4-2	Tindill 2, Bartlett, Smillie	8544			3	6	5	4	7	8						1	2			10	11			9			
				Apps			15	16	41	46	43	38	43	32	14	6	30	5	24	30	6	2	39	20	1	2	2	33	7	8	2	1
				Goals						3		3	8	15	8	4	2						14	1				10		1		

Two own goals

F.A. Cup

		Date	Opponent	Score	Scorers	Att.	Bro E	Hou WG	Sha D	Woo R	Smi RD	Jag GN	Hil A	Hop A	Oli K	Tin H
R1	No	4	West Auckland Town	3-3	Oliver 2, Swindells	2876	3	6	5	4	7	9	11	1 2	10	8
rep		8	WEST AUCKLAND T	2-0	Smillie, Swindells	5383	3	6	5	4	7	9	11	1 2	10	8
R2		25	CARLISLE UNITED	1-2	Swindells	11489	3	6	5	4	7	9	11	1 2	10	8

F.L. Cup

		Date	Opponent	Score	Scorers	Att.	Swi C	Bro E	Hou WG	Sha D	Smi RD	Bar F	Hop A	Oli K	Rin T	Tin H	Woo BW
R1	Se	13	SOUTHPORT	3-2	Oliver 3	4489	2 3	6	5	11	4		1	7	10	9	
R2	Oct	9	WORKINGTON	1-3	Oliver	1977	2 3	6	5		8		11 1	7	9		10

Played in R1: S Mokone (at 8). Played in R2, R Smith (at 4).

Division 3 — Final Table

		P	W	D	L	F	A	W	D	L	F	A	Pts
1	Portsmouth	46	15	6	2	48	23	12	5	6	39	24	65
2	Grimsby Town	46	18	3	2	49	18	10	3	10	31	38	62
3	Bournemouth	46	14	8	1	42	18	7	9	7	27	27	59
4	Queen's Park Rgs.	46	15	3	5	65	31	9	8	6	46	42	59
5	Peterborough Utd.	46	16	0	7	60	38	10	6	7	47	44	58
6	Bristol City	46	15	3	5	56	27	8	5	10	38	45	54
7	Reading	46	14	5	4	46	24	8	4	11	31	42	53
8	Northampton Town	46	12	6	5	52	24	8	5	10	33	33	51
9	Swindon Town	46	11	8	4	48	26	6	7	10	30	45	49
10	Hull City	46	15	2	6	43	20	5	6	12	24	34	48
11	Bradford Park Ave.	46	13	5	5	47	27	7	2	14	33	51	47
12	Port Vale	46	12	4	7	41	23	5	7	11	24	35	45
13	Notts County	46	14	5	4	44	23	3	4	16	23	51	43
14	Coventry City	46	11	6	6	38	26	5	5	13	26	45	43
15	Crystal Palace	46	8	8	7	50	41	6	6	11	33	39	42
16	Southend United	46	10	7	6	31	26	3	9	11	26	43	42
17	Watford	46	10	9	4	37	26	4	4	15	26	48	41
18	Halifax Town	46	9	5	9	34	35	6	5	12	28	49	40
19	Shrewsbury Town	46	8	7	8	46	37	5	5	13	27	47	38
20	BARNSLEY	46	9	6	8	45	41	4	6	13	26	54	38
21	Torquay United	46	9	4	10	48	44	6	2	15	28	56	36
22	Lincoln City	46	4	10	9	31	43	5	7	11	26	44	35
23	Brentford	46	11	3	9	34	29	2	5	16	19	64	34
24	Newport County	46	6	5	12	29	38	1	3	19	17	64	22

1962/63 — 18th in Division 3

League matches

Player columns (left→right): Hill A, Hopper A, Brookes E, Wood R, Winstanley E, Houghton WG, Hosie J, Oliver K, Leighton A, Kerr GAM, O'Hara AE, Bartlett F, Burke T, Earnshaw RI, Edgley BK, Jagger GN, Lawton P, McCarthy RS, Murphy BL, Nicol RBM, Ogley A, Ring T, Smith R

#	Date	Opponent	Score	Scorers	Att	Hill A	Hopper A	Brookes E	Wood R	Winstanley E	Houghton WG	Hosie J	Oliver K	Leighton A	Kerr GAM	O'Hara AE	Bartlett F	Burke T	Earnshaw RI	Edgley BK	Jagger GN	Lawton P	McCarthy RS	Murphy BL	Nicol RBM	Ogley A	Ring T	Smith R
1	Aug 18	SWINDON TOWN	1-1	O'Hara	7083	1	2	3	4	5	6	7	8	9	10	11												
2	21	Brighton & Hove Albion	0-2		15154	1	2	3	4	5	6	7		9	10		8											11
3	25	Peterborough United	2-4	Kerr, O'Hara	12944	1	2	3	4	5	6	7	10	9	8	11												
4	28	BRIGHTON & HOVE ALB	2-0	Leighton, O'Hara	7426	1	2	3	4	5	6	7		9	8	11					10							
5	Sep 1	Notts County	0-2		6347	1	2	3	4	5	6	7		9	8	11					10							
6	4	HALIFAX TOWN	1-0	Leighton	7848	1	2	3	4	5	6	7		9	8	11					10							
7	8	NORTHAMPTON T	1-1	O'Hara	7674	1	2	3	6	5		7		9	8	11					10				4			
8	11	Halifax Town	0-2		3772	1		3	6	5		7		9	8	11						10		2	4			
9	15	Queen's Park Rangers	1-2	Bartlett	11246	1	2	3	6	5		7	10	9		11	8								4			
10	18	Bristol Rovers	2-3	Oliver, O'Hara	10285		2	3	6	5		7	10	9		11	8								4		1	
11	22	HULL CITY	1-2	Leighton	6848	1		3		5	6	7	10	9	8	11								2	4			
12	29	Crystal Palace	2-1	Leighton, Evans (og)	14062	1		3		5	6	7	10	9	8	11								2	4			
13	Oct 2	WREXHAM	2-1	Leighton, Oliver	7484	1		3		5	6	7	10	9	8	11								2	4			
14	5	COVENTRY CITY	2-1	Kerr, Oliver	9025	1	2	3		5	6	7	10	9	8	11									4			
15	13	Bradford Park Avenue	1-1	Oliver	9325	1	2	3		5	6	7	10	9	8	11									4			
16	20	WATFORD	4-1	Leighton 2, Oliver 2	7868	1	2	3		5	6	7	10	9	8	11									4			
17	27	Bristol City	2-5	Kerr, Leighton	10034	1	2	3		5	6	7	10	9	8	11									4			
18	Nov 9	Port Vale	0-1		8798	1	2	3		5	6	7	10	9	8	11									4			
19	17	SHREWSBURY TOWN	1-0	Oliver	7111	1	2	3		5	6	7	10	9	8	11									4			
20	27	BRISTOL ROVERS	4-0	O'Hara 3, Oliver	8782	1	2	3		5	6	7	10	9	8	11									4			
21	Dec 1	SOUTHEND UNITED	2-2	Houghton, Oliver	9280	1	2	3		5	6	7	10	9	8	11									4			
22	8	Colchester United	1-1	Hopper	3547	1	2	3		5	6	7	10	9	8	11									4			
23	15	Swindon Town	1-2	Leighton	10387	1	2	3		5	6		10	9	8	11			7						4			
24	21	PETERBOROUGH UTD.	0-2		9645	1	2	3		5	6	7	10	9	8	11									4			
25	Jan 12	NOTTS COUNTY	3-1	Leighton 2, O'Hara	7719	1	2	3		5	6	7	8	9	10	11									4			
26	Feb 23	Coventry City	0-2		12649	1	2	3	4	5	6	7		9	10	11	8											
27	Mar 12	Watford	0-0		6717	1	2			5	6	7	8	9	10	11								3	4			
28	16	BRISTOL CITY	1-1	O'Hara	6131		2			5	6	7	8	9	10	11								3	4	1		
29	20	Bournemouth	1-1	Leighton	8038		2		4		6		8	9	10	11								3	5	1		7
30	22	Reading	1-4	O'Hara	6455		2			5	6		8	9	10	11								3	4	1		7
31	29	PORT VALE	2-1	Leighton 2	4368	1	2	3	4	5	6	7	8	9	10	11												
32	Apr 6	BOURNEMOUTH	2-2	Leighton, O'Hara	7117	1	2	3	4	5	6	7	8	9	10	11												
33	6	Shrewsbury Town	3-1	Leighton 2, O'Hara	4263	1	2	3	4	5	6	7	8	9	10	11												
34	12	Carlisle United	1-2	Leighton	5944	1		3	4	5	6	7	8	9	10	11								2				
35	13	MILLWALL	4-1	Kerr, Leighton, Oliver, O'Hara	5996			3	4	5	6	7	8	9	10	11								2		1		
36	16	CARLISLE UNITED	2-0	Oliver, Oliphant (og)	8146			3	4	5	6	7	8	9	10	11								2		1		
37	20	Southend United	0-0		6901			3	4	5	6	7	8	9	10	11								2		1		
38	23	Northampton Town	2-4	Leighton, O'Hara (pen)	15939			3	4	5	6	7	8	9	10	11								2		1		
39	27	COLCHESTER UNITED	2-3	Houghton, Rutter (og)	5351			3	4	5	6	7	8	9	10	11								2		1		
40	30	BRADFORD PARK AVE.	1-4	Bartlett	6556	1	2	3	4	5	6	7		9	10	11	8											
41	May 4	Hull City	2-0	Leighton, O'Hara	4923	1		3		5	6		8	9	10	11			7					2	4			
42	8	Wrexham	1-2	Leighton	5006	1		3		5	6		8	9	10	11			7					2	4			
43	10	QUEEN'S PARK RANGERS	0-0		4934	1		3		5	6		8	9		11			7	10				2	4			
44	13	READING	1-0	Earnshaw	5289	1		3		5	6		8	9		11			7	10				2	4			
45	18	Millwall	1-4	Oliver	8521	1		3		5	6	9	8			11			7	10				2	4			
46	22	CRYSTAL PALACE	0-4		3807					5	6				10	11			9	8	7		3	2	4	1		
	Apps					37	29	41	29	45	34	37	35	44	44	45	4	1	7	4	5	1	1	21	29	9	1	3
	Goals						1				2		12	22	4	16	2		1									

Three own goals

F.A. Cup

#	Date	Opponent	Score	Scorers	Att	Hill A	Hopper A	Brookes E	Wood R	Winstanley E	Houghton WG	Hosie J	Oliver K	Leighton A	Kerr GAM	O'Hara AE	Nicol RBM
R1	Nov 3	RHYL	4-0	Kerr 2, Leighton, O'Hara (pen)	10755	1	2	3	6	5		7	10	9	8	11	4
R2	24	CHESTERFIELD	2-1	Oliver 2	17328	1	2	3	6	5		7	10	9	8	11	4
R3	Jan 15	EVERTON	0-3		30011	1	2	3		5	6	7	10	9	8	11	4

F.L. Cup

#	Date	Opponent	Score	Scorers	Att	Hill A	Hopper A	Brookes E	Wood R	Winstanley E	Houghton WG	Hosie J	Oliver K	Leighton A	Kerr GAM	O'Hara AE	Bartlett F	Murphy BL	Nicol RBM
R1	Sep 6	Hartlepools United	1-1	Oliver	2393	1	2	3		5	6	7	10	9		11	8		4
rep	13	HARTLEPOOLS UTD.	2-1	Oliver 2	5130	1		3	6	5		7	10	9		11	8	2	4
R2	25	GRIMSBY TOWN	3-2	Oliver 2, Hosie	5408	1		3	6	5		7	10	9	8	11		2	4
R3	Oct 16	LUTON TOWN	1-2	Leighton	10335	1	2	3	6	5		7	10	9	8	11			4

Division 3 Final Table

		P	W	D	L	F	A	W	D	L	F	A	Pts
1	Northampton Town	46	16	6	1	64	19	10	4	9	45	41	62
2	Swindon Town	46	18	2	3	60	22	4	12	7	27	34	58
3	Port Vale	46	16	4	3	47	25	7	4	12	25	33	54
4	Coventry City	46	14	6	3	54	28	4	11	8	29	41	53
5	Bournemouth	46	11	12	0	39	16	7	4	12	24	30	52
6	Peterborough Utd.	46	11	5	7	48	33	9	6	8	45	42	51
7	Notts County	46	15	3	5	46	29	4	10	9	27	45	51
8	Southend United	46	11	7	5	38	24	8	5	10	37	53	50
9	Wrexham	46	14	6	3	54	27	6	3	14	30	56	49
10	Hull City	46	12	6	5	40	22	7	4	12	34	47	48
11	Crystal Palace	46	10	7	6	38	22	7	6	10	30	36	47
12	Colchester United	46	11	6	6	41	35	7	5	11	32	58	47
13	Queen's Park Rgs.	46	9	6	8	44	36	8	5	10	41	40	45
14	Bristol City	46	10	9	4	54	38	6	4	13	46	54	45
15	Shrewsbury Town	46	13	4	6	57	41	3	8	12	26	40	44
16	Millwall	46	11	6	6	50	32	4	7	12	32	55	43
17	Watford	46	12	3	8	55	40	5	5	13	27	45	42
18	BARNSLEY	46	12	6	5	39	28	3	5	15	24	46	41
19	Bristol Rovers	46	11	8	4	45	29	4	3	16	25	59	41
20	Reading	46	13	4	6	51	30	4	3	16	23	48	40
21	Bradford Park Ave.	46	10	9	4	43	36	4	3	16	36	61	40
22	Brighton & Hove A.	46	7	6	10	28	38	5	6	12	30	46	36
23	Carlisle United	46	12	4	7	41	37	1	5	17	20	52	35
24	Halifax Town	46	8	3	12	41	51	1	9	13	23	55	30

Season 1962/63
Back row: Raynor (Director) Steele J (Manager) Swift, Wood, Gerrard, Hill, Winstanley, Bradbury,
Hopper, Griffiths, Houghton, Turner, Brookes, Rimmington (Trainer), Steele E (Groundsman)
Centre row: Jagger, Bartlett, Leighton, Oliver, Ring, Mulligan
Front row: Shaw, Smith, Kerr, Lawton, Senior, Farnsworth, McCarthy, O'Hara, Green

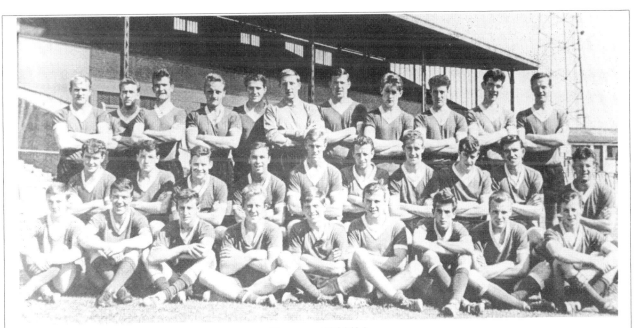

Season 1963/64
Back row: Wood, Mulligan, Murphy, Houghton, Nicol, Hill, Winstanley, Rutherford, Edgley, Craven, Brookes
Centre row: Sheavills, McCarthy, Provan, Murray, Leighton, O'Hara, Lawton, Earnshaw, Hopper, Kerr
Front row: Booker, Farnsworth, Duerden, Howard, Bradbury, Green, Blaydon, Gardiner, Shaw

1963/64 — 20th in Division 3

League matches

#	Date	Opponent	Score	Scorers	Att
1	Aug 24	Colchester United	1-4	O'Hara	3507
2	27	SOUTHEND UNITED	0-1		6203
3	31	MILLWALL	1-1	Leighton	4717
4	Sep 6	LUTON TOWN	3-1	Leighton 2, Murray	5388
5	9	Southend United	1-4	Kerr	10441
6	14	Hull City	2-2	Leighton, O'Hara	8920
7	17	WATFORD	0-0		6536
8	21	BOURNEMOUTH	2-1	Leighton 2	5989
9	27	Wrexham	2-7	Leighton, O'Hara	7820
10	Oct 1	Watford	1-2	Leighton	5612
11	4	QUEEN'S PARK RANGERS	3-1	Leighton 2, Kerr	5791
12	8	OLDHAM ATHLETIC	2-2	Leighton, O'Hara	10433
13	11	Walsall	4-4	Leighton 2, Kerr, O'Hara	9847
14	16	Oldham Athletic	0-2		17114
15	19	BRENTFORD	1-1	Leighton	6775
16	22	Bristol Rovers	1-1	Winstanley	13539
17	26	Shrewsbury Town	1-3	Nicol	6451
18	29	BRISTOL ROVERS	1-2		6542
19	Nov 2	BRISTOL CITY	2-4	Leighton, Briggs (og)	6124
20	9	Port Vale	0-1		9083
21	23	Crewe Alexandra	2-1	Byrne, Leighton	4416
22	30	CRYSTAL PALACE	2-0	Leighton, O'Hara	5539
23	Dec 14	COLCHESTER UNITED	1-1	O'Hara	5145
24	26	COVENTRY CITY	1-1	Byrne	12502
25	28	Coventry City	1-3	Byrne	26922
26	Jan 11	Luton Town	3-2	Byrne 2, Kerr	4555
27	17	HULL CITY	2-2	Houghton, Sheavills	8193
28	Feb 1	Bournemouth	1-4	Kerr	8242
29	8	WREXHAM	3-0	Brookes, Hopper (pen), O'Hara	17186
30	22	WALSALL	1-3	Winstanley	4862
31	29	Reading	1-6	Kerr	7646
32	Mar 3	NOTTS COUNTY	2-1	Houghton, Winstanley	3709
33	7	SHREWSBURY TOWN	2-1	Leighton, Kerr	3655
34	9	Mansfield Town	1-2	O'Hara	8687
35	14	Bristol City	2-5	Leighton, Sheavills	6950
36	20	READING	0-3		3761
37	28	Notts County	1-1	Hopper (pen)	3607
38	30	Peterborough United	2-3	Earnshaw, Kerr	7220
39	31	PETERBOROUGH UTD.	3-2	Byrne 3	4672
40	Apr 4	CREWE ALEXANDRA	1-0	Sheavills	4621
41	11	Crystal Palace	2-1	O'Hara 2	21205
42	13	Millwall	2-4	Leighton 2	11826
43	18	MANSFIELD TOWN	1-1	Leighton	5747
44	20	PORT VALE	0-0		4918
45	25	Brentford	1-1	Leighton	8351
46	27	Queen's Park Rangers	2-2	Byrne, Sheavills	8434

Appearances and Goals (shirt numbers)

Players (columns): Hill A, Hopper A, Brookes E, Nicol RBM, Winstanley E, Houghton WG, Provan AMH, Mulligan PG, Leighton A, Kerr GAM, O'Hara AE, Byrne J, Cochrane H, Earnshaw RJ, Lawton P, Murphy BL, Murray A, Rutherford C, Sheavills JE, Sproates J, Wood R, Williamson R

	Hill A	Hopper A	Brookes E	Nicol RBM	Winstanley E	Houghton WG	Provan AMH	Mulligan PG	Leighton A	Kerr GAM	O'Hara AE	Byrne J	Cochrane H	Earnshaw RJ	Lawton P	Murphy BL	Murray A	Rutherford C	Sheavills JE	Sproates J	Wood R	Williamson R
Apps	31	46	42	8	46	46	3	2	38	41	41	27	5	7	1	4	21	1	39	2	40	15
Goals		2	1	1	3	2			24	9	10	9		1			1		4			

One own goal

F.A. Cup

Rd	Date	Opponent	Score	Scorers	Att
R1	Nov 16	STOCKPORT COUNTY	1-0	Byrne	7577
R2	Dec 7	ROCHDALE	3-1	Kerr 2, Leighton	9431
R3	Jan 4	Scunthorpe United	2-2	Byrne, O'Hara	11060
rep	7	SCUNTHORPE UTD.	3-2	Byrne 2, O'Hara (aet)	21477
R4	25	BURY	2-1	Kerr, Gallagher (og)	21894
R5	Feb 15	MANCHESTER UTD.	0-4		38076

F.L. Cup

Rd	Date	Opponent	Score	Scorers	Att
R1	Sep 4	Darlington	2-2	Kerr, Murray	4690
rep	11	DARLINGTON	6-2	Leighton 2, Houghton, Kerr, Murray, Sheavills	4254
R2	25	Aston Villa	1-3	O'Hara	10679

Division 3 Final Table

Pos	Team	P	W	D	L	F	A	W	D	L	F	A	Pts
1	Coventry City	46	14	7	2	62	32	8	9	6	36	29	60
2	Crystal Palace	46	17	4	2	38	14	6	10	7	35	37	60
3	Watford	46	16	6	1	57	28	7	6	10	22	31	58
4	Bournemouth	46	17	4	2	47	15	7	4	12	32	43	56
5	Bristol City	46	13	7	3	52	24	7	8	8	32	40	55
6	Reading	46	15	5	3	49	26	6	5	12	30	36	52
7	Mansfield Town	46	15	8	0	51	20	5	3	15	25	42	51
8	Hull City	46	11	9	3	45	27	5	8	10	28	41	49
9	Oldham Athletic	46	13	3	7	44	35	7	5	11	29	35	48
10	Peterborough Utd.	46	13	6	4	52	27	5	5	13	23	43	47
11	Shrewsbury Town	46	13	6	4	43	19	5	5	13	30	61	47
12	Bristol Rovers	46	9	6	8	52	34	10	2	11	39	45	46
13	Port Vale	46	13	6	4	35	13	3	8	12	18	36	46
14	Southend United	46	9	10	4	42	26	6	5	12	35	52	45
15	Queen's Park Rgs.	46	13	4	6	47	34	5	5	13	29	44	45
16	Brentford	46	11	4	8	54	36	4	10	9	33	44	44
17	Colchester United	46	10	8	5	45	26	2	11	10	25	42	43
18	Luton Town	46	12	2	9	42	41	4	8	11	22	39	42
19	Walsall	46	7	9	7	34	35	6	5	12	25	41	40
20	BARNSLEY	46	9	9	5	34	29	3	6	14	34	65	39
21	Millwall	46	9	4	10	33	29	5	6	12	20	38	38
22	Crewe Alexandra	46	10	5	8	37	29	1	7	15	21	51	34
23	Wrexham	46	9	4	10	50	42	4	2	17	25	65	32
24	Notts County	46	7	8	8	29	26	2	1	20	16	66	27

1964/65   24th in Division 3

League Results

#	Month	Date	Opponent	Score	Scorers	Att.
1	Aug	22	QUEEN'S PARK RANGERS	0-0		5688
2		25	Bristol City	1-5	Leighton	10491
3		29	Shrewsbury Town	3-3	Byrne 2, Leighton	5260
4	Sep	4	READING	1-1	O'Hara	6103
5		9	Gillingham	0-1		13677
6		12	Southend United	0-2		6131
7		15	GILLINGHAM	1-0	Byrne	5025
8		19	Grimsby Town	2-3	Graham, Leighton	7613
9		25	SCUNTHORPE UNITED	2-0	Byrne, Leighton	6289
10		30	HULL CITY	1-1	Graham	6940
11	Oct	3	Walsall	1-1	Leighton	5047
12		7	Hull City	0-7		7830
13		10	BOURNEMOUTH	2-2	Kerr, Leighton (pen)	4804
14		17	Exeter City	0-3		6313
15		20	WATFORD	4-0	Leighton 2, Kerr, Mancini (og)	4998
16		24	OLDHAM ATHLETIC	0-1		5611
17		26	Mansfield Town	3-4	Leighton 2 (1 pen), Sheavills	8245
18		31	Bristol Rovers	0-1		11773
19	Nov	3	BRISTOL CITY	1-2	Kerr	3982
20		7	BRENTFORD	3-1	Graham 2, Kerr (pen)	4252
21		21	PORT VALE	0-2		5288
22		28	Carlisle United	0-4		6723
23	Dec	11	Queen's Park Rangers	2-3	O'Hara 2	3350
24		18	SHREWSBURY TOWN	6-2	O'Hara 2, Senior 2, Kerr, Leight	2492
25		26	Peterborough United	1-4	O'Hara	8963
26		28	PETERBOROUGH UTD.	3-2	Leighton 2, O'Hara	3395
27	Jan	2	Reading	1-1	Sheavills	6620
28		9	Colchester United	1-4	O'Hara	2824
29		16	SOUTHEND UNITED	1-4	Graham	2898
30		30	LUTON TOWN	3-0	Kerr (pen), Senior, Graham	2989
31	Feb	5	Scunthorpe United	3-2	Kerr 2, Senior	6516
32		13	WALSALL	0-1		2953
33		20	Bournemouth	0-1		5377
34		27	EXETER CITY	0-0		3034
35	Mar	13	BRISTOL ROVERS	0-2		3272
36		16	Watford	1-1	Kerr	6078
37		20	Brentford	0-1		7954
38		26	COLCHESTER UNITED	1-2	O'Hara	3330
39		30	GRIMSBY TOWN	1-0	Swallow	2633
40	Apr	3	Port Vale	0-2		6311
41		7	Luton Town	1-5	Bettany	6112
42		10	CARLISLE UNITED	1-2	Dean (og)	3164
43		16	Workington	0-0		3751
44		17	Oldham Athletic	1-1	Hopper	5731
45		20	WORKINGTON	0-3		2297
46		24	MANSFIELD TOWN	2-3	O'Hara, Kerr	6860

Appearances (shirt numbers)

#	Hill A	Hopper A	Brookes E	Swallow BE	Winstanley E	Cunningham WL	Sheavills JE	Kerr GAM	Leighton A	Byrne J	O'Hara AE	Addy M	Bettany JW	Bradbury A	Callaghan WA	Craven T	Earnshaw RI	Farnsworth PA	Graham M	Murphy BL	Senior RV	Shaw EL	Wilcox A	Williamson R	Wood R
1	1	2	3	4	5	6	7	8	9	10	11														
2	1	2	3	4	5	6	7	8	9	10	11														
3	1	2	3		5	6	7	8	9	10	11														4
4		2	3		5	6	7	8	9	10	11													1	4
5		2	3		5	6	7	8	9	10	11													1	4
6		2	3		5	6	7	8	9	10	11													1	4
7		2	3		5	6	7		9	8	11									10				1	4
8		2	3		5	6	7		9	8	11									10				1	4
9		2			5	6		8	9	10									7		11	3		1	4
10		2			5	6		8	9	10									7		11	3		1	4
11			3		5	6		10	9	8	11								7		2			1	4
12		2			5	6		8	9	10	11								7		3			1	4
13			3		5	6		8	9	10	11								7		2			1	4
14			3	5		6		8	9	10	11								7		2		1		4
15			3	5		6		8	9	4	11								7	10	2		1		
16			3	5		6		8	9	4	11								7	10	2		1		
17			3	5		6	7	8	9	4	11									10	2		1		
18		2		5		6	7	8	9		11									10	3		1		
19		2		5		6	7	8	9	4	11									10			1		
20	1	2	3		5		6	7	8	9									11	10					4
21	1	2	3		5		6	7	8	9									11	10					4
22	1	2	3	5		6	10	7	8	9											11				4
23	1	2	3	5				7	8	9	6									10	11				4
24	1	2	3	5				7	8	9	6									10	11				4
25	1	2	3	5				7	8	9	6									10	11				4
26		2	3	5				7	8	9	6									10	11			1	4
27		2	3	5			9	7	8		6									10	11			1	4
28		2	3	5			9	7	8		6									10	11			1	4
29		2	3	5				7	8		6								9	10	11			1	4
30		2	3	5				7	8		4				6				9	10	11			1	
31		2	3	5				7	8		4				6				9	10	11			1	
32		2	3	5				7	8		4				6				9	10	11			1	
33		2	3	5				8	10			6							7	9	11	4		1	
34		2	3	5				8	10			6							7	9	11	4		1	
35		2	3	5			7	8	9		11	6								10				1	4
36			3	4	5			8			11				6	10			9	2	7			1	
37			3	4	5			8			11				6	10			9	2	7			1	
38			3	4	5			8			11				6	10			9	2	7			1	
39			3	4	5				9		11			8	6				7	2	10			1	
40			3	4	5				9		11	8			6				7	2	10			1	
41			3	4	5		7		9		11		10		6				8	2				1	
42			3		5			8	4		9	6	2		10						11			1	
43			3		5			8	4		9	6	2		10						11			1	
44		9	3		5			8	4		11	6	2		10				7					1	
45			3		5			10	9		11	4	2		6			7						1	
46			3		5			8	9		11	4	2		6		7							1	
Apps	9	30	41	29	26	24	26	42	25	41	41	14	11	1	15	3	1	1	20	22	21	2	6	31	24
Goals		1		1			2	10	13	4	10		2						5		4				

Two own goals

F.A. Cup

Rnd	Month	Date	Opponent	Score	Scorers	Att.
R1	Nov	14	Netherfield	3-1	Byrne, Graham, Kerr	4164
R2	Dec	5	CHESTER	2-5	Byrne, Senior	6674

F.A. Cup appearances:
- R1: Hill 1, Hopper 2, Brookes 3, Swallow 5, Cunningham 6, Kerr 8, Leighton 9, Byrne 7, O'Hara 11, Graham 10, Wood 4
- R2: Hill 1, Hopper 2, Swallow 5, Cunningham 6, Kerr 8, Leighton 9, Byrne 10, O'Hara 11, Murphy 3, Senior 7, Wood 4

F.L. Cup

Rnd	Month	Date	Opponent	Score	Scorers	Att.
R1	Sep	2	LINCOLN CITY	2-1	Byrne 2	4262
R2		23	Leyton Orient	0-3		5146

F.L. Cup appearances:
- R1: Hill 1, Hopper 2, Brookes 3, Winstanley 5, Cunningham 6, Sheavills 7, Kerr 8, Leighton 9, Byrne 10, O'Hara 11, Wood 4
- R2: Hopper 2, Winstanley 5, Cunningham 6, Sheavills 7, Leighton 9, Byrne 8, O'Hara 11, Senior 10, Shaw 3, Williamson 1, Wood 4

Final Table — Division 3

		P	W	D	L	F	A	W	D	L	F	A	Pts
1	Carlisle United	46	14	5	4	46	24	11	5	7	30	29	60
2	Bristol City	46	14	6	3	53	18	10	5	8	39	37	59
3	Mansfield Town	46	17	4	2	61	23	7	7	9	34	38	59
4	Hull City	46	14	6	3	51	25	9	6	8	40	32	58
5	Brentford	46	18	4	1	55	18	6	5	12	28	37	57
6	Bristol Rovers	46	14	7	2	52	21	6	8	9	30	37	55
7	Gillingham	46	16	5	2	45	13	7	4	12	25	37	55
8	Peterborough Utd.	46	16	3	4	61	33	6	4	13	24	41	51
9	Watford	46	13	8	2	45	21	4	8	11	26	43	50
10	Grimsby Town	46	11	10	2	37	21	5	7	11	31	46	49
11	Bournemouth	46	12	4	7	40	24	6	7	10	32	39	47
12	Southend United	46	14	4	5	48	24	5	4	14	30	47	46
13	Reading	46	12	8	3	45	26	4	6	13	25	44	46
14	Queen's Park Rgs.	46	15	5	3	48	23	2	7	14	24	57	46
15	Workington	46	11	7	5	30	22	6	5	12	28	47	46
16	Shrewsbury Town	46	10	6	7	42	38	5	6	12	34	46	42
17	Exeter City	46	8	7	8	33	27	4	10	9	18	25	41
18	Scunthorpe United	46	9	8	6	42	27	5	4	14	23	45	40
19	Walsall	46	9	4	10	34	36	6	3	14	21	44	37
20	Oldham Athletic	46	10	3	10	40	39	3	7	13	21	44	36
21	Luton Town	46	6	8	9	32	36	5	3	15	19	58	33
22	Port Vale	46	7	6	10	27	33	2	8	13	14	43	32
23	Colchester United	46	7	6	10	30	34	3	4	16	20	55	30
24	BARNSLEY	46	8	5	10	33	31	1	6	16	21	59	29

Season 1964-65
Back row: Swallow, Wood, Fidler, Williamson, Winstanley, Hill, Hopper, Green, Craven
Centre: Murphy, Shaw, Senior, Nicholson, Graham, Kerr, Byrne, O'Hara, Addy
Front: Callaghan, Clay, Brookes, Bradbury, Farnsworth, Cunningham, Sheavils

Season 1965-66
Back row: Murphy, Winstanley, Ferguson, Ironside, Hill, Swallow, Brookes, Jackson
Front: Parker, Earnshaw, Bettany, Kerr, Haynes, Hewitt, Brandon

1965/66 — 16th in Division 4

#		Date	Opponent	Score	Scorers	Att	Ironside R	Murphy BL	Brookes E	Ferguson M	Swallow BE	Duerden H	Earnshaw RI	Hayes J	Kerr GAM	Bettany JW	Hewitt R	Adamson KB	Addy M	Hill A	Hobson J	Parker RW	Howard P	Jackson B	Lambert R	McColl D
1	Aug	21	Crewe Alexandra	1-0	Kerr	3645	1	2	3	4	5	6	7	10	9	8	11									
2		24	PORT VALE	1-0	Kerr	3016	1	2	3	4	5	6	7	10	9	8	11									
3		28	BRADFORD CITY	4-2	Kerr 2 (1 pen), Hewitt, Earnshaw	5261	1	2	3	4	5	6	7	10	9	8	11									
4	Sep	3	CHESTERFIELD	0-0		4894	1	2	3	4	5	6	7	10	9	8	11									
5		11	Colchester United	0-4		5083	1	2	3	4	5	6	7	10	9	8	11									
6		13	Port Vale	1-1	Kerr	6573	1	2	3	10	5	6	7		9	8	11							4		
7		17	TRANMERE ROVERS	4-0	Earnshaw, Ferguson, Hewitt, Kerr	6255	1		3	10	5	6	7		9	8	11					2		4		
8		24	Stockport County	0-1		15352	1		3	10	5	6	7		9	8	11					2		4		
9	Oct	1	DARLINGTON	3-1	Bettany, Keeble (og), Ferguson	6800	1		3	10	5	6	7		9	8	11					2		4		
10		6	Chester	3-3	Earnshaw, Ferguson, Kerr	8412	1		3	10	5	6	7		9	8	11					2		4		
11		9	Luton Town	4-5	Ferguson 2, Bettany, Kerr	5948	1		3	10	5	6	7		9	8	11					2		4		
12		15	BARROW	3-0	Earnshaw, Ferguson, Kerr	7922	1		3	10	5	6	7		9	8	11					2		4		
13		20	Torquay United	0-3		5762	1		3	10	5	6			9	8	11					2	7	4		
14		23	Hartlepools United	2-1	Duerden, Kerr	4194	1		3	10	5	6	7		9	8	11					2		4		
15		29	DONCASTER ROVERS	1-5	Hewitt	13358	1	12	3	10	5	6	7		9	8	11					2		4*		
16	Nov	20	Bradford Park Avenue	2-7	Ferguson 2	5833	1		3	10	5	6	7		9	8	11	4				2				
17		23	CHESTER	0-2		2959			3	10		6	7		9	8	11	4		1		2		5		
18	Dec	11	TORQUAY UNITED	1-0	Ferguson	4646			3	10	5	6	7		9	8	11	4		1		2				
19		18	Barrow	5-1	Ferguson 2, Kerr 2, Hewitt	3943			3	10	5	6	7		9	8	11	4		1		2				
20		27	HALIFAX TOWN	1-2	Ferguson	8641			3	10	5	6	7		9	8	11	4		1		2				
21		28	Halifax Town	2-2	Bettany, Ferguson	5410			3	10	5	6	7		9	8	11	4		1		2				
22	Jan	1	LUTON TOWN	3-0	Hewitt, Kerr, Reid (og)	5053			3	10	5			7	9	8	11			1	6	2		4		
23		8	Wrexham	3-6	Kerr, Hewitt, Hayes	4149			3	10	5			7	9	8	11			1	6	2		4		
24		15	HARTLEPOOLS UNITED	2-2	Bettany, Kerr	3471			3	10	5	6		7	9	8	11	4		1		2				
25		29	CREWE ALEXANDRA	0-1		3556			3	10	5			7	9	8	11			1		2		4	6	
26	Feb	5	Bradford City	0-1		4976			3	10	5				9	8	11			1	7	2		4	6	10
27		12	NOTTS COUNTY	1-1	Ferguson	2516			3	6	5			7	9	8	11			1		2		4		10
28		19	Chesterfield	1-3	Kerr	4049			3	4	5	6	7	10	9	8	11			1		2		4		
29		26	COLCHESTER UNITED	1-1	Kerr	3323		3		6	5				10	8	11		4	1		2		7		
30	Mar	5	Notts County	1-0	Earnshaw	5894			3	6	5			7	9	8	11		4	1		2				
31		8	ROCHDALE	5-0	Earnshaw 2, Hayes 2, Bettany	3426			3	6	5			7	10	9	8	11		4	1		2			
32		11	Tranmere Rovers	0-1		6732			3	6	5			7	10	9	8	11		4	1		2			
33		15	ALDERSHOT	2-1	Bettany, Hewitt	4153			3	6	5			7	10	9	8	11		4	1		2			
34		18	STOCKPORT COUNTY	1-2	Hewitt (pen)	4944			3		5			7	10	8	11	9		4	1		2		6	
35		22	Lincoln City	1-4	Addy	2368			3		5			7	10	8	11	9	4	1		2		6		
36		26	Darlington	1-2	Hewitt	5071			3	4	5			7		11	9	6	1	8	2				10
37	Apr	4	Southport	1-3	Bettany	3591			3	6	5			7		8	11	4	1	9	2				10
38		9	Newport County	0-1		2328			3	6	5			7	8		11		4	1	9	2				10
39		11	Rochdale	1-2	Addy	3316			3	9	5			7	8		11		6	1	10	2		4		
40		15	BRADFORD PARK AVE.	1-1	Addy	2057			3	6	5				8		11	9	10	1	7	2		4		
41		23	Aldershot	1-1	Bettany	3657			3		5			7		4	11	9	8	1	10	2		6		
42		26	LINCOLN CITY	0-1		2287			3		5			7	8	4	11	9	1	10	2		6		
43		29	NEWPORT COUNTY	2-2	Ferguson, Hobson	1697			3	9	5			7		8	11		6	1	10	2		4		
44	May	3	Doncaster Rovers	1-2	Hewitt	16494			3	9	5			7		8	11		6	1	10	2		4		
45		10	WREXHAM	3-0	Ferguson 2, Earnshaw	1577			3	9	5			7		8	11		6	1	9	2		4		
46		13	SOUTHPORT	4-0	Addy 2, Hewitt, Hobson	1915			3		5			7	10	8	11		6	1	9	2		4		

	Iron	Mur	Bro	Fer	Swa	Due	Ear	Hay	Ker	Bet	Hew	Ada	Add	Hil	Hob	Par	How	Jac	Lam	McC
Apps	16	8	45	40	45	23	33	26	33	42	46	6	21	30	15	40	1	28	3	5
Goals				17		1	8	3	17	8	11		5		2					

Two own goals

F.A. Cup

		Date	Opponent	Score	Scorers	Att	Ironside R	Brookes E	Ferguson M	Swallow BE	Duerden H	Earnshaw RI	Kerr GAM	Bettany JW	Hewitt R	Adamson KB	Hill A	Parker RW	Jackson B
R1	Nov	13	Lincoln City	3-1	Bettany, Earnshaw, Kerr (pen)	6378	1	3	10	5	6	7	9	8	11	4		2	
R2	Dec	4	GRIMSBY TOWN	1-1	Kerr	8112		3	10	5	6	7	9	8	11		1	2	4
rep		8	Grimsby Town	0-2		10664		3	10	5	6	7	9	8	11		1	2	4

F.L. Cup

		Date	Opponent	Score	Scorers	Att	Ironside R	Murphy BL	Brookes E	Ferguson M	Swallow BE	Duerden H	Earnshaw RI	Hayes J	Kerr GAM	Bettany JW	Hewitt R
R1	Sep	1	Doncaster Rovers	2-2	Earnshaw, Kerr	14309	1	2	3	4	5	6	7	10	9	8	11
rep		7	DONCASTER ROVERS	1-2	Kerr	11946	1	2	3	4	5	6	7	10	9	8	11

Division 4 Final Table

		P	W	D	L	F	A	W	D	L	F	A	Pts
1	Doncaster Rovers	46	15	6	2	49	21	9	5	9	36	33	59
2	Darlington	46	16	3	4	41	17	9	6	8	31	36	59
3	Torquay United	46	17	2	4	43	20	7	8	8	29	29	58
4	Colchester United	46	13	7	3	45	21	10	3	10	25	26	56
5	Tranmere Rovers	46	15	1	7	56	32	9	7	7	37	34	56
6	Luton Town	46	19	2	2	65	27	5	6	12	25	43	56
7	Chester	46	15	5	3	52	27	5	7	11	27	43	52
8	Notts County	46	9	8	6	32	25	10	4	9	29	28	50
9	Newport County	46	14	6	3	46	24	4	6	13	29	51	48
10	Southport	46	15	6	2	47	20	3	6	14	21	49	48
11	Bradford Park Ave.	46	14	2	7	59	31	7	3	13	43	61	47
12	Barrow	46	12	8	3	48	31	4	7	12	24	45	47
13	Stockport County	46	12	4	7	42	29	6	2	15	29	41	42
14	Crewe Alexandra	46	12	4	7	42	23	4	5	14	19	40	41
15	Halifax Town	46	11	6	6	46	31	4	5	14	21	44	41
16	BARNSLEY	46	11	6	6	43	24	4	1	15	31	54	40
17	Aldershot	46	12	6	5	47	27	3	4	16	28	57	40
18	Hartlepools United	46	13	4	6	44	22	3	4	16	19	53	40
19	Port Vale	46	12	7	4	38	18	3	2	18	10	41	39
20	Chesterfield	46	8	9	6	37	35	5	4	14	25	43	39
21	Rochdale	46	12	1	10	46	27	4	4	15	25	60	37
22	Lincoln City	46	9	7	7	37	29	4	4	15	20	53	37
23	Bradford City	46	10	5	8	37	34	2	8	13	26	60	37
24	Wrexham	46	10	4	9	43	43	3	5	15	29	61	35

#	Date		Opponent	Score	Scorers	Att.	Ironside R	Parker RW	Brookes E	Swallow BE	Winstanley E	Addy M	Earnshaw RI	Bettany JW	Barton DR	Bradbury A	Hewitt R	Adamson KB	Briscoe J	Burns EO	Cockburn K	Duerden H	Evans JD	Graham P	Hamstead GW	Hemstock B	Howard P	Moran BJ	Murphy BL	Raggett BC	Thomas BE	Wood RE	Booker M
1	Aug	20	BRENTFORD	0-1		2564	1	2	3	4	5	6	7	8	9	10	11																
2		27	Newport County	0-2		2940	1	2	3	4	5	9		8		10	11																
3		30	BARROW	2-3	Briscoe, Hewitt	2227	1	2	3	4	5	6		8		10		9	7			6											
4	Sep	2	CHESTERFIELD	0-3		3560	1	2	3	4	5	6		8		10		9	7						11								
5		5	Stockport County	1-2	Briscoe	9068		2	3	5		4		8	7				9						11				3	1			
6		10	LUTON TOWN	2-1	Earnshaw, Murphy	2188		2	3	4	5	6	12	8			10		9*						11				3	1			
7		17	Aldershot	2-3	Bettany 2	4292		2	3	4	5	6	9	8	7		10								11				7	1			
8		23	WREXHAM	2-2	Bettany, Hewitt	2900		2	3	4	5	6	7	8	10		9								11					1			
9		27	STOCKPORT COUNTY	1-2	Hamstead	4294		2	3	4	5	6	7	8	10		9								11					1			
10		30	Southend United	0-3		9576		2	3	4	5	6	7	8	10		9								11					1			
11	Oct	8	Rochdale	1-1	Barton	2784		2	3	4	5	6	7	8	10*		9								11					1			12
12		15	SOUTHPORT	0-0		2719		2	3	4	5	6	8	9	10										11		7*			1			12
13		22	Notts County	3-0	Hamstead 2, Briscoe	6373		2	3	4	5	6	7	8	10				9						11					1			
14		24	EXETER CITY	2-1	Bettany, Briscoe	3689		2	3	4	5	6	7	8	10				9						11					1			
15		29	CHESTER	1-2	Briscoe	4474		2	3	4	5	6*	7	8	10				9			12			11					1			
16	Nov	5	Chesterfield	0-1		5260	1	2	3	6	5		7	4	8			10	9						11								
17		12	PORT VALE	1-0	Earnshaw	4823	1	2	3	6	5		7	4	10								8		11							9	
18		16	Exeter City	3-0	Thomas 2, Hamstead	2753	1	2	3		5		7	4	10								6		11							9	
19		19	Crewe Alexandra	2-2	Hamstead, Hewitt	3887	1	2	3		5		7	4	10								6		11							9	
20	Dec	3	York City	3-0	Earnshaw 2, Evans	3413	1	2	3		5		7	4	10								6		11							9	
21		10	LINCOLN CITY	2-1	Hamstead, Thomas	9394	1	2	3		5		7	4	10								6		11							9	
22		17	Brentford	1-3	Evans	4255	1	2	3		5		7	4	10								6		11							9	
23		26	BRADFORD CITY	1-1	Thomas	11192	1	2	3		5		7	4	10								6		11							9	
24		27	Bradford City	1-1	Hewitt (pen)	6828		2	3	5			7	4	10								6		11						9		1
25		31	NEWPORT COUNTY	1-1	Evans	7765		2	3	5			7	4	10								6		11						9		1
26	Jan	14	Luton Town	1-1	Thomas	8287		2	3				7	4	10								6		11						9		1
27		21	ALDERSHOT	1-1	Walker (og)	10105		2	3	5			7	4	10								6	9	11								1
28	Feb	4	Wrexham	2-2	Earnshaw, Graham	9368		2	3	9	5		7		10								6		11	8				4			1
29		11	SOUTHEND UNITED	1-2	Hewitt	7856		2	3	9	5		7		10								6		11	8				4			1
30		15	Bradford Park Avenue	3-1	Earnshaw, Hamstead, T	4962		2	3		5		7		10								6		11					4	9		1
31		18	Hartlepools United	1-1	Evans	6715		2	3		5		7		10					9			6		11					4			1
32		25	ROCHDALE	3-1	Barton, Evans, Thomas	7585		2	3		5		7		10								6		11					4	9		1
33	Mar	4	Southport	0-3		5347		2	3		5		7		10								6		11					4	9		1
34		11	HARTLEPOOLS UNITED	1-2	Earnshaw	6479		2	3		5	12	7		10								8*		11					4	9		1
35		18	NOTTS COUNTY	0-0		5278		2			5		7			4	10					11					8		3	6	9		1
36		25	Barrow	0-2		5342		2			5		7		10	8	6								11				3	4	9		1
37		27	HALIFAX TOWN	4-1	Bradbury 2, Evans, Tho	5354		2			5		7		10	4	6								11				3		9		1
38		28	Halifax Town	1-1	Winstanley	4348		2			5		7		10	4	6						8		11				3		9		1
39	Apr	1	BRADFORD PARK AVE.	2-0	Hamstead, Hewitt	5936		2			5		7		10	4	6						8		11				3		9		1
40		8	Port Vale	1-3	Hewitt	3209		2			5		7		10	4	6						8		11				3		9		1
41		11	TRANMERE ROVERS	2-2	Earnshaw, Evans	5186		2			5		7		10	4	6						8		11				3		9		1
42		15	CREWE ALEXANDRA	1-0	Evans	5899	1	2			5		7		10	4	6						8		11				3		9		
43		22	Chester	0-1		2969	1	2			5		7			4	6		10				8		11				3		9		
44		24	Tranmere Rovers	3-3	Thomas 2, Barton	7362	1	2			5		7		10								8		11				3	4	9		
45		28	YORK CITY	0-1		5213	1	2			5		7		10								8		11				3	4	9		
46	May	6	Lincoln City	1-0	Evans	2860	1	2			5		7		10								8		11				3	4	9		
			Apps				17	46	34	22	41	15	42	27	39	11	41	1	9	3	1	2	25	2	43	1	1	0	14	12	26	29	2
			Goals								1		8	4	3	2	7		5				9	1	8				1		10		

One own goal

F.A. Cup

Rd	Date		Opponent	Score	Scorers	Att.	Ironside R	Parker RW	Brookes E	Swallow BE	Winstanley E	Addy M	Earnshaw RI	Bettany JW	Barton DR	Bradbury A	Hewitt R	Adamson KB	Briscoe J	Burns EO	Cockburn K	Duerden H	Evans JD	Graham P	Hamstead GW	Hemstock B	Howard P	Moran BJ	Murphy BL	Raggett BC	Thomas BE	Wood RE	Booker M
R1	Nov	26	SOUTHPORT	3-1	Thomas 2, Evans	11560	1	2	3		5		7	4	10								6		11							9	
R2	Jan	7	PORT VALE	1-1	Hewitt	13343		2	3		5		7	4	10								6		11						9		1
rep		16	Port Vale	3-1	Bettany, Hewitt, Parker	12784		2	3		5		7	4	10								6		11						9		1
R3		28	CARDIFF CITY	1-1	Evans	21464		2	3		5		7	4	10								6		11						9		1
rep		31	Cardiff City	1-2	Thomas	21020		2	3	5		4	7		10								6		11						9		1

F.L. Cup

Rd	Date		Opponent	Score	Scorers	Att.	Ironside R	Parker RW	Brookes E	Swallow BE	Winstanley E	Addy M	Earnshaw RI	Bettany JW	Barton DR	Bradbury A	Hewitt R
R1	Aug	24	GRIMSBY TOWN	1-2	Hewitt	2495	1	2	3	4	5	6	7	8	9	10	11

		P	W	D	L	F	A	W	D	L	F	A	Pts
1	Stockport County	46	16	5	2	41	18	10	7	6	28	24	64
2	Southport	46	19	2	2	47	15	4	11	8	22	27	59
3	Barrow	46	12	8	3	35	18	12	3	8	41	36	59
4	Tranmere Rovers	46	14	6	3	42	20	8	8	7	24	23	58
5	Crewe Alexandra	46	14	5	4	42	26	7	7	9	28	29	54
6	Southend United	46	15	5	3	44	12	7	4	12	26	37	53
7	Wrexham	46	11	12	0	46	20	5	8	10	30	42	52
8	Hartlepools United	46	15	3	5	44	29	7	4	12	22	35	51
9	Brentford	46	13	7	3	36	19	5	6	12	22	37	49
10	Aldershot	46	14	4	5	48	19	4	8	11	24	38	48
11	Bradford City	46	13	4	6	48	31	6	6	11	26	31	48
12	Halifax Town	46	10	11	2	37	27	5	3	15	22	41	44
13	Port Vale	46	9	7	7	33	27	5	8	10	22	31	43
14	Exeter City	46	11	6	6	30	24	3	9	11	20	36	43
15	Chesterfield	46	13	6	4	33	16	4	2	17	27	47	42
16	BARNSLEY	46	8	7	8	30	28	5	8	10	30	36	41
17	Luton Town	46	15	5	3	47	23	1	4	18	12	50	41
18	Newport County	46	9	9	5	35	23	3	7	13	21	40	40
19	Chester	46	8	5	10	24	32	7	5	11	30	46	40
20	Notts County	46	10	7	6	31	25	3	4	16	22	47	37
21	Rochdale	46	10	4	9	30	27	3	7	13	23	48	37
22	York City	46	11	5	7	45	31	1	6	16	20	48	35
23	Bradford Park Ave.	46	7	6	10	30	34	4	7	12	22	45	35
24	Lincoln City	46	7	8	8	39	39	2	5	16	19	43	31

Season 1966/67
Back row: Rimmington (Trainer) Murphy, Swallow, Brookes, Winstanley, Howard, Booker
Ironside, Naylor, Raggett, Addy, unknown, Steele (Manager)
Centre row: Barton, Earnshaw, Duerden, Boughen, Smart, Parker, Hewitt, Bradbury, Hobson, Bettany, Briscoe
Front row: Seven players sitting - six unknown, Hamstead.

Season 1967/68
Back row: Brookes, Robson, Ironside, Winstanley, Murphy, Graham
Front row: Earnshaw, Evans, Bettany, Taylor, Hamstead

1967/68 — 2nd in Division 4

#	Month	Date	Opponent	Score	Scorers	Att.
1	Aug	19	DONCASTER ROVERS	1-0	Thomas	11305
2		26	Luton Town	0-2		7887
3	Sep	2	SOUTHEND UNITED	1-1	Thomas	6982
4		4	Bradford Park Avenue	1-1	Evans	4428
5		9	Wrexham	0-2		8426
6		15	CHESTERFIELD	0-0		9094
7		23	SWANSEA TOWN	3-0	Hamstead, Hobson, Winstanley	6599
8		26	BRADFORD PARK AVE.	2-0	Hobson, Humes	7884
9		29	Hartlepools United	1-2	Bettany	5002
10	Oct	3	ROCHDALE	1-1	Bettany	4663
11		7	Darlington	2-0	Evans, Thomas	4208
12		14	ALDERSHOT	1-0	Earnshaw	7811
13		21	Workington	1-0	Evans	2433
14		23	Rochdale	0-1		3368
15		28	LINCOLN CITY	2-1	Hewitt 2 (1 pen)	9290
16	Nov	4	Halifax Town	1-1	Winstanley	6762
17		11	BRADFORD CITY	1-0	Thomas	13732
18		13	Southend United	1-4	Thomas	10513
19		18	Crewe Alexandra	3-3	Evans 2, Thomas	6541
20		25	NOTTS COUNTY	3-1	Thomas 2, Smith (og)	8361
21	Dec	2	Port Vale	0-2		3724
22		15	Doncaster Rovers	2-1	Taylor, Thomas (pen)	9364
23		23	LUTON TOWN	2-2	Bettany, Hamstead	8704
24		26	York City	1-1	Hamstead	8132
25		30	YORK CITY	1-0	Bettany	10175
26	Jan	6	Brentford	1-0	Taylor	5176
27		20	Chesterfield	3-2	Evans 2 (1 pen), Howard	16091
28		27	EXETER CITY	2-1	Earnshaw, Robson	11781
29	Feb	3	Swansea Town	1-1	Evans	11069
30		10	HARTLEPOOLS UNITED	4-0	Evans 2, Earnshaw, Robson	12896
31		17	Newport County	0-3		4301
32		24	CREWE ALEXANDRA	3-1	Evans, Earnshaw, Robson	15096
33	Mar	2	Aldershot	1-1	Evans (pen)	6852
34		5	Wrexham	2-2	Evans, Winstanley	14555
35		9	Exeter City	0-2		3840
36		16	WORKINGTON	2-1	Bettany, Hamstead	11427
37		23	Lincoln City	1-0	Hamstead	7772
38		30	HALIFAX TOWN	0-0		11586
39	Apr	6	Bradford City	0-1		12647
40		13	DARLINGTON	1-0	Bradbury	11626
41		15	BRENTFORD	3-0	Bradbury 2, Winstanley	12405
42		20	Notts County	4-1	Bradbury, Earnshaw, Hobson, Rob	8674
43		23	CHESTER	2-1	Bradbury, Hobson	14596
44		26	PORT VALE	2-0	Robson, Winstanley	15913
45	May	4	Chester	1-1	Winstanley	4402
46		11	NEWPORT COUNTY	4-2	Robson 2, Evans, Rowlands (og)	12323

Player appearances (shirt numbers). Columns: Ironside R, Murphy BL, Brookes E, Bettany JW, Winstanley E, Howard P, Earnshaw RI, Evans JD, Thomas BE, Barton DR, Taylor BJ, Arblaster BM, Bradbury A, Briscoe J, Graham P, Hamstead GW, Hewitt R, Hobson J, Humes J, Parker RW, Priestley RM, Raggett BC, Robson J, Wood RE

#	Iro	Mur	Bro	Bet	Win	How	Ear	Eva	Tho	Bar	Tay	Arb	Brad	Bri	Gra	Ham	Hew	Hob	Hum	Par	Pri	Rag	Rob	Woo
1	1	2	3	4	5	6	7	8	9	10	11													
2		2	3	4	5	6	7	8	9	10*	11											12		1
3	1	2	3	4	5	6	7	8	9	10	11													
4	1	2	3		5	6	7	8		10			4	9		11								
5	1	2	3		5	6	7	8		10			4			11			12				9*	
6	1	2	3	4	5	6	7	8		10						11		9						
7	1	2	3	4	5	6	7	8*					10			11		9						
8	1	2	3*	4	5	6	7						10			11		12	9					
9	1		3	4	5	6	7			12			10			11		8	9					
10	1		3	4	5	6	7						10			11		8	9*	2				
11	1		3	4	5	6	7	8	9				10			11				2				
12	1		3	4	5	6	7	8	9				10			11				2				
13	1		3	4	5	6	7	8	9	10						11				2				
14	1		3	4	5	6	7	8	9	10					12	11				2				
15	1	2	3	4	5	6	7	8	9							11	10							
16	1		3	4	5	6	7	11	9							10	8			2				
17	1		3	4	5	6	7	9	11							10	8			2				
18	1		3		5	6	7	9	11	4*						10	8			2				
19	1		3	4	5	6	7	8	9	10						11			7	2				
20	1	2	3	4	5	6	7	8	9	10	11													
21	1	2	3	4	5	6	7*	8	9	12	10													
22	1	2	3	4	5	6	7		9	10						11		8						
23	1	2	3	4	5	6	7		9	10						11		8						
24	1	2	3	4	5	6	7			10					9	11		8						
25	1	2	3	4	5	6	7	8		10						11			9					
26	1		3	4	5	6	7	8		10						11			9	2				
27	1		3	4		6	7	8							5	11				2			9	
28	1		3	4	5	6	7	8								11				2			9	
29	1		3	4	5	6	7	8								11				2			9	
30	1		3	4	5	6	7	8								11				2			9	
31	1		3	4	5	6	7	8							12	11				2			9	
32	1		3	4	5	6	7	8								11				2			9	
33	1		3	4	5	6	7	8								11				2			9	
34	1		3	4	5	6	7	8		10						11				2			9	
35	1		3	4	5	6	7	8								11				2			9	
36	1		3	4	5	6	7	8								11	10			2			9	
37	1		3	4	5	6	7	8								11	10			2			9	
38	1		3	4	5	6	7									11	10	8		2			9	
39	1		3	4	5	6	7				11		10				8			2			9	
40	1		3	4	5	6	7	8			11		10							2			9	
41	1		3	4	5	6	7					1	10			11		8		2			9	
42	1		3	4	5	6	7						10			11		8		2			9	
43	1		3	4	5	6	7						10			11		8		2			9	
44	1		3	4	5	6	7						10			11		8		2			9	
45	1		3	4	5	6	7	12					10			11		8*		2			9	
46	1		3	4	5	6	7	8					10			11				2			9	
Apps	44	46	25	43	45	46	44	34	17	8	23	1	16	1	5	37	8	16	6	21	0	1	20	1
Goals				5	6	1	5	14	9		2		5			5	2	4	1				7	

Two own goals

Match 14: Original player not known (Brookes sub.)
Match 31: Original player not known (Graham sub.)

F.A. Cup

Rd	Month	Date	Opponent	Score		Att.	Players
R1	Dec	9	Chesterfield	0-2		17161	1 2 3 4 5 6 _ 8 9 10 11 ... 7

F.L. Cup

Rd	Month	Date	Opponent	Score	Scorer	Att.	Players
R1	Aug	22	Middlesbrough	1-4	Taylor	15966	_ 2 3 4 5 6 7 8 9 10 11 ... 1

		P	W	D	L	F	A	W	D	L	F	A	Pts
1	Luton Town	46	19	3	1	55	16	8	9	6	32	28	66
2	BARNSLEY	46	17	6	0	43	14	7	7	9	25	32	61
3	Hartlepools United	46	15	7	1	34	12	10	3	10	26	34	60
4	Crewe Alexandra	46	13	10	0	44	18	7	8	8	30	31	58
5	Bradford City	46	14	5	4	41	22	9	6	8	31	29	57
6	Southend United	46	12	8	3	45	21	8	6	9	32	37	54
7	Chesterfield	46	15	4	4	47	20	6	7	10	24	30	53
8	Wrexham	46	17	3	3	47	12	3	10	10	25	41	53
9	Aldershot	46	10	11	2	36	19	8	6	9	34	36	53
10	Doncaster Rovers	46	12	8	3	36	16	6	7	10	30	40	51
11	Halifax Town	46	10	6	7	34	24	5	10	8	18	25	46
12	Newport County	46	11	7	5	32	22	5	6	12	26	41	45
13	Lincoln City	46	11	3	9	41	31	6	6	11	30	37	43
14	Brentford	46	13	4	6	41	24	5	3	15	20	40	43
15	Swansea Town	46	11	8	4	38	25	5	2	16	25	52	42
16	Darlington	46	6	11	6	31	27	6	6	11	16	26	41
17	Notts County	46	10	7	6	27	27	5	4	14	26	52	41
18	Port Vale	46	10	5	8	41	31	2	10	11	20	41	39
19	Rochdale	46	9	8	6	35	32	3	6	14	16	40	38
20	Exeter City	46	9	7	7	30	30	2	9	12	15	35	38
21	York City	46	9	6	8	44	30	2	8	13	21	38	36
22	Chester	46	6	6	11	35	38	3	8	12	22	40	32
23	Workington	46	8	8	7	35	29	2	3	18	19	58	31
24	Bradford Park Ave.	46	3	7	13	18	35	1	8	14	12	47	23

1968/69 10th in Division 3

Player columns (left → right): Ironside R · Parker RW · Murphy BL · Bettany JW · Howard P · Raggett BC · Earnshaw RI · Evans JD · Robson J · Bradbury A · Hamstead GW · Arblaster BM · Barton DR · Booth D · Brookes E · Dean N · Graham P · Hobson J · Loyden E · Ormond JL · Winstanley E · Hewitt R

#	Mon	Date	Opponent	Score	Scorers	Att
1	Aug	10	BARROW	2-3	Bradbury, Evans	10054
2		17	Oldham Athletic	1-1	Earnshaw	5197
3		24	GILLINGHAM	0-1		8646
4		28	Luton Town	1-5	Earnshaw	15899
5		31	Rotherham United	0-0		15058
6	Sep	6	Tranmere Rovers	1-3	Howard	7756
7		14	ORIENT	2-2	Dean, Winstanley	9877
8		17	SOUTHPORT	2-1	Robson, Winstanley	9946
9		21	Torquay United	1-3	Robson	8311
10		23	Plymouth Argyle	0-0		12996
11		28	BRIGHTON & HOVE ALB	4-0	Robson 2, Booth, Earnshaw	9383
12	Oct	5	Shrewsbury Town	0-0		4540
13		8	LUTON TOWN	3-1	Earnshaw, Evans, Hamstead	13019
14		12	WALSALL	0-0		11488
15		18	Hartlepool	1-2	Robson	4658
16		26	READING	1-0	Winstanley	9029
17	Nov	2	Bournemouth	0-3		7569
18		4	Watford	2-1	Robson, Winstanley	10612
19		9	CREWE ALEXANDRA	2-2	Dean, Winstanley	9130
20		23	PLYMOUTH ARGYLE	0-0		7754
21		30	Northampton Town	1-3	Ormond	6195
22	Dec	14	Walsall	0-3		5159
23		21	HARTLEPOOL	2-1	Winstanley 2	7701
24		26	SHREWSBURY TOWN	1-0	Loyden (pen)	11733
25	Jan	11	BOURNEMOUTH	1-0	Evans	10768
26		18	Crewe Alexandra	4-1	Loyden 2, Earnshaw, Evans	5109
27		29	Reading	2-3	Loyden, Winstanley	4775
28	Feb	1	SWINDON TOWN	1-1	Bettany	14160
29		18	Bristol Rovers	2-4	Evans, Loyden (pen)	6781
30	Mar	1	Barrow	1-0	Howard	3553
31		4	BRISTOL ROVERS	4-2	Loyden 2, Bettany, Earnshaw	7932
32		8	OLDHAM ATHLETIC	0-1		10865
33		14	Gillingham	1-1	Loyden	5961
34		21	ROTHERHAM UNITED	0-1		13479
35		25	Swindon Town	0-2		17401
36		29	TRANMERE ROVERS	2-2	Earnshaw, King (og)	6529
37		31	Stockport County	1-1	Hamstead	4261
38	Apr	5	Brighton & Hove Albion	1-4	Dean	11410
39		7	Southport	0-1		4325
40		8	MANSFIELD TOWN	2-0	Evans, Loyden	8334
41		12	TORQUAY UNITED	1-0	Evans	5631
42		14	Mansfield Town	0-0		6190
43		19	Orient	1-1	Robson	3914
44		22	WATFORD	3-2	Winstanley 3	6726
45		25	NORTHAMPTON T	2-1	Loyden, Winstanley	7640
46		29	STOCKPORT COUNTY	2-0	Hamstead, Hobson	7739

Match 8: Original player not known (Bradbury sub.)
Match 35: Original player not known (Evans sub.)

Appearances / Goals summary

	Iron	Park	Murp	Bett	How	Ragg	Earn	Evan	Robs	Brad	Hams	Arbl	Bart	Boot	Broo	Dean	Grah	Hobs	Loyd	Orm	Win	Hew
Apps	36	1	46	35	34	8	39	40	43	33	30	9	3	38	31	12	5	3	22	1	36	3
Goals				2	2		7	7	7	1	3				1	3		1	10	1	12	

One own goal

F.A. Cup

R	Mon	Date	Opponent	Score	Scorers	Att
R1	Nov	16	ROCHDALE	0-0		11414
rep		18	Rochdale	1-0	Dean	7340
R2	Dec	7	Darlington	0-0		7864
rep		10	DARLINGTON	1-0	Winstanley	15062
R3	Jan	4	LEICESTER CITY	1-1	Evans	25099
rep		8	Leicester City	1-2	Loyden (pen)	31814

F.L. Cup

R	Mon	Date	Opponent	Score	Scorers	Att
R1	Aug	14	York City	4-3	Graham 2, Evans, Robson	5280
R2	Sep	3	MILLWALL	1-1	Bradbury	9282
rep		9	Millwall	1-3	Winstanley	15034

Division 3 — Final Table

		P	W	D	L	F	A	W	D	L	F	A	Pts
1	Watford	46	16	5	2	35	7	11	5	7	39	27	64
2	Swindon Town	46	18	4	1	38	7	9	6	8	33	28	64
3	Luton Town	46	20	3	0	57	14	5	8	10	17	24	61
4	Bournemouth	46	16	2	5	41	17	5	7	11	19	28	51
5	Plymouth Argyle	46	10	8	5	34	25	7	7	9	19	24	49
6	Torquay United	46	13	4	6	35	18	5	8	10	19	28	48
7	Tranmere Rovers	46	12	3	8	36	31	7	7	9	34	37	48
8	Southport	46	14	8	1	52	20	3	5	15	19	44	47
9	Stockport County	46	14	5	4	49	25	2	9	12	18	43	46
10	BARNSLEY	46	13	6	4	37	21	3	8	12	21	42	46
11	Rotherham United	46	12	5	6	40	21	4	7	12	16	29	45
12	Brighton & Hove A.	46	12	7	4	49	21	4	6	13	23	44	45
13	Walsall	46	10	9	4	34	18	4	7	12	16	31	44
14	Reading	46	13	3	7	41	25	2	10	11	26	41	43
15	Mansfield Town	46	14	5	4	37	18	2	6	15	21	44	43
16	Bristol Rovers	46	12	6	5	41	27	4	5	14	22	44	43
17	Shrewsbury Town	46	11	8	4	28	17	5	3	15	23	50	43
18	Orient	46	10	8	5	31	19	4	6	13	20	39	42
19	Barrow	46	11	6	6	30	23	4	5	15	26	52	42
20	Gillingham	46	10	10	3	35	20	3	5	15	19	43	41
21	Northampton Town	46	9	8	6	37	30	5	4	14	17	31	40
22	Hartlepool	46	6	12	5	25	29	4	7	12	15	41	39
23	Crewe Alexandra	46	11	4	8	40	31	2	5	16	12	45	35
24	Oldham Athletic	46	9	6	8	33	27	4	3	16	17	56	35

Season 1968/69
Back row: Howard, Bettany, Brookes, Ironside, Winstanley, Parker, Murphy
Front row: Hobson, Evans, Robson, Bradbury, Hamstead

Season 1969/70
Back row: Murphy, Booth, Howard, Arblaster, Sherratt, Winstanley, Raggett, Robson.
Front row: Bettany, Boardman, Evans, Loyden, Bradbury, Hamstead, Dean.

1969/70 — 7th in Division 3

Player columns (in order): Arblaster BM · Murphy BL · Booth D · Bettany JW · Robson J · Howard P · Earnshaw RI · Bradbury A · Dean N · Boardman G · Hamstead GW · Evans JD · Winstanley E · Loyden E · Graham P · Raggett BC · Sherratt B · Brown KG · Barrowclough SI

#	Date	Opponent	Res	Scorers	Att	Arb	Mur	Boo	Bet	Rob	How	Ear	Bra	Dea	Boa	Ham	Eva	Win	Loy	Gra	Rag	She	Bro	Bar
1	Aug 9	BOURNEMOUTH	1-0	Bradbury	10393	1	2	3	4	5	6	7	8	9	10	11								
2	16	Bristol Rovers	3-3	Murphy, Bettany, Evans	7548	1	2	3	4	6	5	7	8		10	11	9							
3	23	STOCKPORT COUNTY	1-0	Winstanley	7869	1	2	3	4	10	6	7			8	11	9	5						
4	26	READING	4-3	Earnshaw 2, Bettany, Evans	8234	1	2	3	4	10	6	7			8	11	9	5						
5	30	Doncaster Rovers	0-1		16671	1	2	3	4	10	6	7			8	11	9	5						
6	Sep 6	WALSALL	2-0	Evans 2	9724	1	2	3	4	11	6	7		9	8		10	5						
7	13	Bury	2-1	Evans, Boardman	4850	1	2	3	4	11	6	7		9	8		10	5						
8	15	Tranmere Rovers	1-0	Booth	4642	1	2	3		11	6	7	4	9	8		10	5						
9	20	ORIENT	1-2	Boardman	11684	1	2*	3	12	11	6	7	4	9	8		10	5						
10	27	Gillingham	3-1	Loyden 2, Earnshaw	5446	1	2	3	4	11	6	7			8		10	5	9					
11	29	Plymouth Argyle	0-0		9909	1	2	3	4	11	6	7		12	8		10*	5	9					
12	Oct 4	BARROW	2-1	Loyden, Boardman	11239	1	2	3	4	11	6	7			8		10	5	9					
13	7	BRISTOL ROVERS	2-0	Robson, Boardman	10235	1	2	3	4	11	6	7			8			5	9	10				
14	11	Bradford City	1-1	Boardman	16224	1	2	3	4	11	6	7			8		10	5	9					
15	18	SOUTHPORT	1-1	Evans	10940	1	2	3	4	11	6	7			8		10	5	9					
16	25	Fulham	0-0		10555	1	2	3	6	11	4	7			8		10	5	9					
17	Nov 1	HALIFAX TOWN	2-0	Pickering (og), Boardman	13453	1	2	3	4		6	7			8	11	10	5	9					
18	8	Luton Town	1-1	Howard	17422	1	2	3	4	5	6	7			8	11	10		9					
19	22	BRIGHTON & HOVE ALB	1-2	Dean (pen)	11460	1	2	3	4		6	7		9	8	11		5		10				
20	26	Torquay United	1-1	Evans	5805	1	2	3	4		6	7	10			11	8	5		9				
21	Dec 2	Rotherham United	0-2		12553	1	2	3	4		6	7			10	11	8	5		12				
22	13	BURY	3-3	Bettany, Evans, Hamstead	9342	1	2*	3	4	5	6	7		9	10	11	8							
23	20	Walsall	2-3	Dean 2	4427	1	2	3	8	6	4	7			10	12	11	5	9*					
24	26	Stockport County	0-1		4991	1	2	3	7*		6	12	4	9	10	11	8	5						
25	27	DONCASTER ROVERS	2-1	Bettany, Dean	17395	1	2		4		6	7		9	10	11	8	5			3			
26	Jan 17	GILLINGHAM	5-1	Loyden 2, Evans 2, Boardman	9092	1	2		4		6	7			8	10			11	9	3			
27	24	Shrewsbury Town	1-1	Earnshaw	5360	1	2		4		6	7			8	10	11	5	9		3			
28	31	Barrow	1-1	Dean	2174	1	2		4		6	7			8	10	11	5	9		3			
29	Feb 7	BRADFORD CITY	3-2	Winstanley, Howard, Loyden	13843	1*	2		4		6	7			8	10	11	5	9	12	3			
30	9	PLYMOUTH ARGYLE	0-1		10729		2	12	4		6	7*			8	10	11	5	9		3	1		
31	14	Bournemouth	1-3	Winstanley	4202		2	12	4		6	7*			8	10	11	5	9		3	1		
32	16	Orient	2-4	Loyden, Dean	10792		2		4		6	7			10	11	8	5	9		3	1		
33	21	FULHAM	3-3	Evans 3	9884		2	6	4			7			10	11	8	5	9	6	3	1		
34	28	Halifax Town	2-0	Loyden, Hamstead	6562		2	3							10	11	8	5	9	6		1		4
35	Mar 3	ROCHDALE	1-0	Evans	9548		2	3			7				10	11	8	5	9	6		1		4
36	7	Brighton & Hove Albion	0-2		15621		2	3			7				10	11	8	5	9	6		1		11*
37	9	Mansfield Town	0-2		7936		2	3	12	7	4				8		10	5	9	6		1		7
38	13	ROTHERHAM UNITED	1-0	Evans	11552		2		4		6				10	11	8	5	9		3	1		7
39	17	SHREWSBURY TOWN	1-1	Hamstead	7786		2		4		6				10	11	8	5	9		3	1		7
40	21	Rochdale	1-1	Hamstead	4887		2	3	4		6	12			10	11	8*	5	9			1		7
41	27	Southport	1-0	Loyden	4516		2		4		6	7			10		8	5	9		3	1		11
42	28	MANSFIELD TOWN	1-1	Booth	8978		2	8	4		6	7			10	11		5	9		3	1		
43	31	LUTON TOWN	2-1	Dean, Hamstead	9988		2		4		6			7	10	8		5	9		3	1		11
44	Apr 4	Reading	2-6	Dean, Hamstead	6924		2		4		6			7	8	11		5	9		3	1	10	11
45	7	TORQUAY UNITED	3-0	Dean, Loyden, Brown	5842	1	2	3	4		6			7	8			5	9				10	11
46	14	TRANMERE ROVERS	1-1	Dean	6174	1	2	3	4		6			7	8			5	9				10	11
		Apps				31	46	35	40	23	41	33	7	24	43	28	37	42	31	7	19	15	5	9
		Goals					1	2	4	1	2	4	1	10	7	6	15	3	10				1	

One own goal

F.A. Cup

Rd	Date	Opponent	Res	Scorers	Att	Arb	Mur	Boo	Bet	Rob	How	Ear	Bra	Dea	Boa	Ham	Eva	Win	Loy	Gra	Rag	She	Bro	Bar
R1	Nov 15	Darlington	0-0		5478	1	2	3	4		6				8	11	10	5	9					7
rep	18	DARLINGTON	2-0	Dean, Graham	13218	1	2	3	4		6			9	8	11		7	5	10				
R2	Dec 4	BARROW	3-0	Loyden 2, Robson	10289	1	2	3	4	7	6				8	10	11	5	9					
R3	Jan 3	Mansfield Town	2-3	Dean, Evans	14387	1	2		4		6	7*		9	10	11	8	5	12		3			

F.L. Cup

Rd	Date	Opponent	Res	Att	Arb	Mur	Boo	Bet	Rob	How	Ear	Bra	Dea	Boa	Ham
R1	Aug 13	HALIFAX TOWN	0-1	9546	1	2	3	4	5	6	7	8	9	10	11

Division 3 Table

		P	W	D	L	F	A	W	D	L	F	A	Pts
1	Orient	46	16	5	2	43	15	9	7	7	24	21	62
2	Luton Town	46	13	8	2	46	15	10	6	7	31	28	60
3	Bristol Rovers	46	15	5	3	51	26	5	11	7	29	33	56
4	Fulham	46	12	9	2	43	26	8	6	9	38	29	55
5	Brighton & Hove A.	46	16	4	3	37	16	7	5	11	20	27	55
6	Mansfield Town	46	14	4	5	46	22	7	7	9	24	27	53
7	BARNSLEY	46	14	6	3	43	24	5	9	9	25	35	53
8	Reading	46	16	3	4	52	29	5	8	10	35	48	53
9	Rochdale	46	11	6	6	39	24	7	4	12	30	36	46
10	Bradford City	46	11	6	6	37	22	6	6	11	20	28	46
11	Doncaster Rovers	46	13	4	6	31	19	4	8	11	21	35	46
12	Walsall	46	11	4	8	33	31	6	8	9	21	36	46
13	Torquay United	46	9	9	5	36	22	5	8	10	26	37	45
14	Rotherham United	46	10	8	5	36	19	5	6	12	26	35	44
15	Shrewsbury Town	46	10	12	1	35	17	3	6	14	27	46	44
16	Tranmere Rovers	46	10	6	7	38	29	4	8	11	18	43	44
17	Plymouth Argyle	46	10	7	6	32	23	6	4	13	24	41	43
18	Halifax Town	46	10	9	4	31	25	4	6	13	16	38	43
19	Bury	46	13	4	6	47	29	2	7	14	28	51	41
20	Gillingham	46	7	6	10	28	33	6	7	10	24	31	39
21	Bournemouth	46	8	9	6	28	27	4	6	13	20	44	39
22	Southport	46	11	6	6	31	22	5	7	11	25	44	38
23	Barrow	46	7	9	7	28	27	1	5	17	18	54	30
24	Stockport County	46	4	7	12	17	30	2	4	17	10	41	23

1970/71   12th in Division 3

No	Date	Match	Score	Scorers	Att	Arblaster BM	Murphy BL	Raggett BC	McPhee J	Winstanley E	Howard P	Booth D	Boardman G	Dean N	Hamstead GW	Kear MP	Lea L	Evans JD	Sharp F	Loyden E	Brown KG	Boughen P	Millar A	Hopkinson A	Earnshaw Rl	Brindle W	Turner P	O'Connor D	Chambers PM
1	Aug 15	FULHAM	0-1		8929	1	2	3	4	5	6	7	8	10	11														
2	22	Bradford City	0-1		8912	1	2	3	4	5	6	12		10			7	8	11*	9									
3	28	BURY	1-1	Evans	7149	1	2		4	5	6	3		10			7	8	11	9									
4	Sep 1	Walsall	2-1	Kear, Winstanley	6755	1	2		4	5	6	3		10		11	7	8	9										
5	4	Tranmere Rovers	2-2	Lea, Evans	5893	1	2		4	5	6	3		10			7	8	9	11									
6	12	ASTON VILLA	1-1	McPhee (pen)	13644	1	2		4	5	6	3		10			7	8	9	11									
7	19	Reading	0-2		6562	1	2		4	5	6	3		10*			7	8	9	11	12								
8	21	Torquay United	1-0	Evans	5818	1	2		4	5	6	3					7	8	11	9	10								
9	26	HALIFAX TOWN	2-2	Evans 2	9667	1	2		4	5	6	3					7	8	11	9	10								
10	29	GILLINGHAM	3-1	Loyden (pen), McPhee, Dean	7585	1	2		4	5	6	3		10			7	8	11	9									
11	Oct 3	Port Vale	1-1	Dean	4490	1	2		4	5	6	3		10			7	8	11	9									
12	10	ROTHERHAM UNITED	2-1	Loyden 2	14563	1	2		4	5	6	3		10			7*	8	11	9	12								
13	17	Fulham	1-1	Lea	12952	1	2	12	4	5	6	3		10			7*	8	11	9									
14	21	Chesterfield	2-4	Winstanley 2	11893	1	2		4	5	6	3		10			7	8	11	9									
15	24	Rochdale	0-1		5462	1	2		4	5	6	3	8*		10		7		11	9					12				
16	31	DONCASTER ROVERS	0-1		9480	1			4	5	6	3	8*		10		7		11	9	10				2				
17	Nov 6	Shrewsbury Town	0-1		4499	1	2		4		6	3	9				8	7	11		5								
18	9	Preston North End	1-3	Dean	11053	1	2		4	9	6	3		10			7	8	11		5								
19	14	SWANSEA CITY	0-0		5364	1	2		4		6	3	8		11			7	9		5								
20	28	PLYMOUTH ARGYLE	2-0	Dean, Winstanley	4903	1	2		10	5	6	3	8	9				7	11		4								
21	Dec 5	Brighton & Hove Albion	2-1	McPhee, Winstanley	7685	1	2	10	4	5	6	3	8					9*	7		12								
22	19	BRADFORD CITY	2-0	Lea, Howard	6173	1	2	12	8	5*	6	3		10	9	11					4								
23	26	Mansfield Town	2-1	Brown, Dean	5939	1	2		5		6	3	8	9	10				11		4								
24	Jan 2	BRISTOL ROVERS	0-4		8773	1	2			5	6	3	8	9	10		7	12	11		4*								
25	9	Gillingham	1-2	Dean	3169	1	2			5	6	3	8	9	10		7				4								
26	16	CHESTERFIELD	1-0	Lea	8291	1	2		4	5	6	3			11		7	9			4								
27	23	WREXHAM	3-1	Boardman, Sharp, Lea (pen)	5130	1	2	12	4	5	6	3		10			7	9	11		8*								
28	Feb 1	Plymouth Argyle	1-2	Evans	5464	1	2		10*	5	6	3	8				7	9	11		4								
29	6	BRIGHTON & HOVE ALB	1-0	Evans	5066	1	2			5	6	3	8				7	10	11		4		12						
30	13	Wrexham	0-1		5372	1	2			5	6	3		10			8	9	11		4				7				
31	20	PRESTON NORTH END	0-1		6848	1	2			5	6	3	8	9			7	12	11		4			10*					
32	26	Doncaster Rovers	0-1		4792	1	2		4	5	6	3		10	8*		7	12	11				9						
33	Mar 6	ROCHDALE	2-2	Lea 2	4872	1	2			5	4	3	8				7	9	11*		12	6	10						
34	9	Torquay United	2-0	Hopkinson, Boardman	3828	1	2			5	6	3		4			7	8	11				9	10					
35	12	Swansea City	2-1	Hopkinson, Sharp	7146	1	2			5	6	3		4			7	8	11				9	10					
36	16	Bristol Rovers	0-3		6832	1	2			5	6	3		4			7	8	11				9	10					
37	20	SHREWSBURY TOWN	2-1	Evans 2	5156	1	2			5	6	3		4			7	8	11				9	10					
38	26	TRANMERE ROVERS	0-0		4637	1	2			5	6	3		4			7*	8	11		12		9	10					
39	Apr 3	Bury	0-0		3242	1	2			5	6	3		4			7	10	11				9	8					
40	10	MANSFIELD TOWN	1-0	Sharp	5292	1	2			5	6	3		4			7	9	11				10	8					
41	12	Aston Villa	0-0		20718	1	2			5	6	3		4			7	8					9	10					
42	13	PORT VALE	1-0	Lea	4837	1	2			5	6	3		4	9		7		11					10			8		
43	17	Rotherham United	0-1		7652	1	2	12		5	6	3		4	9		7		11*					10				8	
44	24	READING	3-0	Winstanley, Booth 2	2975	1	2		5	9	6	8		4			7		11					10					3
45	27	WALSALL	1-2	Booth	3932	1	2		5	9	6	8		4			7		11					10					3
46	May 1	Halifax Town	1-4	Lea (pen)	6332	1	2		5	9	6	8		4			7		11*				12	10					3
Apps						46	45	12	26	43	46	46	33	20	10	6	45	32	43	12	16	8	14	9	2	1	1	3	3
Goals									3	6	1	3	2	6			1	9	9	3	3	1		2					

F.A. Cup

No	Date	Match	Score	Scorers	Att	Arblaster	Murphy	Raggett	McPhee	Winstanley	Howard	Booth	Boardman	Dean	Hamstead	Kear	Lea	Evans	Sharp	Loyden	Brown	Boughen	Millar	Hopkinson
R1	Nov 21	BRADFORD PARK AVE.	1-0	Dean (pen)	7189	1	2		4	5	6	3		10	9		8		11	7				
R2	Dec 12	Rhyl	0-0		5000	1	2		4	5	6	3	8				7		11		9			
rep	15	RHYL	1-1	Lea (aet)	7466	1	2		4	5	6	3	8	9			7		11		10			
rep2	21	Rhyl	0-2		3296	1	2	5	4*		6	3	8	9	11		7		12		10			

Replay 2 at Old Trafford.

F.L. Cup

No	Date	Match	Score	Scorers	Att	Arblaster	Murphy	McPhee	Winstanley	Howard	Booth	Boardman	Dean	Hamstead	Evans	Sharp	Loyden	Boughen
R1	Aug 19	ROTHERHAM UTD.	0-1		8260	1	2	4	5	6	3	8*	10	11	9	12		7

Pos	Team	P	W	D	L	F	A	W	D	L	F	A	Pts
1	Preston North End	46	15	8	0	42	16	7	9	7	21	23	61
2	Fulham	46	15	6	2	39	12	9	6	8	29	29	60
3	Halifax Town	46	16	2	5	46	22	6	10	7	28	33	56
4	Aston Villa	46	13	7	3	27	13	6	8	9	27	33	53
5	Chesterfield	46	13	8	2	45	12	4	9	10	21	26	51
6	Bristol Rovers	46	11	5	7	38	24	8	8	7	31	26	51
7	Mansfield Town	46	13	7	3	44	28	5	8	10	20	34	51
8	Rotherham United	46	12	10	1	38	19	5	6	12	26	41	50
9	Wrexham	46	12	8	3	43	25	6	5	12	29	40	49
10	Torquay United	46	12	6	5	37	26	7	5	11	17	31	49
11	Swansea City	46	11	5	7	41	25	4	11	8	18	31	46
12	BARNSLEY	46	12	6	5	30	19	5	5	13	19	33	45
13	Shrewsbury Town	46	11	6	6	37	18	5	7	11	21	34	45
14	Brighton & Hove A.	46	8	10	5	28	20	6	6	11	22	27	44
15	Plymouth Argyle	46	6	12	5	39	33	6	7	10	24	30	43
16	Rochdale	46	8	8	7	29	26	6	7	10	32	42	43
17	Port Vale	46	11	6	6	29	18	4	6	13	23	41	42
18	Tranmere Rovers	46	8	11	4	27	18	2	11	10	18	37	42
19	Bradford City	46	7	6	10	23	25	6	8	9	26	37	40
20	Walsall	46	10	1	12	30	27	4	10	9	21	30	39
21	Reading	46	10	7	6	32	33	4	4	15	16	52	39
22	Bury	46	7	9	7	30	23	5	4	14	22	37	37
23	Doncaster Rovers	46	8	5	10	28	27	5	4	14	17	39	35
24	Gillingham	46	6	9	8	22	29	4	4	15	20	38	33

Season 1970/71
Back row: Murphy, Boardman, Hamstead, Arblaster, Winstanley, Raggett, Booth, Howard
Front row: McPhee, Dean, Evans, Loyden, Brown, Sharpe, Lea

Season 1971/72
Back row: Steele (Manager) Boardman, Booth, Raggett, Seal, Barker, Arblaster, Murphy,
Brown, Turner, Howard, Rimmington (Coach)
Front row: Waddell, Sharp, Hopkinson, Winstanley, Millar, Lea, Chambers, Dean

1971/72 22nd in Division 3

Player columns (left → right): Barker K, Murphy BL, Booth D, Boardman G, Raggett BC, Howard P, Lea L, Waddell W, Seal J, Millar A, Sharp F, Winstanley E, Chambers PM, Stewart G, Turner P, Brown KG, Martin P, Greenwood PG, Mahoney B, Hopkinson A, Earnshaw RI, Cole R, O'Connor D, Baker C

#	Date	Opponent	Res	Scorers	Att	Bk	Mu	Bo	Bd	Ra	Ho	Le	Wa	Se	Mi	Sh	Wi	Ch	St	Tu	Br	Ma	Gr	Mh	Hp	Ea	Co	OC	Ba
1	Aug 14	WALSALL	4-2	Booth 2, Seal 2	6181	1	2	3	4	5	6	7	8	9	10	11													
2	21	Rotherham United	0-3		7001	1	2	3	4	5	6	7	8	9	10	11													
3	28	SHREWSBURY TOWN	1-3	Hopkinson	5152	1	2	3	4		6	7	8	9	10	11*	5								12				
4	31	TRANMERE ROVERS	0-0		4274	1	2		4		6	7		9	10	11	5								8				
5	Sep 4	Swansea City	0-2		6068	1	2		4		6	7		9	10	11	5	3							8				
6	11	HALIFAX TOWN	1-2	Lea	5992	1	2	3	4		6	8		9	10	11	5										7		
7	18	Bristol Rovers	0-3		9286	1	2	3	4		6		8	9	10	11	5		12								7		
8	25	ROCHDALE	3-3	Seal, Millar, Waddell	5805	1	2	3	7	4		11*	10	9	6	8	5								12				
9	28	ASTON VILLA	0-4		8632	1	2	3	7	4		11	10*	9	6	8	5								12				
10	Oct 2	Brighton & Hove Albion	0-0		12107		2	3	7	4		10		6	8	5	11	1									9*	12	
11	9	CHESTERFIELD	1-4	O'Connor	6603		2	3	6	4		11*		10	8	5		1								7	9	12	
12	16	Walsall	1-1	Waddell	3121		2	3*	8			6		9	10	11	5	4	1							7		12	
13	18	Mansfield Town	0-0		3696		2	8						10	5	6	11	3	1	4						7	9*	12	
14	23	BRADFORD CITY	0-2		6101		2	5	4					9	6	10	11	3	1							7	9*	8	
15	30	Torquay United	2-1	Waddell, Seal	4494		2	6	4				10	9	8	11	5		1	3	7								
16	Nov 6	OLDHAM ATHLETIC	2-1	Brown, Waddell	6126		2	3	11*				9	10	8	7	5		1	4	6	12							
17	13	York City	1-1	Seal	6004		2	3	6				7	8		11	5		1	4	9								
18	27	BOURNEMOUTH	0-0		8548		2	3				7	8	9	10	11	5		1	4	6								
19	Dec 4	Notts County	0-3		12639		2	3	12			11*		9	10	6	5		1	4	7		8						
20	18	SWANSEA CITY	0-1		4273		2	3				7	8	10	6	11	5		1		6		4						
21	27	Bolton Wanderers	0-0		7274		2	3				11		9	10	6	5		1	4	7		8						
22	Jan 1	BRISTOL ROVERS	0-0		4740		2	3				11		9	10	6	5		1	4	7		8						
23	7	Shrewsbury Town	0-1		3344		2	3	6*					9	10	11	5		1	4	7	12	8						
24	15	PLYMOUTH ARGYLE	2-2	Lea, Boardman	3660		2	3	12			10		9		7	5		1	4	8*	11	6						
25	22	Aston Villa	0-2		30531		2	3	8	6		10	12	9*		7	5		1	4		11							
26	29	MANSFIELD TOWN	1-1	Seal	3924		2	3	6*			7	8	9	12	11	5		1	10			4						
27	Feb 5	Blackburn Rovers	0-4		7678		2	3	7			10	8			11	5		1		4		12	6*	9				
28	12	Bradford City	2-0	Lea, Seal	4254		2	3	8			10		9	6	11	5		1		7		4						
29	19	TORQUAY UNITED	0-0		4043		2	3	6			7		9	10	11	5		1		8		4						
30	26	Oldham Athletic	0-6		5784		2	3	8	12				9	7	10*	11		1	5	6		4						
31	Mar 4	YORK CITY	2-1	Mahoney, Boardman	3479		2	3	7			8		10		11	5		1		6		4	9					
32	8	WREXHAM	2-1	Seal, Brown	2185		2	3	7			8		10		11	5		1		6		4	9					
33	11	Chesterfield	0-0		6543		2	3	10			8*		9		11	5		1	12	6		4	7					
34	14	Plymouth Argyle	1-2	Seal	8660		2	3	7*					10		11	5		1	8	6	12	4	9					
35	18	ROTHERHAM UNITED	1-1	Greenwood	7383		2	3	7			8*		10	12	11	5		1		6		4	9					
36	21	PORT VALE	0-0		4048		2	3	7*			8		10	12	11	5		1		6		4	9					
37	25	Halifax Town	0-2		2702		2	3	7			8*		10		11	5		1		6		4	9					
38	Apr 1	BOLTON WANDERERS	1-0	Boardman	4146		2	3	8			12		10		11	5		1		7*		4	9					
39	3	Rochdale	2-0	Seal, Mahoney	3838		2	3	8					10*	6	11	5		1		7	12	4	9					
40	4	BRIGHTON & HOVE ALB	0-1		6772		2	3	8					10*	6	11	5		1		7	12	4	9					
41	8	BLACKBURN ROVERS	0-0		4509		2	3	8					10	6*	11	5		1		7	12	4	9					
42	15	Bournemouth	0-0		13976		2	3	8			6		10		11*	5		1	12	7		4	9					
43	17	Wrexham	0-2		4285		2	3	8	12		6		10		11*	5		1		7		4	9					
44	22	NOTTS COUNTY	2-1	Seal 2	6264		2	3	8			6		10			5		1		7		4	9		11			
45	24	Tranmere Rovers	0-0		3764		2	3	8			6		10			5		1		7		4	9		11			
46	29	Port Vale	0-1		2614		2	3	8	12		6		10			5		1		7		4	9		11*			
		Apps				9	46	45	39	12	6	34	18	43	34	42	42	7	37	17	29	8	27	16	6	9	3	4	1
		Goals						2	3			3	4	12	1							2		1	2	1			1	

F.A. Cup

	Date	Opponent	Res	Scorers	Att	Mu	Bo	Le	Wa	Se	Mi	Sh	Wi	St	Tu	Br	Ma	Gr
R1	Nov 20	Rochdale	3-1	Winstanley 2, Seal	5185	2	3	10	7	9	6	11	5	1	4	8		
R2	Dec 11	CHESTERFIELD	0-0		11537	2	3	8*	12	9	10	11	5	1		6	7	4
rep	15	Chesterfield	0-1		13954	2	3	9	12	10*	6	11	5	1	4	7		8

F.L. Cup

	Date	Opponent	Res	Scorers	Att	Bk	Mu	Bo	Bd	Ra	Ho	Le	Wa	Se	Mi	Sh	Wi	Ea
R1	Aug 18	HARTLEPOOL	0-0		5985	1	2	3	4	5	6	7	8	9	10			11
rep	23	Hartlepool	1-0	Howard	9577	1	2	3	4		6	7	8	9	10	11	5	
R2	Sep 8	Arsenal	0-1		27284	1	2	3	4		6		8	9	10	11	5	7

R1 replay a.e.t.

		P	W	D	L	F	A	W	D	L	F	A	Pts
1	Aston Villa	46	20	1	2	45	10	12	5	6	40	22	70
2	Brighton & Hove A.	46	15	5	3	39	18	12	6	5	43	29	65
3	Bournemouth	46	16	6	1	43	13	7	10	6	30	24	62
4	Notts County	46	16	3	4	42	19	9	9	5	32	25	62
5	Rotherham United	46	12	8	3	46	25	8	7	8	23	27	55
6	Bristol Rovers	46	17	2	4	54	26	4	10	9	21	30	54
7	Bolton Wanderers	46	11	8	4	25	13	6	8	9	26	28	50
8	Plymouth Argyle	46	13	6	4	43	26	7	4	12	31	38	50
9	Walsall	46	12	8	3	38	16	3	10	10	24	41	48
10	Blackburn Rovers	46	14	4	5	39	22	5	5	13	15	35	47
11	Oldham Athletic	46	14	4	8	37	35	6	7	10	22	28	45
12	Shrewsbury Town	46	13	5	5	50	29	4	5	14	23	36	44
13	Chesterfield	46	10	5	8	25	23	8	3	12	32	34	44
14	Swansea City	46	10	6	7	27	21	7	4	12	19	38	44
15	Port Vale	46	10	10	3	27	21	3	5	15	16	38	41
16	Wrexham	46	10	5	8	33	26	6	3	14	26	37	40
17	Halifax Town	46	11	6	6	31	22	2	6	15	17	39	38
18	Rochdale	46	11	7	5	35	26	1	6	16	22	57	37
19	York City	46	8	8	7	32	22	4	4	15	25	44	36
20	Tranmere Rovers	46	9	7	7	34	30	1	9	13	16	41	36
21	Mansfield Town	46	5	12	6	19	26	3	8	12	22	37	36
22	BARNSLEY	46	6	10	7	23	30	3	8	12	9	34	36
23	Torquay United	46	8	6	9	31	31	2	6	15	10	38	32
24	Bradford City	46	6	8	9	27	32	5	2	16	18	45	32

1972/73   14th in Division 4

League matches

#	Mon	Date	Opponent	Score	Scorers	Att	Stewart G	Murphy BL	Chambers PM	Greenwood PG	Winstanley E	Boardman G	Earnshaw RI	Brown KG	Lea L	Sharp F	Mahoney B	Hopkinson A	Butler MA	Pettit RJ	Millar A	Martin P	O'Connor D	Doyle R	Arblaster BM	McMahon K	Dean N	Boyle IR	Senior S	Yates D	Wood CC	Tingay P	Cole R
1	Aug	12	Bradford City	1-3	Lea	3928	1	2	3	4	5	6*	7	8	10	11											9	12					
2		19	CAMBRIDGE UNITED	3-1	Sharp, Boardman, Lea	2808	1	2	3	4	5	6	7	8	10	11											9						
3		25	Stockport County	0-2		3923	1	2	3	4	5	6		8	7	11	12										10*	9					
4		29	DONCASTER ROVERS	4-2	Sharp, Lea, Boardman, Hopkinson	3377	1	2	3	4	5	6			10	11	9	8										7					
5	Sep	2	GILLINGHAM	1-1	Sharp	3113	1	2	3	4	5	6		8	11	10	9										7*	12					
6		9	Southport	0-1		2781	1	2	3	7	5	6		12	10	11	9*	8		4													
7		16	COLCHESTER UNITED	4-0	Greenwood 2, Mahoney 2	2514	1	2	3	7*	5	6			10	11	9	8		4	12												
8		19	Hereford United	2-1	Lea 2	6857	1		3	2	5	6		12	10	11	9	8*		4	7												
9		23	Mansfield Town	1-3	Winstanley	5997	1		3	2	5	6		7	8	11*	9			4	10							12					
10		26	CREWE ALEXANDRA	2-2	Winstanley, Lea	3082	1		3	6	5			8	10	11				4	7						9*	12	2				
11		30	CHESTER	0-0		2998	1		3	6		9		8		11				4	10*	12							5	7			
12	Oct	7	PETERBOROUGH UTD.	3-2	Martin, O'Connor 2	2689	1	2	3	4	5				9	7				6	10	11	8										
13		11	Workington	2-3	Lea 2	1347		2	3	6	5				10	8				4	7	11	9	1									
14		14	Northampton Town	2-2	Martin 2	3013		2	3	6					9	7				4	10*	11	9	1					5	12			
15		21	DARLINGTON	0-2		2961		2	3	6			12		10	8				4	7	11	9	1					5*				
16		24	TORQUAY UNITED	0-0		2460		2	3	6	5		7		10*	8	12			4		11	9	1									
17		28	Aldershot	2-0	Martin, O'Connor	4761		2	3	4	5	6			9	7				8		11	10	1									
18	Nov	4	Crewe Alexandra	0-1		1913		2	3	6	5				10*	8	7	12		4		11	9	1									
19		11	HEREFORD UNITED	0-0		3040		2	3	6	5				8	7	9			4		11	10	1									
20		25	NEWPORT COUNTY	2-1	Lea 2	2278		2	3	4	5				8	7				6	10	11	9	1									
21	Dec	2	Exeter City	1-2	Martin	3882		2	3	4	5				8	7				6	10	11	9	1									
22		8	HARTLEPOOL	2-1	Lea, Mahoney	1897	1	2	3	6	5				8	7*	12			4	10	11	9										
23		16	READING	0-0		2393	1	2	3	6	5				8	7*				4	10	11	12										
24		23	Lincoln City	2-1	Pettit, Earnshaw	4029	1	2	3	4	5		12	7	8	9				6	10	11*											
25		26	MANSFIELD TOWN	1-1	Brown	5900	1	2	3	4	5		7	6	11	9	8				10												
26		30	Cambridge United	1-1	Winstanley	3864	1	2	3	6	5			8	7	4	9*				10		12										
27	Jan	6	STOCKPORT COUNTY	1-3	Mahoney	2864	1	2	3	6	5		7	6	11	9	8*			12	10												
28		13	Torquay United	0-0		1825	1	2	3	6	5				8	11	10			4	12	9	7*										
29		20	Gillingham	1-5	Martin	2550	1		3	6					8	7*	11	9		4	10	12							5	2			
30		27	SOUTHPORT	0-1		2867	1	2	3	6			12	4	8	11*	9			5	10	7											
31	Feb	6	WORKINGTON	1-0	Winstanley	2096	1	2	3	6	5				10	8	11	9					7		4								
32		10	Colchester United	2-1	Lea, Mahoney	3148	1	2	3	6	5				7	9	11	10					8		4								
33		17	BRADFORD CITY	1-2	Butler	4949	1	2	3	6	5				7	8	11	9					10		4								
34		24	Reading	0-0		5560		2	3	10	5				8	7	11		9	6				1	4						1		
35	Mar	2	Peterborough United	3-6	Sharp, Butler, Brown	5253		2	3	10	5				7	8	11		9	6				1	4								
36		6	Bury	1-2	Butler	3283		2	3	10	5				7	8	11	12	9	6				1	4*								
37		10	NORTHAMPTON T	2-0	Chambers, Butler	2244		2	3	10	5				7	8	11		9	6				1	4							1	
38		17	Darlington	0-0		1628		2	3	10	5				7	8	11		9	6				1	4							1	
39		24	ALDERSHOT	0-2		2100		2	3	10	5				7	8*	11	12	9	6				1	4							1	
40		31	Newport County	1-1	Butler	4757		2	3	6	5				8	10	11		9	4				1								1	
41	Apr	6	EXETER CITY	1-1	Butler	1638		2	3	10	5				7	8			9	6			11	1	4							1	
42		14	Hartlepool	4-1	Butler 3, O'Connor	2448		2	3	6	5				10				9	4			11		7	1						1	
43		20	Chester	0-0		2284		2	3	6	5				8	10*			9	4	12		11		7	1						1	
44		21	BURY	0-1		2741		2	3	6	5				8			9	10	4			11		7	1						1	
45		24	LINCOLN CITY	4-1	O'Connor, Hopkinson, Brown, Greenwood	2807		2	3	6	5				8		10	9					11		7	1							4
46		27	Doncaster Rovers	0-0		2721		2	3	6	5*				8		10	9		12			11		7	1							4
Apps							24	42	46	46	42	11	7	32	38	40	23	11	14	34	23	18	20	17	13	5	4	6	2	2	1	8	2
Goals									1	3	4	2	1	3	12	4	5	2	9	1		6	5									

F.A. Cup

	Mon	Date	Opponent	Score	Scorers	Att	Stewart G	Murphy BL	Chambers PM	Greenwood PG	Winstanley E	Boardman G	Earnshaw RI	Brown KG	Lea L	Sharp F	Mahoney B	Hopkinson A	Butler MA	Pettit RJ	Millar A	Martin P	O'Connor D	Doyle R
R1	Nov	18	HALIFAX TOWN	1-1	Lea	4330		2	3	4	5				8	7	9			6	10	11		1
rep		21	Halifax Town	1-2	Kemp (og)	2461		2	3	4	5		12		8	7*	9			6	10	11		1

F.L. Cup

	Mon	Date	Opponent	Score	Scorers	Att	Stewart G	Murphy BL	Chambers PM	Greenwood PG	Winstanley E	Boardman G	Earnshaw RI	Brown KG	Lea L	Sharp F	Dean N	Boyle IR
R1	Aug	16	GRIMSBY TOWN	0-0		4292	1	2	3	4	5	6	7	8	10	11	9	
rep		22	Grimsby Town	0-2		12383	1	2	3	4	5	6	7*	8	10	11	9	12

Division 4 final table

		P	W	D	L	F	A	W	D	L	F	A	Pts
1	Southport	46	17	4	2	40	19	9	6	8	31	29	62
2	Hereford United	46	18	4	1	39	12	5	8	10	17	26	58
3	Cambridge United	46	15	6	2	40	23	5	11	7	27	34	57
4	Aldershot	46	14	6	3	33	14	8	6	9	27	24	56
5	Newport County	46	14	6	3	37	18	8	6	9	27	26	56
6	Mansfield Town	46	15	7	1	52	17	5	7	11	26	34	54
7	Reading	46	14	7	2	33	7	3	11	9	18	31	52
8	Exeter City	46	13	8	2	40	18	5	6	12	17	33	50
9	Gillingham	46	15	4	4	44	20	4	7	12	19	38	49
10	Lincoln City	46	12	7	4	38	27	4	9	10	26	30	48
11	Stockport County	46	14	7	2	38	18	4	5	14	15	35	48
12	Bury	46	11	7	5	37	19	3	11	9	21	32	46
13	Workington	46	15	7	1	44	20	2	5	16	15	41	46
14	BARNSLEY	46	9	8	6	32	24	5	8	10	26	36	44
15	Chester	46	11	6	6	40	19	3	9	11	21	33	43
16	Bradford City	46	11	6	6	42	25	4	5	14	19	40	43
17	Doncaster Rovers	46	10	8	5	28	19	5	4	14	21	39	42
18	Torquay United	46	8	10	5	23	17	4	7	12	21	30	41
19	Peterborough Utd.	46	10	8	5	42	29	4	5	14	29	47	41
20	Hartlepool	46	8	10	5	17	15	4	7	12	17	34	41
21	Crewe Alexandra	46	7	8	8	18	23	2	10	11	20	38	36
22	Colchester United	46	8	8	7	36	28	2	3	18	12	48	31
23	Northampton Town	46	7	6	10	24	30	3	5	15	16	43	31
24	Darlington	46	5	9	9	28	41	2	6	15	14	44	29

Season 1972/73
Back row: Chambers, Millar, Arblaster, Greenwood, Winstanley, Martin
Front row: McMahon, Turner, Dean, Brown, Stewart, Mahoney, Murphy, Sharp

Season 1973/74
Back row: Winstanley, Gorry, Collingwood, Boyle, Cole, Burke, Gill.
Centre row: Murphy, Hopkinson, Millar, Turner, Arblaster, Stewart, Parry, Yates, unknown, Lea.
Front row: Chambers, Greenwood, Mahoney, Brown, Butler, O'Connor, Doyle, Pettit.
Sitting on grass: Both unknown.

1973/74 — 13th in Division 4

League (Division 4)

#	Date		Opponent	Score	Scorers	Att
1	Aug	25	COLCHESTER UNITED	0-1		2717
2	Sep	1	Scunthorpe United	0-3		3612
3		8	MANSFIELD TOWN	1-1	Brown	2487
4		11	Doncaster Rovers	0-1		3070
5		15	Torquay United	1-1	Millar	3583
6		18	LINCOLN CITY	0-1		2778
7		22	STOCKPORT COUNTY	4-0	Lea (pen), Butler, Millar, Manning	2552
8		29	Brentford	1-5	Butler	5010
9	Oct	3	Lincoln City	1-1	Butler	3841
10		6	BRADFORD CITY	2-2	Butler, Manning	4082
11		13	Workington	0-1		1026
12		20	NEWPORT COUNTY	1-1	Manning	2274
13		23	DONCASTER ROVERS	2-0	Manning, O'Connor	3301
14		27	Swansea City	0-2		2669
15	Nov	3	BURY	3-2	Butler 2, Greenwood	3265
16		10	Exeter City	1-6	Butler	4697
17		13	Northampton Town	1-2	Butler	4299
18		17	CREWE ALEXANDRA	2-1	Greenwood, Manning	2483
19	Dec	8	Hartlepool	2-1	Brown, Butler	1101
20		22	BRENTFORD	2-1	Butler 2	2458
21		26	Rotherham United	1-2	Mahoney	6243
22		29	Mansfield Town	2-2	Lea 2	4141
23	Jan	1	SCUNTHORPE UNITED	5-0	Butler 3, Mahoney, Brown	6158
24		5	Gillingham	1-1	Mahoney	6825
25		12	TORQUAY UNITED	1-0	Lea (pen)	5102
26		19	Colchester United	0-2		5793
27		27	CHESTER	1-1	Butler	8511
28	Feb	3	READING	3-2	Butler, Doyle, Mahoney	6218
29		10	Stockport County	1-1	Millar	2776
30		17	WORKINGTON	4-0	Mahoney, Doyle, Butler, Lea	5697
31		23	Bradford City	0-3		5716
32		24	DARLINGTON	1-0	Doyle	6057
33	Mar	3	ROTHERHAM UNITED	1-0	Butler	6490
34		10	SWANSEA CITY	1-0	Butler	4757
35		17	Newport County	0-1		1808
36		20	Reading	0-1		7012
37		23	EXETER CITY	3-0	Doyle, Lea, Mahoney	3284
38		26	GILLINGHAM	3-1	Turner, Millar, Butler	5132
39		30	Bury	0-2		4420
40	Apr	3	Chester	1-3	Butler	2144
41		6	NORTHAMPTON T	0-2		3646
42		13	Crewe Alexandra	1-0	Brown	1491
43		15	Peterborough United	0-3		10328
44		16	PETERBOROUGH UTD.	0-0		4834
45		20	HARTLEPOOL	2-0	Millar, Manning	3555
46		27	Darlington	2-4	Chambers, Brown	2563

Appearances and goals (shirt numbers; * = substitute)

#	Arblaster BM	Murphy BL	Chambers PM	Pettit RJ	Cole R	Greenwood PG	Doyle R	Mahoney B	Butler MA	Millar A	Lea L	Boyle IR	Brown KG	Yates D	O'Connor D	Manning JJ	Hopkinson A	Stewart G	Turner P	Collingwood G	Parry S
1	1	2	3	4	5	6	7	8	9	10	11										
2	1	2	3	4		6	7	8	9	10	11	5									
3	1	2	3			6		4	8	9	10	11	5	7							
4	1		3			6	7		9	10	11	5		4	2	8					
5	1		3			6	4	10*	9	8	11	5	7	2	12						
6	1		3			6	7	8	9	10	11	5		4	2						
7	1		3			6	4	8	7	10	11	5			2	9					
8	1		3			6	4	8	7	10	11	5			2	9					
9	1		3			6	4			10	11	5			2	9	8				
10	1		3			6	4	8*	7	10	11	5		12	2	9					
11			3			6	4	12	8	10	11*	5	7		2			9	1		
12			3			6	4	8	7	10		5		12	2	11*		9	1		
13			3			6	4	8*		10		5		12	2	11		9	1		
14			3	12		6	4			7	11	5		8	2	9		10*	1		
15			3			6	4	8	9	11		5		7	2			10	1		
16			3	9		6	4	8	7	10	12	5		11*	2			12	1		
17			3	5		6	4		7*		10	12		11	2	8		9	1		
18			3	5		6	4	9		11	10			7	2	8			1		
19			3	5		6	4			7	10	8		11	2			9	1		
20			3	5			4	10	7	8	9			11	2			6	1		
21			3			6	4*	9	7	10	8			11	2			5	1	12	
22			5			6*		9	7	10	8			11	2	12			1		
23			5	3				9	7	10	8			11	2			1		6	
24			4	6					9	7	10	8*		11	2	12	5		1	3	
25			5	3		6	4	8	7	11	9			10	2			5	1		
26			5	3		6	4*		9	7	10	8		11	2	12			1		
27			5	3		6	4		9	7	10	8		11	2				1		
28			5*	3		6	4	9	7	10	8			11	2				1		
29		12		3		6	4	9	7*	10	8			11	2			5	1		
30			3			6	4	9	7	10	8			11	2			5	1		
31			3			6	4	10	9	11	8			7	2			5	1		
32			3			6	4	9	7	10	8			11	2			5	1		
33			3					9	7	10	8			11	2			5	1		4
34			3	6				9	7	10	8			11	2			5	1		6
35		4	3					9	7	10*	8			11	2			5	1	6	12
36			5	6			3	9	7	10	8			11	2			4	1		
37			3	6			4	8	7	11	9			10	2			5	1		
38			3	6			4	9	7*	10	8			11	2			5	1	12	
39			3	6		5	4	8	7	10	9			11*	2				1	12	
40			3	5		6	4*	9	7	10	8			11	2				1	12	
41			3	5		6	4	9	7	10	9			11	2				1		
42			3	6		12	4*	8	7	11	9			10					1	2	
43			3	6		5	4	9	7	10	8			11					1	2	
44			3			6	4	8	7	10	9			11	2			5	1		
45			3			6	4	8	7	11	9			10	2			5	1		
46			3	6			4	9	7	10	8*			11	2			5	12		1
Apps	10	11	46	17	1	38	43	41	45	46	41	15	41	41	9	32	1	35	10	2	1
Goals		1				2	4	6	21	5	6		5			1		6	1		

F.A. Cup

#	Date		Opponent	Score	Scorers	Att
R1	Nov	24	Chesterfield	0-0		5505
rep		28	CHESTERFIELD	2-1	Manning 2	3421
R2	Dec	15	BRADFORD CITY	1-1	Butler	6660
rep		19	Bradford City	1-2	Brown	4954

#	Chambers PM	Pettit RJ	Greenwood PG	Doyle R	Butler MA	Millar A	Lea L	Yates D	O'Connor D	Stewart G	Turner P
R1	3	5	6	4	8	11	10	7	2	9	1
rep	3	5	6	4	7	10	8	11	2	9	1
R2	3	5	6	4	7	10	8	11	2	9	1
rep	3	5*	6	4	12	7	10	8		9	1

F.L. Cup

#	Date		Opponent	Score	Scorers	Att
R1	Aug	28	Halifax Town	1-1	Mahoney	2768
rep	Sep	4	HALIFAX TOWN	0-1		4168

#	Arblaster BM	Murphy BL	Chambers PM	Pettit RJ	Cole R	Greenwood PG	Doyle R	Mahoney B	Butler MA	Millar A	Lea L	Boyle IR	Brown KG	O'Connor D
R1	1	2	3	4	5	6	7	8	9	10	11			
rep	1	2	3			6	7	9*	8	10	11	5	4	12

Final Division 4 table

		P	W	D	L	F	A	W	D	L	F	A	Pts
1	Peterborough Utd.	46	19	4	0	49	10	8	7	8	26	28	65
2	Gillingham	46	16	5	2	51	16	9	7	7	39	33	62
3	Colchester United	46	16	5	2	46	14	8	7	8	27	22	60
4	Bury	46	18	3	2	51	14	6	8	9	30	35	59
5	Northampton Town	46	14	7	2	39	14	6	6	11	24	34	53
6	Reading	46	11	9	3	37	13	5	10	8	21	24	51
7	Chester	46	13	6	4	31	19	4	9	10	23	36	49
8	Bradford City	46	14	7	2	45	20	3	7	13	13	32	48
9	Newport County	46	13	6	4	39	23	3	8	12	17	42	45
10	Exeter City	45	12	5	6	37	20	6	3	13	21	35	44
11	Hartlepool	46	11	4	8	29	16	5	8	10	19	31	44
12	Lincoln City	46	10	8	5	40	30	6	4	13	23	37	44
13	BARNSLEY	46	15	5	3	42	16	2	5	16	16	48	44
14	Swansea City	46	11	6	6	28	15	5	5	13	17	31	43
15	Rotherham United	46	10	9	4	33	22	5	4	14	23	36	43
16	Torquay United	46	11	7	5	37	23	2	10	11	15	34	43
17	Mansfield Town	46	13	8	2	47	24	0	9	14	15	45	43
18	Scunthorpe United	45	12	7	3	33	17	2	5	16	14	47	42
19	Brentford	46	9	7	7	31	20	3	9	11	17	30	40
20	Darlington	46	9	8	6	29	24	4	5	14	11	38	39
21	Crewe Alexandra	46	11	5	7	28	30	3	5	15	15	41	38
22	Doncaster Rovers	46	10	7	6	32	22	2	4	17	15	58	35
23	Workington	46	10	8	5	33	26	1	5	17	10	48	35
24	Stockport County	46	4	12	7	22	25	3	8	12	22	44	34

1974/75 — 15th in Division 4

#		Date	Opponent	Res	Scorers	Att	Stewart G	Yates D	Chambers PM	Doyle R	Pickering J	Murphy BL	Butler MA	O'Riley P	Manning JJ	Millar A	Brown KG	Lea L	Mahoney B	Collingwood G	Turner P	Dungworth JH	Peachey JM	Price PW	Pickering MJ	Burke P	Sanderson P	Parry S	Riley G	Otulakowski A
1	Aug	17	EXETER CITY	1-0	Pickering	4979	1	2	3	4	5	6	7	8*	9	10	11	12												
2		24	Swansea City	3-0	Doyle, Mahoney, O'Riley	2421	1	2	3	4	5	6		8	9		7		10	11										
3		31	CHESTER	0-1		6181	1	2	3	4	5	6	12	7	9	10	11*		8											
4	Sep	3	SCUNTHORPE UNITED	2-2	Manning, Mahoney	5603	1	2	3	4	5		7		6	10	11		8	9										
5		7	Rochdale	1-3	Doyle	1376	1	2	3	4	5		7	12	6		11		8	9*	10									
6		13	STOCKPORT COUNTY	2-0	Lea, Butler	5115	1	2	3	4	5	6	7		12		11	8		9*	10									
7		17	CAMBRIDGE UNITED	1-1	Butler	6002	1	2	3	4	5	6	7		9		11	8	12	10*										
8		20	Southport	0-1		2246	1		3	4*	5	6	7	8	9		11		12	10	2									
9		25	Crewe Alexandra	1-1	Butler	4004	1		3	4	5	6	7	10	9		11	8*		12	2									
10		28	NEWPORT COUNTY	2-1	Pickering, Butler	4728	1		3	4	5	6	7		9	10	11	8			2									
11	Oct	1	Scunthorpe United	0-1		2582	1		3	4	5	6	7	12	9	10	11	8*			2									
12		5	WORKINGTON	0-1		4312	1		3	4	5	6	9*		12	10	11	7	8		2									
13		12	Darlington	0-0		2246	1	2	3	4	5	6					11	7	9				8							
14		15	MANSFIELD TOWN	1-3	Mahoney	4923	1	2	3	4		6		12	5*	10	7	11	9				8							
15		19	HARTLEPOOL	2-1	Shoulder (og), Butler	3135	1	2	3			6	7	9		10	11			5			8				4			
16		21	Mansfield Town	1-2	Butler	5291	1	2	3			12	6	8	9	10	11	7									4	5*		
17		26	Reading	3-0	Butler, O'Riley, Dungworth	5973	1	2	3	7	5	6	8	9*		10	11					12	4							
18	Nov	2	BRENTFORD	1-1	Doyle	4158	1	2	3	7	5	6	9	8		10	11						4							
19		9	Bradford City	0-2		4146	1	2	3	7	5	6	9	8*		10	11	12					4							
20		16	LINCOLN CITY	0-2		4567	1	2	3	12	5	6	7	8		10	11	9					4*							
21		30	Shrewsbury Town	1-3	Sanderson	3287		2	3	4	5	6				10	11							8	7		9	1		
22	Dec	7	TORQUAY UNITED	0-1		2861		2	3	4	5	6				10		7						9	8		11	1		
23		14	Exeter City	2-4	Price 2	2916		2	3	4	5	6				10	11	7					9	8				1		
24		21	NORTHAMPTON T	5-1	Brown, Peachey, Price, Yates, Millar	2666	1	2	3	4	5	6				10	11	7					9	8						
25		26	Stockport County	3-0	Price 2, Yates	2389	1	2	3	4	5	6				10	11	7					9	8						
26	Jan	4	SOUTHPORT	3-0	Price 3	4321	1	2	3	4	5	6				10	11	7					9	8						
27		11	Torquay United	1-1	Peachey	2401	1	2	3	4	5					10	11	7					9	8	6					
28		14	Cambridge United	0-2		2906	1	2	3	4	5					10	11	7					9	8	6					
29		18	SHREWSBURY TOWN	1-0	Price	5376	1	2	3	4	5	6				10	11	7					9	8						
30		24	Doncaster Rovers	1-1	Peachey	4153	1	2	3	4	5	6				10	11	7					9	8						
31	Feb	1	BRADFORD CITY	2-2	Butler 2	7492	1	2	3	4	5	6	12			10*	11	7					9	8						
32		8	Brentford	0-3		5080	1	2	3	4	5	6				10								11		7				
33		15	DONCASTER ROVERS	0-1		6451	1	2	3	4	5	6					11	7					9	8	6					
34		22	Lincoln City	0-3		6464		2	3	4	5		7*			10	11	12					9	8	6			1		
35		25	ROTHERHAM UNITED	1-1	Butler	7810	1	2	3	4	5		7			10	12	11					9*	8	6					
36	Mar	1	Chester	1-2	Butler	5160	1	2	3		5		9			11	7	10					4	8	6					
37		8	CREWE ALEXANDRA	1-1	Chambers	3754	1	2	3	4		6	10				7	11				12	9	8*	5					
38		15	Newport County	4-3	Doyle (pen), Butler 3	1773	1	2	3	4	5	10	9				8	7					11		6					
39		22	ROCHDALE	5-3	Doyle (pen), Butler 3, Peachey	3594	1	2	3	4	5	8	10				7	11					9		6					
40		28	Northampton Town	1-2	Price	2594	1	2	3	4	5	7	8				11*	10					9	12	6					
41		31	Rotherham United	0-2		9889	1	2	3	4	5		8			10	11	7					9		6					
42	Apr	5	READING	2-0	Butler, Doyle (pen)	2772	1	2	3	4	5		9			10	7	11						8	6					
43		12	Workington	2-1	Price, Butler	1661	1	2	3	4	5		9*			8	11	7						10	12	6				
44		19	DARLINGTON	1-1	Lea	3037	1	2	3	4	5					11	10	7					9	8	6					
45		22	SWANSEA CITY	1-0	Riley	3014	1	2	3	4	5	7				10	11						9	8	6*				12	
46		26	Hartlepool	3-4	Brown, Price, Peachey	2159	1	2	3	4	5	6		12			7						11	10					9*	8
			Apps				42	41	46	43	43	35	30	14	13	34	44	38	10	12	7	3	25	23	14	2	2	4	2	1
			Goals					2	1	6	2		19	2	1	1	2	2	3			1	5	12			1		1	

One own goal

F.A. Cup

| R1 | Nov | 23 | HALIFAX TOWN | 1-2 | Brown | 5314 | 1 | 2 | 3 | 4 | 5 | 6 | 7* | | | 10 | 11 | 8 | | | | 9 | 12 | | | | | | | |

F.L. Cup

| R1 | Aug | 20 | HALIFAX TOWN | 0-1 | | 5139 | 1 | 2 | 3 | 4 | 5 | 6 | 7 | 12 | 9* | 10 | 11 | 8 | | | | | | | | | | | | |

		P	W	D	L	F	A	W	D	L	F	A	Pts
1	Mansfield Town	46	17	6	0	55	15	11	6	6	35	25	68
2	Shrewsbury Town	46	16	3	4	46	18	10	7	6	34	25	62
3	Rotherham United	46	13	7	3	40	19	9	8	6	31	22	59
4	Chester	46	17	5	1	48	9	6	6	11	16	29	57
5	Lincoln City	46	14	8	1	47	14	7	7	9	32	34	57
6	Cambridge United	46	15	5	3	43	16	5	9	9	19	28	54
7	Reading	46	13	6	4	38	20	8	4	11	25	27	52
8	Brentford	46	15	6	2	38	14	3	7	13	15	31	49
9	Exeter City	46	14	3	6	33	24	5	8	10	27	39	49
10	Bradford City	46	10	5	8	32	21	7	8	8	24	30	47
11	Southport	46	13	7	3	36	19	2	10	11	20	37	47
12	Newport County	46	13	5	5	43	30	6	4	13	25	45	47
13	Hartlepool	46	13	6	4	40	24	3	5	15	12	38	43
14	Torquay United	46	10	7	6	30	25	4	7	12	16	36	42
15	BARNSLEY	46	10	7	6	34	24	5	4	14	28	41	41
16	Northampton Town	46	12	6	5	43	22	3	5	15	24	51	41
17	Doncaster Rovers	46	10	9	4	41	29	4	3	16	24	50	40
18	Crewe Alexandra	46	9	9	5	22	16	2	9	12	12	31	40
19	Rochdale	46	9	9	5	35	22	4	4	15	24	53	39
20	Stockport County	46	10	8	5	26	27	2	6	15	17	43	38
21	Darlington	46	11	4	8	38	27	2	6	15	16	40	36
22	Swansea City	46	9	4	10	25	31	6	2	15	21	42	36
23	Workington	46	7	5	11	23	29	3	6	14	13	37	31
24	Scunthorpe United	46	7	8	8	27	29	0	7	16	14	49	29

Season 1974/75
Back row: Parry, Stewart
(L to R): Doyle, Murphy, Pickering, Gorry, Gill, Chambers, Millar, Butler, Brown, Yates, O'Riley, Manning, Riley, unknown, Lea, Harris, Mahoney, unknown, Turner, unknown, Collingwood, Pickering, Burke

Season 1975/76
Back row: Doyle, Peachey, Burke.
Middle row: Sanderson, Price, Reynolds, Springett, Pickering, Gorry, Butler.
Front row: Walker, Yates, Chambers, Murphy, Brown, McGettigan, Millar, Lea.

1975/76 — 12th in Division 4

#	Mon	Date	Opponent	Score	Scorers	Att	Springett PJ	Yates D	Chambers PM	Doyle R	Burke P	Murphy BL	Millar A	Butler MA	Price PW	Walker PG	Brown KG	Peachey JM	Pickering MJ	Lea L	Harris LH	Gorry MC	Saunders JG	Felton GM	Otulakowski A	Riley G	Butler I	Deere SH
1	Aug	16	WATFORD	1-0	Butler M	3814	1	2	3	4	5	6	7	8	9*	10	11	12										
2		23	Southport	0-0		1230	1		3	4	5	2	7*	8	9	10	11	12	6									
3		30	NORTHAMPTON T	3-1	Butler M 2, Peachey	3649	1		3	4	5	2	11	9	10	8	7*	12	6									
4	Sep	6	Brentford	0-1		5605	1		3	4	5	2	9	10	11*	7	8	12	6									
5		12	CREWE ALEXANDRA	1-1	Butler M	4367	1	2	3	4	5	10*	7	8			11	9	6								12	
6		19	Tranmere Rovers	0-1		2638	1		3	4	5	2	7	8			11	9	6	10								
7		24	DONCASTER ROVERS	0-1		6681	1		3	4	5	2	7	8		10*	12	9	6	11								
8		27	WORKINGTON	0-0		2959	1		3	4	5	2	11	9		8	7*	6	12	10								
9	Oct	4	Bournemouth	1-1	Chambers	4408	1	2	3	4	5		8	7	9	10		6		11								
10		11	Newport County	0-1		3043	1	2	3	4	5		11	10	7	8		12	6		9*							
11		18	READING	4-2	Butler I, Peachey, Price 2	2938	1	2	3	4	5		6	7	8		10	9	6								11	
12		21	EXETER CITY	0-0		3741	1	2	3	4		5	7		8		10	9	6								11	
13		25	Hartlepool	0-1		2350	1	2	3	4	5		6	7	8		11*	9						12			10	5
14	Nov	1	SWANSEA CITY	0-0		2833	1	2	3	4	5	10*	11		8				12	9							7	6
15		5	Torquay United	0-2		1615	1	2	3	4	5	8	7			10	12				9						11*	6
16		8	Darlington	0-2		2066	1	2	3	4	5		11	7					6		8				9			10
17		15	STOCKPORT COUNTY	2-2	Butler M, Otulakowski	2758	1	2	3	4	5		11	7			9		6		10				8			
18		29	HUDDERSFIELD T	2-3	Brown, Price	5131	1			4	5	2	11	7	8		10		6				3		9			
19	Dec	6	Bradford City	1-2	Otulakowski	3285	1		3	4	5	6	11	9*		12	8					2			10	7		
20		20	Cambridge United	1-1	Harris	2180	1		3	4		12		8		10	11		6			9	2	5	7*			
21		26	ROCHDALE	2-1	Brown, Millar	3486	1		3	4		12		8		10*	11		6			9	2	5	7			
22		27	Lincoln City	1-2	Butler M	12074	1			4		2		10	8		11		6			9	3	5	7			
23	Jan	3	SCUNTHORPE UNITED	1-0	Doyle (pen)	2947	1		3	4			11	10	9	7			6			12	5		8			
24		10	Northampton Town	0-5		6132	1		3	4			11*	7	9	10			6			12	2	5	8			
25		17	TRANMERE ROVERS	1-0	James (og)	2813	1	2	3	4			11	8*	10				6			9	12	5	7			
26		23	Crewe Alexandra	1-1	Price	2291	1	2	3	4			10	9	8		11		6					5	7			
27		31	Exeter City	0-2		2449	1	2	3	4			7	10	9	11*			6			12		5	8			
28	Feb	7	TORQUAY UNITED	0-0		2353	1	2	3	4			11*	7	9	10			6			12		5	8			
29		14	Darlington	1-0	Price	2564	1			4	5	2	11		9	10			6			3		7	8			
30		20	Stockport County	1-1	Gorry	2707	1			4	5	2		8	9		11		6			3		7	10			
31		24	Doncaster Rovers	2-2	Felton, Butler M	8250	1			4	5	2		8	9		11		6			3		7	10			
32		28	Hartlepool	3-1	Price, Doyle (pen), Gorry	2772	1			4	5	2		8	9*		11		6			3	12	7	10			
33	Mar	5	Swansea City	1-3	Butler M	2533	1			4	5	2		8	9	12	11		6			3		7*	10			
34		9	BOURNEMOUTH	2-0	Brown, Felton	2674	1			4	5	2		8	9		11		6			3		7	10			
35		13	NEWPORT COUNTY	3-1	Peachey 2, Doyle	2587	1			4	5	2		8			11	9	6			3		7	10			
36		17	Reading	0-0		6709	1		3	4	5	2		8			11	9	6					7	10			
37		20	Huddersfield Town	2-1	Burke, Brown	10049	1		3	4	5	2		8			11	9	6					7	10			
38		27	BRADFORD CITY	1-1	Peachey	5330	1		3	4	5	2		8			11	9	6					7	10			
39		30	CAMBRIDGE UNITED	4-0	Peachey, Price, Brown, Seddon (og)	3190	1			4		2		8			11	9	6			3	5	7	10			
40	Apr	3	Watford	0-1		4203	1			4		2		8			11	9	6			12	3	5	10	7*		
41		7	Workington	7-1	Peachey 3, Price 2 (1p), Saunders, Doyle (p)	894	1			4		2		8			11*	9	6			12	3	5	10	7		
42		10	BRENTFORD	1-1	Doyle (pen)	3877	1			4		2	12			8*	11	9	6				3	5	10	7		
43		17	Rochdale	0-0		1386	1			4		2		7		8*	11	9	6		12		3	5	10			
44		19	LINCOLN CITY	0-1		8697	1			4		2		7			11	9	6		8		3	5	10			
45		20	Scunthorpe United	0-1		4940	1			4		2		7			11	9	6		8		3	5	10			
46		24	SOUTHPORT	2-0	Peachey, Doyle	3119	1			4		2		8			11	9	6		7		3	5	10			
			Apps				46	15	29	46	26	37	29	31	31	13	40	24	41	9	18	22	17	12	31	4	5	4
			Goals						1	6	1		1	8	9		5	10			1	2	1	2	2		1	

Two own goals

F.A. Cup

Rnd	Mon	Date	Opponent	Score	Scorer	Att	Springett	Yates	Chambers	Doyle	Burke	Murphy	Millar	Butler MA	Price	Walker	Brown	Peachey	Pickering	Otulakowski
R1	Nov	22	Marine	1-3	Butler	2400	1	2	3	4	5		7*	9	8	10	12		6	11

F.L. Cup

Rnd	Mon	Date	Opponent	Score	Scorer	Att	Springett	Chambers	Doyle	Burke	Murphy	Millar	Butler MA	Price	Walker	Brown	Peachey	Pickering
R1/1	Aug	19	Huddersfield Town	1-2	Butler	4200	1	3	4	5	2	7*	8	9	10	11	12	6
R1/2		27	HUDDERSFIELD T	1-1	Price	6045	1	3	4	5	2	7	8	9	10	11		6

Division 4 Final Table

	Team	P	W	D	L	F	A	W	D	L	F	A	Pts
1	Lincoln City	46	21	2	0	71	15	11	8	4	40	24	74
2	Northampton Town	46	18	5	0	62	20	11	5	7	25	20	68
3	Reading	46	19	3	1	42	9	5	9	9	28	42	60
4	Tranmere Rovers	46	18	3	2	61	16	6	7	10	28	39	58
5	Huddersfield Town	46	11	6	6	28	17	10	8	5	28	24	56
6	Bournemouth	46	15	5	3	39	16	5	7	11	18	32	52
7	Exeter City	46	13	7	3	37	17	5	7	11	19	30	50
8	Watford	46	16	4	3	38	18	6	2	15	24	44	50
9	Torquay United	46	12	6	5	31	24	6	8	9	24	39	50
10	Doncaster Rovers	46	10	6	7	42	31	9	5	9	33	38	49
11	Swansea City	46	14	8	1	51	21	2	7	14	15	36	47
12	BARNSLEY	46	12	8	3	34	16	2	8	13	18	32	44
13	Cambridge United	46	7	10	6	36	28	7	5	11	22	34	43
14	Hartlepool	46	10	6	7	37	29	6	4	13	25	49	42
15	Rochdale	46	7	11	5	27	23	5	7	11	13	31	42
16	Crewe Alexandra	46	10	7	6	36	21	3	8	12	22	36	41
17	Bradford City	46	9	7	7	35	26	3	10	10	28	39	41
18	Brentford	46	12	7	4	37	18	2	6	15	19	42	41
19	Scunthorpe United	46	11	3	9	31	24	3	7	13	19	35	38
20	Darlington	46	11	7	5	30	14	3	3	17	18	43	38
21	Stockport County	46	8	7	8	23	23	5	5	13	20	53	38
22	Newport County	46	8	7	8	35	33	5	2	16	22	57	35
23	Southport	46	6	6	11	27	31	2	4	17	14	46	26
24	Workington	46	5	4	14	19	43	2	3	18	11	44	21

1976/77 6th in Division 4

#	Date	Opponent	Score	Scorers	Att	Springett PJ	Murphy BL	Gorry MC	Otulakowski A	Burke P	Pickering MJ	Felton GM	Peachey JM	Joicey B	Brown KG	Millar A	Price PW	Harris LH	Saunders JG	Warnock N	Pugh IG	Chambers PM	Lathan IG	Collins JL	Mallender G	Yates D	Wigg RG
1	Aug 21	Brentford	1-0	Millar	3903	1	2	3	4	5	6	7	8	9	10	11											
2	28	NEWPORT COUNTY	2-0	Gorry, Felton	4318	1	2	3	4	5	6	7	8	9	10	11											
3	Sep 4	Swansea City	1-2	Felton (pen)	3132	1	2	3	4	5	6	7	8	9	10	11											
4	11	DARLINGTON	1-1	Joicey	3530	1	2	3	4	5	6	7*	8	9	10	11	12										
5	17	Stockport County	1-2	Price	7923	1	2	3	4	5	6		9	10	11	8	7*	12									
6	25	BRADFORD CITY	2-2	Joicey 2	6609	1	2	3	4	5	6	7*	10	9	8	11		12									
7	Oct 2	HUDDERSFIELD T	2-1	Peachey, Joicey (pen)	7124	1	2	3	4		6		8	9	10	11			5	7							
8	9	Doncaster Rovers	1-2	Joicey	6707	1	2	3	4		6		8	9	10	11		12	5	7*							
9	16	ALDERSHOT	1-0	Joicey (pen)	4012	1	2	3	4		6		8	9	10	11			5	7							
10	19	CREWE ALEXANDRA	2-2	Millar, Harris	4242	1	2	3	4		6		8	9	10	11		12	5	7*							
11	22	Southport	0-1		2308	1	2	3	4	5	6		8	9	10	11		7*		12							
12	26	SOUTHEND UNITED	3-1	Peachey, Joicey 2	4532	1	2	3		5	6		8	9	10	11				7	4*				12		
13	30	Watford	0-1		5313	1	2				6	7	9	8	11	10			5				3			2	
14	Nov 3	Workington	1-0	Joicey	1229	1	2				6	7	9	8	11	10			5				3			2	
15	6	SCUNTHORPE UNITED	5-1	Letheran (og), Peachey 3, Joicey	4595	1	2				6		8	9	11	10			5	7*	12		3			2	
16	9	TORQUAY UNITED	2-1	Pugh, Peachey	5564	1	2				6		9	8	11	10			5	7	10		3			2	
17	13	Cambridge United	0-0		5138	1	2				6		9	8	11	10			5	7	4		3				
18	27	COLCHESTER UNITED	0-1		5814	1	2				6	7	9*	8	4	10	12		5	11			3				
19	Dec 18	HARTLEPOOL	3-0	Joicey 2, Brown	3667	1	2				6		8	9	10	11			5	7	4			3			
20	27	Crewe Alexandra	0-1		3724	1	2				6	7		9	11	10	8*		5		12	4		3			
21	29	HALIFAX TOWN	1-0	Joicey	5893	1	2				6			9	11	10	8		5	7	4			3			
22	Jan 8	Exeter City	0-1		3784	1	2				6	7	9	8	11	10	12		5		4*			3			
23	15	Torquay United	0-1		2141	1	2				6	7		8	4	11		9	5	11				3			
24	22	BRENTFORD	2-0	Pugh, Joicey	4095	1	2				6	7	12	8	11	10	9*		5		4			3			
25	25	Rochdale	3-2	Joicey, Peachey, Mountford (og)	2474	1	2				6	7	9	8	11	10			5		4			3			
26	29	BOURNEMOUTH	3-1	Chambers, Joicey 2	5558	1	2				6	7	9	8	11	10			5		4	3					
27	Feb 8	Scunthorpe United	2-1	Joicey 2	4698	1	2				6	7	9	8	11	10		12	5		4*			3			
28	12	SWANSEA CITY	1-0	Saunders	6750	1	2				6	7	9	8	11	10		12	5		4*			3			
29	19	Darlington	1-2	Saunders	3137	1	2				6	7	9	8	11	10*			5		4		12	3			
30	26	STOCKPORT COUNTY	1-0	Joicey	5828	1	2				6	7	9	8	11	10			5		4	3					
31	Mar 5	Bradford City	0-0		8834	1	2				6	7		8	11	10			5		4	3					9
32	9	WATFORD	1-1	Millar	7581	1	2				6	7		8	11	10			5		4	3					9
33	12	Huddersfield Town	0-1		11659	1	2				6	7*	12	8	11	10			5		4	3					9
34	19	DONCASTER ROVERS	1-1	Saunders	10180	1	2				6		9	8	11	10			5	7	4	3	7*				12
35	26	Aldershot	1-0	Warnock	2789	1	2				6		9	8	11	10			5	7	4			3			
36	28	Newport County	1-1	Peachey	2319	1	2				6		9	8	11	10			5	7	4			3			
37	Apr 2	SOUTHPORT	1-0	Joicey (pen)	4481	1	2				6		9	8	11	10*			5	7	4			3			12
38	9	Halifax Town	1-0	Peachey	3529	1	2				6		9	8	11	10			5	7	4	3					
39	11	WORKINGTON	4-0	Joicey (2 pens), Peachey, Brown	5823	1	2				6		9	8	11	10			5	7	4			3			
40	15	Southend United	1-1	Joicey	4903	1	2				6		9	8	11	10			5	7	4			3			
41	19	Bournemouth	0-1		2247	1	2				6		9	8	11	10			5	7	4			3			
42	22	CAMBRIDGE UNITED	2-1	Peachey 2	9146	1	2				6	7*	9	8	11	10			5		4			3			12
43	29	Colchester United	0-1		5802	1	2				6	7	9	8	11	10			5		4			3			
44	May 3	EXETER CITY	3-4	Felton, Pickering, Joicey	5293	1	2				6	7	9	8	11	10			5		4			3			
45	7	ROCHDALE	2-0	Joicey, Warnock	2531	1	2				6		9	8	11	10			5	7	4			3			
46	14	Hartlepool	2-0	Brown, Warnock	1274	1	2				6		9	8*	11	10			5	7	4			3			12
					Apps	46	46	12	10	8	45	24	41	46	46	45	8	8	40	23	26	9	7	25	1	4	6
					Goals		1				1	3	12	26	3	3		1	1	3	3	3	2	1			

Two own goals

F.A. Cup

R	Date	Opponent	Score	Scorers	Att	Springett	Murphy	Gorry	Otulakowski	Burke	Pickering	Felton	Peachey	Joicey	Brown	Millar	Price	Harris	Saunders	Warnock	Pugh	Chambers	Lathan	Collins
R1	Nov 20	BOSTON UNITED	3-1	Joicey 3 (1 pen)	7294	1	2				6		9	8	11	10	12		5	7*	4	3		
R2	Dec 11	Port Vale	0-3		5451	1	4				6	7	12	8	11	10*	9		5			3		2

F.L. Cup

R	Date	Opponent	Score	Scorers	Att	Springett	Murphy	Gorry	Otulakowski	Burke	Pickering	Felton	Peachey	Joicey	Brown	Millar	Price
R1/1	Aug 14	York City	0-0		2995	1	2	3	4	5	6	7	12	9	11	10	8*
R1/2	17	YORK CITY	0-0		4965	1	2	3	4	5	6	7	8	9	11	10	
rep	24	York City	2-1	Peachey 2	3542	1	2	3	4	5	6	7	8	9	11	10	
R2	Sep 1	West Ham United	0-3		17889	1	2	3	4	5	6	7	8	9	10	11*	12

R1 replay a.e.t.

Division 4 Final Table

		P	W	D	L	F	A	W	D	L	F	A	Pts
1	Cambridge United	46	16	5	2	57	18	10	8	5	30	22	65
2	Exeter City	46	17	5	1	40	13	8	7	8	30	33	62
3	Colchester United	46	19	2	2	51	14	6	7	10	26	29	59
4	Bradford City	46	16	7	0	51	18	7	6	10	27	33	59
5	Swansea City	46	18	3	2	60	30	7	5	11	32	38	58
6	BARNSLEY	46	16	5	2	45	18	7	4	12	17	21	55
7	Watford	46	15	7	1	46	13	3	8	12	21	37	51
8	Doncaster Rovers	46	16	2	5	47	25	5	7	11	24	40	51
9	Huddersfield Town	46	15	5	3	36	15	4	7	12	24	34	50
10	Southend United	46	11	9	3	35	19	4	10	9	17	26	49
11	Darlington	46	13	5	5	37	25	5	8	10	22	39	49
12	Crewe Alexandra	46	16	6	1	36	15	3	5	15	11	45	49
13	Bournemouth	46	13	8	2	39	13	2	10	11	15	31	48
14	Stockport County	46	10	10	3	29	19	3	9	11	24	38	45
15	Brentford	46	14	3	6	48	27	4	4	15	29	49	43
16	Torquay United	46	12	5	6	33	22	5	4	14	26	45	43
17	Aldershot	46	10	8	5	29	19	6	3	14	20	40	43
18	Rochdale	46	8	7	8	32	25	5	5	13	18	34	38
19	Newport County	46	11	6	6	33	21	3	4	16	9	37	38
20	Scunthorpe United	46	11	6	6	32	24	2	5	16	17	49	37
21	Halifax Town	46	11	6	6	36	18	0	8	15	11	40	36
22	Hartlepool	46	8	9	6	30	20	2	3	18	17	53	32
23	Southport	46	3	12	8	17	16	0	7	16	16	49	25
24	Workington	46	3	7	13	23	42	1	4	18	18	60	19

Season 1976/77
Back row: Young (Coach) Yates, Harris, Burke, Saunders, Springett, Peachey,
Joicey, Gorry, Pickering, Iley (Manager)
Front row: Felton, Chambers, Brown, Murphy, Otulakowski, Price, Millar, Riley

Season 1977/78
Back row: Warnock, Joicey, McCarthy, Saunders, Copley, Springett, Peachey, Burke, Wigg, Collier
Front row: Pugh, Chambers, Brown, Collins, Murphy, Price, Millar, Riley

League Matches

No	Month	Date	Opponent	Score	Scorers	Att
1	Aug	20	ROCHDALE	4-0	Murphy (pen), Little, Joicey, Price	3901
2		27	Swansea City	1-2	Wigg	6860
3	Sep	3	NEWPORT COUNTY	1-0	Price	4172
4		6	Darlington	2-0	Price, Wigg	2158
5		10	Aldershot	0-0		3447
6		13	SCUNTHORPE UNITED	3-0	Wigg 2, Price	5888
7		17	WATFORD	1-0	Wigg	6662
8		23	Stockport County	0-3		4743
9		27	Halifax Town	1-1	Collier	2783
10	Oct	1	YORK CITY	2-1	Price, Pugh	4760
11		4	TORQUAY UNITED	2-0	Collier, Joicey	5634
12		8	Doncaster Rovers	1-2	Owens (og)	7971
13		14	GRIMSBY TOWN	1-2	Warnock	6314
14		22	Huddersfield Town	0-2		7583
15		29	HARTLEPOOL UNITED	3-2	Joicey 2 (1 pen), Warnock	4287
16	Nov	4	Southend United	0-0		5612
17		12	BRENTFORD	0-0		4209
18		19	Northampton Town	1-1	Joicey	3131
19	Dec	3	READING	4-1	Little 2, McCarthey, Peachey	4346
20		10	Wimbledon	0-0		2406
21		26	CREWE ALEXANDRA	4-0	Warnock 2, Peachey, Joicey	5730
22		27	Southport	1-1	Higham (og)	2571
23		31	SOUTHEND UNITED	1-1	Price	7609
24	Jan	2	Bournemouth	2-2	Pugh, Hinch	3909
25		7	DARLINGTON	2-1	Hinch, Brown	5791
26		14	Rochdale	1-1	Hinch	2668
27	Feb	7	ALDERSHOT	2-0	Brown, Joicey	5899
28		11	Watford	0-0		13216
29		18	STOCKPORT COUNTY	0-1		6928
30		24	York City	2-1	Little, Hinch	3437
31		28	Newport County	1-3	Warnock	3523
32	Mar	4	DONCASTER ROVERS	0-0		7575
33		7	Scunthorpe United	0-1		4987
34		11	Grimsby Town	0-1		5243
35		18	HUDDERSFIELD T	1-1	Joicey (pen)	8655
36		24	Hartlepool United	2-1	Prendergast, Joicey (pen)	4315
37		25	SOUTHPORT	2-1	Joicey 2	5215
38		27	Crewe Alexandra	1-2	Little	3014
39		31	BOURNEMOUTH	3-0	Warnock, Little, Joicey (pen)	5387
40	Apr	4	HALIFAX TOWN	3-2	Prendergast, Joicey (p), Warnock	6313
41		8	Brentford	0-2		12139
42		11	SWANSEA CITY	0-2		8797
43		15	NORTHAMPTON T	2-3	Saunders, Joicey	3434
44		22	Reading	0-0		3914
45		26	Torquay United	1-3	Little	1845
46		29	WIMBLEDON	3-2	Millar 2 (1 pen), Riley	2642

Appearances and Goals

Players: Springett PI, Murphy BL, Collins JL, Pugh IG, Saunders IG, McCarthy MJ, Little A, Price PW, Peachey JM, Collier GR, Warnock N, Joicey B, Wigg RG, Chambers PM, Brown KG, Hinch JA, Riley G, Millar A, Prendergast MJ, Fox PD, Nixon JC, Yates D

	Spr	Mur	Col	Pugh	Sau	McC	Lit	Pri	Pea	Colr	War	Joi	Wigg	Cham	Brn	Hin	Ril	Mil	Pre	Fox	Nix	Yat
Apps	45	43	37	42	46	46	44	17	24	24	34	36	12	10	24	12	10	9	11	1	10	1
Goals		1		2	1	1	7	6	2	2	7	14	5		2	4	1	2	2			

Two own goals

F.A. Cup

Rnd	Month	Date	Opponent	Score	Scorers	Att
R1	Nov	26	HUDDERSFIELD T	1-0	Warnock	9579
R2	Dec	17	Grimsby Town	0-2		6171

Played in R2: G Copley (at 1).

F.L. Cup

Rnd	Month	Date	Opponent	Score	Scorers	Att
R1/1	Aug	13	Chesterfield	1-4	Pugh	4030
R1/2		16	CHESTERFIELD	3-0	McCarthy, Price, Warnock	3677
rep		23	CHESTERFIELD	0-2 (aet)		8230

Played in R1/1: P Burke (at 5).

Final Table — Division 4

		P	W	D	L	F	A	W	D	L	F	A	Pts
1	Watford	46	18	4	1	44	14	12	7	4	41	24	71
2	Southend United	46	15	5	3	46	18	10	5	8	20	21	60
3	Swansea City	46	16	5	2	54	17	7	5	11	33	30	56
4	Brentford	46	15	6	2	50	17	6	8	9	36	37	56
5	Aldershot	46	15	8	0	45	16	4	8	11	22	31	54
6	Grimsby Town	46	14	6	3	30	15	7	5	11	27	36	53
7	BARNSLEY	46	15	4	4	44	20	3	10	10	17	29	50
8	Reading	46	12	7	4	33	23	6	7	10	22	29	50
9	Torquay United	46	12	6	5	43	25	4	9	10	14	31	47
10	Northampton Town	46	9	8	6	32	30	8	5	10	31	38	47
11	Huddersfield Town	46	13	5	5	41	21	2	10	11	22	34	45
12	Doncaster Rovers	46	11	8	4	37	26	3	9	11	15	39	45
13	Wimbledon	46	8	11	4	39	26	6	5	12	27	41	44
14	Scunthorpe United	46	12	6	5	31	14	2	10	11	19	41	44
15	Crewe Alexandra	46	11	8	4	34	25	4	6	13	16	44	44
16	Newport County	46	14	6	3	43	22	2	5	16	22	51	43
17	Bournemouth	46	12	6	5	28	20	2	9	12	13	31	43
18	Stockport County	46	14	4	5	41	19	2	6	15	15	37	42
19	Darlington	46	10	8	5	31	22	4	5	14	21	37	41
20	Halifax Town	46	7	10	6	28	23	3	11	9	24	39	41
21	Hartlepool United	46	12	4	7	34	29	3	3	17	17	55	37
22	York City	46	8	7	8	27	31	4	5	14	23	38	36
23	Southport	46	5	13	5	30	32	1	6	16	22	44	31
24	Rochdale	46	8	6	9	29	28	0	2	21	14	57	24

1978/79 4th in Division 4

						Springett PJ	Collins JL	Chambers PM	Pugh JG	Saunders JG	McCarthy MJ	Little A	Clarke AJ	Joicey B	Peachey JM	Millar A	Riley G	Prendergast MJ	Speedie DR	Bell DM	Reed G	Graham T	Copley G	Banks IF	Mallender G
1	Aug	19	HALIFAX TOWN	4-2	Joicey 3, Little	5828	1	2	3	4	5	6	7	8	9	10	11*	12								
2		23	Crewe Alexandra	2-0	Clarke, Peachey	2642	1	2	3	4	5	6	7	8		11	10	9								
3		26	Bradford City	2-1	Pugh, Peachey	8341	1	2	3	4	5	6	7	8	12	11	10	9*								
4	Sep	2	YORK CITY	3-0	Millar, Clarke, Pugh	8839	1	2	3	4	5	6	7	8	12	11	10	9*								
5		9	Scunthorpe United	1-0	Little	7767	1	2	3*	4	5	6	7	8	12	11		9		10						
6		12	TORQUAY UNITED	1-2	Clarke	13088	1	2	3*	4	5	6	7	8		11	10	9		12						
7		16	HUDDERSFIELD T	1-0	Clarke	11794	1	2	3	4	5	6	7*	8	10	12	11	9								
8		23	Doncaster Rovers	2-2	Millar, Riley	9380	1	2	3	4	5	6	7	8		10	11	9								
9		26	Darlington	0-0		3475	1	2	3	4	5	6	7	8		11	10	9								
10		30	READING	3-1	Little, Saunders, Pugh	10282	1	2	3	4	5	6	7	8		10	11	9*	12							
11	Oct	7	NORTHAMPTON T	1-1	Clarke	10336	1	2	3	4	5	6	7	8		11	10	9*	12							
12		13	Stockport County	0-0		9054	1	2	3	4	5	6	7	8	12	11*	10	9								
13		17	Aldershot	0-1		3622	1	2	3	4	5	6	7	8	12	11*	10	9								
14		21	WIGAN ATHLETIC	0-0		9841	1	2	3	4	5	6		8	11		10	9*	12	7						
15		28	Newport County	1-1	Bell	4571	1	2	3	4	5	6		7		10*	11	9		12	8					
16	Nov	4	WIMBLEDON	3-1	Bell 2, Riley	11761	1	2	3	4	5	6			8	10	11	9		12	7*					
17		11	York City	1-0	Bell	6900	1	2	3	4	5	6			8	9*	10	7		12	11					
18		18	BRADFORD CITY	0-1		11695	1	2	3	4	5	6			8		10*	9		12	11	7				
19	Dec	9	Rochdale	3-0	Bell, Millar, Clarke	3136	1	2	3	4*	5	6		8			10	9	12		11		7			
20		23	Hartlepool United	1-1	Graham	5956	1	2	3	4	5	6	7				10	9			11		8			
21		26	PORT VALE	6-2	Clarke 3, Little, Graham, Millar	10532	1	2	3	4	5	6	7	8			10	12			11*		9			
22	Jan	31	Torquay United	2-3	Bell, Graham	2654	1	3		2*	5	6	7	8			10	4	12		11		9			
23	Feb	10	Reading	0-1		6915	1	2	3		5	6	4	8			10	7*			11		9			12
24		24	STOCKPORT COUNTY	4-4	Graham 2, Bell 2	9153		2	3		5	6	4	8			10	7			11		9	1		
25		28	Hereford United	1-1	Collins	3120	1	2	3	4	5	6	7	8			10				11		9			
26	Mar	3	Wigan Athletic	1-1	Clarke (pen)	9427	1	2	3	4	5	6	7	8			10*	9			11				12	
27		6	BOURNEMOUTH	1-0	Graham	7599	1	2	3	4	5	6	7	8			10				11		9			
28		10	NEWPORT COUNTY	1-0	Clarke	9428	1	2	3	4	5	6	7	8			10				11		9			
29		13	SCUNTHORPE UNITED	4-1	Graham 3, McCarthy	9309	1	2	3	4	5	6	7	8			10				11		9			
30		24	CREWE ALEXANDRA	3-1	Bell (pen), Pugh, Little	8945	1	2	3	4	5	6	7	8			10				11		9			
31		27	Halifax Town	2-0	Graham, Bell (pen)	5654	1	2	3	4	5	6	7				10	8			11		9			
32		30	PORTSMOUTH	1-1	Graham	12928	1	2	3	4	5	6	7	8*			10	12			11		9			
33	Apr	3	DONCASTER ROVERS	3-0	Clarke, McCarthy, Riley	12082	1	2	3	4	5	6	7	8			10	12			11*		9			
34		7	Bournemouth	2-0	Little, Bell	3265	1	2	3	4	5	6	7				10	8			11		9			
35		12	HARTLEPOOL UNITED	1-0	Bell	11398	1	2	3	4	5	6	7	8			10	4			11		9			
36		14	Port Vale	2-3	Graham, Keenan (og)	5226	1	2	3	4	5	6	7	8			10*	8			11		9		12	
37		16	HEREFORD UNITED	2-1	Bell 2	12260	1	2	3	4	5	6	7	8			10*	12			11		9			
38		21	Grimsby Town	0-2		16138	1	2	3	4	5	6	7	8*			10	12			11		9			
39		24	ALDERSHOT	2-0	Bell (pen), Dungworth (og)	12718	1	2	3	4	5	6	7				8	10	8		11		9			
40		26	Northampton Town	1-0	Bell	3305	1	2	3	4	5	6				10	8	12	7	11		9*			
41		28	ROCHDALE	0-3		12051	1	2	3	4	5	6	10				8	12	7	11		9*			
42		30	DARLINGTON	1-1	Little	10974	1	2	3	4	5	6	7	8*			10	12			11		9			
43	May	2	Huddersfield Town	0-1		9382	1	2	3	4	5	6	7				10	8			11		9			
44		5	Portsmouth	1-0	Bell	8767	1	2	3	4	5	6	7				10	8			11		9			
45		8	GRIMSBY TOWN	2-1	Saunders, Bell	21261	1	2	3	4*	5	6	7				10	8		12	11		9			
46		14	Wimbledon	1-1	Chambers	5794	1	2	3		5	6	7				10	8		4	11		9			
			Apps				45	46	45	42	46	46	40	34	11	13	43	41	9	10	32	1	27	1	2	1
			Goals					1	1	4	2	2	7	12	3	2	4	3			18		12			

Two own goals

F.A. Cup

R1	Nov	25	WORKSOP TOWN	5-1	Clarke, Riley, Bell, Reed 2	10433	1	2	3	4	5	6		8			10	9			11	7				
R2	Dec	16	ROTHERHAM UTD.	1-1	Clarke	15491	1	2	3	4	5	6		8			10	9			11					
rep	Jan	9	Rotherham United	1-2	Forrest (og)	15535	1	2	3	4	5	6	7	8			10	9			11					

F.L. Cup

| R1/1 | Aug | 12 | CHESTERFIELD | 1-2 | Little | 8606 | 1 | | 3 | | 4 | | 6 | 11 | 8 | 5 | | 12 | 7 | 10 | | | | | | |
| R1/2 | | 16 | Chesterfield | 0-0 | | 6278 | 1 | 2 | 3 | 4 | 5 | 6 | 7 | 8 | 9 | 11 | 10 | | | | | | | | | |

Played in R1/1: D Markham (at 2), PW Price (at 9 -substituted).

	P	W	D	L	F	A	W	D	L	F	A	Pts
1 Reading	46	19	3	1	49	8	7	10	6	27	27	65
2 Grimsby Town	46	15	5	3	51	23	11	4	8	31	26	61
3 Wimbledon	46	18	3	2	50	20	7	8	8	28	26	61
4 BARNSLEY	46	15	5	3	47	23	9	8	6	26	19	61
5 Aldershot	46	16	5	2	38	14	4	12	7	25	33	57
6 Wigan Athletic	46	14	5	4	40	24	7	8	8	23	24	55
7 Portsmouth	46	13	7	3	35	12	7	5	11	27	36	52
8 Newport County	46	12	5	6	39	28	9	5	9	27	27	52
9 Huddersfield Town	46	13	8	2	32	15	5	3	15	25	38	47
10 York City	46	11	6	6	33	24	7	5	11	18	31	47
11 Torquay United	46	14	4	5	38	24	5	4	14	20	41	46
12 Scunthorpe United	46	12	3	8	33	30	5	8	10	21	30	45
13 Hartlepool United	46	7	12	4	35	28	6	6	11	22	38	44
14 Hereford United	46	12	8	3	35	18	3	5	15	18	35	43
15 Bradford City	46	11	5	7	38	26	6	4	13	24	42	43
16 Port Vale	46	8	10	5	29	28	6	4	13	28	42	42
17 Stockport County	46	11	5	7	33	21	3	7	13	25	39	40
18 Bournemouth	46	11	6	6	34	19	3	5	15	13	29	39
19 Northampton Town	46	12	4	7	40	30	3	5	15	24	46	39
20 Rochdale	46	11	4	8	25	26	4	5	14	22	38	39
21 Darlington	46	8	8	7	25	21	3	7	13	24	45	37
22 Doncaster Rovers	46	8	8	7	25	22	5	3	15	25	51	37
23 Halifax Town	46	7	5	11	24	32	2	3	18	15	40	26
24 Crewe Alexandra	46	3	7	13	24	41	3	7	13	19	49	26

Season 1978/79
Back row: Millar, Markham, Little, Joicey, Collins, Mallender
Centre row: Young (Coach) Saunders, McCarthy, Copley, Murphy, Springett, Peachey, Rimmington (Physio)
Front row: Chambers, Prendergast, Clarke (Player/Manager) Price, Pugh, Riley

Season 1979/80
Back row: Hunter, Pierce, Springett, Graham
Centre row: Young (Coach) Flavell, McCarthy, Little, Millar, Chambers, Rimmington (Physio) Murphy (Coach)
Front row: Pugh, Bell, Speedie, Clarke (Player/Manager) Glavin, Riley, Collins

1979/80   11th in Division 3

#		Date	Opponent	Score	Scorers	Att	Pierce G	Flavell RW	Collins JL	Glavin RM	Pugh IG	McCarthy MJ	Little A	Clarke AJ	Graham T	Millar A	Bell DM	Banks IF	Dugdale A	Riley G	Reed G	Speedie DR	Chambers PM	Lester MJ	Wormley P	Hunter N	Springett PJ	Aylott TKC	Joyce JP	Evans JP	Cooper N	Parker DH	Downs RD	Campbell WR
1	Aug	18	SHEFFIELD WEDNESDA	0-3		22360	1	2	3	4	5	6	7	8	9	10*	11	12																
2		21	Chesterfield	0-2		7706	1	2	3	4*	10	6	7			12	11		5	8	9													
3		25	READING	2-0	Bell, Glavin	10451	1	2	3	4	10	6	7						5	8	9*													
4	Sep	1	Oxford United	0-1		5120	1	2	3	4	9	6	7			10*	11		5	8		12												
5		8	MANSFIELD TOWN	1-0	Riley	10588	1	2	3	4	9	6	7*			10	11		5	8		12												
6		15	Sheffield United	0-2		20507	1	2		4		6	7		9	10	11		5	8		3												
7		19	Blackburn Rovers	1-0	Glavin	7582	1	2		4	9	6				10	11	7	5	8		3												
8		22	MILLWALL	2-1	Bell, Glavin (pen)	11788	1	2		4		6	7	12	9	10	11		5	8*		3												
9		29	Colchester United	0-0		3376	1	2	5	4	7	6			9	10	11			8		3												
10	Oct	2	BLACKBURN ROVERS	1-1	Glavin (pen)	12460	1	2	5	4	9	6		12		10	11	7*		8		3												
11		6	Brentford	1-3	Glavin (pen)	7292	1	2	5	4		6			9	10		7		8		3	11											
12		9	CHESTERFIELD	0-1		12366	1	2	5	4		6		8			11	7		9*		12	3	10										
13		13	Gillingham	2-0	Lester, Clarke	9132	1	2	6	4	5			8			11	7		9			3	10										
14		20	Carlisle United	1-3	Lester	5156	1	2	4	6	5			10			11	7		9			3	8										
15		23	Bury	2-2	Glavin 2 (1 pen)	4341	1	2	5	4	6			8				7		11		12	3	10	9*									
16		27	CHESTER	1-1	Glavin	9879	1	2		7	4	5		10			12	8		11		3*	9			6								
17	Nov	3	Sheffield Wednesday	2-0	Riley, Lester	23544		2	3	4	11	6		8				7		9			10			5	1							
18		6	Bury	2-1	Lester, Glavin (pen)	11691		2	3	4	11	6		8*				7		9		12	10			5	1							
19		10	EXETER CITY	2-2	Glavin 2 (1 pen)	11739	2*	3	4	11	6	7		8				9		12		10			5	1								
20		17	Hull City	2-0	McCarthy, Hood (og)	8327		2	3	7	6	5		8				10					9		4	1	11							
21	Dec	1	SOUTHEND UNITED	1-2	Clarke	11602		2	3	4	7	6		8				10		12			9*		5	1	11							
22		8	Plymouth Argyle	1-2	Graham	5311		2	3	4	11	6		8			7	5		10					1	9								
23		21	BLACKPOOL	2-1	Clarke, Aylott	8567		2	3	4	11	6		8	10			7						5	1	9								
24		26	Grimsby Town	0-3		14417		2	3	4	12	6		8	10			7		11				5	1	9*								
25		29	Reading	0-7		5728	2*	3	4	11	5		8	9			7		6		10		1		12									
26	Jan	12	SWINDON TOWN	1-2	Banks	10420	1		3	4				9	10		7				6	8		11	2	5								
27		26	OXFORD UNITED	2-0	Glavin, Aylott	9058	1			4				9	12			8				3	10*	7		11	2	5		6				
28	Feb	9	Millwall	2-2	Parker, Aylott	5835	1			4	5				10							3	7	8		11	2		6	9				
29		16	COLCHESTER UNITED	1-2	Glavin (pen)	11309	1			4	6				11					12		3	10*	5		9	2		7	8				
30		23	Gillingham	1-1		5800	1			4	5				9							3	8	7		11	2		6	10				
31	Mar	1	CARLISLE UNITED	1-1	Glavin	10116	1			4	5				10							3	8	7		11	2		6	9				
32		4	ROTHERHAM UNITED	0-0		13186	1			4	6									11		5		9	2		7	8						
33		8	Chester	0-0		5227	1			4	6				11					12		3	10*	5		9		7	2	8				
34		11	Wimbledon	2-1	Glavin, Cooper	2785	1			4	6				12							3	10	5		9		7	2	8				
35		15	BRENTFORD	1-0	Parker	9368	1				6				7							4	3	8		10		5	2	9	11			
36		22	Exeter City	1-2	Aylott	4700	1				6											3	10	5		9		7	2	8	11			
37		25	SHEFFIELD UNITED	0-0		19686	1			4	6											3	10	5		9		7	2	8	11			
38	Apr	4	Blackpool	1-1	Lester	10049	1			4	6				12							3	10	5		9*		7	2	8	11			
39		5	GRIMSBY TOWN	0-1		16433	1			4	5				8*					7		3	10	12		6		2	9	11				
40		7	Rotherham United	1-1	Glavin	9376	1			4	6								9			3	10	5		7	2	8	11				
41		11	WIMBLEDON	4-0	Glavin, Lester, Banks 2	10032	1			4	6						5	9				3	10	5		7	2	8	11					
42		14	Mansfield Town	4-1	Cooper, Parker, Evans, Riley	6789	1			4	6						5	9				3	10			7	2	8	11					
43		19	Southend United	1-2	Glavin	4740	1			4	5						10	9	7			3				6	2	8	11					
44		22	HULL CITY	3-1	Cooper, Glavin (pen), Parker	11016	1			4	6				9							10		3		7	2	8	11					
45		26	PLYMOUTH ARGYLE	0-0		10231	1				6				4			9				3	8	7		5	2	10	11					
46	May	3	Swindon Town	1-0	Riley	8506	1				6				7			9*				3	8	4		5	2	10	11	12				
				Apps			37	25	22	42	20	44	7	13	11	12	14	38	7	27	2	13	32	33	1	24	9	18	8	16	20	19	13	1
				Goals						20	1			3	1		2	3		4				6				4		1	3	4		

One own goal

F.A. Cup

#		Date	Opponent	Score	Scorers	Att																												
R1	Nov	24	HARTLEPOOL UTD.	5-2	Clarke, Glavin 2, Aylott, Leste	12548		2	3	7	6	5		8				10*		12			9		4	1	11							
R2	Dec	18	Chester	0-1		4616		2	3	4		6		8	11			7					10		5	1	9								

F.L. Cup

#		Date	Opponent	Score	Scorers	Att																												
R1/1	Aug	11	Lincoln City	1-2	Riley	6733	1	2	3	4			5	7		9	10	11		8							6							
R1/2		14	LINCOLN CITY	2-1	Bell, Graham	11914	1	2	3	4	5	6	7	8	12	10	11			9*														
R2/1		28	West Ham United	1-3	Glavin	12320	1	2	3	4	9	6	7			10	11		5	8														
R2/2	Sep	4	WEST HAM UTD.	0-2		15898	1	2*	3	4	9	6	7			12	11	10	5	8														

R1/2 a.e.t. Barnsley won 4-3 on penalties

	P	W	D	L	F	A	W	D	L	F	A	Pts
1 Grimsby Town	46	18	2	3	46	16	8	8	7	27	26	62
2 Blackburn Rovers	46	13	5	5	34	17	12	4	7	24	19	59
3 Sheffield Wed.	46	12	6	5	44	20	9	10	4	37	27	58
4 Chesterfield	46	16	5	2	46	16	7	6	10	25	30	57
5 Colchester United	46	10	10	3	39	20	10	2	11	25	36	52
6 Carlisle United	46	13	6	4	45	26	5	6	12	21	30	48
7 Reading	46	14	6	3	43	19	2	10	11	23	46	48
8 Exeter City	46	14	5	4	38	22	5	5	13	22	46	48
9 Chester	46	14	6	3	29	18	3	7	13	20	39	47
10 Swindon Town	46	15	4	4	50	20	4	4	15	21	43	46
11 BARNSLEY	46	10	7	6	29	20	6	7	10	24	36	46
12 Sheffield United	46	13	5	5	35	21	5	5	13	25	45	46
13 Rotherham United	46	13	4	6	38	24	5	6	12	20	42	46
14 Millwall	46	14	3	6	49	23	2	7	14	16	36	45
15 Plymouth Argyle	46	13	7	3	39	17	3	5	15	20	38	44
16 Gillingham	46	8	9	6	28	16	5	5	12	23	33	42
17 Oxford United	46	10	4	9	34	24	4	9	10	23	38	41
18 Blackpool	46	10	7	6	39	34	5	4	14	23	40	41
19 Brentford	46	10	6	7	33	26	5	5	13	26	47	41
20 Hull City	46	11	7	5	29	21	1	9	13	22	48	40
21 Bury	46	10	4	9	30	23	6	5	14	15	36	39
22 Southend United	46	11	6	6	33	23	3	4	16	14	35	38
23 Mansfield Town	46	9	9	5	31	24	1	7	15	16	34	36
24 Wimbledon	46	6	8	9	34	38	4	6	13	18	43	34

FINAL LEAGUE TABLES: 1980/81 - 1985/86

Final League Table 1980/81 Division 3

		Pl.	Home					Away					F.	A.	Pts
			W	D	L	F	A	W	D	L	F	A			
1	Rotherham United	46	17	6	0	43	8	7	7	9	19	24	62	32	61
2	BARNSLEY	46	15	5	3	46	19	6	12	5	26	26	72	45	59
3	Charlton Athletic	46	14	6	3	36	17	11	3	9	27	27	63	44	59
4	Huddersfield Town	46	14	6	3	40	11	7	8	8	31	29	71	40	56
5	Chesterfield	46	17	4	2	42	16	6	6	11	30	32	72	48	56
6	Portsmouth	46	14	5	4	35	19	8	4	11	20	28	55	47	53
7	Plymouth Argyle	46	14	5	4	35	18	5	9	9	21	26	56	44	52
8	Burnley	46	13	5	5	37	21	5	9	9	23	27	60	48	50
9	Brentford	46	7	9	7	30	25	7	10	6	22	24	52	49	47
10	Reading	46	13	5	5	39	22	5	5	13	23	40	62	62	46
11	Exeter City	46	9	9	5	36	30	7	4	12	26	36	62	66	45
12	Newport County	46	11	6	6	38	22	4	7	12	26	39	64	61	43
13	Fulham	46	8	7	8	28	29	7	6	10	29	35	57	64	43
14	Oxford United	46	7	8	8	20	24	6	9	8	19	23	39	47	43
15	Gillingham	46	9	8	6	23	19	3	10	10	25	39	48	58	42
16	Millwall	46	10	9	4	30	21	4	5	14	13	39	43	60	42
17	Swindon Town	46	10	6	7	35	27	3	9	11	16	29	51	56	41
18	Chester	46	11	5	7	25	17	4	6	13	13	31	38	48	41
19	Carlisle United	46	8	9	6	32	29	6	4	13	24	41	56	70	41
20	Walsall	46	8	9	6	43	43	5	6	12	16	31	59	74	41
21	Sheffield United	46	12	6	5	38	20	2	6	15	27	43	65	63	40
22	Colchester United	46	12	7	4	35	22	2	4	17	10	43	45	65	39
23	Blackpool	46	5	9	9	19	28	4	5	14	26	47	45	75	32
24	Hull City	46	7	8	8	23	22	1	8	14	17	49	40	71	32

Final League Table 1981/82 Division 2

		Pl.	Home					Away					F.	A.	Pts
			W	D	L	F	A	W	D	L	F	A			
1	Luton Town	42	16	3	2	48	19	9	10	2	38	27	86	46	88
2	Watford	42	13	6	2	46	16	10	5	6	30	26	76	42	80
3	Norwich City	42	14	3	4	41	19	8	2	11	23	31	64	50	71
4	Sheffield Wed.	42	10	8	3	31	23	10	2	9	24	28	55	51	70
5	Queen's Park Rgs.	42	15	4	2	40	9	6	2	13	25	34	65	43	69
6	BARNSLEY	42	13	4	4	33	14	6	6	9	26	27	59	41	67
7	Rotherham United	42	13	5	3	42	19	7	2	12	24	35	66	54	67
8	Leicester City	42	12	5	4	31	19	6	7	8	25	29	56	48	66
9	Newcastle United	42	14	4	3	30	14	4	4	13	22	36	52	50	62
10	Blackburn Rovers	42	11	4	6	26	15	5	7	9	21	28	47	43	59
11	Oldham Athletic	42	9	9	3	28	23	6	5	10	22	28	50	51	59
12	Chelsea	42	10	5	6	37	30	5	7	9	23	30	60	60	57
13	Charlton Athletic	42	11	5	5	33	22	2	7	12	17	43	50	65	51
14	Cambridge United	42	11	4	6	31	19	2	5	14	17	34	48	53	48
15	Crystal Palace	42	9	2	10	25	26	4	7	10	9	19	34	45	48
16	Derby County	42	9	8	4	32	23	3	4	14	21	45	53	68	48
17	Grimsby Town	42	5	8	8	29	30	6	5	10	24	35	53	65	46
18	Shrewsbury Town	42	10	6	5	26	19	1	7	13	11	38	37	57	46
19	Bolton Wanderers	42	10	4	7	28	24	3	3	15	11	37	39	61	46
20	Cardiff City	42	9	2	10	28	32	3	6	12	17	29	45	61	44
21	Wrexham	42	9	4	8	22	22	2	7	12	18	34	40	56	44
22	Orient	42	6	8	7	23	24	4	1	16	13	37	36	61	39

Final League Table 1982/83 Division 2

		Pl.	Home					Away					F.	A.	Pts
			W	D	L	F	A	W	D	L	F	A			
1	Queen's Park Rgs.	42	16	3	2	51	16	10	4	7	26	20	77	36	85
2	Wolverhampton W.	42	14	5	2	42	16	6	10	5	26	28	68	44	75
3	Leicester City	42	11	4	6	36	15	9	6	6	36	29	72	44	70
4	Fulham	42	13	5	3	36	20	7	4	10	28	27	64	47	69
5	Newcastle United	42	13	6	2	43	21	5	7	9	32	32	75	53	67
6	Sheffield Wed.	42	9	8	4	33	23	7	7	7	27	24	60	47	63
7	Oldham Athletic	42	8	10	3	38	24	6	9	6	26	23	64	47	61
8	Leeds United	42	7	11	3	28	22	6	10	5	23	24	51	46	60
9	Shrewsbury Town	42	8	9	4	20	15	7	5	9	28	33	48	48	59
10	BARNSLEY	42	9	8	4	37	28	5	7	9	20	27	57	55	57
11	Blackburn Rovers	42	11	7	3	38	21	4	5	12	20	37	58	58	57
12	Cambridge United	42	11	7	3	26	17	2	5	14	16	43	42	60	51
13	Derby County	42	7	10	4	27	24	3	9	9	22	34	49	58	49
14	Carlisle United	42	10	6	5	44	28	2	6	13	24	42	68	70	48
15	Crystal Palace	42	11	7	3	31	17	1	5	15	12	35	43	52	48
16	Middlesbrough	42	8	7	6	27	29	3	8	10	19	38	46	67	48
17	Charlton Athletic	42	11	3	7	40	31	2	6	13	23	55	63	86	48
18	Chelsea	42	8	8	5	31	22	3	6	12	20	39	51	61	47
19	Grimsby Town	42	9	7	5	32	26	3	4	14	13	44	45	70	47
20	Rotherham United	42	6	7	8	22	29	4	8	9	23	39	45	68	45
21	Burnley	42	10	4	7	38	24	2	4	15	18	42	56	66	44
22	Bolton Wanderers	42	10	2	9	30	26	1	9	11	12	35	42	61	44

Final League Table 1983/84 Division 2

		Pl.	Home					Away					F.	A.	Pts
			W	D	L	F	A	W	D	L	F	A			
1	Chelsea	42	15	4	2	55	17	10	9	2	35	23	90	40	88
2	Sheffield Wed.	42	16	4	1	47	16	10	6	5	25	18	72	34	88
3	Newcastle United	42	16	2	3	51	18	8	6	7	34	35	85	53	80
4	Manchester City	42	13	3	5	43	21	7	7	7	23	27	66	48	70
5	Grimsby Town	42	13	6	2	36	15	6	7	8	24	32	60	47	70
6	Blackburn Rovers	42	9	11	1	35	19	8	5	8	22	27	57	46	67
7	Carlisle United	42	10	9	2	29	13	6	7	8	19	28	48	41	64
8	Shrewsbury Town	42	13	5	3	34	18	4	5	12	15	35	49	53	61
9	Brighton & Hove A.	42	11	6	4	42	17	6	3	12	27	43	69	60	60
10	Leeds United	42	13	4	4	33	16	3	8	10	22	40	55	56	60
11	Fulham	42	9	6	6	35	24	6	6	9	25	29	60	53	57
12	Huddersfield Town	42	8	6	7	27	20	6	9	6	29	29	56	49	57
13	Charlton Athletic	42	13	4	4	40	26	3	5	13	13	38	53	64	57
14	BARNSLEY	42	9	6	6	33	23	6	1	14	24	30	57	53	52
15	Cardiff City	42	11	3	7	32	27	4	3	14	21	39	53	66	51
16	Portsmouth	42	8	3	10	46	32	6	4	11	27	32	73	64	49
17	Middlesbrough	42	9	8	4	26	18	3	5	13	15	29	41	47	49
18	Crystal Palace	42	8	5	8	18	18	4	6	11	24	34	42	52	47
19	Oldham Athletic	42	10	6	5	33	27	3	2	16	14	46	47	73	47
20	Derby County	42	9	5	7	26	26	2	4	15	10	46	36	72	42
21	Swansea City	42	7	4	10	20	28	0	4	17	16	57	36	85	29
22	Cambridge United	42	4	7	10	20	33	0	5	16	8	44	28	77	24

Final League Table 1984/85 Division 2

		Pl.	Home					Away					F.	A.	Pts
			W	D	L	F	A	W	D	L	F	A			
1	Oxford United	42	18	2	1	62	15	7	7	7	22	21	84	36	84
2	Birmingham City	42	12	6	3	30	15	13	1	7	29	18	59	33	82
3	Manchester City	42	14	4	3	42	16	7	7	7	24	24	66	40	74
4	Portsmouth	42	11	6	4	39	25	9	8	4	30	25	69	50	74
5	Blackburn Rovers	42	14	3	4	38	15	7	7	7	28	26	66	41	73
6	Brighton & Hove A.	42	13	6	2	31	11	7	6	8	23	23	54	34	72
7	Leeds United	42	12	7	2	37	11	7	5	9	29	32	66	43	69
8	Shrewsbury Town	42	12	6	3	45	22	6	5	10	21	31	66	53	65
9	Fulham	42	13	3	5	35	26	6	5	10	33	38	68	64	65
10	Grimsby Town	42	13	1	7	47	32	5	7	9	25	32	72	64	62
11	BARNSLEY	42	11	7	3	27	12	3	9	9	15	30	42	42	58
12	Wimbledon	42	9	8	4	40	29	7	2	12	31	46	71	75	58
13	Huddersfield Town	42	9	5	7	28	29	6	5	10	24	35	52	64	55
14	Oldham Athletic	42	10	4	7	27	23	5	4	12	22	44	49	67	53
15	Crystal Palace	42	8	7	6	25	27	4	5	12	21	38	46	65	48
16	Carlisle United	42	8	5	8	27	23	5	3	13	23	44	50	67	47
17	Charlton Athletic	42	8	7	6	34	30	3	5	13	17	33	51	63	45
18	Sheffield United	42	7	6	8	31	28	3	8	10	23	38	54	66	44
19	Middlesbrough	42	6	8	7	22	26	4	2	15	19	31	41	57	40
20	Notts County	42	6	5	10	25	32	4	2	15	20	41	45	73	37
21	Cardiff City	42	5	3	13	24	42	4	5	12	23	37	47	79	35
22	Wolverhampton W.	42	5	4	12	18	32	3	5	13	19	47	37	79	33

Final League Table 1985/86 Division 2

		Pl.	Home					Away					F.	A.	Pts
			W	D	L	F	A	W	D	L	F	A			
1	Norwich City	42	16	4	1	51	15	9	5	7	33	22	84	37	84
2	Charlton Athletic	42	14	5	2	44	15	8	6	7	34	30	78	45	77
3	Wimbledon	42	13	6	2	38	16	8	7	6	20	21	58	37	76
4	Portsmouth	42	13	4	4	43	17	9	3	9	26	24	69	41	73
5	Crystal Palace	42	12	3	6	29	22	7	6	8	28	30	57	52	66
6	Hull City	42	11	7	3	39	19	6	6	9	26	36	65	55	64
7	Sheffield United	42	10	7	4	36	24	7	4	10	28	39	64	63	62
8	Oldham Athletic	42	13	4	4	40	28	4	5	12	22	33	62	61	60
9	Millwall	42	12	3	6	39	24	5	5	11	25	41	64	65	59
10	Stoke City	42	8	11	2	29	16	6	4	11	19	34	48	50	57
11	Brighton & Hove A.	42	10	5	6	42	30	6	3	12	22	34	64	64	56
12	BARNSLEY	42	9	6	6	29	26	5	8	8	18	24	47	50	56
13	Bradford City	42	14	1	6	36	24	2	5	14	15	39	51	63	54
14	Leeds United	42	9	7	5	30	22	6	1	14	26	50	56	72	53
15	Grimsby Town	42	11	4	6	35	24	3	6	12	23	38	58	62	52
16	Huddersfield Town	42	10	6	5	30	23	4	4	13	21	44	51	67	52
17	Shrewsbury Town	42	11	5	5	29	20	3	4	14	23	44	52	64	51
18	Sunderland	42	10	5	6	33	29	3	6	12	14	32	47	61	50
19	Blackburn Rovers	42	10	4	7	30	20	2	9	10	23	42	53	62	49
20	Carlisle United	42	10	2	9	30	28	3	5	13	17	43	47	71	46
21	Middlesbrough	42	8	6	7	26	23	4	3	14	18	30	44	53	45
22	Fulham	42	8	3	10	29	32	2	3	16	16	37	45	69	36

1980/81 — 2nd in Division 3

#		Date	Opponent	Score	Scorers	Att	New MP	Cooper N	Chambers PM	Glavin RM	Banks IF	McCarthy MJ	Evans IP	Parker DH	Aylott TKC	Lester MJ	Downes RD	Riley G	Boyd G	Hunter N	Joyce IP	Pierce G	Barrowclough SJ	Campbell WR	McHale R	Walker C
1	Aug	16	PORTSMOUTH	1-2	Parker	10253	1	2	3	4	5	6	7	8	9*	10	11	12								
2		19	Hull City	2-1	Banks, Glavin	6978	1	2	3	4*	5	6	7	8		10	11	9	12							
3		23	Gillingham	1-1	Banks (pen)	5222	1	2	3		5	6	7	8		10	11	9	4							
4		30	SHEFFIELD UNITED	2-1	Glavin, Evans	17478	1	2	3	4	5	6	7	8		10	11	9								
5	Sep	6	Rotherham United	0-2		10766	1	2	3	4	5		7	8		10	11	9		6						
6		13	HUDDERSFIELD T	1-0	Glavin	13819	1	2	3	4	5		7	8	12	10	11*	9		6						
7		15	Brentford	1-1	Banks	6935	1	2	3	4	5		7	8		10	11	9		6						
8		20	SWINDON TOWN	2-0	Glavin (pen), Parker	9747	1	2	3	4	5	6	7	8		10	11	9								
9		27	Reading	2-3	Banks, Parker	6102	1	2	3	4	5	6	7	8	12	10	11	9*								
10		30	BRENTFORD	0-1		11227	1	2	3	4	5	6	7	8	12	10	11*	9								
11	Oct	4	CHARLTON ATHLETIC	0-0		9305	1	2	3	4	5	6	7	8	9	10		11								
12		7	Carlisle United	2-2	Lester, Riley	2828	1	2	3	4*	5	6	7	8	9	10		11			12					
13		11	Colchester United	2-2	Parker, Glavin	2749	1	2	3	4*	5	6	7	8	9	10		11			12					
14		18	MILLWALL	2-0	Aylott, Banks (pen)	8693	1		3		5	6	7	8	9	10	11				4	2				
15		21	OXFORD UNITED	1-1	Downes	8991	1		3	4	5	6	7	8	9	10	11					2				
16		25	Plymouth Argyle	3-1	Lester, Riley, Glavin	8911	1		3	4	5	6	7	8*	9	10		12				2				
17	Nov	1	CHESTER	2-0	Aylott, Glavin	9330	1		3	4	5	6	7		9	10	11	8				2				
18		4	CARLISLE UNITED	3-1	Glavin, Aylott, Lester	9191	1		3	4	5	6	7		9	10	11	8				2				
19		8	Exeter City	1-0	Riley	4019	1		3	4	5	6	7		9	10	11	8				2				
20		11	HULL CITY	5-0	Aylott 3, Riley, Banks	11628	1	12	3	4	5*	6	7		9	10	11	8				2				
21		15	Portsmouth	1-0	Riley	14732	1	4	3		5	6	7		9	10	11	8				2				
22		29	FULHAM	2-2	Lester, Banks	9940		4	3		5	6	7		9	10	11	8				2	1			
23	Dec	2	Burnley	1-0	Banks	9109		4	3		5	6	7	8	9	10	11					2	1			
24		6	Newport County	0-0		5537		4	3		5	6	7	8	9	10	11					2	1			
25		20	BLACKPOOL	2-0	Aylott, Parker	10862		10	3	4	5	6	7	8	9		11					2	1			
26		26	Chesterfield	0-0		17169		10	3	4	5	6	7	8	9		11					2	1			
27		27	WALSALL	3-0	Glavin 2, Aylott	14958		10	3	4	5	6	7	8	9		11					2	1			
28	Jan	10	PLYMOUTH ARGYLE	2-1	Lester, Aylott	12355			3	4	5	6	7	8	9	10	11					2	1			
29		16	Fulham	3-2	Aylott, Banks, Parker	5265			3	4	5	6	7	8	9	10	11	12				2	1*			
30		31	GILLINGHAM	3-3	Banks, Parker, Riley	13703	1		3	4	5	6	7	8	9*	10	11	12				2				
31	Feb	7	Huddersfield Town	0-1		28901	1	12	3	4	5*	6	7	8		10	11	9				2				
32		21	READING	2-3	McCarthy, Aylott	13304	1	7	3	4	5				9	10	11	8				2				
33		28	Swindon Town	0-2		8066		4	3			6	7		9	10	11	8*				2	1	5	12	
34	Mar	7	Charlton Athletic	1-1	Banks	9371			3	4	5	6	7	8	9							2	1	11		10
35		21	Millwall	1-1	Glavin	4911			3	4	5	6	7	8	9							2	1	11		10
36		24	Oxford United	1-1	Glavin	4943			3	4*	5	6	7	8	9							2	1	11		10
37		28	BURNLEY	3-2	Glavin, Banks 2 (1 pen)	13689			3*		5	6	7	8	9			12				2	1	11		10
38		31	Sheffield United	1-1	Riley	20369					5	6	7	8	9			3				2	1	11		10
39	Apr	4	Chester	2-2	Parker, Glavin	4863		12			4	5	6	7*	8	9		3				2	1	11		10
40		7	COLCHESTER UNITED	3-0	McHale, Parker 2	13283		7			4	5	6		8	9	11	3				2	1			10
41		10	EXETER CITY	1-0	Cooper	14038		4	3		5	6	7	8	9							2	1			10
42		18	Walsall	1-1	Cooper	6026		4	3	12	5	6	7	8	9*							2	1			10
43		20	CHESTERFIELD	1-1	Banks	17019		4	3		5	6	7	8*	9							2	1			10	12
44		25	Blackpool	0-1		7648		4*	3	9	5	6	7	8								2	1			10	12
45		28	ROTHERHAM UNITED	1-0	Glavin	25935			3	4	5	6	7	8	9*			12				2	1			10
46	May	2	NEWPORT COUNTY	4-1	Parker, Glavin 3	15659			3	4	5	6	7	8			9					2	1			10
			Apps				24	30	43	37	45	43	44	38	37	31	30	32	2	6	33	22	13	1	13	2
			Goals					2		18	14	1	1	11	11	5	1	7							1	

F.A. Cup

		Date	Opponent	Score	Scorers	Att	New MP	Cooper N	Chambers PM	Glavin RM	Banks IF	McCarthy MJ	Evans IP	Parker DH	Aylott TKC	Lester MJ	Downes RD	Riley G	Boyd G	Hunter N	Joyce IP	Pierce G
R1	Nov	22	Chester	2-1	Cooper, Banks	7135	1	4	3		5	6	7		9	10	11	8				2
R2	Dec	13	Rotherham Uunied	1-0	Parker	15426		4	3		5	6	7	8	9	10	11					2	1
R3	Jan	3	TORQUAY UNITED	2-1	Parker 2	14431			3	4	5	6	7	8	9	10	11					2	1
R4		24	ENFIELD	1-1	Aylott	24251	1		3	4	5	6	7	8	9	10	11					2
rep		28	Enfield	3-0	Aylott 2, Glavin	35244	1		3	4	5*	6	7	8	9	10	11	12				2
R5	Feb	14	Middlesborough	1-2	Lester	37557	1	7	3	4	5	6			9	10	11	8				2

R4 replay at White Hart Lane.

F.L. Cup

		Date	Opponent	Score	Scorers	Att	New MP	Cooper N	Chambers PM	Glavin RM	Banks IF	McCarthy MJ	Evans IP	Parker DH	Aylott TKC	Lester MJ	Downes RD	Riley G	Boyd G	Hunter N	Joyce IP	Pierce G
R1/1	Aug	8	Scunthorpe United	1-0	Parker	4550	1	2	3	4	5*	6	7	8	9	10	11				12	
R1/2		12	SCUNTHORPE UTD.	2-1	Banks, Glavin	8430	1	2	3	4	5	6	7	8	9		11	10				
R2/1		26	Mansfield Town	0-0		6294	1	6	3	4	5		7	8		10	11	9				2
R2/2	Sep	2	MANSFIELD TOWN	4-2	Riley, Glavin 3 (1 pen)	10566	1	2	3	4	5	6	7	8		10	11	9				
R3		23	CARDIFF CITY	3-2	Glavin (pen), Parker, Banks	13135	1	2	3	4	5	6	7	8		10	11	9				
R4	Oct	28	West Ham United	1-2	Evans	21548	1		3	4	5	6	7		9	10	11	8				2

R2/2 a.e.t.

Season 1980/81
Back row: Banks, New, McCarthy, Pierce, Parker
Centre row: Young (Youth coach) Wilkinson (Chief scout) Lester, Hunter, Evans, Aylott,
Graham, Murphy (Coach) Rimmington (Physio)
Front row: Cooper, Downes, Chambers, Clarke (Manager) Glavin, Riley, Boyd

Season 1981/82
Back row: New, Horn, Pierce.
Centre row: Collins(Youth coach), Riley, Aylott, Evans, Parker, Joyce, Banks, McCarthy, Rimmington(Physio).
Front row: McHale, Glavin, Downes, Hunter (Manager), Chambers, Cooper, Barrowclough.
Inset: Campbell.

1981/82 — 6th in Division 2

#	Mon	Date	Opponent	Res	Scorers	Att	Horn RI	Joyce JP	Chambers PM	Glavin RM	Banks IF	McCarthy MJ	Evans JP	Parker DH	Aylott TKC	McHale R	Barrowclough SI	Riley G	Campbell WR	Cooper N	Walker C	Law N	Wilkes DA	Birch A	Mann JA	Longden DP
1	Aug	29	SHREWSBURY TOWN	4-0	Aylott 2, Parker, Banks (pen)	13344	1	2	3	4	5	6	7	8	9	10	11									
2	Sep	5	Norwich City	1-1	Parker	12911	1	2	3	4	5	6	7	8	9	10	11									
3		8	Leicester City	0-1		15447	1	2	3	4	5	6	7	8	9*	10	11									
4		12	BOLTON WANDERERS	3-0	Aylott 2, McCarthy	13844	1	2	3	4	5	6	7	8	9	10	11									
5		19	Cambridge United	1-2	Banks	5586	1	2	3	4	5	6	7	8	9	10	11*	12								
6		22	SHEFFIELD WEDNESDAY	1-0	Banks	28870	1	2	3	4	5	6	7	8	9	10	11									
7		26	CARDIFF CITY	0-1		12114	1	2	3	4	5	6	7	8*	9	10	11	12								
8	Oct	3	Watford	1-3	Aylott	10827	1	2	3	4	5	6	7	8	9*	10	11	12								
9		10	Blackburn Rovers	1-2	Banks (pen)	10522	1	2	3	4	5	6	7	8		10	12	9*	11							
10		17	NEWCASTLE UNITED	1-0	Aylott	18477	1	2	3	4	5	6	7	8	9	10			11							
11		24	Chelsea	2-1	Banks, Glavin	15236	1	2	3	4	5	6	7	8	9	10			11							
12		31	ORIENT	1-0	Aylott	13435	1	2	3		5	6	7	8	9	10			11	4						
13	Nov	7	OLDHAM ATHLETIC	3-1	Banks 2 (1 pen), Parker	14918	1	2	3		5	6	7	8	9	10			11	4						
14		14	Rotherham United	4-2	Banks 3 (1 pen), Glavin	18324	1	2	3	4	5	6	7	8	9	10	11									
15		21	WREXHAM	2-2	Parker 2	14544	1	2	3	4	5	6	7	8	9	10	11									
16		24	Sheffield Wednesday	2-2	Parker, Glavin	30861	1	2	3	4	5	6	7	8	9	10	11									
17		28	Charlton Athletic	1-2	Aylott	5553	1	2	3	4	5	6	7		9	10	11				8					
18	Dec	5	CRYSTAL PALACE	2-0	Glavin 2	14877	1	2	3	4	5	6	7		9	10	11				8					
19		12	Queen's Park Rangers	0-1		10972	1	2	3	4	5	6	7		9	10	11				8					
20	Jan	23	Orient	3-1	Walker, Banks, Aylott	3620	1	2	3		5	6	7		9	10	11			4	8					
21		30	CAMBRIDGE UNITED	0-0		13114	1		3	4	5	6	7		9	10	11			2	8					
22	Feb	2	Shrewsbury Town	2-0	Walker, Banks	4392	1		3		5	6	7		9	10				4	8	2	11			
23		6	Bolton Wanderers	1-2	Cooper	11680	1		3		5	6	7		9	10		12		4	8	2	11*			
24		9	WATFORD	0-0		17070	1		3		5	6	7		9	10	11*	12		4	8	2				
25		20	Cardiff City	0-0		4500	1		3		5	6	7	8	9	10	11			4		2				
26		24	NORWICH CITY	0-1		15360	1		3		5	6	7	8*	9	10				4		2		11		
27		27	BLACKBURN ROVERS	0-1		13150	1		3	4	12	6	7		9	10	8		5*			2		11		
28	Mar	6	Newcastle United	0-1		18784	1		3	4	5	6	7		9	10			11*		2			8	12	
29		12	CHELSEA	2-1	Banks, Glavin	12706	1		3	4	5	6	7		9	10					8	2		11		
30		16	LUTON TOWN	4-3	Walker 2, Banks, Evans	14044	1		3	4	5	6	7		9						8	2		11	10	
31		23	GRIMSBY TOWN	3-2	Aylott, Walker, Banks	15383	1		3	4	5	6	7		9						8			11	10	2
32		27	Oldham Athletic	1-1	Glavin	8939	1		3	4	5	6	7*	9	12						8			11	10	2
33	Apr	2	ROTHERHAM UNITED	3-0	Birch 2, Walker	23059	1		3		5	6			9	10					8	7		11	4	2
34		9	Grimsby Town	2-3	Walker 2	12158	1		3	4	5	6									8	7		11		2
35		10	DERBY COUNTY	0-0		13457	1		3	4	5	6	7		9	10				12	8	2		11*		
36		17	Wrexham	0-0		4860	1		3		5	6	7		9	10					8	2		11	4	
37		24	CHARLTON ATHLETIC	1-0	Walker	9287	1		3		5	6	7		9	10					8	2		11	4	
38		28	Derby County	1-0	Walker	11296	1		3		5	6	7		9	10					8	2		11	4	
39	May	1	Crystal Palace	2-1	Walker, Birch	7955	1		3		5	6	7		9	10					8	2		11	4	
40		4	LEICESTER CITY	0-2		15418	1		3		5	6	7		9	10				12	8	2		11	4*	
41		8	QUEEN'S PARK RANGERS	3-0	Birch, Aylott, Walker	10579	1		3		5	6	7		9	10				4	8	2		11		
42		15	Luton Town	1-1	Birch (pen)	14463	1		3		5	6	7		9	10				4	8	2		11		
Apps							42	20	42	27	42	42	40	18	41	40	18	15	7	10	19	19	2	17	10	4
Goals										7	15	1	1	6	11					1	12			5		

F.A. Cup

Rd	Mon	Date	Opponent	Res	Scorers	Att	Horn RI	Joyce JP	Chambers PM	Glavin RM	Banks IF	McCarthy MJ	Evans JP	Parker DH	Aylott TKC	McHale R	Barrowclough SI	Riley G	Campbell WR	Cooper N	Walker C
R3	Jan	5	BLACKPOOL	0-2		13429	1	2	3	4	5	6	7		9	10	11		8*	12	

F.L. Cup (Milk Cup)

Rd	Mon	Date	Opponent	Res	Scorers	Att	Horn RI	Joyce JP	Chambers PM	Glavin RM	Banks IF	McCarthy MJ	Evans JP	Parker DH	Aylott TKC	McHale R	Barrowclough SI	Riley G	Campbell WR	Cooper N	Walker C
R1/1	Sep	2	Peterborough United	3-2	Glavin 2, Joyce	4608	1	2	3	4	5	6	7	8	9	10	11				
R1/2		15	PETERBOROUGH UTD.	6-0	Glavin 2, Parker 2, Aylott, Barrowclough	11198	1	2	3	4	5	6	7	8	9	10	11				
R2/1	Oct	6	SWANSEA CITY	2-0	Riley, Evans	12793	1	2	3	4	5	6	7	8		10	12	9	11*		
R2/2		27	Swansea City	2-3	Glavin, Cooper (aet)	9800	1	2	3	4*	5	6	7	8	9	10	11			12	
R3	Nov	10	BRIGHTON & HOVE A.	4-1	Glavin, McCarthy, Aylott 2	19534	1	2	3	4	5	6	7	8	9	10	11				
R4	Dec	2	MANCHESTER CITY	1-0	Aylott	33792	1	2	3	4	5	6	7		9	10	11				8
R5	Jan	12	Liverpool	0-0		33707	1	2	3		5	6	7		9	10	11			4	8
rep		19	LIVERPOOL	1-3	Walker	29639	1	2	3	12	5*	6	7		9	10	11			4	8

1982/83   10th in Division 2

Date		Opponent	Score	Scorers	Att	Horn RI	Joyce JP	Chambers PM	Ronson W	Banks IF	McCarthy MJ	Souter DD	Walker C	Airey C	Mann JA	Campbell WR	Parker DH	Law N	Barrowclough SJ	Evans IP	Birch A	Glavin RM	Cunningham AE	Ainscow A	Pierce G	Hunter N	Wilkes DA	Moores IR	McGuire MJ	Cross P	Goodison CW	Longden DP	Shutt SJ
Aug	28	Crystal Palace	1-1	Airey	7664	1	2	3	4	5	6	7	8*	9	10	11	12																
Sep	4	OLDHAM ATHLETIC	1-1	Futcher (og)	11909	1	2	3	4	5	6	7		9	10	11	8																
	7	Cambridge United	1-1	Parker	3314	1		3	4		6			9	10	12	8		2	5	7*	11											
	11	Wolverhampton Wan.	0-2		15065	1		3	4		6	12		9	10	7*	8		2	5		11											
	18	BURNLEY	3-0	Glavin 2, Parker	11938	1		3	10	5*	6	7		9			8		2		12	11	4										
	25	Newcastle United	2-1	Glavin, Parker	24522	1		3	10	5	6	7					8		2			11	4	9									
Oct	2	FULHAM	4-3	Banks 2, Glavin, Cunningham	12959	1		3	10	5	6	7					8		2			11	4	9									
	9	QUEEN'S PARK RANGERS	0-1		13270	1		3	10	5	6	7					8		2		12	11*	4	9									
	16	Rotherham United	0-1		13791	1		3	10	5	6	7					8		2		12	11*	4	9									
	19	DERBY COUNTY	1-1	Airey	10343	1	2	3	10	5	6	7		12		8*		4				11	9										
	23	Bolton Wanderers	2-0	Glavin (pen), Birch	7339	1	2	3	10	5	6	7				8						11	4	9									
	30	SHREWSBURY TOWN	2-2	Glavin, Parker	11150	1	2	3	10	5	6	7				9*	8					11	4	12									
Nov	6	Middlesbrough	0-2		11787	1	2	3	10	5	6	7					8	9*				11	4	12									
	13	CHELSEA	1-1	Glavin	13286	1	2	3	10	5	6	7					8	9				11	4										
	20	Grimsby Town	2-1	Glavin, Cunningham	7219	1	2	3		5	6	7			10		8					11	4	9									
	27	LEEDS UNITED	2-1	Campbell, Glavin (pen)	21530	1	2	3		5	6	7				10	8					11	4	9									
Dec	4	Blackburn Rovers	1-1	Campbell	6769	1	2	3	10		6	7					8	9				11	4	5									
	11	CARLISLE UNITED	2-2	Barrowclough, Banks	10229	1	2	3	10	5	6	7					8	4	12		11*		9										
	18	Charlton Athletic	2-3	Glavin, Cunningham	4942		2	3	9	5	6	7					8					11	4		1			10					
	27	SHEFFIELD WEDNESDAY	0-0		23275		2	3	10	5	6						8	7				11	4		1			10					
	28	Leicester City	0-1		14838		2	3	9	5	6						8	7				11	4		1			10					
Jan	1	GRIMSBY TOWN	4-0	Banks, Parker 2, Birch	12318		2	3	9	5							8	7			12	11	4		1			10	6*				
	3	Oldham Athletic	1-1	Parker	8382		2	3	9	5	6						8	7				11	4		1			10					
	15	CRYSTAL PALACE	3-1	Glavin 2, Cunningham	10120		2	3	9	5	6						8	7				11	4		1			10					
	22	Burnley	1-3	Joyce	10358		2	3	9	5	6				10		8	7			11*		4		1		12						
Feb	5	WOLVERHAMPTON W.	2-1	Banks, Parker	13535		2	3	9	5	6						8	7			11		4		1					10			
	19	Queen's Park Rangers	0-3		10271		2	3	9	5	6*						8	7			11		4		1					10			
	26	ROTHERHAM UNITED	2-1	Birch, Parker	13969		2	3	9*	5	6					12	8	7			11		4		1					10			
Mar	5	BOLTON WANDERERS	3-1	Birch, McCarthy, Ronson	10400		2	3	9	5	6					10	8	7			11		4		1								
	12	Shrewsbury Town	1-3	Parker	4024		2	3	9	5		12				10	8	7		6*	11		4		1								
	19	MIDDLESBROUGH	2-0	Birch, Campbell	10681		2	3	9	5	6					10*	8	7			12	11	4		1								
	26	Chelsea	3-0	Hales (og), Cunningham, Park	7223		2	3	9	5	6						8	7			11		10		1				4				
Apr	2	LEICESTER CITY	1-2	McGuire	13278			3	9	5	6		2				8	7			11*		12		1			10	4				
	4	Sheffield Wednesday	1-0	Glavin	22667		2	3	9	5	6						8*	7			11		12		1			10	4				
	9	CAMBRIDGE UNITED	2-3	Cunningham, Glavin	9934		2		9	5	6						12	7			11		10		1				4		3*		
	16	Derby County	1-1	Cunningham	14861		2		9	5	6						8	7			11		12		1			4*				3	
	19	Fulham	0-1		9003			3	9	5	6						8			2	11				1			10				7	4
	23	BLACKBURN ROVERS	2-2	Glavin 2	7617			3	9	5	6		8					7			11		4		1			10			2		
	30	Leeds United	0-0		15346		2	3	9				8					7			11		4		1			10		5			
May	4	NEWCASTLE UNITED	0-5		10958		2	3	9		6		8					7			11*		4		1		12	10		5			
	7	CHARLTON ATHLETIC	0-0		6457	1	2	3		5	6			9							4		10				11		8		7		
	14	Carlisle United	1-1	Glavin	5898	1	2	3	8	5	6			9				7			4		10				11						

	Horn	Joyce	Chambers	Ronson	Banks	McCarthy	Souter	Walker	Airey	Mann	Campbell	Parker	Law	Barrowclough	Evans	Birch	Glavin	Cunningham	Ainscow	Pierce	Hunter	Wilkes	Moores	McGuire	Cross	Goodison	Longden	Shutt
Apps	20	32	40	39	37	39	21	3	11	5	17	32	28	21	2	27	35	29	2	22	1	4	3	7	1	3	1	1
Goals		1		1	5	1			2		3	11				5	17	7						1				

Two own goals

F.A. Cup

Date		Opponent	Score	Scorers	Att	Horn	Joyce	Chambers	Ronson	Banks	McCarthy	Souter	Parker	Law	Birch	Glavin	Cunningham	Pierce
Jan	8	Bradford City	1-0	Glavin	11012		2	3	9	5	6		8	7	11	4	10	1
	29	Cambridge United	0-1		6612		2	3	9	5	6	10*	8	7	11	4	12	1

F.L. Cup (Milk Cup)

Rd	Date		Opponent	Score	Scorers	Att	Horn	Joyce	Chambers	Ronson	Banks	McCarthy	Souter	Walker	Mann	Campbell	Parker	Barrowclough	Birch	Glavin	Cunningham
1	Oct	12	CAMBRIDGE UTD.	2-1	Glavin, McCarthy	8794	1		3	10	5	6	7	9			8	2		11	4
2		26	Cambridge United	3-1	Donaldson (og), Birch, Banks	4500	1	2	3	10	5	6	7				8	9		11	4
3	Nov	9	Sheffield United	3-1	Glavin 2, Kenworthy (og)	25207	1	2	3	10	5	6	7	12			8*	9		11	4
4		30	Sheffield Wednesday	0-1		33354	1	2	3	10	5	6	7				8	9	11		4

Season 1982/83
Back row: Rimmington (Physio) Glavin, Law, McCarthy, Horn, Evans, Pierce,
Banks, Parker, Souter, Collins (Youth coach)
Front row: Campbell, Birch, Longden, Walker, Hunter (Manager) Chambers, Barrowclough, Joyce, Mann

Season 1983/84
Back row: Ogley, Thornton, Knight, Horn, Ironside, Rhodes, Corson, Semley, Smith, Holmes
2nd back: Winstanley (Coach) Goodison, Shutt, Gray, Parker, Airey, Evans, McCarthy,
Cunningham, Law, Campbell, Rimmington (Physio) Collins (Coach)
2nd front: Glavin, Whitehouse, McGuire, Wilkes, Ronson, Hunter (Manager) Chambers, Birch, Fletcher, Joyce
Front row: Peel, Reynolds, Croft, Agnew, Cross, Marshall, Utley, Jeffels, Deakin

1983/84 — 14th in Division 2

#		Date	Opponent	Score	Scorers	Att.	Horn RI	Joyce JP	Chambers PM	Glavin RM	Law N	McCarthy MJ	Wilkes DA	Campbell WR	Ronson W	Cunningham AE	Gray S	May LC	Airey C	McGuire MJ	Findlay JW	Geddis D	Rhodes AC	Fletcher MRJ	Whitehouse D	Semley A	Pickering MJ	Lowe SJ	Johnson DE	Jeffels S	Thomas DG	Futcher P	Plummer CA	Agnew SM
1	Aug	27	FULHAM	3-0	Wilkes 2, Gray	9851	1	2	3	4	5	6	7	8	9	10	11																	
2	Sep	3	Manchester City	2-3	Chambers, Gray	25105	1	2	3	4		6	7	8	9	10	11	5																
3		6	Portsmouth	1-2	Gray	12804	1	2	3	4		6	7	8	9	10	11	5																
4		10	MIDDLESBROUGH	0-2		10039	1	2	3	4		6	7	8*	9	10	11	5	12															
5		17	Shrewsbury Town	2-3	Gray, Cunningham	3857	1	2	3			6	7		9	10	11	5	8	4														
6		24	NEWCASTLE UNITED	1-1	Cunningham	14085		2	3	4		6	7			10	11	5	9	8	1													
7		27	GRIMSBY TOWN	3-1	Gray, Geddis 2	10966		2	3	4		6	7			10	11	5	12	8	1	9*												
8	Oct	1	Cardiff City	3-0	Glavin 2, Geddis	6378		2	3	4		6	7			10	11	5	8		1	9												
9		8	Derby County	2-0	Glavin, Cunningham	12611		2	3	4		6			7	10	11	5	8		1	9												
10		15	HUDDERSFIELD T	2-2	Geddis, Cunningham	14096		2	3	4		6			7	10	11	5	8		1	9												
11		22	LEEDS UNITED	0-2		18236		2	3			6	12	7	4	10	11*	5	8		1	9												
12		29	Crystal Palace	1-0	May	6477		4	3	2		6	7			11	10	5	8			9	1											
13	Nov	5	Sheffield Wednesday	0-2		27758		4	3	12	2	6	7*			11	10	5	8			9	1											
14		12	SWANSEA CITY	3-2	Glavin, Gray 2 (1 pen)	8161		7	3	4	2	6					11	5	10	8		9	1											
15		19	Charlton Athletic	2-3	Geddis, Glavin	4582		7	3	4	2	6					11	5	10	8		9	1											
16		26	BRIGHTON & HOVE ALB	3-1	Gray (pen), Airey 2	7705		4	3		2	6		7			11	5	10	8		9	1											
17	Dec	3	Oldham Athletic	0-1		5475		7	3	4	2*	6		12			11	5	10	8		9	1											
18		10	CHELSEA	0-0		10300		2	3	4	12	6		7	8		11*	5	10			9	1											
19		17	Carlisle United	2-4	Airey, Joyce	4412		7	3	4		6		8				5	10			9	1			2	11							
20		26	CAMBRIDGE UNITED	2-0	McGuire, Law	7486		2	3	4	6			11	8			5	10	7		9	1											
21		28	Blackburn Rovers	1-1	Glavin	8960		2	3	4	6*			11	8			5	10	7		9	1							12				
22		31	MANCHESTER CITY	1-1	Geddis	17148		2	3	4				11	8			5	10*	7		9	1					12	6					
23	Jan	2	Newcastle United	0-1		29842		2	3	4				11	8			5	10*	7		9	1					12	6					
24		14	Fulham	0-1		5085		4	3	2				11	8			5		7		9	1					12	6	10*				
25	Feb	4	CARDIFF CITY	2-3	McGuire, Geddis	7107		2	3	4	6			11	8			5		7		9	1						10					
26		11	Middlesbrough	1-2	Glavin	7480		2*	3	4	6			11	8			5	12	7			1					9						
27		18	CRYSTAL PALACE	1-1	Geddis	6237		3	4	2				11	8			5	9	7			1					10			6			
28		25	Leeds United	2-1	Glavin, Johnson	19132		3	4	2				11	8			5	9	7			1					10			6			
29	Mar	3	SHEFFIELD WEDNESDAY	0-1		20322		12	3	4	2			11	8			5		7			1			9*		10			6			
30		10	Swansea City	0-1		4864		2	3	4	6			11	8			5	10			9	1											
31		13	SHREWSBURY TOWN	3-0	Geddis, Glavin, Campb	5576		2	3	4	6			11				5	10	7		9	1								8			
32		17	Portsmouth	0-3		7030		2	3	4*	6			11		12		5	9	7			1							10	8			
33		31	DERBY COUNTY	5-1	McGuire 2, Plummer, Rons	6500		2	3	4					7			5	12	8		9	1							10	6	11*	
34	Apr	7	Huddersfield Town	1-0	Geddis	9657		2	3*	4				11	7			5	12	8		9	1							10	6		
35		10	Grimsby Town	0-1		6769		2	4*	3				11	7			5	12	8		9	1							10	6		12
36		14	CHARLTON ATHLETIC	2-0	Glavin, McGuire (pen)	6321		2	4	3				11	7			5	9*	8			1							10	6		12
37		21	Cambridge United	3-0	Geddis 2, Ronson	2486		2	4	3				11	7			5	12	8		10*	1								9	6	12	
38		23	BLACKBURN ROVERS	0-0		7123		2	4	3				11	7			5	9*	8			1							10	6	12	
39		28	Brighton & Hove Albion	0-1		8987		2	3	4				11	7			5	9	8			1							10	6		
40	May	5	OLDHAM ATHLETIC	0-1		5539		2	3	4				11	7			5		8		10	1							9	6		
41		7	Chelsea	1-3	Geddis	29541		2	3					11	7			5	4	8		10	1						9		6		
42		12	CARLISLE UNITED	2-1	Geddis, Campbell	4672		2		3				11	7			5		8		10	1					9			4	6		
			Apps				5	40	37	35	31	12	11	31	32	13	17	41	27	36	6	31	31	1	2	4	3	2	4	3	13	10	2	1
			Goals					1	1	11	1		2	2	2	4	8	1	3	5		14							1				1	

F.A. Cup

		Date	Opponent	Score		Att.	Joyce	Chambers	Glavin	McCarthy	Campbell	Ronson	May	Airey	McGuire	Geddis	Rhodes	Lowe
R1	Jan	7	Sheffield Wednesday	0-1		29638	2	3	4	6	11*	8	5	10	7	9	1	12

F.L. Cup (Milk Cup)

		Date	Opponent	Score		Att.	Joyce	Chambers	Glavin	McCarthy	Wilkes	Campbell	Cunningham	Gray	May	Airey	Geddis	Findlay
R2/1	Oct	4	Walsall	0-1		3681	2	3	4	6	7*	12	10	11	5	8	9	1
R2/2		25	WALSALL	0-2		7844	2	3		6	7*	11	10		5	8	9	1

Played in R2/2: SJ Shutt (at 4)

1984/85   11th in Division 2

#	Date	Opponent	Score	Scorers	Att	Rhodes AC	Joyce JP	Chambers PM	Ronson W	May LC	Futcher P	Owen G	Thomas DG	Walsh IP	Geddis D	Campbell WR	Plummer CA	Law N	Agnew SM	Baker CE	McGuire MJ	Jeffels S	Cross P	Wylde RJ	Futcher R	Goodison CW	Gray S
1	Aug 25	Grimsby Town	0-1		6190	1	2	3	4	5	6	7	8	9*	10	11	12										
2	27	CARLISLE UNITED	1-3	Owen	5681	1	2	3	4	5	6	7	8	9	10		11										
3	Sep 1	OLDHAM ATHLETIC	0-1		5121	1	2		4	5	6	7	8		10*	11	9	3	12								
4	4	Notts County	2-0	May, Plummer	4703		2		4	5	6	7	8	9		11	10	3		1							
5	8	Portsmouth	0-0		11509		2		4	5	6		8	9	7	11	10*	3		1		12					
6	15	CARDIFF CITY	2-0	Geddis 2 (1 pen)	4692		2		4	5	6		8	9*	7	11	10	3		1		12					
7	22	Huddersfield Town	1-1	Campbell	6864		2		4	5*	6		8	12	10	11	9	3		1		7					
8	29	WOLVERHAMPTON W.	5-1	Agnew, Geddis 3 (2p), Owen	5566		2		4		6	7	8	12	10	11		3	9*	1		5					
9	Oct 7	Crystal Palace	1-0	Geddis	6261		2		4		6		8	12	10	7		3	9*	1		5	11				
10	13	LEEDS UNITED	1-0	Owen	16199		2		4		6	7	8	9	10*	11	12	3		1		5					
11	20	Brighton & Hove Albion	0-0		10944		2		4		6	7	8	9		11	10	3		1		5					
12	27	CHARLTON ATHLETIC	1-0	Owen	6301		2		4		6	7	8			11	10	3	9	1		5					
13	Nov 10	Middlesbrough	0-0		5231		2		4		6	7	8		10	11	9	3		1		5					
14	13	SHEFFIELD UNITED	1-0	Thomas	13468		2		4		6	7	8		10	11	9	3		1		5					
15	17	SHREWSBURY TOWN	3-1	Geddis 2, Plummer (pen)	6257		2		4		6	7	8		10	11	9	3		1		5					
16	24	Birmingham City	0-0		9505		2		4		6	7	8		10*	11	9	3		1	12	5					
17	Dec 1	FULHAM	1-0	Owen	6742		2		4		6	7	8	9		11	10	3		1		5					
18	8	Wimbledon	3-3	Geddis 2 (1 pen), Owen	2871		2		4		6	7	8		10	11		3		1		5		9			
19	23	Oldham Athletic	1-2	Owen (pen)	5687		2		4		6	7	8			11	12	3		1		5		10	9*		
20	26	Manchester City	1-1	Wylde	27131		2		4	5	6		8	9		11	7	3		1				10			
21	29	NOTTS COUNTY	0-0		7447		2		4	5	6	7	8	12		11	9	3		1				10*			
22	Jan 1	BLACKBURN ROVERS	1-1	Owen (pen)	10628		2		4	5	6	7	8	9		11	10	3		1				10			
23	Feb 2	Wolverhampton Wan.	1-0	Futcher R	6864		2	3	4			7	8			11	12	5		1				10	9*	6	
24	9	PORTSMOUTH	2-2	Campbell, Wylde	7382		2		4		6	7	8			11		3		1				10	9	5	
25	23	Sheffield United	1-3	Owen	16343		2		4		6	7	8			11		3		1				9	10	5	
26	26	MIDDLESBROUGH	1-0	Wylde	6866		2		4			7	8			11		3		1		6		10	9	5	
27	Mar 2	Charlton Athletic	3-5	Futcher R 3	3832		2		4		6	7	8			11		3	10	1		5			9		
28	13	BRIGHTON & HOVE ALB	0-0		5342		2		4	5	6	7	8			11									9	3	10
29	16	Leeds United	0-2		13075		2		4	5	6	7	8	9		11		3	10*	1					12		
30	23	CRYSTAL PALACE	3-1	Campbell, Owen 2	4174	1	2		4	5	6	7	8			11		3	9					10			
31	30	Carlisle United	0-2		2784	1	2		4	5	6	7	8			11		3						10	9		
32	Apr 2	OXFORD UNITED	3-0	Owen 3	6029		2		4	5	6	7	8			11		3	12	1				10	9*		
33	6	MANCHESTER CITY	0-0		12930			3	4	5	6	7	8			11				1				10	9	2	
34	8	Blackburn Rovers	0-0		9322		2	3	4	5	6	7				11				1				10	9		
35	13	HUDDERSFIELD T	2-1	Futcher R, Wylde (pen)	7832		2	3		5	6					11				1		7		10	9	8	4
36	20	Shrewsbury Town	0-2		3148		2		4	5	6	7	8			11		3		1				10*	9		12
37	23	Cardiff City	0-3		3044		2			5	6	7	8			11		3		1	9*			10	12	4	11
38	27	BIRMINGHAM CITY	0-1		6757		2		4	5	6	7	8			11	10*	3		1				12	9		
39	30	GRIMSBY TOWN	0-0		3261		2		4	5		7	8			11		3	10*	1		6			9		12
40	May 4	Fulham	1-1	Plummer	3625		2	3	4			7	8			11	10	5		1		6			9		
41	6	WIMBLEDON	0-0		3053		2		4			7	8			11	10	5*		1		6			9	12	3
42	11	Oxford United	0-4		13195		2		4	5		7	8	10		11				1		6*			9	12	3
		Apps				5	41	7	40	23	36	36	40	16	14	38	26	35	10	37	4	18	1	17	19	12	7
		Goals								1		14	1		10	3	3		1					4	5		

F.A. Cup

Rd	Date	Opponent	Score	Scorers	Att	Rhodes AC	Joyce JP	Chambers PM	Ronson W	May LC	Futcher P	Owen G	Thomas DG	Walsh IP	Geddis D	Campbell WR	Plummer CA	Law N	Agnew SM	Baker CE	McGuire MJ	Jeffels S	Cross P	Wylde RJ	Futcher R	Goodison CW	Gray S
R3	Jan 5	READING	4-3	Futcher R. Owen 2 (1p), Joyce	7272		2		4	5	6	7	8			11		3		1				10	9		
R4	26	BRIGHTON & HOVE ALB.	2-1	Owen, Futcher R	8860		2		4			7	8			11		3		1		5		10	9	6	
R5	Mar 4	Southampton	2-1	Agnew, Owen (pen)	20971		2		4	5	6	7	8			11		3	10*	1		12			9		
R6	10	LIVERPOOL	0-4		19838		2		4	5	6	7	8			11			10*	1					9	3	12

F.L. Cup (Milk Cup)

Rd	Date	Opponent	Score	Scorers	Att	Rhodes AC	Joyce JP	Chambers PM	Ronson W	May LC	Futcher P	Owen G	Thomas DG	Walsh IP	Geddis D	Campbell WR	Plummer CA	Law N	Agnew SM	Baker CE	McGuire MJ	Jeffels S	Cross P	Wylde RJ	Futcher R	Goodison CW	Gray S
R2/1	Sep 25	Grimsby Town	0-3		3577		2	3*	4		6		8	7	10	11	9	5		1		12					
R2/2	Oct 9	GRIMSBY TOWN	1-1	Campbell	5578		2	3	4		6		8	9	10	12	7	5		1		11*					

Season 1984/85
Back row: Wilkes, Airey, May, Law, Geddis, Futcher
Centre row: Winstanley (Coach) Campbell, Gray, Baker, Rhodes, Walsh, Plummer, Clayton (Physio)
Front row: Owen, Ronson, McGuire, Collins (Manager) Thomas, Chambers, Joyce

Season 1985/86
Back row: Plummer, Goodison, Law, Jeffels, Futcher, Gray
Centre row: Winstanley (Coach) Agnew, Wylde, Rhodes, Baker, May, Glavin, Rimmington (Physio)
Front row: Ronson, Campbell, Joyce, Clarke (Manager) Walsh. Owen, Thomas

1985/86 — 12th in Division 2

#	Mon	Date	Opponent	Score	Scorers	Att	Baker CE	Joyce JP	Law N	Thomas DG	Burns K	Jeffels S	Goodison CW	Hirst DE	Walsh IP	Gray S	Campbell WR	Ronson W	Futcher P	Glavin RM	Owen G	Plummer CA	May LC	Cross P	Agnew SM	Ogley MA	McKenzie IE	Jonsson S	Aylott TKC	Kwomya AD
1	Aug	17	Charlton Athletic	1-2	Gray (pen)	4178	1	2	3*	4	5	6	7	8	9	10	11	12												
2		20	BRIGHTON & HOVE ALB	3-2	Thomas 2, Walsh	5051	1	2		4	5	7	3	8	9	10*	11		6	12										
3		24	STOKE CITY	0-0		6588	1	2		4	5	10	3	8	9*		11		6		7	12								
4		26	Norwich City	1-1	Owen	12376	1	2		8	5	10	3		9		11		6	4	7									
5		31	FULHAM	2-0	Owen, Walsh	5197	1	2			5	8*	3	12	9	10	11		6	4	7									
6	Sep	3	Wimbledon	0-1		2351	1	2			5	8	3		9	10	11		6	4	7									
7		7	Carlisle United	1-1	Owen (pen)	2418	1	2			5		3		9	10	11		6	4*	7	12	8							
8		14	SHREWSBURY TOWN	2-0	Campbell, Walsh	4516	1	2		8	5				9	3	11		6		7		4	10						
9		21	GRIMSBY TOWN	1-0	Walsh	5365	1	2		8	5				9	3	11		6		7		4	10						
10		28	Middlesbrough	0-0		2272	1	2		8	5				9	3	11		6		7		4	10						
11	Oct	5	PORTSMOUTH	0-1		7064	1	2		8	5			7	9	3	11		6				4	10						
12		12	Bradford City	0-2		5707	1	2		10	5			8*		3	11		6	4		12	7			9				
13		19	Sheffield United	1-3	Owen (pen)	11167	1	2		10	5					3	11	8	6		7		4			9				
14		27	LEEDS UNITED	3-0	Owen, Hirst, Walsh	8444	1	2		8			4	10	9	3			6		7		11	5						
15	Nov	2	OLDHAM ATHLETIC	1-0	Donache (og)	7118	1	2		8			4	10	9	3			6		7		11	5						
16		9	Blackburn Rovers	3-0	Hirst 2, Walsh	5927	1	2		8			4	10	9	3			6		7		11	5						
17		16	SUNDERLAND	1-1	Hirst	9410	1	2		8			4	10	9	3			6		7		11	5						
18		23	Crystal Palace	0-1		5625	1	2		8	12		4	10	9	3			6		7*			5	11					
19		30	MILLWALL	2-1	Owen (pen), Gray	4340	1	2		8			4	10	9	3	11		6		7			5						
20	Dec	7	Brighton & Hove Albion	1-0	Hirst	8829	1	2		8			4	10		3	9		6		7		11	5						
21		14	CHARLTON ATHLETIC	2-1	Hirst 2	6231	1	2		8			4	10	9	3			6		7		11	5						
22		21	Stoke City	0-0		9895	1	2		8			4	10	9	3			6		7		11	5						
23		26	Huddersfield Town	1-1	Hirst	10575	1	2		8			4	10	9	3			6		7		11	5						
24		28	WIMBLEDON	0-1		9067	1	2		8	12		4	10		3	9		6		7		11*	5						
25	Jan	1	HULL CITY	1-4	Owen (pen)	8363	1	2		8	9		4	10		3			6		7		11	5						
26		11	Shrewsbury Town	0-3		2756	1	2		8				10	9	3	11		6		7			5			4			
27		18	Fulham	0-2		3803	1	2		8			12		9*	3	11		6		7	10		5	4					
28	Feb	1	NORWICH CITY	2-2	Hirst, Thomas	5608	1			4	2			10	9	3			6		7		11	5				8		
29		15	Leeds United	2-0	Walsh 2	11738	1			4	2			10*	9	3	12		6		7		11	5				8		
30	Mar	8	Portsmouth	1-1	Walsh	10426	1	2		4					9	3			6		7		11	5				8	10	
31		15	BRADFORD CITY	2-2	Thomas, Owen (pen)	7512	1	2		4					9	3			6		7*	12	11	5				8	10	
32		22	CARLISLE UNITED	1-2	Walsh	4400	1	2		4					9	3			6		7	12	11*	5				8	10	
33		25	MIDDLESBROUGH	0-0		3827	1	2		4				10	8	3			6		7		11	5						
34		29	Hull City	1-0	Plummer	7903	1	2		4		6		10		3						7	8	5					9	
35		31	HUDDERSFIELD T	1-3	Plummer	5746	1	2		4		3		10			11					7	8	5					9	
36	Apr	6	Oldham Athletic	1-1	Thomas	3974	1	2		4	8		12	10			11*		6		7			5	3				9	
37		8	SHEFFIELD UNITED	2-1	Walsh 2	5451	1	2		4	8			10	11	3			6		7			5					9	
38		12	BLACKBURN ROVERS	1-1	Walsh	4256	1	2		4	8	12		10	11	3			6		7			5					9*	
39		19	Sunderland	0-2		12349	1	2		4			8	10	9	3	11		6		7			5						
40		22	Grimsby Town	2-1	Walsh, Owen	4224	1	2		4		6*	12	9	8	3	10				7			5						11
41		26	CRYSTAL PALACE	2-4	Owen, Walsh	3862	1	2		4	12	6		9	8	10*	11				7		3	5						
42	May	3	Millwall	2-2	Plummer, Owen (pen)	4230	1	2		4		6		9	8	3	11				10	7		5						
Apps							42	40	1	39	22	11	21	28	33	36	29	2	37	6	32	23	36	20	2	2	1	5	9	1
Goals										5				9	15	2	1				11	3							

One own goal

F.A. Cup

Rd	Mon	Date	Opponent	Score	Scorers	Att	Baker CE	Joyce JP	Thomas DG	Burns K	Goodison CW	Walsh IP	Gray S	Futcher P	Owen G	Plummer CA	May LC	Cross P
R3	Jan	13	Bury	0-2		3676	1	2	8	10*	4	9	3	6	7	12	11	5

F.L. Cup (Milk Cup)

Rd	Mon	Date	Opponent	Score	Scorers	Att	Baker CE	Joyce JP	Thomas DG	Burns K	Goodison CW	Hirst DE	Walsh IP	Gray S	Campbell WR	Futcher P	Glavin RM	Owen G	Plummer CA	May LC	Cross P	Ogley MA
R2/1	Sep	25	Newcastle United	0-0		18544	1	2	8	5	3		9		11	6		7		4	10	
R2/2	Oct	7	NEWCASTLE UTD.	1-1	Gray (pen)	10084	1	2	10	5		8*		3	11	6	4	7	12			9

(Newcastle U won on away goals)

1986/87 11th in Division 2

#	Date	Opponent	Res	Scorers	Att	Baker CE	Joyce JP	Cross P	Thomas DG	May LC	Futcher P	Lowndes SR	Bradshaw C	Campbell WR	Gray S	Beresford J	Plummer CA	Wylde RJ	Ogley MA	Agnew SM	Chandler I	Foreman D	Dobbin J	Malcolm PA	Hedworth C	Duggan AJ	Ferry W	Clarke MD	MacDonald J	Jeffels S
1	Aug 23	CRYSTAL PALACE	2-3	Bradshaw, Thomas	4629	1	2	3	4	5	6	7	8	9	10	11														
2	25	Oldham Athletic	0-2		5306	1	2	3	4	5	6	7	8	9*	10	11	12													
3	30	Millwall	0-1		4028	1	2	3	4	5	6	7	8*	12	10	11		9												
4	Sep 2	LEEDS UNITED	0-1		6843	1	2	3	4	5	6	7	8	12	10	11		9*												
5	6	PORTSMOUTH	0-2		4341	1	2	3	4		6	7	8*		10	11	12		5	9										
6	13	Shrewsbury Town	0-1		2435	1	2	3	4		6	7*	8		10		12		5	11	9									
7	20	PLYMOUTH ARGYLE	1-1	May	4163	1	2		4	5	6	7			3	12				11	9*	8	10							
8	27	Grimsby Town	1-0	Gray	4791	1	2	3	4	5	6				10	7				11	9	8								
9	Oct 4	Birmingham City	1-1	Foreman	6427	1	2	3	4	5					10	7				11	12	9*	8							
10	11	BRADFORD CITY	2-0	Gray 2 (1 pen)	6978		2		4	5		7			3	10			6	11	12	9*	8	1						
11	18	Brighton & Hove Albion	1-1	Dobbin	7924		2		4	5		7			3	10			6	11		9	8	1						
12	25	SHEFFIELD UNITED	2-2	Gray 2 (1 pen)	7613		2		4	5		7*			10				6	11	12	9	8	1	3					
13	Nov 1	BLACKBURN ROVERS	1-1	Gray (pen)	4861	1	2		4	5					10				6	11*	12	9	8		3*					
14	8	Reading	0-0		5566	1	2		4	5	6	7			10					12	11	9	8		3*					
15	15	DERBY COUNTY	0-1		8283	1	2		4	5	6	7*			10					12	11	9	8		3					
16	22	Ipswich Town	0-1		10158	1		3	4	5		7			10	11			2			9	8*				6	12		
17	29	WEST BROMWICH ALB.	2-2	Lowndes, Beresford	5750	1		3	4	5		7*			6	11	8		2			9							12	10
18	Dec 13	SUNDERLAND	1-0	Gray	5535	1			4	5	6				3	11			2			7	9						8	10
19	20	Portsmouth	1-2	Ferry	9568	1			4	5	6				3	11			2	8		7					9		9*	10
20	26	STOKE CITY	0-2		7436	1		3	4	5	6				11	7			2			8							12	10
21	27	Derby County	2-3	Chandler, Gray	17574	1			4	5	6				3				2	7	9	8						11		10
22	Jan 1	Hull City	4-3	Chandler 3, Duggan	4879	1		3	4		6				5				2	8	9	7*				12		11		10
23	3	OLDHAM ATHLETIC	1-1	MacDonald	8101	1		3	4	5	6				7				2	8	9							11		10
24	24	Crystal Palace	1-0	MacDonald	6011	1	2	3	4	5	6				7					8			9		12			11		10*
25	Feb 7	MILLWALL	1-0	Dobbin	5461	1	2	3	4	5	6				7*					8			9		12			11		10
26	14	Leeds United	2-2	Sheridan (og), Dobbin	14196	1	2	3	4		6								5	8			9		7			11		10
27	24	GRIMSBY TOWN	1-0	MacDonald	5136	1	2	3	4		6				5					8			9		7			11*		10
28	28	Plymouth Argyle	0-2		9588	1	2	3			6				5	12			4	8			9		7			11*		10
29	Mar 3	SHREWSBURY TOWN	2-1	MacDonald, Gray	4718	1	2				6				5	12			4	8	7*		9		3			11		10
30	7	Sheffield United	0-1		8971	1	2				6				5	7				8			9		3			11		10
31	14	BRIGHTON & HOVE ALB	3-1	MacDonald, Wylde, Gray	4733	1	2		4		6				5	3		7		8			9					11		10
32	21	Bradford City	0-0		9648	1	2		4		6				5	3		7		8			9					11		10
33	28	BIRMINGHAM CITY	2-2	Wylde 2	4688	1	2		4		6				5	3		7		8			9		12			11*		10
34	31	Huddersfield Town	2-2	MacDonald, Thomas	7569	1	2		4		6				5	3		7		8			9					11		10
35	Apr 4	READING	2-0	Wylde, Gray	4285	1	2		4		6				5	3		7		8*			9					11		10
36	11	Blackburn Rovers	2-4	Clarke, MacDonald	7320	1	2		4		6				5	3		7					9		12			11		10
37	18	HULL CITY	1-1	Wylde	5607	1	2		4		6				5			7		8			9		3			11		10
38	20	Stoke City	2-1	Thomas, Clarke	7260	1	2		4		6				5			7		8			9		3			11		10
39	25	IPSWICH TOWN	2-1	Thomas, Wylde	5536	1	2		4		6				5	12		7					9		3*			11		10
40	May 2	West Bromwich Albion	1-0	Clarke	6361	1	2		4		6					8		7					9		3			11	10	5
41	4	HUDDERSFIELD T	0-1		8564	1	2		4		6				10	8		7					9		3*	12		11		5
42	9	Sunderland	3-2	Dobbin, Wylde, Thomas	19059	1	2		4		6				5	3		7		8*			9					11	10	12
		Apps				39	34	18	40	22	36	15	6	4	40	27	3	15	17	33	12	16	30	3	20	2	4	23	25	3
		Goals							5	1		1	1		11	1		7			4	1	4			1	1	3	7	

One own goal

F.A. Cup

Rd	Date	Opponent	Res	Scorers	Att	Baker CE	Joyce JP	Cross P	Thomas DG	May LC	Futcher P	Lowndes SR	Bradshaw C	Campbell WR	Gray S	Beresford J	Plummer CA	Wylde RJ	Ogley MA	Agnew SM	Chandler I	Foreman D	Dobbin J	Malcolm PA	Hedworth C	Duggan AJ	Ferry W	Clarke MD	MacDonald J	Jeffels S
R3	Jan 10	Caernarfon Town	0-0		2630	1		3	4	5	6				7				2	8	9							11		10
rep	26	CAERNARFON TOWN	1-0	Wylde	8530	1		3	4	5	6				7			10	2	8	9							11		
R4	31	Aldershot	1-1	Agnew	4772	1	2	3	4	5	6				7					12	8	9						11*		10
rep	Feb 3	ALDERSHOT	3-0	May 2, Thomas	9784	1	2	3	4	5	6				7					12	8	9						11		10*
R5	21	Arsenal	0-2		28,302	1	2	3	4	5	6									8		9			7			11		10

F.L. Cup (Littlewoods Challenge Cup)

Rd	Date	Opponent	Res	Scorers	Att	Baker CE	Joyce JP	Cross P	Thomas DG	May LC	Futcher P	Lowndes SR	Bradshaw C	Campbell WR	Gray S	Beresford J	Plummer CA	Wylde RJ	Ogley MA	Agnew SM	Chandler I	Foreman D	Dobbin J	Malcolm PA	Hedworth C	Duggan AJ	Ferry W	Clarke MD	MacDonald J	Jeffels S
R2/1	Sep 23	TOTTENHAM HOTSPUR	2-3	Gray 2 (1 pen)	9979	1	2	3	4	5	6	7*			10	12				11	9	8								
R2/1	Oct 8	Tottenham Hotspur	3-5	Beresford, May, Chandler	12299	1	2	3*	4	5	6^				10	8			12	11	7	9			13					

Full Members Cup

Rd	Date	Opponent	Res	Scorers	Att	Baker CE	Joyce JP	Cross P	Thomas DG	May LC	Futcher P	Lowndes SR	Bradshaw C	Campbell WR	Gray S	Beresford J	Plummer CA	Wylde RJ	Ogley MA	Agnew SM	Chandler I	Foreman D	Dobbin J	Malcolm PA	Hedworth C	Duggan AJ	Ferry W	Clarke MD	MacDonald J	Jeffels S
R1	Sep 16	Sunderland	1-1	Gray	6904	1	2	3	4	5	6	7			10	12				11	9	8*								

Lost 7-8 on penalties a.e.t.

FINAL LEAGUE TABLES: 1986/87 - 1991/92

Final League Table 1986/7 Division 2

		Pl.	Home					Away					F.	A.	Pts
			W	D	L	F	A	W	D	L	F	A			
1	Derby County	42	14	6	1	42	18	11	3	7	22	20	64	38	84
2	Portsmouth	42	17	2	2	37	11	6	7	8	16	17	53	28	78
3	Oldham Athletic	42	13	6	2	36	16	9	3	9	29	28	65	44	75
4	Leeds United	42	15	4	2	43	16	4	7	10	15	28	58	44	68
5	Ipswich Town	42	12	6	3	29	10	5	7	9	30	33	59	43	64
6	Crystal Palace	42	12	4	5	35	20	7	1	13	16	33	51	53	62
7	Plymouth Argyle	42	12	6	3	40	23	4	7	10	22	34	62	57	61
8	Stoke City	42	11	5	5	40	21	5	5	11	23	32	63	53	58
9	Sheffield United	42	10	8	3	31	19	5	5	11	19	30	50	49	58
10	Bradford City	42	10	5	6	36	27	5	5	11	26	35	62	62	55
11	BARNSLEY	42	8	7	6	26	23	6	6	9	23	29	49	52	55
12	Blackburn Rovers	42	11	4	6	30	22	4	6	11	15	33	45	55	55
13	Reading	42	11	4	6	33	23	3	7	11	19	36	52	59	53
14	Hull City	42	10	6	5	25	22	3	8	10	16	33	41	55	53
15	West Bromwich A.	42	8	6	7	29	22	5	6	10	22	27	51	49	51
16	Millwall	42	10	5	6	27	16	4	4	13	12	29	39	45	51
17	Huddersfield Town	42	9	6	6	38	30	4	6	11	16	31	54	61	51
18	Shrewsbury Town	42	11	3	7	24	14	4	3	14	17	39	41	53	51
19	Birmingham City	42	8	9	4	27	21	3	8	10	20	38	47	59	50
20	Sunderland	42	8	6	7	25	23	4	6	11	24	36	49	59	48
21	Grimsby Town	42	5	8	8	18	21	5	6	10	21	38	39	59	44
22	Brighton & Hove A.	42	7	6	8	22	20	2	6	13	15	34	37	54	39

Final League Table 1987/88 Division 2

		Pl.	Home					Away					F.	A.	Pts
			W	D	L	F	A	W	D	L	F	A			
1	Millwall	44	15	3	4	45	23	10	4	8	27	29	72	52	82
2	Aston Villa	44	9	7	6	31	21	13	5	4	37	20	68	41	78
3	Middlesbrough	44	15	4	3	44	16	7	8	7	19	20	63	36	78
4	Bradford City	44	14	3	5	49	26	8	8	6	25	28	74	54	77
5	Blackburn Rovers	44	12	8	2	38	22	9	6	7	30	30	68	52	77
6	Crystal Palace	44	16	3	3	50	21	6	6	10	36	38	86	59	75
7	Leeds United	44	14	4	4	37	18	5	8	9	24	33	61	51	69
8	Ipswich Town	44	14	3	5	38	17	5	6	11	23	35	61	52	66
9	Manchester City	44	11	4	7	50	28	8	4	10	30	32	80	60	65
10	Oldham Athletic	44	13	4	5	43	27	5	7	10	29	37	72	64	65
11	Stoke City	44	12	6	4	34	22	5	5	12	16	35	50	57	62
12	Swindon Town	44	10	7	5	43	25	6	4	12	30	35	73	60	59
13	Leicester City	44	12	5	5	35	20	4	6	12	27	41	62	61	59
14	BARNSLEY	44	11	4	7	42	32	4	8	10	19	30	61	62	57
15	Hull City	44	10	8	4	32	22	4	7	11	22	38	54	60	57
16	Plymouth Argyle	44	12	4	6	44	26	4	4	14	21	41	65	67	56
17	Bournemouth	44	7	7	8	36	30	6	3	13	20	38	56	68	49
18	Shrewsbury Town	44	7	8	7	23	22	4	8	10	19	32	42	54	49
19	Birmingham City	44	7	9	6	20	24	4	6	12	21	42	41	66	48
20	West Bromwich A.	44	8	7	7	29	26	4	4	14	21	43	50	69	47
21	Sheffield United	44	8	6	8	27	28	5	1	16	18	46	45	74	46
22	Reading	44	5	7	10	20	25	5	5	12	24	45	44	70	42
23	Huddersfield Town	44	4	6	12	20	38	2	4	16	21	62	41	100	28

Final League Table 1988/89 Division 2

		Pl.	Home					Away					F.	A.	Pts
			W	D	L	F	A	W	D	L	F	A			
1	Chelsea	46	15	6	2	50	25	14	6	3	46	25	96	50	99
2	Manchester City	46	12	8	3	48	28	11	5	7	29	25	77	53	82
3	Crystal Palace	46	15	6	2	42	17	8	6	9	29	32	71	49	81
4	Watford	46	14	5	4	41	18	8	7	8	33	30	74	48	78
5	Blackburn Rovers	46	16	4	3	50	22	6	7	10	24	37	74	59	77
6	Swindon Town	46	13	8	2	35	15	7	8	8	33	38	68	53	76
7	BARNSLEY	46	12	8	3	37	21	8	6	9	29	37	66	58	74
8	Ipswich Town	46	13	3	7	42	23	9	4	10	29	38	71	61	73
9	West Bromwich A.	46	13	7	3	43	18	5	11	7	22	23	65	41	72
10	Leeds United	46	12	6	5	34	20	5	10	8	25	30	59	50	67
11	Sunderland	46	12	8	3	40	23	4	7	12	20	37	60	60	63
12	Bournemouth	46	13	3	7	32	20	5	5	13	21	42	53	62	62
13	Stoke City	46	10	9	4	33	25	5	5	13	24	47	57	72	59
14	Bradford City	46	8	11	4	29	22	5	6	12	23	37	52	59	56
15	Leicester City	46	11	6	6	31	20	2	10	11	25	43	56	63	55
16	Oldham Athletic	46	9	10	4	49	32	2	11	10	26	40	75	72	54
17	Oxford United	46	11	6	6	40	34	3	6	14	22	36	62	70	54
18	Plymouth Argyle	46	11	4	8	35	22	3	8	12	20	44	55	66	54
19	Brighton & Hove A.	46	11	5	7	36	24	3	4	16	21	42	57	66	51
20	Portsmouth	46	10	6	7	33	21	3	6	14	20	41	53	62	51
21	Hull City	46	7	9	7	31	25	4	5	14	21	43	52	68	47
22	Shrewsbury Town	46	4	11	8	25	31	4	7	12	15	36	40	67	42
23	Birmingham City	46	6	4	13	21	33	2	7	14	10	43	31	76	35
24	Walsall	46	3	10	10	27	42	2	6	15	14	38	41	80	31

Final League Table 1989/90 Division 2

		Pl.	Home					Away					F.	A.	Pts
			W	D	L	F	A	W	D	L	F	A			
1	Leeds United	46	16	6	1	46	18	8	7	8	33	34	79	52	85
2	Sheffield United	46	14	5	4	43	27	10	8	5	35	31	78	58	85
3	Newcastle United	46	17	4	2	51	26	5	10	8	29	29	80	55	80
4	Swindon Town	46	12	6	5	49	29	8	8	7	30	30	79	59	74
5	Blackburn Rovers	46	10	9	4	43	30	9	8	6	31	29	74	59	74
6	Sunderland	46	10	8	5	41	32	10	6	7	29	32	70	64	74
7	West Ham United	46	14	5	4	50	22	6	7	10	30	35	80	57	72
8	Oldham Athletic	46	15	7	1	50	23	4	7	12	20	34	70	57	71
9	Ipswich Town	46	13	7	3	38	22	6	5	12	29	44	67	66	69
10	Wolverhampton W.	46	12	5	6	37	20	6	8	9	30	40	67	60	67
11	Port Vale	46	11	9	3	37	20	4	7	12	25	37	62	57	61
12	Portsmouth	46	9	8	6	40	34	6	8	9	22	31	62	65	61
13	Leicester City	46	10	8	5	34	29	5	6	12	33	50	67	79	59
14	Hull City	46	7	8	8	27	31	7	8	8	31	34	58	65	58
15	Watford	46	11	6	6	41	28	3	9	11	17	32	58	60	57
16	Plymouth Argyle	46	9	8	6	30	23	5	5	13	28	40	58	63	55
17	Oxford United	46	8	7	8	35	31	7	2	14	22	35	57	66	54
18	Brighton & Hove A.	46	10	6	7	28	27	5	3	15	28	45	56	72	54
19	BARNSLEY	46	7	9	7	22	23	6	6	11	27	48	49	71	54
20	West Bromwich A.	46	6	8	9	35	37	6	7	10	32	34	67	71	51
21	Middlesbrough	46	10	3	10	33	29	3	8	12	19	34	52	63	50
22	Bournemouth	46	8	6	9	30	31	4	6	13	27	45	57	76	48
23	Bradford City	46	9	6	8	26	24	0	8	15	18	44	44	68	41
24	Stoke City	46	4	11	8	20	24	2	8	13	15	39	35	63	37

Final League Table 1990/91 Division 2

		Pl.	Home					Away					F.	A.	Pts
			W	D	L	F	A	W	D	L	F	A			
1	Oldham Athletic	46	17	5	1	55	21	8	8	7	28	32	83	53	88
2	West Ham United	46	15	6	2	41	18	9	9	5	19	16	60	34	87
3	Sheffield Wed.	46	12	10	1	43	23	10	6	7	37	28	80	51	82
4	Notts County	46	14	4	5	45	28	9	7	7	31	27	76	55	80
5	Millwall	46	11	6	6	43	28	9	7	7	27	23	70	51	73
6	Brighton & Hove A.	46	12	4	7	37	31	9	3	11	26	38	63	69	70
7	Middlesbrough	46	12	4	7	36	17	8	5	10	30	30	66	47	69
8	BARNSLEY	46	13	7	3	39	16	6	5	12	24	32	63	48	69
9	Bristol City	46	14	5	4	44	28	6	2	15	24	43	68	71	67
10	Oxford United	46	10	9	4	41	29	4	10	9	28	37	69	66	61
11	Newcastle United	46	8	10	5	24	22	6	7	10	25	34	49	56	59
12	Wolverhampton W.	46	11	6	6	45	35	2	13	8	18	28	63	63	58
13	Bristol Rovers	46	11	7	5	29	20	4	6	13	27	39	56	59	58
14	Ipswich Town	46	9	8	6	32	28	4	10	9	28	40	60	68	57
15	Port Vale	46	10	4	9	32	24	5	8	10	24	40	56	64	57
16	Charlton Athletic	46	8	7	8	27	25	5	10	8	30	36	57	61	56
17	Portsmouth	46	10	6	7	34	27	4	5	14	24	43	58	70	53
18	Plymouth Argyle	46	10	10	3	36	20	2	7	14	18	48	54	68	53
19	Blackburn Rovers	46	8	6	9	26	27	6	4	13	25	39	51	66	52
20	Watford	46	5	8	10	24	32	7	7	9	21	27	45	59	51
21	Swindon Town	46	8	6	9	31	30	4	8	11	34	43	65	73	50
22	Leicester City	46	12	4	7	41	33	2	4	17	19	50	60	83	50
23	West Bromwich A.	46	7	11	5	26	21	3	7	13	26	40	52	61	48
24	Hull City	46	6	10	7	35	32	4	5	14	22	53	57	85	45

Final League Table 1991/92 Division 2

		Pl.	Home					Away					F.	A.	Pts
			W	D	L	F	A	W	D	L	F	A			
1	Ipswich Town	46	16	3	4	42	22	8	9	6	28	28	70	50	84
2	Middlesbrough	46	15	6	2	37	13	8	5	10	21	28	58	41	80
3	Derby County	46	11	4	8	35	24	12	5	6	34	27	69	51	78
4	Leicester City	46	14	4	5	41	24	9	4	10	21	31	62	55	77
5	Cambridge United	46	10	9	4	34	19	9	8	6	31	28	65	47	74
6	Blackburn Rovers	46	14	5	4	41	21	7	6	10	29	32	70	53	74
7	Charlton Athletic	46	9	7	7	25	23	11	4	8	29	25	54	48	71
8	Swindon Town	46	15	3	5	38	22	3	12	8	31	33	69	55	69
9	Portsmouth	46	15	6	2	41	12	4	6	13	24	39	65	51	69
10	Watford	46	9	5	9	25	23	9	6	8	26	25	51	48	65
11	Wolverhampton W.	46	11	6	6	36	24	7	4	12	25	30	61	54	64
12	Southend United	46	11	5	7	37	26	6	6	11	26	37	63	63	62
13	Bristol Rovers	46	11	9	3	43	29	5	5	13	17	34	60	63	62
14	Tranmere Rovers	46	9	9	5	37	32	5	10	8	19	24	56	56	61
15	Millwall	46	10	4	9	32	32	7	6	10	32	39	64	71	61
16	BARNSLEY	46	11	4	8	27	25	5	7	11	19	32	46	57	59
17	Bristol City	46	10	8	5	30	24	3	7	13	25	47	55	71	54
18	Sunderland	46	10	8	5	36	23	4	3	16	25	42	61	65	53
19	Grimsby Town	46	7	5	11	25	28	7	6	10	22	34	47	62	53
20	Newcastle United	46	9	8	6	38	30	4	5	14	28	54	66	84	52
21	Oxford United	46	10	6	7	39	30	3	5	15	27	43	66	73	50
22	Plymouth Argyle	46	11	5	7	26	26	2	4	17	16	38	42	64	48
23	Brighton & Hove A.	46	7	7	9	36	37	5	4	14	20	40	56	77	47
24	Port Vale	46	7	8	8	23	25	3	7	13	19	34	42	59	45

Season 1986/87
Back row: Thomas, Agnew, Cassey, Duggan, Baker, Gray, Bell, Kiwomya
2nd back: Winstanley (Coach) Plummer, Hirst, May, Malcolm, Wylde, Futcher, Ogley, Rimmington (Physio)
2nd front: Goodison, Cross, Owen, Clarke (Manager) Joyce, Hedworth, Beresford
Front row: Harber. Thompson, Wardle, Sidlow, Marshall

Season 1987/88
Back row: Dobbin, Foreman, Robinson, Baker, Ogley, Agnew, Coatsworth
Centre row: Winstanley (Coach) Futcher, Chandler, Hedworth, Malcolm, Jeffels, Wylde, Duggan, Rimmington (Physio)
Front row: Beresford, Clarke M, Lowndes, MacDonald, Clarke A (Manager) Joyce, Gray, Thomas, Cross.

1987/88 — 14th in Division 2

#	Date		Opponent	Score	Scorers	Att	Baker CE	Joyce JP	Beresford J	Thomas DG	Gray S	Futcher P	Wylde RI	Agnew SM	Dobbin J	MacDonald J	Clarke MD	Lowndes SR	Jeffels S	Cross P	Robinson MJ	Broddle JR	McGugan PI	Foreman D	Coatsworth G	Hedworth C	Currie DN	Rees AA	Blair A	Rolph DG	Tiler C
1	Au	16	LEEDS UNITED	1-1	Wylde	9778	1	2	3	4	5	6	7	8	9*	10	11	12													
2		18	Blackburn Rovers	1-0	MacDonald	6708	1	2		4	5	6	7	8		10	11*	9		3	12										
3		22	Millwall	1-3	Lowndes	5918	1	2		4	5	6	7	8		10	11*	9		3		12									
4		29	CRYSTAL PALACE	2-1	Wylde, MacDonald	4853	1	2	3*	4	5	6	7	8		10	11*			12	13										
5		31	Bournemouth	2-1	MacDonald, Lowndes	7486	1	2	3	4	5	6	7	8		10	11	9													
6	Se	5	PLYMOUTH ARGYLE	2-1	Wylde 2 (1 pen)	6976	1	2		4	5	6	7	8		10	11	9		3											
7		12	Aston Villa	0-0		12621	1	2	12	4	5	6	7	8		10	11*	9		3											
8		15	SWINDON TOWN	0-1		7773	1	2		4	5	6	7	8		10	11	9		3											
9		26	Oldham Athletic	0-1		5853	1	2	12	4	5	6	7	8		10*	11*	9		3											
10		29	SHEFFIELD UNITED	1-2	Agnew	10203	1	2	12	4	5	6	7	8		10	11*	9		3*		13									
11	Oct	3	Ipswich Town	0-1		10993	1	2	12	4	5	6	7*	8		10		9		3		13									
12		10	Leicester City	0-0		8669	1	2	7	4	5	6		8		10		9		3		11									
13		17	HULL CITY	1-3	Lowndes	7310	1	2	7	4	5	6		8	13	10*		9		3		11*	12								
14		20	READING	5-2	MacDonald 2, Wylde, Joyce, Richardson (og)	4396	1	2	11	4	5	6	7	8		10		9		3											
15		24	Manchester City	1-1	Thomas	17063	1	2	11*	4	5	6	7	8	12	10		9		3											
16		31	STOKE CITY	5-2	MacDonald, Wylde 2, Dobbin, Lowndes	5908	1	2		4	11	6	7		8	10*		9		3		5	12								
17	No	3	Birmingham City	0-2		6622	1	2		4	11	6	7*		8	10*		9		3		13	5	12							
18		7	BRADFORD CITY	3-0	Gray, Lowndes, Wylde	11569	1	2		4	11	6	7		8	10		9		3		13	5	12							
19		14	Huddersfield Town	2-2	MacDonald, Gray	8629	1	2		4	11	6	7		8	10		9		3			5								
20		21	SHREWSBURY TOWN	2-1	Lowndes, Thomas	5364	1	2	11	4	5	6	7	8		10		9		3			5								
21		28	Middlesbrough	0-2		12732	1	2	11	4		6		8	7	10		9		3			5								
22	De	5	WEST BROMWICH ALB.	3-1	Agnew 2, Foreman	5395	1	2	11	4		6		8		10		9		3*		12	5	7							
23		19	MILLWALL	4-1	Agnew 2 (1p), McGugan, Broddle	5011	1			4		6		8		10*	12	9		3		11	5	7	2						
24		26	OLDHAM ATHLETIC	1-1	Thomas	8676	1		10*	4		6	13	8			12	9		3		11	5	7*	2						
25	Jan	1	Crystal Palace	2-3	Agnew, Lowndes	8563	1		10	4		6		8				9		3		11	5	7	2						
26		2	ASTON VILLA	1-3	Gray	11542	1		10	4		6		8				9		3		11	5	7	2						
27		16	Leeds United	2-0	Foreman 2	19043	1	2	12	4		6		8*	10			9		3		11	5	7							
28	Fe	13	BLACKBURN ROVERS	0-1		8972	1	2	11	4		6	7	8		10*		9		3		12	5								
29		20	Sheffield United	0-1		11861	1	2	11*	13		6		8*	4	12		9		3		10	5	7							
30		27	IPSWICH TOWN	2-3	Currie 2	6512	1	2	11	4		6		8*	10			9		3		12	5				7				
31	Ma	5	Hull City	2-1	Dobbin, Beresford	7622	1		4			6			8	10	9	12	3			5				2*	7	11			
32		8	BOURNEMOUTH	2-1	Beresford, Lowndes	6140	1		4			6			8	10*	9	2	3			12	5				7	11			
33		12	LEICESTER CITY	1-1	Rees	7447	1	2	4*	13		6			8	10*	9	3				12	5				7	11			
34		15	Swindon Town	0-3		7558	1	2		4		6			8	10*	9	3				12	5				7	11			
35		19	Stoke City	1-3	Rees	7929	1	2	10	4		6					9	3				5					7	11	8		
36		26	MANCHESTER CITY	3-1	Joyce, Beresford, Hinchcliffe (og)	9061	1	2	10	4		6					9	3				5					7	11	8		
37	Apr	2	Bradford City	1-1	Thomas	15098	1	2	10*	4		6					9	3				5		12			7	11	8		
38		4	HUDDERSFIELD T	1-0	Currie	7950	1	2	10*	4		6					9	3				5		12			7	11	8		
39		9	Reading	1-2	Hicks (og)	5039	1	2	10	4		6					9	3				5			12		7	11	8*		
40		15	Plymouth Argyle	0-0		8059	1	2	10	4							9	6	3			5			12		7	11*	8		
41		23	BIRMINGHAM CITY	2-2	Currie 2	4949	1	2	10*	4					8	12	9	6	3			5					7	11			
42		30	Shrewsbury Town	1-1	Lowndes	4712	1	2	3	4		6				10	11*	9				5		8*			7	12			
43	Ma	2	MIDDLESBROUGH	0-3		13240	1	2	3	4		6				10*	11	9				5	13	8*			7	12		3	12
44		7	West Bromwich Albion	2-2	Currie 2	8473	1	2	10	4							9	6*				5		8			7	11		3	12

| | | | | | Apps | | 44 | 38 | 34 | 42 | 20 | 41 | 20 | 25 | 16 | 33 | 14 | 44 | 7 | 38 | 3 | 19 | 29 | 9 | 6 | 5 | 15 | 14 | 6 | 2 | 1 |
| | | | | | Goals | | | 2 | 3 | 4 | 2 | | 8 | 6 | 2 | 7 | | 9 | | | | 1 | 1 | 4 | | | 7 | 2 | | | |

Three own goals

F.A. Cup

	Date		Opponent	Score	Scorers	Att	Baker CE	Joyce JP	Beresford J	Thomas DG	Gray S	Futcher P	Wylde RI	Agnew SM	Dobbin J	MacDonald J	Clarke MD	Lowndes SR	Jeffels S	Cross P	Robinson MJ	Broddle JR	McGugan PI	Foreman D	Coatsworth G
R3	Jan	9	BOLTON WANDERERS	3-1	Broddle 2, Beresford	9667	1	2	10	4		6		8				9		3		11	5	7	
R4		30	BIRMINGHAM CITY	0-2		13219	1	2		4		6		8	10*	12		9		3		11	5	7*	13

F.L. Cup (Littlewoods Challenge Cup)

	Date		Opponent	Score	Scorers	Att	Baker CE	Joyce JP	Beresford J	Thomas DG	Gray S	Futcher P	Wylde RI	Agnew SM	Dobbin J	MacDonald J	Clarke MD	Lowndes SR	Jeffels S	Cross P	Broddle JR	McGugan PI
/1	Se	8	WEST HAM UNITED	0-0		10330	1	2	12	4	5	6	7	8		10	11*	9		3		
/2	Oct	6	West Ham United	5-2	Agnew 2 (1 p), Beresford, Lowndes, MacDon'	12403	1	2	7	4	5	6		8		10		9		3	11	
R3		27	SHEFFIELD WEDNESDAY	1-2	Agnew	19439	1	2	11*	4	5	6	7	8*	13	10		9		3		12

R2/2 a.e.t.

Full Members Cup (Simod Cup)

	Date		Opponent	Score	Scorers	Att	Baker CE	Thomas DG	Gray S	Futcher P	Wylde RI	Agnew SM	Dobbin J	MacDonald J	Cross P	Broddle JR	Coatsworth G
R1	No	18	Chelsea	1-2	MacDonald	8501	1	4	11	6	7	9	8	10	3	5	2

1988/89 — 7th in Division 2

#	Mon	Date	Opponent	Score	Scorers	Att	Baker CE	Joyce JP	Beresford J	Dobbin J	McGugan PJ	Futcher P	Lowndes SR	Agnew SM	Cooper SB	Currie DN	Thomas DG	MacDonald J	Clarke MD	Broddle JR	Shotton M	Foreman D	Marshall C	Rees AA	Robinson MJ	Tiler C
1	Aug	27	Oldham Athletic	1-1	Cooper	6551	1	2	3	4	5	6	7*	8	9	10	11	12								
2		29	SWINDON TOWN	1-1	Lowndes	6034	1	2	3	4	5	6	7	8	9	10	11									
3	Sep	3	STOKE CITY	1-0	Agnew	5682	1	2	3*		5	6	7	8	9	10	4	12	11*	13						
4		10	Hull City	0-0		5654	1	2	3	11		6	7	8	9	10	4				5					
5		17	CHELSEA	1-1	Dobbin	6942	1	2	3	11		6	7	8	9		4	10*			5	12				
6		21	Leeds United	0-2		17364	1	2	3	11		6	7	8	9	10	4				5					
7		24	MANCHESTER CITY	1-2	Shotton	9300	1	2	3	11		6	7*	8	9	10	4				5		12			
8	Oct	1	Birmingham City	5-3	Beresford, Broddle, Currie, Rees, Lowndes	4892	1	2	3	12		6	7	8*		10	4			11	5			9		
9		5	Brighton & Hove Albion	1-0	Currie (pen)	7327	1	2	3			6	7	8	12	10	4			11	5			9*		
10		8	WEST BROMWICH ALB.	2-1	Currie, Thomas	5674	1	2	3	13	6*		7*	8	12	10	4			11	5			9		
11		15	Blackburn Rovers	1-2	Mail (og)	9316	1	2	3	13		6	7*	8*	12	10	4			11	5			9		
12		22	IPSWICH TOWN	2-0	Cooper 2	6325	1	2	3	8		6	12	13	9	10*	4			11	5			7*		
13		25	Watford	0-4		10356	1	2	3	8		6	7*	12	9		4			11	5			10		
14		29	PLYMOUTH ARGYLE	3-1	Cooper, Thomas, Dobbin	5485	1	2	3	8		6			9		4	10		11	5			7		
15	Nov	5	Crystal Palace	1-1	Broddle	7768	1	2	3*	8	12	6			9		4	10		11	5			7		
16		12	BRADFORD CITY	0-0		8838	1	2		8	3	6			9	10*	4	12		11	5			7		
17		19	Portsmouth	0-3		10001	1	2		8	3	6	9			10	4			11	5			7		
18		26	BOURNEMOUTH	5-2	Currie 4 (1 pen), Dobbin	4937	1	2		8	3	6				10	4	7		11	5			9*	12	
19	Dec	3	Oxford United	0-2		4449	1	2		8	3	6	12	13		10	4	7*		11	5			9*		13
20		10	WALSALL	1-0	Broddle	5173	1	2	3	8	5*	6			12	9	10	4		11				7*		13
21		17	LEICESTER CITY	3-0	Currie (pen), McGugan, Agnew	6477	1	2	3	8	5	6	7		9	10	4			11						
22		26	Sunderland	0-1		21994	1	2	3	12	5	6	7	8*	9*	10	4			11					13	
23		31	Shrewsbury Town	3-2	Currie (p), Lowndes, Moyes (og)	4401	1	2	8		5	6	7		9	10	4	12		11	3*			7*		
24	Jan	2	HULL CITY	0-2		9879	1	2	3	12	5	6			9	10	4	8		11						
25		14	Swindon Town	0-0		10201	1	2	3	8	5	6	7		9	10				11		4				
26		21	OLDHAM ATHLETIC	4-3	Lowndes, Skipper (og), Currie 2 (1p)	7684	1	2	3*	4	5	6	7	8	9	10				11		12				
27	Feb	4	BRIGHTON & HOVE ALB	2-2	Cooper, Agnew	12498	1	2	3		5*	6		8	9	10				11	12	4		7		
28		11	West Bromwich Albion	1-1	Lowndes	12650	1	2	3		5	6	7	8	9					11	10	4				
29		21	Ipswich Town	0-2		10261	1	2	3	4	5*	6	7*	8	9	10				13	12					
30		25	BLACKBURN ROVERS	0-1		8777	1	2	3	4		6		8	9	10		11*		12	5			7		
31		28	WATFORD	2-2	MacDonald, Shotton	6163	1	2		4		6		8		10		11	3	9	5			7		
32	Mar	4	Bradford City	2-1	Currie (pen), MacDonald	11085	1	2	3	4		6		8		10		11		9	5			12	7	
33		11	CRYSTAL PALACE	1-1	MacDonald	7055	1	2		4		6		8		10		11	3*	9	5				7	
34		19	LEEDS UNITED	2-2	Agnew, Robinson	11575	1	2		4		6	9	8		10*		11		3			12		7	5
35		25	Stoke City	1-1	Currie (pen)	10209	1	2		4		6	9	8	12	10		11		3					7*	5
36		27	SUNDERLAND	3-0	Robinson, Cooper, Dobbin (pen)	8070	1	2		4		6	9	8	12	10		11		3	5	13			7	
37	Apr	1	Chelsea	3-5	McLaughlan (og), Dobbin, Agnew	15986	1	2		4		6	9	8	12	10		11*		3	5	13			7*	
38		8	SHREWSBURY TOWN	1-0	MacDonald	5252	1	2		4		6		8	9*	10		11		3	5	12			7	
39		11	Leicester City	1-0	Lowndes	7266	1	2		4		6	7	8	9	10		11		3	5					
40		15	BIRMINGHAM CITY	0-0		6464	1	2		4		6	7	8	9	10*		11		3	5			12		
41		22	Manchester City	2-1	Cooper (og), Shotton	21274	1	2		4		6	9	8		10		11		3	5				7	
42		25	PLYMOUTH ARGYLE	2-1	Currie, Shotton	5468	1	2		4		6	9	8		10		11		3	5			7*		
43		29	Bournemouth	2-3	O'Driscoll (og), Shotton	5520	1	2		4		6	9	8	12	10		11		3	5				7*	
44	May	1	OXFORD UNITED	1-0	Evans (og)	5940	1	2		4				8	9	10*		11		3	5	12			7	6
45		6	PORTSMOUTH	1-0	Currie (pen)	5718	1	2		4		6	12	8	9*	10		11		3	5				7	
46		13	Walsall	3-1	MacDonald, Currie, Agnew	3966	1			4		6	9	8		10		11		3	5				7	2
			Apps				46	45	27	41	20	41	33	39	35	41	24	32	3	38	37	5	1	17	18	4
			Goals						1	5	1		6	6	6	16	2	5		3	5			1	2	

Seven own goals

F.A. Cup

Rd	Mon	Date	Opponent	Score	Scorers	Att	Baker CE	Joyce JP	Beresford J	Dobbin J	McGugan PJ	Futcher P	Lowndes SR	Agnew SM	Cooper SB	Currie DN	Thomas DG	MacDonald J	Clarke MD	Broddle JR	Shotton M	Foreman D	Marshall C	Rees AA	Robinson MJ	Tiler C
R3	Jan	7	CHELSEA	4-0	Thomas, Agnew 2, Currie	13241	1	2	3	8	5	6	7*		9	10	4*		11	13			12			
R4		28	Stoke C	3-3	Currie 2, MacDonald	18592	1	2	3	4	5	6	7	8	9	10		11								
rep		31	Stoke C	2-1	MacDonald, Cooper	21086	1	2	3	4	5	6	7*	8	9	10		11				13		12*		
R5	Feb	18	EVERTON	0-1		32551	1	2	3	4	5	6	7	8	9	10		11*		12						

F.L. Cup (Littlewoods Challenge Cup)

Rd	Mon	Date	Opponent	Score	Scorers	Att	Baker CE	Joyce JP	Beresford J	Dobbin J	McGugan PJ	Futcher P	Lowndes SR	Agnew SM	Cooper SB	Currie DN	Thomas DG	MacDonald J	Clarke MD	Broddle JR	Shotton M	Foreman D	Marshall C	Rees AA	Robinson MJ	Tiler C
R2/1	Sep	27	WIMBLEDON	0-2		5194	1	2	3		5	6	7	8		10	4			11				9		
R2/2	Oct	12	Wimbledon	1-0	Currie	2259	1	2	3	10	4	5	11		8	6				9				7		

Full Members Cup (Simod Cup)

Rd	Mon	Date	Opponent	Score	Scorers	Att	Baker CE	Joyce JP	Beresford J	Dobbin J	McGugan PJ	Futcher P	Lowndes SR	Agnew SM	Cooper SB	Currie DN	Thomas DG	MacDonald J	Clarke MD	Broddle JR	Shotton M	Foreman D	Marshall C	Rees AA	Robinson MJ	Tiler C
R1	Nov	9	Millwall	1-1	Broddle	3330	1	2		8"	3	6	9	12				4*	10	11	5			7	13	

Lost 0-3 on penalties a.e.t.

Season 1988/89
Back row: Rolph, Futcher, Wardle, Sidlow, Baker, Cross, Coatsworth
Centre row: Winstanley (Coach) Currie, Robinson, Rees, Tiler, McGugan, Duggan,
Cooper, Clarke M, Dobbin, Ross, Barlow (Coach) Nile (Physio)
Front row: Broddle, Beresford, MacDonald, Thomas, Marshall, Clarke A (Manager)
Joyce, Foreman, Agnew, Bond, Lowndes

Season 1989/90
Back row: Lowndes, Cooper, Shotton, Tiler, McGugan, Futcher, Foreman, Broddle
Centre row: Winstanley (Coach) Rees, Cross, Currie, Wardle, Baker, Banks, Dobbin,
Nile (Physio) Fogg (Youth coach)
Front row: MacDonald, Robinson, Agnew, Clarke (Manager) Joyce, Thomas, Archdeacon

1989/90 19th in Division 2

#	Date		Opponent	Score	Scorers	Att	Baker CE	Tiler C	Broddle JR	Dobbin J	Shotton M	Futcher P	Lowndes SR	Agnew SM	Cooper SB	Currie DN	Robinson MI	MacDonald J	Banks IF	Wardle IS	Foreman D	Archdeacon OD	Cross P	Dunphy S	Smith MC	McCord BJ	Marshall C	Taggart GP	Glover EL	Gray P	Thomas DG	Saville AV	Fleming JG
1	Aug	19	Ipswich Town	1-3	Lowndes	12025	1	2	3	4	5	6	7	8	9	10	11																
2		26	BRIGHTON & HOVE A.	1-0	Currie	6283	1	2	3	4	5*	6	7	8	9*	10	11	12	13														
3	Sep	2	Plymouth Argyle	1-2	MacDonald	7708	1		3	4	2	6	7	8	12	10	11	9*	5														
4		5	STOKE CITY	3-2	Agnew, Cooper, Lowndes	8584	1	12	3	4	2	6*	7	8	9	10	11		5														
5		9	MIDDLESBROUGH	1-1	Shotton	10535			3	4	2	6	7	8	9	10	11		5	1													
6		16	Swindon Town	0-0		6540			3	4	2	6	7*	8	9			10	5	1	12	11											
7		23	BRADFORD CITY	2-0	Agnew, Foreman	8992		2		4	5	6		8		10	11		7	1	9		3										
8		26	WOLVERHAMPTON W.	2-2	Currie 2	10161		2		4	5	6		8	12	10	11		7	1	9*		3										
9		30	Blackburn Rovers	0-5		8415		2		4	5	6		8		10	11		7	1	9		3										
10	Oct	7	Oldham Athletic	0-2		6769				5	4	2	6	8	9				7	1		11*	12	3									
11		14	PORT VALE	0-3		6475	1			3	4	2	6	7	8	9	10	11*	5			12											
12		17	SHEFFIELD UNITED	1-2	Agnew	16629	1			2	4	6		8		10			7			9	11	3	5								
13		21	Oxford United	3-2	Banks 2, Foreman	3865	1			2	4	6		8		10			7		9		11	3	5								
14		28	LEICESTER CITY	2-2	Archdeacon, Currie (pen)	6856	1			2	4	6		8		10			7		9		11	3	5								
15		31	Sunderland	2-4	Currie, Tiler	14368	1	3		2	4	6		8*		10		13	7			12	9	11	5*								
16	Nov	4	PORTSMOUTH	0-1		5524	1	12		2	4	6*		8		10		13	7*	1	9		11	3	5								
17		11	West Bromwich Albion	0-7		9317		5		2	6			8	12	10	7*	11*	4	1		9	3	13									
18		18	NEWCASTLE UNITED	1-1	Currie	10475	1			2	5			8	9	10			4			11	3		6	7							
19		25	Hull City	2-1	Cooper, Currie	5715	1			2	5			8	9	10			4			11	3		6	7							
20	Dec	2	IPSWICH TOWN	0-1		6097	1			2	5		4*	8	9	10						12	11	3	6	7							
21		9	Stoke City	1-0	Cooper	10055	1			2	5		4	8	9	10						11	3		6	7							
22		16	Bournemouth	1-2	Lowndes	5506	1		11	2	5		4	8	9				10*				3		6	7	12						
23		26	WATFORD	0-1		7357	1		7	2	5		4	8		10			9			12	11*	3*	6		13						
24		30	LEEDS UNITED	1-0	Foreman	14841	1		11	2	5	3	4	8		10			9		7				6*								
25	Jan	1	West Ham United	2-4	Dobbin, Archdeacon	18391	1	13	7*	2	5	4		8	12	10			9			11	3		6								
26		13	Brighton & Hove A.	1-1	Taggart	6856	1			2	5	4	7	8	9*	10			11			3		6				12					
27		20	PLYMOUTH ARGYLE	1-1	Smith	7224	1			2	5	4	7	8*			13		11*	12			6					3	9	10			
28	Feb	3	Bradford City	0-0		9923	1			2*	5	4			10	11		7	12			6						3	9	8*	2		
29		10	SWINDON TOWN	0-1		7179	1				5	4	13	10	11*		7		12			6						3	9	8*		12	
30		24	HULL CITY	1-1	Cooper	8901	1	6			4	2	10	11	7*		8*		13		5							3	9			12	
31	Mar	3	Newcastle United	1-4	Agnew	18999	1	6			4	2*	10	11	7		8		13		5							3	9			12	
32		10	Wolverhampton Wan.	1-1	Agnew (pen)	15995	1	6			4		10	11	7*		8				5			2				3	9			12	
33		17	OLDHAM ATHLETIC	1-0	Milligan (og)	10598	1	6			4	13	10	11*	7*		8	1*			5			2				3	9			12	
34		19	Port Vale	1-2	Banks	7036	1	6			4		10	11	7		8				5							3	9			9	2
35		24	Sheffield United	2-1	Agnew, Saville	15472	1				4		10	11*	13		8*				5		6	7				3				9	2
36		31	OXFORD UNITED	1-0	Smith	7096	1				4		10	11*			8				5		6	7				3				9	2*
37	Apr	3	Blackburn Rovers	0-0		8713	1	4					10	11*	13		8*				5		6	7				3				9	2
38		7	Leicester City	2-2	Cooper, Agnew	8620	1	4					10	11	12		8*				5		6	7				3				9	2
39		10	SUNDERLAND	1-0	McCord	11141	1	4					10	11	8*						5		6	7				3				9	2
40		14	WEST HAM UNITED	1-1	Taggart	10344	1	4					13	10	11*		8				5		6	7*				3				9	2
41		17	Watford	2-2	Lowndes, Agnew (pen)	7289	1	4					11*	10			8				5		6	7				3				9	2
42		21	BOURNEMOUTH	0-1		7415	1	4*					13	11	10		8*				5		6	7				3				9	2
43		25	Leeds United	2-1	O'Connell, Archdeacon	31663	1	4					7*	11	10		8				13		5	6*				3				9	2
44		28	WEST BROMWICH ALB.	2-2	O'Connell, Saville	10334	1	4					6	11*	10		8				12		5					3		6	11*	9	2
45	May	2	Middlesbrough	1-0	Smith	17015	1	4					7		8						5							3		6	8*	9	2
46		5	Portsmouth	1-2	Saville	8315	1						4	12*	10				13				11	5				3		6	8*	9	2

| | | | | | | Apps | 37 | 21 | 20 | 28 | 29 | 29 | 24 | 46 | 30 | 24 | 24 | 4 | 37 | 9 | 17 | 21 | 36 | 6 | 25 | 16 | 2 | 21 | 8 | 3 | 3 | 15 | 12 |
| | | | | | | Goals | | 1 | | 1 | 1 | | 4 | 8 | 5 | 7 | | 1 | 3 | | | 3 | 3 | | 3 | 1 | | 2 | | | | 3 | |

One own goal

F.A. Cup

Rd	Date		Opponent	Score	Scorers	Att																											
R3	Jan	6	Leicester City	2-1	Currie, Lowndes	16278	1			2	5	4	7	8*	9*	10			12		13	11	3		6					3	9	10*		
R4		27	IPSWICH TOWN	2-0	Taggart, Cooper	14440	1	12		2	5	4	7	8	11							6						3	9	10*			
R5	Feb	18	Sheffield United	2-2	Smith, Cooper	33113	1				5	4	2	10	11		7*		8		13		12	6*				3	9				
rep		21	SHEFFIELD UNITED	0-0		27672	1	6			4	2	10	11			7		8				5					3	9				
rep2	Mar	5	SHEFFIELD UNITED	0-1		26560	1	6			4	2*	10	11			7*		8		13	5						3	9				

Both R5 replays a.e.t.   Played in R5 second replay: JM Deehan (at 12)

F.L. Cup (Littlewoods Challenge Cup)

Rd	Date		Opponent	Score	Scorers	Att																											
R2/1	Sep	19	BLACKPOOL	1-1	Archdeacon	7515			3	4	2	6	7	8	9			10*	5	1	12	11											
R2/2	Oct	3	Blackpool	1-1	Briggs (og)	5251			5	4*	2	6		8	9	10	11		7	1		12	3										

Blackpool won 5-4 on penalties, a.e.t.

Full Members Cup (Zenith Data Systems Cup)

Rd	Date		Opponent	Score	Scorers	Att																											
R1	Nov	28	LEEDS UNITED	1-2	Dobbin	6136	1	12	7	2	5	6	13	8	9	10			4*			11*	3										

1990/91   8th in Division 2

#	Date		Opponent	Score	Scorers	Att	Baker CE	Fleming IG	Taggart GP	McCord BJ	Joyce JP	Smith MC	Banks IF	Cooper SB	Saville AV	Agnew SM	Archdeacon OD	Tiler C	O'Connell BJ	Robinson MJ	Connelly D	Rammell AV	Dobbin J	Gridelet PR	Marshall C	Deehan JM	Rimmer SA	Cross P
1	Aug	25	BRIGHTON & HOVE ALB	2-1	Cooper, Smith	6955	1	2	3	4	5	6	7	8	9	10	11											
2	Sep	1	Millwall	1-4	Banks	10114	1	2	3	4		5	7	8	9*	10	11	6	12									
3		8	OLDHAM ATHLETIC	0-1		11257	1	2	3	4		5*		8	9	10	11	6	12	7								
4		15	Blackburn Rovers	2-1	Saville, Rammell	7665	1	2	3	4		5		8*	9*		11	6	12	7	10	13						
5		18	Notts County	3-2	McCord, Saville, O'Connell	7187	1	2*	3	4		5		8"	9	10	11	6	12	7		13						
6		22	PORT VALE	1-1	Archdeacon (pen)	8533	1	2*	3	4		5		8"	9	10	11	6	12	7	10*	13						
7		29	Charlton Athletic	1-2	Rammell	4455	1	2	3	4		5		8*	9	10	11	6	12	7*		13						
8	Oct	2	IPSWICH TOWN	5-1	Taggart, Archdeacon, Rammell, Agnew, Saville	6934	1		3	4		5	2		9	10	11*	6	7	12		8						
9		6	OXFORD UNITED	3-0	Rammell, Saville, O'Connell	6776	1		3	4		5	2		9	10	11	6	7			8						
10		13	Portsmouth	0-0		8701	1		3	4		5	2		9	10*	11	6	7			8						
11		20	West Bromwich Albion	1-1	Cooper	9577	1	5	3	4			2	12	9		11	6	7		12	10	8*					
12		23	Sheffield Wednesday	1-1	Rammell	23079	1	5	3	4			2		9		11	6	7			10	8					
13		27	SWINDON TOWN	5-1	O'Connell, Agnew 2 (1p), Rammell 2	7690	1	5	3*	4	12		2		9	10	11	6	7				8					
14	Nov	3	Middlesbrough	0-1		18470	1	5	3	4			2*	12	9	10	11	6	7				8					
15		7	Bristol Rovers	1-2	Banks	4563	1	5*	3	4			2	12	9	10	11	6	7				8					
16		10	LEICESTER CITY	1-1	O'Connell	8581	1	5	3	4			2	12	9	10*	11	6	7				8					
17		17	Newcastle United	0-0		15556	1	5		4		3	2	9*			11	6	7		12	10*	8	13				
18		24	WOLVERHAMPTON W.	1-1	Saville	9267	1	5			8*	3	2	9			11	6	7		12		8	13				
19	Dec	1	Watford	0-0		7839	1	5			8	3	2	9*			11	6	7		12	10		4				
20		15	Brighton & Hove Albion	0-1		5829	1	5	3	4*			2*		9	10	11	6	7		12	8		13				
21		22	WEST HAM UNITED	1-0	Smith	10348	1	4	3			5	2*		9	10	11	6	7		12	8*				13		
22		26	Plymouth Argyle	1-1	Rammell	5668	1	4*	3			5	2		9	10	11	6	7			8				12		
23		29	Hull City	2-1	Agnew, Deehan	7916	1	4	3			5	2		9	10	11	6	7			8*				12		
24	Jan	1	BRISTOL CITY	2-0	Rammell, Taggart	8961	1	4	3			5	2		9	10	11	6	7			8*				12		
25		12	MILLWALL	1-2	Agnew	7857	1	3				5*	2		9	10	11	6	7		13	8				12		
26		19	Oldham Athletic	0-2		13849	1	3		4*		5	2		9	10	11	6	7			8		12				
27	Feb	23	Leicester City	1-2	Smith	9027	1	4	3			5	2		9	10	11	6	7			8		12				
28		26	BRISTOL ROVERS	1-0	Saville	6197	1	4	3			5	2		9	10	11	6	7			8						
29	Mar	2	WATFORD	2-1	Saville, Rammell	6755	1	4	3*			5*	2		9	10	11	6	7		12	8*		13				
30		9	Wolverhampton Wan.	5-0	Saville, Rammell, Stancliffe (og), Robinson, Agnew	15671	1	3				5	13		9	10	11	6	7"	12		8		13			12	
31		16	CHARLTON ATHLETIC	1-1	O'Connell	6373	1	3	2*				13		9	10	11	6	7"	12		8					4	5*
32		19	PORTSMOUTH	4-0	Saville 2, Rimmer, Agnew	4921	1	3					2		9	10*	11	6	7*	5		8					4	12
33		23	Oxford United	0-2		4689	1	3					8*	2*	9	10	11	6	7	5		12	13				4	
34		30	PLYMOUTH ARGYLE	1-0	Agnew (pen)	6142	1	3				5			9	10	11	6	7			8	2				4	
35	Apr	1	West Ham United	2-3	Saville, O'Connell	24607	1	3				5			9	10	11	6	7			8	2					
36		6	HULL CITY	3-1	O'Connell 2, Rammell	6859	1	3				5			9	10	11	6	7	4		8*	2*			13	12	
37		9	NOTTS COUNTY	1-0	O'Connell	9801	1	3				5			9	10	11	6	7	4*		8	2				12	
38		13	Bristol City	0-1		12081	1	4	3*			5			9	10	11	6	7	12		8	2*					
39		15	Port Vale	1-0	Saville	6939	1	3				5			9	10	11	6	7	2	12	8					13	
40		20	WEST BROMWICH ALB.	1-1	Deehan	9594	1	3				5			9	10*	11	6	7	2*	12	13				8	4	
41		23	BLACKBURN ROVERS	0-1		8648	1	3		13		5			9		11	6	7	2*	12	10				8*	4	
42		25	Ipswich Town	0-2		7570	1	3				5*	2		9	10	11	6	7		12	10				8*	4	
43		27	Sheffield Wednesday	1-3	Smith	30693	1	3	12	2*		5	4		9*	10	11	6	7			8					13	
44	May	4	Swindon Town	2-1	Tiler, Smith	9531	1	2	3			5	4		9	10	11	6	7			8*					12	
45		7	NEWCASTLE UNITED	1-1	Smith	9534	1	2	3*			5	4		9	10	11	6	7			8					12	
46		11	MIDDLESBROUGH	1-0	Tiler	14494	1	2	3			5	4		9	10	11	6	7			8						
			Apps				46	44	30	24	3	37	33	12	45	38	45	45	45	22	9	40	14	4	1	11	15	2
			Goals						2	1		6	2	2	12	8	2	2	9	1		12				2	1	

One own goal

F.A. Cup

							Baker	Fleming	Taggart	McCord	Joyce	Smith	Banks	Cooper	Saville	Agnew	Archdeacon	Tiler	O'Connell	Robinson	Connelly	Rammell	Dobbin	Gridelet	Marshall	Deehan	Rimmer	Cross
R3	Jan	6	LEEDS UNITED	1-1	Deehan	22424	1	4	3			5*	2		9	10	11	6	7			8				12		
rep		9	Leeds United	0-4		19773	1	4	3			5*	2*		9	10	11	6	7	12		8				13		

F.L. Cup (Rumbelows Cup)

							Baker	Fleming	Taggart	McCord	Joyce	Smith	Banks	Cooper	Saville	Agnew	Archdeacon	Tiler	O'Connell	Robinson	Connelly	Rammell	Dobbin	Gridelet	Marshall	Deehan	Rimmer	Cross
R1/1	Aug	28	Wigan Athletic	1-0	Cooper	2144	1	2	3	6		4	7	8	9	10	11	5										
R1/2	Sep	4	WIGAN ATHLETIC	0-1		4558	1	2	3	4		5	7*	8	9	10*	11	6		13	12							
R2/1		26	Aston Villa	0-1		14471	1	2	3	4		5		8*	9	10	11	6	7		12							
R2/2	Oct	9	ASTON VILLA	0-1		13924	1		3	4		5*	2		9	10	11	6	7	12		8						

R1/2 won 4-3 on penalties, a.e.t.

Full Members Cup (Zenith Data Systems Cup)

							Baker	Fleming	Taggart	McCord	Joyce	Smith	Banks	Cooper	Saville	Agnew	Archdeacon	Tiler	O'Connell	Robinson	Connelly	Rammell	Dobbin	Gridelet	Marshall	Deehan	Rimmer	Cross
R1	Nov	21	West Bromwich Albion	5-3	Robinson, Smith, Banks 3	4452	1	5			7	3	2				11		8	10				4	6	9*		12
R2	Dec	18	Sheffield Wednesday	3-3	Archdeacon 2, Connelly	5942	1	5	3	4*	12		2		9	10*	11	6	7		13	8						
Nqf	Jan	30	NOTTM. FOREST	2-1	Rammell, O'Connell	6692	1	4	3			5	2		9	10	11	6	7			8						
Nsf	Mar	13	EVERTON	0-1		10287	1	3	2*			5	13		9	10	11	6	7	12		8					4	

R2 won 4-2 on penalties, a.e.t.

Season 1990/91
Back row: O'Connell, Burton, Saville, Wardle, Whitehead, Baker, Smith, Connelly, Fleming
Centre row: Benson (Chief Scout) Deehan (Coach) Lowndes, Cooper, Hoyle, Tiler, Taggart, McGugan,
Dobbin, Joyce, Winstanley (Youth coach) Nile (Physio)
Front row: Marshall, Banks, Beaumont, Cross, Machin (Manager) Agnew, Archdeacon, McCord, Robinson

Season 1991/92
Back row: Wilkinson, Hoyle, Rammell, Taggart, Whitehead, Butler, Pearson, Smith, Saville, Gridelet
Centre row: Nile (Physio) O'Connell. Liddell, Eaden, Burton, Banks, Bishop, Graham,
Bullimore, Williams, Davis, Winstanley (Youth coach)
Front row: Deehan (Coach) Jackson, Fleming, McCord, Robinson, Machin (Manager) Marshall,
Archdeacon, Connelly, Cross, Benson (Chief scout)

1991/92 — 16th in Division 2

#					Att	Whitehead PM	Bishop CD	Williams GI	Banks IF	Davis SP	Taggart GP	O'Connell BJ	Rammell AV	Pearson JS	McCord BJ	Graham DWT	Fleming JG	Connelly D	Smith MC	Butler LS	Robinson MJ	Cross P	Redfearn ND	Currie DN	Archdeacon OD	Saville AV	Bullimore WA	Whitworth NA	Liddell AM
1	Aug	17	Plymouth Argyle	1-2 Pearson	6352	1	2	3	4	5	6	7	8	9	10*	11	12												
2		20	SUNDERLAND	0-3	12454	1	2	3	4	5	6*	7	8	9		11"	10	12	13										
3		24	BRIGHTON & HOVE ALB	1-2 O'Connell	6066	1	2		4	5	6	7	8	9*		12	10	11	3										
4		27	Port Vale	0-0	6299		10		4		6	7	8	9			11		5	1	2	3							
5		31	Swindon Town	1-3 Banks	7732		10		4		6	7	8	9*		12	11		5	1	2	3							
6	Sep	3	WATFORD	0-3	6500		10		4	5	6	7	8	9		11*	2			1	12	3							
7		7	Derby County	1-1 Saville	10559		2		4*		6	7	8"			12	3		5	1				9	10	11	13			
8		14	IPSWICH TOWN	1-0 Currie	6786				4		6	7		12			3		5	1	2		8	10	11	9*			
9		17	LEICESTER CITY	3-1 Rammell, Taggart, Redfearn (pen)	9318				4		6	7		9			3		5	1	2		8	10*	11	12			
10		21	Tranmere Rovers	1-2 Banks	8462				4		6	7*		9	10		3		5	1	2		8		11	12			
11		28	MILLWALL	0-2	6544				4*		6	7		9			3		5	1	2		8	10	11	12			
12	Oct	5	Wolverhampton Wan.	2-1 Saville, O'Connell	14082		12				6	7		9		11	4			1	2		8	10*	3	5			
13		12	PORTSMOUTH	2-0 Taggart, Graham	6579		12				6	7		9	10	11	4			1	2		8		3*	5			
14		19	BRISTOL CITY	1-2 Currie	6566			13			6	7		9*		11	4	12		1	2		8	10	3	5"			
15		26	Cambridge United	1-2 Rammell	5534			9			6	7				11	4	12	5	1	2		8	10*	3				
16	Nov	2	Oxford United	1-0 Redfearn	3420			9*			6	7				11	4		5	1	2		8	12	3		10		
17		5	MIDDLESBROUGH	2-1 Rammell, Taggart	6525			9			6	7				11	4		5	1	2		8	10	3				
18		9	BRISTOL ROVERS	0-1	6688		5	9			6	7				11	4*	12		1	2		8	10	3				
19		16	Blackburn Rovers	0-3	13797		13	9*			6	7		12		11	4		5	1	2		8	10*	3				
20		23	Southend United	1-2 Saville	5060		10				6					11	4*		5	1	2		8	12	3	9	7		
21		30	NEWCASTLE UNITED	3-0 Saville, Robinson, Rammell	9702		3				6					10*	2		5	1	7		8	12	11	9	4		
22	Dec	7	Charlton Athletic	1-1 Redfearn (pen)	4581		3				6					12	2		5	1	7		8	10*	11	9	4		
23		14	GRIMSBY TOWN	4-1 Currie, Archdeacon 2, Saville	6856		3	13			6					12	2		5	1	7		8"	10*	11	9	4		
24		22	Watford	1-1 Robinson	7522		3				6					12	2		5	1	7		8	10*	11	9	4		
25		26	PORT VALE	0-0	8843		3				6					12	2		5	1	7		8	10	11	9	4*		
26		28	SWINDON TOWN	1-1 Rammell	8357		3	13			6				10		2*		5	1	7		8	12	11	9*	4		
27	Jan	1	Sunderland	0-2	16125		3*	13			6					10	2		5	1	7		8	12	11	9	4*		
28		11	Brighton & Hove Albion	1-3 Currie	6107		3				6	7*		9		12			5	1	2"		8	10	11	13	4		
29		18	PLYMOUTH ARGYLE	1-3 Saville	5374		3			5	6	7				12	2"	13		1			8	10	11	9	4*		
30	Feb	1	Bristol City	2-0 Archdeacon, O'Connell	9508		3	8			6	7		9			4		5	1	2			10	11				
31		8	CAMBRIDGE UNITED	0-0	6196		3	8			6	7*		9			4		5	1	2			10	11	12			
32		15	SOUTHEND UNITED	1-0 O'Connell	5328		3*	8			6	7		9*			4		5	1	2		13	10	11	12			
33		22	Newcastle United	1-1 Currie	27382		3*	8				7"					4	13	5	1	2			9	10	11	12	6	
34		29	CHARLTON ATHLETIC	1-0 Archdeacon	6050		3	8				7				12	4*	13	5	1	2			10	11	9*		6	
35	Mar	7	Grimsby Town	1-0 Archdeacon	6913		3	8	4			7							5	1	2			10	11	9		6	
36		14	OXFORD UNITED	1-0 Currie	5436		3	8	4			7							5	1	2			9	10	11		6	
37		21	Bristol Rovers	0-0	5641		3	8	4			7							5	1	2			9	10	11		6	
38		28	BLACKBURN ROVERS	2-1 Smith, Rammell	13337		3	8	4			7				12			5	1	2			9	10*	11		6	
39		31	Ipswich Town	0-2	14157		3	8*	4"			7				10		13	5	1	2			9	12	11		6	
40	Apr	4	DERBY COUNTY	0-3	10127		3*	8				7				10	4	13	5	1	2			9	12	11		6"	
41		11	Leicester City	1-3 Currie	14438		3	8"				7*				12	4		5	1	2			9	10	11	13	6	
42		13	Middlesbrough	1-0 Redfearn	12743		3					7*				12	4		5	1	2			9	10	11	8	6	
43		18	TRANMERE ROVERS	1-1 Archdeacon	5811		3"	13				7*				10	4	12	5	1	2			9	11		8	6	
44		22	Millwall	1-1 Rammell	5703		3				6				10*	12	4		5	1	2			9	11	7	8		
45		25	WOLVERHAMPTON W.	2-0 Bullimore, Rammell	7244		12				6				10	3*	4		5	1	2			9	11	7	8		
46	May	2	Portsmouth	0-2	11169		3				6*				10		4	12	5	1	2			9	11	7*	8		13
Apps						3	28	17	26	9	38	36	37	10	3	21	42	3	38	43	41	3	36	37	40	22	18	11	1
Goals								2			3	4	8	1		1			1		2		4	7	6	6	1		

F.A. Cup

					Att	Whitehead PM	Bishop CD	Williams GI	Banks IF	Davis SP	Taggart GP	O'Connell BJ	Rammell AV	Pearson JS	McCord BJ	Graham DWT	Fleming JG	Connelly D	Smith MC	Butler LS	Robinson MJ	Cross P	Redfearn ND	Currie DN	Archdeacon OD	Saville AV	Bullimore WA	Whitworth NA	Liddell AM
R3	Jan	4	Norwich City	0-1	12189		3				6			9	10		2		5*	1	7		8	12"	11	13	4		

F.L. Cup (Rumbelows Cup)

					Att	Whitehead PM	Bishop CD	Williams GI	Banks IF	Davis SP	Taggart GP	O'Connell BJ	Rammell AV	Pearson JS	McCord BJ	Graham DWT	Fleming JG	Connelly D	Smith MC	Butler LS	Robinson MJ	Cross P	Redfearn ND	Currie DN	Archdeacon OD	Saville AV	Bullimore WA	Whitworth NA	Liddell AM
R2/1	Sep	24	Blackpool	0-1	4123				4		6	7		9		10*	3		5	1	2		8		11	12			
R2/2	Oct	8	BLACKPOOL	2-0 O'Connell, Pearson	6315		13				6	7		9		11"	4	12		1	2		8	10	3	5*			
R3		29	Middlesbrough	0-1	9381			9			6	7				11	4*	13	5	1	2		8	10*	3		12		

Full Members Cup (Zenith Data Systems Cup)

					Att	Whitehead PM	Bishop CD	Williams GI	Banks IF	Davis SP	Taggart GP	O'Connell BJ	Rammell AV	Pearson JS	McCord BJ	Graham DWT	Fleming JG	Connelly D	Smith MC	Butler LS	Robinson MJ	Cross P	Redfearn ND	Currie DN	Archdeacon OD	Saville AV	Bullimore WA	Whitworth NA	Liddell AM
R1	Oct	2	Leicester City	3-4 Archdeacon, Currie, Saville (aet)	3995		4*	13			6	7"		9		11	3			1	2		8	10	12	5			

1992/93 13th in Division 1 (Divisions re-numbered)

#		Date	Opponent	Score	Scorers	Att	Butler LS	Robinson MJ	Taggart GP	Bishop CD	Fleming JG	Bullimore WA	Currie DN	Rammell AV	Pearson JS	Redfearn ND	Archdeacon OD	Liddell AM	Smith MC	Graham DWT	Burton MA	O'Connell BJ	Robinson J	Biggins W	Godfrey W	Williams GJ	Watson DN	Davis SP	Whitehead PM	Hendon IM	Jackson CD	Gridelet PR	Bennett T	Feeney MA
1	Aug	16	WEST HAM UNITED	0-1		6798	1	2	3	4	5	6	7	8*	9	10	11	12																
2		22	Portsmouth	0-1		11473	1	2	3	4	5	6*	12	8*	9	10	11	7	13															
3		29	MILLWALL	0-0		4795	1	2*	3	4	5	6*	8	12	9	10	11	7	13															
4	Sep	1	WOLVERHAMPTON W.	0-1		6906	1	2	3	4	5	6*	8*	12	9	10	11	7	13															
5		5	Notts County	3-1	Taggart, Liddell, Archdeaco	6205	1	13	3	4	5		12	8	9	10	11	7*		2		6*												
6		12	DERBY COUNTY	1-1	Rammell	8412	1		3	4	5			8	9	10	11	7*		2		6	12											
7		19	PETERBOROUGH UTD.	1-2	Liddell	5275	1		3	4	5		13	8	9	10	11	7	2*			6	12											
8		26	Bristol City	1-2	O'Connell	8041	1	2	3	4	5	12	13		9	10	11	7*				6*	8											
9	Oct	3	Leicester City	1-2	Biggins	12290	1		5	4*	2			8	9	10	11	13				6*	12	3	7									
10		10	LUTON TOWN	3-0	Biggins 2, Pearson	5261	1	2		4	5	6		8*	9	10*	11							12	3	7	13							
11		17	Oxford United	0-0		4422	1	2		5	4		6	8*	9	10	11							12	7									
12		24	BRENTFORD	3-2	Biggins, Pearson 2	4928	1	2		5	4	3		8*	9	10	11					6		7	12									
13		31	Swindon Town	0-1		8069	1	2		5	4	3		12	9	10	11	8*				6		7										
14	Nov	3	Bristol Rovers	5-1	*See below	5013	1	2		5	4	3		8*		10	11	9*				6		7	12									
15		7	Watford	0-1		6193	1	2		5	4	3*		8		10	11	9				6		7	12									
16		14	Cambridge United	2-1	Biggins 2	3963	1	2		5	4	3	12		9	10	11	8*				6		7										
17		21	BIRMINGHAM CITY	1-0	Currie	5603	1	2		5	4	3	12		9	10	11	8*				6		7										
18		28	CHARLTON ATHLETIC	1-0	Biggins	5851	1	2		5	4	3	12		9	10	11	8*				6		7										
19	Dec	5	Sunderland	1-2	Sampson (og)	17403	1	2		5	4	3*	12	8		10	11	9				6		7										
20		13	NEWCASTLE UNITED	1-0	O'Connell	13263	1	2		5	4			8	9*	10	11	12				6		7										
21		19	Southend United	0-3		3629	1	2		5	4	3*	12	8		10	11	9*				6		7				13						
22		26	Grimsby Town	2-4	Taggart, Currie	8242	1	2		5	4	3	7	8*		10	11	9*				6		12				13						
23		28	TRANMERE ROVERS	3-1	Currie, Rammell, Redfearn	8204	1	2		5	4	3	9	8		10	11			12		6		7*										
24	Jan	9	Peterborough United	1-1	Rammell	6542	1	2		5	4	3	9*	8	12	10	11					6		7										
25		16	BRISTOL CITY	2-1	O'Connell 2	5423	1	2		5	4	3	9	8		10	11					6		7										
26		27	Wolverhampton Wan.	0-1		11342	1	2*		5	4	3	7	8	9	10	11					6				12								
27		30	PORTSMOUTH	1-1	Archdeacon	6551	1	2		5	4	3	7	8	9	10	11					6												
28	Feb	6	West Ham United	1-1	Rammell	14101	1	2		5	4	3	7*	8	9	10	11	12				6												
29		10	Derby County	0-3		13096		2		5	4	3	7	8		10	11					6		12	9*			1						
30		20	Millwall	4-0	Archdeacon 2, Biggins 2	8032		2		5		3	9	8		10	11					6		7				1	4					
31		27	Luton Town	2-2	O'Connell, Currie	7595		2		5		3	9	8		10	11					6		7				1	4					
32	Mar	6	LEICESTER CITY	2-3	Rammell 2	9282		2*		5	4	3*	9	8		10	11	13				6		7				12	1					
33		9	CAMBRIDGE UNITED	2-0	Biggins, Redfearn	5445				5		3	9	8		10	11	2*		12		6		7				4	1					
34		13	Watford	2-1	Biggins 2	5785				5	2	3	12	9	8*	10	11					6		7				4	1					
35		16	NOTTS COUNTY	0-0		6372				5	2	3	8	9		10	11					6		7				4	1					
36		21	SUNDERLAND	2-0	Biggins 2	7297				5	2	3		9	8	10	11			12		6		7				4	1	8*				
37		23	Birmingham City	0-3		12664				5	2	3	13	9*		10						11	6	7		12		4*	1	8				
38		27	BRISTOL ROVERS	2-1	Graham, Archdeacon	5220				5	4	3	13	9		10*	11					8	6*	7	12			1	2					
39	Apr	3	Charlton Athletic	0-0		6154				5	4	3	8	12		10						9*	6*	11	7	13		1	2					
40		7	Newcastle United	0-6		29513				5	4	3	8*	9		10				13		6*	11	7				1	2	12				
41		10	GRIMSBY TOWN	0-2		4990				5	4	3	13	12		10						9	6	7				11*	1	2*		8		
42		12	Tranmere Rovers	1-2	Taggart	6436				5	4	3		8*		10						9*	6	7		12		11	1		13	2		
43		17	SOUTHEND UNITED	3-1	Williams 3	3855				4	3		13			10						9	2	7	11	1	5			8*		6*	12
44		24	OXFORD UNITED	0-1		5588				5	4	3	12			10						9	6	2	7	1					8*		
45	May	1	Brentford	1-3	Williams	7958				5	4*	3	8			10						9*	6	2	7			1					13
46		8	SWINDON TOWN	1-0	Williams	6031				5	4	3	12	8		10	13					9	6	2*		11*		1					

Played in game 14: D Connelly (13)
Scorers in game 14: Robinson, Taggart, O'Connell, Redfearn, Rammell

	Apps	28	29	44	43	46	17	35	30	22	46	38	21	4	15	5	40	8	34	8	8	5	11	13	6	3	2	2	2
	Goals		1	4				4	7	3	3	5	2		1		6		14		5								

One own goal

F.A. Cup

		Date	Opponent	Score	Scorers	Att	Butler	Robinson MJ	Taggart	Bishop	Fleming	Bullimore	Currie	Rammell	Pearson	Redfearn	Archdeacon	Liddell	Smith	Graham	Burton	O'Connell	Robinson J	Biggins	Godfrey	Williams	Watson	Davis	Whitehead	Hendon	Jackson	Gridelet	Bennett	Feeney
R3	Jan	13	Leicester City	2-2	Whitlow (og), Redfearn	19137	1	2	5	4	3			9	8	12	10	11				6		7*										
rep		20	LEICESTER CITY	1-1	Archdeacon	15423	1	2	5	4	3*	13	9	8*	12	10	11					6		7										
R4		24	WEST HAM UTD.	4-1	Rammell 3, Redfearn	13716	1		5	4	3		9	8	12	10	11					6		7*							2			
R5	Feb	13	Manchester C	0-2		32807	1	2	5	4	3*		7	8		10	11	9*				6		13		12								

R3 replay won 5-4 on penalties, a.e.t.

F.L. Cup (Coca Cola Cup)

		Date	Opponent	Score	Scorers	Att	Butler	Robinson MJ	Taggart	Bishop	Fleming	Bullimore	Currie	Rammell	Pearson	Redfearn	Archdeacon	Liddell	Smith	Graham	Burton	O'Connell
R1/1	Aug	19	Grimsby Town	1-1	Redfearn	3927	1	2	3	4	5	6		8	9	10	11	7				
R1/2		25	GRIMSBY TOWN	1-1	Liddell (aet)	4636	1	2	3	4	5	6*	13	8*	9	10	11	7				12

Grimsby T won 5-3 on penalties

Anglo-Italian Cup

		Date	Opponent	Score	Scorers	Att	Butler	Robinson MJ	Taggart	Bishop	Fleming	Bullimore	Currie	Rammell	Pearson	Redfearn	Archdeacon	Liddell	Smith	Graham	Burton	O'Connell
PR	Sep	15	Notts County	1-1	O'Connell	2115	1		3	4	5			8	9	10	11*	7	2			6	12
PR		29	DERBY COUNTY	1-2	Taggart	3960	1	2	5	4			12	9		10*	11	7*				6	8	3		13

FINAL LEAGUE TABLES: 1992/93 - 1997/98

Final League Table 1992/93 Division 1 (Formerly Division 2)

		Pl.	Home					Away					F.	A.	Pts
			W	D	L	F	A	W	D	L	F	A			
1	Newcastle United	46	16	6	1	58	15	13	3	7	34	23	92	38	96
2	West Ham United	46	16	5	2	50	17	10	5	8	31	24	81	41	88
3	Portsmouth	46	19	2	2	48	9	7	8	8	32	37	80	46	88
4	Tranmere Rovers	46	15	4	4	48	24	8	6	9	24	32	72	56	79
5	Swindon Town	46	15	5	3	41	23	6	8	9	33	36	74	59	76
6	Leicester City	46	14	5	4	43	24	8	5	10	28	40	71	64	76
7	Millwall	46	14	6	3	46	21	4	10	9	19	32	65	53	70
8	Derby County	46	11	2	10	40	33	8	7	8	28	24	68	57	66
9	Grimsby Town	46	12	6	5	33	25	7	1	15	25	32	58	57	64
10	Peterborough Utd.	46	7	11	5	30	26	9	3	11	25	37	55	63	62
11	Wolverhampton W.	46	11	6	6	37	26	5	7	11	20	30	57	56	61
12	Charlton Athletic	46	10	8	5	28	19	6	5	12	21	27	49	46	61
13	BARNSLEY	46	12	4	7	29	19	5	5	13	27	41	56	60	60
14	Oxford United	46	8	7	8	29	21	6	7	10	24	35	53	56	56
15	Bristol City	46	10	7	6	29	25	4	7	12	20	42	49	67	56
16	Watford	46	8	7	8	27	30	6	6	11	30	41	57	71	55
17	Notts County	46	10	7	6	33	21	2	9	12	22	49	55	70	52
18	Southend United	46	9	8	6	33	22	4	5	14	21	42	54	64	52
19	Birmingham City	46	10	4	9	30	32	3	8	12	20	40	50	72	51
20	Luton Town	46	6	13	4	26	26	4	8	11	22	36	48	62	51
21	Sunderland	46	9	6	8	34	28	4	5	14	16	36	50	64	50
22	Brentford	46	7	6	10	28	30	6	4	13	24	41	52	71	49
23	Cambridge United	46	8	6	9	29	32	3	10	10	19	37	48	69	49
24	Bristol Rovers	46	6	6	11	30	42	4	5	14	25	45	55	87	41

Final League Table 1993/94 Division 1

		Pl.	Home					Away					F.	A.	Pts
			W	D	L	F	A	W	D	L	F	A			
1	Crystal Palace	46	16	4	3	39	18	11	5	7	34	28	73	46	90
2	Nottingham Forest	46	12	9	2	38	22	11	5	7	36	27	74	49	83
3	Millwall	46	14	8	1	36	17	5	9	9	22	32	58	49	74
4	Leicester City	46	11	9	3	45	30	8	7	8	27	29	72	59	73
5	Tranmere Rovers	46	15	3	5	48	23	6	6	11	21	30	69	53	72
6	Derby County	46	15	3	5	44	25	5	8	10	29	43	73	68	71
7	Notts County	46	16	3	4	43	26	4	5	14	22	43	65	69	68
8	Wolverhampton W.	46	10	10	3	34	19	7	7	9	26	28	60	47	68
9	Middlesbrough	46	12	6	5	40	19	6	7	10	26	35	66	54	67
10	Stoke City	46	14	4	5	35	19	4	9	10	22	40	57	59	67
11	Charlton Athletic	46	14	3	6	39	22	5	5	13	22	36	61	58	65
12	Sunderland	46	14	2	7	35	22	5	6	12	19	35	54	57	65
13	Bristol City	46	11	7	5	27	18	5	9	9	20	32	47	50	64
14	Bolton Wanderers	46	10	8	5	40	31	5	6	12	23	33	63	64	59
15	Southend United	46	10	5	8	34	28	7	3	13	29	39	63	67	59
16	Grimsby Town	46	7	14	2	26	16	6	6	11	26	31	52	47	59
17	Portsmouth	46	10	6	7	29	22	5	7	11	23	36	52	58	58
18	BARNSLEY	46	9	3	11	25	26	7	4	12	30	41	55	67	55
19	Watford	46	10	5	8	39	35	5	4	14	27	45	66	80	54
20	Luton Town	46	12	4	7	38	25	2	7	14	18	35	56	60	53
21	West Bromwich A.	46	9	7	7	38	31	4	5	14	22	38	60	69	51
22	Birmingham City	46	9	7	7	28	29	4	5	14	24	40	52	69	51
23	Oxford United	46	10	5	8	33	33	3	5	15	21	42	54	75	49
24	Peterborough Utd.	46	6	9	8	31	30	2	4	17	17	46	48	76	37

Final League Table 1994/95 Division 1

		Pl.	Home					Away					F.	A.	Pts
			W	D	L	F	A	W	D	L	F	A			
1	Middlesbrough	46	15	4	4	41	19	8	9	6	26	21	67	40	82
2	Reading	46	12	7	4	34	21	11	3	9	24	23	58	44	79
3	Bolton Wanderers	46	16	6	1	43	13	5	8	10	24	32	67	45	77
4	Wolverhampton W.	46	15	5	3	39	18	6	8	9	38	43	77	61	76
5	Tranmere Rovers	46	17	4	2	51	23	5	6	12	16	35	67	58	76
6	BARNSLEY	46	15	6	2	42	19	5	6	12	21	33	63	52	72
7	Watford	46	14	6	3	33	17	5	7	11	19	29	52	46	70
8	Sheffield United	46	12	9	2	41	21	5	8	10	33	34	74	55	68
9	Derby County	46	12	6	5	44	23	6	6	11	22	28	66	51	66
10	Grimsby Town	46	12	7	4	36	19	5	7	11	26	37	62	56	65
11	Stoke City	46	10	7	6	31	21	6	8	9	19	32	50	53	63
12	Millwall	46	11	8	4	36	22	5	6	12	24	38	60	60	62
13	Southend United	46	13	2	8	33	25	5	6	12	21	48	54	73	62
14	Oldham Athletic	46	12	7	4	34	21	4	6	13	26	39	60	60	61
15	Charlton Athletic	46	11	6	6	33	25	5	5	13	25	41	58	66	59
16	Luton Town	46	8	6	9	35	30	7	7	9	26	34	61	64	58
17	Port Vale	46	11	5	7	30	24	4	8	11	28	40	58	64	58
18	Portsmouth	46	9	8	6	31	28	6	5	12	22	35	53	63	58
19	West Bromwich A.	46	13	3	7	33	24	3	7	13	18	33	51	57	58
20	Sunderland	46	5	12	6	22	22	7	6	10	19	23	41	45	54
21	Swindon Town	46	9	6	8	28	27	3	6	14	26	46	54	73	48
22	Burnley	46	8	7	8	36	33	3	6	14	13	41	49	74	46
23	Bristol City	46	8	8	7	26	28	3	4	16	16	35	42	63	45
24	Notts County	46	7	8	8	26	28	2	5	16	19	38	45	66	40

Final League Table 1995/96 Division 1

		Pl.	Home					Away					F.	A.	Pts
			W	D	L	F	A	W	D	L	F	A			
1	Sunderland	46	13	8	2	32	10	9	9	5	27	23	59	33	83
2	Derby County	46	14	8	1	48	22	7	8	8	23	29	71	51	79
3	Crystal Palace	46	9	9	5	34	22	11	6	6	33	26	67	48	75
4	Stoke City	46	13	6	4	32	15	7	7	9	28	34	60	49	73
5	Leicester City	46	9	7	7	32	29	10	7	6	34	31	66	60	71
6	Charlton Athletic	46	8	11	4	28	23	9	9	5	29	22	57	45	71
7	Ipswich Town	46	13	5	5	45	30	6	7	10	34	39	79	69	69
8	Huddersfield Town	46	14	4	5	42	23	3	8	12	19	35	61	58	63
9	Sheffield United	46	9	7	7	29	25	7	7	9	28	29	57	54	62
10	BARNSLEY	46	9	10	4	34	28	5	8	10	26	38	60	66	60
11	West Bromwich A.	46	11	5	7	34	29	5	7	11	26	39	60	68	60
12	Port Vale	46	10	5	8	30	29	5	10	8	29	37	59	66	60
13	Tranmere Rovers	46	9	9	5	42	29	5	8	10	22	31	64	60	59
14	Southend United	46	11	8	4	30	22	4	6	13	22	39	52	61	59
15	Birmingham City	46	11	7	5	37	23	4	6	13	24	41	61	64	58
16	Norwich City	46	7	9	7	26	24	7	6	10	33	31	59	55	57
17	Grimsby Town	46	8	10	5	27	25	6	4	13	28	44	55	69	56
18	Oldham Athletic	46	10	7	6	33	20	4	7	12	21	30	54	50	56
19	Reading	46	8	7	8	28	30	5	10	8	26	33	54	63	56
20	Wolverhampton W.	46	8	9	6	34	28	5	7	11	22	34	56	62	55
21	Portsmouth	46	8	6	9	34	32	5	7	11	27	37	61	69	52
22	Millwall	46	7	6	10	23	28	6	7	10	20	35	43	63	52
23	Watford	46	7	8	8	40	33	3	10	10	22	37	62	70	48
24	Luton Town	46	7	6	10	30	34	4	6	13	10	30	40	64	45

Final League Table 1996/97 Division 1

		Pl.	Home					Away					F.	A.	Pts
			W	D	L	F	A	W	D	L	F	A			
1	Bolton Wanderers	46	18	4	1	60	20	10	10	3	40	33	100	53	98
2	BARNSLEY	46	14	4	5	43	19	8	10	5	33	36	76	55	80
3	Wolverhampton W.	46	10	5	8	31	24	12	5	6	37	27	68	51	76
4	Ipswich Town	46	13	7	3	44	23	7	7	9	24	27	68	50	74
5	Sheffield Utd.	46	13	5	5	46	23	7	8	8	29	29	75	52	73
6	Crystal Palace	46	10	7	6	39	22	9	7	7	39	26	78	48	71
7	Portsmouth	46	12	4	7	32	24	8	4	11	27	29	59	53	68
8	Port Vale	46	9	9	5	36	28	8	7	8	22	27	58	55	67
9	Queens Park Rgs.	46	10	5	8	33	25	8	7	8	31	35	64	60	66
10	Birmingham City	46	11	7	5	30	18	6	8	9	22	30	52	48	66
11	Tranmere Rovers	46	10	9	4	42	27	7	5	11	21	29	63	56	65
12	Stoke City	46	15	3	5	34	22	3	7	13	17	35	51	57	64
13	Norwich City	46	9	10	4	28	18	8	2	13	35	50	63	68	63
14	Manchester City	46	12	4	7	34	25	5	6	12	25	35	59	60	61
15	Charlton Athletic	46	11	8	4	36	28	5	3	15	16	38	52	66	59
16	West Bromwich A.	46	7	7	9	37	33	7	8	8	31	39	68	72	57
17	Oxford United	46	14	3	6	44	26	2	6	15	20	42	64	68	57
18	Reading	46	13	7	3	37	24	2	5	16	21	43	58	67	57
19	Swindon Town	46	11	6	6	36	27	4	3	16	16	44	52	71	54
20	Huddersfield Town	46	10	7	6	28	20	3	8	12	20	41	48	61	54
21	Bradford City	46	10	5	8	29	32	2	7	14	18	40	47	72	48
22	Grimsby Town	46	7	7	9	31	34	4	6	13	29	47	60	81	46
23	Oldham Athletic	46	6	8	9	30	30	4	5	14	21	36	51	66	43
24	Southend United	46	7	9	7	32	32	1	6	16	10	54	42	86	39

Final League Table 1997/98 PremierDivision

		Pl.	Home					Away					F.	A.	Pts
			W	D	L	F	A	W	D	L	F	A			
1	Arsenal	38	15	2	2	43	10	8	7	4	25	23	68	33	78
2	Manchester Utd.	38	13	4	2	42	9	10	4	5	31	17	73	26	77
3	Liverpool	38	13	2	4	42	16	5	9	5	26	26	68	42	65
4	Chelsea	38	13	2	4	37	14	7	1	11	34	29	71	43	63
5	Leeds United	38	9	5	5	31	21	8	3	8	26	25	57	46	59
6	Blackburn Rovers	38	11	4	4	40	26	5	6	8	17	26	57	52	58
7	Aston Villa	38	9	3	7	26	24	8	3	8	23	24	49	48	57
8	West Ham United	38	13	4	2	40	18	3	4	12	16	39	56	57	56
9	Derby County	38	12	3	4	33	18	4	4	11	19	31	52	49	55
10	Leicester City	38	6	10	3	21	15	7	4	8	30	26	51	41	53
11	Coventry City	38	8	9	2	26	17	4	7	8	20	27	46	44	52
12	Southampton	38	10	1	8	28	23	4	5	10	22	32	50	55	48
13	Newcastle United	38	8	5	6	22	20	3	6	10	13	24	35	44	44
14	Tottenham Hot.	38	7	8	4	23	22	4	3	12	21	34	44	56	44
15	Wimbledon	38	5	6	8	18	25	5	8	6	16	21	34	46	44
16	Sheffield Wed.	38	9	5	5	30	26	3	3	13	22	41	52	67	44
17	Everton	38	7	5	7	25	27	2	8	9	16	29	41	56	40
18	Bolton Wanderers	38	7	8	4	25	22	2	5	12	16	39	41	61	40
19	Barnsley	38	7	4	8	25	35	3	1	15	12	47	37	82	35
20	Crystal Palace	38	2	5	12	15	39	6	4	9	22	32	37	71	33

Season 1992/93

Back row: Taggart, Rammell, Gridelet, Currie, Butler, Watson, Godfrey, Davis, Bishop, Robinson
Centre row: Wadsworth (Coach) Winstanley (Youth coach) Mercer, Bullimore, Burton, Eaden,
Robinson, O'Connell, Pearson, Benson (Chief scout) Stafford (Physio)
Front row: Connelly, Morgan, Graham, Smith, Machin (Manager) Fleming, Archdeacon, Redfearn, Liddell

Season 1993/94

Back row: Currie, Moses, Williams, Watson, Butler, Robinson, Rammell, Bishop
Centre row: Walker (Youth coach) Winstanley (Coach) Feeney, Bryson, Hanby, O'Connell, Graham,
Fleming, Burton, Taggart, Biggins, Bullock, Stafford (Physio)
Front row: Gregg, Archdeacon, Liddell, Wilson (Player/coach) Anderson (Player/manager)
Snodin, Eaden, Redfearn, Morgan

1993/94   18th in Division 1

#		Date	Opponent	Res	Scorers	Att	Butler LS	Fleming JG	Snodin G	Wilson DJ	Taggart GP	Anderson VA	O'Connell BJ	Redfearn ND	Bryson JIC	Biggins W	Archdeacon OD	Graham DWT	Currie DN	Robinson J	Bishop CD	Watson DN	Eaden NJ	Rammell AV	Liddell AM	Jackson CD	Boden CD	Williams GI	Payton AP	Sheridan DSD
1	Aug	14	WEST BROMWICH ALB.	1-1	Anderson	12940	1	2	3	4	5	6	7	8	9*	10	11	12												
2		17	Peterborough United	1-4	Currie	5875	1	2	3	4	5	6	7	8		10	11		9*	12										
3		21	Watford	2-0	Biggins, Bryson	5937	1	2	3	4	5	6	7	8	9*	10	11					12								
4		24	MIDDLESBROUGH	1-4	Anderson	10597	1	2	3	4	5	6	7	8*	9	10	11		12											
5		28	BIRMINGHAM CITY	2-3	Redfearn, Anderson	7241	1	2	3*	4	5	6	7	8	9	10	11				12									
6	Sep	4	Millwall	0-2		8004		2		4		6	7	8	9	10	11				5	1	3*	12						
7		11	NOTTM. FOREST	1-0	Archdeacon (pen)	13270		2		4	5	6	7	8		10	11				3	1		9						
8		18	Tranmere Rovers	3-0	Rammell,Redfearn,O'Connell	6755		2		4	5	6	7	10	9		11				3	1		8						
9		25	LEICESTER CITY	0-1		10392		2		4	5	6	7	10	9		11*				3	1		8	12					
10	Oct	2	Luton Town	0-5		6201		2		4	5	6	7*	10	9*		11				3	1	13	8	12					
11		9	CHARLTON ATHLETIC	0-1		5186		2		4	5	6	7	10	9		11				3	1			8"	13				
12		16	Bristol City	2-0	Bryson, Redfearn	6923		2		4		6	7*	8	9	10					5	1	11	12			3			
13		23	SOUTHEND UNITED	1-3	Redfearn (pen)	5240		2		4			7	8	9*	10					5	1	6	12	11		3			
14		30	Stoke City	4-5	Redfearn,O'Connell,Bryson,Archd'n	14691	1	2		4		6*	7	10	9		12				5		11	8*	13		3			
15	Nov	2	Oxford United	1-1	Redfearn	4065	1	2		4			7	10	9		11				5		6	8*			3	12		
16		7	GRIMSBY TOWN	1-2	O'Connell	5942	1	2		4		6	7	8	9	10	11				5*			12			3			
17		13	Wolverhampton Wan.	1-1	Biggins	18355	1	2		4		6	7	8	9	10	11				5		3							
18		20	CRYSTAL PALACE	1-3	Redfearn	5384	1	2		4		6	7	8	9*	10	11				5		3"		12			13		
19		27	BOLTON WANDERERS	1-1	Jackson	6755	1	2		4	5		7	8			11			12	6		3		9*				10	
20	Dec	4	Grimsby Town	2-2	Payton, Redfearn	5283	1	2		4	5		7	8			11				6		3	9	12				10	
21		11	PETERBOROUGH UTD.	1-0	Payton	6424	1	3		4	5		7	8			11				6		2	9					10	
22		19	West Bromwich Albion	1-1	Payton	16062	1	3		4	5		7	8			11				6		2	9					10	
23		27	DERBY COUNTY	0-1		11562	1	3		4	5		7	8			11				6		2	9					10	
24	Jan	1	PORTSMOUTH	2-0	O'Connell, Redfearn	6328	1	3		4	5		7	8			11				6		2	9					10	
25		3	Sunderland	0-1		19096	1	3			5		7	8			11				6		2	9	12				10	4*
26		15	BRISTOL CITY	1-1	Rammell	5222	1	3		4	5		7	8			11				6		2	9					10	
27		22	Charlton Athletic	1-2	Payton	7286	1	3		4	5		7	8			11				6		2	9					10	
28	Feb	5	Southend United	3-0	Eaden, Redfearn, Rammell	4101	1	3		4	5		7	8			11				6		2	9					10	
29		12	STOKE CITY	3-0	Rammell, Redfearn, Taggart	7551	1	3		4	5		7	8			11				6		2	9					10	
30	Mar	1	Notts County	1-3	Payton	6297	1	3	13	4	5		7*	8			11*				6		2	9	12				10	
31		5	Birmingham City	2-0	O'Connell, Rammell	15382	1	3		4	5	6	7	8			11						2	9					10	
32		12	TRANMERE ROVERS	1-0		6203	1	3		4	5	6	7	8			11						2	9					10	
33		16	Nottingham Forest	1-2	Taggart	20491	1	3		4	5		7	8			11				6		2	9					10	
34		19	Leicester City	1-0	Payton	15640	1	3		4	5*		7	8			11				6		2	9	12				10	
35		26	LUTON TOWN	1-0	Payton	6289	1	3		4	5			8			11				6		2	9	7				10	
36		29	SUNDERLAND	4-0	Eaden, Liddell, Payton, Rammell	10042	1	3		4	5			8			11				6		2	9	7				10	
37	Apr	2	Derby County	0-2		14968	1	3		4	5			8			11*				6		2	9	7				10	
38		4	NOTTS COUNTY	0-3		6827	1	3	11	4	5			8							6		2	9	7*				10	12
39		9	Portsmouth	1-2	Redfearn (pen)	7005	1	3	11		5	6	7	8									2*	9	12			13	10	4*
40		12	WATFORD	0-1		4380	1	3*	13	4	5	6					11						2	9	7			12	10*	
41		16	OXFORD UNITED	1-0	Williams	4874	1	3		4	5			8			11				6		2	9				7	10	
42		23	Crystal Palace	0-1		20522	1	3		4	5			8			11				6		2	9	7	12		10*		
43		26	Middlesbrough	0-5		6368	1	3		4	5		7	8			11				6		2	9					10	
44		30	WOLVERHAMPTON W.	2-0	O'Connell, Payton	11329	1	3		4	5		7	8			11				6		2	9					10	
45	May	3	MILLWALL	0-1		5059	1	3		4	5		7	8			11				6		2	9	12				10*	
46		8	Bolton Wanderers	3-2	Bishop, Payton 2	11661		3	13	4	5			8			11*				6	1	2	9*	7			12	10	
Apps							37	46	11	43	38	20	38	46	16	13	42	2	3	1	38	9	37	34	22	4	4	9	25	3
Goals											2	3	6	12	3	2	2		1		1		2	6	1	1		1	12	

F.A. Cup

		Date	Opponent	Res	Scorers	Att	Butler LS	Fleming JG	Snodin G	Wilson DJ	Taggart GP	Anderson VA	O'Connell BJ	Redfearn ND	Bryson JIC	Biggins W	Archdeacon OD	Graham DWT	Currie DN	Robinson J	Bishop CD	Watson DN	Eaden NJ	Rammell AV	Liddell AM	Jackson CD	Boden CD	Williams GI	Payton AP	Sheridan DSD
R3	Jan	8	Bromsgrove Rovers	2-1	Rammell, Archdeacon	4893	1	3		4	5		7*	8			11				6		2	9	12				10	
R4		29	Plymouth Argyle	2-2	Payton, Taggart	12760	1	3		4	5		7	8			11				6		2	9					10	
rep	Feb	9	PLYMOUTH ARGYLE	1-0	O'Connell	10913	1	3		4	5		7	8			11				6		2	9					10	
R5		19	Oldham Athletic	0-1		15685	1	3		4	5		7	8			11				6		2	9					10	

F.L. Cup (Coca Cola Cup)

		Date	Opponent	Res	Scorers	Att	Butler LS	Fleming JG	Snodin G	Wilson DJ	Taggart GP	Anderson VA	O'Connell BJ	Redfearn ND	Bryson JIC	Biggins W	Archdeacon OD	Graham DWT	Currie DN	Robinson J	Bishop CD	Watson DN	Eaden NJ	Rammell AV	Liddell AM	Jackson CD	Boden CD	Williams GI	Payton AP	Sheridan DSD
R2/1	Sep	21	PETERBOROUGH UTD.	1-1	Archdeacon (pen)	4549		2		4	5	6	7	10	9		11				3	1		8						
R2/2	Oct	5	Peterborough United	1-3	Bryson	3533		2		4	5	6	7	10	9*		11				3	1	13		8*	12				

R2/2 a.e.t.

Anglo-Italian Cup

		Date	Opponent	Res	Scorers	Att	Butler LS	Fleming JG	Snodin G	Wilson DJ	Taggart GP	Anderson VA	O'Connell BJ	Redfearn ND	Bryson JIC	Biggins W	Archdeacon OD	Graham DWT	Currie DN	Robinson J	Bishop CD	Watson DN	Eaden NJ	Rammell AV	Liddell AM	Jackson CD	Boden CD	Williams GI	Payton AP	Sheridan DSD
PR	Sep	7	Middlesbrough	0-3		5173	1			4				10	9		3				6	5		2	8			11*		12
PR		14	GRIMSBY TOWN	2-1	Archdeacon, O'Connell	1627					5		7	8		10	11*				3	6	1	2	9"	13	12			4

Played in first game: MJ Bullock (at 7)

1994/95 — 6th in Division 1

No	Date	Opponent	Res	Scorers	Att	Watson DN	Eaden NJ	Fleming JG	Wilson DJ	Taggart GP	Bishop CD	O'Connell BJ	Redfearn ND	Rammell AV	Payton AP	Snodin G	Davis SP	Liddell AM	Bullock MJ	Jackson CD	Sheridan DSD	Archdeacon OD	Butler LS	Moses AP	Shotton M	Hurst G
1	Aug 13	DERBY COUNTY	2-1	Rammell 2	8702	1	2	3	4	5	6	7	8	9	10	11										
2	20	Charlton Athletic	2-2	Payton, Davis	8167	1	2	3	4	5	6	7*	8	9	10	11	12									
3	27	READING	0-2		4771	1	2"	3	4	5		7*	8	9	10	11	12	13								
4	30	Port Vale	1-2	O'Connell	7228	1	2	3"	4	5	6	7	8	9	10	11*	12	13								
5	Sep 3	Burnley	1-0	Payton	11989	1	2	3	4	5		7	8	9	10	11	6									
6	10	WATFORD	0-0		4251	1	2	3	4	5		7	8	9	10*	11	6	12								
7	13	NOTTS COUNTY	1-1	Rammell	3928	1	2	3	4	5		7	8	9	10*	11	6	12								
8	17	Sunderland	0-2		16145	1	2	3*	4	5	2	7	8	9	10	11	6	12								
9	24	Oldham Athletic	0-1		7941	1	13	3	4	5	2*	7	8	9*	10	11	6	12								
10	Oct 1	SWINDON TOWN	2-1	Redfearn 2	3911	1	2	3	4	5	6		8		10*	11	7	12		9						
11	8	SOUTHEND UNITED	0-0		3659	1	2	3	4	5		7*	8	12			6	13		9"	11					
12	16	Sheffield United	0-0		12317	1	2	3	4	5		7	8	9	10		6				11					
13	22	WEST BROMWICH ALB.	2-0	O'Connell, Redfearn	5082	1	2	3	4	5		7	8	9	10		6				11					
14	29	Luton Town	1-0	Rammell	7212	1	2	3	4	5		7	8	9	10		6				11					
15	Nov 1	Tranmere Rovers	1-6	Rammell	5592	1	2	3	4	5		7	8	9	10*		6				11*	13				
16	5	STOKE CITY	2-0	O'Connell, Sheridan	5117	1	2	3	4	5		7	8				6	10		9"	11					
17	19	Millwall	1-0	Liddell	7040		2	3	4*	5		7	8	12			6	10		9"	11	13	1			
18	26	BOLTON WANDERERS	3-0	Eaden, Davis, Redfearn	8507		2	3		5		7*	8	12			6	10		9	11	4	1			
19	Dec 3	West Bromwich Albion	1-2	Jackson	13921		2"	3		5		7*	8	13			6	10	12	9	11	4	1			
20	7	BRISTOL CITY	2-1	Liddell, Archdeacon	4305		2	3		5		7*	8	13			6	10	12	9"	11	4	1			
21	10	CHARLTON ATHLETIC	2-1	Redfearn, Liddell	5466		2	3		5		7	8	9			6	10			11	4	1			
22	17	Derby County	0-1		13205		2	3		5		7	8	9			6	10	12		11	4*	1			
23	26	GRIMSBY TOWN	4-1	Payton 3, Liddell	8669		2	3		5		7	8	9			6	10	4		11		1			
24	27	Portsmouth	0-3		6751		2	3		5"	13	7	8	12	9*		6	10	4		11		1			
25	31	WOLVERHAMPTON W.	1-3	Redfearn (pen)	9250		2	3		5		7	8	12			6	10	4		11*		1			
26	Jan 14	LUTON TOWN	3-1	Redfearn, Liddell 2	4808	1	2	3	4			7	8	9			6	10			11			5		
27	Feb 4	Bristol City	2-3	Rammell, Wilson	6408	1	2	3	4			7*	8	9				10	12		11			5	6	
28	11	TRANMERE ROVERS	2-2	Rammell, Redfearn	5506	1	2	3"	4	5		7	8	9		13		10*	12		11				6	
29	18	Bolton Wanderers	1-2	Liddell	12463	1	2	3"	4	5		7*	8	9		13	6	10	12		11					
30	21	MILLWALL	4-1	Redfearn 2, Payton 2	4730	1	2	3	4	5		7*	8"	9		13	6	10	12		11					
31	25	Swindon Town	0-0		8636	1	2	3	4*	5		7	8	9			6	10	12		11					
32	Mar 7	BURNLEY	2-0	Taggart, Payton	5537	1	2	3	4	5		7	8"	9		13	6	10	12		11*					
33	11	Reading	3-0	O'Connell, Taggart, Payton	7556	1	2	3	4	5		7		9			6	10	8		11					
34	14	Middlesbrough	1-1	Payton	19655	1	2	3	4	5		7		9			6*	10	8		11	12				
35	18	PORT VALE	3-1	Liddell 2, Sheridan	6878	1	2	3	4	5		7		12	9			10*	8		11	6*		13		
36	21	Watford	2-3	Liddell 2	6883	1	2	3*	4	5		7		12	9			10	8		11			6		
37	24	SUNDERLAND	2-0	Shotton, Payton	7804	1	2	3	4	5		7			9			10	8		11				6	
38	Apr 1	Notts County	3-1	O'Connell, Wilson, Liddell	6834	1	2	3	4	5		7			9			10	8		11				6	
39	8	Wolverhampton Wan.	0-0		26385	1	2	3	4	5		7		12	9			10*	8		11				6	
40	12	Stoke City	0-0		10734	1	2	3	4	5		7		12	9			10*	8		11				6	
41	15	PORTSMOUTH	1-0	Payton	6825	1	2	3	4*	5		7		12	9	11	6	10	8							
42	17	Grimsby Town	0-1		7277	1	2	3		5		7	4	12	9		6	10*	8		11					
43	22	MIDDLESBROUGH	1-1	Liddell	11782	1	2	3				7	4		9		6	10*	8		11				5	12
44	29	SHEFFIELD UNITED	2-1	O'Connell 2	10844	1	2	3				7	4		9		6	10	8		11				5	
45	May 2	OLDHAM ATHLETIC	1-1	Taggart	9383	1	2	3"		5		7	8		9		6	10*	4	12	11					13
46	7	Southend United	1-3	Redfearn	6451	1	2	3*	4"	5		12	8	10	9		6	13		7	11					
				Apps		37	45	46	34	41	8	45	39	24	43	14	36	39	29	8	35	9	9	4	8	2
				Goals			1		2	3		7	11	7	12		2	13		1	2	1			1	

F.A. Cup

	Date	Opponent	Res		Att	Watson DN	Eaden NJ	Fleming JG	Wilson DJ	Taggart GP	Bishop CD	O'Connell BJ	Redfearn ND	Rammell AV	Payton AP	Snodin G	Davis SP	Liddell AM	Bullock MJ	Jackson CD	Sheridan DSD	Archdeacon OD	Butler LS	Moses AP
R3	Jan 7	ASTON VILLA	0-2		11469	1	2	3*	4"			7	8	12	9		6	10	13		11			5

F.L. Cup (Coca Cola Cup)

	Date	Opponent	Res	Scorers	Att	Watson DN	Eaden NJ	Fleming JG	Wilson DJ	Taggart GP	Bishop CD	O'Connell BJ	Redfearn ND	Rammell AV	Payton AP	Snodin G	Davis SP	Liddell AM	Bullock MJ	Jackson CD
R1/1	Aug 17	Darlington	2-2	Taggart, Redfearn	2207	1	2	3	4	5	6	7	8	9	10	11				
R1/2	23	DARLINGTON	0-0		3263	1	2*	3	4	5	6	7"	8	9	10	11	12	13		
R2/1	Sep 20	Newcastle United	1-2	Redfearn	27208	1		3	4	5	6	7	8	9*	10	2	11	12		
R2/2	Oct 5	NEWCASTLE UNITED	0-1		10992	1	2	3*	4	5	11	7	8	13	10		6	12		9"

R1/2 won on away goals rule, a.e.t.

Season 1994/95

Back row: Jackson, Hanby, Davis, Butler, Fearon, Taggart, Watson, Moses, Rammell, Hurst
Centre row: Shotton (Reserve coach) Winstanley (Coach) Field, Fleming, Payton, Liddell, Eaden, Burton, Bennett, Brooke, Bochenski, Jones, Rimmington (Kit Manager), Stafford (Physio)
Front row: Snodin, Bullock, O'Connell, Wilson (Player/Manager) Redfearn, Sheridan, Archdeacon, Feeney

Season 1995/96

Back row: Jones, Hanby, Jackson, Hamer, O'Connell, Hurst, Davis, Bennett, Bishop, Fearon, Beckett
Centre row: Smith (Physio) Winstanley (Coach) Clyde, Brooke, Rammell, Sollitt, Butler, Watson, Taggart, Liddell, Burton, Walker (Youth coach) Shotton (Reserve coach)
Front row: Feeney, Perry, Gregory, Redfearn, Eaden, Fleming, Wilson (Player/Manager) Payton, Archdeacon, Bullock, Sheridan, Moses, Bochenski

1995/96 — 10th in Division 1

#	Date	Opponent	Score	Scorers	Att.	Watson DN	Eaden NJ	Davis SP	Bishop CD	Viveash AL	Kane PJ	Bullock MJ	Redfearn ND	Payton AP	Liddell AM	Archdeacon OD	Rammell AV	Fleming JG	Shirtliff PA	Sheridan DSD	Butler LS	Jackson CD	Bochenski S	Shotton M	Moses AP	Molby J	De Zeeuw A	Hurst G	O'Connell BJ	Regis D	Jones S	Van der Velden C	Ten Heuvel L
1	Aug 12	Crystal Palace	3-4	Davis, Viveash, Liddell	12166	1	2	3	4	5	6	7*	8	9	10	11	12																
2	19	OLDHAM ATHLETIC	2-1	Redfearn (p), Payton	8793	1	2	5	6		4	12	8	9	10*	11	7	3															
3	26	Watford	3-2	Davis, Rammell 2	8049	1	2	5	6		4	12	8	9	10*	13	7			3"	11+	14											
4	29	TRANMERE ROVERS	2-1	Davis, Payton	9816	1	2	5	6		4	12	8	9*	10		7			3	11												
5	Sep 2	BIRMINGHAM CITY	0-5		11121	1	2		6	5*		7	8	9	10	4				3	11	12											
6	9	Millwall	1-0	Redfearn	9272	1	2	5	6			12	8	9	10	4				3	11	7*											
7	12	Huddersfield Town	0-3		14635	1	2	5	6			10	8	9		4		12		3	11"	7*	13										
8	17	SHEFFIELD UNITED	2-2	Davis, Payton	7150		2	5				12	8	9*	10	4				3"	11	1					6		13				
9	23	DERBY COUNTY	2-0	Liddell 2	8929	1	2	5	6			7*	8	9	10	11				4	12				3								
10	30	Charlton Athletic	1-1	Redfearn	11198	1	2	5	6			12	8	9	10*	11	7*			4	13				3								
11	Oct 7	LEICESTER CITY	2-2	Bullock, Payton	13669	1	2	5	6			12	8	9"		11	7		13	4		10			3*								
12	14	Norwich City	1-3	Eaden	14002	1	2	5*	6			13	8	9		11	12		7	4		10			3								
13	21	PORT VALE	1-1	Archdeacon	7332	1	2	5*				7	8	13		11			14			9"			3				4+				
14	28	Sunderland	1-2	Liddell	17024	1	2	5				7	8	9	10	11	12			4				6*	3								
15	Nov 4	WOLVERHAMPTON W.	1-0	Redfearn	9668	1	2	5				12	8	9	10*	11	7		3	4							6						
16	11	Grimsby Town	1-3	Davis	6455	1	2	5				12	8	9	10*	11	7		3	4							6						
17	18	Reading	0-0		6695	1	2	5				7	8	9	10	11			3	4							6						
18	21	PORTSMOUTH	0-0		6194	1	2	5				7	8	9"	10*	11	12		3	4							6		13				
19	25	LUTON TOWN	1-0	Redfearn	6437	1	2	5				7	8	9	10*	11	12		3	4							6						
20	Dec 2	Leicester City	2-2	Payton 2	15129	1	2	5				7*	8	9	10*	11	12		3	4							6		13				
21	9	Derby County	1-4	Rammell	14415	1	2					7	8	9	10*	11	12		3	4*					5		6		13				
22	16	CHARLTON ATHLETIC	1-2	Payton	5534	1	2					12	8	9*	7	11	10		3	4*					5		6		13				
23	22	Ipswich Town	2-2	Liddell, De Zeeuw	12047	1	2						8	12	7*	11	10		3	4					5		6		9				
24	26	STOKE CITY	3-1	Redfearn, Lid'll, Ram'll	9229	1	2	5					8	12	7*	11	10		3	4							6		9				
25	Jan 1	Southend United	0-0		6537	1	2	5					8		7	11	10		3	4*					12		6		9				
26	13	Oldham Athletic	1-0	Payton	6029	1	2	5					8	11	7		10		3	4*					12		6		9				
27	20	CRYSTAL PALACE	1-1	Liddell	6637	1	2	5				12	8	10	7	11			3*	4							6		9				
28	Feb 3	WATFORD	2-1	Payton, Archdeacon	5966	1	2	5				4	8	10	7*	11	12		3								6		9				
29	10	Tranmere Rovers	3-1	Redfearn (p), Payton 2	6376	1	2	5				4	8	10	7	11*			3	12							6		9				
30	20	Birmingham City	0-0		14168	1	2	5				4	8	10	7				3	11							6		9				
31	24	Sheffield United	0-1		14584	1	2	5*	12			4	8	10	7				3	11"							6		9	13			
32	27	MILLWALL	3-1	Payton 2, Liddell	6366	1	2					4	8	10	7	5			3	11							6		9*	12			
33	Mar 2	Stoke City	0-2		12655	1	2					4	8	10	7	5			3	11							6	12	9*				
34	9	IPSWICH TOWN	3-3	Redfearn 2(1p), Liddell	7666	1	2						8	10	7	5			3	11							6		9			4	
35	16	West Bromwich Albion	1-2	Payton	12645	1	2					12	8	10	7	5			3*	11							6		9	13		4*	
36	19	HUDDERSFIELD T	3-0	Eaden, Redfearn, Arch'	10660	1	2					12	8	10	7*	11			3	4					5		6		9*	13			
37	23	SOUTHEND UNITED	1-1	Payton	6727	1	2					12	8	10	7	11			3*	4					5		6		9*	13			
38	30	Port Vale	0-3		7358	1	2					12	8	10	7"				3	4					5		6		9	13		11*	
39	Apr 2	NORWICH CITY	2-2	Redfearn, Payton	6420	1	2					3	8	10						4					5		6	12	9	7*		11	
40	6	SUNDERLAND	0-1		13189	1	2					11	8	10	7				3	4					5*		6		12	13		9*	
41	8	Wolverhampton Wan.	2-2	Payton, Moses	23789	1	2					11	8	10	7				3*	4					5		6		12	13		9	
42	13	READING	0-1		5440	1	2					11	8	10*	7	4			3"						5		6	12	8	9	3		
43	20	Portsmouth	0-0		8734	1	2					7		10*	11					4					5		6	12	8	9	3		
44	27	Luton Town	3-1	Redfearn 2, O'Connell	6194	1	2					11	8		10	3				4					5		6		7	9*		12	
45	30	WEST BROMWICH ALB	1-1	Regis	6979	1	2					11	8		10	3				4					5		6		7*	9*		12	13
46	Ma 4	GRIMSBY TOWN	1-1	Redfearn	6056	1	2					11*	8		10	12				4					5		6	13				3	7 9*
		Apps				45	46	27	13	2	4	41	45	40	43	38	20	3	32	41	3	8	1	2	24	5	31	5	25	12	4	7	3
		Goals					2	5		1		1	14	17	9	3	4								1		1		1	1			

F.A. Cup

#	Date	Opponent	Score	Scorers	Att.	Watson DN	Eaden NJ	Davis SP	Bishop CD	Viveash AL	Kane PJ	Bullock MJ	Redfearn ND	Payton AP	Liddell AM	Archdeacon OD	Rammell AV	Fleming JG	Shirtliff PA	Sheridan DSD	Butler LS	Jackson CD	Bochenski S	Shotton M	Moses AP	Molby J	De Zeeuw A	Hurst G	O'Connell BJ	Regis D	Jones S	Van der Velden C	Ten Heuvel L
R3	Jan 8	OLDHAM ATHLETIC	0-0		9751	1	2	5				12	8	13	7*	11	10		3	4*							6		9				
rep	23	Oldham Athletic	1-2	Redfearn	6670	1	2	5*				12	8	10	7	11			4			13			3		6		9*				

F.L. Cup (Coca Cola Cup)

#	Date	Opponent	Score	Scorers	Att.	Watson DN	Eaden NJ	Davis SP	Bishop CD	Viveash AL	Kane PJ	Bullock MJ	Redfearn ND	Payton AP	Liddell AM	Archdeacon OD	Rammell AV	Fleming JG	Shirtliff PA	Sheridan DSD	Butler LS	Jackson CD	Bochenski S	Shotton M	Moses AP	Molby J	De Zeeuw A	Hurst G	O'Connell BJ	Regis D	Jones S	Van der Velden C	Ten Heuvel L
R2/1	Sep 19	Huddersfield Town	0-2		8264	1	2	5	3			7	8	9	10	4			11						6*	12							
R2/2	Oct 3	HUDDERSFIELD T	4-0	Payton 3, Rammell	8192	1	2	5	6			12	8	9		11	7		4	10					3*								
R3	24	ARSENAL	0-3		18429	1	2	5*	6			7	8	9	10	11	12		4						3								

1996/97 2nd in Division 1

#	Mon	Date	Opponent	Score	Scorers	Att	Watson DN	Eaden NJ	Appleby MW	Bosancic J	Davis SP	De Zeeuw A	Marcelle CS	Redfearn ND	Wilkinson P	Liddell AM	Thompson N	Sheridan DSD	Moses AP	Regis D	Bullock MJ	van der Velden C	Shirtliff PA	Ten Heuval L	Hurst G	Hendrie IG	Jones S
1	Aug	17	West Bromwich Alb.	2-1	Marcelle, Liddell	18561	1	2	3	4*	5	6	7*	8	9	10	11	12	13								
2		25	HUDDERSFIELD T.	3-1	Wilkinson, Redfearn, Marcelle	9787	1	2	3	4*	5	6	7	8	9	10	11	12									
3		28	READING	3-0	Sheridan, Liddell2	7523	1	2	3	4	5	6		8	9	10	11	7									
4	Sep	7	Manchester City	2-1	Marcelle 2	26464	1	2	3		5	6	7	8	9*	10	11	4		12							
5		10	STOKE CITY	3-0	Davis, Thompson, Liddell	11696	1	2	3	12	5	6	7	8	9*	10	11	4*		13							
6		14	QUEENS PARK RANGERS	1-3	Wilkinson	13003	1	2	3		5	6	7	8	9	10*	11	4*		13	12						
7		21	Oldham Athletic	1-0	Redfearn (pen)	7043	1	2	3		5	6	7	8	9	10*	11				12						
8		28	GRIMSBY TOWN	1-3	Liddell	8833	1	2	3	4+	5	6	7*	8	9	10	11*			13	12	14					
9	Oct	1	Ipswich Town	1-1	Redfearn (pen)	9041	1	2	3		5	6		8	9	10	11*			12	7*	4			13		
10		12	CRYSTAL PALACE	0-0		9183	1	2	3		5	6		8	9	10		4	11							7*	
11		15	OXFORD UNITED	0-0		6337	1	2	3		5	6		8	9	10		4								7*	11
12		19	Bradford City	2-2	Liddell, Davis	11477	1	2*	3		5	6	12	8	9	10*		4								7	11
13		25	BOLTON WANDERERS	2-2	Redfearn 2 (1 pen)	9413	1	2	3		5	6	12	8	9	10		4								7	11*
14		29	Port Vale	3-1	Hendrie, De Zeeuw, Marcelle	5231	1	2	3	12	5	6	13	8	9	10*		4*								7	11
15	Nov	2	Wolverhampton Wan.	3-3	De Zeeuw, Redfearn (pen), Eaden	22840	1	2	3		5	6	12*	8	9*	10		4				13				7	11
16		12	NORWICH CITY	3-1	Moses, Wilkinson, Hendrie	9697	1	2	3	12	5	6		8	9	10		4	5							7*	11
17		16	Swindon Town	0-3		10837	1	2*	3			6	13	8	9	10*		4	5							7	11
18		23	PORTSMOUTH	3-2	Wilkinson, Hendrie, Davis	7449	1	2	3	13	5	6	12	8	9	10*	11*	4								7	
19		30	Bolton Wanderers	2-2	Redfearn 2 (1 pen)	16852	1	2	3	4	5	6	10*	8	9			11								7	
20	Dec	3	Birmingham City	0-0		24004	1	2	3	4*	5	6	10	8	9			11								7	12
21		7	SOUTHEND UNITED	3-0	Hendrie, Wilkinson 2	7483	1	2	3*	4*	5	6	10	8	9			11			12					7	13
22		14	TRANMERE ROVERS	3-0	Hendrie, Wilkinson, Redfearn (pen)	8513	1	2		4	5	6	10*	8	9	12		3	13		11*					7	
23		21	Sheffield United	1-0	Hendrie	24384	1	2		4	5	6	10	8*	9			11					3			7	12
24		26	Stoke City	0-1		19025	1	2	3	4*	5	6	10+		9	12		11	14		13					7	8*
25		28	MANCHESTER CITY	2-0	Bosancic (pen), Moses	17159	1	2	3	4	5	6			9	12		11	8							7*	
26	Jan	11	Queens Park Rangers	1-3	Redfearn	12058	1	2		4	5*	6	10	8	9*	13		11			12		3			7	
27		18	IPSWICH TOWN	1-2	Liddell	9872	1	2		12		6	10+	8	9	7	5*	4	3		11*			14			13
28		28	Grimsby Town	3-2	Hendrie 3	6323	1	2	3*					8	9+	10*		4	5		12	6		14		7	13
29	Feb	1	Norwich City	1-1	Eaden	17001	1	2	3				12	8	9	10*	11	4	5			6				7	
30		8	PORT VALE	1-0	Hendrie	12246	1	2		11		6	12	8	9*	10		4	5		3					7	
31		15	Charlton Athletic	2-2	Hendrie 2	9104	1	2		11*		6	12	8	9	10*		4	5		3					7	13
32		22	WOLVERHAMPTON WAN.	1-3	Sheridan	18024	1	2*		4*		6	12	8	9	13		11	5			14	3+			7	10
33	Mar	1	Southend United	2-1	Redfearn 2	4855	1	2	3			6	12	8	9			4	5		11*					7	
34		4	SWINDON TOWN	1-1	Redfearn	8518	1	2	3*			6	12	8	9	13		4	5		11					7*	10
35		7	SHEFFIELD UNITED	2-0	Hendrie, Eaden	14668	1	2	3			6	10	8	9		11	4	5							7	
36		15	Tranmere Rovers	1-1	Wilkinson	7347	1	2		12		6	10	8	9*		13	4*	5		14		3			7	11+
37		22	Huddersfield Town	0-0		14754	1	2	6				10	8	9		12	3	4	5	11					7*	
38		28	WEST BROMWICH ALB.	2-0	Redfearn, Thompson (pen)	12087	1	2	3			6	10*	8	9*	12	11	4	5		13					7	
39		31	Reading	2-1	Holsgrove (og), Liddle	10244	1	2	3*	12		6	10	8	9		11	4	5							7	
40	Apr	5	BIRMINGHAM CITY	0-1		13092	1	2	3*			6	10*	8	9	12	11	4	5							7	
41		12	CHARLTON ATHLETIC	4-0	Marcelle, Thompson 2, Hendrie	11701	1	2	3			6	10*	8	9*	12	11	4	5							7	
42		15	OLDHAM ATHLETIC	2-0	Hendrie, Marcelle	17476	1	2	3	8*		6	10		9	12	11		5				4			7	
43		19	Crystal Palace	1-1	Thompson (pen)	20006	1	2	3*			6	10	8	9		11	4	5		12					7	
44		22	Portsmouth	2-4	Redfearn 2	8328	1	2				6	10*	8	9	12	11	4	5		13		3*			7	
45		26	BRADFORD CITY	2-0	Wilkinson, Marcelle	18605	1	2				6	12	8	9	10*		3	4	5	11*		13			7	
46	May	4	Oxford United	1-5	Redfearn	8693	1	2		12		6	13	8	9		11	4*	5		10		3*			7	
			Apps				46	46	35	25	24	43	40	43	45	38	24	41	28	4	28	2	13	2	1	36	18
			Goals					3		1	3	2	8	17	9	8	5	2	2							15	

One own goal

F.A. Cup

	Mon	Date	Opponent	Score	Scorers	Att	Watson DN	Eaden NJ	Appleby MW	Bosancic J	Davis SP	De Zeeuw A	Marcelle CS	Redfearn ND	Wilkinson P	Liddell AM	Thompson N	Sheridan DSD	Moses AP	Regis D	Bullock MJ	van der Velden C	Shirtliff PA	Ten Heuval L	Hurst G	Hendrie IG	Jones S
R3	Jan	14	OLDHAM ATHLETIC	2-0	Bullock, Marcelle	9936	1	2		4*		6	10+	8	9	13	5	12	3		11					7*	14
R4		25	Queens Park Rangers	2-3	Redfearn, Hendrie	14317	1	2	3+	4*		6	10*	8	9	14		11	5		12					7	13

F.L. Cup (Coca Cola Cup)

	Mon	Date	Opponent	Score	Scorers	Att	Watson DN	Eaden NJ	Appleby MW	Bosancic J	Davis SP	De Zeeuw A	Marcelle CS	Redfearn ND	Wilkinson P	Liddell AM	Thompson N	Sheridan DSD	Moses AP	Regis D	Bullock MJ	van der Velden C	Shirtliff PA	Ten Heuval L	Hurst G	Hendrie IG	Jones S
R1/1	Aug	20	Rochdale	1-2	Wilkinson	2426	1	2	3	4*	5	6	7*	8	9	10	11	12		13							
R1/2	Sep	3	ROCHDALE	2-0	Redfearn, Wilkinson	5638	1	2	3	4*	5	6	12	8	9	10	11*	7									
R2/1		17	GILLINGHAM	1-1	Onuora (og)	4491	1	2	3	4*	5	6	7	8	9	10*	11			13	12						
R2/2		24	Gillingham	0-1		5666	1	2	3	12	5	6	7*	8	9					13	10	4*			11		

Season 1996/97
Back row: Shotton (Reserve Coach) Winstanley (Coach) Shirtliff, Davis, Moses, Wilkinson, Watson, Sollitt,
Ten Heuvel, de Zeeuw, Thompson, Liddell, Walker (Youth Coach)
Front row: Tarmey (Physio) Appleby, Marcelle, Sheridan, Jones, Bullock, Wilson (Manager),
Redfearn, Eaden, Bosancic, Hendrie, Smith (Physio)

Season 97/98
Back row: Smith(Physio), McClare, Hudson, Morgan, Wilkinson, Bullock T., Leese, Watson,Davis, Hume, Bagshaw, Sheridan, Tarmey(Physio)
Centre row: Winstanley (Coach) Jones D., Prendergast, Beckett, Perry, Rose, Gregory, Shenton,
de Zeeuw, Tinkler, Ten Heuvel, Moses, Thompson, Rimmington (Kit Manager), Shotton (ReserveCoach)
Front row: Shirtliff,Marcelle,Liddell,Eaden, Bullock M., Redfearn, Wilson (Manager), Appleby, Hendrie,Bosancic,Krizan,Hristov, Walker(Y'outh Coach)

1997/98   19th in Premiership

#	Mon	Date	Opponent	Score	Scorers	Att	Watson	Eaden	Barnard	Moses	Shirtliff	De Zeeuw	Tinkler	Redfearn	Bullock MJ	Hendrie	Wilkinson	Marcelle	Hristov	Liddell	Appleby	Sheridan	Leese	Ward	Ten Heuvel	Krizan	Thompson	Bosancic	Markstedt	Morgan	Fjortoft	Jones
1	Aug	9	WEST HAM U.	1-2	Redfearn	18667	1	2	3	4	5*	6	7	8	9+	10	11"	12	13	14												
2		12	Crystal Palace	1-0	Redfearn	21547	1	2	3	4		6		8	9	10	11				5	7										
3		24	CHELSEA	0-6		18177	1	2	3	4		6	7	8	9	0	11	12	13			5*										
4		27	BOLTON W.	2-1	Tinkler, Hristov	18661	1*	2	3	4		6	7	8	13	10			9*	11+	14		5	12								
5		30	Derby County	0-1		27232		2	3*	4		6	7	8		13	14		9*	11+	10		5	12	1							
6	Sep	13	ASTON V.	0-3		18649		2	3	4		6	7*	8	13					11+	9"		5	12	1		10	14				
7		20	Everton	2-4	Redfearn, Barnard	32659			3	4	5	6	7+	8	14				13	12	11	2*	9				10*					
8		23	Wimbledon	1-4	Tinkler	7688	1		3	4		6	7*	8	10				12	13	11"	2	9					5				
9		27	LEICESTER C.	0-2		18660			3	4		6	7*	8	12				13		11"	2	9	1		10		5				
10	Oct	4	Arsenal	0-5		38049	1	13	7	2*		6	4	8	12					14	11+		9*		10			5	3			
11		20	COVENTRY C.	2-0	Ward, Redfearn (pen)	17476	1	2	7	13		4		8	9*				12	11"		6		10				5	3			
12		25	Manchester U.	0-7		55142	1	2	7	12		4		8	9	13				11"			6	10				5*	3+	14		
13	Nov	1	BLACKBURN R.	1-1	Bosancic	18687	1	12	14	2	5	4		8	9	10				11"	13	6*				3+		7				
14		8	Southampton	1-4	Bosancic (pen)	15018	1	2	14	6	5*	4	8		9	10*				11		12			13	3+	7					
15		22	Liverpool	1-0		41011	1		2	3	6	4	7	8	9	13				11*	12		1	10*				5				
16		29	LEEDS UTD.	2-3	Liddell, Ward	18690		2	3	12	4	7	8	9*					14	11+	13		1	10				6*	5			
17	Dec	8	Sheffield Wed.	1-2	Redfearn	29086	1	2	3	6			8	13	12				11"	4*	9		1	10				5	7			
18		13	NEWCASTLE U.	2-2	Redfearn, Hendrie	18694	1	2	3	6			9	8	14	13			11"	4+	12		1	10				5	7*			
19		20	Tottenham H.	0-3		28232	1	2	3	6		4	9	8	12				13	11"	7		1	10				5*				
20		26	Bolton Wands.	1-1	Hristov	25000	1	2	3	5		4	7	8				12	9*	11"	13	6		10							
21		28	DERBY CO.	1-0	Ward	18686	1	2	3	5		4	7	8	13				9*	11"	12	6		10							
22	Jan	10	West Ham Utd.	0-6		23714	1	2	9				7	8	14			13	11+	4*	6			10		5*				12	3	
23		17	CRYSTAL PAL.	1-0	Ward	17831	1	2	3				7	8				9		12	6			10				5	4	11*		
24		31	Chelsea	0-2		34442	1	2	3	5		4		8	9	13				14	6*			10		7+			12	11*		
25	Feb	7	EVERTON	2-2	Fjortoft, Barnard	18654	1	2	3	5		4		8	9	12			13					10		7			6*	11*		
26		21	Coventry City	0-1		20262	1	2		5				8	9*	12		13	14			6+		10		7		4		11*		3
27		28	WIMBLEDON	2-1	Fjortoft 2	17172	1	2	3	5			12	8	9					13				10		7*		4*	6	11		
28	Mar	11	Aston Villa	1-0	Ward	29519	1	2	3*	5			13	8	9				12					10		7			6	11		4
29		14	SOUTHAMPTON	4-3	Ward, Jones, Fjo'ft, Redf'n (pen)	18366	1	2	3	5			14	8	9				13	12*				10*		7			6	11	4+
30		28	LIVERPOOL	2-3	Redfearn 2 (1pen)	18687	1	2	3					8	9*	0	14	13	5					7		12			6	11*	4
31		31	Blackburn R.	1-2	Hristov	24179	1	2	3	5				8	9*	12*	11	14	13					7					6		4+
32	Apr	4	Leeds United	1-3	Hristov	37749	1	2	3	5				8	9*	12	11							7					6	13	4*
33		11	SHEFFIELD W.	2-1	Ward, Fjortoft	18692	1	2		5		6		8	9	11*								10		3			7	12	4
34		13	Newcastle Utd.	1-2	Fjortoft	36534	1	2		5		6	12	9+	13			14						10		3*			7	11*	4
35		18	TOTTENHAM H.	1-1	Redfearn	18692	1	2	3	5		6	7*	8	9	12			13					10						11	4*
36		25	ARSENAL	0-2		18691	1	2	3	5		6	7*	8	9	14	10*							12		13				11	4
37	May	2	Leicester City	0-1		21293	1	2	3	5		6	7*	8	13	9			14					10		12				11	4*
38		10	MANCHESTER U.	0-2		18694	1	12	3	5				8	9			11"		2*	7			10					6	13	4
			Apps				30	35	35	35	4	26	25	37	33	20	4	20	23	26	15	26	9	29	2	12	3	17	7	11	15	12
			Goals						2				2	10		1			4	1		8				2				6	1

F.A. Cup

Rnd	Mon	Date	Opponent	Score	Scorers	Att	Watson	Eaden	Barnard	Moses	Shirtliff	De Zeeuw	Tinkler	Redfearn	Bullock MJ	Hendrie	Wilkinson	Marcelle	Hristov	Liddell	Appleby	Sheridan	Leese	Ward	Krizan	Bosancic	Morgan	Fjortoft	Jones
R3	Jan	3	BOLTON W.	1-0	Barnard	15042	1	2	3	5		4	7	8	12				9*	11"	13		6	10					
R4		24	Tottenham H.	1-1	Redfearn (pen)	28722	1	2	3	5		4	7*	8		11"	9			13			6	10		12			
rep	Feb	4	TOTTENHAM H.	3-1	Ward, Redfearn, Barnard	18220	1	2	3	5		4		8	9	11							10	7		6			
R5		15	Manchester U.	1-1	Hendrie	54700	1	2				4*	8	9	11		13	12				3	7	6					
rep		25	MANCHESTER U.	3-2	Jones 2, Hendrie	18655	1		3	5			8	9+	11"	14	12	2*	13			10	7	4		6			6
R6	Mar	8	Newcastle U.	1-3	Liddell	36695	1	2	3	5		4"	8	12	9*	13	11		7			10		6					

F.L. Cup (Coca-Cola Cup)

Rnd	Mon	Date	Opponent	Score	Scorers	Att	Watson	Eaden	Barnard	Moses	Shirtliff	De Zeeuw	Tinkler	Redfearn	Bullock MJ	Hendrie	Marcelle	Hristov	Liddell	Appleby	Sheridan	Leese	Ward	Thompson	Bosancic	Markstedt
R2/1	Sep	16	Chesterfield	2-1	Redfearn (pen), Ward	6318		2	3	4	5		7	8					11*		9	1	10	12	6	
R2/2		30	CHESTERFIELD	4-1	Lid'll, Redf'n, Sher'n, Hri'ov	8417			3	4		6	7	8+	12		14	13	11"	2*	9	1	10		5	
R3	Oct	14	SOUTHAMPTON	1-2	Liddell	9019	1	2	7			4		8*	9		12	13	11"		6		10		5	3

PLAYERS - SQUAD NUMBERS

1	David Watson	11	Neil Thompson	22	Georgi Hristov
2	Nicky Eaden	12	Andy Liddell	23	Ales Krizan
3	Matty Appleby	13	Lars Lees	24	Darren Barnard
4	Darren Sheridan	14	Martin Bullock	25	Ashley Ward
5	Adie Moses	15	Jovo Bosancic	26	Tony Bullock
6	Arjan de Zeeuw	16	Steve Davis	27	Chris Morgan
7	John Hendrie	17	Laurens Ten Heuvel	28	Luke Beckett
8	Neil Redfearn	18	Scott Jones	29	Peter Markstedt
9	Paul Wilkinson	19	Peter Shirtliff	30	Jan Aage Fjortoft
10	Clint Marcelle	20	Dave Regis	31	Sean McClare
		21	Eric Tinkler		

ADVANCED SUBSCRIBERS

Philip Kerr, Darton, Barnsley
Mark Nottingham, Monk Bretton
D.J. Penty, Pontefract
Martyn D. Moxon, Barnsley
Mr. A. Bower, Barnsley
Danny Auckland, Brampton, Barnsley
Janine and Peter Jones, Barnsley
Matt and Mark Norman
Stephen Shaw, Oakwell, Barnsley
E.A. Gill, Dodworth, Barnsley
Arthur Gill, Lewden, Worsbrough Dale
Andy Waddington, Meadow St., Barnsley
John Garbett, Portslade, Sussex
Michael Holt, Gilroyd, Barnsley
Paul Davies, Hemsworth, W.Yorks.
Joan & Dave Winstanley
Andy Flesher, Birdwell, Barnsley
Eric Broadhead, Hull
Alan & Denise Bagshaw, Mexborough
Philip Sharp, Barnsley
Wayne Peter Smith, Wath
Alan & Janet Lockwood, Dodworth
Roy White, Wombwell
Gareth Davies, Gosport, Hampshire
Alan Whiteley, Barnsley
D.J. Brady, Harlington
Stephen Roy Sutton, Rawmarsh
David Franks, High Hoyland
Tony Moran, Hemsworth
Richard Phillipson, Embsay, Skipton
The Parr Family, Croydon
Bob Davies, Warwickshire
Keith Marsh, Gosport, Hants.
Martin Humphries, Swinton
S. Milner, Oakworth, Keighley
Lee Dooling, Athersley, Barnsley
Timothy Cannon
G. Richard Northern, Cawthorne
Gerald Popplewell, Staincross, Barnsley
Bernard Hinchcliffe, Horbury, Wakefield
David Bamforth, Barnsley
John Roebuck, Fitzwilliam
Mark Jackson, Barnsley
Steve Holroyd, Barnsley
David Slater, Silkstone Common
Gary Simpson, Perth, Australia
Syd Bates
Robert Booth, Wilthorpe
Peter Schofield, Oxspring
Albert Day, Pontefract

Robert Day, Pontefract
K. Golding
P. Brook
Rhys Owen, Oakwell, Barnsley
Scott Hollinshead, High Wycombe
Stewart Hardman, Thurnscoe, Rotherham
Roy Whittaker, Monk Bretton
Glen Scholey, Wakefield
Eddie Arnold, Hemsworth
Terrence Lowe, Kendray
John White, Harlow, Essex
Paul Bamford, Hutton, Preston
David Wood, Bedford
Nigel & Stephen Harper, Featherstone
Albert Allan Fitzwilliam, Pontefract
James Ritchie, Gawber, Barnsley
Brian Gill, Barnsley
Kev Golding, Normanton
Gordon Howard, Barnsley
Katie Sherfield, Barnsley
J. Platts, Crewe, Cheshire
Richard Roper, Barnsley
M.J. Harley, Millhouse Green
George, Alfred, Gray, Knottingley
John Ennis
Anthony McHale, Normanton
Mr. Sagar, Barnsley
Mick Wright, Watford
Stephen Sutton, Barnsley
Neil Hartup, York
John Osbourne, Ossett, Wakefield
Kevin Roper, Dodworth, Barnsley
Richard Foster, Hemsworth, Pontefract
Paul B. Mann, Gawber
Joseph Birkbeck, Barnsley
A.M. Filak, Loosley Row
Terry Bowman, Bessacar, Doncaster
William Rowland Hill, Wetherby
Laurence and Lisa Harte
Trevor O'Connor, Worsbrough
Sam, From Mr. Cadswell
Jane Utley, Worsbrough, Barnsley
Len Hanson, Wombwell
David Wroe, Grimethorpe, Barnsley
Gerard Pearson, Eccles, Lancs.
Doug Dixon, Marlow, Bucks.
Roger, Eamon, Nevyn, Gavin
Paul and Sue Rowlands
Bryan, Harry, Michael Wright
Matthew James Smith

Dave Feeny, Hood Green
Richard Oxley, Stoke Row
John Kenneth, Wellburn, Havercroft
Hilary James, Brierley
Wendy Blackburn, Worsbrough Dale
William, David Tucker, Hemingfield
Jane & Mark Greaves, Cawthorne
Kevin Smith
Terry Smith
Diana Gilfillan, Barnsley
Ralph Mallinson, London
Ronald Howell, Cudworth
Andrew Wilson, Penistone, Barnsley
John Clarke, Barnsley
Chris Kenchington, Barnsley
Neil and James Turton
John Brayford, Newlodge, Barnsley
Michael White, Queensway, Barnsley
Jim Stanton, South Kirby
Paul, Claire Galvin, Pogmoor
John Coyne, Cudworth
Norman Turton, Royston, Barnsley
Gerald Bottomley, Birdwell, Barnsley
Trevor Blackburn, Darfield, Barnsley
Matthew Spencer, Darfield, Barnsley
J. Puddephatt, Silkstone, Barnsley
George & Elizabeth Dutton, Tamworth
Martyn Brown, Goole
Diane Mellor, Birdwell, Barnsley
Richard Senior, Silkstone, Barnsley
Christopher O'Brien, Darfield
Ian Thomas, Portsmouth
Chris Corke, Hoylandswaine, Barnsley
Rhys Corke, York Red
Alister & Jenny Carr, York
Tony Raikes, South Elmsall
Roger and Shirley Montague
Stephen John Healey, Silkstone
Jon Taylor, Barnsley
Alan Pickles, Royston
Robert Crowe, Royston, Barnsley
J.S. Rollinson, Ossett
Andrew Hinchcliffe, Barnsley
John Wilson Banks, Royston
Fred Davies, Skelmanthorpe, Huddersfield
David Deaves, Hallgreen, Wakefield
C & L Sabey, Ossett
Colin Levitt, Hoyland, Belmont
John Turner, South Hiendley
Johnny "Wig" Lister, South Hiendley

Les Potts, Cudworth
Sam Goulding, Jersey
David Cooper, Penistone Reds
Jerry Fisher, Hoyland Common
Alan Bloore, Chairman Supporters Club
Rob Bland, Beverley, East Yorks.
Richard Bland, Sheffield
Frank Race, Darton, Barnsley
Richard Martin Gillespie
John, Julie, Natalie Nuttall
Curtis Ledger, Leeds
Alison Saxby, Bapaume, France
Albert Mason, Marsden, W. Yorks.
Sarah Taylor, Smithies, Barnsley
Jack, Marilyn, Amy, Joe.
Les Coles, Athersley, Barnsley
Roy Bowran, Mapplewell, Barnsley
Stuart Wallace, Little Houghton
Alice Jepson (1901-1996)
Ernest Jepson (Match Sec. 1939-54)
Sue and Emma Darton
Stephen Sharp, Barnsley
Alan Beaumont, Arnside, Cumbria
Graham Beaumont Arnside, Cumbria
Michael Stuart, Marsden, Barnsley
Stephen Wroe, Allendale Rd, Barnsley
Marcus Wroe, Allendale Rd, Barnsley
The Davies', Caerfyrddin Cymru
Andrew Horsfield, Silkstone
The Tunnicliffe Family, Epworth
Barrie Kay, Bottesford, Scunthorpe
Joy and Andy, Rawmarsh
James Robert Brown, Barugh
Donald L. Birkinshaw, Gawber
Chris Burrows, Barnsley
Louis Hall, Pontefract
Ray Brammer, Ellesmere Port
Colin, Wendy & John Ding
Stephen Bramall, Victoria, Hepworth
John Garrity, Staincross
James Rae, Worsbrough, Barnsley
Benny Hill (Sheffield)
Simon Gill, Bolton Yorkshireman
Clive and Anne Wood, Royston
Lord Mason of Barnsley
Wayne Bateman, Bentley, Doncaster
Dave Swales, Nottingham Branch
William I. Moss, Dodworth, Barnsley
John Ward, Worsbrough Common
Lynn, Barry, Miriam Adam
Gareth Williams, Mapplewell, Barnsley
Jon Cutts, Penistone
Dennis Ryal, Cudworth

David John Clemit, Barnsley
Alan Potter, Kexborough, Barnsley
Ian Parker, Royston, Barnsley
Wayne Parkes, Swinton, Yorkshire
Keith & Pam Grummett, Brierley
Graham & Rosemary Wraith, Thurnsoe
Cathrine Williams, Silkstone Common
Ian Richard Marsden, Darfield
Darren Wall, Dodworth, Barnsley
Geoff Brown, Wollongong, Australia
Peter Middleton, Grimethorpe
Mark Bell, Pogmoor, Barnsley
Roy Lunn, Worsbrough, Barnsley
David Robinson, Wombwell, Barnsley
Ian Jones, Hoyland, Barnsley
David J. Barr, Monk Bretton
Keith Waddington, Wombwell, Barnsley
David Mann, Wickersley, Rotherham
Dr. Julie Greensill, Liverpool
Mrs. Michelle Neal, Hoyland
Debbie Griffiths, Wilthorpe
Ashley Blandamour, Barnsley
Jonathan Richard Eyre, Barnsley
Ian Glover, Perth
Desmond Herring, Dodworth
Andrew Blakeley, Ryhill, Wakefield
Phil Grain, Chapletown, Sheffield
Kerry and Abbey Guest
Bryan Utley, Hoyland
Ian Phillips, Wakefield Road
Simon Limb, London
Richard Limb, Manchester
Chris Limb, Tavistock
Andrew Limb, Scarborough
Andrew Ward, Cockerham, Cumbria
Simon Reed, Doncaster
Nick Reed, Loughton, Essex
Anita Ainsworth, Swinton, Rotherham
Geoffrey Whittaker, Monk Bretton
Samuel Wright, Bolton-on-Dearne
Neil John Firth, Derby
David Wright, Barnsley
Alf Wood, Upton, Pontefract
Mary Horne, Monk Bretton
Raymond Fereday, Shafton, Barnsley
Reg. Lee, Shafton, Barnsley
Glynn Fereday, Shafton, Barnsley
Sian Louise Cartledge
David Andrew Philip Cartledge
Mark Parr, Northallerton
David Lees, Abergavenny
John Pickering, Woodlesford, Leeds
Glyn Owen, Armley, Leeds

David Barraclough, Hemsworth, Pontefract
Teifion Whitham, Darton, Barnsley
Mr. J.A. Dennis, Barnsley
Mr. D. Sokell, Wombwell, Barnsley
A.J.& P Fulton-Robb, Newbury, Berks.
Paul Henley, Fulflood, Winchester
Stanley Brooks, Barnburgh, Yorkshire
Stephen Brooks, Barnburgh, Yorkshire
Neil Taylor, Barnsley
Malcolm R. Stothard, Cudworth
Matthew Rhodie, Gawber, Barnsley
Andrew & Richard Clutton, Crofton
Happy Birthday Robert Hickey
Duncan Thompson, Bessacar, Doncaster
Paul Vincent, Wath-upon-Dearne
Sue Jones, Wavertree, Liverpool
Leonard W. Long, Retford, Notts.
Thomas Schofield, Royston
Ian Schofield, Royston
Neil Addy, Carlton
Natalie Addy, Carlton
Roger Priest, Hoyland Common
Adrian Oddy, Barnsley
Gary Cooper, Carlton, Barnsley
Paul Denton, Kirkhamgate, Wakefield
Carol Bird, Brampton Bierlow
Craig Sykes, Darfield, Barnsley
Elizabeth Perry, Staincross, Barnsley
Ken and Ann Murtagh
John William Hobson, Barnsley
Graham Hutchinson, Shafton, Barnsley
John & Mary Moralee
Mike Crow, Harlington, Doncaster
Mark Nile, Mapplewell, Barnsley
Garry Rawson, Hoyland, Barnsley
Andrew Hunt, Denby Dale
Vincent & Paul Stothard, Bucks.
Nigel Garrett
David Wood, Filey
Jayne Brooks, Brierley, Barnsley
Steve Fletcher of Pocklington
Darren Webster, Barnsley
Stephen Blakeley, Cawthorne, Barnsley
Alan Blakeley, Royston, Barnsley
David Bass, South Elmsall
Steven Tune, Blackrock, Dublin
Tony & Paul Bennett, Monk Bretton
Laura Batterham, Barnsley
Angela Walmsley, Barnsley
Carol Chapman, Gawber, Barnsley
Tony Ennis, Cudworth, Barnsley
Steven O'Connor, Worsbrough, Barnsley
Mick Lagdon, Mapplewell

Patrick Walker & Pam Bowman
Gary Rose, Darfield, Barnsley
Vicky & David Hodge, Halifax
Lucy Ryalls, Hereford
Darren and Matthew Hayes
C.F. Darfield
Laurence & Lynette Mace, Worsbrough Dale
Alexandra Kilburn, Barnsley
Ian Birdsall, Carlton, Worksop
Trevor Pearce, Royston, Barnsley
Phil Allen, Royston, Barnsley
Paul & Stuart Cole, Barnsley
Paul McEnhill, Skelmanthorpe, Huddersfield
Jason Law, Darfield
Michael Masters Golborne, Warrington
John Hibbard, Leicestershire
Walter Hibbard, Barnsley
Andrew G. Parr, Ealing
Edwin Parr, Penistone
Keith Howlett, Coventry, Warwickshire
Malcolm Birdsall, Carlton, Worksop
Andrew Birdsall, Carlton, Worksop
Jack Peel, Wath-upon-Dearne
Kenny Gough, Barnsley
John Lythe, Wombwell
Daniel Haig, Cudworth, Barnsley
Ron Parker, Wombwell, Barnsley
David Staniforth, Monk Bretton
Anthony Dean, Worsbrough Dale
Miss Diane Waterhouse, Skelmanthorpe
Mr. Charles Davies, Hoyland
Harold Luckman, Broughton, Chester
Ernest Goodman, Dodworth, Barnsley
Mark Ellis, Barnsley
Ernest Picton, Wath
Richard Pickering, Karen Robert
Amy, David, Jeff, Barnsley
Glen Banks, Darton, Barnsley
Neil Hornby, Wombwell, Barnsley
Eugene Botham, Little Houghton
Mark Booth, Cundy Cross
Stuart Manley, Stadium Manager
Matthew Stringer, Thornbury, Bristol
Ian Teesdale, Kexborough, Barnsley
Malcolm Moyes, Editor BRTO
Andrew Kevin Burns, Wakefield
Ron Parker, Wombwell, Barnsley
Ian D. Thompson, 40 years young
Glen Hyde, Dodworth, Barnsley
Maureen & Trevor Carr, Barnsley
James & Mark Carr, Barnsley
Mick Davison, Harrogate
Colin & David Farnsworth, Royston

Hazel Hornsby, Skipton
Barry & Joan Jackson, Cawthorne
Kate and Alex Andrews
Robin Nettleton, Gawber, Barnsley
Barbara Ridge and Family
Stephen Thompson, Monk Bretton
Adrian Thompson, Monk Bretton
Graeme Hind, Outlane, Huddersfield
Philip A. Bowman, Geneva, Switzerland
Paul Darlow, Gilroyd, Dodworth
Brian Dickinson (Worsborough Red)
John Brian Dickinson (Athersley Red)
Tracey and Mick Dodd
Pete Doherty, Bolton-on-Dearne
John Peters, Dodworth, Barnsley
Stephen John Stafford, Dodworth
Don Sykes, South Kirby
Chris & Jane Patzelt, Dodworth
Geoffrey William North, Grimethorpe
Paul McClure, Shafton
David Coupe, Normanton
John & Nigel Webster, Elsecar
Joan & Don Desbro, Cudworth
John Moorhouse, Bridlington
Claire Whitehead, Stairfoot, Barnsley
Sally Hibbert, Honeywell, Barnsley
K. Payne, Wath-on-Dearne
Gareth Park, Barnsley
Ian Jowitt, Birdwell, Barnsley
Arthur Bower, Barnsley
Tim Bower, Barnsley
Tony Bower, Carnforth, Lancashire
Gemma Caves, Wilthorpe, Barnsley
Paul Collins, Barnsley
Jim Connor, Westlake Village, California
Julie Dennis, Orpington, Kent
Sarah Dennis, Wallington, Surrey
Peter Handley, Barnsley
Herbert Mollart, Wakefield
Andy Moore, Wallington, Surrey
Derek Pickering, Oxnard, California
Vic Randerson, Hull
Gerry Slater, Thousand Oaks, California
John Williams, Neath
Alan Beaumont, Chatham
Mr.L.A. Zammit, Fareham
Graham Spackman
Gordon Macey (Q.P.R.Historian)
G. Painter - Castle Cary
Raymond Shaw
Paul Johnson, Birmingham City
Chas. Sumner
Steve Emms

David Keats, Thornton Heath
Ray Bickel
Stephen Kieran Byrne
John Lyne, Highbury 1936
G.S. Briggs
Peter Cogle, Aberdeen
G.T. Allman, Essington
Fred Lee, Plymouth Argyle
Chris. Marsh, Chesterfield
Moira and Frederick Furness
Richard Pepper
Philip H. Whitehead
Mr. J. Holbrook
B.H. Standish
Richard Wells
Dave Windross, York City
J. Ringrose
Bob Lilliman
Jonny Stokkeland, Kvinesdal, Norway
Robert M. Smith
Raymond Koerhuis, Notherlands
Martin Simons, Belgium
Simon Johnson, Felixtowe, Suffolk
Geoffrey Wright
John & James Davies
David J. Godfrey
Roger Wash
A & J.A. Waterman
A.N. Other
Richard Stocken
Donald Noble, Dunkeld, Perthshire
Christer Svensson
Derek Grimshaw
Kevin Grimshaw
Phil Hollow
Mick McConkey, Luton
David and Matthew Fleckney
David Jowett
Mr. S. Metcalfe
John Gdula
Trond Isaksen, Norway
John Rawnsley
Willy Østby
David Morgan
Phil Newport, Birmingham
David Yates, Guisley
Peter Baxter
Grant E. Reynolds, Australia
Richard Lane, Norwell, Notts.
Örjan Hansson
R.H. White, Saudi Arabia
C.Phillips, Buckinghamshire
Arran & Nicholas Matthews